Thomas Townsend

The honors of the Empire State in the War of the Rebellion

Thomas Townsend

The honors of the Empire State in the War of the Rebellion

ISBN/EAN: 9783337274498

Printed in Europe, USA, Canada, Australia, Japan

Cover: Foto ©ninafisch / pixelio.de

More available books at **www.hansebooks.com**

THE

HONORS OF THE EMPIRE STATE

— IN THE —

WAR OF THE REBELLION

BY

THOMAS S. TOWNSEND,

Compiler of "THE LIBRARY OF NATIONAL RECORDS."

NEW YORK:
A. LOVELL & CO., 3 EAST 14TH STREET.
1889.

DEDICATED

TO THE MEMORY OF THE ELEVEN HUNDRED COMMISSIONED OFFICERS OF THE VOLUNTEER REGIMENTS OF THE STATE OF NEW YORK WHO WERE KILLED, OR DIED FROM THE EFFECTS OF WOUNDS RECEIVED, OR DISEASE CONTRACTED, IN DEFENCE OF THE GOVERNMENT DURING THE WAR OF THE REBELLION, AND WHOSE NAMES, TOGETHER WITH PARTICULARS OF THEIR DEATH, APPEAR AT THE CLOSE OF THIS VOLUME.

"IT is rather for us to be here dedicated to the great task remaining before us, that from these honored dead we take increased devotion to that cause for which they gave the last full measure of devotion."—*Lincoln's Gettysburg Speech.*

PREFACE.

A CAREFUL study of the records of the War of the Rebellion, long since convinced the author and compiler of this volume that due credit had never been given to the sacrifices and sufferings, the patriotism and devotion of the Empire State in the great struggle for preserving the Union. The conspicuous part taken by New York in all the great movements of the war; her magnificent contributions to the armies of the Union; her hearty coöperation in all the financial measures of the Government; her generous aid in alleviating the miseries of the conflict,—these things were, of course, known, and had been in many ways recorded and commented upon. But no single and intelligent effort had thus far been made to bring all the facts together in a compact form, or to present concisely the brilliant record made by the State in the various forms of activity necessary to the suppression of the Rebellion.

It is the aim of the author to give just that general glance at New York's share in the honors and privations of the struggle, and to show briefly, but decisively, what a conspicuously honorable and glorious part she had in the triumph of the Union. In a volume of ordinary size this record can be traced only in outline, but the object of the author will be attained, if he succeeds in presenting to the reader an intelligent idea of the importance of the work done and the honors achieved by the Empire State in "the greatest war that ever strained the power or tested the strength of any government."

It is the hope of the author that his labors may merit the commendation of his fellow-citizens, and that they may find in the following pages a grateful reminder of an honorable past and a new incentive to pride in their native State.

NEW YORK, July 4, 1889.

CONTENTS.

CHAPTER I.
INTRODUCTION 11

CHAPTER II.
FORT SUMTER 17

CHAPTER III.
THE PRESIDENT'S CALL FOR TROOPS . . 21

CHAPTER IV.
THE MARCH OF THE SEVENTH REGIMENT . . 26

CHAPTER V.
THE UNION SQUARE MEETING—REVOLUTIONARY FEELING REVIVED—ACTION OF THE CLERGY 34

CHAPTER VI.
COLUMBIA COLLEGE—THE COLLEGE OF THE CITY OF NEW YORK AND THE UNIVERSITY OF THE CITY OF NEW YORK 38

CHAPTER VII.
THE MEDICAL PROFESSION 44

CHAPTER VIII.
THE BAR AND THE JUDICIARY . . . 51

CHAPTER IX.
THE METROPOLITAN PRESS . . . 54

CHAPTER X.

THE INFLUENCE OF WOMAN—THE SANITARY, CHRISTIAN AND ALLOTMENT COMMISSIONS, AND THE UNION LEAGUE CLUB ... 58

CHAPTER XI.

THE MERCHANTS AND BANKERS ... 66

CHAPTER XII.

THE PATRIOTISM OF NEW YORK CITY ... 77

CHAPTER XIII.

EUROPEAN HOSTILITY—MR. BEECHER'S SERVICES ABROAD—FOREIGNERS IN THE UNION ARMY ... 82

CHAPTER XIV.

NEW YORK SOLDIERY—CONSPICUOUS INSTANCES OF GALLANTRY ... 86

CHAPTER XV.

HOW NEW YORK LED IN MANY WAYS ... 89

CHAPTER XVI.

NEW YORK AT GETTYSBURG ... 93

CHAPTER XVII.

HONORS WON IN BATTLE BY NEW YORKERS ... 106

CHAPTER XVIII.

NEW YORK IN THE NAVY ... 112

CHAPTER XIX.

COLORED TROOPS AND THE RIOT IN NEW YORK ... 120

CHAPTER XX.

NEW YORK'S LOSSES IN THE WAR—CONCLUSION ... 125

APPENDIX NO. I.

ONE THOUSAND NEW YORK HEROES—AND HOW THEY DISTINGUISHED THEMSELVES ... 129

PAGE

APPENDIX NO. II.

NEW YORK REGIMENTS.
- STATE MILITIA 229
- CAVALRY 253
- ARTILLERY 267
- ENGINEER 281
- VOLUNTEER INFANTRY 283

APPENDIX NO. III.

OUR HONORED DEAD 373

THE HONORS OF THE EMPIRE STATE.

CHAPTER I.

INTRODUCTION.

The extraordinary events that lately aroused attention throughout the world towards American affairs—the great conflict that convulsed the foundations of American society, while incidentally affecting the rights and interests of all mankind, may well revive occasional recollections concerning those memorable days, and especially of the part borne by the Empire State, in a war unparalleled in the history of the civilized world for its magnitude and its intensity.

It has become a habit to say that the War of the Rebellion is forgotten, because the minds of the people are occupied with new incidents and events. But this is not, and ought not to be true, for though we have ceased to talk of the war as a subject of immediate and pressing interest, yet as the most valuable and trying experience in the history of the Nation it can never be lost sight of. When we consider the multitudinous incidents of the decade between 1860 and 1870; when we reflect upon the vast variety of important and exciting subjects included in the history of our civil war, it may not be considered an exaggeration to say that the events of that decade alone, comprise more material for history interesting to mankind, than all that is recorded of the transactions of the previous 240 years,—for it was a period like some great tragedy, into which were crowded the events of centuries. We can, therefore, appreciate far better now than ever before, the language uttered in the New York Chamber of Commerce in April, 1861, when James Gallatin, himself the son of a statesman prominent in establishing American freedom, urged his countrymen to arouse to the full importance of the crisis, prophetically exclaiming, that "history will make faithful record of our proceedings, and that that record will be consulted by future generations for encouragement, for instruction, and for warning throughout all time."

And well may we also remember the words of the gallant Theodore Winthrop, a former member of the Seventh Regiment of the New York National Guard (himself one of the earliest martyrs of the battle-field), when his patriotic spirit uttered a hope, in his last hours, "that some of his countrymen would keep careful record of passing events as we were making history hand over hand."

But neither Gallatin, Winthrop, nor any other of the far-seeing men of that early day, could then have formed any adequate conception of the long duration, vast proportions, and far-reaching consequences of the warfare thus forced upon the Nation; hostilities that cost the country, North and South, the loss of 500,000 lives, the wounding and premature death of hundreds of thousands more, and the creation of a public debt out of nothing, which imposed on the American people a burden as great as that accumulated by England in 120 years—a sum of dollars equal to more than twice the number of inhabitants on this planet.

We all know with what honest pride the descendants of our revolutionary ancestry glory in the services rendered by their forefathers in establishing our national independence. Men and women, who can thus point to the struggle that resulted in making this a nation, may well appreciate the sacrifices of those whose blood and services were spent in preserving that nationality, especially as the War of the

Rebellion involved a loss of life and treasure a thousand-fold greater than the Revolutionary War. The example of Trinity Church in some degree exemplifies this praiseworthy feeling. That corporation has within a few years deemed it due to a patriotic ancestry, to erect a noble monument in the most conspicuous portion of Broadway, to commemorate the services and sufferings of the 11,000 revolutionary patriots who perished miserably in British prisons in New York City. Nearly three times as many of our gallant volunteers (out of 270,000 who were prisoners during the war) perished by starvation and other horrors in the prison-pens of Andersonville and Libby, Salisbury and Belle Isle, rather than secure life and liberty by abandoning the flag they had sworn to defend. Of this number 46,000 New York soldiers suffered confinement, of whom 5546 died in Southern prisons, or one sixth of the whole number.

Trinity Church, by the monument it has erected, teaches the great lesson that forgiveness and forgetfulness are widely different things, and now, although charity and reconciliation are happily healing all wounds, Heaven may not forgive us, if we fail to remember the friends who defended us after unexampled efforts in preserving our National independence.

To the calm observer in a future age, aye! even to the coolest judgment in our own time, it may well seem like desperation to have contended against such complicated horrors as beset the country in 1861. There is a celebrated mountain-pass in Switzerland over which the traveller is conducted blindfold. It is said that he would lose his footing, with his reason, at a glimpse of the fearful abyss beneath. In like manner, had not God dealt with the American people, in withholding from them a premonition of the whirling maelstrom of carnage and bloodshed that lay before them, the boldest minds might have doubted the possibility of preserving our National existence, even with the loss of 300,000 heroic soldiers, and an expense to the Government and the loyal States of a sum estimated by the Secretary of the Treasury in 1880, at $12,000,000,000—ten times as much as England spent in her six years of war with Napoleon Bonaparte.

The most capacious minds of Europe, schooled to the uttermost limit in all the wisdom of the past, called the war a madness. It was a madness, if estimated by any material standard. But the loyal people of the United States had a hidden strength, which the world did not understand. It was faith. The people felt as if by an inspiration from Heaven, that the moral elements of the National cause made it irresistible. It was this which carried them through the struggle. Ten times their physical strength would not have kept them up in the absence of this sovereign faith. "Never before had the Government been thrown upon an Administration in such total wreck and ruin," said Horace Greeley. "It was as if a fleet cast ashore on Fire Island in a storm, beaten upon by the waves, and dismantled by the winds, had been hastily committed to the care of fresh officers to do what they could to rescue it from total destruction."

The forlorn condition to which the republic was reduced in 1861, was depicted by the Hon. Charles Francis Adams in language brief and vivid enough to be easily understood, and clearly remembered. "It was," said Mr. Adams, "only by a little contrivance, by passing through Baltimore in disguise, at an unexpected midnight hour that Mr. Lincoln succeeded in defeating the plot that had been formed for the seizure of his person, and to disable the country from arriving at the constitutional organization of the Executive Department. He came to Washington, and was qualified as President. But President of what? He looked around him on all branches of the Government, and everything seemed to be shaking under him. He looked to the organization of his own immediate Executive Department, and he found, wherever he touched, it was unsound. So ingeniously had the poison of rebellion been disseminated through all the ramifications of the Government, that treachery was cropping out at all points. He had to begin with a thorough scrutiny of men ; from those occupying the uppermost seats down to almost the lowest place. The President looked upon the foreign department of his government, and when he cast his eyes abroad, there was not to be found one single individual in the foreign service of the Government, who sympathized with him in his feelings or his difficulties. Nay, more, there was in the service of the Government (with the exception of some cautious individual who did not choose to commit himself) scarcely a person who was not practically disseminating distrust of the Government under which he was serving. Not a few of those produced a very considerable effect in almost every country in Europe, in creating the opinion, which became prevalent, that the complete subversion of the old system was at hand, and that a new one was inevitable.

"Very shortly after the election of Mr. Lincoln, he did me the honor to designate me as the individual to represent the country at the British Court. I reached London in about two months after the inauguration of the President. On my arrival, the first news that met me was, that 'three distinguished Commissioners' had come out from the Rebel authorities, and were at that time in London.

"I had the pleasure of learning also, that those Commissioners had confidently announced among their friends, that before I should reach London, the Government and Capitol at Washington would be in their hands; consequently I should stand no chance of being received by the British government as the representative of the United States. That is simply a specimen of the mode in which that class of persons labored throughout Europe, and it required much time and effort from that day forward, to inspire the different countries of Europe with a tolerable share of confidence in our power to maintain the Government of the United States. Let me go a step farther. When the war broke out the President looked around to see where was the military organization upon which he had to rely for the support of his coercive measures, and he found here, too, that so vigorously had treason worked itself through all the channels of military organization, that there was not one man out of three who could be trusted. He found one set of men who were, and who ultimately proved themselves to be, traitors. He found another set of men who were timid and lukewarm; and did not know whether they would support the Government, and he found still another set, who had been in the service so long, and who had arrived at such an age, that however excellent their disposition, they could not well be relied upon in the field on account of physical disability."

Such was the condition of public affairs that confronted President Lincoln at the very threshold of his term of office, and how prophetic were his words before leaving his Western home—that a duty rested upon him which was perhaps greater, than that which had devolved upon any other man since the days of Washington. But Lincoln was evidently raised up by the Divine Providence for the accomplishment of a great and sublime mission, and gathering up his manhood, with a calm dignity and a childlike trust in God, he went forth to give his labor and his life for his country.

CHAPTER II.

FORT SUMTER.

The gloomy winter of 1860-61 was passed in vain attempts to avert the catastrophe impending on the Nation, by measures of conciliation with respect to slavery. This was the exclusive subject of conversation and debate in the National Legislature and the Peace Congress, the engrossing topic of the journals, political meetings, and social circles throughout the country. Impartial records show that loyalists of all parties, anxious to preserve peace, as long as peace could be preserved without dishonor to themselves, and without destruction to their Government, made efforts to preserve peace, almost as remarkable as was their subsequent energy in defending the Nation after warfare had been forced upon them.

Actuated by a spirit of magnanimity, Mr. A. A. Low, in the spring of 1861, accompanied a respectable delegation from New York and Brooklyn, bearing to the capital of the Nation a petition signed by 40,000 citizens. They placed this petition in the hands of Mr. Seward, and desired him to use his large influence in persuading the representatives of the people to tender to the States of the South such concessions as might bring back their fealty and love for the Union. It was the wish of the committee that the memorial, as presented, should shadow forth such concessions on the part of the representatives of New York, as would satisfy the various opinions held among them, and if these were declined, "an appeal to arms and to the God of Hosts was all that was left to them." The appeal was met with insults, and Mr. Mason, of Virginia, who frequently interrupted Mr. Seward, said that his state had been arming for over a year.

Finally the Rebels seized the property of the United States—they seized its forts, its ships and its treasures. They fired upon the flag of the "Star of the West," and the Secretary of War, at Montgomery, threatened that by the 1st of May the Confederate flag should float over the Capitol at Washington, and in due time over Faneuil Hall. Boston. They told us that if we gave them a blank paper and a pencil, to write the terms of a new compact, they would not agree to it, and they announced that they were aiming to establish a Republic whose corner stone should be slavery. "They could not afford to wait for some overt act on the part of Mr. Lincoln," said Mr. Toombs, of Georgia, "for it would be fatal to the South, as a political power based upon slavery, to permit the experiment."

On the 11th of April, 1861, while Jefferson Davis and members of his Cabinet were discussing the propriety of immediately opening fire upon Fort Sumter, Mr. Gilchrist, a member of the Alabama Legislature, appeared before them and said: "Unless you sprinkle fire in the face of the people of Alabama they will be back in the old Union in less than ten days." This warning, possibly, may have stimulated the ambitious leaders of the revolt to hasten the consummation of that treasonable act, by which they hoped to commit the Southern States irretrievably to rebellion.

On the same day, orders were given for General Beauregard to open fire upon Fort Sumter,—the very stones of whose foundation came from the granite hills of the North, carried and put there by the money of the Nation. The dawn of April 12, 1861, was just breaking over the city of Charleston, revealing to that inglorious band that had in charge the ruthless deed, the walls of Sumter, surmounted by the yet unsullied splendors of our National ensign. The clock marks the hour of half-past four, when the sullen boom of a gun, fired by Col. George S. James, awoke from uneasy slumbers the hopeful patriot and determined traitor. Those gloomy echoes had not died away, when a second gun, fired by Lieut. W. H. Gibbs, confirmed the mournful truth that peace no longer lingered in the land. Soon came a third shot, fired by Edmund Ruffin, of Virginia (who, on the day of the surrender of Lee in 1865, fired a bullet through his own head), and then "freedom banished, sighed a long farewell."

Major Anderson, the representative of the Federal authority, with his little band of patriotic soldiers garrisoned the Federal fortress, now the target of insurgent artillery, and for thirty-four hours did they maintain their defence against this unholy and unequal attack. Their flag had been shot down, and though from that moment the Rebels concentrated their fire on the staff to prevent its being replaced, yet New York's first volunteer, Peter Hart, was there, who, reckless of the fast falling messengers of death, nailed it to the staff, while the cheers of his comrades arose above the smoke that enveloped them. He had been permitted to enter the fort by Governor Pickens, only on condition that he would not fight. But, though true to his pledge, his patriotism and bravery found opportunity for demonstration in the noble deed above mentioned. Peter Hart still lives, at this time, holding an humble position in the New York post office. Honorable allusion should also be made to the first martyr in the unhappy strife, who lost his life, not by the murderous shot of insurgent cannon, but by the premature discharge of a gun used in saluting the flag, as the little band of heroes marched out of the fort. He, too, was a New Yorker; his name, the first on the great roll of fame, was Daniel Hough. He had served his country for two terms in the Mexican war, and left surviving him an aged mother, two sisters and a brother, who, at the time of his death, were living in New York City. A month after his death, his brother William appeared before the

National Committee of the Common Council, and represented that the family, in poor circumstances, desired aid to have his body, which had been buried within the walls of Sumter, removed to his native city. A committee was appointed to confer with Major Anderson on the subject, but the object never was accomplished.

On Sunday afternoon, April 13, Major Anderson issued from his charred and battered fortress, his flag in shreds, his garrison smoke-begrimed, hungry, and worn down with fatigue. Fort Sumter had surrendered! and the flag that our fathers of the Revolution carried for seven weary years, through evil and through good report, through the snows and frosts of winter, and the heats and droughts of summer, until at last they brought it out at Yorktown over a captured army and a land made free and independent forever—that flag, which had never been trailed in the dust before a foreign power, had now given place to the flag of the Southern Confederacy.

The bombardment of Sumter awoke strange echoes, and touched chords long silent in the American heart. It was an act that was to close a volume in the history of the country and open a new one, in which were to be recorded the sacrifices, the heroic deeds, the unprecedented bravery of the American people for the preservation of the National Union, as well as the miseries, carnage, desolation and times of deep discouragement, closing with the declaration that the Union emerged out of all these trials in her full integrity and without the loss of a single star from the flag.

CHAPTER III.

THE PRESIDENT'S CALL FOR TROOPS.

The Rebel cannon were yet thundering in triumph over captured Sumter, when popular feeling in the loyal States crowded the electric lines with telegrams, proffering to President Lincoln all the aid required in men and money, for repelling the warfare thus forced upon the Nation. Whatever doubts swayed other minds, the President clearly saw his duty and fearlessly discharged it. His memorable proclamation of April 15, 1861, calling for 75,000 volunteers, was quickly followed by an uprising of the North which showed that a call for five-fold the force would have been answered with equal promptness. "Have we a country to save, and shall we save it?" asked the President, and wherever the words of his proclamation were read, the patriotic fire kindled in every heart, and from cities, towns and villages, all over the country, the lightning flew to bear their clear and quick response. The hardy farmers, mechanics and laborers, vied with the merchants and bankers in generous demonstrations. Capital and labor were never more signally exemplified in coöperation for the public defence. They gathered from the farm, from the workshop, from the factory ; young men of fortune left luxurious homes for the camp and the field; native and foreign born alike came forward with a common enthusiasm—all were seen rallying beneath a common flag, and exclaiming with one heart and voice, "The American Union, it must and shall be preserved, cost what it may of treasure and of blood." Surely if the voice of the people can ever be accounted as the inspiration of God, that which came to us in the united tones of the great mass of statesmen and jurists, historians and scholars, philosophers and poets, warriors and spiritual guides, must be so accepted. By the side of the Union stood Bancroft and Motley, Sparks and Palfrey, who had made the history of its free institutions their peculiar study. The harps of Bryant and Longfellow, Whittier, Holmes and Lowell were strung to the music of the Union, to inspire the hearts of the people, and nerve their arms. If we turned abroad, Gasparin, Laboulaye and Langel were seen stemming the tide of Imperial hostility in France, while John Stuart Mill, Professor Newman, Goldwin Smith, Richard Cobden and John Bright were vindicating in England the cause of the Union against the calumnies of its foes.

Fort Sumter capitulated on the 13th of April, 1861. On the 16th the President's call for troops reached Albany—the birthplace of the American Union. It was there that the first distinct movement towards a union of the Colonies, looking to strength and protection from united counsel and combined efforts, first took place. It was in defence of that city, at the battle of Saratoga, that the stars and stripes, emblems of State and National sovereignty, were displayed for the first time upon our National banner, under whose folds, in devotion to its sacred import, the greatest army ever amassed by king or emperor, was now, in the fifteenth war in which Americans had been engaged, about to decide by the arbitrament of arms, whether the Nation should live or die.

The emergencies of this critical period, the necessity for instantaneous action in supplying money, soldiers and provisions for relieving the Government, may be illustrated by the simple fact, that the National authorities at Washington were actually cut off from all ordinary peaceable connection with the people of the North, on whom they had to rely for rescue from the enemies by whom they were blockaded almost as closely as was the little band of Major Anderson at Fort Sumter. Success at Charleston instantly stimulated Rebel hostilities against Washington; and the pet project of Henry A. Wise, of Virginia, in 1857, was now about to be carried out by the attempted capture of the National capital.

In preparing for the intended assault, the Rebels not only severed the connection by railroad and telegraph northward, but actually picketed the roads, so as to prevent the surrounding farmers from supplying the Washington markets, and forbade Baltimore merchants to sell flour and other provisions to the officers of the Government. So that, if instantaneous relief had not been sent from New York, the capital might have been quickly reduced by starvation, if not previously captured by the Rebel army. *There was not a moment to be lost.* The danger of starvation, as well as the Rebel army, was rapidly approaching, and before the lightning lines were cut, the last telegram was sent by Secretary Stanton to Thurlow Weed on the night of the 18th of April, urging the chartering of steamers and the sending of troops and provisions to save the threatened capital. It will surprise many to learn that the Governor of the State of New York was actually compelled to resort to stratagem to inform President Lincoln that every practicable effort was being made to forward the required troops and provisions. The reader may well desire the name of the person that gallantly braved death as a spy, by volunteering to act as secret messenger between the State Government and the President in this critical difficulty. It was Edward B. Hill, only son of Nicholas Hill, an eminent lawyer of Albany, who, by devious routes and various disguises, fortunately succeeded in assuring President Lincoln personally, that the siege of Washington would quickly be raised by the troops rallying everywhere throughout the State.

The name of this patriotic young man and his peculiar

service to the country, should not be forgotten. When romance shall throw its glamour over the events of the war (if romance can add anything to the stern reality of such a history) some future Cooper may well irradiate the name of young Hill as a worthy counterpart of the celebrated Harvey Birch, who rendered a peculiar service to General Washington while the latter was organizing troops around New York City to aid in securing our National independence—though the gallant young Hill was not spared, like Harvey Birch, to witness the success of the cause for which he risked ignominious death as a spy having fallen heroically soon after in one of the battles in Virginia.

For many anxious days the capital was defended by only a little band of brave and gallant men under command of Cassius M. Clay. Of this handful many were New Yorkers, among them Gen. Daniel Butterfield (subsequently the hero of the battle of Resaca),

GEN. J. H. HOBART WARD,	NEHEMIAH LATHROP,
RAY W. POTTER,	GEORGE B. VAN BRUNT,
JAMES W. NYE,	CHARLES A. CLARK,
SAMUEL P. DINSMORE,	SILAS B. DUTCHER,
JOHN O. DONNELL,	WILLIS PATTEN,
WILLIAM PORTER,	JOHN G. CAMP,
B. F MUDGETT,	GEORGE S. GREGORY,
D. D. CONNOVER,	JAMES G. SLAIGHT,
JOHN N. GENIN,	HUGH TYER,
JAMES MILLWARD,	WILLIAM L. LOCKWOOD.

The imminent danger of the capital stimulated the already sufficiently-excited feelings and efforts of the city's population, and some of its energetic citizens were actually engaged at sunrise on the following morning in arousing sleepers to the necessity of despatching at least one ship-load of provisions to Washington. In answer to that appeal, the Hon. James S. Wadsworth assumed at once the whole responsibility of chartering and loading a steamer with provisions and accompanying it to Washington. Mr. Wadsworth immediately thereafter sought active duty as a soldier, and New York laid no nobler sacrifice on the altar of National integrity than when the gallant Wadsworth fell while nobly leading his division at the battle of the Wilderness. There was no instance in the war of a more high-toned surrender of comfort, fortune and life itself to principle, than that afforded in General Wadsworth's career. Possessed of enormous wealth, occupying the highest social position attainable in this country, accustomed to a life of ease and personal enjoyment, he joined the army because he believed the cause of the Union to be the highest in which the sword was ever drawn, and because he could not rest at ease in his own house while others were fighting the battle of human liberty and republican government. The patriotism of General Wadsworth was also exemplified in his son, Capt. Craig W Wadsworth, who served with the most distinguished gallantry in the cavalry branch of the service.

CHAPTER IV

THE MARCH OF THE SEVENTH REGIMENT.

WITH an enthusiasm such as this country had never before known, the regiments of the National Guard from New York City and Brooklyn now sprang to arms: and the only rivalry among them was concerning the hour and the minute when they should be placed under marching orders. And not only in 1861, but also in 1862 and 1863 these two cities furnished all the militia regiments, with the exception of the Twenty-fifth from Albany and an Ulster County regiment, in response to the three calls of the Governor for troops to march to the defence of the capital. In fact, the National Guard of New York and Brooklyn essentially constituted the National Guard of the State, and its onerous and arduous duties almost entirely fell upon them.

Language cannot sufficiently describe the feelings with which the population turned out to witness the departure of the Seventh Regiment on its line of march through the city for the scene of action. At the head of the regiment marched Col. Marshall Lefferts with his Staff, consisting of Major, Alexander Shaler; Adjutant, J. H. Liebenau; Captain of Engineers, Egbert L. Viele; Quartermaster, Locke W. Winchester; Surgeon, Timothy M. Cheeseman; Surgeon's Mate, John C. Dalton; Chaplain, Sullivan H. Weston; Paymaster, Meredith Howland; Ordnance Officer, William Patton; Assistant Quartermaster, John A. Baker; Military Secretary, Charles J. McClenachan; Commissary Sergeant, L. L. S. Clearman; R. G. Guide, Oscar Ryder; L. G. Guide, Joseph J. Morrison. Non-commissioned Staff: Robert C Rathbone,

Sergeant-Major; John H. Draper, Ordnance Sergeant; Simon C. Scott, Color Bearer; Thomas H. Pierce, Color Bearer.

The popular excitement was intensified by the news flying in "extras," as the regiment was passing through the streets, showing the difficulties which the Massachusetts Sixth Regiment had encountered from the murderous mob then controlling Baltimore. Although the Seventh, on leaving New York, expected to force a passage through Baltimore, it was made known at Philadelphia, that the authorities at Washington found it expedient to order all troops to hurry instantly to the capital with full ranks—without the delay or loss that might result from fighting their way through Baltimore. The Mayor of Baltimore, backed by Governor Hicks, of Maryland, had protested against any further movement of troops through that city. The President and General Scott agreed in a temporizing policy anxious to get reinforcements to Washington without incurring losses of life or time—*however galling* it might be to deviate from the usual route. The paramount object then was to get speedy relief in defending the capital; and hence the policy was adopted of getting around Baltimore with troops, till the safety of Washington was secured, and loyal forces could be spared to force a passage through that city or over its ruins.

This deviation from the common route, this going round Baltimore, instead of through that city, was specially annoying to the members of the Seventh Regiment, from the fact that, during a recent visit to Baltimore, they had received the hospitalities of the Baltimore regiments, and they were "anxious to see whether the same men had become their enemies, and the enemies of their country at the same time." It may be added here, that it was soon after learned that the Baltimoreans had actually made special preparations to meet the members of the Seventh on their present expedition, having, among other things, turned out its artillery regiment with ten cannon before sunrise on the morning when the Seventh was first expected on its march for Washington—"*horses all harnessed, guns waiting in the streets*, all ready, at a moment's call, to attack the Seventh Regiment, and welcome its members with *bloody hands to hospitable graves*,"—for which *benevolent* purpose, the Baltimore *American* said that Col. Pettigrew, in Charleston, was raising a mounted rifle regiment, to be specially pitted against the New York Seventh.

The Eighth Massachusetts Regiment passed through New York some hours before the Seventh Regiment started for Washington. Beyond Philadelphia, the obstacles in the path of both regiments were the same; but the commander of the former resolved to try the railroad as far as it was not yet torn up, while the Seventh chartered a steamer from Philadelphia for Annapolis. The Massachusetts troops found the railroads torn up south of the Susquehanna River, but fortunately found the large ferry-boat commodious enough to take the regiment down to Annapolis. Unluckily, by bad pilotage or treachery, the boat grounded on a mud-bank near Annapolis, where the Massachusetts troops, though anxious to be foremost on the way to Washington, saw the steamer of the Seventh pass ahead, towards and alongside of the renowned frigate "Constitution," then used as a school-ship for the Naval Academy at Annapolis—which time-honored war ship, like the Naval Academy itself, was thus saved from falling into the hands of the Secessionists, who were prowling in the neighborhood, preparing to capture both the academy and the vessel.

The Mayor of Annapolis, like his brother Mayor at Baltimore, protested against the landing of the New York and Massachusetts troops. In accordance with the views of his line officers, Colonel Lefferts replied, that the Seventh would force its way, if necessary, through Annapolis to Washington, and that, for the bloodshed which the Annapolis Corporation predicted, they must be responsible *who should oppose the march of his regiment.*

The pressing necessity for speed in reaching Washington, required that all the troops should be quickly placed ashore in marching order, and after the Seventh Regiment was landed at the Government dock in Annapolis, its steamer was sent back to relieve the Massachusetts Eighth from its unfortunate predicament.

It is not necessary to particularize the difficulties that beset the troops in repairing the railroad, which had been partly broken up by Rebels lurking in the woods around Annapolis and along the line of march towards Washington. Suffice it to say, that the arrival of the Seventh, as the vanguard of the New York troops, along with the Massachusetts Eighth, was hailed by the Governmental officers and the loyal Washingtonians, with a degree of satisfaction that can better be imagined than described.

The aid so promptly supplied by troops, as well as by money and provisions from New York, induced President Lincoln and General Scott to say to the New York Union Defence Committee, that " *the safety of the National capital* and the preservation of the archives of the Government, at a moment when both were seriously menaced, *may fairly be attributed to the prompt and efficient action of the State and City of New York.*"

Having accomplished all that was required of it during its thirty days term of service, and other troops having been brought into the service for the further prosecution of the war, the Seventh Regiment returned home, with the hearty thanks of the President and General Scott, and with the warm salutations of the people of New York, expressed through the press and otherwise. Nobly did the Seventh vindicate the truth of General Scott's response to Colonel Lefferts' entreaty that the regiment might be allowed to continue in the service after its term had expired. "Colonel," said General Scott, "yours is a regiment of officers." No less than 650 officers in the Volunteer service during the war, received their military education in the school of the Seventh. Of these, six rose to the rank of Major-General—Alexander Shaler, Abram Duryea, Lewis T. Barney, Schuyler Hamilton, Joseph E. Hamblin and John McNeill. Twenty-five became Brigadier-Generals. They were William Henry Browne, Edward Jardine, Edward L. Molineaux, Jacob E. Duryea, William H. Lawrence, Gilbert H. McKibben, Henry E. Tremain, John C. Wright, H. S. Gansevoort, John Hendrickson, John H. Oley, R. N. Bowerman, Charles A. Hartwell, Allan Rutherford, F. E. Trotter, Samuel B. Jones, William Gurney, William B. Barton, Robert Nugent, E. E. Graves, N. B. McLaughlin, J. Frederick Pierson, Egbert L. Viele, Joseph J. Morrison and O. H. Hart.

The visitor to Central Park will be interested in viewing the monument erected there to the memory of the following fifty-eight men of the Seventh Regiment, who lost their lives in the defence of their country:

ALDEN, CAPTAIN HENRY H., 42d Regiment, killed at the battle of Balls Bluff.

ADDIS, LIEUTENANT–COLONEL THOMAS J., 39th Regiment.

ARNOLD, CAPTAIN HENRY, 47th Regiment, killed in action, February 20, 1864.

BAKER, LIEUTENANT JOHN A., 147th Regiment.

BISSELL, CAPTAIN GEORGE W., 90th Regiment.

BOGERT, LIEUTENANT A. S., 65th Regiment, died June 2, 1862.

BROWN, LIEUTENANT MILNOR, 124th Regiment, killed at Gettysburg, July 2, 1863.

CHAPMAN, LIEUTENANT–COLONEL ALFORD B., 57th Regiment, killed at the Wilderness, May 5, 1864.

COWDRY, CAPTAIN EDWARD A., 95th Regiment.

DRAYSON, SERGEANT FORDRED.

ELLSWORTH, CAPTAIN ASHER M., 165th Regiment, died at Port Hudson, August 14, 1863.

FARNHAM, COLONEL NOAH L., 11th Regiment, died of wounds received at the battle of Bull Run.

FLEET, SERGEANT AUGUSTUS.

GADSDEN, ADJUTANT CHARLES A., 9th Regiment, killed at the battle of Camden, April 19, 1862.

HURST, CAPTAIN FREDERICK, 48th Regiment, died July 31. 1863, of wounds received at Fort Wagner.

HARRISON, CAPTAIN EDWARD, 74th Regiment, killed at the battle of Bristow Station, August 27, 1862.

HICKS, JR., CAPTAIN HENRY W., 165th Regiment.

HART, MAJOR ROBERT McD., 159th Regiment, killed at the battle of Cedar Creek, October 19, 1864.

KELTY, CAPTAIN EUGENE.

KINGSLAND, LIEUTENANT WM. H., 25th Regiment.

KEESE, PRIVATE J. LAWRENCE, accidentally killed while with the 7th Regiment on its march to Washington in 1861.

LE FORT, CAPTAIN GEORGE, 73d Regiment, killed in action, May 20, 1864.

LEWIS, COLONEL GEORGE W., 3d Cavalry.

LENT, CAPTAIN LOUIS H., 48th Regiment, killed in action on Morris Island, July 10, 1863.

Moies, Lieutenant John E.
Miller, Major Lindley M. H.
Morey, Captain George A., 74th Regiment, died June 23, 1862.
Mellick, Captain Simon A., 7th Cavalry.
Miller, Lieutenant Silas A.
Milligan, Captain Samuel G., 2d Cavalry, died May 28, 1862.
Mallon, Colonel James E., 42d Regiment.
O'Brien, Captain Fitz James.
Parmelee, Adjutant Lewis O.
Phipps, Gurdon S.
Plume, Captain I. Henry.
Prentiss, Major Clifton K.
Russell, Captain Theodore, 61st Regiment.
Radcliffe, Captain H. G.
Savage, Henry F.
Stevens, Lieutenant-Colonel George H.
Sands, Captain Henry A., 103d Regiment, mortally wounded at Antietam.
Seabury, Captain Robert.
Staples, Captain Wright.
Shaw, Colonel Robert G., 54th Massachusetts Regiment, killed in the assault on Fort Wagner.
Starr, Colonel Samuel H., 5th New Jersey Regiment.
Smedberg, Lieutenant Charles J.
Trenor, Captain J. J., 61st Regiment, killed at Fair Oaks, June 1, 1862.
Tremaine, Lieutenant Walter R., 132d Regiment, died December 25, 1862.

Timolat, Lieutenant Henry N.
Tucker, Lieutenant-Colonel George, 78th Regiment.
Tracy, Lieutenant Frederick A.
Van Postley, Lieutenant De.
Van Nostrand, James H.
Van Duzer, Lieutenant Charles F., 8th Cavalry.
Williams, Captain Wm. J., 56th Regiment, killed at Fair Oaks, May 30, 1862.
Winthrop, Major Theodore, killed at Big Bethel.
Wheeler, Captain William.
Welles, Private Edward B.

CHAPTER V

THE UNION SQUARE MEETING—REVOLUTIONARY FEELING REVIVED—ACTION OF THE CLERGY.

THE echoes of Sumter's guns had hardly died away when the people of New York assembled on the 20th of April, 1861, at Union Square, in the largest meeting ever held on this continent, and then and there pledged themselves, not only to this generation, but to all who should come after them, bearing their names and partaking their blood, that the cause of Constitutional Government should be upheld at every hazard. How would the nerves of Gouverneur Morris, one of those stern old fathers, who on the 14th of June, 1777, in Congress assembled, first established the Stars and Stripes as the flag of the Union—how would his nerves have been thrilled, could he have foreseen how eighty-four years afterwards, the people of New York would rally to its defence against domestic treason in that very Union Square which he, in 1807, stamped indelibly upon the Island of Manhattan—to bear the name and to be forever consecrated to the memory of that glorious Union which he had labored so successfully to call into being. "This meeting," said the Hon. Wm. M. Evarts, in 1864, when efforts were being made to secure aid for the orphans of the soldiers, " was responsible for the vigor, for the magnitude, the sufferings and bereavements of the war, and we invoke the aid and support of this great community, simply in redemption of that pledge so made, that the orphans that the war might make, should be adopted by their country." The spirit of Gouverneur Morris and of those other great names who laid the foundations of our government, found fitting commentary in the patriotic gallantry of their descendants. The four signers of the Declaration of Independence from the State of New York were all honorably represented by their great-grandsons on the battle-fields of the Rebellion: General William Floyd, by Capt. John Gelston Floyd, Jr., of the 145th Regiment; Lewis Morris, by Col. Lewis O. Morris, of the Seventh Heavy Artillery Regiment, killed at the battle of Coal Harbor; Francis Lewis, by Lieut. Manning Livingston, of the Regular Army, killed at the battle of Gettysburg (Lieutenant Livingston was also a great-grandson of Robert R. Livingston, one of the committee appointed to prepare the Declaration of Independence, and who also, on the 24th of March, 1783, informed General Washington that peace had been declared); Philip Livingston, by Capt. Stephen Van Rensselaer Cruger, of the 150th Regiment, and Lieut. Killian Van Rensselaer, of the Thirty-ninth Regiment. Captain Cruger was wounded at the battle of Resaca and left on the field for dead. He was soon after promoted for his gallantry. Gen. Samuel R. Webb, who wrote the order for promulgating the Declaration of Independence, and was Grand Marshal on the occasion of the inauguration of President Washington, was honorably represented on the battle-field by four of his grandsons, Gen. Alexander S. Webb, who was twice wounded, as his grandfather had been before him; Gen. George W Morrell, Maj. Robert Webb and Capt. Watson Webb, of the Regular Army. The first Chief Justice of the United States, John Jay, was worthily represented by his great-grandson, Col. William Jay, who served with distinction on the staffs of Generals Sykes and Meade; and his father, the Hon. John Jay, was active all through the war in promoting the interests of the Government and the welfare of the soldiers. How forcibly do these patriotic illustrations indicate the truth of the sentiment, eloquently expressed by the late President Garfield in his oration on "The Life and Services of General Thomas."

"Each individual," said the late President, "possesses forces and qualities that may date back centuries, and find their origin in the life and deeds of remote ancestors— forces, the germs of which, enveloped in the awful mystery of life, have been transmitted silently from generation to generation."

The patriotic spirit pervaded all classes of society. The clergy of all denominations showed in their language and actions, that they vividly realized the responsibilities resting on all right-minded men in redressing the calamities of their country. "All denominations share in the inspiration," said the editor of the *World*.

The National ensign was firmly fixed upon the top of the cross on the lofty steeple of Trinity by Thomas Davidson. Before an assemblage of many thousand persons he ascended the steeple step by step until he reached the top. There he stood on the cross, placing his cap upon the top, amidst the cheers of the multitude. From the pulpit of the old North Dutch Church, whose steeple looked down upon armies of Red Coats in 1776, a venerable minister bid his hearers take up arms, and declared himself ready to go with them. Pastors, so numerous that they cannot here be enumerated, offer their services as chaplains—not a few descend from the desk and enroll themselves as soldiers. Whole companies are formed from single churches and go forth with solemn approbation of their spiritual fathers. The Churchman fraternizes at last with the dissenter: they go together in a common cause and with a common faith. The stern Presbyterian, like the old Covenanter, or like the Revolutionary "Jersey Blue," puts on his harness. The Methodist, undaunted pioneer, is in the van, with his cheery, practical faith. The Baptist, most indomitable of religionists, takes his place beside his less literal brother. The venerated pastor of the Old Brick Church opens the great popular meeting with an invocation, and from another stand, an honored divine calls out to the crowd, "Why are you not on your way to Washington?" Archbishop Hughes writes to the chairman: "The Stars and Stripes have been my flag and shall be so to the end," whereupon 7000 sons of Erin press the recruiting ranks.

Trinity Church, faithful to its traditions of loyalty and patriotic sacrifices, was forward in encouraging the work of subscription and enlistment, the clergy of the parish being themselves well represented in the field. Dr. Higbee had a son in the navy; Dr. Vinton had two brothers in the army; Dr. Oglesby, a son; Dr. Dix, a father and a brother, while Dr. Weston was chaplain of the Seventh Regiment. The Rev. Dr. Gillette, of the Calvary Baptist Church, was honorably represented by his son, Col. James Gillette, who was brevetted for gallant conduct at Gettysburg; the Rev. Spencer H. Cone, by his son, Col. Spencer W Cone, of the Sixty-first regiment, the father of "Kate Claxton." The Rev. Dr. Thompson, of the Tabernacle Church, and the Rev. Dr. William I. Buddington, of the Congregational Church, should be especially remembered for the assistance they gave our wounded soldiers at the battle of Resaca, as should also be the invaluable service rendered our cause in Europe by the Rev. Dr. McClintock. The Methodist Episcopal Clergy had a noble representative in the person of Capt. Pelatiah Ward, formerly pastor at Ellenville. At the second battle of Bull Run, he seized the colors of his regiment (the Eightieth), which had been shot down, and while in the act of cheering his men on to renewed efforts, was mortally wounded. Seven Chaplains of the Volunteer regiments from the Empire State died of disease contracted while in the discharge of their duty. They were the Rev. R. O. Dwyer, Second Cavalry; the Rev. Wm. H. Gilder, Fortieth Infantry; the Rev Orlando N. Benton, Fifty-first Regiment and the Rev. Anthony Zyla, Fifty-eighth Regiment.

CHAPTER VI.

COLUMBIA COLLEGE—THE COLLEGE OF THE CITY OF NEW YORK AND THE UNIVERSITY OF THE CITY OF NEW YORK.

IT is not wonderful that the spirit shown by the religious organizations should manifest itself in the colleges, and other institutions for intellectual and moral improvement.

Columbia College, mindful of her Revolutionary fame, was true to her teachings. "Her traditions and the history of the past," said the Hon. Hamilton Fish, "are those of patriotism and love of country. In her earlier days, her numbers few, and the noise of war upon us, she gave freely of her wisdom and her blood. The names of Jay, Hamilton, Morris, Livingston and Benson are among the records of the earlier history of our country." So in the War of the Rebellion, Columbia College secured for herself an enduring record among the institutions most honored by the services of their sons in the army and navy. Over one hundred of her surviving and widely-scattered graduates (one sixth of the whole number) were among the earliest and most distinguished in the field and other branches of the service—a large proportion, when the disqualifying ages and professions are taken into account, and conclusively proves that in no other class of our countrymen was the sense of duty and loyalty to the cause more conspicuous. She was represented in every arm of the service, from Gen. Phil Kearny, of the class of '33, who fell at Chantilly by the bullets of the Sixteenth Georgia Regiment, to Color-Serg. Theodore Parkman, of the Forty-fifth Massachusetts Regiment, who fell in the engagement at Whitehall, North Carolina, December 16, 1862. "In the days of the struggle which preceded the conflict with Great Britain," said Mr. Fish, "an assemblage was held in the city of New York to denounce the Boston Port Bill. Speakers of eminence, men of age had been enlisted, and had exhausted, as they thought, the subject in denouncing the tyranny of the government. A pale stripling, weak in figure, but intellectual in countenance, arose and addressed the assemblage. At first a feeling of surprise at the audacity of a child following a man of learning, when a subject was supposed to be exhausted, pervaded the assemblage. Soon, however, they became interested in the earnestness, argument and power of the boy, who for more than an hour held them in thrall by his eloquence and persuasiveness. He brought forth reasons which his superiors in years and experience had failed to bring forth, and when at the close he released them, the cry went around: 'Who is he?' The answer was, a collegian—Alexander Hamilton. That voice of wisdom and patriotism came from Columbia College, and did more to arouse the public sentiment of the city, then loyal to the crown, than came from any other quarter." Lofty niches in the temple of fame may Columbia claim for its illustrious dead, and prominent on the honorable roll will be found recorded, besides the name of General Kearny, Col. Orlando W Morris, of the Sixty-sixth New York Regiment, killed at the battle of Coal Harbor, whose gallantry in previous battles had been recognized by his fellow citizens by the presentation to him of a sword at the Metropolitan Fair a short time before his death; Lieut-Col. William Cary Massett, of the Sixty-first Regiment, killed at the battle of Fair Oaks, and Capt. Thomas Colden Cooper, of the Sixty-seventh Regiment, killed at the battle of the Wilderness.

No less than five of Columbia's graduates, including Phil Kearny, became general officers: Henry E. Davies, Jr., Stewart L. Woodford, Thomas Swords and Edward E.

Potter. Twenty-two of the graduates served in the Seventh Regiment, six in the Seventy-first, nine in the Twenty-second and the remainder in smaller numbers in other regiments.

It was a graduate of Columbia, the late Col. J. Watts de Peyster, Jr., chief of artillery of the Second Division of the Sixth Corps, who, at the battle of Chancellorsville, fought his guns with such skill and bravery in covering the retreat, that the corps was enabled to effect a successful withdrawal. Colonel de Peyster was a brother of Col. Johnston Livingston de Peyster, who first raised the Stars and Stripes over the capitol of the Confederate States, when the Union troops entered the city of Richmond in 1865, and was also a brother of the late Maj. Frederick de Peyster, Jr., who, like his brother J. Watts, died of disease contracted in the service of his country. All these gallant men were sons of the historian, J. Watts de Peyster, who was himself educated at Columbia College.

Several of the graduates of Columbia served in the Medical Department, and it was represented in the Sanitary Commission by the late Dr. Cornelius R. Agnew, Dr. Oliver W Gibbs, and Mr. George T. Strong. The whole moral force of the college was actively exerted in behalf of the Union. Dr. F. A. P. Barnard, who was chosen President in 1864, had suffered for his loyalty while teaching in the South, and made his way North through the Confederate lines only after many hardships and detentions. The early and devoted services of Prof. Francis Lieber, in connection with the work of the Loyal Publication Society, did much towards strengthening the patriotic impulses of the North. The generous labors, too, of President Charles King, President Barnard's predecessor, and Prof. William G. Peck, in every loyal enterprise, are enough to show that the Faculty of Old Columbia were not backward in sustaining the cause for which so many of its graduates were battling on land and sea. President King had himself been a military man ; in his earlier years he was the first colonel of the Second State Militia Regiment, known as "The Washington Guard," organized in 1824. A Columbia graduate, who, like President Barnard, suffered in the South for his convictions, was the Rev. Cecil Duncan, who stood out boldly against disunion, and was forced at last to fly from New Orleans, leaving his family behind him.

The city's two other conspicuous institutions of learning—the College of the City of New York, and the University—were as prompt to come to the defence of the Union as Columbia College. When the news was received that Fort Sumter was fired upon, one of the students of the College of the City of New York. Gilbert M. Elliott, unfurled the Stars and Stripes from the top of the college building, and in an address declared that he would defend his country's honor with his life's blood. He kept his promise faithfully, for at the battle of Lookout Mountain, while in command of his regiment, the 102d New York, after exhibiting the most extraordinary bravery, he fell dead from the bullet of a sharpshooter. For his gallantry in the same battle, and in the same regiment, another graduate of the college deserves to be ranked among the heroes of the war—Lieut. Phineas C. Kingsland. A soldier whose name ranks high among the leading spirits of the great struggle, Gen. Henry E. Tremain, was a graduate of the college. General Tremain was an aide to General Sickles, and, throughout the battle of Chancellorsville, was everywhere seen where the danger was greatest, animating the troops with his presence and carrying out the orders of his chief. Among the graduates of the college who rose to high rank through force of merit, was Lieut. James L. Van Buren, who was promoted to the rank of Brigadier-General, and died in the service. Maj. Edward F. Young, of the Fourth Heavy Artillery, has a place, also, on the roll of honor, dying in 1863 of disease contracted while in the discharge of his duty. Lieut. William Cullen Bryant Gray and Lieut.

Edward Wightman, both graduates of the college, also lost their lives in the Union armies. Among the graduates who served with credit in the Medical Department of the army, were: Dr. Howard Pinkney, Surgeon of the Eighty-third Regiment; Dr. Samuel N. Fiske, of the Twenty-fifth; Dr. Benjamin Ellis Martin, of the Fifth (Duryea's Zouaves), and that most eminent and successful surgeon—Dr. Robert F. Weir.

Judge Advocate Asa B. Gardener, formerly lieutenant in the Thirty-first Regiment, also received his education at the College of the City of New York, as did Capt. David D. Terry, of the 176th; Capt. Eugene Douglass, of the Forty-seventh; Capt. Rodney G. Kimball, of the Forty-fourth; Capt. Benjamin F. Lee, of the 126th; Capt. Thorndike Saunders, of the Fifty-seventh; Capt. James M. Tripp, of the Thirty-ninth; Lieut. Dennis F Sullivan, of the Sixty-ninth; Lieut. Richard P. Strong, of the 139th, and Capt. Wm. H. Sanger.

The University of the City of New York—the smallest of the three colleges, did its ample share towards supporting the Government, both at home and in the field.

A spirit of active patriotism was clearly shown at the very outset of the Rebellion, and on the 3d of May, 1861, the American flag was raised from the roof of the building by Captain Jones, who, while in command at Harper's Ferry a short time before, set fire to the Arsenal, so as to prevent the arms therein from falling into the hands of the enemy. On the same day the gallant Baker, then a United States Senator, and soon to meet his death at Ball's Bluff, delivered an eloquent address, calling upon the students to do their part in defence of their country. Twenty patriotic young men soon responded to the call for volunteers. Of these, the author has records only of the following: Col. Gouverneur Carr (now an attaché of the New York *Tribune*), who became captain in " Duryea's Zouaves," from which position he was promoted for gallantry to be major of the 165th

Regiment; Lieut. Hanson C. Gibson and Capt. Wm. W. Stephenson, both of whom were officers in the 165th, with their classmate, Colonel Carr; Lieut. John Townsend Connolly, of the 182d; Lieut. Charles W Woolsey; Lieut. Walter R. Marsh, of the Fifteenth (Engineers); Private James L. Millard, of the Thirteenth; Chaplain Jesse Brush, of the 158th; Surg. Henry N. Fisher; Serg. Samuel B. Parish. Second Kansas Cavalry, and Capt. H. W T. Mali, of the Twentieth Massachusetts.

CHAPTER VII.

THE MEDICAL PROFESSION AND THE BAR.

No less prompt and spirited than that of the clergy and the scholarly classes, was the response of the medical profession. The surgeon's duty is not, as is often supposed, one of slight exposure, for he is often called to render his humane offices in the very fore-front of battle, and although ardently devoted to his profession, he had not, like his brother officers, the incentive of promotion and recognition for distinguished services, for he was unable to gain any higher rank than that in which he first entered the army; whether as surgeon of a regiment or medical director of a corps, he remained always a major. But notwithstanding the hardships, the dangers, and the comparative obscurity of the service, the call for troops filled at once the ranks of the Surgical Staff with volunteers of the highest character and standing. When the assistant-surgeon of the Seventh Regiment resigned, just before its departure for the war, Prof. John C. Dalton, of the College of Physicians and Surgeons, with but a moment's notice, announced to his numerous class his desire to serve his country, and sprung into the vacant position in the ranks, with the same spirit that took Israel Putnam from the field he was ploughing, or that sent Dr. Joseph Warren with a Major-General's commission in his pocket into the ranks of Bunker Hill.

The medical men of New York, of all classes and schools, veterans and students, offered their services to the country with an enthusiasm that could not be surpassed. Professors, such as the noble Dalton and Dr. Gordon Buck, Dr. Alex. B. Mott, Dr. Thomas M. Markoe, Dr. William Detmold, Dr. Finnell, Dr. Carnochan, Dr. James R. Wood, Dr. John P Garrish, Professor Parker and Dr. Abraham J. Berry, forsook their chairs to render what aid they could in relieving the miseries of a soldier's life.

At home, Dr. Frank H. Hamilton (whose son, Col. Theodore B., of the Sixty-second Regiment, acquitted himself with the greatest gallantry at the battle of Chancellorsville), Dr. Bradford R. Wood, Dr. Rufus King Browne, Dr. Sandford B. Hunt, and many others, gave their services in preparing undergraduates for the duties of assistant-surgeons in the field. At an improvised meeting of students, held in the amphitheatre of Bellevue, the illustrious ex-president of the College of Physicians and Surgeons, the venerable Stephens, burst forth into exclamations of patriotic devotion that brought fountains of water to the eyes of men unused to tears. "Oh, that I were a young man again," said he, and the grand old doctor actually seemed for a moment to be carried back three-quarters of a century, and his countenance was radiant with the ever youthful heroism that could be aroused only by such a cause.

Among medical men, cowardice is the one unpardonable sin. They are trained under a code of ethics which allows no man, under any circumstances, to turn his back upon danger. The same courage that made them rush into the deadly atmosphere of Norfolk and Chicago, at the call of suffering, and which fills every hospital and city where the plague rages fiercest with hosts of recruits, now also draws to the most dangerous branch, even of army service, the finest intellect and the highest skill and science of an unselfish profession.

"New York," said the late Dr. John Swinburne, of Albany, Medical Superintendent for the State Troops, in his official report for 1863, "has made the best selection of surgeons for her regiments of any State in the Union. For this judicious and extraordinary selection," continued Dr. Swinburne, "we are indebted to Surgeon-General Vanderpoel, of whom the medical profession of the State may well be proud."

The first surgical operation under fire, performed during the war, was made by a New York surgeon—the late Dr. Rufus H. Gilbert, of the Fifth Infantry. Dr. Gilbert, it will be remembered, subsequently became famous as the projector of the elevated railroad system.

Forty-five surgeons belonging to the armies of the Union were killed, and seventy mortally wounded. Of this number only three belonged to the volunteer regiments from the Empire State—William H. Rulison, of the Ninth Cavalry; Otto Shenk, of the Forty-sixth Infantry, and John Hurley, of the Sixty-ninth. Twenty-eight New York surgeons died of disease contracted while in the discharge of their duty. They were:

ROLLIN T. BAKER, 12th Cavalry;
JOHN F. ROBINSON, 15th Cavalry;
LEWIS F. BAKER, 6th Artillery;
BYRON L. FLOWER, 9th Artillery;
CONRAD JOACHIM, 15th Artillery;
EDWARD MOELLER, 15th Artillery;
ASA B. SNOW, 1st Engineers;
RICHARD H. PALMER, 10th Infantry;
CHARLES H. WILCOX, 21st Infantry;
JOSEPH B. ARTHERLY, 22d Infantry;
STEPHEN GRISWOLD, 38th Infantry;
MICHAEL E. FOYE, 38th Infantry;
CHARLES E. HALSEY, 40th Infantry;
THOMAS H. SAWYER, 43d Infantry;
GEORGE H. LEONARD, 51st Infantry;

Taylor Elmore, 137th Infantry;
Richard W Faucett, 155th Infantry;
Samuel H. Brown, 174th Infantry;
William P. Bush, 61st Infantry;
John M. Forsher, 66th Infantry;
Richard H. Hinman, 67th Infantry;
Daniel P Van Vleek, 128th Infantry;
Patrick R. Brannigan, 99th Infantry;
Johnson Clarke, 99th Infantry;
Frederick H. Pettit, 106th Infantry;
Charles Mitchel, 110th Infantry;
Charles E. Washburn, 113th Infantry;
Henry A. Collier, 120th Infantry.

The war experience of many a medical man proved to be the foundation of his future success, and many volunteer surgeons have since attained a most enviable position in their profession, among whom may be mentioned, the well-known and distinguished surgeon—Dr. Robert F. Weir; also Dr. Andrew H. Smith, of the Forty-third Regiment; Dr. Charles E. Hackley, of the Second Cavalry, who was honorably mentioned in General Kilpatrick's report of the great cavalry expedition in 1863, under General Stoneman; Dr. Richard S. Connelly, of the 123d, who, at the battle of Chancellorsville, took his station in the hottest of the fight, and dressed the wounded where they fell; Surg. Alexander A. Edmerston, of the Eighteenth; Surg. Martin S. Kittenger, of the 100th; Surg. George McAllister, of the Seventy-first; Surg. Owen Munson, of the Fifth, and Surg. John D. Osborne, of the Forty-second, all of whom voluntarily remained with our wounded soldiers on the battle-field, rather than desert their suffering comrades; Surg. George C. Bennett, of the Seventh Cavalry, who acquitted himself with conspicuous credit on the battle-field; Surgs. Theodore Artand and Felix Petard, of the Fifty-fifth, who were honorably mentioned in Colonel de Trobriand's report of the battle of Williamsburg; Surg. William L. Harding, of the Ninth, honorably mentioned in Colonel Kimball's reports of the battles of South Mountain and Antietam; Surg. George H. Humphreys, of the Ninth, commended in Colonel Kimball's report of the battle of South Mills; Surg. John S. Jemison, of the Eighty-sixth, who was unremitting in his care and skilful treatment of those under his charge at the Second Battle of Bull Run; Surg. Charles J. Nordguist, of the Eighty-third, who was presented with a gold watch as a mark of appreciation for the services rendered by him in the discharge of his professional duties; Surg. Frank Ridgway, of the Seventy-third, who constantly exposed himself to danger at the battle of Williamsburg, in his endeavors to relieve his bullet-stricken comrades; Dr. J. W Robinson, of the Eighty-second, who was especially conspicuous in the prosecution of his labors at the battle of Seven Pines, and has been reported "missing" since 1862; Surg. Henry Root, of the Fifty-eighth, who gained great credit for the hardships and dangers sustained by him at the battle of Chancellorsville; Surg. Truman H. Squire, Eighty-ninth Regiment, alluded to in honorable terms by Colonel Kimball in his report of the battle of South Mills; Surg. J. G. Porteous, 118th Regiment, of whom Gen. Butler said in General Orders: "Surg. Porteous deserves the highest credit for his bravery and attention to his duties, being the only surgeon in the Second Brigade, Eighteenth Corps, who advanced with his regiment in the charging column at the battle of Chapin's Farm;" and Surg. George de Landre, 158th Regiment, of whom General Butler said: "While under fire, Surgeon de Landre worked faithfully night and day dressing the wounds of those who required attention, without reference to the corps to which they belonged;" Surg. B. Ellis Martin, Fifth Regiment, honorably acquitted himself at the battle of Big Bethel;

Surg. Alfred Powell, Eighty-second Regiment, who nobly surrendered himself to the rebels rather than desert his wounded comrades at the battle of Bull Run; Surg. Wm. F. Swalm, Eighty-fourth Regiment, honorably mentioned in Medical Director King's Report of the battle of Bull Run; Assistant Surg. Joseph E. West, Fourteenth Regiment, who had charge of most of the hospitals in the Army of the Potomac, and was especially thanked by the Medical Bureau for his zeal and skill in the care of the patients under him; Surg. Francis M. Wright, Seventh Cavalry Regiment, who acquitted himself nobly in engagements near Suffolk; Surg. Joseph M. Homiston, Eighty-fourth Regiment, honorably mentioned in Medical Director King's report of the battle of Bull Run; Surg. Roger W Pease, Tenth Cavalry, whose services were so highly appreciated that he was promoted to be Medical Director of the Cavalry Corps of the Army of the Potomac; Surg. Nelson D. Fergerson, Eighth Cavalry, who was captured while in the discharge of his duties and suffered the torments of a Rebel prison; Surg. Alfred D. Wilson, Third Light Artillery; Surg. Frank W Benjamin, Third Artillery; Surg. Archibald F Mudie, Third Artillery; Surg. George E. McDonald, Twelfth Cavalry; Surg. John M. Palmer, Eighty-fifth Regiment, and Surg. Pitkin B. Rice, 132d Regiment, who battled bravely with the pestilence in North Carolina, in 1863.

To be also mentioned for their constant devotion to the sick and wounded in hospitals and on the field, are: Dr. Aaron P Dalrymple, of the First Engineers; Dr. Robert Ormiston, of the Thirteenth State Militia Regiment, and now one of Brooklyn's most eminent practitioners; Dr. Thomas M. Flandreau, of the 146th; Surg. J. B. W Bidlack, of the Sixty-second; Dr. John W Hunt, of the Tenth; Dr. Julius A. Skilton, of the Eighty-seventh; Dr. Samuel R. Elliott, of the Sixty-third; Dr. Frederick A. Castle; Dr. Armand Dufloo, of the Twenty-fifth; Dr. O. Sprague Paine, of the Second Artillery; Dr. William Balser, of the Fifteenth Artillery; Dr. Benjamin Howard, of the Third Artillery; Dr. George V Skiff, of the Twelfth Infantry; Dr. Sylvanus S. Mulford, of the Thirty-third; Dr. John H. Thompson, of the Fortieth; Dr. W O. McDonald, of the Sixty-fifth; Dr. Charles S. Wood, of the Sixty-sixth; Dr. Henry E. Crampton, of the Ninety-third; Dr. Stephen G. Champlin; Dr. Robert A. Cameron; Dr. Abraham S. Cox; Dr. George M. Sternberg, Dr. Joseph H. Stewart, Dr. S. Fleet Speir, of Brooklyn, and Dr. Joseph Lawrence Hicks, of the First Regiment, now a leading physician of Flushing, L. I.

CHAPTER VIII.

THE BAR AND THE JUDICIARY.

WHILE the different professions furnished many heroes and victims to the war, the Bar gave the most. But this was no new connection between the court and the field. In the Revolution the Bar took the lead in the cause of the country. The greatest judge of the Supreme Court of the United States, John Marshall, had been a soldier, and the earliest commanding general of our Revolutionary army, Artemus Ward, was afterwards a judge. It was, therefore, right that the Bar should again take the lead in defending the Union and upholding the majesty of the law. "It was by virtue of the law," said an eminent jurist, "that the soldier was enlisted; by virtue of the law that regiments were formed and armies organized and marshalled; by virtue of the law that there was the tread of armed men among us, and that the drum rattled and even that the cannon roared to save and protect the Constitution. It was because the Rebels violated and trampled upon the Constitution that we, who sustained and supported it, brought them to account by the arbitrament of arms."

On the 22d of April, 1861, a meeting of the members of the Bar was held in New York City, and not only were resolutions supporting the Government passed, but the sum of $30,000 was quickly subscribed, to aid in preparing the regiments for the field. Judge Edmonds, in a patriotic address, said that he was himself once a colonel, and although over sixty-five years old, he felt the fire of youthful blood running through his veins, and was still able to take charge of any military organization of which the members of the Bar might honor him with the command. Several of the best regiments that went to the war were officered by well-known members of the Bar, and most of these legal heroes distinguished themselves nobly, and the civil profession to which they belonged received some part of the lustre of their military achievements.

From the long list of gallant men whose names adorn the records of the New York Bar, may be mentioned Gen. Francis C. Barlow, of whom General Caldwell, in his official report of the battle of Antietam, said: "Whatever praise is due to the most distinguished bravery, the utmost caution and quickness of perception, the greatest promptitude and skill in handling troops under fire, is justly due to General Barlow"; Gen. Henry A. Barnum, who after acquitting himself with the utmost gallantry in the battles on the Peninsula, led his regiments with great skill and bravery at Gettysburg and Lookout Mountain, where he was badly wounded; Gen. Daniel E. Sickles, who was brevetted brigadier-general in the Regular Army for bravery at Fredericksburg and major-general for gallant conduct at Gettysburg; Gen. Henry W Slocum, formerly colonel of the Twenty-seventh Regiment; Gen. Calvin E. Pratt, formerly colonel of the Thirty-first, who was wounded while gallantly leading his regiment into action at the battle of Gaines Mills; Gen. Ferris Jacobs, who, while major of the Third Cavalry Regiment, was selected to proceed with his command and destroy the costly structure in North Carolina, known as the Rocky Mount Railroad Bridge, a task he accomplished in the most admirable manner; Gen. Benjamin F Tracy, colonel of the 109th, and now Secretary of the Navy; Gen. George H. Sharpe, formerly colonel of the 120th; Gen. William J. Nagle, the eldest of four brothers, all of whom enlisted in the service; Gen. Frederick Townsend, of Albany, to whose efficiency as adjutant-general is due the fact that the State sent so many troops to the field, and whose subsequent career in the army was in the highest degree honorable; Gen. William E. Strong; Gen. David Stuart; Gen. John Cochrane, formerly colonel of the Sixty-fifth; Col. Lewis Benedict, of the 162d; Col. Wm. H. McMahon; Lieut.-Col. George W Arrowsmith, of the 157th, killed at the battle of Gettysburg; Gen. James C. Rice, formerly colonel of the Forty-fourth Regiment, killed at the battle of Spottsylvania, and whose last words were "Turn me over, that I may die with my face to the enemy"; Col. William O. Stevens, of the Seventy-second, killed at the battle of Chancellorsville; Col. David S. Cowles, of the 128th, killed at the battle of Port Hudson; Col. Lionel A. Sheldon, of the Forty-second Ohio; Col. Jesse C. Smith; Col. Samuel A. Rice, of the Thirty-third Iowa; Col. Robert G. Ingersoll, of the Eleventh Illinois Cavalry, and Col. Charles H. Larrabee, of the Twenty-fourth Wisconsin. Among the officers of a lower rank, whose record for gallantry reflects credit upon the profession to which they belonged, were Maj. Charles McL. Knox, of the Ninth New York Cavalry, one of the most active, zealous and valuable cavalry officers in the army; Lieut. Philip L. Wilson, of the Fifth Regiment; Capt. Frederick Scoville, of the Eighth Cavalry; Lieut. Albert Wyckoff, and Lieut. Edward Carrington, of the 143d Regiment, the latter killed in action on March 6, 1865.

CHAPTER IX.

THE METROPOLITAN PRESS.

THE public press should be mentioned as among the foremost influences and powerful agencies in preserving the National Union, by arousing attention to the dangers of the times, and in furnishing materials for their history. Never was such opportunity presented for journalistic enterprise, and never was any great responsibility more readily and successfully encountered. There is a class of persons who affect to speak contemptuously about "newspaper statements," but as nearly all our history must now come through newspaper channels, for nothing escapes newspaper notice, it may be well for them to reflect upon the words of one of our leading statesmen when consecrating the battlefield of Gettysburg.

"The astonishingly minute, accurate, and graphic accounts of the battle contained in the journals of the day," said Edward Everett, "prepared from personal observation, by reporters who witnessed the scenes and so often shared the perils which they described, will readily supply the deficiency of my condensed statements. And where can we find greater accuracy," continued Mr. Everett, "than in the leading newspapers? The error which one journal makes is very speedily corrected by the others, and in this age of inquiry and debate, if truth ever emerges from the well in which she is said to abide, it is to clothe herself in print." Carlyle said: "The newspapers constitute the essence of all history," and Daniel Webster expressed his sense of their importance when he said: "If you want to find genuine history, you must look for it in the newspapers and in private letters."

The energy, liberality and ability of the editorial corps of the principal city journals during the War of the Rebellion, more than realized all that Gallatin and Winthrop hoped for, when urging their countrymen to keep careful record of passing events for the instruction of future ages. The metropolitan journals were all ably represented by regular and occasional correspondents, amid all the scenes of active warfare, and the expenses of the *Herald*, though disproportionately large, may be especially mentioned, as indicating something of the great outlay which other leading journals readily assumed; since that paper alone maintained a corps of over sixty war correspondents at an expense of about half a million dollars. The story of the class of men, which the exigencies of the war called into existence for the second time in this country,—army correspondents,—if faithfully told, would comprise many creditable chapters in the history of the Rebellion. Faithful to the journals they represented, untiring in the pursuit of such news as the public required, and sharing all the hardships and dangers of campaign life, without military rank or honors, they not infrequently played the double part of soldiers and civilians with infinite credit to themselves and the profession to which they belonged.

The accounts of movements and battles, by some of those correspondents, often surpassed in clearness and accuracy the official reports, and some of them equalled Victor Hugo's description of the battle of Waterloo. They were written by gentlemen of education, who were perfectly competent to describe a tactical or strategical movement, such as Mr. Whitelaw Reid, Mr. Edmund C. Stedman, now the "banker poet," Maj. George F. Williams, Mr. George W Smalley, Mr. Henry Villard, now the famous railroad magnate, Mr. E. A. Paul, Col. Finley Anderson, Mr. William Swinton, Mr. George Crounse, Mr. W F. G. Shanks, Mr.

John Russell Young, Mr. Truman A. Merriman, Mr. Amos J. Cummings, Mr. D. P. Conyngham, Mr. S. T. Buckley, Mr. John A. Connery, Mr. Galen A. Osborne, Mr. L. A. Hendricks, Mr. George H. Hart and Mr. G. E. P Doyle. Such are a few of the men to whom the future historian will be indebted for the most valuable material in preparing a history of the great rebellion. Official reports do not, and never did, convey to the general reader a comprehensive and correct idea of the nature of a great battle. Wellington's reply to Edward Everett, that he could no more describe Waterloo, than he could tell him of all that was occurring in the ball-room where they stood, illustrates the imperfection of official reports.

As an indication of the enterprise and accuracy of the metropolitan press, the following statements from the Confederate press is very convincing. On the 29th of November, 1864, the Richmond *Examiner* said: "The authorities are mistaken in supposing that they deprive the enemy of much information by keeping it out of the press. The New York *Herald*, of the twenty-first, received yesterday, is a proof of the fact. They know more of the affairs in Georgia than we could tell them, and they get the Georgia papers long before they come to Richmond."

In August, 1861, there was great excitement in Richmond, caused by the receipt of a New York journal containing an account of the military forces of the Confederacy. So detailed and so accurate was the report that the Confederate Congress proposed to order an investigation, on the ground that no one in a subordinate position could have prepared such a paper for the New York press. During 1864, the Richmond *Examiner* said: "There have been instances in which the speculations of the New York press have been the real shadows of coming events. The assignment of Gen. Joseph E. Johnston to the command of our armies in Northern Virginia, and the removal to that quarter of a large body of his veteran troops. was not known in Richmond beyond the circle of the initiated of the war office, yet we see the whole of our plans, as regards our campaign of invasion, spread before the world in the columns of a leading New York journal."

CHAPTER X.

THE INFLUENCE OF WOMAN—THE SANITARY, CHRISTIAN AND ALLOTMENT COMMISSIONS, AND THE UNION LEAGUE CLUB.

THE enthusiasm that pervaded all portions of the community was nowhere more remarkable than among the ladies of New York. It would be interesting to trace the development of woman through the leading events that have marked the progress of our country's history. "Woman's influence," said the Rev. Dr Storrs, " was instrumental in the discovery of this continent; it really flashed out upon Columbus, from the dark eyes of the girl he followed in the streets of Lisbon, though he was unconscious of it. This continent, from its grace and delicacy of outline has been considered the feminine representative of the continents, in comparison with the more massive breadth of the eastern. It might be called woman's sphere; for here she is especially protected; here she has the benefits of free government, free institutions."

While the male portion of the population were counselling for the public defence, a notice appeared, calling on the ladies generally to meet in the Church of the Puritans, to organize a society for furnishing hospital materials and make other humane provisions for aiding the soldiers who might become sick and wounded during the struggle between the Government and its assailants. This was the first step in the movement that finally culminated in the great meeting of three thousand ladies in the Cooper Institute, the call for which was signed by:

Mrs. General Dix,
Mrs. Gerard Stuyvesant,
Mrs. Merritt Trimble,
Mrs. Peter Townsend,
Mrs. Astor,
Mrs. Charles Butler,
Mrs. Marquand,
Mrs. Hamilton Fish,
Mrs. Judge Daly,
Mrs. Henry Lawrence,
Mrs. Aspinwall,
Mrs. Amos R. Eno,
Mrs. William M. Evarts,
and many others.

"This assemblage of ladies," said the *Herald*, "was one of the grandest and most noble sights that it is possible for the eye to rest on. Upwards of three thousand philanthropic ladies assembled for the purpose of adopting a plan of concerted action—devoting themselves to the cause of the suffering soldiers and their bereaved relatives and friends. Among those thousands of Spartan women were many whose delicacy of physique showed that they had been nurtured in the lap of luxury. What a noble sight it was to see many of those ladies offering to place themselves in the imminent perils of the battle-field, to attend to the wants of the bullet-stricken and sword-pierced soldiers—and when all hope is lost; when his life is on the wing from the field of carnage to the valley of peace—to lean over him like a ministering angel, and pour such balm into his bursting heart as will send him on his long journey in a sublime dream to elysian happiness? Woman's mission is not war, but peace, and she will appear on the battle-fields of the Rebellion not in the character of an Amazon, but as an angel of mercy—a messenger of deliverance—a comforter in the hour of need, and in the last moments of the dying soldier; in charity and meekness she will pursue her glorious work of alleviating human suffering when no other hand than hers is near to give help and succor, and she will do this without the prospect of fee and reward, in the pure goodness of her heart."

A long list could be made of those Nightingales of New

York, conspicuous among whom were Mrs. Dr. Edward Vanderpoel, Mrs. Susan B. Edson, Mrs. Anna E. Garrish, Mrs. Caroline M. Kirkland, Miss Cornelia Hancock, of Albany, Miss S. E. Hall, Mrs. Isaac Palmer, Miss Clara Rapke, Mrs. S. M. Barnum, Miss Susan K. Dwyer, Miss Mary A. Stanley, Mrs. Young, of Ithaca, known in the Grand Army as "Aunt Becky" Young, Mrs. Joseph Howland, Miss Woolsey, Mrs. S. H. Gibbons, Mrs. E. J. Russell, Mrs. R. H. Spencer and Miss Dada. If Massachusetts can claim Charlotte Cushman, to whose memory the nation owes a debt of gratitude for the service she rendered our cause in Europe, New York can point with equal pride to the late Miss Mary L. Booth. At the very opening of the war Miss Booth translated Count de Gasparin's "Uprising of a Great People," and in a fortnight afterward it went over the country like a trumpet-blast. "It was a whole phalanx in the cause of human freedom," said Charles Sumner, and President Lincoln took pains to send her a personal letter of thanks for what she had done in giving fresh heart to the American people. "The value of what she did," says Miss Harriet Prescott Spofford, in a recent sketch, "was fully recognized, and it has been everywhere felt and acknowledged that her part in kindling and upholding the earnestness of the people was not surpassed by the efforts of any one man, or woman, during the years of the war."

The Cooper Union meeting soon bore practical fruit. The impetus there given to the movement for the relief of the suffering soldiers, was strong enough to lead to the formation of a Woman's Central Relief Association, which took charge of all the preparations for work in the field. Thousands of wounded soldiers owe their lives to the aid furnished by this public-spirited body of women; for by their efforts the whole hospital service was strengthened and made more efficient. The headquarters of the association remained in New York. On the board of managers were these well-known ladies:

Mrs. Hamilton Fish,   Mrs. H. Bayles,
Mrs. Cyrus W Field,   Mrs. N. D. Sewell,
Mrs. Charles P Kirkland, Mrs. G. L. Schuyler,
Mrs. Dr. Bayard,   Mrs. C. Griffin,
Mrs. Charles Abernethy,   Mrs. Laura Doremieux,
Mrs. V Botta.

" The American Sanitary Commission "—the great organization which left its humane impress on the thousand scenes of suffering on the battle-field and in the hospitals, and which established a model for philanthropic effort in meliorating the horrors of warfare throughout the world—was one of the glorious results of the benevolent impulses that actuated the patriotic movements of the ladies of New York. Never was such exemplary care bestowed on the victims of warfare, as was given by this excellent association, wherever its services and supplies were most needed. It is memorable, not only for the good it accomplished directly, but also for its effect in stimulating benevolent people everywhere to render aid in similar humanitarian ways. The exemplary fidelity and economy with which the whole enterprise was managed, was acknowledged by all who were most conversant with its operations, and probably never was an equally large amount—about five millions of dollars by the parent society and two millions more by auxiliaries, making a total of seven millions of dollars—spent in benevolence more wide-spread and in ways whereby vast armies were benefitted in hospitals and battle-fields. The periodical reports and the final history of the Sanitary Commission are worthy monuments to its excellent officers, and the late Rev. Henry W Bellows, as its president, the late Dr. Cornelius R. Agnew, the late Mr. George T. Strong, Dr. Charles J. Stillé, Gen. George W Cullum and the Rev. Gordon Winslow, need no other claim on general respect than is furnished by the record of their zealous and laborious services in promoting this benevolent enterprise. The great services rendered by the Sanitary Commission, and by other benevolent societies in which the ladies were efficient auxiliaries, were strikingly presented by General Meade when alluding particularly to the immense number of wounded soldiers in the three days' battle of Gettysburg. "It has been my duty," said General Meade, "to make inquiry as to the practical working and benefit of the United States Sanitary Commission, and it affords me great pleasure to bear testimony, so far as the Army of the Potomac is concerned, to the inestimable benefits and blessings conferred by this noble association on the suffering and sick and wounded soldiers. A few facts in connection with this point may be of interest to you. At the battle of Gettysburg the number of wounded of our army alone, amounted to nearly fourteen thousand; those of the enemy left on the field, were estimated by our medical officers as amounting to eight thousand. This would make in all, twenty-two thousand suffering beings, requiring immediate care and attention to save life. Few people can realize such large numbers," continued the General, "but if I tell them that should they fill and pack your Academy of Music, (which holds 3500 people) six times, and then imagine every soul in this immense crowd wounded, they will have some idea of the great work for humanity on the battle-field of Gettysburg."

The gentlemen who conceived, organized and controlled the United States Sanitary Commission were also the originators of the Union League Club. The Rev. Henry W Bellows, in his history of the club, says: "It is the child of the Sanitary Commission. Professor Walcott Gibbs was the first to suggest that the idea on which the Sanitary Commission was founded needed to take on the form of a club, which should be devoted to the social organization of the sentiment of "unconditional loyalty" to the Union, and he chose Mr. Frederick Law Olmsted as the first person to be consulted and advised with, and the latter at length became the corner-stone of the Union League Club.

The club soon had the opportunity of repaying the Sanitary Commission for its parentage, for the whole membership became ardent and active supporters of the commission, and the great Metropolitan Fair, which poured over a million dollars into the treasury, was organized in its club house. The influence of the club was manifested in many ways. The conferences of the directors of banks and trust companies at the club house, led to the joint action of the banks and the Secretary of the Treasury in negotiating Government bonds, a service often acknowledged by Mr. Chase himself.

One of the most beneficial arrangements for promoting the welfare of soldiers and the comfort of their families, was the "Allotment Commission"—an excellent adjunct of the Sanitary Commission. While the latter provided for the relief of wounded soldiers in active service and in hospitals, the former arranged for securing the pay of the volunteers and forwarding it to the women and children at home. The promptness and fidelity with which vast sums of money were thus received from the soldiers and paid over to their families, is one of the most satisfactory features of those troubled times. It cost much severe labor and zealous effort to make it understood through the army, that the Allotment Commission would attend without compensation to this arduous service; but when fully comprehended, the soldiers generally gave requisite authority to the commission to collect all or most of their pay and forward it to their families. The effects were most salutary. The soldier became more economical in avoiding needless expense when he knew that every dollar thus saved by him would thus immediately promote the comfort of those he had left at home. It required extraordinary exertion on the part of the commission to accomplish their benevolent work for a considerable period after the war begun, as their progress was impeded by wintry weather and by almost impassable roads. Nearly one hundred of the State regiments were personally visited by some or all of the commission, from the necessity of explaining the law to the officers and men—by addressing company after company, and obtaining signatures to its rolls, authorizing the commissioners to collect the monthly pay. The service thus rendered by the commissioners was at least equally important as any that could ordinarily be given in discharging soldierly duty, and the success of their philanthropic operations may be measurably understood from the fact that, in their very first annual report, it was shown that the sums collected and paid over to the families and friends of volunteers reached the large total of over $5,000,000 in a single year. These are a few of the facts connected with the Allotment Commission—the labors of which were facilitated by the aid of Col. George Bliss, Jr., —then Paymaster-General of the State. But foremost in the scale of merit and honor are the Allotment Commissioners themselves—the late Theodore Roosevelt, William E. Dodge, Jr., and Theodore B. Bronson, upon whom devolved the principal labor in the discharge of these most arduous duties.

Never before was such exemplary care taken of the spiritual as well as the physical welfare of soldiers, as was bestowed upon the armies of the Union by the Sanitary, Allotment and Christian Commissions (the late William E. Dodge, active in all patriotic and philanthropic works, being president of the New York branch of the latter). Six thousand delegates from the Christian Commission went to the front to render assistance to the sick and wounded, and during the war millions of Bibles and religious papers were distributed among the soldiers. Such works as were done by these commissions, had been done nowhere else in the world, and it would be safe to say, that these three commissions combined doubled the efficiency of our army. Search history through, and it will be discovered that not one of these purely benevolent institutions, owing their existence, as they do, to no reasons of state, can be found until we come to modern times. It was one of the new ideas evoked by this war—one of those great facts which illustrates how God is continually in all time, "from seeming evil, still educing good."

CHAPTER XI.

THE MERCHANTS AND BANKERS.

On the day previous to the great meeting in Union Square, the merchants of New York assembled in the Chamber of Commerce, to defend the honor of an insulted government and an outraged flag. Merchants, like the clear-seeing, practical men that they are, have in every period of our history distinguished themselves by their self-sacrificing patriotism. To them belongs the credit of sustaining the government in its dangers and perils, and to them in fostering and extending our commerce we owe our present greatness and prosperity. "The greatness and power of this commercial city," said the Hon. William M. Evarts, "has been the result of the Union," and Daniel Webster declared that "it was the mercantile classes, that carried through the Union in 1788." It is not known as well as it should be, that nine of the fifty-six signers of the Declaration of Independence were men bred to mercantile pursuits. From the beginning to the end of the war—from the capture of Fort Sumter, through all the trying scenes that marked the checkered strife, down to the surrender of Lee at Appomattox—the merchants, as a body, in the Chamber of Commerce, and individually, as members of, and contributors to, various patriotic associations, did their duty and their whole duty, with a degree of firmness that formed a glorious chapter in the records of commercial history.

There is sometimes a power behind the throne greater than the throne itself, and the extent to which Secretary

Chase and President Lincoln relied for counsel and practical assistance upon such public-spirited New Yorkers as Isaac Sherman and Mr. Silas M. Stilwell, vindicates the truth of the sentiment. Besides Mr. Sherman and Mr. Stilwell, the following-named gentlemen may also be mentioned as among the leading citizens of the metropolis, who, in various ways, assisted the Government in those dark days of trouble: Mr. William E. Dodge (also represented in the field by his son, Gen. Charles C Dodge, who, while colonel of the Seventh New York Cavalry, was the hero of a brilliant expedition into North Carolina); Mr. Stewart Brown, the father of that gallant young hero, Lieut. Milnor Brown, of the 124th Regiment, killed at the battle of Gettysburg; Mr. A. A. Low, Mr. Adrian Iselin, Mr. John A. Stevens, Mr. Moses Taylor, Mr. James Gallatin, Mr. John E. Williams, Mr. George S Coe, Mr. Jonathan Sturges, Mr. Peletiah Perit, Mr. Marshall O Roberts, Mr. James Punnett, Mr. Thomas Tileston, Mr. James M. Morrisson, Mr. Reuben W. Howes, Mr. Joseph Lawrence, Mr. John D. Jones, Mr. J. D. Vermilye, Mr. Harvey Fisk, Mr. Charles H. Russell, Mr. Peter Cooper, Mr. Morris K. Jesup, Mr. Isaac H. Bailey, Mr. Moses H Grinnell, Mr. John A. Stewart, Mr. Seth B. Hunt, Mr. Wilson G. Hunt, Mr. Henry G. Stebbins, Mr. W H. De Forest, Mr. Samuel Sloan, Mr. Jackson S. Schultz, Mr. William H. Aspinwall, Mr. S. B. Chittenden, Mr. Carlisle Norwood, Mr. James Boorman, Mr. Henry T. Vail, Mr. William F Havemeyer, Mr. Charles H. Marshall, Mr. August Belmont, Mr. Robert B. Minturn, Mr. Morris Ketchum, Mr. James W Beekman, Mr. Royal Phelps, Mr. Shepard Knapp, Mr. William H. Johnson, Mr. Henry Clews, Mr. Amos R. Eno (Mr Eno was represented in the war by his son Col. Amos F Eno, who served on the staff of Gen. John S Phelps); Mr. Daniel F Appleton, Mr. Oliver Hoyt, Mr. Fletcher Harper, Mr. Elliot F. Cowdin, Mr. R. H. McCurdy and Mr. Le Grand B. Cannon.

At the celebration of the centennial anniversary of the

founding of the Chamber of Commerce, after narrating the prominent acts and resolutions of that body during its first hundred years (for that institution is a few years older than our Nation), the orator of the occasion, John Austin Stevens, Jr., "capped the climax" of its prominent public service, by referring emphatically to the zealous spirit with which the members of the Chamber sustained the Government during the darkest hours of its necessities, and all through the war. "The early years of the Chamber of Commerce," said Mr. Stevens, "were marked by its spirited devotion to American freedom. So its century of life has closed upon years of devotion with equal spirit, to the maintenance of the freedom which was then gained—devotion manifested zealously, from the commencement down to the overthrow of the most formidable rebellion that ever strained the power, or tested the strength, of any government. Here was lighted, on the 19th of April, 1861, that patriotic fire which spread with electric flash to the farthest eastern homestead on the Atlantic shores and to the most distant cabin of the Western prairies. Should the eventful history of this Chamber close with this evening, the record of its hundred years will ever stand an honor to New York merchants, and the children and children's children of its members will point with just pride to their names upon its rolls."

The prompt and spirited action of the Chamber of Commerce might well be taken as an indication of the course of the bankers and business men generally. Any account of the war would be deficient in a most essential point, if it failed to refer early and steadily to the prompt and persevering support afforded by the bankers of New York, when monied aid was instantaneously required, to equip the multitudes of gallant men who were thronging towards the battle-field. The value of any services in public or private life should be estimated by the difficulties under which those services are rendered. Never was there a period in the history of any country so unpropitious for negotiating loans as was the time when the New York bankers assembled to devise means for replenishing the bankrupt National Treasury; and who can forget the forlorn condition of that treasury, when Secretary Howell Cobb (secretly aiding the Confederates, whom he afterwards openly joined) had so crippled its pecuniary resources, and so seriously impaired the National credit, that even a paltry ten million loan could not be readily effected—though it was a mere two-penny affair when compared with the thousands of millions required during the succeeding four years. Although the late Secretary Cobb did all that he could to destroy public confidence, by intimating a doubt whether a ten million loan could ever be repaid, " as the Union was about falling to pieces," the spirit of the New York capitalists could not be repressed, and when the Administration of President Lincoln appealed for aid, through the new Secretary, Chase, the outlines of a financial system were devised by the aid of New York bankers, enabling the Administration to sustain the armies then flocking to its standard. The assertion of a well-known writer has become proverbial "that, under the rule of men entirely great, the pen is mightier than the sword;" but the condition of this Republic at the commencement of hostilities, if not the very salvation of the Union itself, furnishes one of the many evidences of the fact, that " the purse " is sometimes mightier than pen and sword combined. In our own country, as well as in the foreign nations, from which larger loans are commonly derived by Americans, there were serious doubts concerning our ability to maintain a treasury adequate for gigantic warfare, and the minds of even many loyalists were measurably swayed by similar doubts, touching the ability of our political system to provide the vast sums required for sustaining a long war. George Peabody, then a well-known banker in London, wrote that " the anticipation of a conflict between the North and South has already destroyed confidence in the United States Government stocks and in many of the State securities, and millions have within a few months been sent home for a market in consequence."

The London *Times* exclaimed that "no financial pressure that ever threatened, is equal to that which now hangs over the United States," and declared that "national bankruptcy is not an agreeable prospect, but it is the only one presented by the existing state of American finances." The New York *Herald* early appreciated the efforts of our bankers to coöperate with Secretary Chase in raising loans, but mentioned the depressed condition of financial affairs on the 10th of April, 1861, by saying; "Now that civil war is commenced, it seems an unfortunate time for Mr. Chase to throw five millions in treasury notes on the market, and capitalists will be afraid to touch them at par, especially as owing to the operation of the Morrill tariff, there is no prospect of revenue to pay those notes when they become due, and there is no other security to back them."

As some prominent public men supposed that the difficulties would be speedily overcome, it is not wonderful that financial arrangements, like our military affairs, should have been managed on a correspondingly limited scale down to the date of the Bull Run disaster and the second virtual siege of the city of Washington. It was in this forlorn condition that the National Government turned towards the Commercial Metropolis for relief—for instantaneous relief—and for future help, adequate to the demands incident to a contest, which it was now generally conceded must be of long duration and immense cost.

It was while news of a most appalling character was convulsing the public mind respecting the Bull Run affair, that Secretary Chase invited a meeting of New York bankers, on the evening of August 8, 1861, to devise measures for permanent financial operations, as well as for means of immediate relief. This consultation was held at the house of Mr. John J. Cisco, Assistant Treasurer of the United States. Never was a meeting of business men convened under circumstances more memorable. The sturdiest hearts could not avoid showing profound depression concerning the calamities overhanging the Nation.

During the discussion which ensued, Mr. George S. Coe, President of the American Exchange Bank, suggested the practicability of uniting the banks of the North by some organization that would combine them into an efficient and inseparable body for the purpose of advancing the capital of the country upon Government bonds in large amounts; and through their clearing-house facilities and other well-known expedients, to distribute them in smaller sums among the people in a manner that would secure active coöperation among the members in this special work, while in all other respects each bank could pursue its independent business. This suggestion met with the hearty approbation of the assembled company and arrested the earnest attention of the secretary. At his request it was presented to the consideration of the banks, at a meeting called for that purpose at the American Exchange Bank on the following day.

The plan, enlarged and modified, finally included the banks of Boston and Philadelphia. Mr. John A. Stevens, the President of the Bank of Commerce, the largest and most important financial institution in the country, was requested by Mr. Secretary Chase to form a Treasury Note Committee to float the Government loans. Mr. Chase named John A. Stevens, Moses Taylor, James Gallatin, John E. Williams and George S. Coe, of New York. Of this committee John Austin Stevens, Jr., son of the president, was the confidential secretary. Its business was the general advisement of the Secretary of the Treasury as to the financial policy of the Government. Its hope was to maintain specie payments by a skilful accumulation and husbanding of the metallic circulation of the country.

The report of the committee, prepared by the secretary, Mr. Coe, was received with general approval at the next meeting of the bankers, when a committee was appointed to invite concurrence from banks that were not represented at the meeting, and it is to the honor of all concerned, that every bank thus invited, promptly concurred in the course recommended for meeting the emergencies of the Government.

* The result of the conference was a pledge of the banking interests of New York, Boston, and Philadelphia, to take $150,000,000 of treasury notes in three instalments of $50,000,000 each and to pay for them in gold. Of this loan, New York City furnished $105,000,000. Massachusetts not being satisfied with the terms, refused to take her full proportion, and New York made up the deficiency. This loan nearly equalled the aggregate capital of all the banks of the loyal states, and was $15,000,000 more than the cost to the colonies of the Revolutionary War. Early in 1862, Secretary Chase reported, that of the $260,000,000 advanced in loans to the Government, New York had contributed $210,000,000. The assistance of the bankers was further shown in a way that should be particularly appreciated by the citizens of New York. What could the corporation, or the Board of Supervisors, have done in organizing troops, were it not for the prompt coöperation of the banks? The chairman of the committee for raising volunteers, Mr. Orison Blunt, was compelled to borrow several millions of dollars on what purported to be the bonds of the city (bonds issued without any legal authority whatever)—the worthlessness of which were well known to all the bankers, but who trusted to future legislative action for legalizing their issue. Without this timely assistance from the banks, it would have been impracticable to recruit so promptly the large forces sent to the war from the Commercial Metropolis. In fact, on a calm review of the condition of things in that most gloomy period, it is no exaggeration to

say, that the people of the whole Union are indebted to the wisdom, patriotism and liberality of the New York bankers, coöperating with prompt military movements, for the preservation of the Union. It was well remarked at the time, and subsequent developments strengthen the assertion, that the New York bankers, by promptly furnishing the sinews of war, were the sole barriers against National bankruptcy and ruin. Their praises were sounded everywhere, and they should never be forgotten in after times.

After Secretary Chase had obtained his first loan from the New York banks, the London *Times* said that he had "coerced" $50,000,000 from the banks, but that he would not fare so well on the London Exchange. But from that time, his demands were all met at home, without borrowing a dollar from the London or any other foreign exchange; till at the end of the war there had been furnished to the National Government over four thousand millions of dollars, exclusive of the expenditures by states, cities, counties and towns, for war purposes, amounting to at least one thousand million dollars more, showing an aggregate of $5,000,000,000 contributed by the people of the Northern States within a period of five years, and this for purposes of the war alone, exclusive of the ordinary expenses of the Government—a sum which represented in greenbacks of one dollar each, would girdle the earth twenty-three times. It affords gratifying evidence of the recuperative powers of this Nation to add, that two-thirds of the National debt has been paid, and we shall no doubt in a few years claim from the London *Times*, all the praise so doubtingly promised to us in September, 1863, when it said: "No pressure that ever threatened, is equal to that which now hangs over the United States, and it may safely be said that if through future generations they faithfully meet their liabilities, they will fairly earn a fame that will shine throughout the world."

Richard Cobden asked: "Why is it that the American states have laughed to scorn the prediction of all our writers on finance, who told them that they could not go on with the war for six months, without coming to Europe for a loan? How is it that they have deceived and disappointed the whole of Europe? It is because the American people have never allowed their Government to make a war expenditure in time of peace. That is the whole secret. They were spending for the purposes of their Government from fifteen to seventeen millions sterling a year when the war broke out, and the savings then made have enabled them to go through this terrific strain. Take ten millions of savings for forty years with compound interest, and see what a fabulous amount it will come to. This is what America did."

The first United States Government bonds were purchased by residents of New York City, R. L. & A. Stuart, Bond No. I having been purchased by the late Mr. Alexander Stuart. It was a New York banker, Mr. Silas M. Stilwell, who first recommended to Secretary Chase, the Treasury Note, or Greenback, system. It was a New Yorker, Mr. Elbridge T. Spaulding, of Buffalo, who first suggested the National Banking law, which had worked so well in the State of New York, and with slight modifications it was adopted by the General Government—the secretary, in one of his official reports, acknowledging the precedence of New York State over all others on the subject of finance.

The first contribution made by a private citizen for the defence of the Nation was made by a New Yorker—Col. John Jacob Astor, when he liberally furnished the means to purchase the tug-boat "Yankee," which was sent to the relief of the garrison at Fort Sumter. The pioneer in the noble and righteous work of extending relief to the poor families of our volunteers, was Mr. John Anderson, of New York City. When the comptroller advertised for a loan of

$500,000 for the purpose mentioned, Mr. Anderson immediately responded, by presenting his check for $10,000.

In many other indirect ways, was the liberality of New York's citizens shown from time to time. A fund was raised for the relief of the operatives in Lancashire, England, who, though suffering intensely from the cutting off of the cotton supplies for the English mills, were still under the influence of John Bright and a few other stanch friends of the North. Valuable testimonials were gotten up for Admiral Farragut, General Grant and General Sherman, and $200,000 were raised for the relief of the sufferers in East Tennessee. It is to the credit of Mr. John Austin Stevens, Jr., that he initiated the movement that resulted in this substantial assistance. But this was only one of the many important enterprises organized by this public-spirited citizen. Money was also sent to aid the Unionists of Western North Carolina, and when Sherman captured Savannah, a large subscription was taken for the sufferers there. In short, every demand that patriotism could make found a willing response in New York City. One effect of this generous and patriotic effort to sustain the Nation's credit, was to gain for New York an enormous reputation for financial stability, and its municipal securities at once established themselves beyond question, New York having, since 1865, been easily at the head of American cities in the matter of public credit.

Before the war, some men imagined that all the old National spirit was perishing out of the hearts of the American people—that the passion for money-getting was operating as a fatal canker to patriotism and every heroic sentiment. Carlyle merely embodied a prevalent European feeling when he exclaimed: "My friend, brag not yet of our American cousins. Their quantity of cotton, dollars, industry and resources, I believe to be almost unspeakable; but I can by no means worship the like of those. What great human soul? what great thought? what great noble thing that one could worship and admire has been produced there? None! The American cousins have yet done none of these things." It could not now be said that right and liberty were of less significance than dividends and dollars, for did not the action of our people prove that under all the hard work and rage for material progress and development, there was a capacity nowhere equalled for great actions, and great sacrifices—that love of country glowed as intensely here and inspired as pure an enthusiasm as among any people that ever figured in history?

CHAPTER XII.

THE PATRIOTISM OF NEW YORK CITY.

It was fortunate for the cause and the honor of the city of New York that the choice of mayor for the term running through the years of 1862 and 1863, fell upon a citizen so well qualified for the emergency as George Opdyke, whose services among bankers and business men had been so prompt and persevering in stimulating measures for organizing the forces requisite for sustaining the Government. It was a pleasant feature of Mayor Opdyke's course, that while encouraging his fellow citizens in their patriotic efforts, he seized every proper opportunity for rendering credit to old political opponents, who had promptly buried partisan feelings in their zeal for sustaining the Union. This characteristic was happily exemplified in a speech near the close of 1862, before the war was half over.

The following extract from the address referred to, is worthy of particular notice for its allusion to the patriotic course of the people of all parties in this city.

"There has been from the beginning of the war," said the Mayor, "a moral sublimity in the patriotism of the citizens of New York which has never received the appreciative notice it deserves. A moral sublimity which I may with entire propriety refer to, since it has found its highest illustration in the conduct of those to whom I am politically opposed. This is a Democratic city; most decidedly so, as we all know who have read the returns of recent elections. The leaders of the Rebellion were also Democrats, who had, prior to the outbreak of the war, acted in harmony and concert with that party here. Nor is it any secret that the prime movers of the Rebellion, counting on the strong ties of party organization and political sympathy, expected, yes, confidently relied on, the continued sympathy and support of their political friends in the North, and especially on their friends in this city Thank God ! they were mistaken. They found to their cost, that they had sadly underestimated the patriotism of the Northern heart. The first gun fired on Sumter, over which the old flag waved, severed in an instant every partisan tie, and, under the prompting of an earnest patriotism, every honest Democrat at once rallied to the support of an Administration to which he had been until then opposed, and it was here, in this city, that the patriotic movement of the Northern Democracy was inaugurated. Sir, those of us who were original friends and supporters of the Administration, can scarcely appreciate the sacrifice thus made by its political opponents. We have but to consider the misleading influence of party prejudice, and the bitterness engendered by party contests, to enable us to judge something of the depth and strength of the patriotic impulse by which they were moved. Nor was it mere lip-service that the Democracy gave the cause. They volunteered with alacrity ; they gave their money freely ; the city government, which was chiefly in their hands, appropriated $1,000,000 to fit out regiments and speed them to the field,—it appropriated $2,000,000 for the relief of the families of volunteers, and provided hospitals for the sick and wounded. In view of these facts, so creditable to the city, and to the party which cast two-thirds of the votes, and which acted thus nobly in support of an Administration whose election it opposed, I have a right to say, that the city of New York is thoroughly loyal, and that she will never hesitate to contribute freely of her strength and her resources to uphold the Union, and to aid in crushing out this atrocious Rebellion." Mayor Opdyke's tribute to the loyalty of the Democratic masses in New York was fully deserved. There were no stancher friends of the Union than many of its political leaders in the Metropolis, who had voted and worked against the Republican candidates in 1860. The war had wiped out party lines on all questions affecting the suppression of the Rebellion. Democrats joined with Republicans in holding up the hands of the President, and on the vital issues of supporting the war there was no division of sentiment in Democratic New York. Among those who made themselves honorably conspicuous at home as "War Democrats," may be mentioned James T. Brady, James B. Brady, Charles P Daly, John Van Buren, Richard Schell, Abram S. Hewitt, Edward Cooper, Francis B. Cutting (Mr. Cutting was represented in the army by his son, General William Cutting. who served on the Staff of General Burnside), Henry Bergh, Elbridge T. Gerry, James A. Roosevelt. John Kelly, John T. Agnew, J. Willis James, Isaac Bell, John D. Townsend, Samuel D. Babcock, Robert M. Knapp, Wm. C. Prime. Augustus Schell, John T. Hoffman, S. L. M. Barlow, Daniel Lord, Wm. Allen Butler, John R. Brady, Hiram Ketchum, William Butler Duncan, Manton Marble, David M. Stone, and Andrew J. Colvin of Albany, who, in the Legislature of 1861, rallied the war Democrats for the defence of the Union.

It is due to the truth of history, however, to state that though there was an immense preponderance of loyal sentiment among the great mass of citizens of all parties, there was actually a smouldering element among a "dangerous class," that only awaited some strong wind to burst into conflagration, as was afterwards shown in the so-called draft riots of 1863. In view of this threatening danger, let us turn towards one branch of the city government, on which largely depended the question whether troops from other States would be allowed to pass quietly through its streets, and whether any of our city regiments could safely be spared to accompany them in the early movements for defending the capital. It was evidently an essential part of the rebel schemes to create in New York City, just such a state of things as prevailed in Baltimore, where mobs were arranged to murder Abraham Lincoln, on his way to enter upon the Presidency. Writers in the *Journal of Commerce* expressed apprehensions, said to be then widely felt by property holders on this subject, that efforts had been made to dissuade the officers of some of the city's regiments from marching for the defence of Washington, as their absence would leave the city open to mob violence. But the reorganization of the New York Police Department, under a law of 1860, about which Mayor Wood bitterly complained in his telegram to General Floyd, of Georgia, happily rendered the new police system fit to discharge the delicate and important duties of this trying crisis. The new law facilitated the appointment of that excellent superintendent, the late John A. Kennedy, a gallant Southerner, born in Maryland, but whose devotion to the Union flag was paramount to mere local attachments, or prejudices. It is worthy of special remembrance that the newly-appointed superintendent infused his loyal spirit to such an extent through the newly, organized police, that public order was secured, and the domestic affairs of New York presented a marked contrast to the turbulence that disgraced his native Baltimore. But for this salutary change in the spirit of the police, it would evidently have been almost impracticable for our city regiments to have left home to temporarily defend the National capital. Indeed, it is evident that nothing but the overwhelming loyalty of the citizens generally, prevented an attempt by Rebel agents and sympathizers to seize the navy yard and the forts around New York harbor—in readiness for which purposes commissions, or promises of commissions, in the Confederate service were evidently scattered among officials in our city government, including some prominent military men, who were stationed in corporation offices, ready to take command whenever an insurrection should occur in this city But the spontaneous uprising among our citizens warned these officers to escape like fugitives in the night, as the contemplated insurrectionary movement could not then have been successful, and they soon afterwards turned up at the South in their true colors, as full-fledged generals in the Confederate armies. A single one of the warnings by the leading journals may be here quoted, as among the many indications of danger from local conspiracies.

The *Herald*, of January 17, 1861, said: "It is rumored and believed in certain circles, that a large military force is being enrolled in this city for the purpose of seizing on the forts in the harbor, as soon as civil war breaks out in Charleston, or anywhere else at the South. It is said that from three thousand to five thousand men have already been enlisted under various pretexts;—some for the purpose of assisting the South; some for the purpose of protecting the city, and some for the purpose of acting as a defensive corps in the event of the secession of the city from the State—(a course recommended by Mayor Wood in 1860). All these pretences have been used for the purpose of getting together this force, but it is believed that the real object is what we have stated, the seizure of the harbor defences."

CHAPTER XIII.

EUROPEAN HOSTILITY—MR. BEECHER'S SERVICES ABROAD—
FOREIGNERS IN THE ARMY.

THE feeling existing among the aristocratic classes of Europe in regard to America when the war began, will make appropriate a brief reference to the attitude of England towards us from the beginning to the close of the contest. That contest was kept alive by means of military stores and ammunition manufactured in British workshops and smuggled into Rebel ports by the blockade runners of Great Britain. The guns with which the Rebels waged the war, the money with which they paid and clothed their troops, and even the very clothes themselves, to a great extent, were free gifts of the people of Great Britain. Our commerce was swept from the ocean by armed vessels built in English ship-yards and fitted out in her ports. Two hundred and eighty-five of our vessels were captured by the "Alabama" and other cruisers. One hundred and fifty-eight were destroyed by the "Alabama" alone, the estimated value of which, with their cargoes, was $2,600,000, for which, by the terms of the Treaty of Washington, $15,000,500 was awarded as compensation to be paid by the government of Great Britain to the United States. These acts, and others for which the government of Great Britain was morally responsible, certainly prolonged the war at least two years, and doubtless added $1,500,000,000 to the National debt. Had the South been given directly to understand that she would not receive the moral support of England or France, there would have been no war, for the Rebels expected to draw their main strength from British favor and assistance, and the arrangements made by the Confederates to procure vessels, arms and military supplies in Great Britain, on the basis of the cotton crop of the South for 1860, was well known in Downing Street, London. When questions involving the destruction of the Union were being discussed on all sides by the monarchies of Europe, the faithful and statesmanlike manner in which the Hon. William H. Seward served the Nation during all these trying ordeals, signally manifested the wisdom of President Lincoln's selection for the office of Secretary of State.

It is proper here also to refer to the great services rendered to the Government by a citizen of Brooklyn, whose eloquence and convincing arguments, ultimately caused a revolution in the popular feeling of the United Kingdom in favor of the National cause; reference, of course, is made to the late Rev Henry Ward Beecher. No representative of the loyal States had been able to arouse any thing like the interest that was taken in Mr. Beecher's addresses, and no better evidence of the power of his eloquence need be asked, than the earnest efforts made by the Rebel sympathizers, after his first address, to shut his mouth by force. Nothing but the fear of him, or rather of the truths coming from his lips, could have raised such a tempest of opposition, and there was not a more heroic achievement, on any of our battle-fields, than the successful delivery of his great speech against the odds which opposed it, at Exeter Hall, London, in 1863.

But while aristocratic England was against America, the England of Milton, Hampden, and Cromwell, was mainly with her, and aside from the politicians who made of statesmanship a trade, those whose souls were imbued with the love of humanity and who desired the triumph of constitutional law and freedom, were all enlisted in the earnest support of the Government. "Be sure that the heart of England has always been right," said the Rev. Newman

Hall, of London. "There have been hundreds, if not thousands, of public meetings enthusiastically for Union and emancipation; not one has been convened for sympathy with the South."

As New York City receives nearly all the vast throngs of immigrants who seek refuge on our shores, and as it was falsely said that the Northern armies were most largely recruited from foreigners, it is proper to mention that although great benefit was derived from the general loyalty of the foreign-born element in our population, there were in the whole Union armies only five per cent of unnaturalized foreigners and ten per cent of naturalized citizens, thus showing that native-born Americans constituted fully eighty per cent of all the loyal forces. This statement explodes the falsehoods to the effect that the Secessionists were overborne by foreign mercenaries. But this must not be understood as under-estimating the value of the assistance afforded by the Irish and German citizens, who constitute the great mass of our foreign-born inhabitants. Edward Everett, when addressing a war meeting in Boston in 1862, said: "There is no one element of strength, which is more important to the country than the cordial support of her adopted citizens of the various foreign nationalities. The Irish alone are probably equal in number to the entire population of the Union during the Revolutionary War—there being at least three millions of Irish birth and lineage in the United States, and the cordial sympathy of three millions of true and loyal hearts, contributing a fair proportion to our armies, warrant us in believing that if, on some hard-fought field, should the doubtful day be about to turn against us, the Irish brigade, as of old at Fontenoy, would rush to the rescue, with 'the terrible war-cry of 'Fag-a-balla,' and would sweep the foes of the Union before them like chaff before the wind."

Some of the best officers in the Union Army were foreigners, and America can never forget the gleam of pure friendship that flashed from the swords of her foreign benefactors on the battle-fields of the Rebellion. England gave to the Union Gen. John W Fuller and Gen. William H. Powell. Although the Union had an enemy in Napoleon III., the people of France were always her friends, and they were represented in the great struggle by the Prince de Joinville, the Duc de Chartres, the Comte de Paris, General de Trobriand and Gen. Alfred N Duffie. The Prince de Joinville was also represented in the Navy by his son, the Duc de Penthieve.

Germany was faithful to the standard of the Union and contributed to her cause many valuable officers, among them, Gen. Franz Sigel, Gen. August V Kautz and Gen. Schimmelfennig, who commanded the forces that first entered the city of Charleston, in 1865; Gen. Adolph von Steinwehr and Gen. Lewis Blenker; Prussia, Gen. Peter J. Osterhaus, Gen. Frederick Solomon, Gen. August Willich, Baron von Steuben, Gen. Carl Schurz and Gen. George von Schack, formerly of the Seventh Volunteer Infantry Regiment; Hungary, Gen. Alexander Asboth, Gen. Julius H. Stahel and Gen. Albin Schoepf; Russia, Gen. John B. Turchin; Spain, Gen. Edward Ferrero; Sweden, Gen. John McArthur and Maj. Frederic Rosencrantz; Poland, General Kryzanowski; Ireland, General Shields, Gen. Thomas W Sweeny, Gen. Michael R. Lawler, Gen. Patrick E. Connor, Gen. Thomas A. Smyth, Gen. Patrick H. Jones and Gen. Thomas Francis Meagher; Scotland, Gen. Daniel McCraig McCallum, the manager of our military railroads; Col. David Ireland, of the One Hundred and Thirty-seventh New York Regiment; Maj. John M. Farquhar, of the Eighty-ninth Illinois; Lieut. Daniel Kerr, of the One Hundred and Seventeenth Illinois; Capt. James B. White, Thirtieth Indiana, and Col. David B. Henderson, of the Forty-sixth Iowa—all four of the officers last mentioned, who served with honorable distinction on the battle-fields of the Rebellion, afterwards becoming members of the United States House of Representatives.

CHAPTER XIV

NEW YORK SOLDIERY—CONSPICUOUS INSTANCES OF GALLANTRY.

The gorgeous blossoming of patriotism, which, upon the fall of Sumter, burst forth all over the loyal States, found fruitage during the ensuing four years, in the mustering into service of 2,500,000 men—a larger army than that with which Napoleon overran Europe, overthrew kingdoms and empires, and revolutionized the political systems of one-half of Christendom. To that great army, the State of New York contributed 475,000—more than one-sixth of the entire national force. In all civil convulsions it is the heart of the commercial system that suffers most. The very conditions which made New York the most prosperous of American cities in the ordinary course of events, caused her to suffer the most of all when that course was interrupted. But notwithstanding this, the city of New York stood foremost in defending the Union, voting the first dollar voted by any city for the equipment of troops, furnishing the national Government with three quarters of the money necessary to raise and support its armies, and contributing to those armies 116,000 men, not including 20,000 furnished for three months—all at an expense to the city of $14,500,000, nearly four times as much as the cost to the state of the Revolutionary War. Thirty-five thousand of the sons of the city of Brooklyn went forth to fight the battles of the Union—a larger number in proportion to her population, than was contributed by the city of Boston; thus was the Athens of America eclipsed by the City of

Churches. It was the boast of a Senator from Massachusetts, at the commencement of the war, that "New York was being dragged at the wheels of the chariot of Abraham Lincoln;" but it is more than probable that had it not been for the devotion of the Empire State, Massachusetts would have been dragged at the wheels of the chariot of Jefferson Davis, for it is safe to assume that had it not been for the patriotism of the State of New York, the result of the struggle would have been different in every respect.

The historian will never have to record greater heroism than was displayed by the soldiers from the Empire State on the battle-fields of the Rebellion. It was said by an eminent authority, that no soldiers in the world showed more spirit and endurance. There was no loyal army, the shouts over whose victories did not drown the dying sigh of some son of New York. There was scarcely a battle-field that was not moistened with his blood, and hardly an official report that did not bear witness to his courage and devotion. In many of the New York regiments, says Col. Wm. F. Fox, in his article on "The Chances of Being Hit in Battle," "the percentage of killed and wounded in certain actions, exceeded the loss of the heroic Light Brigade in the famous charge at Balaklava."

"The war developed the fact," said General Sherman, "that the boys from the city could stand more fatigue and hardship and marching than the country boys. The boys from the country were stronger always, but they were used to a regular life, and when they got into the army, the irregularities of the life, its hardships and exposures, weakened and finally killed many a strong young farmer boy, while the boys from the city, being used to irregular hours and irregular living, could stand any amount of hardship without going under."

The old world at first sneered at the idea of anything respectable in warfare being effected by men who were not professionally bred to military duties, and Von Moltke's definition of our war was, "The wrangling of two armed mobs." But our foreign critics soon abandoned that notion and were bewildered by the falsification of their own predictions. The London *Times* frankly acknowledged that the events of American warfare baffled all its earlier calculations. "The whole of this dreadful fighting," said the *Times*, "has been done by volunteers without as much training as our British riflemen; yet those new companies, without professional skill or regimental traditions,—with captains snatched from the counter, or the store, and with generals who were attorneys a few months before,—are fighting with as much obstinacy as Napoleon's Old Guard." The London *Times* must have forgotten that the most successful general of the War of 1812 was a lawyer, Andrew Jackson, and that the most successful of Napoleon's marshals were frequently unlearned soldiers from the ranks.

CHAPTER XV

HOW NEW YORK LED IN MANY WAYS.

To New York State must be given the credit of being first in many striking deeds and incidents of the contest. The first successful military movement of the war was made under the direction of a New York general, John A. Dix, who in July, 1861, sent General Lockwood into Accomac and Northampton Counties, Virginia, with orders to occupy those counties and drive the Rebels out.

The credit of organizing the first movement for the raising of volunteers, has been very generally awarded to General Butler, who issued a call for a meeting of the officers of the Sixth Massachusetts Regiment to be held at Lowell, on the 21st of January, 1861; but the records show that the honor is justly due to Capt. Allan Rutherford, of New York City, who issued a call for a meeting of volunteers to aid in defence of the Government, to be held at the Mercer House, ten days before General Butler's appeal was made public.

It was a New Yorker, Gen. John Cochrane, a grandson of Surg.-Gen. John Cochrane, of Washington's Staff, who first publicly urged the arming of the slaves.

It was a citizen of New York, Gen. Hiram Walbridge, who first pointed out to President Lincoln the importance of securing Port Royal and Beaufort, South Carolina, and this advice was acknowledged by the President in a letter of thanks to Mr. Walbridge.

It was upon the suggestion of the Hon. Thurlow Weed, in 1861, that Gen. Wm. Tecumseh Sherman, then president of a college, was invited by the Government to exchange his position for the camp and field.

The first gun fired in defence of the Union, was fired from Fort Sumter by a New Yorker, Capt. (Gen.) Abner Doubleday, of the First United States Artillery.

The conspicuous gallantry of the soldiers from the State of New York, adorn the records of all sections of the loyal States. "The admirable defence of Mumfordsville, Ky., in 1862, which frustrated General Bragg's plan for the reconquest of the Western Border States," said General de Peyster, "was made by a son of New York—Col. John T. Wilder, of the Seventeenth Indiana Regiment." General de Peyster might also have added that Colonel Wilder (commanding a brigade) had the honor of giving the city of Chattanooga the first hostile shot it received at the time General Rosecrans marched on that place in August, 1863.

It was a son of a member of the New York Bar—Maj. Frank J. White,—who, while in command of a batallion of prairie scouts, captured the city of Lexington, Mo. Major White was one of four patriotic citizens, who had the foresight to perceive the dangers that lay before the country, and, with Captain Rutherford, issued the first call for volunteers in New York City to prepare to defend the Government.

The grand old symbol of the Republic was first raised over Vicksburg, in July, 1863, by a New Yorker—Col. William E. Strong, of the Twelfth Wisconsin Regiment.

The first to hoist the Stars and Stripes over the Rebel fort at Roanoke Island, was the Fifty-first New York, under command of Col. Edward Ferrero, and its colors were also the first to wave over the Capitol at Jackson, Miss. It was a son of New York, Col. Philip Sidney Post, now a member of Congress, who, as colonel of the Fifty-ninth Illinois, often led that splendid regiment to victory, and in recognition of his services was promoted to the rank of Brigadier-General.

The fortunes of the day were decided at the battle of

Fair Oaks, by a brilliant charge of the "Irish Rifles"—the Thirty-seventh New York. The only Rebel flag captured at Fair Oaks was taken by "The United States Chasseurs," Sixty-fifth New York, Col. John Cochrane, who was soon after promoted to the rank of Brigadier-General. The Sixty-fifth is also entitled to the distinction of having furnished three Brigadier-Generals to the army—one more than was contributed by any other volunteer infantry regiment from the State.

The 102d New York was the first to dash across the crest in the attack on Lookout Mountain, "which made them," said General Geary, "the heroes of that battle."

The first to spill their blood on the breastworks of the enemy at Yorktown, were the soldiers of the "Mozart" (Fortieth) Regiment, Col. Thomas W Egan, and they were also the first to plant the New York State colors on the breastworks of Fort Magruder.

The first Union banner to float over Fort Fisher in January, 1865, was the flag of the 117th New York, Col. Rufus Daggett, who for his gallantry was promoted to the rank of Brevet Brigadier-General.

The Stars and Stripes were first raised over the Court House at Atlanta, Ga., when General Sherman captured the city, by the Sixtieth New York and 111th Pennsylvania Regiments.

The first flag to float over the ruins of the Rebel fort at the time of the explosion of the mine in front of Petersburg, July 30, 1864, was that of the Fourteenth New York Heavy Artillery, during a charge led by Capt. Charles H. Houghton, who for his gallantry was promoted to Brevet Major in 1865.

The Twelfth New York State Militia, led by Col. Daniel Butterfield, was the first regiment to set foot on the soil of the old Dominion, in 1861, and was the first to receive an attack after the army of invasion crossed into Virginia.

The 131st New York, Col. Nicholas W Day, is said

to have saved the fortunes of the day at the battle of Winchester, September 19, 1864.

In May, 1864, when General Meade called for the reports of the battles in which the regiments and batteries of the Army of the Potomac had been engaged, that they might be inscribed on the flags, Battery D, First New York Artillery, Capt. Geo. B. Winslow, bore off the palm.

CHAPTER XVI.

NEW YORK AT GETTYSBURG.

NEW YORK turned the tide of battle at Gettysburg, and the Empire State will ever remember that that glorious success, secured chiefly by the unexampled steadiness and bravery of her private soldiers, will ever signalize and seal to their honor the truth, that the many disasters our arms had previously sustained were not to be laid to the charge of the rank and file. Distinguished military officers have ascribed the chief credit of our warfare to the private soldiers, whose energies always rose with the necessity for action, and declared that "thinking" bayonets often secured victory when military science despaired of success. General Grant said in 1863: " My sympathies are with every movement which aims to acknowledge our indebtedness to the private soldiers—the countless, nameless, often disregarded heroes of the musket and bayonet—to whose true patriotism, patient endurance, and fiery courage in the day of danger, we, who are generals, owe victory and the country will yet owe its salvation."

As Gettysburg has been called the "soldiers' battle," the author cannot refrain from recalling to the minds of his readers how signally in this great crisis New York sustained her heroic fame. In this battle two hundred and sixty loyal regiments were engaged, of which number eighty-seven regiments and batteries were from the Empire State. Of the nineteen infantry divisions six were led by New York officers, and of the seventy brigade organizations, twenty-one were under command of New York generals, or colonels. Of General Meade's eighty-two commanders, the following twenty were natives of the State of New York. Major-Generals: Romeyn B. Ayres, Daniel Butterfield, Francis C. Barlow, Henry Baxter, Joseph B. Carr, Thomas C Devin, Abner Doubleday, Charles K. Graham, Wesley Merritt, Thomas H. Ruger, Daniel E. Sickles, Henry W Slocum, Robert O. Tyler, James S. Wadsworth, Gouverneur K. Warren; Brigadier-Generals: William R. Brewster, Marsena R. Patrick, John C. Robinson, Alexander S. Webb and J. H. Hobart Ward.

The relative strength of the two armies was nearer equal than ever before, and larger numbers were actually engaged. The losses far surpassed those of any other battle ever fought on this continent, the Union loss reaching 23,000, and the Confederate loss about 28,000.

In results, Gettysburg has been called the decisive battle of the war, breaking the backbone of the Rebellion. Its loss would have left the Confederates no hindrance to their march on Philadelphia and New York, and possibly through European recognition might have lost to the nineteenth century the cause of freedom. But it must not be assumed for an instant that substantially all the fighting our soldiers did was done at Gettysburg. Gettysburg was merely a sample of what came before and followed after. It was only a specimen of a frequent experience of the men who carried the salvation of the country in the barrels of their rifles during those terrible four years of conflict.

The results of the battles of Fredericksburg and Chancellorsville, followed by the depletion of the Union army by the mustering out of the short-term troops, while active conscription at the South had added largely to the Rebel army, all conspired to raise the confidence of the leaders at Richmond, and they plainly saw that if their experiment of war was to have any other effect than final exhaustion through the superior resources of the North, that now was the opportunity for such an aggressive stroke as must, if any effort on their part could do so, secure the end for which they had raised their fratricidal hands.

General Lee had come to feel an almost boundless confidence in his army, and his army shared in no small degree in the elation. They were well equipped and provided in everything but food, and their necessities in this respect gave additional incentive to the grand movement now contemplated—the invasion of the North. On the evening of Monday, June 15, 1863, Governor Seymour received a telegram from Washington calling for 20,000 militia to resist the threatened invasion. His order was issued the next morning, and the great metropolis was again alive with military excitement. On Wednesday, the 17th, the regiments of the National Guard began to leave, the Seventh, Colonel Lefferts, in the van: followed by the Eighth, Col. Joshua M. Varian; the Seventy-first, Col. Benjamin L. Trafford; the Eleventh, Col. J. Maidhoff; the Twenty-second, Col. Lloyd Aspinwall; the Thirty-seventh, Col. Charles Roome; the Fifth, Col. Louis Berger; the Fourth, Col. Daniel W Teller: the Sixty-ninth, Col. James Bagley; the Fifty-fifth, Col. Eugene Le Gal; the Twelfth, Col. William G. Ward; the Eighty-fourth, Col. Frederick A. Conkling; the Thirteenth, Col. John B. Woodward; the Fifty-sixth, Col. Michael Bennett; the Twenty-third, Col. William Everdell; the Sixth, Col. Joel W. Mason: the Forty-seventh, Col. Meserole: the Fifty-second, Col. Matthew T. Cole; the Twenty-first, Col. Wright: the Fifty-sixth, Lieut.-Col. John Quincy Adams, and the Seventy-fourth, Col. Watson A. Fox.

On the 22d of June General Lee advanced up the Cumberland valley, reaching Chambersburg in force on the 27th. For several days the Rebel army marched through Maryland and Pennsylvania unopposed, and made extensive levies of money and supplies from the panic-stricken population. On the 25th and 26th General Hooker crossed the Potomac, and failing to obtain expected reinforcements from the garrison at Harper's Ferry, owing to the adherence of the authorities at Washington to the policy of ample protection for the Federal capital, resigned his command on the 27th of June. His place was promptly filled, on the 28th, by the appointment of Gen. George G. Meade, from the Fifth Corps. Thanks to the good discipline of the army and to the fact that the new chief was taken from it, and knew its condition and had its confidence, so great a change in such an emergency had no evil consequences. For this fortunate result, however, great credit is due to his Chief of Staff, Gen. Daniel Butterfield,—for General Meade has said: "But for the efficient assistance my Chief of Staff so heartily rendered, I hardly know how I should have gotten through with the new and arduous duties imposed on me."

The army accordingly moved on as if no change had occurred. On the morning of the 29th of June, General Meade put his army in motion to the northward, to intercept, as soon as possible, the invaders, though ignorant of their present position. Lee was just then ready to cross the Susquehanna and seize Harrisburg, but becoming aware that his communications with the Potomac were menaced, he abandoned that project, and began to concentrate, with a view to preserving his line of retreat. It has been satisfactorily ascertained that the 14,000 New York militia, abandoning their business and their homes at an hour's notice, and boldly confronting the enemy, deterred their further progress through Pennsylvania and doubtless saved Harrisburg from capture. On General Ewell's retreat from Harrisburg, through Carlisle, towards Lee's main army, the Twenty-second New York State Militia Regiment, with Col. Lloyd Aspinwall at its head, had the advance of the pursuing division, supporting Capt. Rufus King's battery. The Twenty-second took possession of Carlisle and replaced Lee's flag, which they hauled down, with the celebrated Carlisle flag, which is now in the armory of the regiment.

"The first men," said Colonel Aspinwall in his report, "to enter Carlisle, were the men of the Twenty-second, and the first Stars and Stripes raised over the place was raised by a member of the regiment." The Thirty-seventh New York State Militia, Col. Charles Roome, also claims the honor of having been the first to enter Carlisle, but where both regiments did so well, the honors may be equally divided.

The point to which General Lee was now calling his commanders was Gettysburg—a quiet hamlet about to rise into fame as the scene of the grandest encounter of modern days. On Wednesday, July 1, General Buford's cavalry, a few miles west of Gettysburg, suddenly encountered the advance of the Confederate army At ten o'clock on that summer morning a musket shot was fired by the Rebels against Buford's picket line—this was the opening shot of the great battle of Gettysburg. The gallant General Reynolds with a force of 8000 men arrived just in time to support Buford, who was hard pressed by two divisions of Gen. A. P Hill's corps, numbering from twenty to thirty thousand men. Here, that day, on Willoughby Run, was fought what was in itself a great battle, in one respect, perhaps the greatest battle of the war,—that is, in the number of losses as compared with the forces engaged,—the Union losses, in killed, wounded and missing reaching nearly ten thousand. Until about one o'clock the action had been sustained on the Union side by the First Corps alone, and General Doubleday said : "That Corps fought with a determination such as I had never seen equalled." At one o'clock new actors appeared upon the stage. Hill was reinforced by a division under General Pender, while the Eleventh Corps, under General Howard, came to the assistance of the First Corps. A division of the Eleventh Corps, commanded by Gen. Francis C. Barlow, numbering about eight thousand men, was soon attacked by a force three times that number, under Gen. Jubal Early, and although General Barlow fought his division with such skill and bravery as to win the admiration even of his opponents, he found it impossible to keep his command to its work, and was himself severely wounded, and fell into the hands of the enemy. The Confederate force which the First and Eleventh Corps engaged, was enough to have crushed them, and though by sheer bravery and desperation the soldiers of the Union began the day with a series of successes, they were at last compelled to yield—but not until two-thirds of the men of the First Corps were killed, wounded or captured, and "had it not been for the marvellous bravery of this corps," said General Meade, "the position would have been lost, and with it the country." Such a tribute from such a source adds additional lustre to the records of the following New York regiments, and their commanders, who, with their companions from other States, constituted the heroic First Corps: Seventy-sixth Regiment, Maj. Andrew J. Grover, killed; Ninety-fifth Regiment, Col. George H. Biddle, wounded; One Hundred Forty-seventh Regiment, Lieut. Col. Francis C. Miller, wounded; Eighty-fourth Regiment, Col. Edward B. Fowler; Ninety-fourth Regiment, Col. Adrian R. Root, wounded; One Hundred and Fourth Regiment, Col. Gilbert G. Prey; Eighty-third Regiment, Col. Joseph A. Moesch; Ninety-seventh Regiment, Col. Charles Wheelock; Eightieth Regiment, Col. Theodore B. Gates; First Light Artillery, Capt. Gilbert H. Reynolds.

The remnants of the two corps beat a retreat finally through the town of Gettysburg to Cemetery Ridge, on the southern edge of the village. Here a part of the Eleventh Corps had been left in reserve, and behind breastworks hurriedly thrown up preparations for another stand were made. Towards evening reinforcements began to arrive, and during the night almost the whole Army of the Potomac was brought on the field. The Confederate forces also came up in full strength and were posted on the Ridge on which the desperate first day's battle had been fought so heroically by the First and a part of the Eleventh Corps. The night was spent in getting in readiness for the next day's battle, and in gathering up the wounded who so thickly strewed the field.

The record of New Yorkers, who shed their life's blood on the first day of the battle of Gettysburg, includes the following commissioned officers: Theodore Blume, of the First Independent Battery, the only artillery officer from the State killed in the three days' battle; Capt. Robert B. Everett, Capt. Robert Story, Lieut. Philip Keeler and Lieut. Robert G. Noxon, of the Seventy-sixth Regiment; Capt. Joseph S. Corbin and Lieut. George W Brankstone, of the Eightieth Regiment; Capt. Thomas W Quirk and Lieut. Charles A. Clark, of the Eighty-third Regiment; Lieut. Rush P Cady, Lieut. James H. Stiles and Lieut. William J. Morren, of the Ninety-seventh Regiment; Lieut. Henry I. Palmer, of the One Hundred and Thirty-fourth Regiment; Lieut. William P Schenck, Lieut. David G. Van Dusen, Lieut. Guilford D. Mace, Lieut. Daniel McAssy, of the One Hundred and Forty-seventh Regiment; Lieut. Col. George W Arrowsmith, Capt. Jason K. Backus, Capt. George A. Adams, Capt. Harrison Frank and Lieut. Randall D. Lower, of the One Hundred and Fifty-seventh Regiment.

The morning of July 2d, the second day of the battle, found the Union army, with the exception of the Sixth Corps, encamped on Cemetery Ridge—a line of hills extending south from Gettysburg about three miles, terminating in a high rocky peak, named Round Top, the less elevated portion of which is called Little Round Top. Had it not been for the desperate bravery with which the First Corps, on the day previous, held on to the Ridge west of the town, we would have been unable to gain this position,—Cemetery Ridge,—in itself a tower of strength, and the ensuing battle would have been fought elsewhere, and under most discouraging circumstances. To the west, a mile or less distant, is Seminary Ridge, on which the Confederate army was posted. Between these ridges lay a cultivated and undulating valley—such was the scene of this grand encounter.

Meade's position, though not one of his selection, and occupied by our retreating columns of the First and Eleventh Corps before his arrival, because it lay in their way, was in every respect an advantageous one for defence. Lee had no alternative but to assume the offensive, for which he was rendered the more ready by his success on the day before. The whole day up to four o'clock was consumed in preparations, the Union army making good use of the time in throwing up defensive works. At that hour Longstreet's corps made a desperate effort to carry Little Round Top—a prize eagerly coveted by both combatants. His column charged with reckless fury upon the Union left, which covered Round Top, but they were met with a valor and fortitude that defied their utmost efforts. Barnes' division of the Fifth Corps, however, suddenly gave way, and could not be rallied, when Gen. Samuel K. Zook, formerly Colonel of the Fifty-seventh New York Regiment, who has been called the hero of this day's battle, volunteered with his brigade to take Barnes' place. When his men reached the ground, Barnes' disorganized troops impeded the advance of the brigade. "If you can't get out of the way," cried Zook, "lie down and we will march over you." Barnes ordered his men to lie down, and the chivalric Zook and his splendid brigade, in which were the Fifty-second and Sixty-sixth New York Regiments, under the personal direction of General Birney, did march over them, right into the breach. Zook soon fell mortally wounded, and half his brigade perished with him.

After one of those fearful struggles, illustrating whatever there is of the savage and terrible in war, Little Round Top was successfully held by our troops, although at a heavy sacrifice of officers and men. A truthful picture of those thousands of brave men in deadly encounter, would bring before the reader instances of a most daring assault, met by a steadiness and bravery so unflinching as to exalt the men engaged to the highest grade of military renown. The results of the day were inconclusive, though within the brief space between four o'clock and nightfall were compressed a magnitude of military operations, a grandeur and diversity of exploits, and a devastation of noble lives that makes the day one of the most memorable in the history of warfare. The commissioned officers of the New York regiments, whose lives were then yielded up to the honor of their country, were: Col. George L. Willard, of the 125th regiment; Lieut. Robert Evans, of the 108th; Lieut. Emil Frost, of the 119th; Capt. Lansing Hollister, Capt. Ayers G. Barker, Lieut. Michael E. Creighton, Lieut. Frederick Freelewick, Lieut. Jason Carle and Lieut. John R. Burhaus, of the 120th (a regiment that, with the exception of the Twenty-fourth Michigan, lost the largest number of commissioned officers killed outright, in the three days' battles, of any regiment in the army); Capt. Norman F. Weer, of the 123d; Col. A. Van Horn Ellis (son of Dr. Samuel C. Ellis), Maj. James Cromwell, Capt. Isaac Nichols, and Lieut. Milnor Brown, of the 124th; Lieut. John H. Van Emburg and Lieut. Henry W Hallett, of the 137th, Col. Patrick H. O'Rorke and Lieut. Charles P Klein, of the 140th; Lieut. Theodor Paush and Lieut. Adolph Wagner, of the Thirty-ninth; Lieut. Wm. H. H. Johnson, of the Fortieth; Maj. Edward Venuti, of the Fifty-second; Adjutant Louis Deitrich, of the Fifty-eighth; Lieut. Myron D. Stanley, of the Sixtieth; Lieut. Franklin K. Garland, of the Sixty-first; Capt. Henry V Fuller, Lieut. Alfred H. Lewis, Lieut. Willis G. Babcock and Lieut. Ira S. Thurber, of the Sixty-fourth; Capt. Otto Friederich, of the Sixty-eighth; Lieut. Chas A. Foss, of the Seventy-second; Capt. Eugene C. Shine, Lieut. Wm. L. Herbert and Lieut. George Dennen, of the Seventy-third; Lieut. Col. James Huston and Capt. Jonah C. Hoyt, of the Eighty-second, Capt. John N. Warner, of the Eighty-sixth; Adjutant Wm.

McClelland, of the Eighty-eighth; Capt. George H. Ince and Capt. Elijah T. Munn, of the Sixty-sixth, and Adjutant J. V Upham, of the 102d.

The issues depending upon that now-approaching Friday, July 3d, were too vast, too momentous to give sleep to the eyelids of the council of commanders which late that evening assembled, and not even the brief duration of the darkness of that solstitial night afforded rest to the brave men on whose fidelity and courage hung the destinies of the century. That council, not disheartened by the fearful losses we had sustained, and knowing that the advantages the Rebels had gained were rather apparent than substantial, voted to fight it out at Gettysburg. Scarcely for break of day could wait the anxious heart of Gen. Henry W Slocum, of New York, on whom had rested the responsibilities of the Union right. The bulk of his command had been drawn off to reinforce the Union left on the evening of July 2d, and in its absence Ewell's corps had taken possession of the Federal lines on Culp's Hill. Having spent the night in bringing up powerful artillery against the breastworks where Ewell had placed his troops, at four o'clock General Slocum opened a heavy fire. This elicited from the enemy a most furious charge, which for desperation and recklessness scarcely has a parallel. But the Union forces presented an impenetrable front, and coolly delivering a terrific fire, strewed the ground with dead in fearful numbers.

After a close contest the abandoned portion of our line was recovered by a charge of Geary's division, the original positions on Culp's Hill were reëstablished, and the right wing made secure. Being thus thwarted in his plans against the flanks of the Union army, Lee resolved to stake his all upon the centre. After the struggle had ceased upon the right, there was for some hours a deep silence, indicating that some weighty design was in preparation by the enemy. About noon this silence was broken by the roar of the Confederate artillery, all of Lee's batteries uniting in an attempt to uncover the Union centre, preparatory to a charge by the flower of Longstreet's veterans under General Pickett. For more than an hour the Rebel guns poured on Cemetery Ridge a furious and unremittent shower of shells —the steadiest and most continuous fire ever maintained by the Confederate artillery. The Union batteries were not slow to answer the first attack, and the earth almost shook under the terrible and unbroken thunder of over three hundred guns. Finally the rebel fire slackened and then ceased altogether. The moment had come for Pickett's hazardous assault, the last forlorn hope of Confederate victory. Soon, across the fields, was seen moving the solid mass of Pickett's division, its three brigades led by Kemper, Garnett and Armisted. On they came with compact ranks, three lines deep—not a tree, scarce a shrub to impede their advance. They seemed to have gathered up all their strength and determination for one fierce convulsive effort that should sweep away all resistance.

The entire weight of the Rebel army was now thrown against the Second Corps, in which New York was represented by her Thirty-ninth, Forty-second, Fifty-second, Fifty-seventh, Fifty-ninth, Sixty-first, Sixty-third, Sixty-fourth, Sixty-sixth, Sixty-ninth, Eighty-second, Eighty-eighth, One Hundred and Eighth, One Hundred and Eleventh, One Hundred and Twenty-fifth and One Hundred and Twenty-sixth regiments. This devoted corps bore the brunt of the onslaught, and merits the honors of the victory. Pickett's splendid division of Longstreet's corps, in front, with the best of A. P Hill's veterans in support, came steadily, and as it seemed, resistlessly sweeping up. At last they were in point-blank range, and then came the order for our troops to fire, when from thrice six thousand guns issued a sheet of smoky flame—a crash of leaden death. The first Confederate line literally melted away, but on came the second line not less resolute. Pickett's division now thrust itself up to Hancock's line, and the full strength of this attack fell upon the brigade commanded by Gen. Alexander S. Webb, now president of the College of the City of New York.

"The movement," says Swinton, "was certainly as critical as can well be conceived, but the personal bravery and skill of General Webb, aided by the cool appreciation and quick action of General Hancock, caused the repulse and rout of the assailants," and with the repulse of Pickett's attack the last hope of Confederate victory perished. As a token of his appreciation of General Webb's magnificent conduct on this memorable day, he was presented by General Meade with a bronze medal.

Thus ended the great battle of Gettysburg, and there was fulfilled the prophecy, made thirty years before the war, by William H. Seward, "that slavery was opening up before our people a graveyard, to be filled with brothers falling in mutual political combat." Here, in this battle,—the second bloodiest battle that had occurred in one hundred years, the grand old Army of the Potomac vindicated its claim to immortal fame. This army was never in favor at the War Department; it rarely, if ever, had heard a word of official commendation after a success, or of sympathy, or encouragement, after a defeat. It had been led to battle oft, to victory but seldom, but now

"Like some tall cliff that rears its awful form
Swells from the vale and midway leaves the storm,
Though round its base the rolling clouds are spread;
Eternal sunshine settles on its head."

But this signal victory was not won without great cost. Of the dead that were identified and buried in the National Cemetery, over one-third were New York soldiers, and nearly one thousand nameless dead fell in the ranks of the New York troops. Of the wounded officers and men, New York had nearly one-third, and of the total losses, the same proportion, 6,777, is to the credit of the Empire State. Out of 247 officers killed, New York claims seventy-seven, fourteen more than at Antietam, where she sustained her next greatest loss in the war. The names of the commissioned officers from the Empire State, who, on the third day of the battle, consecrated the scenes of their patriotic devotion with their life's blood, were: Capt. William H. Gilfillan, of the Forty-third; Capt. William H. Chester, of the Seventy-fourth; Capt. Ambrose N Baldwin, of the Eightieth; Capt. John Mead, of the One Hundred and Second; Lieut. Joseph B. Day, Lieut. John Cranston, and Lieut. John H. McDonald, of the Eighty-second; Lieut. Carl V Amiet and Lieut. Dayton T. Card, of the One Hundred and Eighth; Lieut. John H. Drake, Lieut. Augustus W Prosens and Lieut. Erastus M. Granger, of the One Hundred and Eleventh; Lieut. Edward H. Ketchum, of the One Hundred and Twentieth, said to have been the first officer killed on the third day; Capt. Ephraim Wood, of the One Hundred and Twenty-fifth; Capt. Oscar C. Williams, of the One Hundred and Thirty-seventh; Col. Eliakim Sherrill, Capt. Isaac Shimer, Capt. Orin J Herendeen, Capt. Charles M. Wheeler, and Lieut. Jacob Sherman, of the One Hundred and Twenty-sixth.

But the heroic deeds of those brave men have not perished; the sentiments their lives and death inspire will be the most precious inheritance of those who are to be the hope of coming years.

CHAPTER XVII.

HONORS WON IN BATTLE BY NEW YORKERS.

The bravery of New York soldiers on the field of battle is strikingly shown by a glance at the list of awards for the capture of Confederate battle-flags. Of the three hundred medals of honor given by the War Department for the capture of flags, eighty, or more than one quarter, were presented to soldiers from the Empire State, and of this number, forty-one, or one half, were awarded to members of the twenty-five cavalry regiments. To take from the enemy a color, is to take it red with the blood of more than one who had died before its capture became possible. For a soldier to show an enemy's flag, won by his individual prowess, is a proof that he has done and dared everything, —all that may become a man.

The first Confederate flag captured in the war was taken by a New Yorker—Col. Elmer E. Ellsworth, at the Marshall House, Alexandria, Va. The first Confederate flag captured on the battle-field, was taken at the battle of Williamsburg by a native of New York City, Lieut. John N. Coyne, of the Seventieth New York Volunteers, known as the First Regiment Excelsior Brigade.

The names of the men whose conspicuous gallantry in capturing the enemy's colors reflects such credit on the Empire State, are given, as they deserve to be, in full. The honors are pretty evenly divided between officers and privates. Here is the list of the medal-winners:

Anderson, C. W., Private, 1st Cavalry, Waynesboro, March 2, 1865.

Bowen, C. B., Corporal, 1st Dragoons, Winchester, Va., September 19, 1864.
Begley, T., Sergeant, 7th Heavy Artillery, Coal Harbor, June 3, 1864.
Burk, M., Private, 125th Regiment, Spottsylvania, May 12, 1864.
Burton, Christopher C., Captain, 22d Cavalry, Waynesboro, March 2, 1865.
Bickfeld, H. H., Corporal, 8th Cavalry, Waynesboro, March 2, 1865.
Buckley, D., Private, 136th Regiment, Peach Tree Creek, July 20, 1864.
Brewer, William I., Private, 2d Cavalry, Sailor's Creek, April 6, 1865.
Benjamin, J. F., Corporal, 2d Cavalry, Sailor's Creek, April 6, 1865.
Brown, Morris, Jr., Captain, 126th Regiment, Gettysburg, July 3, 1863. Killed June 22, 1864.
Burke, T., Sergeant, 5th Cavalry, Hanover Court House, June 30, 1862.
Connors, J., Private, 43d Regiment, Fisher's Hill, September 22, 1864.
Cullen, T., Corporal, 82d Regiment, Bristoe Station, October 14, 1863.
Compson, Hartwell B., Major, 8th Cavalry, Waynesboro, March 2, 1865.
Carman, W., Private, 1st Cavalry, Waynesboro, March 2, 1865.
Crowley, M., Private, 1st Cavalry, Waynesboro, March 2, 1865.
Calkin, J. S., Sergeant, 2d Cavalry, Sailor's Creek, April 6, 1865.
Dare, George H., Sergeant, 126th Regiment, Gettysburg, July 3, 1863.
Dockham, W. C., Private, 121st Regiment, Sailor's Creek, April 6, 1865.

Davis, T., Private, 2d Heavy Artillery, Sailor's Creek, April 6, 1865.
Edwards, D., Private, 146th Regiment, Five Forks, April 1, 1865.
Everson, Private Adelbert, 185th Regiment, Five Forks, April 1, 1865.
Freeman, A., Private, 124th Regiment, Spottsylvania, May 12, 1864.
Ford, George W., Lieutenant, 88th Regiment, Sailor's Creek, April 6, 1865.
Goheen, C. A., Sergeant, 8th Cavalry, Waynesboro, March 2, 1865.
Gribbon, James H., Lieutenant, 2d Cavalry, Sailor's Creek, April 6, 1865.
Gifford, B., Private, 121st Regiment, Sailor's Creek, April 6, 1865.
Goettel, P., Private, 149th Regiment, Lookout Mountain, November 24, 1863.
Hill, J., Sergeant, 14th Heavy Artillery, Petersburg, July 30, 1865.
Harvey, H., Corporal, 22d Cavalry, Waynesboro, March 2, 1865.
Hagerty, Asel, Private, 61st Regiment, Sailor's Creek, April 6, 1865.
Jones, William, Sergeant, 73d Regiment, Spottsylvania, May 12, 1864.
Judge, F. W., Sergeant, 79th Regiment, Knoxville, November, 29, 1863.
Kelley, T., Private, 6th Cavalry, Front Royal, August 16, 1864.
Kuder, Andrew, Lieutenant, 8th Cavalry, Waynesboro, March 2, 1865.
Kelley, D., Sergeant, 8th Cavalry, Waynesboro, March 2, 1865.
Kenyon, S. P., Private, 24th Cavalry, Sailor's Creek, April 6, 1865.

Kline, Private H., 40th Regiment, Sailor's Creek, April 6, 1865.
Klauss. A., Corporal, 15th Artillery, Five Forks, April 1, 1865.
Kappesser, P., Private, 149th Regiment, Lookout Mountain, November 24, 1863.
Leslie, F., Private, 4th Cavalry, Front Royal, August 15, 1864.
Larish, A. J., Sergeant, 1st Dragoons, Winchester, September 19, 1864.
Love, George M., Colonel, 116th Regiment, Cedar Creek, October 19, 1864.
Ladd, George, Private, 22d Cavalry, Waynesboro, March 2, 1865.
Lutes, F W., Corporal, 111th Regiment, Petersburg, March 31, 1865.
Mandy, H. J., Sergeant, 4th Cavalry, Front Royal, August 15, 1864.
Meech, G. E., 6th Cavalry, Winchester, September 19, 1864.
Murphy, H., Corporal, 158th Regiment, Chapin's Farm, September 29, 1864.
Marsh, A., Sergeant, 64th Regiment, Spottsylvania, May 12, 1864.
Miller, J., Private, 8th Cavalry, Waynesboro, March 24, 1865.
Morris, William, Sergeant, 1st Cavalry, Sailor's Creek, April 6, 1865.
Miller, F., Private, 2d Cavalry, Sailor's Creek, April 6, 1865.
Murphy, T. J., Sergeant, 146th Regiment, Five Forks, April 1, 1865.
McEnroe, Patrick, Sergeant, 6th Cavalry, Winchester, September 19, 1864.
Niven, Robert, Lieutenant, 8th Cavalry, Waynesboro, March 2, 1865.

Norton, John R., Lieutenant, 1st Cavalry.
Newman, Wm. H., Lieutenant, 86th Regiment, Amelia Springs, April 6, 1865.
O'Brien, P., Private, 1st Cavalry, Waynesboro, March 2, 1865.
Parks, J., Private, 9th Cavalry, Cedar Creek, October 19, 1864.
Pittman, G. J., Sergeant, 1st Cavalry, Sailor's Creek, April 6, 1865.
Payne, J. C., Corporal, 2d Cavalry, Sailor's Creek, April 6, 1865.
Potter, N. F., Sergeant, 149th Regiment, Lookout Mountain, November 24, 1863.
Reynolds, George, Private, 9th Cavalry, Winchester, September 19, 1864.
Russell, C. L., Corporal, 93d Regiment, Spottsylvania, May 12, 1864.
Read, Mort A., Lieutenant, 8th Cavalry, Appomattox Station, April 8, 1865.
Riddle, Randolph R., Lieutenant, 61st Regiment, Sailor's Creek, April 6, 1865.
Scofield, D. S., Sergeant, 5th Cavalry, Cedar Creek, October 19, 1865.
Schlachta, G., Private, 73d Regiment, Spottsylvania, May 12, 1864.
Savacoal, Edwin, Captain, 1st Cavalry, Sailor's Creek, April 6, 1865.
Sava, J. E., Saddler, 8th Cavalry, Sailor's Creek, April 6, 1865.
Schmal, G. W., Blacksmith, 24th Cavalry, Paine's Cross Roads, April 5, 1865.
Schubert, F., Sergeant, 43d Regiment, Petersburg, April 2, 1865.
Simmons, J., Private, 2d Artillery, Sailor's Creek, April 6, 1865.
Shipley, R. F., Sergeant, 140th Regiment, Five Forks, April 1, 1865.

Tompkins, G. W., Corporal,, 124th Regiment, Petersburg, April 2, 1865.
Wells, T. M., Bugler, 6th Cavalry, Cedar Creek, October 19, 1864.
Walsh, J., Corporal, 5th Cavalry, Cedar Creek, October 19. 1864.
Westerhald, W., Sergeant, 52d Regiment, Spottsylvania. May 12. 1864.
Wall, J., Private, 126th Regiment, Gettysburg, July 3, 1863.
Wiley, J., Sergeant, 59th Regiment, Gettysburg, July 3, 1863.
Weeks, J., Private. 152d Regiment. Spottsylvania, May 12, 1864.
Winnegar, William W., Lieutenant, 1st Dragoons, Five Forks, April 1, 1865.

CHAPTER XVIII.

NEW YORK IN THE NAVY.

LET the reader now glance at the record of the American Navy and see what was done by that arm of the service, which proved to be a most potent diplomatist in preventing foreign interference with our domestic affairs. When Secretary Welles received the seals of office from Isaac Toucey, Mr. Buchanan's Secretary of the Navy, he found the department in the most feeble and deplorable condition of any branch of the Government,—without vessels, or armament, or men, and without legal authority to increase or strengthen either. The entire Navy consisted of forty-six vessels, one-half of them out of commission, and only twenty-three left for service, nearly all of which were on squadron duty abroad, so that only four were available for home defence. Secretary Welles soon set to work to create a navy. Every steam engine factory in the land was at once engaged to produce marine machinery. Every shipyard, public and private, was taxed to its utmost capacity ; and at one time twenty-five thousand hammers were at work night and day in our navy yards, and every forge and furnace in the country was at white-heat on our iron-clads and gun-boats, and the ordnance which was to man them. Starting with four vessels only, the number was increased in nine months to two hundred and twenty-six, and at the end of four years to six hundred and seventy-one, almost as many ships as we had seamen in the service at the commencement of the war.

Although nearly three hundred and fifty officers traitorously deserted the service, it should be remembered that the whole South was not disloyal, but that in our navy about one third of the officers belonged to slaveholding territory yet remained faithful to the Union. The reader is reminded that notwithstanding the large defection of officers in both the army and navy, when secession first commenced, political life was a much better school for treason than military or naval life; for while the South gave to the political councils of the nation no Unionists more conspicuous than Andrew Johnson and Mr. Hamilton, of Texas, there were one hundred officers in the regular army, all of whom were born in States that seceded, and more than half of whom were graduates of West Point. Thus it will be seen that the disloyalty of West Point was not as great as is generally supposed. In the navy about one-third of the officers came from slaveholding States, yet remained faithful to the Union; while one-eighth of the Union army, or 300,000 men, were contributed by the Southern States. Very few people realize what it cost a Southerner to sustain the old flag, when every one was rushing blindly into treason and secession; but time and history will yet hold up for universal admiration many a Southern hero of that kind whose name has not yet reached the public ear.

Tennessee gave to the navy Admiral Farragut, and to the army, Gen. Samuel P. Carter and Gen. Alvan C. Gillem; Virginia, Com. Napoleon B. Harrison, and to the army Gen. George H. Thomas, "the Rock of Chickamauga," Gen. Lawrence P Graham, Gen. John D. Stevenson, Gen. John Newton, and J. J. S. Hassler, a son of Commodore Hassler, of Virginia, who was one of four persons who issued the first call for the raising of troops in New York City, to defend the Government; Florida, Gen. John R. McIntosh; Georgia gave to the Union army Gen. John M. Cuyler; Alabama, Gen. William Birney; North Carolina, Gen. Solomon Meredith and Admiral James H. Spotts; Louisiana, Com. Edward Barrett; Mississippi, Col. Benjamin F. Davis, of the Eighth New York Cavalry; South Carolina, Commander Steedman, Commander Percival Drayton and Commander John P Bankhead, of the "Pembina."

One of the most valued nurses in the Union army was also from South Carolina—Mrs. Jane R. Munsell, who severed every tie with treason at the outset, and found her just recompense in healing the wounds of patriotic soldiers.

No action during the war shed more lustre upon our arms, or was attended with graver consequences to the country and its commerce, than the exploit of John A. Winslow—a native of North Carolina, and Commander of the United States steamer "Kearsage," under whose guns the privateer "Alabama" went down on the 19th of June, 1864, off Cherbourg.

The embarrassments caused by desertion were but temporary. Better men from the merchant marine promptly volunteered their services to fight the battles of the Union, and about seven thousand five hundred of those gallant tars received appointments, and were employed in the service. But while in this time of need so many officers resigned and proved false to the Government that had pampered them, not one common soldier, or sailor, was known to have abandoned his flag, although during the four years of the war two hundred and sixty were executed for desertion. When the disadvantages are considered under which the navy labored at the commencement of the war, we may claim the credit of having achieved a series of results surpassing in magnitude and importance the record of any navy in any country. Let Norfolk, Hatteras, Roanoke Island, Port Royal, Pensacola, the Rio Grande, Fort Henry, Fort Donaldson, Island No. 10, Memphis, Vicksburg, Port Hudson, Fort Jackson, Fort St. Philip, Fort Fisher, the city of New Orleans, Mobile, and the shattered fragments of Sumter, bear witness to the activity and efficiency of the American Navy.

"This was the only war in modern times," said Mr.

Whitney, late Secretary of the Navy, "in which naval operations on a great scale have been carried on. It was the only war in which rams, torpedoes, iron-clads, and steam blockades have been employed. All that is known of naval war to-day dates from the war of 1861."

The State of New York, ranking as a right arm in bringing the great conflict to a successful issue, can boast of a glorious record in the naval portion of its history. Of the 122,000 enlistments, 48,000 men from the State of New York were in every scene of danger and duty.

Along the Atlantic and the Gulf, on the Tennessee, the Mississippi and the Rio Grande, under Dupont, Dahlgren, Foote, Farragut and Porter, the sons of the Empire State bore their part and paid the debt of patriotism and valor. Three thousand and twenty-five naval officers perished in battle, or died during the war of disease contracted in the service, of whom eight hundred and eighty-seven were from the State of New York.

When the Administration was so greatly in need of large additions to its navy, Commodore Vanderbilt came forward and presented his magnificent ship, the "Vanderbilt," costing $800,000, as a free gift to the Government. He thus placed his name at the head of the list of those who made magnificent donations, and in recognition of the gift Congress presented him with a gold medal. The Commodore was also represented in the army by his son, the late Capt. George W Vanderbilt, of the regular army, who participated in the siege of Corinth by General Halleck, with whom he entered the city in triumph, but soon after contracted a disease from which he finally died.

One of the most important contributions ever made by individuals at their own risk in defending this, or any other, nation, was made by citizens of New York, in an utterly unexpected manner in one of the most critical periods of the war. On the 8th of March, 1862, when our fleet of steamers and sailing-craft had landed the Army of the Potomac, under General McClellan, on the Peninsula, the sudden appearance of the Rebel ram "Merrimac," near Old Point Comfort, threatened serious derangement of the plans of that officer's campaign. Here occurred the first naval engagement on record between iron and wooden vessels, in which the gallantry of the "Cumberland" will be forever remembered—her flags floating defiantly, and her noble crew, including John Bracken, of New York City, delivering their shots from the port-holes, as the ship sank in the deep sea.

Readers of Scott's novels will have a vivid recollection of the tournament in Ivanhoe, where an endangered cause was saved from destruction by the sudden advent of the Black Knight—an unknown warrior, whose diminutive appearance seemingly precluded all hope that he could successfully contend against an apparently overwhelming adversary. But a parallel on a far mightier scale was to be furnished on the following morning by a little vessel of insignificant appearance as she steamed into Hampton Roads. It was the "Monitor"—looking like a "cheese-box, on a raft,"—designed and built by the late Capt. John Ericsson, of New York, and constructed at their own expense and risk by the Hon. John A. Griswold and the Hon. John F Winslow, of New York, with the Hon. C. S. Bushnell, of Connecticut. The "Merrimac" came forth again to the contest, and after one of the most desperate conflicts recorded in naval history, we had the satisfaction of beholding the little "Monitor" the victor, and the "Merrimac" slowly withdraw from the contest. Had it not been for the genius that conceived the "Monitor," and the public spirit that prompted the manufacturers to peril reputation and money in her construction, the "Merrimac" could readily have sunk all the vessels that had landed the Army of the Potomac on the Peninsula, and Fortress Monroe might have been lost to the Union. When it is remembered that the "Monitor" was private property until after the victory was achieved, and was then sold to the Government for $275,000 (less than had been paid for the engines alone of many a third-class gunboat), we may fairly rank such men as Mr. Griswold, Mr. Winslow and Mr. Bushnell, among the heroes and saviors of the country, as well as the generals who commanded our armies. On the long roll of gallant officers whose names adorn the records of the American Navy, New York can point with special pride to such men as Com. John L. Worden, who commanded the "Monitor" in her engagement with the "Merrimac," and who, in 1861, was captured by the Confederates and became the first prisoner of war; Lieut. William B. Cushing (born in Wisconsin, but appointed to the navy from New York) the hero of the "Albemarle" fight, and who had three brothers in the service, two of whom were killed while exhibiting the greatest bravery; Lieutenant Wood, the inventor of the torpedo that destroyed the "Albemarle"; Lieut.-Com. Pierre Gouraud, the marksman of the "Montauk," and the young officer who received the Rebel Admiral Buchanan's sword at the capture of Mobile; Commander Melancthon Smith (a descendant of the Nestor of the New York Bar), who fought his ship in the attack upon Port Hudson, until she was riddled with shot and then destroyed her; Commander David Constable, who was personally complimented by President Lincoln for his gallant conduct in leading with his steamer the attacking forces in the ascent of the James River, and the bombardment of Fort Darling; Commander William E. Le Roy, one of the heroes of the battle of Mobile Bay; Com. Henry W. Morris, who participated with Farragut, in the passing of Forts Jackson and St. Philip, and in the attack upon the Chalmette batteries, the Admiral testifying to the faithfulness and ability of the commodore, who obtained a record in the war such as any officer might be proud of; Commander Homer C. Blake, who was presented with a sword in recognition of the courage and skill displayed by him in an engagement with the privateer "Alabama;" Commander Jonathan W. Wainwright, who lost his leg while in the defence of the city of Galveston, and Commander William B. Renshaw, who destroyed his vessel, and himself with her, rather than allow her to fall into the hands of the Rebels at the time of the recapture of Galveston in 1863.

Commander Theodorus Bailey, when ordered to the Southwest Pass, to co-operate in the expedition against New Orleans, found upon his arrival that his vessel, the "Colorado," could not go over the bar, and although suffering from the effects of a recent surgical operation, requested permission of Admiral Farragut to participate as a volunteer. So great was the confidence of the Admiral in his skill and bravery, that he placed him second in command, and the records of the war show how well he performed his duty during the memorable engagement with the forts, and subsequently in his conference with the Rebel authorities at New Orleans.

The records of the war are crowded with proofs of the skill and bravery of New York officers, and conspicuous on the honorable roll will be found the names of Commanders

EDWARD E. POTTER,	CHARLES A. BABCOCK,
THOMAS H. EASTMAN,	ROBERT W. SHUFELDT,
CHARLES H. BALDWIN,	ALEXANDER C. RHIND,
LEONARD PAULDING,	GEORGE M. RANSOM,
THOMAS PATTISON,	WILLIAM F. SPICER,
S. P. QUACKENBUSH,	SOMERVILLE NICHOLSON,
JOHN N. QUACKENBUSH,	JOHN S. BARNES,
FRANCIS A. ROE,	MONTGOMERY SICARD,
STEPHEN B. LUCE,	CHARLES S. NORTON,
WILLIAM C. WEST,	ROBERT L. PHYTHIAN,
GEORGE W. YOUNG,	JAMES H. STRONG,

Edmund W Henry,　　　J. R. Madison Mullany,
Ralph Chandler,　　　C. R. P Rodgers,
L. Howard Newman,　　Stephen D. Trenchard,
Henry Wilson,　　　　Foxhall A. Parker,
A. E. K. Benham,　　　Egbert Thompson,
Robert L. May,　　　　Robert Townsend,
Henry Erben,　　　　　John M. B. Clitz,
Edward P. McCrea,　　George H. Cooper,
George Bacon,　　　　Daniel L. Braine,
Lester A. Beardslee,　Andrew Bryson,
Edward Simpson,　　　Selim E. Woodworth,
Milton Haxtun,　　　　Lewis A. Kimberly,
　　　　　H. N. T. Arnold.

CHAPTER XIX.

COLORED TROOPS—AND THE RIOT IN NEW YORK CITY.

ONE hundred and eighty thousand colored troops served during the war,—the largest negro force ever mustered into the service of any government. Three colored regiments were organized under the auspices of the Union League Club, for which purpose $18,000 was contributed by the members. They were known as the Twentieth, Twenty-sixth and Thirty-first United States Colored Troops. "Considering," said the Rev. Dr. Bellows, in his history of the club, "that the whole number of negroes capable of bearing arms in the State, in 1863, was only six thousand, and that fifteen hundred of these had previously volunteered in regiments out of the State, the success of the club was very striking." On the 5th of March, 1864, the first of these regiments, the Twenty-sixth, under command of the late Col. Nelson B. Bartram, marched down Fifth Avenue and Broadway in solid platoons, to the strains of martial music, and were everywhere saluted with the acclamations and plaudits of countless beholders. Eight months before these same men could not have shown themselves in the most obscure streets of the city without fear of instant death. The African race had been literally hunted down like wild beasts; when caught, they were shot in cold blood, or hung to the nearest lamp posts. Their homes were pillaged, the Asylum which Christian charity had provided for their children was burned, and there was no limit to the persecution, save the physical impossibility of finding further material on which the mob could wreak its vengeance. How astonishingly has all this been changed! The negro troops secured for themselves a record in the war that will insure for them and their race the respect and honor which was needed to make their freedom valuable to them, and which, for us, freely and generously to give proves that we have become emancipated from the demoralizing influences of slavery.

Consider for a moment the debt America owed to Africa. "There had been landed on this Western Continent, on the West Indies and South America and in the United States," said the Hon. Charles Sumner, "15,500,000 African slaves, and for every slave reaching those shores another had perished, either on the voyage, or in the process of procuring and bringing them down to the coast in Africa. We had, therefore, thirty millions as the round number, lost to Africa, by the institution of slavery." "This institution," said the Hon. R. M. T. Hunter, of Virginia, in the United States Senate, in 1860, "is the very keystone of the mighty arch which sustains our social superstructure. Knock that out, and the mighty fabric, with all it upholds topples and tumbles to its fall." Could Mr. Hunter have looked into the future, with what horror would he have seen, within five years, that very "keystone of the mighty arch" knocked out by the entrance of a brigade of negro soldiers into the city of Richmond, and with what amazement would he have seen colored troops first occupy the capital of a Confederacy, of which, in the days of its hoped-for supremacy, African Slavery was to be the very corner-stone.

No words can state too strongly the debt of gratitude which the city owed to the handful of policemen who breasted the fury of the ferocious mob during the three days of July, 1863, when the life of a negro depended entirely on the security of his hiding-place. There have been other abominations of the sort in America, but nothing that began to be as infernal as this. From the very first day of the riot, a vileness and depravity of spirit was shown by the mob scarcely to be paralleled in any civilized land since the

French Reign of Terror. During the first day of the riot the police bore the whole brunt of the storm, and it was to the unflinching courage and admirable tenacity with which they resisted step by step the fury of the mob, that the citizens owed the check that was finally put upon its depredations. Less than fifteen hundred policemen, scattered over the city, without any warning of the coming tempest, were suddenly required to face and withstand a raging mob of tens of thousands of reckless and infuriated madmen, who taking advantage of the absence of all our militia regiments that were again, for the third time, at the seat of war, endeavored to aid the Confederate cause and to minimize the advantages our arms were gaining in the field. The Richmond correspondent of the New York *Tribune* said, "I knew, as did everyone connected with the Rebel War Department, as early as the 6th of July, that there would be a bloody riot in New York. We were led by letters from Copperheads in New York, however, to believe that instead of being a mere riot, there would be a tremendous insurrection; that the Peace-men were organized, and that the forts and arsenals would be seized, the Abolitionists massacred and the metropolis itself threatened with destruction."

That the club is mightier than the musket in the suppression of a mob, was proven by the experiences of those three days of riot. It has been said that there is no instance on record in which an efficient police force has not scattered the mobs they were sent against, while it was also noticeable that the mob fought far more desperately, and with greater success, against the soldiers than the police. Bullets have an unaccountable propensity to kill the wrong person, but clubs rarely reach any but the right heads; hence the terrible exasperation that invariably follows the use of the former in all crowded communities.

Occasions make the reputation of heroes. This apothegm is true as regards the conduct of the police. From the time when Superintendent Kennedy went alone among the mob, barely escaping with his life, the police force distinguished themselves by their supreme courage, devotion and fidelity to the cause of peace and good order, of the Union, and the laws. And each and all of these brave men deserve to have their names perpetuated in the annals of the State and city of New York, for those who were living in the midst of those exciting days cannot forget how much the city was indebted to the constaut vigilance, bravery and skill of Commissioners Thomas C. Acton and John G. Bergen; Inspectors George W Dilks, James Leonard, Daniel Carpenter and John W Folk ; Captains Theron S. Copeland, Jacob B. Warlow, G. W Walling, Jeremiah Petty, Jacob L. Siebring, T. C. Davis, Jacob J. Mount, Theron R. Bennett, John Jourdan, Christopher Dixon, Thomas Steers, J. J. Williamson, C W Caffry, H. Heddon, S. Brower, John Cameron, Henry C. Scott, Henry Hutchings, James Todd, Nathaniel W Mills, Thomas W Thorne, John C. Helme, John F. Dickson, F. C. Speight, J. Hartt, James Z. Bogart, A. S. Wilson, and Officers John A. Crocker, Stephen B. Smith, John Mangin, Harry Whittemore, John Walsh, Stephen Blackwood, Hiram Chandler and Henry Dippel (killed).

Many of these brave men were severely injured and some are still suffering from the effects of wounds received while defending the lives and property of those committed to their care.

Col. Joel B. Erhardt, after serving with distinction for two years as an officer of that famous regiment, the First Vermont Cavalry, resigned, and returned to his native State. During the riots he was made a provost-marshal, and while in the discharge of his duty he was severely wounded, and came near losing his life. He is now Collector of the Port of New York.

After Superintendent Kennedy was disabled, Commissioner Thomas C. Acton assumed command of the police, and there was no better evidence of the weight of the responsibility that rested upon this faithful guardian of the public interests than the fact, that for one hundred hours he never closed his eyes in sleep, nor had scarcely an opportunity to obtain a change of clothing. Mr. Acton still lives—hale and hearty—and is at this time President of the Bank of New Amsterdam.

CHAPTER XX.

NEW YORK'S LOSSES IN THE WAR—CONCLUSION.

The grand total of all the Union losses from the attack on Sumter to the close of the war, amounted to 9,000 commissioned officers and 285,000 men, equal to the entire number that composed our armies in the Revolutionary War. Eleven hundred commissioned officers of New York regiments were killed, mortally wounded, or died of disease while in the service of their country; and of this number nearly one-half, or 543, belonged to the organizations from the city of New York. Fourteen thousand five hundred New York soldiers were killed, or died of wounds received in battle, and 17,500 died of disease contracted in the service during the four years of the war, thus showing a grand total of 33,000 from the Empire State, who sacrificed their lives during the War of the Rebellion.

The records also show that the Eighth Heavy Artillery Regiment, organized at Lockport, and the Eighty-fifth Infantry, organized in New York City, contributed the largest number of commissioned officers to that mighty roll of fallen heroes. The first commissioned officers from the New York City regiments killed outright in battle, were Col. James Cameron and Capt. David Brown, of the Seventy-ninth State Militia (Highlanders), who shed their blood at the first battle of Bull Run, and the last commissioned officer from a New York City regiment killed in battle was Lieut. William Malcolm, of the Sixty-first, who fell on the 6th of April, 1865. Col. William F. Fox, formerly of the 107th New York Regiment, in his article on "The Chances of Being Hit in Battle," says: "Only thirty-five infantry regiments, in the armies of the Union, lost over two hundred officers and men killed and wounded in battle. Of these thirty-five, five were from the State of New York, viz.: the Fortieth, Forty-eighth, Sixty-ninth and 121st. Of the five mentioned, the Sixty-ninth, an Irish Regiment, lost the largest number—259." The Sixty-ninth also furnished the youngest colonel from the Empire State—Col. Denis F Burke, who proved himself a most gallant officer and was honorably mentioned in the official reports.

Twenty-five hundred battles and skirmishes took place during the four years of the war, and one-half of all the sacrifices occurred in the principal battles, which numbered thirty-one in all. When the news of some of these great battles reached Paris, men asked if giants had broken loose, who thus fought battles, not of days, but of weeks, and piled up slaughter in the face of which the bloodiest fights of Europe seem pale and unsanguinary. The losses of the Army of the Potomac alone, at the Wilderness, Spottsylvania, and Coal Harbor, equalled in number those of the whole allied army which fought on the plains of Waterloo for the liberties of Europe and the very existence of England.

The remains of over three hundred thousand private soldiers now rest in more than eighty cemeteries, located mostly in those States, that they gave their lives to save to the Union. Of this number only 172,000, a little over one-half, have been identified; and that many have been enabled to pay the last honors to those whose fate would otherwise have remained unknown, is due to the thoughtful care and personal exertions of Miss Clara Barton.

The battles in which our heroes fell were not fought in a corner, but upon the Lookout Mountain of human hope; and if it be true that the spirits of departed friends are cognizant of what is done upon the earth, then we may imagine the blue vault above us peopled with the spirits of our soldier brothers, whose bones lie mouldering back to dust in the places where they fell, but whose heroic deeds are enshrined forever in the memories of mankind.

But while we venerate the memory of the dead, let us not forget the living. They, too, offered up their lives, although the sacrifice was not required, and their valor helped to win the day for which their comrades shed their blood. While in other lands a single battle might have secured the triumph of the Right, they had to risk their lives in twenty-five hundred different engagements. They had to rise superior to the disastrous perils of the Peninsula; to encounter the enemy with renewed courage at Manassas, and, undismayed by that reverse, to assail him determinedly at Antietam and brave destruction at Fredericksburg.

They buried their thousands of dead under the shadow of Marye's Heights and went to meet an equal loss at Chancellorsville. They did not rest upon their laurels at Gettysburg, but marched on to the terrible carnage of the Wilderness, the slaughter of Coal Harbor, the weary months of toil and fighting around Richmond, and the death grapple with the rebellion between Petersburg and Appomattox.

We would have had no centennial to celebrate, if the flag, during those four years of blood and death and perils, had not been defended with such instances of individual heroism, such immolation on the altar of patriotism, even to the sacrificing of whole families, as crowd the records of the American Civil War.

New York had her full share in the brilliant deeds, the sacrifices, the perils and the glories of those years of constant struggle. One hundred million dollars were expended by the State and local authorities in raising troops, including bounties and sanitary supplies. Her regiments were an important factor in every campaign—honorably conspicuous in nearly all the battles and bearing their part in the losses and sufferings of all.

Individual commands were constantly making brilliant

records for gallant service, and scarcely a single organization can be said to have brought discredit on the Empire State. In Appendix No. 2 are given indications of the courage and devotion shown by New York regiments, as well as a brief glance at the salient points in the records of the various commands raised by that State for the prosecution of the war.

A volume, too, could be filled with the special acts of daring; the striking individual achievements; the gallantry of both men and officers. In another appendix, No. 1, substantial lists are given of New Yorkers who won honorable distinction on the field of battle. These thousand instances or so, stand for a greater body of unknown, or unrecorded, achievements of courage, sacrifice, and devotion which will make the Civil War ever glorious in American history. And in these inspiring annals, the Empire State can always look for a fresh impulse to genuine patriotism.

One of the most interesting Greek manuscripts that has come down to us, and is still in a good state of preservation, contains a list of Athenian youths who left home to meet the invader and lay down their lives in defence of their country. Perhaps three thousand years have rolled over this memorial, and yet it outlives whole cities of brick and marble. May this record of the sons of New York, telling of immortal deeds, be read three thousand years hence in the archives of the Empire State.

APPENDIX I.

SOME OF NEW YORK'S HEROES,

AMONG THE LOWER OFFICERS AND IN THE RANK AND FILE.

"Whoe'er amidst the sons of reason, valor, liberty and virtue, displays distinguished merit, is a Noble of nature's own creating."

THOMSON'S Coriolanus.

Many names will be found in the list who afterwards attained to higher rank by promotion, or have gone down to honored graves in later stages of the service, or since the close of the war.

The reference at the end of each paragraph in this roll of honorably mentioned New York Soldiers, is to the detailed data in the Author's "LIBRARY OF NATIONAL RECORDS."

Ten thousand acts of heroism the most worthy of praise, often while the least paraded, have not been made public and thus brought within reach of the Compiler.

ALLASON: CAPTAIN ROBERT F., 38th Regiment. Honorably mentioned in Colonel Farnsworth's Report of the battle of Bull Run. Vol. 11, page 61.

ABBOTT: LIEUTENANT THOMAS, 42d Regiment. Honorably mentioned in Lieutenant Colonel Mooney's Report of the battle of Ball's Bluff. Vol. 14, page 140.

ARNOULD: LIEUTENANT J., 55th Regiment. Honorably mentioned in General Peck's Report of the battle of Seven Pines. Vol. 21, page 359.

ARMES: CAPTAIN GEORGE A., 2d Artillery; on the occasion of a reconnoissance in December, 1864, on the Vaughn Road to Hatcher's Run, the conduct of Captain Armes was specially commended by General Miles. Vol. 51, page 203.

ANDERSON: PRIVATE BRUCE, 142d Regiment. He volunteered to advance with the head of the column and cut the palisading at the time of the assault on Fort Fisher. Vol. 52, page 380.

ADAMS: CAPTAIN HENRY J., 118th Regiment. General Butler said, "Captain Adams and Lieutenant Gibbs were the first men in the redoubts (Chapin's Farm), and are commended for their presence of mind in turning the enemy's guns to bear upon them." Vol. 49, page 456.

ARCHER: SERGEANT LESTER, 96th Regiment. Honorably mentioned by General Butler for his gallantry in placing the colors of his regiment on Battery Harrison. (Chapin's Farm.)
Vol. 49, page 456.

ARTHUR: MAJOR WILLIAM, 4th Artillery. He gallantly commanded his men in the brilliant action of May 19, 1864, at Spottsylvania. Vol. 44, page 356.

AXTELL: MAJOR NATHANIEL G., 142d Regiment. In the engagement at Drury's Bluff, May, 1864, Major Axtell was severely wounded, but persisted in keeping on duty, and went through the fight in gallant style. Vol. 44, page 413.

AVERY: LIEUTENANT-COLONEL ROBERT, 102d Regiment. This gallant officer went to the war as a Captain; he won his way to the Lieutenant-Colonelcy, and at Chancellorsville received a wound in the jaw from which he recovered just in time to lead the left wing at the battle of Lookout Mountain, where it took more prisoners than it had men in its ranks.
Vol. 49, page 68.

AVERY: MAJOR M. HENRY, 10th Cavalry. In the engagement at Deep Bottom, Va., July, 1864, Major Avery, during a most critical situation, gathered together some fifteen of his men and made desperate efforts to save from capture Battery A, 2d U. S. Artillery. He charged repeatedly the advancing column of the enemy, but notwithstanding all his efforts and the loss of most of his men, he was compelled to retire.
Vol. 46, page 570.
Major Avery also distinguished himself by a brilliant dash into Drainesville and Leesburg. Vol. 24, page 429.

ASHBY: LIEUTENANT-COLONEL CHARLES, 54th Regiment. Honorably mentioned in Gen. Carl Schurz's Report of the battles of Groveton and second Bull Run. Vol. 25, page 58.

AVERY: LIEUTENANT WILLIAM B, 1st Marine Artillery. Acquitted himself with great bravery at the battle of Tranter's Creek. Vol. 21, page 252.

AVERY: CAPTAIN ROBERT, 102d Regiment. His conduct at the battle of Cedar Mountain, spoken of in the highest terms of praise. Vol. 23, page 295.

AYRES: CAPTAIN CONWAY W., 9th Cavalry. At the battle of Beverly Ford, or Brandy Station, he participated with honor in one of the most daring and brilliant dashes on record. (Killed in action, September 19, 1864.) Vol. 33, page 266.

ANDREWS: BUGLER WILLIAM, 48th Regiment. A boy sixteen years old, previously wounded at Fort Wagner, took a rifle and fired sixty rounds; applying to Major Coan for more ammunition, he went back into the battle and fought gallantly until it was ended. Vol. 42, page 271.

ARNOLD: A. A., 78th Regiment. Honorably discharged the service in order to enable him to receive promotion.
Vol. 30, page 246.

ARROWSMITH: CAPTAIN GEORGE. Formerly of the 26th Regiment, promoted by General Tower for gallantry displayed on the battle field of Bull Run. Vol. 24, page 148.

ALEXANDER: LIEUTENANT WILLIAM, 1st Cavalry. Honorably mentioned in General Kearny's Report of the Cavalry fight at Sangster's Station. Vol. 18, page 424.

ALDEN: MAJOR ALONZO, 169th Regiment. He saw arduous duty in the 38th New York, entering that command on its formation as Second Lieutenant of Company I, and afterwards promoted to the Adjutancy, the duties of which position he discharged with great faithfulness. He was appointed Major of the 169th at the special instance of Hon. James Forsyth and his coadjutors of the Troy War Committee. Vol. 25, page 97. Lieutenant-Colonel Alden acquitted himself with great distinction at the battle of Drury's Bluff. Vol. 44, page 337.

ALBRIGHT: JACOB, 37th Regiment. His name inscribed on the Roll of Honor and to wear the Kearny Cross for gallant conduct at the battle of Chancellorsville. Vol. 32, page 372.

ADAMS: COLONEL JULIUS W., 67th Regiment. Behaved admirably at the battle of Seven Pines. He sat on his horse smoking his pipe during the engagement, and gave his orders with the coolness of a veteran. Vol. 21, page 100.

ADAMS: LIEUTENANT-COLONEL ALEXANDER D., 27th Regiment. He led the gallant 27th on the occasion of a brilliant charge at the battle of Gaines' Mills. Vol. 22, page 648.

ALLEN: SERGEANT-MAJOR MARTIN, 67th Regiment. Wounded at the battle of Seven Pines. He did his duty nobly, rallying his regiment around their standard, and leading them forward when nearly every officer was either killed or had retired to the rear. His services were noticed and appreciated by his commanding officer, who rewarded him by promotion before he left the field. Vol. 21, page 348.

BROWN: CAPTAIN FRANCIS C., 13th Cavalry. Acquitted himself bravely on the occasion of an expedition to the Rapidan, and an encounter with Early's forces, September, 1864.
Vol. 48, page 435.

BEARDSLEY: MAJOR WM. E., 6th Cavalry. The hero of a brilliant affair with three hundred and fifty men under Mosby at the time of the fight at Berryville, September, 1864. Beardsley had only seventy-five men. Vol. 48, page 183.
At the battle of Crooked Run, Major Beardsley led a squadron of his regiment in a brilliant charge. Vol. 47, page 365.

BURGESS: CORPORAL, 13th Cavalry. Promoted for bravery in a fight which resulted in the wounding of the guerilla Mosby, September, 1864. Vol. 48, page 482.

BUSH: CAPTAIN WM. W., 28th Regiment. The first Volunteer of the war. On the 15th of April, 1861, Captain Bush was in the telegraph office at Lockport, when Lincoln's first call for troops was issued. Hearing the call as it went over the wire, he rushed down to his place of business, and five minutes after enlisted, twenty minutes later he had nineteen men enrolled for his company of the 28th Regiment. Captain Bush was very daring; saw severe service in the war, went through many battles, and survived the horrors of Libby Prison. Twenty years later he was president of the Twelfth Army Corps. Vol. 84, page 720.

BRITTON: CAPTAIN RUSSELL A., 19th Cavalry. In an engagement near Winchester, Va., 1864, he especially distinguished himself by his coolness and bravery. Vol. 47, page 365.

BRADSHAW: LIEUTENANT CLINTON, 71st Regiment. Gen. George C. Thomas commanding at Washington, July, 1864, at the time of Jubal Early's raid, said, "As the exigency which called for the services of troops to defend Washington has gone by, I desire publicly to thank Lieutenant Bradshaw." Vol. 46, page 376.

BEADLE: LIEUTENANT MARCUS, 123d Regiment. Formerly of the United States army. Distinguished for bravery at Wilson's Creek, and at the battles of Dug Spring, Pilot Knob, Island No. 10, and at Corinth. Mentioned by Colonel McDougal as the best example of coolness and courage as marking the conduct of the officers of the 123d. Vol. 33, page 110.

BURKE: LIEUTENANT WILLIAM H., 3d Cavalry. Complimented for his gallantry in the action near Washington, N. C. Vol. 31, page 391.

BURKE: PRIVATE, 5th Cavalry. Acquitted himself heroically at the battle of Hanover, Pa. Vol. 34, page 210.

BURTIS: LIEUTENANT-COLONEL CHARLES H., 74th Regiment. He was with his gallant regiment in the various battles on the Peninsula, and fought not only wisely, but too well, as the fatigue he underwent resulted in illness, which compelled him to resign. Vol. 25, page 267.

BULL: LIEUTENANT-COLONEL JAMES M., 126th Regiment. Honorably mentioned in Colonel Kimball's Report of the battle of Antietam. Vol. 24, page 556.

BROWER: LIEUTENANT GEORGE II., 71st Regiment. General George C. Thomas commanding at Washington, July, 1864, at the time of Jubal Early's raid said: "As the exigency which called for the services of troops to defend Washington, has gone by, I desire publicly to thank Lieutenant Brower." Vol. 46, page 376.

BUSH: MAJOR ROBERT P., 185th Regiment. He participated with honor in many noted engagements and was for a time a prisoner of war. Vol. 54, page 206.

BIGLER. CORPORAL TERRENCE, 7th Artillery. At the battle of Coal Harbor, June 3, 1864, in the charge of Barlow's division, the colors of the 26th Virginia Regiment were captured in the Rebel works by Corporal Bigler. Vol. 45, page 122.

BUNDY: LIEUTENANT HENRY, 13th Battery. At the battle of Peach Tree Creek, Ga., July 21, 1864, the indomitable Bundy handled his battery with wonderful skill and bravery.
Vol. 47, page 93.

BROWN: CAPTAIN JOHN A., 85th Regiment. "He commanded with great credit the forces that garrisoned Fort Gray during the siege of Plymouth, N. C." Vol. 43, page 357.

BURROWS: LIEUTENANT JABEZ, 9th Cavalry. At the battles of Beverly Ford and Brandy Station, he participated with honor in one of the most daring and brilliant dashes on record.
Vol. 33, page 266.

BURNS: CAPTAIN MICHAEL W., 73d Regiment. Honorably acquitted himself at the battle of Williamsburg.
Vol. 20, page 318.
He was complimented for his bravery by General Hooker and every field officer in the brigade. Vol. 28, page 339.
Captain Burns commanded the regiment at the battle of Gettysburg. His behavior was most gallant and he won the admiration of all. Vol. 34, page 296.

BURNS: SERGEANT HUGH W. His name ordered to be inscribed on the Roll of Honor, and to wear the Kearny Cross for gallant conduct at Chancellorsville. Vol. 32, page 372.

BURT: CAPTAIN FRANK, 89th Regiment. He voluntarily led his company across the Rappahannock in boats, in order to dislodge the Rebel sharpshooters, and thus enable our engineers to build the bridges that our troops might cross and take the city of Fredericksburg at the time it was attacked by General Burnside. Vol. 27, page 254.

BUCKLEY: JOHN H., 51st Regiment. Promoted for bravery on the battle-field of Newbern. Vol. 20, page 176.

BUTLER: HENRY, 3d Cavalry. The hero of a daring act in North Carolina. The Major of the regiment determined to call on some one to volunteer and swim the Neuse River—then after swimming it, to board a Rebel gunboat. To do this daring deed, Henry Butler volunteered. He undressed, ran down the bank and swam to the opposite side. He then started to get a fire-brand at the burning bridge, when the enemy opened fire on him. Butler instantly turned and ran for the river, followed by a couple of the enemy, jumped into the water, was again fired upon, and finally reached his old position without injury. Vol. 27, page 450.

BURTON: LIEUTENANT JAMES W., 7th Cavalry. One of the heroes of a fight eighteen miles from Suffolk. Vol. 32, page 442.

BAILEY: MAJOR EZRA H., 1st Cavalry. He was for some time an active orderly on General Torbert's Staff. His promotion was a reward for meritorious services in the field.
Vol. 52, page 345.
Captain Bailey was the first Cavalry volunteer on the Union side. Vol. 84, page 719.

BARNEY: LIEUTENANT-COLONEL ALBERT M., 142d Regiment, one of the heroes of Fort Fisher. Vol. 52, page 291.

BYRNE: COLONEL JAMES J., 18th Cavalry. He greatly distinguished himself by industry and gallantry during General Davidson's raid from Baton Rouge to Pensacola. He was on the General's Staff. Vol. 52, page 254.

BARTON: COLONEL WM. B., 48th Regiment. He commanded a brigade under General Brooks, and was one of the leading actors in the successful destruction of the Petersburg and Richmond Railroad in May, 1864. Vol. 44, page 139.

BULL: LIEUTENANT WM. S., 12th Battery. This gallant officer acquitted himself with the greatest bravery on the 22d of June, 1864, when the Rebels attacked and captured his battery in front of Petersburg. Vol. 45, page 482.

BYRNE: LIEUTENANT JOHN J., 36th Regiment. Especially distinguished for meritorious conduct during the storming of the heights of Fredericksburg. Vol. 32, page 308.

BYRNE: SERGEANT, 9th Regiment. Honorably mentioned in Colonel Kimball's Report of the battles of South Mountain and Antietam. Vol. 25, page 7.

BENEDICT: LIEUTENANT-COLONEL LEWIS J., 73d Regiment. Honorably mentioned in the *Tribune's* report of the battle of Williamsburg. Vol. 20, page 261.

BEARD: Major Oliver T., 48th Regiment. Honorably mentioned in General Viele's Report of the capture of Fort Pulaski.
Vol. 20, page 378.

BERCHAND or BURCHANCE: Hiram, 4th Regiment. At the battle of Antietam he lost his regiment amid the confusion attendant upon a great battle, and requested Lieutenant Munn, of the 66th New York, to take him in his command. He was accepted, and fell into the ranks with his men and fought bravely through that terrible deadly struggle. Vol. 25, page 107.

BATTERSBY: Lieutenant-Colonel Jenyns C., 1st Cavalry. When Sheridan in 1864 set out from Winchester to join Grant, his way was obstructed by the Rebels under Rosser, at the bridge over North River, near Mt. Crawford. The 1st, under Lieutenant-Colonel Battersby, was ordered to swim the river a mile above the bridge, and charge the Rebels in flank, which they did in fine style, driving them out of their works.
Vol. 84, page 96.

BAKER: Major Charles C., 39th Regiment. Major Baker was wounded at the battle of Spottsylvania Court House, May 18, 1864. He had commanded his regiment with great bravery through all the severe contests of the army from the battle of the Wilderness, May 5. Vol. 44, page 384.

BAGG: Major Egbert, 117th Regiment. One of the wounded heroes of Fort Fisher. Vol. 52, page 301.

BROWNE; Sergeant Edward, 62d Regiment. In the affair at Salem Heights, Chancellorsville, in May, 1863, Sergeant Browne, who was at the time only Corporal, persisted in holding up the colors of his regiment, although severely wounded, until he was peremptorily ordered to the hospital. In 1886 Sergeant Browne was one of the Judges in the city of New York.
Vol. 87, page 206.

BUTLER: Lieutenant-Colonel Benjamin C., 93d Regiment. He fought in nine different engagements, in all of which he behaved with distinguished gallantry. Vol. 53, page 151.

BOERCKEL: Sergeant Geo. W., Co. F, 47th Regiment. General Butler says: "For gallantry and good conduct he was recommended for promotion." Vol. 49, page 456.

BAKER: PRIVATE SILAS, 142d Regiment. He volunteered to advance with the head of the column and cut down the palisading at the time of the assault on Fort Fisher.
Vol. 52, page 380.

BRADY, JR.: LIEUTENANT JOHN, 38th Regiment. Honorably mentioned in Colonel Farnsworth's Report of the battle of Bull Run. Vol. 11, page 61.

BROWNELL: FRANK E., 11th Regiment. The avenger of the noble Ellsworth's death. Vol. 11, page 236.

BELLINGER: CHRISTOPHER, 78th Regiment. Honorably discharged the service in order to enable him to receive promotion. Vol. 30, page 246.

BROTHERS: SERGEANT JOHN, 88th Regiment. One of those meritorious and distinguished soldiers of General Birney's division, selected for gallantry as a recipient of the Kearny Cross. Vol. 32, page 544.

BRONDHART: JOHN, 88th Regiment. His name ordered to be inscribed on the Roll of Honor, and to wear the Kearny Cross, for gallant conduct at the battle of Chancellorsville.
Vol. 32, page 372.

BRASLIN: SERGEANT THOMAS, 40th Regiment. His name ordered to be inscribed on the Roll of Honor, and to wear the Kearny Cross for gallant conduct at Chancellorsville.
Vol. 32, page 372.

BRAGG: LIEUTENANT HENRY M., 139th Regiment. Promoted for special gallantry to Aide-de-camp to General Gilmore.
Vol. 40, page 148.

BAKER: COLONEL BENJAMIN F., 43d Regiment. He led the regiment with coolness, skill and courage, through all the battles on the Peninsula and Pope's campaign. Vol. 25, page 167.

BAGLEY: LIEUTENANT JAMES, 69th Regiment, N. Y. S. M. Honorably mentioned in General Sherman's Report of the battle of Bull Run. Vol. 11, page 169.

BYRNE: JAMES G., 71st Regiment. Promoted for bravery on the battle-field of Bull Run. Mr. Byrne was formerly an employee in the *Herald* Office. Vol. 11, page 54.

BARTLETT: Major Joseph J., 27th Regiment. Honorably mentioned in General Porter's Report of the battle of Bull Run.
Vol. 11, page 221.

BRITTON: Captain George T., 38th Regiment. Honorably acquitted himself at the battle of Bull Run. Vol. 10, page 132.

BOWE: Major Peter, 42d Regiment. Honorably mentioned in Lieutenant-Colonel Mooney's Report of the battle of Ball's Bluff. Vol. 10, page 532.

BRUNNER: Corporal, 5th Regiment. Honorably mentioned in General Butler's Report of the battle of Big Bethel.
Vol. 9, page 285.

BARKER: Lieutenant John G., 36th Regiment. Especially distinguished for meritorious conduct during the storming of the heights of Fredericksburg. Vol. 32, page 308.

BARKER: Lieutenant Elmer I., 5th Cavalry. Deserves particular mention for his gallantry in a fight with Mosby's guerillas. Vol. 33, page 2.

BARKER: Sergeant, 2d Cavalry. Behaved splendidly during the series of cavalry fights in October, 1863. Vol. 37, page 484.

BARRY: Private, 1st Artillery. Honorably acquitted himself at the battle of Williamsburg. Vol. 20, page 318.

BARTHOLOMEW: Lieutenant T. L., 9th Regiment. Honorably mentioned in Colonel Kimball's Report of the battle of South Mills. Vol. 20, page 146.

BARNETT: Lieutenant Wm. G., 9th Regiment. Honorably mentioned in Colonel Kimball's Report of the battle of South Mills.
Vol. 20, page 146.

BAILEY: Lieutenant Perrin C., 9th Cavalry. At the battle of Beverly Ford or Brandy Station he participated with honor in one of the most daring and brilliant dashes on record.
Vol. 33, page 266.

BARTRAM: Colonel Nelson B., 17th Regiment. From the second battle of Bull Run to the expiration of the term of his enlistment he commanded the regiment. The Army of the Potomac did not produce a more meritorious or efficient officer. He was in 1864 Colonel of the 20th United States Colored Regi-

ment. Colonel Bartram died in 1887, and at the time of his death was an officer in the New York Custom House.
Vol. 40, page 336.

BARTON: COLONEL WILLIAM, 48th Regiment. Commanded a brigade at the battle of Olustee, Fla., and had two horses shot under him. Vol. 41, page 367.

BARRAS: LIEUTENANT SAMUEL A., 126th Regiment. He showed such coolness while endeavoring to rally his wavering companies at the battle of Harper's Ferry, as to attract the attention of Colonel Miles. Vol. 24, page 410.

BAIRD: LIEUTENANT-COLONEL WILLIAM H., 126th Regiment. On the occasion of a reconnoissance of the Army of the Potomac in February, 1864, he won the highest commendation from his superior officers for an exhibition of gallantry seldom witnessed on the battle-field. It will be remembered that he was dismissed for misbehavior in the presence of the enemy at Harper's Ferry. Assured of his innocence of the charge of cowardice, he was reinstated by the President and promoted by the Governor. Vol. 41, page 109.

BOYLE: LIEUTENANT JAMES A., 12th Regiment. His firmness, fidelity and fearlessness made him an invaluable officer.
Vol. 33, page 539.

BENNETT: SERGEANT-MAJOR J. D., 40th Regiment. His name ordered to be inscribed on the Roll of Honor, and to wear the Kearny Cross for gallant conduct at the battle of Chancellorsville. Vol. 32, page 372.

BARTHAUR: WILLIAM C., 100th Regiment. One of the heroes who charged up to the parapet of Fort Wagner on the 28th of July, 1863, and was badly wounded on the occasion.
Vol. 35, page 321.

BELL: SERGEANT JOHN, 73d Regiment. Promoted to Lieutenant for gallant conduct on the field. Vol. 30, page 17.

BENNETT: THOMAS, 99th Regiment. One of the heroes on board the "Congress" who participated in the fight with the "Merrimac." Vol. 18, page 232.

BABCOCK: LIEUTENANT HORACE B., 9th Artillery. After being shot down at the battle of West Point, he supported himself against a tree and urged on his men, until from loss of blood he fell exhausted. Vol. 20, page 437.

BARTO: LIEUTENANT BENNETT G., 125th Regiment. Entitled to distinguished credit for his gallantry in leading one hundred men across the river at Morton's Ford, in February, 1864.
Vol. 41, page 192.

BENNETT: SERGEANT EDWARD. At the battle of Gettysburg he took twenty-five Rebel prisoners belonging to the 5th Texas Regiment. He told them to surrender and they refused. "Co. F, fall on," he cried out. The men did not wait a second call, but surrendered at once. Vol. 34, page 421.

BENHAM: SERGEANT LEONARD, 83d Regiment. Honorably discharged the service in order to receive promotion.
Vol. 30, page 246.

BASSFORD: MAJOR ABRAM, 14th Cavalry Regiment. Alluded to in complimentary terms by General Wool for his gallantry and good conduct during the riot in New York.
Vol. 34, page 574.
At Cane River, La., he commanded his regiment in gallant style. Vol. 43, page 217.

BEECHER: LIEUTENANT HENRY B., 67th Regiment. Son of the late Rev. Henry Ward Beecher. Lieutenant Beecher acquitted himself with great gallantry in North Carolina.
Vol. 27, page 484.

BEECHER: LIEUTENANT LIND, 3d Cavalry. Complimented for his gallantry in action near Washington. Vol. 31, page 391.

BECKER: CAPTAIN GILBERT W., 2d Veteran Cavalry. He was shot through the neck at the battle of Pleasant Hill, but vaulted into his saddle as soon as his wound was dressed, and remained with his command during the entire day.
Vol. 43, page 333.

BIRDSEYE: LIEUTENANT MORTIMER B., 149th Regiment. Promoted by the Governor to First Lieutenant in the 2d New York Cavalry for gallant conduct in the battles before Chattanooga. Vol. 40, page 164.

BLAKE: LIEUTENANT JOHN J., 88th Regiment. General Meagher in his Report of the battle of Fredericksburg says: "Lieutenant Blake displayed courage and soldiership of the highest order, but in doing so, only continued to display those qualities which have brilliantly characterized his conduct in nine desperate engagements. Vol. 27, page 526.

BOYD: CAPTAIN WM. H., 1st Cavalry. He did yeoman service in watching the approach of the rebels towards Carlisle, Penn. He was brave, active and energetic, and was constantly to be found at his post. Vol. 33, page 543.
At one time when the regiment was pursued just before the Gettysburg campaign, Captain Boyd captured in some of the fights more than twice his own number.
Vol. 85, page 273.

BOUTELLE: CAPTAIN GEORGE V., Formerly of the 2d Regiment, and who served for two years with the greatest credit, appointed Major of the 21st New York Cavalry, on account of his enlarged experience and his military acquirements.
Vol. 37, page 395.

BOUGHTON: CAPTAIN HORACE, 13th Regiment. He served with distinction in nearly all the battles in which the armies of Virginia and of the Potomac were engaged, and was commissioned by Governor Morgan Lieutenant-Colonel of the 143d Regiment. Vol. 25, page 433.

BOICE: LIEUTENANT THEODORE A., 5th Cavalry. Acquitted himself heroically at the battle of Hanover.
Vol. 34, page 210.
In October, 1863, while riding in the direction of Aldie, Va., he suddenly came upon a party of cavalry, dressed in our uniform, and numbering about a dozen men. Upon riding up they surrounded him and ordered him to deliver up his arms. Handing over his sword and revolver he rode with them until they came in sight of another party, when the Lieutenant drew a revolver from his boot, shot three of the guerillas and made his escape. They fired upon him, wounding him five times, but not mortally. Vol. 37, page 506.

BROOKS: THOMAS B., 1st Engineer Regiment. To Captain Brooks is due all the credit of pushing our zigzags and parallels up to within speaking distance at Fort Wagner. By day and by night, through driving rain storms and drifting clouds of sand, under fire of shell and round shot, this able officer persisted in his work, allowing no danger to repel and no difficulty or accident to dishearten, but with cheerful and encouraging words toiled on until he saw his hard task accomplished. Vol. 35, page 566.

BROOKS: CORPORAL J. HOWARD, 1st Engineer Regiment. One of those soldiers who entered Fort Wagner and planted our flag upon its parapet at the time of its capture. Lieutenant Brooks died of wounds August 5, 1864.
Vol. 36, page 264.

BRADLEY: CAPTAIN JAMES H., 31st Regiment. Wounded, and acquitted himself with glory on the Peninsula.
Vol. 22, page 206.

BROWN: MAJOR JOHN CARTER, of the *Les Enfants Perdue* Regiment. Presented with an elegant sword by the members of his regiment, as a testimonial of their regard for him as a soldier and a man.
Vol. 23, page 315.

BROWN: LIEUTENANT-COLONEL WILLIAM HENRY, 31st Regiment. He acquitted himself with so much bravery at the battle of West Point, that on the day of the action, the officers of the regiment unbeknown to him, signed a unanimous application for his promotion and dispatched it to Governor Morgan. He also displayed remarkable courage and bravery at Bull Run.
Vol. 22, page 487.
At the battle of Chancellorsville, Lieutenant-Colonel Brown commanded the 2d brigade of the 3d division of Sedgwick's corps, and acquitted himself with skill and bravery. He is one of the heroes of that battle who will bear honorable scars to the day of his death.
Vol. 32, page 276.

BROWN: COLONEL PHILIP P., JR., 157th Regiment. At the battle of Gettysburg he held an isolated position of particular peril.
Vol. 34, page 71.

BROWN: SERGEANT HENRY K., 40th Regiment. His name ordered to be inscribed on the Roll of Honor, and to wear the Kearny Cross for gallant conduct at the battle of Chancellorsville.
Vol. 32, page 372.

BROWN: CAPTAIN JOHN A., 85th Regiment. He was in command of Fort Gray, N. C., when it was attacked by the rebels in 1864. In three assaults he repulsed the enemy in the most determined manner.
Vol. 43, page 303.

BREWSTER: ELIJAH, 73d Regiment. Distinguished himself while on a boat excursion to secure supplies for General Sickles.
Vol. 17, page 149.

BREWSTER: Colonel William R., 73d Regiment. He rose from a sick bed and led the gallant Excelsior Brigade at the battle of Locust Grove or Mine Run, Nov. 27th, 1863, and by his presence inspired his men with the utmost enthusiasm.
Vol. 39, page 56.

BRIGGS: Captain Leroy H., 36th Regiment. Especially mentioned for meritorious conduct during the storming of the heights of Fredericksburg. Vol. 32, page 308.

BRAINERD: Captain Wesley, 50th Engineer Regiment. Acquitted himself heroically while assisting to bridge across the Rappahannock, in order that our troops might cross and capture the city of Fredericksburg. Vol. 27, page 230.

BRODERICK: Sergeant John, 37th Regiment. His name ordered to be inscribed on the Roll of Honor, and to wear the Kearny Cross for gallant conduct at Chancellorsville.
Vol. 32, page 372.

BROWNING: Captain Thomas H., 36th Regiment. Especially distinguished for meritorious conduct during the storming of the heights of Fredericksburg. Vol. 32, page 308.

BARTLETTE: Captain Charles G., 5th Regiment. Honorably mentioned in Colonel Kilpatrick's Report of the battle of Big Bethel. Vol. 9, page 284.

BALDWIN: Captain Charles F., 84th Regiment. Honorably mentioned in General Porter's Report of the battle of Bull Run. Vol. 11, page 221.

BOWER: Lieutenant Wm. H., 1st Artillery. He was a most gallant officer and lost an arm at Rappahannock Station in June, 1863. He then resigned his position and was placed in command of a detachment of the Reserve Corps.
Vol. 49, page 327.

BIRDSALL: "Archie," 65th Regiment (a mere youth). At the battle of Cedar Creek he captured a number of Rebels at the imminent peril of his life. Vol. 50, page 134.

CROCKER: Lieutenant George H., 3d Artillery. At the battle of Honey Hill, Lieutenant Crocker succeeded to the command of Battery B after the wounding of Lieutenant Wildt. The brave Crocker had an eye shot out, but he wrapped a handkerchief round his head and fought his guns for an hour after the hurt. Captain Mesereau says of him in his Report: "I never saw one display such cool judgment and bravery as he did during the entire engagement. Vol. 85, page 154.

COOLEY: CAPTAIN ALFRED, 156th Regiment. Captain Cooley succeeded Captain Hoyt in command of the regiment at the battle of Cedar Creek. When Sergeant Decker fell with the colors, Captain Cooley, seeing their perilous condition, as the surest way of saving them, stripped them from the staff.

Vol. 51, page 191.

CONLIN: CAPTAIN BENJAMIN F., 155th Regiment. The *Herald* of November 2d, 1864, said: "At the time of the battle of the Boydtown Road, October, 1863, two members of General Hancock's Staff—namely, Lieutenant-Colonel Smith and Major Mitchell—were riding down the road in the direction of General Egan. But the enemy was yet in possession of the road, and Egan was cut off. They saw the guns which the enemy in advance had captured, but in his flight abandoned. Colonel Smith took two companies of the First Maine and a small detachment of the First Massachusetts Heavy Artillery, and, hauling off the guns by hand, returned them to the commander of the battery. Major Mitchell went on towards General Egan, but soon encountered the remnant of a Rebel regiment holding as prisoners several of our men. One of them was a Lieutenant Conlin, of the One Hundred and Fifty-fifth New York, who rushed out from among them and shouted: ' Major, I'm a prisoner. You can capture all of them!' Major Mitchell immediately wheeled his horse, and, dashing up the road, soon returned with the Thirty-sixth Wisconsin, of Colonel Rugg's brigade, with which he captured all that body of the enemy, and, in doing so, captured Lieutenant Conlin and his fellow prisoners. ' The tables were turned, and Conlin, seizing the swords of the Rebel officers who had previously captured him, his face covered with blood from a blow a rebel hit him with his musket when the Lieutenant was endeavoring to escape, came up the road with a bundle of Rebel swords under his arm. With the remnant of that Rebel regiment which Major Mitchell and the Thirty-sixth Wisconsin captured, they got a Rebel color—the color of the Twenty-sixth North Carolina Regiment. It is difficult to say to whom the honor of capturing the flag belongs, I believe that Conlin claims it. The general impression is that he is entitled to the honor, and to him it was finally awarded." For his bravery on this and other occasions he was, upon the recommendation of General Hancock, promoted to Commissary of Subsistence, with the rank of Captain. Captain Conlin still lives, and is an officer connected with the Brooklyn post office.

CARROLL: CAPTAIN JOHN J., 20th Cavalry. A most skilful and gallant officer. He commanded the expedition in October, 1864, to North Carolina, for the purpose of breaking up illicit traffic. Vol. 49, page 390.

CAMPBELL: LIEUTENANT GEORGE F., 118th Regiment. Aide to General Burnham. General Butler says: "He carried an order to the assaulting column when near the brow of Fort Harrison, under a heavy fire—a most gallant act."
Vol. 49, page 456.

CURRY: SERGEANT JOHN, 47th Regiment. Battle of Chapin's Farm, General Butler says "he was promoted to First Lieutenant in the 36th Regiment of United States Colored troops for gallant behavior in the assault, and for rallying his men."
Vol. 49, page 456.

COOPER: PRIVATE E. H., 142d Regiment. He volunteered to advance with the head of the column and cut down the palisading at the time of the assault on Fort Fisher.
Vol. 52, page 380.

CHAPIN: PRIVATE ALRIC. 142d Regiment. In the assault on Fort Fisher, he volunteered to approach to a point considerably in advance of the skirmish line, which he did, and valuable information in regard to the ditch was gained.
Vol. 52, page 380.

CODMAN: PRIVATE JAMES, 142d Regiment. He volunteered to advance with the head of the column and cut down the palisading at the time of the assault on Fort Fisher.
Vol. 52, page 380.

CABE. PRIVATE WM. 142d Regiment. He volunteered to advance with the head of the column and cut down the palisading at the time of the assault on Fort Fisher. Vol. 52, page 380.

COAN: LIEUTENANT-COLONEL WM. B., 48th Regiment. One of the heroes of Fort Fisher. Vol. 52, page 301. At Fort Wagner, Colonel Coan acquitted himself heroically. Vol. 55, page 73.

CREIGER: LIEUTENANT-COLONEL JOHN A., 11th Regiment. Honorably mentioned in Colonel Ward's Report of the battle of Bull Run. Vol. 11, page 61.

CAMBRELING: LIEUTENANT CHURCHILL C., 5th Regiment. Honorably mentioned in General Butler's Report of the battle of Great Bethel. Vol. 9, page 285.

COLVIN: LIEUTENANT-COLONEL JAMES A., 169th Regiment. General Ames in his Report of the assault on Fort Fisher says: Lieutenant-Colonel Colvin behaved in the most gallant manner, and rendered efficient service in collecting and arranging troops which had become separated from their comrades in the charge, and in leading them to positions where important advantages were gained. Vol. 52, page 380.

CURTIS: LIEUTENANT JAMES M., 71st Regiment. General George C. Thomas commanding at Washington, July, 1864, at the time of Jubal Early's raid, said, "As the exigency which called for the services of troops has gone by, I desire publicly to thank Lieutenant Curtis. Vol. 46, page 376.

CRENEY: LIEUTENANT-COLONEL JAMES, 95th Regiment. In the charge on the works before Petersburg, June, 1864, Lieutenant-Colonel Creney, after being twice wounded, refused to be carried from the field, saying to those who were anxious to assist him—"Go forward and take the enemy's works." Colonel Creney was in 1865 promoted to Brevet Brigadier-General. Vol. 46, page 297.

CHADDOCK: CAPTAIN WILLIAM H., 112th Regiment. After Lieutenant-Colonel Carpenter was wounded at the battle of Drury's Bluff, May 16, 1864, Captain Chaddock, senior Captain, assumed command of the regiment and led it with great gallantry and courage. Vol. 44, page 337.

CLARKE: CAPTAIN WM. C., 79th N. Y. S. M. He was presented with an elegant medal by the members of his company, as a tribute to his soldierly qualities while the regiment was in active service. Vol. 46, page 44.

CLAASSEN: COLONEL PETER J., 132d Regiment. The success of the expedition, sent out from Batchelor's Creek, N. C., in June, 1863, was mainly due to Colonel Claassen, who was in command of the entire force. Colonel Claassen had long before demonstrated that he possessed rare qualities to command. Vol. 46, page 60.

CROWE: LIEUTENANT CORNELIUS J., 5th Artillery. At the time of the engagement at Snicker's Gap, in December, 1862, the gallant Captain dashed across the Shenandoah River, with thirty of his men, and charged upon the Rebels on the opposite side. The water was deep and the current swift.
Vol. 27, page 19.

CROSS: COLONEL NELSON. 67th Regiment. Entitled to the credit of leading his regiment with great gallantry in the successful attack upon and capture of Marye's Heights, Chancellorsville. Vol. 32, page 282.

CRAWFORD: SERGEANT THOMAS, 40th Regiment. His name ordered to be inscribed on the Roll of Honor, and to wear the Kearny Cross for gallant conduct at the battle of Chancellorsville. Vol. 32, page 372.

CARUTHERS: PRIVATE, 8th Cavalry Regiment. At the battle of Beverly Ford and Brandy Station, he killed the man who shot his Captain. Vol. 33, page 266.

COSTER: CAPTAIN JOHN, 1st Regiment. This gallant officer whom General Kearny characterized as a "most noble fellow," was fearfully wounded in the jaw in one of the battles on the Peninsula. "His conduct," said General Kearny, "deserves high mention." He was a brother of Colonel Charles R. Coster, of the 134th Regiment.

COLE: CAPTAIN GEORGE W., 3d Cavalry. Acquitted himself heroically at the battle of Kinston. He was subsequently promoted to the Colonelcy of the 2d United States Colored Cavalry. Vol. 27, page 365.

CRAFT: PRIVATE, 82d Regiment. Privates Craft and Hayes were on picket (on the Peninsula) behind two old chimneys. The Rebels opened fire on them, tearing down the chimneys over their heads. The men escaped from the ruins uninjured, and continued to hold their posts until relieved. With such men guarding the outposts, there was no danger of surprise.
Vol. 21, page 347.

CRANDELL: Colonel Levin, 125th Regiment. Honorably mentioned in General Owen's Report of the affair at Morton's Ford in February, 1864. Vol. 41, page 187.

CULLEN: Corporal Thomas, 82d Regiment. He took the flag of the 28th North Carolina from the hands of the Rebel bearer at the battle of Bristow Station, in October, 1863.
Vol. 37, page 350.

CUFF: Captain William, 158th Regiment. General Peck, in General Orders, says: "Great credit is due Captain Cuff, for the efficient services he performed on the occasion of an expedition in March, 1864, for the purpose of capturing vessels of the enemy engaged in contraband trade. Vol. 43, page 303.

COGSWELL: Colonel Milton, 42d Regiment. Presented with a sword by the Common Council of the city of New York. On the scabbard is the motto used by Colonel Cogswell at the battle of Ball's Bluff: "Men, we'll cut our way through to Edwards Ferry." Vol. 30, page 254.

CURTIS: Captain Levi, 5th Cavalry Regiment. Captain Curtis and two other members of the 5th Cavalry participated in the first charge on cavalry made during the war, and especially distinguished themselves. It took place near Woodstock, Va.
Vol. 42, page 314.

CURTIS: Captain Martin N., 16th Regiment. (The tallest man in the army, six feet six inches high.) He rallied his men three times after being wounded at the battle of West Point. (Promoted to Brigadier-General.) Vol. 20, page 258.

CURTIN: Sergeant John, 40th Regiment. His name ordered to be inscribed on the Roll of Honor, and to wear the Kearny Cross for gallant conduct at the battle of Chancellorsville.
Vol. 32, page 372.

CURRIE: Colonel Leonard D. H., 133d Regiment. Honorably mentioned for his gallant conduct at Port Hudson, June 14, 1863. Vol. 33, page 560.

COSGROVE: Corporal James, 37th Regiment. His name ordered to be inscribed on the Roll of Honor, and to wear the Kearny Cross for gallant conduct at the battle of Chancellorsville.
Vol. 32, page 372.

COONEY: SERGEANT PATRICK, 37th Regiment. His name ordered to be inscribed on the Roll of Honor, and to wear the Kearny Cross for gallant conduct at the battle of Chancellorsville.
Vol. 32, page 372.

COLLINS: SERGEANT JOHN, 37th Regiment. His name ordered to be inscribed on the Roll of Honor, and to wear the Kearny Cross for gallant conduct at the battle of Chancellorsville.
Vol. 32, page 372.

COULTUR: CORPORAL CLARENCE S., 123d Regiment. At the battle of Chancellorsville, he was severely wounded in the head and arm, but bravely continued to fight until again struck in the head, which rendered him senseless.
Vol. 33, page 110.

COSSUM: SERGEANT FREDERICK, 75th Regiment. During the assault upon the enemy's works at Port Hudson, in June, 1863, he was wounded and went to the rear three successive times, returning each time again to the fight, and was only finally carried from the field after receiving five wounds.
Vol. 33, page 519.

COX: COLOR SERGEANT JAMES, 47th Regiment. His cool and heroic conduct at the battle of Olustee, Fla., February, 1864. Although he had received a ball in the body (hardly an inch from the heart), and another in his thigh, he never let the fact be known, but remained bare-headed, facing the enemy, advancing and then slowly falling back with the colors, as ordered from time to time. The enemy never saw the back of Sergeant Cox. Vol. 42, page 76.
He was honorably mentioned by General Butler for his gallantry at Chapin's Farm, and recommended for promotion.
Vol. 49, page 456.

CROCKER: CAPTAIN GEORGE A., 6th Cavalry. One of the heroes of a reconnoissance and brilliant skirmish under General Geary into Virginia. Vol. 26, page 29.

CONWAY: CHAPLAIN THOMAS W., 9th Regiment. Honorably mentioned in Colonel Kimball's Report of the battle of South Mills, S. C. Vol. 20, page 146.

CARTWRIGHT: LIEUTENANT THOMAS W., 5th Regiment. He was wounded and acquitted himself with glory in the battles on the Peninsula. (Died of wounds received in action December, 1862.) Vol. 22, page 206.

CAHILL: CORPORAL LAWRENCE, 69th Regiment. As his men were being decimated and disheartened at Fredericksburg, he shouted in a stentorian voice: "Stand to it, boys, while a man remains." Vol. 27, page 384.

CALDWELL: SERGEANT WILLIAM, 51st Regiment. Commissioned by Governor Seymour for bravery on the field and meritorious conduct. Vol. 31, page 295.

CARSTEN: M. G., 99th Regiment. One of the heroes of a brilliant affair on the Nansemond River, by which the transports "Commerce" and "Swan" were piloted past the Rebel batteries and arrived safely at Fortress Monroe.
Vol. 32, page 1.

CELLIER: SERGEANT F., 55th Regiment. Honorably mentioned in Colonel de Trobriand's report of the battle of Williamsburg.
Vol. 20, page 303.

CHAPMAN: CORPORAL, 126th Regiment. Honorably mentioned as having been conspicuous for his bravery at the battle of Harper's Ferry. Vol. 24, page 410.

CHASE: LIEUTENANT A. SIDNEY, 5th Regiment. Promoted for gallantry on the battle-field. Vol. 25, page 134.

CHURCH: SERGEANT HARVEY, 5th Artillery. Promoted to Second Lieutenant by Governor Seymour, for gallantry and devotion to duty. Vol. 40, page 201.

CHAMBERS: SERGEANT WILLIAM H., 5th Regiment. Promoted for gallantry on the battle-field. Vol. 25, page 97.

CASHEN: LIEUTENANT JOHN C., 14th Cavalry. He deserves special and honorable mention for his gallantry and bravery in the series of brilliant skirmishes in Louisiana early in April, 1864. Vol. 43, page 332.

CAVANAGH: MAJOR JAMES, 69th Regiment. While most ably and daringly supporting his colonel he fell severely wounded. Never was there a truer heart, never was there a sounder or brighter brain." See General Meagher's report.
Vol. 27, page 525.

CALLAWAY: JOSEPH, 99th Regiment. One of the heroes on board the "Congress" who participated in the fight with the "Merrimac." Vol. 18, page 232.

CAMERON: LIEUTENANT AUGUST, 83d Regiment. One of the heroes of the battle of Fredericksburg. Vol. 27, page 523.

CONWAY: PRIVATE, 1st Artillery. Honorably acquitted himself at the battle of Williamsburg. Vol. 20, page 318.

COOK: CAPTAIN EDWIN F., 2d Cavalry. Honorably mentioned in Colonel Kilpatrick's report of the battle of Falmouth.
Vol. 19, page 533.

CLIFFORD: EDWARD, 40th Regiment. His name ordered to be inscribed on the Roll of Honor, and to wear the Kearny Cross for gallant conduct at the battle of Chancellorsville.
Vol. 32, page 372.

CHALMERS: LIEUTENANT HUGH, 146th Regiment. Presented with a sword by his company, as a token of their regard for him as an officer and a man. Died of wounds received in action June 9, 1864. Vol. 42, page 177.

COOK: CAPTAIN JOHN, 91st Regiment. This brave and veteran officer served under General Scott during the Mexican War, and although sixty-four years of age, he forsook home, family and the comforts of life, and again obeyed the call of his country, and while bravely leading his company in the assault upon Port Hudson, he fell with his right arm badly shattered.
Vol. 35, page 307.

COOPER: LIEUTENANT E. C., 9th Regiment. Honorably mentioned in Colonel Kimball's report of the battle of South Mills, N. C. Vol. 20, page 146.

COLTON: SERGEANT GEORGE A., 3d Cavalry. The brave sergeant led a little party of four men in a brilliant charge against forty of the Confederates at Tranter's Creek, N. C.
Vol. 21, page 252.

COON: CAPTAIN MARCUS, 2d Cavalry. Conspicuous for his dashing bravery in the fight near Upperville, Va., June, 1863.
Vol. 33, page 441.

CONNELLY: LIEUTENANT EDWARD, 69th N. Y. S. M. Acquitted himself heroically at the battle of Bull Run.
Vol. 23, page 546.

CONNELLY: LIEUTENANT HENRY M., 158th Regiment. He is entitled to great credit for the bravery and skill exhibited during a brilliant dash into Jones and Onslow Counties, N. C., in February, 1864. Vol. 41, page 219.

CHARLES: COLONEL EDMUND C., 42d Regiment. One of the heroes of White Oak Swamp, where he was badly wounded and taken prisoner. Vol. 22, page 534.

CHATFIELD: LIEUTENANT-COLONEL HARVEY S., 78th Regiment. Presented with an elegant sword as a mark of esteem for him as a soldier and a friend. Vol. 41, page 372.

CHESTER: CAPTAIN WILLIAM H., 74th Regiment. Acquitted himself with honorable distinction at the battle of Oak Grove on the Peninsula. Vol. 22, page 187.

CHILD: LIEUTENANT CHARLES, 9th Regiment. Honorably mentioned in Colonel Kimball's Report of the battle of South Mills, N. C. Vol. 20, page 146.

CLYMER: SERGEANT JOSEPH N., 40th Regiment. Promoted to Second Lieutenant for splendid action on the battle-field.
Vol. 28, page 76.

CAMPBELL: COLOR-SERGEANT "SANDY," 79th Regiment, wounded at the battle of Chantilly. It was when Campbell fell that General Stevens seized the colors, and calling to his brave Highlanders to follow, that he received his fatal wound.
Vol. 24, page 195.

CARR: COLONEL JOSEPH B., 2d Regiment. Appointed a Brigadier-General for meritorious services on the battle-field.
Vol. 24, page 201.

CARPENTER: SERGEANT M. V. B., 4th Regiment. He behaved in the most gallant manner in the midst of a galling fire of the enemy at Antietam. Vol. 25, page 36.

CONNOR: SERGEANT, 9th Regiment. Honorably mentioned in Colonel Kimball's Report of the battles of Antietam and South Mountain. Vol. 25, page 7.

CORNELL: CORPORAL, 9th Regiment. Honorably mentioned in Colonel Kimball's Report of the battle of Antietam.
Vol. 25, page 579.

EGOLF: CAPTAIN JOSEPH, 125th Regiment. He took an active and heroic part in all the battles of Grant's campaign, losing an arm at the battle of Ream's Station, where he was left for dead upon the field, and was finally captured and taken to Richmond. Vol. 50, page 333.

DONALDSON: LIEUTENANT JOHN L., 9th Regiment. Honorably mentioned in Colonel Kimball's Report of the battle of South Mills, N. C. Vol. 20, page 146.

DONALDSON: CAPTAIN WALTER A., 71st Regiment. Having been compelled by wounds to retire to the Invalid Corps, he was complimented by a letter regretting his retirement, signed by every officer of the Excelsior Brigade. Vol. 38, page 211.

DAVENPORT: LIEUTENANT FREDERICK, 89th Regiment. One of the heroes who volunteered to cross the river in boats, in order to dislodge the Rebel sharpshooters and thus enable our engineers to build the bridges, that the troops might cross and take the city of Fredericksburg at the time it was attacked by Burnside. Vol. 27, page 254.

DARLING: JOHN EDWARD, New York Mounted Rifles (7th Cavalry). One of the heroes of the gallant and successful scouting expedition sent out from Suffolk, Va., in May, 1863.
Vol. 32, page 308.

DASH: MAJOR DANIEL D., 100th Regiment. One of the heroes of the battle of Fort Wagner. Vol. 34, page 752.

DANDY: COLONEL GEORGE B., 100th Regiment. Wounded during the siege of Charleston in 1863. He was about giving an order when a shell exploded in a pile of bricks, a fragment of one striking his leg and causing a contusion. He lay unconscious for a few moments, then rose, received medical attention and remained at the front till his regiment was relieved. He is an officer much esteemed for his military accomplishments.
Vol. 36, page 153.
On the 21st of June, 1864, Colonel Dandy made two brilliant charges, and was complimented for his bravery by General Howell. Vol. 45, page 464.

DAVIS: MAJOR EDWIN P., 153d Regiment, formerly of the 62d New York. He was presented with an elegant sword by the officers and privates of the 62d. On the scabbard is inscribed, "The hero of Williamsburg, Fair Oaks, Turkey Bend, Malvern Hill."
Vol. 26, page 91.

He was brevetted Brigadier-General for meritorious services.
Vol. 51, page 331.

DAVIS: LIEUTENANT WILLIAM, 163d Regiment. Promoted on the battle-field of Fredericksburg for bravery. Vol. 27, page 477.

DENNETT: CAPTAIN GEORGE M., 38th Regiment. Honorably mentioned in Lieutenant-Colonel Birney's Report of the battle of Fredericksburg. Vol. 27, page 487.

DEVIN: COLONEL THOMAS C., 6th Cavalry. On General Burnside's evacuation of Fredericksburg, the 6th Cavalry, under Colonel Devin, formed part of his rear guard. For ably performing this most arduous duty, Colonel Devin received merited acknowledgment from General Burnside. Vol. 40, page 161.

DE MASURE: CAPTAIN LOUIS, 55th Regiment. Honorably mentioned in Colonel de Trobriand's Report of the battle of Williamsburg. Vol. 20, page 303.

DE ST. JAMES: LIEUTENANT ALBERT, 55th Regiment. Honorably mentioned in Colonel de Trobriand's Report of the battle of Williamsburg. Vol. 20, page 303.

DE BEVOISE: MAJOR WILLIAM H., 84th Regiment. He commanded the regiment at the battle of Antietam, and conducted himself in the same gallant manner which had characterized him in every battle in which his regiment had participated.
Vol. 24, page 637.

DERN: LIEUTENANT GEORGE F., 3d Cavalry. Acquitted himself with great bravery at the battle of Washington, N. C.
Vol. 24, page 324.

DEWS: SERGEANT EDWIN, 9th Regiment. Honorably mentioned in Colonel Kimball's Report of the battles of South Mountain and Antietam. Vol. 25, page 7.

DENNEN: SERGEANT THOMAS, 73d Regiment. Promoted for gallant conduct on the field. Lieutenant Dennen was killed at the battle of Chancellorsville, May 3, 1863. Vol. 30, page 17.

DEMPSEY: CAPTAIN JOHN W., 82d Regiment. Presented with a sword by the officers of his regiment, as a token of respect for him as a patriot, an officer and a gentleman.
Vol. 39, page 135.

DeFOREST: Colonel Jacob J., 81st Regiment. The gallant Colonel enrolled the first and last man, and was desperately wounded at Fair Oaks. Vol. 42, page 24.

DICKEL: Colonel Christian, 4th Cavalry Regiment. Honorably alluded to by General Fremont, for his gallant services during the engagements in the Shenandoah Valley.
Vol. 22, page 550.

DICKSON: Captain Campbell, 9th Cavalry. At the battle of Beverly Ford and Brandy Station Captain Dickson participated with honor in one of the most daring and brilliant dashes on record. Vol. 33, page 266.

DONOGHUE: Captain Timothy, 36th Regiment. Especially distinguished for meritorious services during the storming of Fredericksburg. Vol. 32, page 308.

DONAVAN: Sergeant, 37th Regiment. His name ordered to be inscribed on the Roll of Honor, and to wear the Kearny Cross for gallant conduct at Chancellorsville. Vol. 32, page 372.

DOWNING: Adjutant-Major A., 7th Cavalry. Acquitted himself nobly in engagements with the Rebels near Suffolk, Va.
Vol. 26, page 16.

DOWNING: Captain Obadiah J., 2d Cavalry. One of the heroes of a great cavalry fight at Culpepper, Sept. 13, 1863.
Vol. 37, page 484.

DONALD: Captain Alfred A., 73d Regiment. Honorably acquitted himself at the battle of Williamsburg.
Vol. 20, page 318.

DOWNEY: Captain "Jack," 11th Regiment. At Bull Run he was wounded and taken prisoner. It was near the close of the fight that he received his wound. Up to that moment he was one of the leaders of the gallant Zouaves, and participated in all of the attacks made by the regiment upon the overwhelming force of the enemy. Vol. 23, page 587.

DOBKE: Lieutenant-Colonel Adolphus, 45th Regiment. Presented with a sword by the merchants of the Third Ward of New York City, for his faithful services as a policeman before, and a gallant officer during the war. Vol. 42, page 226.

DRISCOLL: CORNELIUS, 37th Regiment. His name ordered to be inscribed on the Roll of Honor, and to wear the Kearny Cross for gallant conduct at the battle of Chancellorsville.
Vol. 32, page 372.

DUFFY: CORPORAL MICHAEL, 37th Regiment. His name ordered to be inscribed on the Roll of Honor, and to wear the Kearny Cross for gallant conduct at Chancellorsville. Vol. 32, page 372.

DWIGHT: COLONEL WILLIAM, 70th Regiment. A braver soldier or a more efficient officer never handled a sword.
Vol. 21, page 35.

DYE: SERGEANT WILLIAM, 5th Regiment. He participated in the first cavalry charge made during the war, and especially distinguished himself. Vol. 42, page 314.

DAYTON: MAJOR OSCAR V., 62d Regiment. Honorably mentioned in General Peck's Report of the battle of Seven Pines.
Vol. 21, page 359.

DANIEL: CAPTAIN J. TOWNSEND, 36th Regiment. Recommended to the President by his Colonel for a brevet commission as Major, for gallant and meritorious conduct and general high military bearing, which was endorsed by Generals Devins, Couch and Hooker. He was in thirteen battles and skirmishes, in all of which he distinguished himself.
Vol. 33, page 109.

DAVIES: MAJOR HENRY E., 2d Cavalry. Son of Judge Davies of New York. Honorably mentioned in Colonel Kimball's Report of the battle at Falmouth, Va. Vol. 19, page 533.
Acquitted himself with honorable distinction on the occasion of an engagement with Stuart's Rebel Cavalry near Fredericksburg. Vol. 22, page 570.
Honorably mentioned in Colonel Kilpatrick's Report of the operations of his command, in connection with the great expedition of General Stoneman in May, 1863.
Vol. 32, page 206.
At the battle of Culpepper Major Davies led the 1st Brigade in a rapid charge. The Brigade had the advance and kept it throughout the day. Promoted to Brigadier-General, September 16, 1863. Vol. 36, page 472.

DI CESNOLA: COLONEL LOUIS P., 4th Cavalry. At the battle of Crooked Run, Va., August 16, 1864, Colonel Di Cesnola greatly distinguished himself. Headed by the gallant Colonel sword in hand, the regiment made a charge under a perfect sheet of leaded fire, and drove the enemy back. Vol. 47, page 463.

DAY: COLONEL NICHOLAS W., 131st Regiment. At a critical moment during the battle of Winchester, September 19, 1864, when by a repulse of a large portion of the 19th Corps, the right center of the line of battle was weakened, and, perhaps, the fate of the day imperilled, Colonel Day seized the colors, rushed to the front, bravely supported by the Color-Sergeant and Color-Guard, and rallied the regiment out to nearly the line from which it had just retreated. Vol. 84, page 348.

DRAKE: COLONEL JEREMIAH C., 112th Regiment. He led his regiment and the 8th Maine in a splendid charge upon the enemy on the 16th of May, 1864, at the time Beauregard surprised General Heckman's Brigade in a dense fog on the morning of that day. Colonel Drake died from the effects of wounds, received June 2, 1864. Vol. 44, page 324.

DIVINE: LIEUTENANT MICHAEL, 65th Regiment. At the battle of the Opequan, September 19, 1864, he was always in front of the lines encouraging the boys by his bravery and example.
Vol. 49, page 135.

DOHERTY: LIEUTENANT EDWARD P., 16th Cavalry. Acquitted himself bravely on the occasion of an expedition to the Rapidan and an encounter with Early's forces, September, 1864.
Vol. 48, page 435.

DAUCHY: LIEUTENANT GEORGE K., 12th Battery. He commanded the battery at Ream's Station with great bravery and skill.
Vol. 47, page 463.

DELACY: LIEUTENANT-COLONEL WILLIAM; 164th Regiment. This brave officer was wounded several times, but returned after each hospital discharge to do battle for the flag. He rose to Brevet Brigadier-General. Vol. 87, page 445.

DUMONT: LIEUTENANT THEODORE S., 5th Regiment. Honorably acquitted himself at the battle of Big Bethel.
Vol. 10, page 200.

DURYEA: LIEUTENANT JACOB, 5th Regiment. Honorably mentioned in General Butler's Report of the battle of Big Bethel.
Vol. 9, page 285.

DOBIE: CAPTAIN JAMES H., 6th Regiment. Honorably acquitted himself at the battle of Santa Rosa Island.
Vol. 13, page 462.

DAGGETT: COLONEL RUFUS, 117th Regiment. Honorably. mentioned in General Ames' Report of the attack on Fort Fisher.
Vol. 52, page 203.

DAWSON: COLOR-SERGEANT TOM, 48th Regiment. For coolness and courage at the battle of Chapin's Farm, Sergeant Dawson was recommended by General Butler for promotion.
Vol. 49, page 456.

DECKER: SERGEANT PHILIP, 156th Regiment. When Corporal Green fell with the colors at the battle of Cedar Creek, Decker immediately raised them from the ground, and, with the colors in one hand and a musket in the other, floated them defiantly over the heads, as it were, of the enemy. Decker fell badly wounded.
Vol. 51, page 191.

DUNN: LIEUTENANT JAMES H., 160th Regiment. Promoted to the rank of Captain for gallant and meritorious services.
Vol. 49, page 286.

DIPPEL: AUGUST, 155th Regiment. ("The Andersonville Kid.") He was the youngest prisoner of the Andersonville pen. He enlisted as a drummer at the age of fourteen; soon after he took a musket and fought bravely until captured at Coal Harbor.
Vol. 85, page 115.

EATON: CAPTAIN THOMAS B., 169th Regiment. In July, 1864, Captain Eaton received his second shoulder bar. Captain Eaton first served as Lieutenant and Provost Marshal at Chain Bridge in 1862, and, subsequently, as a Staff officer in the military families of General R. S. Foster and the late Colonel J. C. Drake. He was an industrious and efficient officer.
Vol. 47, page 150.

EATON: SERGEANT JAMES M., 7th Cavalry. Colonel Dodge asked for volunteers to cross Black River, and three men—Sergeant Eaton, Corporal Pintler and Private Van Duser, volunteering, were selected for the purpose. Nobly and gallantly they spurred their horses in the dark and treacherous looking water, and plunged through and gained the opposite bank.
Vol. 26, page 16.

EDWARDS: Sergeant W., 40th Regiment. His name ordered to be inscribed on the Roll of Honor, and to wear the Kearny Cross for gallant conduct at Chancellorsville.
Vol. 32, page 372.

EDWARDS: Lieutenant Nathaniel M., 1st Engineers. Lieutenant Edwards and Captain McKenna entitled to great credit for conducting the celebrated "Marsh" Battery, used during the siege of Charleston. Vol. 36, page 186.

EDSALL: T. A., 27th Regiment. This young officer is the hero of a series of extraordinary escapes from the Confederate army. He was imprisoned, got free, and was hunted by bloodhounds, but finally reached home in safety. Vol. 40, page 128.

ESTELLE: Quartermaster-Sergeant Charles. General George C. Thomas commanding at Washington, July, 1864. at the time of Jubal Early's raid said: "As the exigency which called for the services of troops has gone by, I desire publicly to thank Sergeant Estelle." Vol. 46, page 376.

EVARTS: Private Charles B., 6th Cavalry. Son of the Hon. Wm. M. Evarts. This young man was at college, but reading in the papers of the daring and seemingly romantic deeds of the 6th New York Cavalry, he ran away from school and enlisted in the regiment as a private soldier, his father being at the time in Europe. He served faithfully and with much credit during the campaign of 1864, and on the return of the regiment from the Lynchburg raid, he was commissioned a Lieutenant by President Lincoln. Mr. Evarts is now a member of the law firm of Evarts, Southmayd & Choate. Vol. 84, page 96.

EGAN: Colonel Thomas W., 40th Regiment. After Lieutenant-Colonel Egan's honorable release from unjust imprisonment, General McClellan wrote a letter to Governor Morgan, requesting that Lieutenant-Colonel Egan be promoted to Colonel of his regiment. This was accompanied by a letter from General Heintzleman, in which he said: "The promotion would only be a small reparation for the injustice he has suffered." General Kearny says: "He has always led his regiment with bravery and distinction, and merits the appointment. The appointment was made, and Colonel Egan led his regiment into action at Savage's Station and contributed largely to the glorious result. Vol. 22, page 136.

ELLIOTT: CAPTAIN CHARLES B., 73d Regiment. Honorably acquitted himself at the battle of Williamsburg.
Vol. 20, page 38.

ELLIOTT: LIEUTENANT HENRY H., 9th Regiment. Colonel Cahill says in his Report of the battle of Baton Rouge: "Of his coolness and intrepidity in action, every officer in the battle can bear witness." Vol. 23, page 338.

ELLERBECK: LIEUTENANT ROBERT E., 6th Cavalry. One of the heroes of a reconnoissance and brilliant skirmish under General Geary into Virginia. Vol. 26, page 29.

EDDY, JR.: MAJOR EDWARD, 47th Regiment. At the battle of Olustee, Fla., Major Eddy assumed command of the regiment after Colonel Moore and Captain McDonald were wounded, and his conduct in bringing off the regiment, and aiding in covering the retreat, was the theme of universal admiration. Major Eddy was for some time on the staff of General Seymour, as Assistant Inspector-General. Vol. 42, page 76.

ELFWING: CAPTAIN NERE A., 48th Regiment. Acquitted himself gallantly in the storming of Fort Wagner. He had been in the Swedish Army. Vol. 34, page 753.

EMMETT: LIEUTENANT TEMPLE, 88th Regiment (Aide to General Meagher). Brilliantly distinguished himself in all the great battles before Richmond. Killed August 9, 1862.
Vol. 22, page 414.

ENNIS: CAPTAIN JOHN, 14th Cavalry. Deserves special mention for his gallantry and bravery in the series of brilliant skirmishes in Louisiana, early in April, 1864. Vol. 43, page 332.

ENTWISTLE: CAPTAIN JAMES, 176th Regiment. At the battle of Fisher's Hill, September 22, 1864, a curious strife manifested itself between two gallant regiments, the 28th Iowa and the 176th New York. Both were charging directly up the hill at the Rebel batteries, and each determined to win the trophy of victory by the possession of some of the guns. Bravely they struggled and well, but fortune favored the New Yorkers, and two companies of the 176th under Captain Entwistle, formerly Adjutant of Wilson's Zouaves, succeeded in striking the pike about half way up the hill, just ahead of the Iowans, and dashing on gained the summit and took possession of five pieces of cannon and some small guns which the Rebels had been in too much haste to remove. Vol. 49, page 352.

ELLISON: CAPTAIN JOHN S., 12th Cavalry Regiment. Presented with a sabre, sash, belt and pistol by the officers under his command. Vol. 40, page 3.

ELLIS: LIEUTENANT DEWITT C., 7th Cavalry Regiment. One of the heroes of a brilliant expedition into North Carolina, rivalling that of Havelock's in India. Vol. 21, page 57.

ELLIS: CAPTAIN M. H., 175th Regiment. Honorably and bravely acquitted himself in the battles which occurred during the march of General Banks from Brashear City to Opelousas, La.
Vol. 32, page 488.

FULLER: LIEUTENANT CHAS. A., 61st Regiment. He was wounded at Gettysburg, while acquitting himself with great gallantry.
Vol. 54, page 206.

FISK: CAPTAIN HENRY C., 65th Regiment. He commanded the regiment at the battle of the Opequan, September 19, 1864, with great skill and bravery. Vol. 49, page 155.

FRENCH: LIEUTENANT-COLONEL WINSOR B., 77th Regiment. Acquitted himself with great distinction in an assault upon the Rebels on the evening of July 12, 1864, when Jubal Early's forces attacked the northern defences of Washington.
Vol. 46, page 287.

FARNUM: COLONEL J. EGBERT, 70th Regiment. Appointed a Colonel in the Reserve Corps. There were but twenty-four colonels in this corps, and the appointment of Colonel Farnum was the worthy reward of three years active service in which he won an honorable record, and honorable wounds.
Vol. 47, page 27.

Colonel Farnum was especially mentioned for his coolness and daring courage at the battle of Chancellorsville.
Vol. 32, page 301.

FARRAND: CAPTAIN HIRAM, 1st Engineer Regiment. He was honorably alluded to by General Butler for his energy and efficiency in constituting the line of intrenchments on the line of the 18th Army Corps, receiving a very severe wound in the discharge of his duties. (Chapin's Farm.)
Vol. 49, page 456.

FITZGIBBON: LIEUTENANT JOHN J., 47th Regiment. Battle of Chapin's Farm, September 29 and 30, 1864, General Butler says: "He had honorable mention for gallantry in both assaults on the enemy's works, and was recommended for promotion." Vol. 49, page 456.

FOWLER: COLONEL EDWARD B., 84th Regiment (14th New York State Militia). General Doubleday in "The Campaigns of the Civil War" says: "The skill and energy of Colonel Fowler at the battle of Gettysburg were of great service to me."

FARMER: LIEUTENANT GEORGE E., 6th Cavalry. At the battle of Cedar Creek, October 19, 1864, Lieutenant Farmer with his regiment made a dashing charge across the bridge, under a terrific fire from the enemy on the other side—a crossing, however, was effected, and the Rebels driven from the opposite bank. Vol. 49, page 425.

FINNIGAN: CORPORAL MICHAEL, 118th Regiment. General Butler says: "He was reported for his cool and humorous courage in capturing a rebel, forcing him to stand on the parapet, face the enemy and give three hearty cheers for the Union." (Chapin's Farm). Vol. 49, page 456.

FERGUSON: CAPTAIN ASA H., 49th Regiment. To him more than to any other man are we indebted for the capture of prize steamer "Ladona," laden with a cargo of nearly a million of dollars. The navy is given one half the value of this prize. Captain Ferguson *not one cent*. Vol. 23, page 548.

FARNESWORTH: COLONEL ADDISON, 79th Regiment. Wounded while gallantly leading a brigade of General Stevens's division in one of the battles under Pope in Virginia. He is one of the volunteer officers who have shown themselves worthy of the highest confidence of the Government. When the rebellion broke out he was one of the first to take his place as a volunteer beside the old flag, as Lieutenant-Colonel of the "Scott Life Guard," 38th Regiment, from which he was promoted to the Colonelcy of the 79th. Vol. 24, page 31. Colonel Farnesworth was honorably mentioned in General Ward's Report of the battle of Bull Run.
Vol. 11, page 61.

FERRIS: LIEUTENANT FRANCIS, 2d Cavalry. Honorably mentioned in Colonel Kilpatrick's Report of the battle of Falmouth, Va.
Vol. 19, page 533.

FARRELL: Corporal, 9th Regiment. Honorably mentioned in Colonel Kimball's Report of the battles on the Peninsula, and South Mountain and Antietam. Vol. 25, page 7.

FARRELL: Sergeant, 99th Regiment. Honorably acquitted himself in a brisk skirmish near Suffolk, Va. Vol. 32, page 70.

FORBES: Captain William T., 102d Regiment, (of General Geary's Staff). Recommended for promotion for gallantry, during the storming of Lookout Mountain.
Vol. 39, page 77.

FORD: Captain George W., 50th Engineers. Captains Ford, McDowell, and Major Magruder, superintended the erection of the bridges across the Rappahannock, at the time of the attack on Fredericksburg. Vol. 27, page 236.

FOLEY: Sergeant Charles, 37th Regiment. His name ordered to be inscribed on the Roll of Honor, and to wear the Kearny Cross for gallant conduct at Chancellorsville.
Vol. 32, page 372.

FITZGERALD: Captain Louis, 40th Regiment. This officer served in the battles on the Peninsula; was wounded at Williamsburg and at Fair Oaks, and was highly complimented by the late General Kearny, who placed him on his Staff. In the battle of Fredericksburg, for his efficiency, he was complimented in the Official Reports. Captain Fitzgerald is now Brigadier-General in command of the New York State Militia.
Vol. 29, page 2.

FIELD: Lieutenant William F, 3d Artillery. Acquitted himself with great skill and bravery at the battle of Washington, N. C. Vol. 24, page 324.

FIELDS: Corporal, 9th Regiment Honorably mentioned in Colonel Kimball's Report of the battles of South Mountain and Antietam. Vol. 25, page 7.

FOSTER: Sergeant Clark C., 37th Regiment. His name ordered to be inscribed on the Roll of Honor, and to wear the Kearny Cross for gallant conduct at Chancellorsville.
Vol. 32, page 372.

FOUR: Captain Jean J., 55th Regiment. Honorably mentioned in Colonel de Trobriand's Report of the battle of Williamsburg. Vol. 20, page 303.
Acquitted himself with honor at the battle of Seven Pines.
Vol. 21, page 255.

FORBES: Sergeant, 9th Regiment. Honorably mentioned in Colonel Kimball's Report of the battles of South Mountain and Antietam. Vol. 25, page 7.

FRANK: Colonel Paul, 52d Regiment. At the battle of Auburn, 1863, the regiment wavered, and was falling back, when Colonel Frank, who commanded the 3d brigade, rode in their front and rallied them, crying out, "Stand, boys, and follow me!" Vol. 37, page 204.

FREDOLPH: Lewis, 88th Regiment. His name ordered to be inscribed on the Roll of Honor, and to wear the Kearny Cross for gallant conduct at Chancellorsville. Vol. 32, page 372.

FUNK: Color-Sergeant Ernst, 163d Regiment. Promoted on the battle-field of Fredericksburg for bravery.
Vol. 27, page 477.

FITZSIMMONS: Major Charles, 3d Cavalry. A brave and daring officer—was captured twice in a desperate skirmish near Trenton, N. C., and although wounded, managed to escape.
Vol. 20, page 673.

FLAGLER: Frank, 3d Cavalry. One of the heroes of Tranter's Creek, where he was captured by the Rebels.
Vol. 21, page 252.

FLEMING: Lieutenant James H., 9th Regiment. Honorably mentioned in Colonel Kimball's Report of the battle of South Mills, N. C. Vol. 20, page 146.

GRUB: Private G. M., 159th Regiment. Recommended to the Secretary of War for a medal for gallant conduct at the battle of Chapin's Farm. Vol. 49, page 456.

GILL: Sergeant, 65th Regiment. At the battle of Cedar Creek, October, 1864, he rushed out amidst a party of Rebels and ordered them to surrender or be shot. They gave themselves up, one lieutenant and four privates. Vol. 50, page 134.

GURNEY: COLONEL WILLIAM, 127th Regiment. At the battle of Honey Hill, S. C., November, 1864, he was conspicuous for his gallantry. Colonel Gurney was promoted to Brevet Brigadier-General in 1865. Vol. 51, page 146.

GREEN: COLOR-SERGEANT C. T., 156th Regiment. At the battle of Cedar Creek, he carried the state colors of the regiment. His name deserves a place on the Roll of Honor.
Vol. 51, page 191.

GATES: COLONEL THEODORE B., 80th Regiment. Colonel Gates succeeded to the command of the regiment after the fall of Colonel Pratt, killed at Manassas, and until November 23, 1864, when he resigned, led the van in every onslaught, encouraging his troops by his noble daring in the fight; while in hospital and camp their welfare and comfort were always insured by his sympathy and forethought. General Doubleday in "Campaigns of the Civil War" says, "The skill and energy of Colonel Gates at the battle of Gettysburg were of great service to me." Vol. 51, page 189.

GIBBS: LIEUTENANT NELSON J., 118th Regiment. General Butler says: "Lieutenant Gibbs and Captain Adams were the first men in the redoubts (Chapin's Farm), and are commended for their presence of mind in turning the enemy's guns to bear upon them. Vol. 49, page 456.

GRAHAM: COLOR-SERGEANT SAMUEL, 158th Regiment. He was recommended to the Secretary of War for a medal by General Butler for conspicuous gallantry and bravery in the assault upon the second line of works, at the battle of Chapin's Farm, and was promoted to first Lieutenant in the United States colored troops. Vol. 49, page 456.

GRAHAM: LIEUTENANT ALEXANDER, 79th Regiment. Honorably mentioned in Colonel David Ireland's Report of the affair at Lewinsville. Vol. 12, page 153.

GOODENOUGH: LIEUTENANT ROLLIN A., 84th Regiment. Honorably mentioned in General Porter's Report of the battle of Bull Run. Vol. 11, page 221.

GILLETTE: LIEUTENANT DANIEL G., 176th Regiment. Son of Rev. A. G. Gillette, of New York. One of the few who made gallant resistance to the foe at the battle of Brashear City, but was captured by the enemy.   Vol. 34, page 197.

GORMAN: CORPORAL OWEN, 37th Regiment. His name ordered to be inscribed on the Roll of Honor, and to wear the Kearny Cross for gallant conduct at the battle of Chancellorsville.
Vol. 32, page 372.

GORDON: LIEUTENANT WILLIAM H., 61st Regiment. Especially commended for his brave conduct and good qualities, by Lieutenant-Colonel Broady, in his Report of the battle of Chancellorsville.   Vol. 32, page 351.

GALLOWAY: RUFUS, 123d Regiment. At the battle of Chancellorsville he fought on, after being shot in the head, until a ball in the arm entirely disabled him.   Vol. 33, page 110.

GALLAGHER: JOHN, 73d Regiment. Distinguished himself while on a boat excursion to secure supplies for General Sickles.
Vol. 17, page 149.

GARRIGAN: CORPORAL THOMAS, 38th Regiment. Lieutenant-Colonel Birney in his Report of the battle of Fredericksburg, says: "Corporal Garrigan was especially noticed for his bravery in the face of the enemy.   Vol. 27, page 487.

GARRISON: CORPORAL, 40th Regiment. His name ordered to be inscribed on the Roll of Honor, and to wear the Kearny Cross for gallant conduct at the battle of Chancellorsville.
Vol. 32, page 372.

GARRARD: MAJOR JEPTHA, 3d Cavalry Regiment. One of the principal heroes of General Foster's expedition against Kinston and Goldsboro, N. C. Promoted to Colonel 1st United States Colored Cavalry.   Vol. 28, page 581.

GARVIE: SERGEANT W., 88th Regiment. His name ordered to be inscribed on the Roll of Honor, and to wear the Kearny Cross for gallant conduct at Chancellorsville.   Vol. 32, page 372.

GARING: SERGEANT GRILLON, 88th Regiment. His name ordered to be inscribed on the Roll of Honor, and to wear the Kearny Cross for gallant conduct at Chancellorsville.
Vol. 32, page 372.

GEIN: SERGEANT LOUIS H., 55th Regiment. Honorably mentioned in Colonel de Trobriand's Report of the battle of Williamsburg. Vol. 20, page 303.

GEISS: LIEUTENANT WILLIAM T., 175th Regiment. Bravely acquitted himself in the battles which occurred during the march of General Banks' forces from Brashear City to Opelousas, La. Vol. 32, page 488.

GARRETT: SERGEANT, 3d Cavalry Regiment. At the battle of Kinston, a gallant thing was done by Sergeant Garrett. It was important for General Foster to ascertain whether a certain bridge below Kinston had been destroyed, or was in condition to permit of the passage of artillery. Sergeant Garrett was detailed for this duty, aided by four men. His instructions were to dash on, and creep through the Rebel troops, and as quickly as possible obtain the desired information. Several small parties of the enemy were dashed through without molestation, the Rebels supposing the Sergeant to belong to their own side, when one of his men reported a party of forty or fifty Rebels just ahead in one place and that he could not make his way through. The Sergeant promptly replied, "I have been ordered to go to that bridge and I'll be damned if I don't," and he did, and returned to his company to receive the congratulations of his commanding officer for his success. Vol. 27, page 434.

GARRARD: LIEUTENANT JOHN C., 158th Regiment. Entitled to great credit for his skill and bravery during the brilliant dash into Jones and Onslow Counties, in February, 1864. Promoted May 11, 1865, to Captain and A. Q. M. Vol. 41, page 219.

GERE: LIEUTENANT EUGENE B., 5th Cavalry. A force of seventy men under Lieutenant Gere and Lieutenant Penfield surprised and routed the Rebel Cavalry and took possession of Orange Court House, in 1862, after General Crawford had been driven back with the main column. Vol. 42, page 314.

GEIP: JACOB, 88th Regiment. His name ordered to be inscribed on the Roll of Honor, and to wear the Kearny Cross for gallant conduct at Chancellorsville. Vol. 32, page 372.

GFANMULLER: CAPTAIN F. S., 55th Regiment. Honorably mentioned in General Peck's Report of the battle of Seven Pines. Vol. 21, page 359.

GILL: CHARLES, 99th Regiment. On board the "Congress," and participated in the fight with the Rebel steamer "Merrimac."
Vol. 18, page 232.

GOLDEN: JAMES, 99th Regiment. On board the "Congress," and participated in the fight with the Rebel steamer "Merrimac."
Vol. 18, page 232.

GOURAND: ADJUTANT GEORGE E., 3d Cavalry. (Formerly engaged with Messrs Tiffany & Co.) Gallantly acquitted himself on the occasion of a brilliant dash of the "Van Allen Cavalry." Vol. 19, page 130.
Captain Gourand and Lieutenants Williams and Cole volunteered to take a boat's crew and run through the blockade at Washington, N. C., with despatches. It was an extremely hazardous feat and their bravery and daring should be remembered. Vol. 31, page 127.
Promoted for special gallantry, to Aide-de-camp to General Foster. Vol. 40, page 148.

GODFREY: LIEUTENANT GEORGE W., 4th Regiment. Acquitted himself with great gallantry at the battle of Antietam.
Vol. 25, page 89.

GRAHAM: COLONEL SAMUEL, 5th Artillery. He won golden opinions for promptness and ability, displayed in the discharge of all duties he was called upon to perform, and especially for the defence of Harper's Ferry in July, 1863.
Vol. 48, page 360.

GRAY: LIEUTENANT ROBERT A., 82d Regiment. Gallantly led the second bayonet charge at Seven Pines, where he was badly wounded. Vol. 21, page 359.

GARDNER: MAJOR GEORGE H., 5th Cavalry Regiment. "One of the bravest and best officers in the service. He acquitted himself with great distinction during Banks' campaign in the Shenandoah Valley. Afterwards, with a few companies of cavalry and a section of artillery he successfully held Bolivar Heights, near Harper's Ferry, against the attacks of Ashby's cavalry. In recognition of his services he was made chief of cavalry by General Stahl. Vol. 40, page 314.

GREGORY: ADJUTANT BENJAMIN F., 2d Cavalry. Honorably mentioned in Colonel Kilpatrick's Report of a successful expedition to Hanover Junction, Va. "A braver and more eager soldier never met an enemy." Vol. 22, page 642.

GRIBBEN: Sergeant, 2d Cavalry. Honorably mentioned in Colonel Kilpatrick's Report of a successful expedition to Hanover Junction. "A braver and more eager soldier never met an enemy." Vol. 22, page 642.

GRAHAM: Lieutenant George W., 24th Battery. General Foster in his Report of the Battles of Kinston and Whitehall, says: "I must particularly mention the conduct of Lieutenant Graham, acting as aide to Colonel Hickman. Throughout the entire march he was conspicuous for his venturesome courage, and at Goldsboro, in company with Lieutenant B. N. Mann, 17th Massachusetts, advanced and fired the bridge, under the fire of the enemy's infantry and artillery." Vol. 28, page 193.

GRANGER: Lieutenant Charles M., 88th Regiment. Presented with a sword as a tribute to his bravery and coolness on the field of battle. Vol. 28, page 495.

GRANNISS: Lieutenant F. W., 61st Regiment. Especially commended for his excellent conduct and soldier-like qualities, by Lieutenant-Colonel Broady in his Report of the battle of Chancellorsville. Vol. 32, page 351.

GRINTON: Captain Henry, 2d Cavalry. Behaved splendidly during the series of cavalry fights in October, 1863, at Bristow Station. Vol. 37, page 484.

GROWER: Major Wm. T. C., 17th Regiment. During General Sherman's expedition from Vicksburg, the Major acted as a Brigadier-General. He is a tactician of very high order, and as he is one who immediately bears the stamp of a gentleman, he could not but impress those with whom he came in contact. Vol. 37, page 48.

GREENE: Lieutenant Joseph A., 9th Regiment. During the bombardment of Hamilton, N. C., Lieutenant Greene with his company was on the gunboat "Ceres," rendering valuable assistance. Early in the action the Lieutenant was wounded in the leg, and was brought on deck, where he lay during the remainder of the action, loading guns for his men, and speaking words of good cheer to them. Vol. 22, page 488.

GREEN: Major A. P., 13th Cavalry. Distinguished himself in several engagements with the enemy. Vol. 29, page 158.

GREEN: CAPTAIN AUGUST P., 5th Cavalry. During Banks' Shenandoah campaign, Captains Green and Pratt escorted Hampton's battery into Winchester, at night. Vol. 42, page 314.

GUION: COLONEL GEORGE M., 148th Regiment. Formerly Captain in the 33d New York. He was all through the Peninsula campaign and acted bravely. Vol. 39, page 88.

GUTHRIE: SERGEANT GEORGE L., 5th Regiment. Promoted for gallantry on the field. Vol. 25, page 97.

HALL: LIEUTENANT-COLONEL JAMES F., 1st Engineers (Serrills Engineers). Honorably mentioned in General Benham's Report of the capture of Fort Pulaski. Vol. 19, page 357. During the battle of Olustee, Fla., he was zealously engaged in inspiring our troops with confidence when the day seemed to be lost, in exhorting the timid and driving up the cowards. He rallied the troops and held them up to their work at all points of the field, and did valuable service in every way.
Vol. 42, page 187.

HARHAUS: COLONEL OTTO, 2d Cavalry. One of the heroes of the Cavalry fight at Culpepper, September, 1863.
Vol. 36, page 472.

HASSLER: MAJOR FERDINAND R., 13th Artillery. Distinguished himself in the campaigns on the Peninsula. Governor Seymour afterwards promoted him to the Majority of the 13th Artillery. Vol. 38, page 32.

HAZLEY: CAPTAIN JAMES, 89th Regiment. He voluntarily led his company across the Rappahannock River in boats, in order to dislodge the Rebel sharpshooters, and thus enable our engineers to build the bridges that our troops might cross and take the city of Fredericksburg at the time it was attacked by General Burnside. Vol. 27, page 254.

HANCOCK: COLOR-SERGEANT GEORGE, 36th Regiment. Especially distinguished for meritorious conduct during the storming of the Heights of Fredericksburg (Chancellorsville).
Vol. 32, page 308.

HARDY: SERGEANT S. P., 73d Regiment. Promoted for gallantry.
Vol. 30, page 17.

HARDER: SERGEANT PHILIP M., 40th Regiment. His name ordered to be inscribed on the Roll of Honor, and to wear the Kearny Cross for gallant conduct at the battle of Chancellorsville. Vol. 32, page 872.

HASTY: CAPTAIN CHARLES, 2d Cavalry. One of the heroes of the great Cavalry fight at Culpepper, September, 1863.
Vol. 36, page 472.

HORNE: BUGLER, 9th Regiment. Honorably mentioned in Colonel Kimball's Report of the battles of South Mountain and Antietam. Until wounded, he sounded the various commands with as much coolness as on parade. Vol. 25, page 7.

HENRY: CHARLES, 99th Regiment. One of the heroes of a brilliant affair on the Nansemond River, by which the transports "Commerce" and "Swan" were piloted past the Rebel batteries and arrived safely at Fortress Monroe.
Vol. 32, page 1.

HENRY: ADJUTANT JAMES, 37th Regiment. Honorably mentioned in General Kearny's Report of the battle of Seven Pines.
Vol. 21, page 426.

HARRINGTON: CAPTAIN HENRY, 42d Regiment. Honorably mentioned in Colonel Mooney's Report of the battle of Ball's Bluff.
Vol. 14, page 140.

HOUGHTON: MAJOR CHARLES H., 14th Artillery. The hero of Fort Stedman, March, 1865. He was permanently disabled.
Vol. 87, page 634.

HOUGH: PRIVATE, 14th Artillery. The man who served the last watch at Fort Stedman, that foggy morning of March 25, 1865, when the fort was surprised, was Private Hough.
Vol. 87, page 634.

HOYT: PRIVATE GEORGE, 142d Regiment. He volunteered to advance with the head of the column and cut down the palisading at the time of the assault on Fort Fisher.
Vol. 52, page 380.

HODGES: SERGEANT, 9th Regiment. Honorably mentioned in Colonel Kimball's Report of the battles of South Mountain and Antietam. Vol. 25, page 7.

HOUSTAIN: MAJOR JOHN B., 132d Regiment. His sufferings in Rebel prisons and escape therefrom, is worthy of remembrance. Vol. 38, page 137.

HOPPER: SERGEANT ROBINSON, 88th Regiment His name ordered to be inscribed on the Roll of Honor, and to wear the Kearny Cross for his gallantry at Chancellorsville. Vol. 32, page 372.

HULL: CAPTAIN WALTER C., 2d Cavalry. Behaved splendidly during a series of cavalry fights in October, 1863, at Bristow Station. Promoted to Colonel and killed at Cedar Creek, November 12, 1864. Vol. 37, page 484.

HULL: MAJOR HARMON D., 5th Regiment. Promoted for gallantry on the battle-field. Vol. 25, page 97.

HUSTON: LIEUTENANT-COLONEL JAMES, 82d Regiment. After the battle of Fredericksburg, General Sumner shook hands with the brave Lieutenant-Colonel and said: "I can depend on you, sir, and your regiment. God bless you all." Killed in action July 2, 1863. Vol. 27, page 522.

HUDSON: LIEUTENANT-COLONEL HENRY W., 82d Regiment. Honorably acquitted himself at the battle of Seven Pines. Vol. 22, page 283.
He participated with honor in all the battles fought by the Army of the Potomac from First Bull Run to April, 1864. Vol. 43, page 189.

HUTTON: WILLIAM, 123d Regiment. Wounded in the engagement at Chancellorsville, but instead of going to the hospital, remained with his company, and was conspicuous for his bravery. Vol. 33, page 110.

HUGGINS: ADJUTANT CHARLES, 47th Regiment. Behaved gallantly at the battle of Olustee, Fla. Vol. 42, page 76.

HEARN: JOSEPH, 5th Cavalry. One of the heroes of the battle of Front Royal. Vol. 20, page 547.

HEADLEY: JOHN O., 148th Regiment. Honorably mentioned in General Wistar's Report of the conflagration and explosion at Yorktown, in December, 1863. Vol. 30, page 309.

HOWLAND: COLONEL JOSEPH, 16th Regiment. He acted with great gallantry at Bull Run, and at West Point displayed consummate coolness and promptitude. Colonel Howland sacrificed everything on the altar of his country, seeking only the approval of a good conscience. He asked no other reward.
Vol. 20, page 408.

HALSTEAD: CAPTAIN EMINEL P., 2d Artillery. Honorably mentioned in General Doubleday's Report of the battle of South Mountain. Vol 25, page 159.

HALSTEAD: CAPTAIN RICHARD F., 42d Regiment. Promoted for special gallantry to Aide-de-Camp to General Sedgwick.
Vol. 40, page 148.

HANLEY: CAPTAIN TIMOTHY, 9th Cavalry. At the battle of Beverly Ford, he participated with honor in one of the most daring and brilliant dashes on record. Vol. 33, page 266. At the battle of Crooked Run, Captain Hanley exhibited the greatest skill and bravery. Vol. 47, page 455.

HALL: WILLIAM, 99th Regiment. One of the heroes of a brilliant affair on the Nansemond River, by which the transports "Commerce" and "Swan" were piloted past the Rebel batteries and arrived safely at Fortress Monroe. Vol. 32, page 1.

HAWKINS: COLONEL RUSH C., 9th Regiment. Honorably mentioned in General Reno's Report of the battle of South Mills or Camden. Vol. 20, page 106.

HAMILTON: CAPTAIN EDGAR A., 7th Cavalry. One of the heroes of a brilliant expedition into North Carolina.
Vol. 21, page 57.

HARMON: CAPTAIN SAMUEL M., 27th regiment. A brave and skilful officer, who acquitted himself in the most heroic manner at Bull Run, West Point, Fair Oaks, and Gaines' Mills, and at the subsequent battles before Richmond. Vol. 23, page 128.

HARMON: LIEUTENANT WILLIAM H., 7th Cavalry. Acquitted himself nobly in the engagements near Suffolk, Va.
Vol. 26, page 16.

HARDING: LIEUTENANT FRANCIS L., 99th Regiment. Honorably acquitted himself in a brisk skirmish with the enemy near Suffolk. Vol. 32, page 70.

HAMMELL: CAPTAIN WILLIAM W., 9th Regiment. Honorably mentioned in Colonel Kimball's Report of the battle of South Mills. Vol. 20, page 146.

HAMMELL: LIEUTENANT-COLONEL JOHN S., 66th Regiment. Honorably acquitted himself and was mentioned in Colonel Moore's Report of the battle of Chancellorsville. He was promoted to Brevet Brigadier-General, March 1, 1865. Vol. 32, page 577.

HANNES: QUARTERMASTER-SERGEANT, 9th Regiment. Honorably mentioned in Colonel Kimball's Report of the battles of South Mountain and Antietam. Vol. 25, page 7.

HAYMAN: COLONEL S. B., 37th Regiment. He acted in the most gallant manner on the occasion of a brilliant charge of the regiment at the battle of Williamsburg. Vol. 20, page 454. Honorably mentioned in General Kearny's Report of the battle of Seven Pines. Vol. 24, page 426.

HUDD: JOHN, 78th Regiment. Honorably discharged the service in order to enable him to receive promotion.
Vol. 36, page 246.

HUGHES: LIEUTENANT-COLONEL JAMES G., 39th Regiment. Honorably mentioned in General Owen's Report of the affair at Morton's Ford in February, 1864. Vol. 41, page 187.

HUSON: CAPTAIN WILLIAM, 12th Regiment. He acquitted himself so heroically upon the battle-field in front of Richmond that the Major of the regiment clapped him on the back and complimented him for his bravery. Vol. 23, page 64.
He was also the hero of a creditable and noteworthy piece of scouting at the time of the battle of Chancellorsville.
Vol. 32, page 205.

HORNER: LIEUTENANT JAMES B., 9th Regiment. Honorably mentioned in Colonel Kimball's Report of the battles of South Mountain and Antietam. Vol. 25, page 7.

HUBBELL: MAJOR WILSON, 62d Regiment. Honorably mentioned in General Wheaton's Report of the battle of Chancellorsville. Killed at Coal Harbor, June 3, 1864. Vol. 32, page 283.

HUNT: COLONEL LEWIS C., 92d Regiment. Recommended by General Foster for promotion to Brigadier-General for gallant conduct at Kinston. Vol. 27, page 365.

HUSK: COLONEL LEWIS W., 111th Regiment. Honorably mentioned in General Owen's Report of the affair at Morton's Ford in February, 1864.   Vol. 41, page 187.

HORTON: LIEUTENANT CHARLES S., 99th Regiment. One of the heroes of a brilliant affair on the Nansemond River.
Vol. 31, page 474.

HOFFMAN: LIEUTENANT WILLIAM. Promoted for gallantry on the battle-field.   Vol. 25, page 97.

HOFFMAN: COLONEL HENRY C., 23d Regiment. Honorably mentioned in General Doubleday's Report of the battle of Pea Ridge.   Vol. 19, page 70.

HOLT: LIEUTENANT-COLONEL THOMAS, 70th Regiment. At the battle of Wapping Heights, he seized the colors of the regiment as they fell from the hands of the wounded color-bearers. Colonel Holt on the march, or in action, was ever ready to assist any that were exhausted by fatigue or sickness, and at times during the heavy marches, marched in the ranks himself, and let the boys ride his horses, and even carried the knapsack of one of his regiment, who was almost tired out.
Vol. 35, page 198.

HAYES: JEREMIAH, 82d Regiment. Privates Hayes and Craft were on picket (on the Peninsula) behind two old chimneys. The Rebels opened fire on them, tearing down the chimneys over their heads. The men escaped from the ruins uninjured and continued to hold their posts until relieved. With such men guarding the outposts, there was no danger of a surprise.
Vol. 21, page 347.

HARRING: LIEUTENANT ABRAM P., 132d Regiment. Had not eleven men of the 132d under Lieutenant Harring, in the block-house at Batchelor's Creek, withstood a Rebel army for over an hour, Newbern would have been captured by the rebels.
Vol. 41, page 136.

HALL: SERGEANT FRED. P., 55th Regiment. Honorably mentioned in Colonel de Trobriand's Report of the battle of Williamsburg.
Vol. 20, page 303.

HARRIS: SERGEANT, 2d Cavalry. Honorably mentioned in Colonel Kilpatrick's Report of a successful cavalry expedition to Hanover Junction. A braver or more eager soldier never met an enemy.   Vol. 22, page 642.

HART: Captain Orson H., 70th Regiment. Acquitted himself with honorable distinction at the battle of Oak Grove.
Vol. 22, page 187.
Especially mentioned for his cool and daring courage at the battle of Chancellorsville. Vol. 32, page 301.

HART: Captain William G., 88th Regiment. Acting Assistant Adjutant-General of the Irish Brigade. General Meagher in his Report of the battle of Fredericksburg says: "He exercised a bright coolness and intelligent courage while steadying the men for the attack." Vol. 27, page 525.

HART: Captain William, 4th Cavalry. One of the heroes of the brilliant cavalry battle at Kelly's Ford. Vol. 30, page 337. Killed at Raccoon Ford, September 16, 1863.
Vol. 30, page 337.

HILL: Sergeant James S., 14th Artillery Regiment. At the battle of the Crater he took a regimental battle-flag by force.
Vol. 87, page 631.

HAMILTON: Sergeant Andrew, 47th Regiment. Battle of Chapin's Farm, General Butler says: "For gallantry and coolness in the assault he was recommended for promotion."
Vol. 49, page 456.

HOTCHKISS: Private D. C., 112th Regiment. In the assault on Fort Fisher, he volunteered to approach to a point considerably in advance of the skirmish line, which he did, and by this step valuable information in regard to the ditch was gained. Vol. 52, page 380.

HENRY: Captain Edmund S., 127th Regiment. Honorably mentioned in General Foster's General Orders, relative to the affair at Forts Johnson, Simpkins, S. C., in July, 1864.
Vol. 50, page 382.

HOLBROOK: Captain Melton T., 173d Regiment. Promoted to Lieutenant-Colonel for meritorious services in the Red River Campaign and in the Shenandoah Valley. Vol. 51, page 489.

HOGG: Major George, 2d Artillery. On the occasion of a reconnoissance on the Vaughn road to Hatcher's Run, December, 1864, Major Hogg commanded the regiment, and his conduct was especially commended by General Miles.
Vol. 51, page 203.

HOYT: CAPTAIN JAMES J., 156th Regiment. Captain Hoyt commanded the regiment at the battle of Cedar Creek, and was equal to the emergency as an efficient and brave officer; amidst the hottest of the action, he could be seen, sword in hand, encouraging his men, not only by his words but by his own exemplary conduct. Vol. 51, page 191.

HARRIS: ARNOLD G., He enlisted in the 21st Regiment from Buffalo, and was transferred to the navy, being given command of a gunboat on the James River. He volunteered to go into the Confederate camp as a spy, and before long was high in the confidence of the authorities at Charleston. He was intrusted with important dispatches to General Beauregard at Richmond, and the commander kept him for some time at his own quarters. Harris was given a dinner by General Beauregard, and when the yacht "Wanderer" was fitted out as a dispatch ship to run the blockade he was placed in command. Important dispatches to the European agents of the Confederates were placed in a tin case, which he was to drop overboard if captured. George N. Saunders was on board, and when the attempt was made to run the blockade, Harris was at the helm. He steered the yacht alongside a Yankee cruiser, and when captured, dropped overboard a duplicate of the tin dispatch case. Harris died in 1888. Vol. 54, page 294.

HEARY: ADJUTANT JAMES J., 6th Regiment. He saved the regimental colors in the fight on Santa Rosa Island.
Vol. 13, page 572.

HAMBLIN: LIEUTENANT THOMAS S., 38th Regiment. Honorably mentioned in Colonel Farnsworth's Report of the battle of Bull Run. Vol. 11, page 61.

HOWARD: LIEUTENANT JOHN B., 84th Regiment. Honorably mentioned in General Porter's Report of the battle of Bull Run. Promoted to Captain and Quartermaster June 30, 1862.
Vol. 11, page 221.

HENBERER: CAPTAIN CHARLES E., 6th Regiment. Distinguished himself in the fight on Santa Rosa Island.
Vol. 13, page 477.

HAMBLIN: COLONEL JOSEPH H., 65th Regiment. When General Upton assumed command of the division after the death of General Russell at the battle of the Opequan, Colonel Hamblin took command of General Upton's brigade, and was always where the bullets flew the thickest, and had his horse shot from under him; still he continued undaunted to cheer his men on, himself setting the noble example. Colonel Hamblin was promoted to Brigadier-General in 1865.

Vol. 49, page 155.

HERMANCE: CAPTAIN WM. L., 6th Cavalry. At the battle of Crooked Run, he led a squadron of his regiment in a gallant charge with great bravery. Vol. 47, page 463.

HARROWER: CAPTAIN HENRY G., 86th Regiment. General Hancock in his complimentary order in reference to the midnight surprise of September 10, 1864, near Petersburg, says: "Great credit is due to Captain Harrower, commanding the picket during the following night, under whose direction the new line was strengthened and properly connected.

Vol. 48, page 396.

HAMMOND: COLONEL JOHN, 5th Cavalry. After the battle of Shepherdstown, Va., August 25, 1864, General McIntosh thanked him for the handsome manner in which he had behaved. And in the battle for the possession of the Weldon Railroad his conduct was so magnificent as to place him very high on the Roll of Fame.

Vol. 47, page 504. See also, Vol. 48, page 204.

He also acquitted himself honorably in an engagement with Mosby's guerillas in 1863. Vol. 32, page 99.

HUTCHINSON: WM., 79th N. Y. S. M. This brave fellow carried the colors of the regiment off the field of Manassas and through the battles of Chantilly, South Mountain and Fredericksburg, where he gave them up on being appointed First Sergeant of Co. C. Vol. 47, page 2.

HOLMES: LIEUTENANT ANSEL, 16th Artillery. He distinguished himself by sighting a gun for a Rebel caisson, which he completely demolished, killing and wounding four Rebels. The action elicited much praise, and General "Baldy" Smith remarked that if there were any more officers of the 16th Artillery of the same sort, he wanted them right away.

Vol. 45, page 94.

ISRAELS: LIEUTENANT LEHMAN, 55th Regiment. Honorably mentioned in General Peck's Report of the battle of Seven Pines.

Vol. 21, page 350.

IRVINE: Lieutenant Colonel William, 10th Cavalry. One of the heroes of the great cavalry exploit under General Stoneman, at the time of the battle of Chancellorsville.
Vol. 39, page 213.

IRELAND: Colonel David, 137th Regiment. On the second day of the battle of Gettysburg he was especially conspicuous for his bravery and skill. Died September 10, 1864—of disease, at Atlanta, Ga. Vol. 34, page 94.

JAMES: Samuel, 99th Regiment. One of the heroes on board the "Congress" and participated in the fight with the steamer "Merrimac." Vol. 18, page 232.

JACKSON: Captain Robert, 36th Regiment. Especially distinguished for meritorious conduct during the storming of the Heights of Chancellorsville. Vol. 32, page 308.

JARDINE: Major Edward, 9th Regiment. Honorably mentioned in Colonel Kimball's Report of the battle of South Mills.
Vol. 20, page 146.
He commanded the 89th Regiment at the battle of Antietam and proved himself abundantly competent for the responsibility. Vol. 25, page 7.
He was honorably mentioned in General Butler's Report of the capture of Fort Hatteras. Vol. 12, page 13.

JOCKNICK: Captain George F., 3d Cavalry. Acquitted himself with great skill and bravery at the battle of Washington.
Vol. 24, page 324.

JUDD: Captain Seymour L., 89th Regiment. He voluntarily led his company across the Rappahannock River in boats, in order to dislodge the Rebel sharpshooters and thus enable our engineers to build the bridges that our troops might cross and take the city of Fredericksburg at the time it was attacked by General Burnside. Vol. 27, page 254.

JUDGE: Sergeant Francis U., 79th Regiment. At the battle of Fort Sanders (siege of Knoxville) when the battle flag of a Georgia regiment was raised upon the parapet, he rushed out among the bullets and tearing it down, carried it through the embrasure, a prize to his comrades. Vol. 39, page 237.

JENKINS: Lieutenant Daniel E., 51st Regiment. Commissioned by Governor Seymour for bravery on the field and meritorious conduct. Killed in action at the battle of the Wilderness, Va., May 6, 1864. Vol. 31, page 295.

JEHL: MAJOR FRANCIS; 55th Regiment. Honorably mentioned in Colonel de Trobriand's Report of the battle of Williamsburg.
Vol. 20, page 303.

JOHNSON: CAPTAIN DAVID R., 51st Regiment. Honorably mentioned in Colonel Ferrero's Report of the engagement at Roanoke Island. (Died of wounds received in action March 19, 1862.) Vol. 17, page 283.

JOHNSON: CAPTAIN ROBERT T., 72d Regiment. If the country rewards her heroes, Captain Johnson's name will stand among the foremost. Promoted September, 1862, to Major 144th Regiment. Vol. 21, page 70.

JOHNSON: SAMUEL, 123d Regiment. While the regiment was engaged at close quarters at the battle of Chancellorsville, he rushed forward, captured and brought in two prisoners.
Vol. 33, page 110.

JONES: CAPTAIN ABRAM, 1st Cavalry. Honorably mentioned in General Kearny's Report of the cavalry fight at Sangster Station. Vol. 18, page 421.
The hero of a gallant fight at McConnellsburg.
Vol. 34, page 181.
One of the heroes of a brilliant skirmish at Smithfield, September, 1863. Vol. 36, page 412.

JONES: COLONEL FRANK, 31st Regiment. He led his regiment in the attack and capture of Marye's Heights.
Vol. 32, page 393.

JONES: LIEUTENANT P. O., 2d Cavalry. One of the heroes of a great cavalry fight at Culpepper, June, 1863.
Vol. 36, page 472.

JOHNSON: COLONEL CHARLES A., 25th Regiment. The battle of Hanover Court House was opened by the 25th, the gallant Colonel displaying great skill and bravery in leading his regiment against the enemy. He is entitled to credit for distinguished services at Chancellorsville. Vol. 20, page 568.

JOHNSON: SERGEANT, 9th Regiment. Honorably mentioned in Colonel Kimball's Report of the battles of South Mountain and Antietam. Vol. 25, page 7.

JACOBSOHN: Sergeant, 9th Regiment. Honorably mentioned in Colonel Kimball's Report of the battles of South Mountain and Antietam. Vol. 25, page 7.

JAMESON: Major William, 4th Regiment. Acquitted himself with great gallantry at the battle of Antietam.
Vol. 25, page 89.

JEFFREY: Alexander, Battery B, Light Artillery. At Gettysburg he was wounded in the head. The surgeon ordered him to the hospital, but after a field dressing, he returned to his guns and stood by them until the fight was over, when he betook himself to the hospital again. Vol. 53, page 409.

JOURDAN: Major James, 84th Regiment. Honorably mentioned in General Porter's Report of the battle of Bull Run.
Vol. 11, page 221.

JONES: Lieutenant Jeptha A., 84th Regiment. Honorably mentioned in General Porter's Report of the battle of Bull Run.
Vol. 11, page 221.

JACKSON: Lieutenant Henry C., 27th Regiment. Honorably mentioned in General Porter's Report of the battle of Bull Run. Vol. 11, page 221.

JOHNSON: Lieutenant-Colonel Nathan J., 115th Regiment. He was wounded at the battle of Chapin's Farm September 29, 1864, while carrying the colors of his regiment, which he seized from the color-sergeant, who was killed.
Vol. 48, page 43.

KETCHUM: Captain Edward N., 176th Regiment. Commanded the Pioneers of the 3d Brigade of General Grover's Division, 19th Corps, at the battle of Fisher's Hill, September 22, 1864. He received honorable mention in the official reports. Armed with a Spencer repeating rifle, none were more efficient in keeping the Rebels close behind their works.
Vol. 49, page 352.

KANE: Corporal, 13th Cavalry. He inflicted what was supposed to be a mortal wound upon the guerilla Mosby.
Vol. 51, page 517.

KEARNS: Corporal, 1st Regiment. At the battle of Gaines Mills, an officer mounted on a white horse rode up to the 1st, and ordered it to cease firing. His appearance was like that of a

well-known field officer of an associated regiment, and he was mistaken by some for him, but upon his coming within fifty yards he was recognized as a Confederate officer and shot dead by Corporal Kearns, one of the color-guard.
Vol. 86, page 500.

KOENIG: PRIVATE JULIUS B., 115th Regiment. Orderly, at Brigade Headquarters, battle of Chapin's Farm. General Butler says: "He carried the brigade flag with extraordinary zealousness in the hottest part of the action and is recommended to the War Department for a medal."
Vol. 49, page 456.

KELLOGG: CAPTAIN ROWLAND C., 118th Regiment. He commanded a company with skill and bravery in many important engagements.
Vol. 54, page 406.

KEEFE: JOHN D., 69th N. Y S. M., honorably acquitted himself at the battle of Bull Run.
Vol. 10, page 545.

KREUTZER: LIEUTENANT-COLONEL WILLIAM, 98th Regiment. Participated with great gallantry in the first attack made by the 18th Corps on the works of Petersburg, June 15th, 1864.
Vol. 45, page 505.

KINSEY: LIEUTENANT-COLONEL WM. B., 161st Regiment. Honorably mentioned in Admiral Porter's Report for the assistance he rendered in effecting the release of the gunboats at Alexandria, La., May, 1864.
Vol. 44, page 484.

KELLY: LIEUTENANT-COLONEL JAMES, 69th Regiment. He captured the Rebel General Pettigrew at the battle of Seven Pines.
Vol. 21, page 110.

KELLY: COLONEL PATRICK, 88th Regiment. General Meagher in his Report of the battle of Fredericksburg, says: "Colonel Kelly displayed a courageous soldiership, which I have no words with all my partiality for him, adequately to describe." Col. Kelly was killed in action near Petersburg, Va., December 13, 1862.
Vol. 27, page 126.

KELLY: SERGEANT DANIEL I., 37th Regiment. His name ordered to be inscribed on the Roll of Honor, and to wear the Kearny Cross for gallant conduct at the battle of Chancellorsville.
Vol. 32, page 312.

KEYES: ALEXANDER, 99th Regiment. One of the heroes on board the "Congress" who participated in the fight with the Rebel steamer "Merrimac." Vol. 18, page 232.

KOENIG: CAPTAIN EMIL, 58th Regiment. Honorably mentioned in General Schurz's Report of the battles of Groveton and Second Bull Run. Vol. 25, page 58.

KING: LIEUTENANT THEODORE F., 158th Regiment. He is entitled to great credit for the skill and bravery exhibited by him during the brilliant dash into Jones and Onslow Counties in February, 1864. Vol. 41, page 219.
General Peck in General Orders, says: "Great credit is due him for the efficient services performed on the occasion of an expedition in March, 1864, for the purpose of capturing vessels of the enemy engaged in contraband of war."
Vol. 43, page 303.

KIMBALL: MAJOR EDWARD A., 9th Regiment. Honorable mention is made of Major Kimball in General Shields' Report of the battle of Winchester. Vol. 19, page 217.
Also in an account of the battle of South Mills.
Lieutenant-Colonel Kimball was killed by General Corcoran April 12, 1863. Vol. 20, page 94.

KRAMM: LIEUTENANT ADAM, 55th Regiment. Honorably mentioned in General Peck's Report of the battle of Seven Pines.
Vol. 21, page 359.

KEYSER: LIEUTENANT HENRY, 5th Regiment. Promoted for gallantry on the battle-field. Vol. 25, page 97.

KEECH: CAPTAIN WILLARD, 61st Regiment. Especially commended for his brave conduct and soldierlike qualities by Colonel Broady, in his Report of the battle of Chancellorsville.
Vol. 32, page 351.

KECH: COLOR-SERGEANT PETER J., 115th Regiment. Distinguished himself by his coolness and courage at the battle of Olustee, Fla. Advancing his colors to the front, he waved them defiantly in the face of the enemy immediately opposite to a Rebel color-bearer who was hiding himself behind a tree. Nearly all the color-guard were shot down. Sergeant Kech escaped. His gallantry was noticed and applauded by the General and his Staff. Vol. 42, page 271.

KIRK: MAJOR WILLIAM A., 57th Regiment. He participated with honor in sixteen engagements, including Antietam, Fredericksburg and Gettysburg. Died of wounds received at Petersburg, July 20, 1864. Vol. 41, page 350.

KAVANAGH: CAPTAIN JOHN, 63d Regiment. General Meagher issued a special order complimenting Captain Kavanagh for his bravery during a general attack on the pickets of the brigade on the 19th of June, near Richmond. Killed in action at Antietam, September 17, 1862. Vol. 21, page 506.

KAVANAGH: LIEUTENANT WILLIAM J., 7th Cavalry. A brave and worthy officer. Vol. 27, page 481.

KAVANAGH: SERGEANT JOHN, 88th Regiment. His name ordered to be inscribed on the Roll of Honor, and to wear the Kearny Cross for gallant conduct. Vol. 32, page 372.

KELLY: PETER, 69th N. Y S. M. Distinguished himself at Bull Run, was wounded, captured, and afterwards made his escape. Vol. 15, page 1.

KLINGSOEHR: LIEUTENANT VICTOR, 9th Regiment. Honorably mentioned in Colonel Kimball's Report of the battle of Wauhatchie. Vol. 41, page 309.

KENNEDY: SERGEANT CHARLES W., 156th Regiment. In one of the battles under General Banks in Louisiana, our forces fell back about twenty feet, when Kennedy advancing to the front, waved his musket as an officer would his sword, and impulsively shouted: "Let's try it again, boys! We'll have it this time," and the gallant fellow, bounding forward, the rest followed with a yell, when the ditch, obstructions, and guns were passed in a moment, and the next instant the abatis was taken. Vol. 31, page 434.

KEATING: SERGEANT. Honorably mentioned in Colonel Kimball's Report of the battles of South Mountain and Antietam.
Vol. 25, page 187.

KEATING: MAJOR GEORGE, 174th Regiment. He commanded the regiment in the battle of Donaldsonville and acquitted himself with conspicuous gallantry. Vol. 35, page 187.

KNAPP: CAPTAIN JACOB W., 19th Cavalry (formerly 130th Infantry), the hero of a brilliant charge, described as being only equalled by the charge of Captain Tompkins at Fairfax, and excelling anything of the kind during the campaign of the Army of the Potomac. Vol. 38, page 191.

KORWIN: SERGEANT JOSEPH, 55th Regiment. Honorably mentioned in Colonel de Trobriand's Report of the battle of Williamsburg. Vol. 20, page 303.

KROM: CAPTAIN ABRAM H., 5th Cavalry. Acquitted himself with great gallantry in an engagement with Mosby guerillas at Warrenton Junction, where he was wounded on the 3d of May, 1863. Vol. 32, page 99.
As a token of the high estimation in which he was held by his comrades, he was presented with an elegant sword.
Vol. 32, page 412.

KRUGER: CAPTAIN CHARLES W., 4th Regiment. Acquitted himself with great gallantry at the battle of Antietam.
Vol. 25, page 89.

KNOSKE: LIEUTENANT EDWARD G., 4th Regiment. Acquitted himself with great gallantry at Antietam.

KRETZLER: ALFRED, 162d Regiment. One of those meritorious soldiers of General Birney's division, selected for his gallantry as a recipient of the Kearny Cross. Vol. 32, page 544.

KNOX: LIEUTENANT EDWARD M., 15th Battery. A gallant soldier wounded at Gettysburg. He received the most complimentary notices for his gallantry while in action, from his superior officers. Vol. 35, page 247.

LEONARD: MAJOR JOHN, 72d Regiment. Especially mentioned for his cool and daring courage at the battle of Chancellorsville.
Vol. 32, page 301.

LEWIS: CORPORAL EUGENE, 1st Cavalry. After the fall of Lieutenant Hidden at Sangster Station, he took command of the fourteen men and fought like a tiger. Vol. 18, page 265.
Honorably mentioned in General Kearny's Report of the fight.
Vol. 18, page 421.

LE FORT: LIEUTENANT GEORGE, 73d Regiment. Promoted for gallant conduct on the field. Captain Le Fort was killed in action May 20, 1864. Vol. 30, page 17.

LEON: CORPORAL, 74th Regiment. He was shot through the thigh at Williamsburg and refused to allow the surgeon to attend him, until the others were cared for. Leon served under Garibaldi as a captain in former years.

LEAHY: CAPTAIN LAWRENCE, 9th Regiment and subsequently of the 16th Cavalry. Honorably mentioned in Colonel Kimball's Report of the battles of South Mountain and Antietam.
Vol. 20, page 146.
He acquitted himself honorably in an encounter with Early's forces in 1864. Vol. 48, page 435.

LEDLIE: COLONEL JAMES H., 3d Artillery. Honorably mentioned for the skilful manner in which he operated his pieces at the battle of Kinston. Promoted December 24, 1862, to Brigadier-General. Vol. 27, page 365.

LATTIN: SERGEANT CHARLES, 37th Regiment. His name ordered to be inscribed on the Roll of Honor, and to wear the Kearny Cross for gallant conduct at Chancellorsville.
Vol. 32, page 373.

LE BAIRE: CAPTAIN ADOLPH, 9th Regiment. Honorably mentioned in Colonel Kimball's Report of the battle of South Mills. Vol. 20, page 146.
Also in the Colonel's Report of the battles of South Mountain and Antietam. Vol. 20, page 146.

LOCKWOOD: LIEUTENANT JOHN J., 120th Regiment He handled his men admirably when attacked by an overwhelming force of Rebels in October, 1863, near Madison Court House. Killed in action May 5, 1864. Vol. 37, page 291.

LOWE: WALTER, 99th Regiment. One of the heroes of an affair on Nansemond River. Vol. 32, page 1.

LUM: ADJUTANT DYER D., 14th Cavalry. Deserves special mention for his gallantry and bravery in the series of brilliant skirmishes in Louisiana, in April, 1864. Vol. 43, page 332.

LORD: COLONEL NEWTON B., 35th Regiment. Colonel Lord commanded the regiment in eight different engagements and proved himself a brave and competent officer. He entered the service as captain, and by his gallantry won the chief command of his regiment. Vol. 29, page 505.

LOUNSBURY: CAPTAIN WILLIAM H., 74th Regiment. Especially mentioned for his cool and daring courage at Chancellorsville.
Vol. 32, page 301.

LEE: CAPTAIN JOHN C., 99th Regiment. Honorably mentioned in Captain Hymes' Report of the opening of Nansemond River.
Vol. 21, page 400.
He commanded the Harbor Police of Norfolk; was with General Graham at the time of the affair at Smithfield, and was placed in command of the force on the "Smith Briggs," and made one of the most brilliant fights of the war against great odds, and subsequently had to swim for his life, or be hung by the Rebels, who offered a prize for his head. Vol. 41, page 85.

LEDDY: CAPTAIN THOMAS, 69th Regiment. Presented with an elegant sword by the members of the regiment, as a token of their appreciation of his bravery and courage in the battles before Richmond.
Vol. 24, page 163.

LINSON: SERGEANT LYMAN S., 143d Regiment. Honorably discharged the service in order to enable him to receive promotion.
Vol. 60, page 246.

LEWIS: LIEUTENANT-COLONEL GEORGE W., 3d Cavalry Regiment. A gallant soldier whose name belongs to Kinston, Whitehall and Goldsboro.
Vol. 28, page 581.

LEE: LIEUTENANT JOHN D., 7th Cavalry. One of the heroes of a brilliant expedition into North Carolina.
Vol. 21, page 57.

LYONS: JOHN D., 37th Regiment. His name ordered to be inscribed on the Roll of Honor, and to wear the Kearny Cross for gallant conduct at the battle of Chancellorsville.
Vol. 32, page 372.

LYNCH: JOHN, 37th Regiment. Presented with a Kearny Medal for his brave and gallant conduct.
Vol. 35, page 180.

LAWRENCE: LIEUTENANT JOHN T., 73d Regiment. Promoted for gallant conduct on the field.
Vol. 30, page 17.

LANSING: COLONEL H. S., 17th Regiment. Entitled to special credit for the bravery and skill displayed in reconnoitering Stonewall Jackson's position on the Peninsula.
Vol. 22, page 199.

LANE: Major James C., 102d Regiment. His conduct at the battle of Cedar Mountain is spoken of in the highest terms of praise.   Vol. 23, page 295.
His intrepidity at Cedar Mountain, won for him the title of "Fighting Major."   Vol. 25 page 59.
The record of the 102d is his record, and one of which he has a right to be proud. Colonel Lane was wounded at Gettysburg, and did not hesitate to brave death in a dozen battles.
   Vol. 40, page 422.

LAPHAM: Captain Daniel W., 9th Cavalry. Exhibited the greatest bravery and skill at the battle of Crooked Run, Va., August 16, 1864.   Vol. 47, page 463.

LUBY: Captain Timothy, 15th Engineer Regiment. The bridge thrown across the James River to Strawberry Plains in July, 1864, was constructed by Captain Luby.   Vol. 46, page 576.

LIPPINCOTT: Lieutenant Adon, 48th Regiment. Battle of Chapin's Farm. General Butler says: "He had special mention for gallant conduct in two assaults and was recommended for promotion.   Vol. 49, page 456.

LIMBACK: Sergeant John A., 83d Regiment. At the time of the engagement at Harper's Ferry, Limback, with an advanced party of the regiment forded the Potomac River and in the face of a fire from Stuart's Cavalry, climbed up a flag-staff and nailed the Stars and Stripes to the head.   Vol. 86, page 546.

LITTLE: Lieutenant John L., 127th Regiment. Honorably mentioned in General Foster's General Orders relative to the affair at Forts Johnson and Simpkins, S. C., in July, 1864.
   Vol. 50, page 382.

LITTLE: Major Edward H., 127th Regiment. Honorably mentioned in General Foster's General Orders, relative to the affair at Forts Johnson and Simpkins, S. C., in July, 1864.
   Vol. 50, page 382.

LONSWAY: Private Joseph, 20th Cavalry. On the occasion of an expedition into North Carolina to break up illicit traffic, in October, 1864, a gallant and heroic deed was performed by Private Lonsway. It becoming necessary to cross the river, and the Rebels having secured the flat-boat which is used to ferry men and teams across, and fastened it to the opposite bank, Lonsway volunteered to secure the boat, and having received permission to do so from Captain Carroll, he gallantly swam the stream under a galling fire from the enemy and not only escaped injury but also brought back the flat-boat amidst shouts and plaudits from his companions.

Vol. 49, page 390.

LUDLOW: ADJUTANT LEFFERT L., 84th Regiment. Honorably mentioned in General Porter's Report of the battle of Bull Run. Vol. 11, page 221.

LEOSER: MAJOR CHARLES McK., 11th Regiment. Honorably mentioned in Colonel Ward's Report of the battle of Bull Run.
Vol. 11, page 61.

LAZELLE: COLONEL H. M., 16th Cavalry. Colonel Lazelle commanded an expedition to the Rapidan in September, 1864, and acquitted himself with great skill and gallantry.
Vol. 48, page 435.

MINNES: LIEUTENANT SAMUEL, 10th Regiment. At one of the battles of the Wilderness May 6, 1864, he, with a few other members of the regiment, attempted to capture a Confederate flag, and was shot through the body. The surgeons pronounced the wound fatal, but his will-power was so strong that it carried him finally. through. For his gallantry on this occasion he was especially mentioned in General Orders from the War Department. When he received the wound, he made a vow that he would be the first wounded man to return to the regiment, and on June 29, following, reported back, but really unfit for duty, thus being the first one back. At Strawberry Plains, July, 1864, he was slightly wounded twice but refused to leave the field. At Hatcher's Run and Boydtown Plank Road, October 27, 1864, he crossed the stream waist deep with his colors, crossing the field which was enfiladed by artillery and infantry fire, and planted his colors on the Confederate breastworks. Here again, he received official notice, and was recommended for a War Department medal. A Second Lieutenant's commission was conferred upon him. At the battle, he was shot through the right hand and also through the left thigh, which confined him several weeks to the hospital. Upon his return he was promoted to First Lieutenant, served to the end of the war and was mustered out July 8, 1865.

Vol. 87, page 678.

MEYER: MAJOR FRANCIS X., 117th Regiment. Major Meyer says, his was the first flag to wave over the parapets of Fort Fisher. Vol. 52, page 426.

MORGAN: PRIVATE D. H., 42d Regiment. He volunteered to advance with the head of the column and cut down the palisading at the time of the assault on Fort Fisher.
Vol. 52, page 380.

MERRILL: PRIVATE GEORGE, 142d Regiment. He volunteered to advance with the head of the column and cut down the palisading at the time of the assault ou Fort Fisher.
Vol. 52, page 380.

McDUFF: PRIVATE W. J., 142d Regiment. He volunteered to advance with the head of the column and cut down the palisading at the time of the assault on Fort Fisher.
Vol. 52, page 380.

MEAGHER: SERGEANT THOMAS, 158th Regiment. General Butler says: "He led a section of his men on the enemy's works at the battle of Chapin's Farm, and was wounded while scaling the parapet. He was recommended for a medal.
Vol. 49, page 450.

MOLINEUX: COLONEL EDWARD L., 159th Regiment. He commanded a brigade at the battle of Winchester, September 19, 1864, and acquitted himself with the greatest distinction. One month later he was promoted to the rank of Brevet Brigadier-General. Vol. 49, page 352.

MULHALL: LIEUTENANT HENRY, 169th Regiment. Promoted to the rank of Captain for gallant and meritorious services.
Vol. 49, page 286.

MERRELL: LIEUTENANT CHARLES D., 169th Regiment. Promoted to the rank of Captain for gallant and meritorious services.
Vol. 49, page 286.

MILLER: PRIVATE WALTER L., 21st Cavalry. Officially reported for capturing the Rebel officer in command of the artillery at the battle of Nineveh, November 12, 1864.
Vol. 50, page 384.

MORRISON: COLONEL DAVID, 79th Regiment. He carried his regiment through nearly all the fiery ordeals for three years of the war—a regiment that covered itself with glory.
Vol. 50, page 451.

He was the first to mount the parapet and scale the walls of a Rebel fort at Secessionville, S. C. Vol. 21, page 528.

McGRATH: SR., CAPTAIN EUGENE, 5th Artillery. Promoted to a Majorship for gallant and meritorious services at the battle of the Opequan. This gallant officer served in the Mexican war. He was wounded at Second Bull Run. Vol. 52, page 345.

McDONALD: CAPTAIN JOSEPH M., 47th Regiment. General Butler recommended him for promotion for the gallant manner in which he commanded his regiment after the colonel was wounded at the battle of Chapin's Farm. Vol. 47, page 456. He also behaved with great bravery at the battle of Olustee, Fla. Vol. 42, page 76.

MATTHEWS: LIEUTENANT JOHN, 11th Regiment. Honorably acquitted himself at the battle of Bull Run.
Vol. 10, page 463.

MURPHY: QUARTERMASTER CHARLES J., 38th Regiment. Honorably mentioned in Colonel Farnesworth's Report of the battle of Bull Run. Vol. 11, page 61.

McKNIGHT: CAPTAIN GEORGE F., 12th Independent Battery. At Petersburg, June 22, 1864, four of his guns were captured. McKnight stood by his guns and his colors till a Rebel flag flaunted beside his own, and there was but one man left with him. Vol. 45, page 523.

McDOUGALL: COLONEL CLINTON D., 111th Regiment. Colonel McDougall commanded a brigade in the 1st Division, 2d Corps, in the assault on the works at Petersburg, June 17, 1864, and greatly distinguished himself. Colonel McDougall was promoted to Brevet Brigadier-General in 1865.
Vol. 45, page 538.

MULCAHY: MAJOR THOMAS, 139th Regiment. Participated with great gallantry in the first attack made on the enemy's ranks at Petersburg, June 15, 1864, by the 18th Corps.
Vol. 45, page 505.

MARSHALL: COLONEL ELISHA G., 14th Artillery. In the assault on the Rebel works at Petersburg after the mine explosion, July 30, 1864, Colonel Marshall commanded with great bravery the brigade that took the lead. Vol. 47, page 32.

MENKE: CAPTAIN ISAAC, 17th Regiment. The chief hero of the battle near Decatur, Ala., 1864. Vol. 44, page 366.

MORRISON: COLONEL JOSEPH J., 16th Artillery. He went to the war as Captain of Co. A, 9th State Militia, and served with it through General Patterson's campaign. After his return home, he organized a light battery with which, as Captain he joined the 3d New York Light Artillery, and fought under Burnside and General Hooker through the North Carolina campaigns, distinguishing himself at Kinston, Whitehall and Goldsboro. At the latter place his battery was charged upon by three South Carolina regiments which he repulsed with a loss of 700 men. Vol. 44, page 47.

McCONIHE: COLONEL JOHN, 169th Regiment. He acquitted himself with great gallantry and distinction in the battles of Drury's Bluff and Walthal Junction. Killed in action at Coal Harbor, June 1, 1864. Vol. 44, page 337.
In March, 1864, he was said to be the youngest Colonel in the army. Vol. 43, page 58.

McKNIGHT: CAPTAIN GEORGE F., 12th Battery. This gallant officer acquitted himself with the greatest bravery on the 22d of June, 1864, when the Rebels attacked and captured his battery in front of Petersburg. Vol. 45, page 482.

MARKSMAN: CORPORAL JAMES, 73d Regiment. Promoted for gallant conduct. Lieutenant Marksman was killed in action July 3, 1863. Vol. 30, page 17.

MARTIN: JESSE, 5th Regiment. Honorably mentioned by Surgeon Charles B. White for his conduct while acting as hospital attendant after the Peninsula battles. Vol. 22, page 502.

MARTIN: LIEUTENANT THOMAS R., 5th Regiment. Promoted for gallantry on the battle-field. Vol. 25, page 97.

MAHONEY: PHILIP, 38th Regiment. Honorably mentioned in General Birney's Report of the battle of Fredericksburg.
Vol. 27, page 487.

MAGRUDER: MAJOR JAMES A., 15th Engineer Regiment. Major Magruder, Captains Ford and McDowell superintended the erection of the bridges across the Rappahannock, at the time of the attack on Fredericksburg by General Burnside.
Vol. 27, page 230.

MAYES: LIEUTENANT JOHN, 3d Cavalry. Captured by the Rebels in a fight near Trenton. He displayed great bravery on the occasion. Killed at Stony Creek, Va., May 7, 1864.
Vol. 20, page 473.

MURPHY: COLONEL JOHN McL., 15th Engineer Regiment. Few names are better entitled to a place on our bright roll of fame. Among the very first to volunteer for his country, his skill and bravery contributed equally to our success in many engagements. Vol. 21, page 520.

MURPHY: COLONEL MATHEW, 182d Regiment. Complimented on the battle-field, near the Blackwater, by General Corcoran, for his gallantry. He was mortally wounded in 1865.
Vol. 29, page 2.

MILLER: LIEUTENANT W. D. W., 66th Regiment. Promoted for special gallantry to Captain and Aide-de-camp.
Vol. 40, page 148.

MILLER: LIEUTENANT MERRITT B., 125th Regiment. He led one hundred men across the river at Morton's Ford, and is entitled to distinguished credit for his gallantry. Died June 26, 1864, of wounds received in action. Vol. 41, page 192.

MARTINDALE: LIEUTENANT FRANKLIN G., 1st Cavalry. At the head of twenty-five men, he was the hero of a brilliant performance in June, 1863. Vol. 33, page 590.

MARION: PHILIP, 2d Regiment. Honorably mentioned by Surgeon Charles White for his conduct while acting as hospital attendant after the Peninsula battles. Vol. 22, page 562.

MAJOR: CORPORAL D. H., 40th Regiment. His name ordered to be inscribed on the Roll of Honor, and to wear the Kearny Cross for gallant conduct at Chancellorsville.
Vol. 32, page 372.

MATTHESON: COLONEL RODERICK, 32d Regiment. Acquitted himself with honor at West Point. Killed October 2, 1862.
Vol. 20, page 437.

MAYAN: SERGEANT JOSEPH, 55th Regiment. Honorably mentioned in Colonel de Trobriand's Report of the battle of Williamsburg. Vol. 20, page 303.

13

MARTIN: MAJOR WILLIAM B., 9th Cavalry. At the battle of Beverly Ford, in June, 1863, he was ordered to take a squadron and drive the Rebels out of the bushes. This he most gallantly did, though it was right in the teeth of the enemy's artillery, and he was met by a perfect storm of canister.
Vol. 33, page 201.

MANN: CAPTAIN NEHEMIAH H., 4th Cavalry. At the battle of Aldie, finding his squadron hesitate in a charge, he plunged alone into the enemy's ranks. The result was a sabre gash, a pistol wound, and a horse killed, but the men were inspired and rushed to victory. Killed in action, August 16, 1864.
Vol. 33, page 465.

MERRITT: CAPTAIN HENRY A. D., 5th Cavalry. One of the heroes of the cavalry fight at Beverly Ford, June, 1863. He was wounded while gallantly leading his men.
Vol. 33, page 230.

MENDENHALL: LIEUTENANT JOHN B., 99th Regiment. Honorably acquitted himself in a brisk skirmish near Suffolk.
Vol. 32, page 70.

MEYER: CAPTAIN PHILIP, 55th Regiment. Honorably mentioned in Colonel de Trobriand's Report of the battle of Williamsburg.
Vol. 20, page 303.

MEYERS: MAJOR RUSSELL, 32d Regiment. Promoted for his bravery on many a hard fought field.
Vol. 32, page 519.

MEARA: SERGEANT J. O. Honorably mentioned in Colonel de Trobriand's Report of the battle of Williamsburg.
Vol. 20, page 303.

MILADOLPHSKY: 88th Regiment. His name ordered to be inscribed on the Roll of Honor, and to wear the Kearny Cross for gallant conduct at Chancellorsville.
Vol. 32, page 544.

MIX: COLONEL SIMON H., 3d Cavalry. This gallant soldier's name belongs to the battles of Kinston, Whitehall and Goldsboro.
Vol. 28, page 581.
He may be justly styled the chief hero of the battle of Washington, N. C. Killed at Petersburg, Va., June 15, 1864.
Vol. 24, page 372.

MITCHELL: CAPTAIN J. F. B., 2d Cavalry. One of the heroes of the great fight at Culpepper, September, 1863.
Vol. 36, page 472.

McVICAR: Lieutenant-Colonel Duncan, 6th Cavalry. The hero of a splendid dash with one hundred and nine of his men on the 13th of December, at Garrett's Ford, where he encountered the enemy's pickets, driving them in under his batteries and to their reserves without losing a man. Killed in action at Spottsylvania Court House, Va., April 30, 1863.
Vol. 28, page 123.

McKENNA: Captain Charles P., 1st Engineers. Entitled to the credit of constructing the celebrated "Marsh" Battery used during the siege of Charleston. Vol. 36, page 186.

McMASTERS: Captain Zolman J., 5th Cavalry Regiment. Acquitted himself with great gallantry in an engagement with Mosby's guerillas at Warrenton Junction. Died September 24, 1863, of disease. Vol. 32, page 99.

McQUADE: Colonel James, 14th Regiment. He acquitted himself with great credit and distinction both as Colonel of his regiment and Brigadier-General (pro tem.) in many of our principal battles, and on the Peninsula his gallantry was especially conspicuous. Vol. 22, page 158.

McREYMOLDS: Colonel Andrew T., 1st Cavalry. Commanding a brigade at Berryville, June, 1863. He proved himself worthy of all confidence as a military leader. Vol. 33, page 413.

McKECHNIE: Lieutenant Robert, 9th Regiment. Honorably mentioned in Colonel Kimball's Report of the battle of South Mills. Vol. 20, page 146.
Also in the Colonel's Report of the battles of South Mountain and Antietam. Vol. 25, page 7.
He conducted himself on several occasions with so much gallantry as to win the esteem and confidence of his superior officers, and the employees of the New York *Herald*, to which he was formerly attached, presented him with a splendid testimonial of their regard. Vol. 29, page 195.

McGUINN: Captain Luke, 5th Cavalry. Acquitted himself heroically at the battle of Hanover Court House. Killed in the battle of the Wilderness, May 5, 1864. Vol. 34, page 210.

McGEE: Captain James E., 69th Regiment. At Antietam the gallant Captain remained on the field until his company was reduced to five men beside himself, and carried the colors in his own hand. Vol. 25, page 544.

McDONALD: Corporal Thomas, 79th Regiment. Honorably acquitted himself at the battle of Bull Run.
Vol. 16, page 50.

McDERMOTT: Sergeant James, 73d Regiment. Promoted for gallant conduct. Vol. 30, page 17.

McGREGOR: Colonel John D., 4th Regiment. Acquitted himself gallantly at Antietam. Vol. 25, page 80.

McCARTHEY: Captain Charles, 175th Regiment. Honorably acquitted himself in the battles which occurred during the march of General Banks' forces from Brashear City to Opelousas, La. Vol. 32, page 488.

McCUTCHEON: Sergeant Charles, 2d Cavalry. Honorably mentioned in Colonel Kilpatrick's Report of a successful expedition to Hanover Junction. Vol. 22, page 642.

MORRIS: Sergeant William, 88th Regiment. His name ordered to be inscribed on the Roll of Honor, and to wear the Kearny Cross for gallant conduct at the battle of Chancellorsville.
Vol. 32, page 372.

MORRIS: Lieutenant Edward H., 62d Regiment. General Wheaton was unreserved in his commendations of Lieutenant Morris, who at Chancellorsville commanded forty-five men deployed as skirmishers, in front of the right of his brigade. By his skill and judgment, the advance of the enemy's masses was delayed and time given to move off the brigade. Had a less discreet officer been in his position, the whole brigade would undoubtedly have been captured. As it was Lieutenant Morris was made a prisoner. Vol. 32, page 150.

MULCAHY: Sergeant John, 57th Regiment. At the risk of his own life, he succeeded in recovering the body of Lieutenant-Colonel Parisen on the field of Antietam. Vol. 24, page 562.

MURRAY: William, 57th Regiment. One of those distinguished soldiers selected for gallantry as a recipient of the Kearny Cross. Vol. 32, page 544.

MAGHIE: Sergeant William, 7th Cavalry. One of the heroes of a fight eighteen miles from Suffolk. Vol. 32, page 442.

McNAMARA: HUGH, 36th Regiment. Honorably mentioned by Surgeon Charles White for his conduct while acting as hospital attendant, after the Peninsula battles.
Vol. 22, page 562.

McNARY: LIEUTENANT-COLONEL W H., 158th Regiment. He commanded the regiment in the successful expedition to Bear Inlet, in December, 1863, and was honorably mentioned by Colonel Jourdan. Vol. 40, page 120.

MILLER: SERGEANT W J., 40th Regiment. His name ordered to be inscribed on the Roll of Honor, and to wear the Kearny Cross for gallant conduct at the battle of Chancellorsville.
Vol. 32, page 372.

MOYNE: SERGEANT W., 40th Regiment. His name ordered to be inscribed on the Roll of Honor, and to wear the Kearny Cross for gallant conduct at the battle of Chancellorsville.
Vol. 32, page 544.

MOTT: COLONEL THADDEUS P., 14th Cavalry. General Wood, in a letter, complimented him on his gallantry and good conduct during the riot in New York, which he says entitled him to the thanks of a grateful city. Vol. 34, page 574.

MOSELY: LIEUTENANT WILLIAM W., 149th Regiment. Promoted for special gallantry to Aide-de-camp. Vol. 40, page 148.

MORTON: LIEUTENANT GEORGE C., 5th Cavalry. He participated in the first charge on cavalry during the war, and especially distinguished himself. Vol. 42, page 314.

MORTON: LIEUTENANT CHARLES E., 2d Cavalry. Honorably mentioned in Colonel Kilpatrick's Report of the battle of Falmouth. Vol. 19, page 533.

MOORE: MAJOR JOHN, 79th N. Y. S. M. This gallant old soldier was twice wounded at the First and Second Battles of Bull Run. Vol. 38, page 471.

MORAN: SERGEANT PETER, 37th Regiment. His name ordered to be inscribed on the Roll of Honor, and to wear the Kearny Cross for gallant conduct at Chancellorsville. Vol. 32, page 372.

MORAN: SERGEANT MICHAEL, 38th Regiment. The first man to plant the Stars and Stripes on the Rebel fortifications at Yorktown. Vol. 26, page 17.

MOLL: SERGEANT ROBERT, 88th Regiment. His name ordered to be inscribed on the Roll of Honor, and to wear the Kearny Cross for gallant conduct at the battle of Chancellorsville.
Vol. 32, page 372.

MORGAN: SERGEANT C. F., 88th Regiment. His name ordered to be inscribed on the Roll of Honor, and to wear the Kearny Cross, for gallant conduct at the battle of Chancellorsville.
Vol. 32, page 372.

MORGANS: MAJOR MORGAN, JR., 176th Regiment. At the capture of Brashear City, he distinguished himself by his gallantry and bravery.
Vol. 35, page 187.

McIRWIN: CAPTAIN SAMUEL, 2d Cavalry. Honorably mentioned in Colonel Kilpatrick's Report of the battle of Falmouth.
Vol. 19, page 533.
Honorably mentioned in Colonel Kilpatrick's Report of the operations of his command in connection with the great cavalry expedition of General Stoneman, May, 1863.
Vol. 32, page 206.
One of the heroes of the great fight at Culpepper.
Vol. 36, page 472.

McIVER: CAPTAIN, 69th N. Y. S. M. "He was the first to go on the battle-field of Bull Run; was the last to leave the field, and when the panic took place did not move, but looked where the colors of the 69th were, and there he stood awaiting orders.
Vol. 23, page 546.

McKEAN: COLONEL JAMES B., 77th Regiment. Acquitted himself with distinction in the skirmish at Mechanicsville.
Vol. 20, page 538.

McMANUS: SERGEANT JAMES, 37th Regiment. His name ordered to be inscribed on the Roll of Honor, and to wear the Kearny Cross for gallant conduct at the battle of Chancellorsville.
Vol. 32, page 372.

McMAHON: JAMES, 5th Cavalry. In the first charge made on cavalry, which was by the 5th New York Cavalry near Woodstock, McMahon killed four Rebels with his own sabre and was made a Corporal on the spot, by order of General Hatch.
Vol. 42, page 314.

MORRISON: Captain Thomas G., 61st Regiment. Especially commended for his excellent conduct at Chancellorsville. Died of wounds received May 8, 1864.   Vol. 32, page 351.

McCOY: Colonel James W., 22d Regiment. Although wounded in the head on the morning of the battle of Antietam, he promptly reported for duty next day when he heard that a fight was impending.   Vol. 24, page 638.

McCARTY: Sergeant Dennis, 38th Regiment. Honorably mentioned in General Birney's Report of the battle of Fredericksburg.   Vol. 27, page 487.

MULLIGAN: Captain Samuel G., 2d Cavalry. Honorably mentioned in Colonel Kilpatrick's Report of the battle at Falmouth. Died at Elizabeth, N. J., of disease, May 28, 1862.
Vol. 19, page 533.

MURRAY: Captain John B., 15th Engineer Regiment. Afterwards became Colonel of the 148th. He acquitted himself with great distinction in many battles.   Vol. 39, page 88.

NOONAN: Corporal Wm., 47th Regiment. Battle of Chapin's Farm. General Butler says: "When the color-bearer was shot, he seized the colors and bore them through the fight, for which act of courage and meritorious conduct he was appointed Second Lieutenant in a regiment of colored troops."
Vol. 49, page 456.

NICHOLS: Lieutenant-Colonel George F., 118th Regiment. General Butler says: "Lieutenant-Colonel Nichols deserves honorable mention for the gallant manner with which he captured with a small number of men two redoubts on the right of Fort Harrison while the main assault was being made, and also for his cool conduct of the skirmish line in the general assault.   Vol. 49, page 456.

NICHOLS: Colonel George S., 9th Cavalry. After the battle of Cedar Creek we pursued the enemy up to the base of Fisher's Hill, where Colonel Nichols with his gallant regiment charged the Rebels again and drove them back, leaving a considerable portion of their wagon train in our hands, which we secured.
Vol. 49, page 425.

NEAFIE: Lieutenant-Colonel Alfred, 156th Regiment. At the battle of Cedar Creek, October 19, 1864, Colonel Neafie was division officer of the day, and on the picket line in front of the 19th Corps when the firing commenced. With the reserve picket he held the enemy's skirmish line in check until overwhelmed by superior numbers and flanked, when he was compelled to retire within the earthworks. Vol. 50, page 6.

NORMAN: Captain Alfred S., 6th Regiment. Honorably acquitted himself at the battle of Santa Rosa Island.
Vol. 13, page 462.

NEWBY: Major Wm., 6th Regiment. Honorably acquitted himself at the battle on Santa Rosa Island. Vol. 13, page 463.

NORTON: Quartermaster Chas. B., 50th Engineers. On the occasion of a presentation to President Lincoln, the President said to him: "I am pleased to meet a quartermaster who thought more of his soldiers than he did of himself."
Vol. 54, page 1.

O'BEIRNE: Captain James R., 37th Regiment. After four years of the hardest kind of service, during which he was wounded several times, the ball in one instance passing clear though the body at the lungs, giving him the rare distinction of a wound and recovering, similar to those of General Shields, in Mexico, he was promoted to Brigadier-General. Vol. 84, page 351.

O'DOHERTY: Patrick, 74th Regiment. Colonel Parmly and Captain Minor bear testimony that this soldier did his duty faithfully up to the time of his discharge. Vol. 43, page 296.

ONDERDONK: Sergeant, 5th Regiment. Honorably mentioned in General Kilpatrick's Report of the battle of Big Bethel.
Vol. 9, page 284.

PENET: Captain John D., 144th Regiment. At the battle of Honey Hill, November, 1864, he had his leg shattered, but continued cheering his men while his leg was temporarily bandaged.
Vol. 51, page 146.

NAGLE: Captain William J., 88th Regiment. He resigned a situation in the Custom House, for which he received $1,300 per annum, and raised a company for the 88th, which cost him $1,000. All that was left of the company after the battle of Fredericksburg was two sergeants and three men. He was in every battle of the war, and had four brothers in the field.
Vol. 27, page 384.

Honorably alluded to in General Meagher's Report of the battle of Fredericksburg. Vol. 27, page 526.

NEEDHAM: FRANCIS, One of the heroes on board the "Congress" and participated in the fight with the "Merrimac."
Vol. 18, page 232.

NEAR: ORDERLY-SERGEANT CHARLES R., 163d Regiment. Promoted on the field of Fredericksburg for bravery.
Vol. 27, page 477.

NELSON: MAJOR PETER, 66th Regiment. Honorably mentioned in Colonel Morris' Report of the battle of Chancellorsville.

NEVIN: COLONEL DAVID J., 62d Regiment. Mr. Nevin left New York with his regiment in the capacity of Captain, immediately after the First Bull Run battle. The regiment was stationed on the Potomac, above Washington. They had been there but a few days when it was discovered that neither Colonel, Lieutenant-Colonel, nor Major was with the regiment. Under this situation of affairs, the regiment demanded that Captain Nevin should take the command. He acted in that capacity for several weeks, but, finding that the labor of three field officers was more than he could stand, he sent in his resignation. This was received by General Peck, who stated that he would send it to General McClellan, with a request that the application be rejected. Some ten days afterwards, General Mansfield rode up to Captain Nevin and stated that he was directed by General McClellan to return the document, as good officers were too scarce to lose, and to request him to remain in the regiment, and that he would be promoted. He was soon after made Lieutenant-Colonel. At Fair Oaks the colonel was killed; Lieutenant-Colonel Nevin then took command, and received special commendation from General Peck for his gallantry. He was immediately commissioned as Colonel; was through the Seven Days Fight, although then quite unwell, and at Malvern Hill was so anxious to do all that was in his power, that although unable to sit up all day, yet rode up to the field in an ambulance, and there took command of his regiment and acquitted himself with great credit. After the removal of McClellan a conspiracy was discovered against this soldier by his superior officers, and Governor Seymour was called upon to see that justice was done to one of whose services the State might well be proud. Vol. 30, page 186.

NICHOL: CORPORAL, 3d Cavalry. Acquitted himself with great skill and bravery at the battle of Washington, N. C.
Vol. 24, page 324.

NOTT: COLONEL CHARLES C., 176th Regiment. In the attack on Brashear City, La., by the Rebels in June, 1863, Colonel Nott, although he had been sick for nearly three months, mounted his horse to endeavor to rally his men, but fell twice.
Vol. 32, page 187.
Colonel Nott is now one of the Judges of the Court of Claims.

NUGENT: COLONEL ROBERT, 69th Regiment. One of the heroes of Malvern Hill. Vol. 22, page 124.
General Meagher in his Report of the battle of Fredericksburg says: "Colonel Nugent acted with signal bravery, leading, as he did, the column into the field with a brilliancy of bearing worthy of the historic reputation attached in Europe to the name he bears. His demeanor and the high spirit he displayed, his words and looks, all were such as could not fail to encourage and incite his men on that day." Vol. 27, page 526.

O'CONNELL: SERGEANT JOHN, 37th Regiment. His name ordered to be incribed on the Roll of Honor, and to wear the Kearny Cross for gallant conduct at Bull Run. Vol. 32, page 372.

OSBORN: SERGEANT JOHN W., 150th Regiment. Honorably discharged in order to enable him to receive promotion.
Vol. 30, page 246.

ONDERDONK: MAJOR BENJAMIN F.. 7th Cavalry. One of the heroes of a brilliant expedition into North Carolina.
Vol. 21, page 57.

OEHL: HENRY, 62d Regiment. Displayed remarkable bravery and coolness when attacked by some two hundred Rebels near the White Oak Swamp. Vol. 21, page 52.

OSBORNE: CAPTAIN THOMAS W., 1st Artillery. Honorably acquitted himself at Williamsburg. Vol. 20, page 318.

O'NEIL: MAJOR JOSEPH, 63d Regiment. General Meagher in his Report of the battle of Fredericksburg says, "Major O'Neil was as true that day as he has ever been."
Vol. 27, page 525.

OLONE: LIEUTENANT H. F., 69th N. Y. S. M. At the First battle of Bull Run, his bravery was surpassed by none.
Vol. 25, page 235.

PEARCE: Major Charles E., 16th Artillery. His bravery and the encouragement he gave his men in battle on the Darbytown Road, October 7, 1864, deserves remembrance.
Vol. 49, page 283.

PRINCE: Major Frederick W., 16th Artillery. His bravery and the encouragement he gave his men in battle on the Darbytown Road, October 7, 1864, deserves remembrance.
Vol. 49, page 283.

PORTEOUS: Private S. R., 142d Regiment. He volunteered to advance with the head of the column and cut down the palisading at the time of the assault on Fort Fisher.
Vol. 52, page 380.

PER LEE: Colonel Samuel R., 114th Regiment. Colonel Per Lee received three wounds: one through the neck, one in the arm, and another in the side, which exposed the lung. Notwithstanding this complication of wounds he rode on horseback from Winchester to Harper's Ferry. Vol. 48, page 473.

PIERCE: Major Henry I., 96th Regiment. Participated with great gallantry in the first attack made on the works at Petersburg, June 15, 1864, by the 18th Corps. Vol. 45, page 505.

PIPER: Colonel Alexander, 10th Artillery. Participated with great gallantry in the first attack made on the works of the enemy at Petersburg, June 15, 1864, by the 18th Army Corps.
Vol. 45, page 505.

PIERCE: Lieutenant-Colonel Francis E., 108th Regiment. Conspicuous for noble bearing in the great charge by Hancock's Corps, near Spottsylvania Court House, May 12, 1864.
Vol. 44, page 374.

POWERS: Colonel Charles J., 108th Regiment. Conspicuous for noble bearing in the great charge by Hancock's Corps, near Spottsylvania Court House, May 12, 1864.
Vol. 44, page 374.

PALMER: Lieutenant-Colonel Jeremiah, 2d Artillery. He gallantly commanded his men in the brilliant action of May 19, 1864, at Spottsylvania Court House.

POTTER: Major James D., 38th Regiment. Honorably mentioned in Colonel Farnsworth's Report of the battle of Bull Run.
Vol. 11, page 169.

PAYNE: CAPTAIN LEWIS S., 100th Regiment. During the siege of Charleston (July, 1863), he succeeded in reaching the parapet of Fort Wagner and inspecting unmolested the interior. He is one of the best and most successful scouts in the army.
Vol. 35, page 93.

PATTOON: MAJOR ALEXANDER G., 7th Cavalry. One of the heroes of a fight eighteen miles from Suffolk. Vol. 32, page 442.

PARISEN: CAPTAIN OTTO W., 9th Regiment. Honorably mentioned in Colonel Kimball's Report of the battle of South Mills. Vol. 20, page 146.
Also in the Colonel's Report of the battles of South Mountain and Antietam. Vol. 25, page 7.
Presented with a gold medal. On one side is the inscription: "Highwood Guard to Captain Otto W Parisen, esteemed as our Orderly Sergeant and chivalric soldier."
Vol. 25, page 235.

PARSONS: LIEUTENANT CHARLES B., 1st Engineers. One of the heroes of the siege of Charleston. Vol. 36, page 186.

PARKS: LIEUTENANT WILLIAM A., 6th Cavalry. One of the heroes of a reconnoisance and brilliant skirmish into Virginia.
Vol. 26, page 29.

PENDERGRAST: LIEUTENANT JEFFREY, 38th Regiment. Honorably mentioned in Colonel Birney's Report of the battle of Fredericksburg. Vol. 27, page 487.

PEEL: SERGEANT WASHINGTON, 40th Regiment. His name ordered to be inscribed on the Roll of Honor, and to wear the Kearny Cross for gallant conduct at Chancellorsville. Lieutenant Peel was killed near Petersburg, September 20, 1864.
Vol. 32, page 372.

PENFIELD: CAPTAIN JAMES A., 5th Cavalry. Acquitted himself with great gallantry in an engagement with Mosby's guerillas at Warrenton Junction. Vol. 32, page 98.

PELL: LIEUTENANT JOHN H., 4th Regiment. Honorably acquitted himself at Antietam. Vol. 25, page 89.

PHELPS, JR.: COLONEL WALTER, 22d Regiment. Colonel Phelps assumed command of the 1st Brigade of the Army of the Potomac, known as the Iron Brigade, on the 14th of Sep-

tember, 1862, and led it in the brilliant charge at South Mountain, and in many of the subsequent battles fought by the Army. Every general of the corps recommended Colonel Phelps to the President for promotion. These recommendations were endorsed by General Hooker in flattering terms.
Vol. 33, page 111.

PIERSON: LIEUTENANT-COLONEL CHARLES H., 43d Regiment. Deserving of special praise for his gallantry at the battle of Williamsburg. Vol. 20, page 188.

PROST: LIEUTENANT JOSEPH, 55th Regiment. Honorably mentioned in Colonel de Trobriand's Report of the battle of Williamsburg. Vol. 20, page 303.

PURDY: LIEUTENANT JAMES H., 59th Regiment. Promoted to a Captaincy for gallant conduct at the battle of Antietam.
Vol. 26, page 85.

PURDY: CAPTAIN LOVELL, 70th Regiment. He was wounded at Williamsburg, and at Gettysburg he was wounded three times, but instead of retiring from the field, preferred remaining with the few gallant men left of his company.
Vol. 40, page 49.

PURTELL: CAPTAIN MICHAEL D., 73d Regiment. He acted as Lieutenant-Colonel at the battle of Gettysburg, and acquitted himself nobly. Killed in action May 10, 1864.
Vol. 35, page 195.

PELL: CAPTAIN ABIJAH S., 47th Regiment. Behaved gallantly at Olustee, Fla. Promoted November 26, 1864, to Major, 8th United States Colored Troops. Vol. 42, page 76.

PERKINS: JOHN R., 123d Regiment. At the battle of Chancellorsville he was shot in the thigh by a rifle ball, and was sent to the surgeon to have the wound dressed, but seeing others there worse than himself yet unattended, returned to his company and commenced firing again, when the line fell back. On account of weakness and loss of blood he was unable to get away, and was taken prisoner. Vol. 33, page 110.

PERLEY: LIEUTENANT HENRY C., 9th Regiment. Honorably mentioned in Colonel Kimball's Report of the battle of South Mills, N. C. Vol. 20, page 168.

PINTLER: CORPORAL J. H., 7th Cavalry. Colonel Dodge asked for volunteers to cross the Blackwater River, and Corporal Pintler, Sergeant Eaton and Private Van Duser volunteering, were selected for that purpose. Nobly and gallantly they spurred their horses in the dark and treacherous-looking water and plunged through and gained the opposite bank.
Vol. 26, page 16.
He was terribly wounded during a reconnoisance to Juni. A braver man never sat in the saddle. Vol. 27, page 380.

PINCKNEY: LIEUTENANT GEORGE E., 131st Regiment. The hero of a fight with guerillas on the Atchafalaya River, March, 1864. Vol. 42, page 391.

PLUM: LIEUTENANT FRANCIS M., 2d Cavalry. Honorably mentioned in Colonel Kilpatrick's Report of a successful expedition to Hanover Junction. He was a son of the late Elias Plum, of Troy. Vol. 22, page 642.

POTTER: LIEUTENANT-COLONEL ROBERT B., 51st Regiment. Honorably mentioned in the *Tribune's* account of the battle of Newbern. Promoted to Brigadier-General March 13, 1863. General Potter died recently. Vol. 18, page 372.

POWELL: LIEUTENANT FRANK, 9th Regiment. Honorably mentioned by Colonel White in his Report of the battle of Pea Ridge. Vol. 18, page 565.

PRATT: CAPTAIN WILLIAM P., 5th Cavalry Regiment. During Banks' Shenandoah campaign, Captains Pratt and Green escorted Hampton's Battery into Winchester at night.
Vol. 42, page 314.

PRATT: LIEUTENANT JOSEPH, 4th Regiment. Acquitted himself with great gallantry at Antietam. Vol. 25, page 89.

QUIRK: CAPTAIN THOMAS W., 83d Regiment. One of the heroes of the battle of Fredericksburg. He was killed at Gettysburg July 1, 1863. Vol. 20, page 547.

QUINN: JOHN, 5th Cavalry. One of the heroes of the battle of Port Royal. Vol. 20, page 547.

QUIN: CAPTAIN JOHN, 4th Regiment. Great credit is due him for the manner in which he stuck by his company at Antietam. He had for some time been suffering with rheumatism, notwithstanding which, he marched to the battle at the head of his company, and remained until relieved. Vol. 25, page 89.

QUINN: Sergeant Henry, 88th Regiment. His name ordered to be inscribed on the Roll of Honor, and to wear the Kearny Cross for gallant conduct at the battle of Chancellorsville.
Vol. 32, page 342.

QUAY: Captain John, 125th Regiment. In the affair at Morton's Ford, Va., February, 1864, a hundred men were called for as skirmishers to cross the ford, and these men were gallantly led by Captain Quay. Killed in action April 2, 1865.
Vol. 41, page 192.

QUINLAN: Major James, 88th Regiment. One of the heroes of Malvern Hill. Vol. 22, page 124.
In the absence of the lieutenant-colonel, the 88th was most intelligently and gallantly maintained by Major Quinlan all through the tempestuous march from Fair Oaks to Malvern Hill. Vol. 22, page 573.
Honorably alluded to in General Meagher's Report of the battle of Fredericksburg. Vol. 27, page 526.

QUARTERMAN: Captain George H., 74th Regiment. Badly wounded at Williamsburg where he acquitted himself most gallantly. Vol. 20, page 360.

QUACKENBOS: Captain Edward M., 36th Regiment. Honorably alluded to in General Keyes' Report of the battle of Seven Pines for the assistance rendered by him during the battle. Died of disease in New York City, August 20, 1862.
Vol. 22, page 242.

RHEIMS: Lieutenant Leon, 3d Battery. Honorably mentioned in an account of the battle of Lee's Mills. Lieutenant Rheims is now a well-known merchant in New York City.
Vol. 19, page 396.

RICHARDS: Lieutenant Edwin F., 59th Regiment. Promoted to Captain. He was a very meritorious officer and served in all the battles in which the regiment was engaged.
Vol. 40, page 316.

ROEMER: Captain Jacob, 34th Battery. The works at College Hill were erected, partially completed, and handsomely defended by that brave officer—Captain Roemer—during the siege of Knoxville. He was one of the last artillery officers in the service. Vol. 40, page 346.

RYDER: CORPORAL RICHARD C., 40th Regiment. Corporal Ryder was highly complimented for his daring and bravery while acting as Color-Bearer at Oak Grove. Vol. 22, page 19. Promoted to Second Lieutenant for splendid action on the battle-field. Vol. 28, page 336.

ROGERS: LIEUTENANT PHILIP C., 55th Regiment. Acquitted himself with honor at the battle of Seven Pines.
Vol. 21, page 255.

ROWE: LIEUTENANT FREDERICK A., 99th Regiment. One of the heroes of a brilliant exploit on the Nansemond River.
Vol. 31, page 474.

RODEN: SERGEANT MICHAEL, 47th Regiment. At the battle of Olustee, Fla., he conducted himself nobly.
Vol. 42, page 76.

ROBERTS: LIEUTENANT JOHN, 175th Regiment. Formerly of the 71st N. Y. S. M. Among the first to rush to the defence of the national capital in 1861, and with the gallant 71st acquitted himself heroically on board steamer "Freeborn," in her engagement with the Rebel batteries at Aquia Creek and again in the First Bull Run battle acquitted himself with great gallantry. Vol. 27, page 116.

ROBERTS: CORPORAL. Honorably mentioned in Colonel Kimball's Report of the battles of South Mountain and Antietam.
Vol. 25, page 7.

ROSA: COLONEL RUDOLPH, 46th Regiment. Honorably mentioned in General Stevens' Report of the battle of Secessionville.
Vol. 34, page 47.

RIDER: CAPTAIN HENRY W., 12th Regiment. His firmness, fidelity and fearlessness made him an invaluable officer.
Vol. 33, page 539.

RYAN: WILLIAM. Distinguished himself while on a boat excursion to secure supplies for General Sickles. Vol. 17, page 149.

RAYMOND: LIEUTENANT JASPER N., 2d Cavalry. One of the heroes of the spirited cavalry skirmish at Aldie, Va., June, 1863. Vol. 33, page 386.

RADCLIFFE: W R., 99th Regiment. One of the heroes on board the "Congress" who participated in the fight with the Rebel steamer "Merrimac."

RICE: LIEUTENANT-COLONEL JAMES C., 44th Regiment. General Butterfield in a letter to General Williams, dated July 2, 1862, said: "In consideration of the bravery and heroic conduct upon three battle-fields, I would most urgently recommend the commanding general to designate Lieutenant-Colonel Rice as Colonel of the regiment, made vacant by the resignation of Colonel Stryker." Vol. 22, page 431.
At Gettysburg he commanded the 3d brigade of Barnes' division, after acting Brigadier-General Vincent was wounded, and inspired his troops with the greatest enthusiasm. Promoted to Brigadier-General August 17, 1863.
Vol. 34, page 120.

REED: THOMAS, 3d Cavalry. One of the heroes of Tranter's Creek, where he was captured by the Rebels. Vol. 21, page 252.

REID: ALEXANDER, 123d Regiment. While the regiment was engaged at close quarters at Chancellorsville, he rushed forward, captured, and brought in two prisoners. Page 110.

REDDY: CORPORAL JAMES, 37th Regiment. His name ordered to be inscribed on the Roll of Honor, and to wear the Kearny Cross for gallant conduct at the battle of Chancellorsville.
Vol. 32, page 372.

RANDOLPH: SERGEANT ALFRED, 2d Cavalry. Honorably mentioned in Colonel Kilpatrick's Report of a successful expedition to Hanover Junction. Vol. 22, page 642.

ROBINSON: SERGEANT, 65th Regiment. Color-Bearer of the regiment. At the time the regiment was about to disband, Colonel Hamblin, after thanking the regiment for the gallantry it had always shown, presented Sergeant Robinson with a splendid blue cross, as a token of his admiration for the gallant manner in which he had borne the flag of his country on all the battle-fields in which the regiment had been engaged.
Vol. 48, page 203.

REVELL: LIEUTENANT WILLIAM A., 13th Cavalry Regiment. Acquitted himself bravely on the occasion of an expedition to the Rapidan, and an encounter with Early's forces, September, 1864. Vol. 48, page 435.

14

RAFFERTY: LIEUTENANT-COLONEL THOMAS, 71st Regiment. For the last fourteen months of the regiment's term of service, he was in command. He was an excellent officer and has been faithful to all trusts. Vol. 46, page 281.

RAULSTON: LIEUTENANT-COLONEL JOHN B., 81st Regiment. Participated with great gallantry in the first attack made on the Rebel works at Petersburg, June 15, 1864, by the 18th Corps. Vol. 45, page 505.
At the battle of Fair Oaks, in 1862, Captain Raulston unsupported held an important position for two hours.
Vol. 41, page 390.

REMINGTON: CAPTAIN GEO. W., 2d Cavalry. He greatly distinguished himself during General Davidson's raid through Mississippi in December, 1864. Vol. 58, page 405.

RYAN: THOMAS C. H., 13th Cavalry. Promoted to Second Lieutenant for his bravery in the fight at Culpepper.
Vol. 49, page 155.

REEVES: CAPTAIN JAMES H., 3d Regiment. One of the heroes of Fort Fisher, where he lost a leg. Vol. 52, page 291.

ROOK: CORPORAL DANIEL T., 156th Regiment. He bore the flag of the regiment in the battle of Cedar Creek, and his name deserves a place on the Roll of Honor. Vol. 51, page 191.

RANDALL: LIEUTENANT-COLONEL GEORGE M., 14th Artillery. One of the heroes of the battle of the Crater, July 31, 1864. Also one of the heroes of Forts Steadman and Haskill.
Vol. 87, page 635.

SHEA: PRIVATE JOSHUA, 92d Regiment. He was recommended by General Butler for a medal, for gallant conduct in bringing the wounded from the field, under a heavy fire at the battle of Chapin's Farm. Vol. 49, page 456.

SMITH: LIEUTENANT CLARK, 169th Regiment. Promoted to the rank of Captain for gallant and meritorious services.
Vol. 49, page 286.

SUESS: CAPTAIN JOHN L., 1st Engineer Regiment. Honorably mentioned by General Butler for his energy in prosecuting the works which enabled our forces to hold Fort Harrison.
Vol. 49, page 456.

SCHILLING: PRIVATE JOHN, 150th Regiment. Recommended to the Secretary of War for a medal, for gallant conduct at the battle of Chapin's Farm.　　　　Vol. 49, page 456.

SHEPPARD: CAPTAIN MORRIS F., 16th Artillery. His bravery and the encouragement he gave his men in the battle on the Darbytown Road October 7, 1864, deserves remembrance.
　　　　Vol. 49, page 283.

SMITH: LIEUTENANT EDWIN R., 169th Regiment. Promoted to the rank of Captain for gallant and meritorious conduct.
　　　　Vol. 49, page 286.

SCOFIELD: SERGEANT DAVID H., 5th Cavalry. At the battle of Cedar Creek, October, 1864, he captured the battle colors of Kershaw's division of Longstreet's corps. General Sheridan gave him thirty-five days furlough as a reward for his bravery.
　　　　Vol. 50, page 134.

SMITH: COLONEL JOHN F., 112th Regiment. One of the heroes of Fort Fisher.　　　　Vol. 52, page 291.

SKELLIE: CORPORAL EBENEZER, 127th Regiment. General Butler says: "He took the colors of the regiment when the color sergeant fell, and carried them through the first charge (battle of Chapin's Farm). At the second charge, after all the color guard were killed or wounded, he carried the colors to the enemy's works, where he fell wounded.　Vol. 49, page 416.

SMITH: MAJOR ELIPHAS, 56th Regiment. On all occasions under the fire of the enemy, he showed unflinching bravery and coolness.　　　　Vol. 52, page 309.

SUMNER: COLONEL E. V., 7th Cavalry. (Son of Major-General Sumner.) Too much credit cannot be given to Colonel Sumner for his display of real courage and skill in manœuvring troops in the fight on the Darbytown Road, October 7, 1864. Promoted to Brevet Brigadier-General in 1865.
　　　　Vol. 49, page 171.

SCOTT: MAJOR RUFUS, 19th Cavalry. In the battle at Newtown, Va., August 16, 1864, Major Scott commanded the regiment, which, although confronted by superior numbers, alone and unsupported, fought nobly for an hour and a half.
　　　　Vol. 47, page 329.

SCOTT:—ORDERLY SERGEANT, 85th Regiment. He was one of the bravest men in the regiment. At one time in 1864 he went outside of the fort at Plymouth and passed an open field to within thirty or forty rods of the rebel line, loading and firing as he went. There was only one Rebel that returned his fire. Scott would wave his cap at him every time he fired.

STANDRING: CAPTAIN JOHN T., 5th Artillery. On the 21st of July, 1864, Captain Standring led a gallant charge, and drove three hundred and fifty Rebel sharpshooters out of the town of Bolivar, Va. Vol. 46, page 437.

STEGMAN: MAJOR L. R., 102d Regiment. Colonel Lane being sick in the hospital at the time of the battle near Pine Hill, Ga., Major Stegman led the regiment into battle.
Vol. 46, page 142.

STRAY: JOHN, 1st Engineer. He was presented by General Gilmore with a bronze medal for valorous conduct, of which, we believe, but thirty-nine in all were ever distributed.
Vol. 44, page 243.

SHAW: CAPTAIN JOHN G., 79th N. Y. S. M. Honorably acquitted himself at the battle of Bull Run. Vol. 10, page 609.

SPERLING: LIEUTENANT J., 71st N. Y. S. M. Honorably acquitted himself at the battle of Bull Run. Vol. 14, page 272.

SINCLAIR: LIEUTENANT JAMES B., 79th Regiment. Honorably mentioned in an account of the battle of Bull Run.
Vol. 13, page 289.

SCOTT: PRIVATE W., 6th Regiment. Honorably mentioned in Colonel Wilson's Report of the battle on Santa Rosa Island.
Vol. 14, page 6.

SAXTON: SERGEANT-MAJOR CHARLES T. Honorably mentioned in connection with the battles of Port Hudson and the Red River and Shenandoah Valley campaigns.
Vol. 54, page 406.

SAVERY: CAPTAIN JOHN E., 75th Regiment. He was wounded at Port Hudson, while bravely leading his men.
Vol. 54, page 206.

SMITH: PRIVATE Co. G., 13th Cavalry. Promoted for bravery in a little fight which resulted in the wounding of the guerilla Mosby. Vol. 48, page 482.

STEVENS: CAPTAIN SAMUEL, 1st Cavalry. He received General Ewell's sword at the battle of Sailor's Creek.
Vol. 84, page 562.

SMITH: CAPTAIN JOSEPH H., 97th Regiment. In the battle for the possession of the Petersburg and Weldon Railroad, Captain Smith came face to face with a Rebel captain, who insisted on his surrender, and on his refusal, attempted to run him through with a bayonet. Parrying the bayonet thrust with his sabre he got out of the captain's way and escaped.
Vol. 47, page 416.

SARTELLE: SERGEANT HENRY, 132d Regiment. In the battle of Chancellorsville he was shot through the arm (after firing over forty rounds). After the wound was dressed by the surgeon he returned to his company and continued firing with his revolver, the fight being then at close quarters, and did not leave until ordered to do so.
Vol. 33, page 110.

SAWYER: CAPTAIN THOMAS J., 47th Regiment. At the battle of Olustee, Fla., 1864, he behaved with extraordinary bravery. At one time running the colors a hundred yards in advance of the line, calling on the boys to "Rally round the flag." The gay captain in the thickest of the bullet storm very energetically expressed his opinion that he could "lick" any Rebel in the fight.
Vol. 42, page 76.

SAVAGE: LIEUTENANT-COLONEL HENRY F., 25th Regiment. Though his arm was broken early in the engagement at Hanover Court House, he determined not to forsake his regiment, and with heroism worthy of record he rode back and front of his men, stimulating them to deeds of valor, until finally he fainted from loss of blood and fell from his horse.
Vol. 20, page 568.

SALISBURY: SERGEANT WILLIAM H., 99th Regiment. Honorably acquitted himself in a brisk skirmish near Suffolk, Va.
Vol. 32, page 70.

SAVACOAL: SERGEANT, EDWIN F., 1st Cavalry. One of the bravest men in the army. He alone captured seventy prisoners and afterwards killed the notorious guerilla Captain Blackford. Captain Savacoal died June 3, 1865, of wounds received in action at Sailor's Run, Va.
Vol. 41, page 247.

SANGER: LIEUTENANT WM. H., 2d Cavalry. One of the heroes of a brilliant expedition into North Carolina. Vol. 21, page 57.

SAMMON: COLONEL SIMON, 115th Regiment. Wounded at the battle of Olustee, Fla., in February, 1864, while gallantly leading his regiment. Vol. 42, page 10.

SCOTT: LIEUTENANT JAMES, 47th Regiment. He behaved gallantly at Olustee, Fla. Captain Scott was killed at Fort Fisher, February 11, 1865. Vol. 42, page 76.

SCHAEFFER: SERGEANT JACOB, 88th Regiment. His name ordered to be inscribed on the Roll of Honor, and to wear the Kearny Cross for gallant conduct at Chancellorsville.
Vol. 32, page 372.

SCHMIDT: CAPTAIN ADOLPH, 14th Cavalry. The hero of a brilliant fight with the Rebels near Pensacola, Fla., in April, 1864.
Vol. 43, page 220.

SCHULTZ: SERGEANT JULIUS C., 37th Regiment. His name ordered to be inscribed on the Roll of Honor, and to wear the Kearny Cross for gallant conduct at the battle of Chancellorsville. Vol. 32, page 372.

SCHEFFELIN: MAJOR WM. H., 7th Cavalry. Acquitted himself nobly in an engagement with the Rebels near Suffolk, Va.
Vol. 26, Page 16.

SCHOONMAKER: SERGEANT-MAJOR LEONARD S., 51st Regiment. Commissioned Lieutenant by Governor Seymour for meritorious conduct and bravery on the field. Vol. 31, page 395.

SHELDON: LIEUTENANT OSCAR, 3d Cavalry. Honorably mentioned for his gallantry at Kinston, N. C. Vol. 27, page 435.

SHORT: LIEUTENANT JOHN P., 73d Regiment. Promoted to Captain for gallant conduct. Vol. 30, page 17.

SHINE: LIEUTENANT EUGENE C., 73d Regiment. Promoted to Captain for gallant conduct. Vol. 30, page 17.

SHAURMAN: LIEUTENANT-COLONEL NELSON, 90th Regiment. He commanded the regiment in the assault upon Port Hudson. He was a thorough soldier and would not send his regiment where he would not go himself. Vol. 34, page 295.

SHAFER: Lieutenant William B., 2d Cavalry. Behaved splendidly during the series of Cavalry fights in October, 1863, at Bristoe Station. Vol. 37, page 484.

SEELY: Lieutenant Israel R., 47th Regiment. Promoted to a Captaincy. He earned his promotion through all the grades of rank. Vol. 25, page 295.

SEARING: Sergeant, 9th Regiment. Honorably mentioned in Colonel Kimball's Report of the battles of South Mountain and Antietam. Vol. 25, page 7.

SETON, Jr., Captain Wm., 4th Regiment. Acquitted himself with great gallantry at the battle of Antietam. Vol. 25, page 89.

SHILLINGLAW: Captain Robert T., 79th Regiment. Honorably acquitted himself at Bull Run. Vol. 16, page 50.

SHOEMAKER: Private, 1st Artillery. Honorably acquitted himself at the battle of Williamsburg. Vol. 20, page 318.

SHANLEY: Captain Timothy S., 69th Regiment. Presented with an elegant sword by his companions in arms as a testimonial of their regard for him as a soldier and a man.
Vol. 23, page 180.

SEAMAN, Jr: Treadwell, 83d Regiment. Honorably discharged the service to enable him to receive promotion.
Vol. 30, page 246.

SERRELL: Colonel Edward W., 1st Engineers. Honorably mentioned in General Benham's Report of the capture of Fort Pulaski. Vol. 19, page 357.
Honorably mentioned in General Wright's Report of the battle of Secessionville. Vol. 22, page 336.
Honorably mentioned in General Brannon's Report of the battle of Frampton. Vol. 26, page 179.

SEARS: Captain Alfred F., 1st Engineer Regiment. Honorably mentioned in General Viele's Report of the capture of Fort Pulaski. Vol. 19, page 430.
Honorably mentioned in General Stevens' Report of the battle of Secessionville. Vol. 22, page 321.

SEYMOUR: Captain Allen M., 2d Cavalry. Honorably mentioned in Colonel Kilpatrick's Report of a successful Cavalry expedition to Hanover Junction. Vol. 22, page 642.

SHERRILL: COLONEL ELIAKIM, 126th Regiment. In the battles resulting in the capture of Harper's Ferry, Colonel Sherrill was conspicuous for his skill and bravery. Dismounting from his horse, and with revolver in each hand, he rallied his wavering troops, calling upon his boys to stand by him, until he was shot in the mouth by a musket ball and carried to the rear. Colonel Sherrill was killed at the battle of Gettysburg, July 3, 1863. Vol. 24, page 410.

SHALER: COLONEL ALEXANDER, 65th Regiment. Honorably mentioned in General Newton's Report of the battle of Fredericksburg. Vol. 28, page —.
In the attack on Marye's Hill, at a critical juncture, he rallied his column with magnificent gallantry, and brought it up to the work once more, and took it on up the hill. Promoted to Brigadier-General, May 26, 1863.
Vol. 32, page 69.

SMITH: LIEUTENANT PETER J., 37th Regiment. Honorably mentioned in General Kearny's Report of the battle of Seven Pines.
Vol. 21, page 426.

SMITH: CAPTAIN JOHN, 4th Regiment. Acquitted himself with great gallantry at Antietam. Vol. 25, page 89.

SMITH: CAPTAIN JOHN, 88th Regiment. Honorably mentioned in General Meagher's Report of the battle of Fredericksburg.
ol. 27, page 526.

SMITH: SERGEANT FRIEND A., 38th Regiment. Honorably mentioned in General Meagher's Report of the battle of Fredericksburg. Vol. 27, page 487.

SMITH: CAPTAIN THOMAS, 73d Regiment. Acting Major at the battle of Gettysburg, and behaved splendidly.
Vol. 35, page 195.

SMITH: LIEUTENANT BERNARD N., 169th Regiment. Appointed Brigade Quartermaster on the staff of General Foster. He went out as a private in the beginning of the war, in the 44th New York Regiment, and was severely wounded in the face and neck, immediately subsequent to which he was promoted to a Lieutenancy for his bravery, and later became Captain.
Vol. 37, page 395.

SMITH: LIEUTENANT JOHN A., 47th Regiment. Behaved gallantly at the battle of Olustee, Fla. Killed in action, May 7, 1864.
Vol. 42, page 76.

SMITH: CAPTAIN SOLOMON P., 115th Regiment. Honorably mentioned in General Hatch's General Orders, No. 19, for the brave and skilful manner in which he commanded a party of twenty-five men in a hazardous and daring expedition from Pilatka, Fla., in March, 1864. Vol. 43, page 262.

SOEST: COLONEL CLEMENS, 29th Regiment. Honorably mentioned in Colonel Schurz's Report of the battles of Groveton and Second Bull Run. Vol. 25, page 58.

SPILLAN: SERGEANT T., 37th Regiment. His name ordered to be inscribed on the Roll of Honor, and to wear the Kearny Cross for gallant conduct at the battle of Chancellorsville.
Vol. 32, page 372.

SQUIER: LIEUTENANT CHARLES W., 74th Regiment. He displayed conspicuous gallantry at the battle of Williamsburg.
Vol. 21, page 48.

STILES: SERGEANT, 9th Regiment. Honorably mentioned in Colonel Kimball's Report of the battles of South Mountain and Antietam. Vol. 25, page 7.

STUART: COLONEL CHARLES B., 50th Engineer Regiment. Honorably mentioned for his valuable services in connection with General Woodbury's Engineer Brigade during the great battles on the Peninsula. Vol. 22, page 268.

STUART: CAPTAIN LEWIS J., 62d Regiment. General Wheaton was unreserved in his commendations of Captain Stuart, at Chancellorsville, whose skill and judgment aided very materially in saving his brigade from capture.
Vol. 32, page 150.

STUART: LIEUTENANT ROBERT, 2d Cavalry. One of the heroes of a spirited skirmish at Aldie, Va., June, 1863. Died September 22, 1863. Vol. 33, page 386.

STUART: CAPTAIN JOHN, 51st Regiment. He won the commendation of his superiors in a long series of fights.
Vol. 29, page 547.

STEVENS: CAPTAIN HAZARD, 79th Regiment. He was conspicuous throughout the battle of Secessionville.
Vol. 21, page 528.

Wounded at the battle of Chantilly while gallantly leading on his men. Vol. 24, page 195.

STEPHENS: CORPORAL, 9th Regiment. Honorably mentioned in Colonel Kimball's Report of the battles of South Mountain and Antietam. Vol. 25, page 7.

SIMPSON: CORPORAL, 21st Regiment. The plucky corporal was too smart for the boasting guerilla Mosby. He was the personification of bravery. Vol. 43, page 12.

SIMMS: CAPTAIN SAMUEL H., 51st Regiment. Honorably mentioned in Colonel Ferrero's Report of the engagement at Roanoke Island. Killed in action at Petersburg, Va., July 30, 1864.
Vol. 17, page 283.

SIEBERT: LIEUTENANT LOUIS, 7th Cavalry. One of the heroes of a brilliant expedition into North Carolina. Promoted to Captain and Acting Assistant Adjutant-General, May 22, 1863.
Vol. 21, page 57.

SMITH, JR.: MAJOR ABEL, 3d Regiment. Honorably mentioned in Colonel Hyne's Report of the opening of the Nansemond River.
Vol. 21, page 400.
Honorably mentioned in General Kearny's Report of the capture of Ponchatoula, La. He was also Lieutenant-Colonel of the 165th, and died June 23, 1863, of wounds received before Port Hudson. Vol. 21, page 906.

STADPOLE: PATRICK, 87th Regiment. His name ordered to be inscribed on the Roll of Honor, and to wear the Kearny Cross for gallant conduct at the battle of Chancellorsville.
Vol. 32, page 372.

SUITER: COLONEL JAMES A., 34th Regiment. Honorably acquitted himself at the battle of Seven Pines. Vol. 22, page 283.

SUTCLIFFE: CORPORAL, 99th Regiment. Honorably acquitted himself in a brisk skirmish with the enemy near Suffolk.
Vol. 32, page 70.

TAYLOR: COLONEL NELSON, 72d Regiment. He led the Excelsior Brigade in the Virginia battles under Pope, and was rewarded for his gallantry by promotion to the rank of Brigadier-General.

TALCOTT: LIEUTENANT EDWARD N. K., 1st Engineer Regiment. One of the heroes of the siege of Charleston.
Vol. 36, page 186.

TERREY: CAPTAIN FRANCIS A., 170th Regiment. Presented with a sword by the officers and men of his regiment, as a testimonial of their appreciation of him as a man and a soldier.
Vol. 38, page 147.

THOMAS: LIEUTENANT ISAAC, 80th Regiment. He shot a color-bearer at the battle of Antietam and brought off his colors.
Vol. 25, page 341.

THOMAS: LIEUTENANT GEORGE W., 3d Artillery Regiment. One of the officers under Burnside to whom is due the capture of Fort Macon. Vol. 20, page 64.

THOMPSON: CAPTAIN AMBROSE, 137th Regiment. Chief Quartermaster of General Shields' division. He was thanked in general orders by the commanding general at the head of the army, for his efficiency in the various positions in which he was placed. Vol. 19, page 230.

THOMPSON: LIEUTENANT LAWRENCE H., 73d Regiment. Promoted to Lieutenant for gallant conduct on the field.
Vol. 30, page 17.

THOUROT: LIEUTENANT-COLONEL LOUIS, 55th Regiment. Honorably mentioned in Colonel de Trobriand's Report of the battle of Williamsburg. Vol. 20, page 303.

THORPE: CAPTAIN GOULD H., 165th Regiment. Honorably mentioned in Colonel Clark's Report of the capture of Ponchatoula. Vol. 31, page 406.

TILLOTSON: CAPTAIN CHARLES W., 99th Regiment (Union Coast Guard). Honorably acquitted himself at the battle of Roanoke Island. Vol. 7, page 263.
Honorably mentioned in General Foster's Report of the battle of Newbern. Vol. 19, page 40.

TIBBITTS: COLONEL WILLIAM B., 2d Regiment. Colonel Tibbitts entered at the beginning of the war as a Captain of a company of his own raising, and for gallantry on the battle-field was promoted to the Colonelcy of the 21st Cavalry.
Vol. 25, page 97.
This cool, fearless, educated and experienced officer displayed the highest possible gallantry at Big Bethel, Bristoe Station and Chancellorsville. Vol. 35, page 66.

TIGHE: LIEUTENANT RICHARD F., 163d Regiment. Promoted on the battle-field of Fredericksburg. Vol. 27, page 477.

TRAVER: CORPORAL GEORGE. 88th Regiment. His name ordered to be inscribed on the Roll of Honor, and to wear the Kearny Cross for gallant conduct at the battle of Chancellorsville.
Vol. 32, page 372.

TREADWELL: CAPTAIN WILLIAM A., 14th Artillery Regiment. Presented with a sword by the members of his company, as a mark of their appreciation of his services as a soldier and their esteem for him as a man. Vol. 40, page 189.

TYLER: LIEUTENANT-COLONEL ROCKWELL. 56th Regiment. "During all the engagements with the enemy he commanded the regiment, and all praise is unnecessary, for every one knows he is as good a soldier as there is in the army."
Vol. 53, page 309.

TRAVIS: LIEUTENANT-COLONEL EDMUND R., 6th Artillery. He gallantly commanded his men in the brilliant action of May 19, 1864, at Spottsylvania Court House. Vol. 44, page 356.

THOMAS: CORPORAL JOSEPH, 158th Regiment. At the battle of Chapin's Farm, September 30, 1864, Corporal Thomas captured a Rebel flag. He took it at great risk and without help from any one. General Butler offered him a commission by way of reward. The corporal said he was too young for such an honor and responsibility. Vol. 49, page 100.

UPTON: COLONEL EMORY. 121st Regiment. He commanded a brigade at Rappahannock Station, November, 1863, and was one of the principal heroes of that brilliant affair. Promoted to Brigadier-General July 4, 1864.

VAN PETTEN: LIEUTENANT COLONEL JOHN B., 160th Regiment. At the battle of Winchester, Lieutenant-Colonel Petten had a bullet through his thigh, but refused to give up the command of his regiment until the fighting was over. As he led off at the head of it General Emery said to him: "Colonel, you are going into a hot fire, you had better dismount." "Can't walk, sir," replied the Colonel, pointing to his bandaged thigh. Vol. 86, page 597.

VAN RENSSELAER: LIEUTENANT W V., 50th Engineer Regiment. His services during the war were of the greatest value.
Vol. 286, page 233.

VON KLEISER: Captain Alfred, 30th Battery. Acquitted himself with great gallantry and distinction at the battle of Piedmont, Va., June, 1864. Vol. 45, page 337.

VAN BROCKLIN: Brevet Major Martin, 50th Engineer Regiment. General Warren in his congratulatory orders in reference to the raid on the Weldon Railroad, in December, 1864, alludes in honorable terms to Major Van Brocklin's efficiency and promptness in the management of the pontoon train.
Vol. 51, page 284.

VEDDER: Brevet Major Commodore Perry, 154th Regiment. He has an honorable record for gallantry at Lookout Mountain, Chancellorsville and the siege of Savannah.
Vol. 54, page 206.

VON SCHACK: Colonel George, 7th Regiment. He was honorably mentioned by Generals Hancock, Humphreys, Caldwell, and others, for gallantry and soldierly qualities.
Vol. 53, page 400.

VAN WINKLE: Corporal, 148th Regiment. General Butler says Corporal Van Winkle was recommended to receive a medal for distinguished gallantry at the battle of Chapin's Farm, in taking a position in advance of the skirmish line within short distance of the enemy's gunners, and driving the cannoneers from their guns. Vol. 9, page 456.

VAN DUSER: Corporal, 9th Regiment. Honorably mentioned in Colonel Kimball's Report of the battles of South Mountain and Antietam. Vol. 25, page 7.

VANDERGRUFF: N. G., 99th Regiment. One of the heroes of a brilliant affair on the Nansemond River, by which the transports "Commerce" and "Swan" were piloted past the Rebel batteries and arrived safely at Fortress Monroe.
Vol. 32, page 1.

VOSS: Corporal, 40th Regiment. His name ordered to be inscribed on the Roll of Honor, and to wear the Kearny Cross for gallant conduct at the battle of Chancellorsville.
Vol. 32, page 372.

VAN ARNSBURG: Colonel George, 45th Regiment. Honorably mentioned for his bravery in many battles, and at Gettysburg he commanded the 1st Brigade, 3d Division, 11th Corps.
Vol. 35, page 14.

VAN VOORHEES: Lieutenant-Colonel Koert S., 137th Regiment. One of the heroes of the battle of Wauhatchie, October, 1863. Vol. 38, page 92.

VENUTI: Captain Edward, 52d Regiment. One of the first cases under the recent laws conferring full citizenship for one year's faithful services in the army. Killed in action near Gettysburg, July 2, 1863. Vol. 25, page 608.

VERNON: George R. Promoted to Second Lieutenant in the 14th United States Infantry, for gallant and meritorious services.
Vol. 31, page 51.

VERMILYEA: Lieutenant Isaac D., 1st Cavalry Regiment. He is entitled to the greatest praise for the manner in which he led his men in a brilliant affair with a party of Rebels at Perry's Ferry in May, 1863. Killed in action at Piedmont, Va., June 5, 1864. Vol. 32, page 543.

VINTON: Colonel Francis L., 43d Regiment. Deserving of especial praise for his gallantry at the battle of Williamsburg. Promoted March 13, 1863, to Brigadier-General.
Vol. 20, page 188.

VOSBURGH: Lieutenant Philo, 36th Regiment. Especially distinguished for meritorious conduct during the storming of Fredericksburg heights. Vol. 32, page 308.

WOOD, Jr.: Colonel James, 136th Regiment. He commanded a brigade at the battle of Peach Tree Creek, Ga., July 20, 1864, and did all that was required of him, as might be expected from so excellent a commander. Vol. 46, page 511.

WELLS: Private James, 6th Cavalry, battle of Gettysburg, 3d day. "At this tumultuous moment, we witnessed a deed of heroism such as we are apt to attribute only to the Knights of the olden times. General Hancock mounted, and accompanied by his staff, with the corps flag flying in the hands of the brave Irishman, Private Wells, started at the right of his line, and slowly rode along the terrible crest to the extreme left of his position, while shot and shell roared and crashed around him, and every moment tore great gaps in the ranks at his side." Vol. 84, page 232.

WINSLOW: Colonel Cleveland, 5th Regiment. At the battle of Coal Harbor, June 2, 1864, Colonel Winslow was wounded in

the first assault, but after the wound was dressed, resumed his place at the head of his regiment. He was that sort of man who stuck to his regiment and to fighting, as long as he could hold a sword and ride a horse.
Vol. 45, page 113.

WRIGHT: CAPTAIN JOHN G., 51st Regiment. Honorably mentioned in Colonel Ferrero's Report of the engagement at Roanoke Island. Vol. 17, page 283.

WOODS: LIEUTENANT, 8th New York State Militia. Honorably mentioned in General Butler's Report of the battle of Big Bethel. Vol. 9, page 285.

WEISS: LIEUTENANT-COLONEL FRANCIS, 20th Regiment. Honorably acquitted himself at the capture of Forts Hatteras and Clark, N. C. Vol. 12, page 119.

WILKINSON: CAPTAIN ARTHUR, 74th Regiment. Honorably mentioned in General Graham's Report of a reconnoissance to Mathias Point. Vol. 14, page 256.

WALSH: CORPORAL JOHN, 5th Cavalry. At the battle of Cedar Creek, 1864, he recaptured the colors of the 15th New Jersey Infantry, that had been captured from the regiment early in the day. General Sheridan gave him thirty-five days furlough as a reward for his gallantry. Vol. 50, page 134.

WOODMAN: CAPTAIN CHARLES H., 65th Regiment. Conspicuous for his gallantry at the battle of Cedar Creek, October, 1864.
Vol. 50, page 134.

WARD: COLONEL (now General) J. H. HOBART, 38th Regiment. Honorably mentioned in the *Tribune's* Report of the battle of Williamsburg. Vol. 20, page 261.
General Birney, in his Report, says: "To Colonel Ward fell the good fortune to lead the most important charges of the day." Vol. 20, page 331.
Honorably mentioned in General Heintzleman's Report of the battle of Fair Oaks, where he acted as Brigadier-General.
Vol. 29, page 124.

WALSH: LIEUTENANT JAMES J., 36th Regiment. In the attack upon Marye's Heights, the column faltered, but was rallied handsomely by Lieutenant-Colonel Walsh.
Vol. 32, page 69.

Honorably mentioned in General Keyes' Report of the battle of Fair Oaks (Seven Pines) for the assistance rendered him during the battle. Vol. 22, page 242.

WARDNER: CHAPLAIN NATHAN, 96th Regiment. He was especially commended by General Butler for charging with his regiment, in the advancing column, ready to administer the last consolations to the dying. Vol. 49, page 456.

WELLES: PRIVATE HENRY, 148th Regiment. General Butler says: "He was recommended to receive a medal for distinguished gallantry at the battle of Chapin's Farm, in taking a position in advance of the skirmish line, within short distance of the enemy's gunners, and driving the cannoneers from their guns." Vol. 49, page 456.

WHITMAN: CAPTAIN GEORGE W., 51st Regiment. Honorably mentioned in the Official Report of the Mine Explosion and also for his long previous career of skill and courage as a soldier. Vol. 49, page 529.

WESTON: CAPTAIN H. JAMES, 127th Regiment. Honorably mentioned in General Foster's General Orders relative to the affair at Forts Johnson and Simpkins, S. C., in July, 1864. Vol. 50, page 382.

WALLING: LIEUTENANT WILLIAM H., 142d Regiment. At the time of the assault upon Fort Fisher, N. C., December 25, 1864, Lieutenant Walling captured a Rebel flag from the outer bastion of the enemy. Vol. 51, page 482.

WILBER: LIEUTENANT JOHN J., 65th Regiment. At the battle of the Opequan, September 19, 1864, he was always in front of the lines, encouraging the boys by his bravery and example. Vol. 49, page 135.

WHITCOMB: SERGEANT WM. H., 5th Cavalry. Sergeant Whitcomb greatly distinguished himself by his bravery at the battle of Shepherdtown, Va., August 25, 1864. When the fire was the hottest and the lines wavering, as if in uncertainty, he rode his horse boldly to the front of our line, and then by word and example cheered and encouraged his faltering comrades. Sergeant Whitcomb also distinguished himself at Buckland Mills under Kilpatrick, and at Todd's Tavern in the Wilderness, where he was wounded. Vol. 47, page 504.

WIEDRICH: COLONEL MICHAEL, 15th Artillery. The regiment under his command was universally accorded the honor by their comrades of having saved the day on the 18th of August. 1864, in the action on the Weldon Railroad, by a courageous charge just at the right time.
Vol. 47, page 511.

WARREN: COLONEL GOUVERNEUR K., 5th Regiment. Promoted to Brigadier-General on recommendation of General McClellan, for distinguished conduct at Gaines Mills.
Vol. 24, page 643.

WALRATH: MAJOR EZRA L., 115th Regiment. With imperturbable cheerfulness, and the cool courage which distinguished him, he moved along the line of his men at the battle of Olustee, Fla., cheering and encouraging his soldiers. His shoulder strap was cut away by a bullet, but he soon replaced it with the device proper to a Lieutenant-Colonel.
Vol. 42, page 10.

WANNAMAKER: SERGEANT GEORGE W., 5th Regiment. Promoted to Lieutenant for gallantry in the field.
Vol. 25, page 97.

WEBSTER: LIEUTENANT ALMER P., 9th Regiment. Honorably mentioned in Colonel Kimball's Report of the battle of South Mills, N. C. Vol. 20, page 259.
Honorably mentioned in Colonel Kimball's Report of the battles of South Mountain and Antietam.
Vol. 25, page 7.

WEST: CAPTAIN ROWLAND R., 12th Cavalry. The hero of a brilliant engagement at Greenville, N. C., November 25, 1863.
Vol. 39, page 108.

WEBBER: CHARLES F., 84th Regiment. Formerly an employee of the New York Herald, acquitted himself gallantly at the battle of Chancellorsville. ol. 34, page 118.

WHEELOCK: COLONEL CHARLES, 97th Regiment. General Doubleday in "The Campaigns of the Civil War," says: "Colonel Wheelock on the first day of the battle of Gettysburg was cut off during the retreat of Robinson's division and took refuge in a house. A Rebel Lieutenant entered and called upon him to surrender his sword. This he declined to do, whereupon the Lieutenant called in several of his men, formed them in line, took out his watch, and said to the Colonel: "You are an old, g ay-headed man, and I dislike to kill you, but if you don't give up that sword in five minutes, I shall order those men to blow your brains out." When the time was up the Colonel still refused to surrender. A sudden tumult at the door called the Lieutenant off for a moment; when he returned the Colonel had given the sword to a girl in the house who had asked him for it, and she secreted it between two mattresses. He was then marched to the rear, but being carelessly guarded, escaped the same night and returned to his regiment. In the battle of August 19, 1864, for the possession of the Weldon Railroad, Colonel Wheelock commanded a brigade with great skill and bravery, and in fact saved the day for a portion of the line. The Colonel died January 21, 1865, of disease. Vol. 47, page 416.

WHEELER: CAPTAIN WILLIAM, 4th Regiment. Acquitted himself gallantly at the battle of Antietam. Vol. 25, page 89.

WHEELER: CAPTAIN WILLIAM, 13th Independent Battery. A splendid sword presented to him by the battery as a token of their high appreciation of him as a man and a soldier. Killed in action near Marietta, Ga., June 22, 1864.
Vol. 42, page 169.

WHITE: MAJOR AMOS H., 5th Cavalry Regiment. Particularly distinguished himself at the battle of Hanover, Pa.
Vol. 34, page 210.
He acquitted himself nobly in the severe fights along the Rappahannock in October, 1863. Vol. 37, page 250.

WILLIAMS: CAPTAIN GEORGE C., 55th Regiment. At the battle of Seven Pines, when the regiment broke, the gallant Captain found himself without a company to be any longer captain of. He inquired for the 62d Regiment—chased it as it was advancing in line of battle, and begged the privilege of fighting through the action with it, and he did so most gallantly.
Vol. 21, page 283.

WILBUR: CAPTAIN R. H., 102d Regiment. Recommended for promotion for gallantry during the storming of Lookout Mountain. Vol. 30, page 77.

WOODWARD: JAMES, 84th Regiment. Formerly an employee of the New York *Herald*, wounded, and acquitted himself with gallantry at Gettysburg. Vol. 34, page 117.

WHITING: Captain James R., 9th Regiment. Honorably mentioned in Colonel Kimball's Report of the battles of South Mountain and Antietam. Vol. 25, page 7.

WADLEIGH: Sergeant. A. G., 40th Regiment. His name ordered to be inscribed on the Roll of Honor, and to wear the Kearny Cross for gallant conduct at Chancellorsville.
Vol. 32, page 372.

WALSH: Corporal Joseph, 88th Regiment. His name ordered to be inscribed on the Roll of Honor, and to wear the Kearny Cross for gallant conduct at Chancellorsville.
Vol. 32, page 372.

WALTON: Lieutenant Thomas, 40th Regiment. His name ordered to be inscribed on the Roll of Honor, and to wear the Kearny Cross for gallant conduct at the battle of Chancellorsville.

WALKER: Lieutenant James, 4th Regiment. Acquitted himself with great gallantry at the battle of Antietam.
Vol. 25, page 89.

WAINWRIGHT: Colonel William P., 76th Regiment. Honorably mentioned in General Doubleday's Report of the battle of South Mountain. Vol. 25, page 159.

WALL: Captain John, 3d Artillery. He was in command of the Fort at Washington, N. C., at the time the place was besieged by the Rebels, and behaved with distinguished gallantry throughout the entire attack. Vol. 31, page 384.

WALTERS: Captain Charles C., 2d Cavalry. A braver man and more eager soldier never met an enemy. Killed at Rapidan Station, Va., August 18, 1862. Vol. 22, page 642.

WILSON: Sergeant Philip L., 5th Regiment. Promoted for gallantry on the battle-field to Lieutenant.
Vol. 25, page 97.

WILSON: Lieutenant Harper, 36th Regiment. Especially distinguished for meritorious conduct during the storming of Fredericksburg. Vol. 32, page 318.

WILSON: Sergeant Alphonso, 145th Regiment. Honorably mentioned in General Wister's Report of the conflagration and explosion at Yorktown, in December, 1863.
Vol. 39, page 389.

WILLIS: CAPTAIN MARTIN, 74th Regiment. One of the heroes of the battle of Williamsburg, where he was taken prisoner.
Vol. 23, page 534.

WILCKEN: LIEUTENANT CHARLES L., 1st Engineers. One of the heroes of the siege of Charleston. Died October 10, 1864, at Newbern, N. C., of disease. Vol. 36, page 186.

YORK: LIEUTENANT JOSEPH S., 5th Regiment. Honorably mentioned in General Kilpatrick's Report of the battle of Big Bethel. Vol. 9, page 284.

YORK: CAPTAIN ROBERT P., 114th Regiment. He performed distinguished services in the battles of the Opequan and Cedar Creek. At the battle of the Opequan, while bearing the national ensign as a rallying point for our troops, he was struck in the throat with a spent ball, which for a short time rendered him almost speechless. He was promoted to Lieutenant-Colonel of the 75th Regiment. Vol. 52, page 345.

APPENDIX II.
NEW YORK REGIMENTS
STATE MILITIA, CAVALRY, ARTILLERY, ENGINEER, AND VOLUNTEER INFANTRY.

STATE MILITIA.

SECOND REGIMENT.—The regiment was known in the army as the Eighty-second Volunteer Infantry.
—See Record of the Eighty-second.

FIFTH REGIMENT.—The Fifth was composed almost exclusively of Germans, and was one of the first to leave for the seat of war, under command of Col. Lewis Berger. The regiment received great praise for the cutting out of the Smith's Point lightship. At the First Battle of Bull Run it formed part of General Patterson's command. On their way home from the war they were attacked in Baltimore by the mob, and some of the members were injured. In June, 1863, the regiment again volunteered their services to the government, and under their old commander, Colonel Berger, advanced to the front, and as in 1861 rendered good service at Fenwick, Pa. After faithful performance of all that was required of them they returned home, and were on duty in New York at the time of the draft riots.

SIXTH REGIMENT.—"Governor's Guard." The Sixth, like the Fifth, was composed largely of Germans. The officers were, Col. James C. Pinckney, subsequently Colonel of the Sixty-sixth Volunteer Infantry; Lieut.-Col. Samuel K. Zook, who, later in the war commanded the Fifty-seventh Infantry, from which position he was promoted to Brigadier-General, and was killed at the battle of Gettysburg; Maj. Milton G. Rathbun, Adjt. Joel W Mason, Chaplain Charles H. Phillips. In 1862 the regiment again went to the front under command of Col. Joel W. Mason. During this, their second term of service, the Sixth performed all the duties required of them with a willingness and fidelity to entitle them to the respect and thanks of all their friends at home. Again, in June, 1863, when General Lee invaded the North, the regiment joined the forces arrayed to repel his further advance. The regiment was assigned the duty of guarding the Monocacy Bridge. They were encamped on the very ground occupied by Lee and Jackson at the time of the battle of Antietam. The position was placed under the command of Colonel Mason. The Sixth afterwards moved to the Relay House, and did good service in guarding the road to Washington.

SEVENTH REGIMENT.—The regiment dates its origin from August 6, 1824, when the Marquis de Lafayette, the commander of the National Guard of Paris, was received by the First Division, New York State Militia. On that day Captains Hawley, Telfair, Curtis and Simons, who commanded four companies in the Eleventh Regiment, resolved to organize a new regiment, which resulted in the formation of the Seventh. Previous to the year 1847, the regiment was known as the Twenty-seventh Regiment. As early as the 14th of January, 1861, in anticipation of coming troubles, Maj. (General) Alexander Shaler, offered a resolution before the board of officers, which was unanimously adopted, that the Seventh were ready to perform any duty that they might be called on by the Governor to perform. The prompt response of the regiment, and its services during the war have already been narrated in Chapter IV

EIGHTH REGIMENT.—" Washington Greys." The regiment claims to be the oldest organized regiment in the service—it being a little over one hundred years since it was organized. The Boston Ancient and Honorable Artillery is supposed to be the oldest organization, but it is contended that the latter is an independent organization, similar to New York's Old Guard; is very limited in its membership, and does not constitute a full regiment. Nor has it for many years had any relation to the State Militia of Massachusetts. The regiment left for the seat of war on the 23d of April, 1861, one thousand strong. The men were mostly mechanics, hard working fellows, with no money to spare and families to provide for; Col. George Lyons, himself, left sick members of his family behind him. Many a man joined the ranks who had sanctified the cause by some great personal sacrifice. A stand of colors was presented to the regiment by Dr. Darrow, on behalf of Mrs. Charles C Crawford, Mrs. Charles Chandler and Mrs. Charles A. Secor. The flag had been made by Mrs. Secor thirty-three years before, and was highly valued by the family. The ladies sent it, however, with the regiment, of which Mrs. Secor's son was a member. The regiment went to Baltimore, where one hundred of the men, in company with one hundred members of the Sixth Massachusetts, were delegated to perform the specific work of capturing the celebrated Winans' Steam Gun, which they did effectually and efficiently. The regiment next took part in the capture of a lightship. The Eighth occupied General Lee's house as their headquarters for some time. At the first battle of Bull Run the regiment suffered severely, as they always maintained an unbroken front. When the regiment returned home they were addressed by Governor Morgan, as follows: "The city and state of New York are duly grateful to you for your very efficient services in defence of our country and our flag. You have performed your duty and covered yourselves with glory." Many members of the Eighth were promoted to positions in other regiments. The Forty-seventh Volunteers had a large number from the Eighth in its ranks as officers and privates. The First and Second Ira Harris Cavalry and the Sixty-ninth Infantry had also a number from the Eighth. On the 29th of May, 1862, the regiment, 895 strong, marched for the second time to the seat of war. The regiment was, on this occasion, presented with a flag by Messrs. Tiffany & Co. The officers were Col. Joshua M. Varian, Lieut.-Col. Obed F. Wentworth, Adjt. David B. Keeler, Maj. Leander Buck. Major Buck was presented with an elegant sword, which he received with a few appropriate remarks, saying: "If the sword was disgraced, they would never see the disgracer." The regiment was on duty at Yorktown. Their duties were arduous, but they were performed to the perfect satisfaction of the commanding officer. After their return home, November 19, 1862, the five members of the regiment who died during their last term of service were buried with appropriate honors. Their names were:

Hugh J. Hopkins, Co. G, buried at Calvary Cemetery.
Thomas W Burns, Co. K, buried at Calvary Cemetery.
Charles P. Albans, Co. I, buried at Greenwood.
Henry Richards, Co. A, buried at Bridgeport, Conn.
Charles E. Lawrence, Co. H, buried at Fordham, N. Y.

On the 17th day of June, 1863, the regiment left for the third time in defence of the country. They went to Harrisburg, and bivouacked one mile from the city. Colonel Varian reported to General Couch, and was ordered to move his regiment across the Susquehanna and occupy the partially finished entrenchments, which order was complied with. On the 19th, Colonel Varian was ordered to take the regiment to Shippensburg, for the purpose of holding the enemy in check should he advance. From Shippensburg the regiment was ordered to Scotland, and on the 21st to Chambersburg. The enemy entering Chambersburg, the regiment retreated to Carlyle. The enemy still advancing, General Knipe ordered the Eighth to move forward and take possession of a very strong position, known as Rocky Ridge, which they did. Here the regiment remained until 9 P. M. when it was ordered to fall back to Kingston. The majority of the men were asleep when the orders came, but they were quickly awakened, and in five minutes they were moving along the Kingston road. The enemy still following, orders were given for the regiment to move towards Carlyle, and take position; this was done. From Carlyle they were ordered to Oyster Point, where General Couch said the Eighth and Seventy-first regiments had accomplished everything that had been required of them, and that they had returned from one of the most successful expeditions he had ever seen accomplished, according to the number engaged in it, viz.: Advancing fifty-two miles beyond all defences and support in case of an attack; holding the enemy in check for the period of six days, thereby giving our forces ample time to prepare their defences, and also allowing the farmers of the Cumberland Valley an opportunity to run off their stock, thus making General Lee's raid a profitless expedition. It was said that the Eighth did more real arduous duty and underwent more fatigue and deprivations than any other militia regiment that had left home. They were in the advance from the first hour they entered the state of Pennsylvania. They marched 170 miles of the roughest travelling that can be imagined, through valleys, up mountains and down again, and the greater part of the time amid rain and mud, with scarcely a pleasant day while away from home. The regiment was drawn up in line of battle five times, on two of which occasions Colonel Varian was Acting Brigadier-General, and Lieutenant-Colonel Wentworth was in command of the regiment. When drawn up in line of battle at Oyster Point, where the Rebels attacked them, the commanding general of the division, upon arriving on the ground, refused to take the command until the movements planned by Colonel Varian were all completed. When the regiment returned home, Colonel Varian was presented with a magnificent sword, upon which is the following inscription: " Presented to Col. J. M. Varian, Eighth Regiment, N. Y. S. N. G., by the officers and members of his command, as a testimony of their great respect for him as a brave soldier and worthy citizen,—July 30, 1863."

NINTH REGIMENT.—This was a three years' regiment and was known as the Eighty-third Volunteers. The Ninth were among the first to volunteer, but as false promises were held out to them, numbers of recruits having left lucrative positions, were compelled to join other regiments or wait for the final orders for the Ninth to leave. By great exertions, and not until after the corps had volunteered for three years, were their services finally accepted. The regiment was composed chiefly of American young men, and comprised as intelligent a set of troops as left the city. The officers were Col. John W Stiles, formerly of the Eighth N. Y. S. M.; Lieut.-Col. W H. Halleck, for many years commander of the "City-Guard;" Surgeon N. F W. Fisher, who discarded all his business and friends to accompany the regiment; Maj. E. L. Stone, Adjt. J. B. Coppinger, Sergeant of Engineers, George Merrill. This is the gentleman who was the claimant in the great Merrill will case, which recently attracted so much attention in New York. The Ninth was the first regiment to go through Baltimore without arms. They went to Camp Cameron and stayed there a month, then led the advance up the Maryland side of the Potomac.

ELEVENTH REGIMENT.—This regiment was formerly known as the Second Regiment, "Washington Guard," and was raised in 1824 by Capt. Charles Mapes, of the 142d Regiment of ununiformed militia. The first Colonel of the regiment was Charles King, since President of Columbia College. The regiment had varying success until 1849, when Colonel Bostwick was placed in command. He was ably supported by Lieut.-Col. John E. Bendix (during the war Colonel of the Tenth New York Volunteers), and Maj. Edward Ferrero (who rose from Colonel of the Fifty-first to the rank of Major-General). The regiment, the only rifle corps in 1861, in the First Division, made strenuous efforts through their commander, Col. Joachim Maidhof (a merchant of New York), to be mustered into the service at the earliest possible day. Colonel Maidof wrote to General Scott on the 28th of May, 1861, stating that the regiment was anxious to volunteer for the term of six months. On the 30th of May, the Secretary of War wrote to the Colonel that the quota of the State was full, and that it would be impossible to accept any more troops. On the 28th of May, 1862, the regiment left for the field. The officers were Colonel Maidhof (formerly of the Fifth Regiment), Lieut.-Col. William B. Weinberger, Maj. George A. Raymond, Adjt. Frederick Vilmar. On the 18th of June, 1863, the regiment went to the war for the second time. On the 3d of July they arrived at Carlisle. During the greater part of its campaign, Colonel Maidhof was in command of a brigade. The following extract from a report will show the estimation in which the Eleventh was regarded by its commanding officer: "All duties, however severe, were performed with a cheerful alacrity, and, although they never encountered the enemy in action, their fortitude in bearing immeasurable hardships of hunger, and exposure to the inclement elements, bear attestation to their possession of all the qualities requisite to the character of the soldier."

TWELFTH REGIMENT.—"Independence Guard." The Twelfth left for the war on the 21st of April, 1861, about 850 strong. The officers were Col. Daniel Butterfield, who subsequently became one of the most famous of the major-generals, and was the chief hero of the battle of Resaca; Lieut.-Col. William G. Ward, Maj. Henry A. Bostwick, Adjt. Frederick T. Locke, who was later in the war promoted to the rank of Brigadier-General for gallant and meritorious service, Engineer Benjamin S. Church, Surg. A. Henry Thurston, Chaplain M. B. Smith. In the ranks marched Private Francis C. Barlow, who also rose to the rank of Major-General, and won a record for bravery and soldierly qualities surpassed by none; Captain Ryder also became a Brigadier-General. About seventy-five officers were furnished to the volunteer army from the ranks of the Twelfth. In 1887 Cap. William H. Murphy was the only survivor in active service with the regiment who went to war in 1861. The Twelfth was the first regiment to cross the Long Bridge into Virginia, and Major Church is said to have been the first of the line to reach the opposite shore. The crossing of the bridge was a grand and impressive spectacle. The moon was full and the sky cloudless. Silently, solemnly and firmly, the troops marched across the river, no sound to disturb the solemnity but that of their own footsteps—the order and firmness of which heightened the effect. The line of the regiment extended along the whole aqueduct, and the Constitution was proclaimed by the advance of the Twelfth on the right bank by the time the rear of it had moved from the left bank of the river .

The regiment suffered severely in the battle of Bull Run. It was one of the regiments sent to reinforce General Patterson. During its absence two deaths occurred among the members which cast a gloom over the regiment. They were Thomas Benbow and Private Morris. General Banks in his order directing the return home of the regiment, said: " The Commanding General takes occasion upon the issue of this first order to make acknowledgment to the Twelfth for the service it has rendered, and the fidelity with which it has discharged all the duties of citizen soldiers, especially in the exemplary conduct, its readiness for service, correct discipline, and prompt obedience to orders." In 1862 the regiment went to the front for the second time, with William G. Ward, for Colonel, Livingston Satterlee, Lieutenant-Colonel; Henry A. Bostwick, Major; E. Ellery Anderson, Adjutant. When its three months term of service had expired, the regiment volunteered to remain until the threatened danger to Harper's Ferry was over. Their offer was accepted, and the regiment was among those captured and paroled by "Stonewall" Jackson. New York should remember with pride those who so nobly remained to uphold her honor in the face of the enemy. (Their names may be found on page 229, of volume xxvi. of Townsend's "Library of National Records.") But it was melancholy to see the regiment march up Broadway without their arms, and reflect that the fine weapons with which they marched down Broadway four months before, had been given up into the hands of the enemy, to be used in slaughtering their own comrades.

Before leaving for home, General Wool addressed the following letter to Colonel Ward: "Before you return with your regiment to the Empire City, I wish, in bidding you a cordial farewell, to express my high appreciation of the patriotic conduct which the Twelfth has shown during this, the most perilous time of our beloved country. Being placed in a position of unusual responsibility and danger, you and your brave men have nobly fulfilled the expectations which your Commanding General entertained of you, and I hereby tender my thanks to every officer and soldier in your regiment, but especially to yourself, for the promptness with which you responded to my call, and setting aside all thoughts of safety, home and comfort, remained faithful to your post as true American patriots." The regiment arrived home on the 19th of September. Only one death occurred during its second term of service, that of Private Daniel J. Wright, whose loss was much lamented. On the 20th of June, 1863, the regiment advanced to the defence of the nation for the third time. They went to Fenwick, Perry Co., Pa., and did picket duty on the mountains. It was tough work at first, sleeping on the ground with nothing but a piece of coarse muslin and a blanket to shelter them; but the boys soon got used to it. Maj. Charles McL. Knox, who acquitted himself with great honor in the Ninth Cavalry, was formerly a member of the Twelfth, as was Lieut. Alexander B. Elder, of the Tenth Volunteer Infantry, and many others who became famous in connection with the volunteer regiments during the war. In the ranks of the Twelfth was a fierce fanatic, who, at one time, shot through the legs a companion who was teasing him. He was often seen on picket duty with a musket in one hand and a Bible in the other. This man was Boston Corbett, who shot Booth—the assassin of President Lincoln.

THIRTEENTH REGIMENT.—This is a Brooklyn regiment and left for the war on the 24th of April, 1861. The officers were Col. Abel Smith, Lieut.-Col. Robert B. Clark, Major Willetts, Adjutant Johnson, Chaplain Rev. William Lee. On the 9th of June, Companies A, F, and D, left Annapolis in two steamers and proceeded to Easton, where they attacked the armory. The Confederate General Thomas, in command of the armory, finally demanded to know to whom he should surrender. The answer was: "The demand is made in the name of Abraham Lincoln, President of the United States, to Abel Smith, Colonel of the Thirteenth Regiment, New York State Militia." The surrender was made, the armory opened and the military stores captured. Soon after the return home of the regiment, Colonel Smith died, October, 1861. He was one of the first to respond to the call of his country, and was commander of the post at Annapolis, while his regiment was there. He was reorganizing his regiment for the war, at the time he met with an accident which caused his death. In the attack on the armory at Easton, Private Ceasar Meisel, a gallant soldier, was killed, and his body was brought home and buried in Greenwood. The 78th and 83d Volunteer Regiments, were largely recruited from the 13th, as was also the 91st ("McClellan Chasseurs").

In 1862 when the regiments of the National Guard were again called upon to go to the front, the Thirteenth went forward the second time, under command of Col. Robert B. Clark, with John B. Woodward as Lieutenant-Colonel, Samuel K. Boyd, Major, and William McKee, Adjutant. The regiment did picket duty at Suffolk during nearly their entire term of service; while in the performance of this duty, Guysbert V Holt, of Brooklyn—a most estimable young soldier, was shot through the head while he was on his way back to camp. The Thirteenth went out the third time, when Lee invaded the North in 1863, and served most of the time at Fenwick, Perry Co., Pa. During this campaign it was commanded by Col. John B. Woodward.

FOURTEENTH REGIMENT.—The Fourteenth was known as the Eighty-fourth Volunteer Infantry.—See Record of Eighty-fourth.

SEVENTEENTH AND EIGHTEENTH.—On the evening of July 3, 1863, the captains of Companies A and H, of the Eighteenth Regiment received orders for their commands to report immediately at Yonkers, there to join their regiment, and to proceed at once to the seat of war. With promptness and alacrity the companies assembled and made arrangements to move on the 4th of July to Yonkers, where the Seventeenth and Eighteenth were to rendezvous. Arriving at Yonkers the soldiers' life began, but its dreariness was relieved by the glorious news of the fall of Vicksburg. On the 8th, the Seventeenth and Eighteenth moved to New York City, and thence by cars to Philadelphia and Baltimore, at which city they arrived after having been thirty hours on the road from Yonkers. Here they reported to General Schenck, who ordered them to Fort Marshall, recently evacuated by the Eighth New York. Colonel James Ryder of the Eighteenth was placed in command of the post, and by his dignified deportment made many friends.

NINETEENTH REGIMENT.—The regiment left Newburg for the seat of war on the 4th of June, 1862. The officers were Col. William R. Brown, Lieut.-Col. James Low, Maj. David Jagger, Adjt. William M. Hathaway, Surg. George S. Little. They were accompanied to Jersey City by Gen. S C. Parmenter and his Staff officer—Paymaster Brewster. They were fully armed and equipped with the best of military material, and were not in any way inferior to other New York regiments that had gone before them. The regiment was on duty in Baltimore during its term of service. After its return home the regiment was reorganized for nine months service under its worthy Colonel Brown, and was known as the 168th Volunteer Infantry. Previous to the departure of the regiment in February, 1863, Colonel Brown was presented with a magnificent sword by his friends in Orange county.

TWENTIETH REGIMENT.—"Ulster County Regiment." After numerous disappointments the regiment reached New York on the 28th of April, 1861, and left that city on the 8th of May for the war. The officers were Col. George W Pratt, Lieut.-Col. Hiram Schooumaker, Maj. Theodore B. Gates, Adjt. J. B. Hardenburgh, Surg. C. Leonard Ingersoll, Chaplain Rev. C. B. Darrach. The regiment, in connection with the Brooklyn Thirteenth, did good service during its three months in the vicinity of Alexandria. Upon its return home the regiment re-enlisted for three years, and was known as the Eightieth Volunteer Regiment. Of the fallen heroes of this regiment there may be found in the Presbyterian Cemetery, at Matteawan, the grave of a brave and gallant soldier, Private Hugh Wallace.—See Record of Eightieth Infantry.

TWENTY-FIRST REGIMENT.—On the 26th of June, 1863, the regiment left Poughkeepsie for the seat of war. The officers were Col. Joseph Wright, Lieut.-Col. James Kent, of Fishkill, Maj. Charles

Fitchett. Adjt. James E. Schram, Quartermaster Joseph H. Marshall, Surg. Edward H. Parker, Chaplain Rev. G. M. McEckron. The regiment went to Baltimore, and at the time of the battle of Gettysburg formed part of the left wing of the Army of the Potomac, under command of General Schenck. At first they were held in readiness to repulse the enemy, who were menacing Baltimore, but no fighting occurred. After that, they assisted the New York Seventh in guarding and transporting the 16,000 Rebel prisoners that had arrived at Baltimore, who were captured by Grant at Vicksburg. Company H was from Fishkill Landing, and was known as the "Denning Guard." named in honor of the late William H. Denning, a wealthy citizen of that place, who had manifested great interest in the company in many generous ways. The company was commanded by Capt. H. H. Hustis, and Lieuts. Samuel Underhill, William N. Anthony and David K. Tillott.

TWENTY-SECOND REGIMENT.—On the 22d of April, 1861, the "White Ball Club," a company composed of young men of good family, called a meeting of its members and other citizens, for the purpose of forming a drill club, whose special province it should be, in the absence of the regular militia who had gone to the war, to defend the lives and property of the citizens of New York. At this meeting Mr. George DeForest Lord presided, and an organization was effected, the gentlemen present forming themselves into a drill company. Thirty names were signed to the roll, including those of William E. Dodge, Jr., A. W. Parsons, Jr., Henry A. Oakley, now president of the Howard Insurance Company, Henry J. Howland and Charles Trumbull White. The regiment was then known as the "Union Greys," and it was not until 1864 that it became part of the National Guard, when the law required all militia regiments to connect themselves with the National Guard. The "Union Greys" were accordingly incorporated in the regular State Militia, and became known as the Twenty-second Regiment. In July, 1862, the regiment was called into active service and ordered to Harper's Ferry. It went at once to the front under command of Col. James Monroe, a graduate of West Point, with Lloyd Aspinwall for Lieutenant-Colonel, J. Henderson Grant, Adjutant, James Renwick, Jr., Engineer, and the Rev. John Cotton Smith, Chaplain. While in camp at Harper's Ferry, Colonel Monroe died of typhoid fever, brought on by exposure and fatigue, and thus was taken from the regiment one whom all had learned to love, and in whom the confidence of the members was at once enthusiastic and profound. One of the last wishes of Colonel Monroe, which was also entertained by every member of the regiment, was that he might at least be spared to ride at the head of the Twenty-second when they returned home. But he fell, like Vosburg and Ellsworth, not in the field where it was his ambition to confront danger, but a victim to disease contracted while on duty. The arrival of large numbers of raw recruits from Ohio, Illinois and Indiana, necessitated the breaking up of the regiment for a time, and the detailing of its men as drill-masters. After four months' service in Virginia the regiment returned home, under command of Colonel Aspinwall, who succeeded the lamented Monroe. In June, 1863, the regiment was again ordered to the front, and upon their arrival at Harrisburg was mustered into the service in General "Baldy" Smith's Division. In General Smith's advance from Harrisburg to Waynesboro, through Carlisle, the regiment, with Colonel Aspinwall at its head, had the advance of the division, supporting Capt. Rufus King's battery The regiment took part in the fight with Fitz Hugh Lee, at Sporting Hill, three miles from Harrisburg, and then advancing to Carlisle it was ascertained when four miles from that place, that Lee had taken possession of the town. The Twenty-second proposed to attack and drive the Rebels out of Carlisle, and accordingly the boys went in on a run and Lee vacated. The Twenty-second now took possession of the place and replaced Lee's flag, which they hauled down, with the celebrated Carlisle flag, which may now be seen in the armory of the Twenty-second. General "Baldy" Smith arrived with his Staff an hour later, and at six in the evening Fitz Hugh Lee sent in a flag of truce and demanded the surrender of the town and the troops in it. This was refused and the Confederates surrounded the place and shelled it all night. At four o'clock in the morning, the Rebels set fire to the government barracks outside the town, and then retreated through Papertown to South Mountain. From Carlisle the regiment was ordered to Waynesboro, where they arrived on the night of the day that Lee left on his retreat from Gettysburg. The Twenty-second assisted in garrisoning the town, relieving part of Sedgwick's Sixth Corps, and thus became part of the Army of the Potomac. After remaining a week at Waynesboro they were ordered to Harper's Ferry, but while on the march they heard of the riots in New York, and received orders to return home immediately. Colonel Aspinwall in a letter summing up the operations of his regiment, says: "The regiment were on foot thirteen hours the day before, participating in the affair at Sporting Hill, marched nineteen miles on the day of the bombardment, and were in motion the whole night during the shelling of the town, having had no rations served them for forty-eight hours, excepting an interrupted bite on the market place of Carlisle." "The first men," said Colonel Aspinwall, "to enter Carlisle, were the men of the Twenty-second; and the first Stars and Stripes raised over that place was by a member of the Twenty-second." The regiment was made up of young men belonging to the first families of New York, and here again we find Fishkill represented in the Twenty-second by two sons of the Hon. Henry E. Davies. William G. and Julien T. Davies; thus it will be seen that no less than four sons and one brother of Judge Davies are referred to in these regimental records. Upon the return home of the regiment, Captain Howland was presented with a sword as a mark of appreciation of the ability with which he commanded his company.

TWENTY-THIRD REGIMENT.—This was the first regiment to leave Brooklyn for the war in 1863, when the call was made for troops to repel Lee's invasion of the North. The regiment left on the 18th of June. Before their departure, General Smith, commanding the Eleventh Brigade, to which the Twenty-third was attached, issued an order complimenting the regiment on the alacrity with which they obeyed the call for troops, having prepared themselves within the brief space of forty-eight hours, fully armed and equipped and prepared for any emergency. The officers were Col. William Everdell, Jr., Lieut.-Col. John A. Elwell, Engineer J. H. Frothingham, Surg. Dr. A. D. Wilson.

TWENTY-FIFTH REGIMENT.—This fine regiment was recognized as the crack corps of Albany. The regiment was among the first in the United States service, being the third regiment from the State in 1861 under the call of the President. The Twenty-fifth built the fort known as Fort Albany, on the Virginia side of the Potomac, acknowledged to be one of the finest defences of Washington. It also had the honor of capturing the first two prisoners captured by the Army of the Potomac. The regiment served its term of three months and fifteen days. It left for the war on the 22d of April. The officers were Col. Michael K. Bryan, Lieut.-Col. James Sarft, Maj. David Friedlander, Adjt. J. Van Zaunt, Chaplain Rev. John M. Kimball. Company G is the oldest company in the State, and was quartered on Governor's Island during the war of 1812. The men did not have an opportunity of signally distinguishing themselves in battle, it having been detailed in the reserve for the defence of the capital. They occupied a prominent position in the reserve and were the advanced post. A large number of the men were anxious to get back that they might join the volunteer regiments. On the 4th of June, 1862, the regiment arrived in New York, on their way to the war for the second time. By command of Governor Morgan, they carried the following inscription on their regimental standard: "Washington, April, 1861." The regiment did picket duty at Suffolk during nearly their entire second term of service, and were mustered out on the 28th of August. Many of the members having expressed a desire to volunteer in the Third Regiment, Colonel Alford issued an order to that effect, with the additional information that the State as well as the United States bounty would be paid to all who would so enlist. The regiment came home with much regret at not having had a chance to strike a blow for their country. A large number of men of the Twenty-fifth re-enlisted in the Fourth Regiment of the Corcoran Legion (175th Volunteers), of which Colonel Bryan was elected Colonel, and the official personnel of the 175th did not vary materially from that of the Twenty-fifth. The brave Colonel Bryan was killed in the action at Port Hudson, where he exhibited dauntless bravery; always at the post of duty, he set an example which his brave men emulated. He fell in the prime of life, and in the midst of usefulness for a cause he devotedly loved.

TWENTY-EIGHTH REGIMENT.—This is a Brooklyn regiment and was composed of the best class of German citizens. The regiment left for the war on the 30th of April, 1861. The officers were Col. Michael Bennett (who was unable to accompany the regiment on account of an accident which resulted in temporarily injuring him). Lieutenant-Colonel Burns, in command: Surgeon, Dr. Rice; Chaplain, Rev. Mr. Zaft. Before the regiment left there was an interesting display of patriotism by the young ladies of Brooklyn Heights Seminary (one of whom, Miss Mollie Fancher, has since become the famous invalid of Brooklyn). They unfurled a beautiful flag at their chapel in Montague Street, where speeches were made by Professor West, Rev. Dr. Storrs, and others. Although it was not the fortune of the Twenty-eighth to participate in the battle of Bull Run, the position they occupied was a most important one, commanding as it did the passage of the Potomac by way of the Georgetown Bridge. Had Beauregard pursued his advantage on Sunday afternoon, and made a dash at Washington, it would have fallen to the lot of the Twenty-eighth to take a prominent part in disputing the passage of the Potomac, and they would doubtless have displayed the traditional bravery which their countrymen have earned on many a hard fought field of the old world. The regiment left as a monument of their industry, Fort Bennett, named in honor of the Colonel—one of the chains of defensive works around Washington,

16

which was constructed by them. In 1862 the regiment went to the war for the second time, and again in June, 1863, they went to Harrisburg, and on both occasions were complimented for their faithful services and quick attention to orders.

THIRTY-SEVENTH REGIMENT.—The Thirty-seventh was organized in September, 1861, by the governor, and the line officers duly commissioned. On the 18th of September, Mr. Charles Roome was elected Colonel of the regiment—a gentleman acknowledged to be a good officer and fully competent to lead his men. The formation of the regiment was first proposed by Mr. Roome and Mr. Monell (who became Lieutenant-Colonel) at the commencement of our national difficulties, and when the city of New York was left in a defenceless and unprotected state by the withdrawal to the seat of war of a large number of our volunteer militia. The principal object then was to raise a regiment for the protection of the city in case of need. So successful was the recruiting for the regiment, and so superior was the material of which it was being formed, that the original plan was abandoned, and a permanent organization under the State Militia law was decided on. The officers were to a large extent taken from the Seventh. In May, 1862, the regiment volunteered their services and were sworn in May 27, for three months. The officers were Colonel Roome, Lieut.-Col. C. L. Monell, Major Ossian D. Ashley, Adjt. Charles M. Catlin, Engineer Henry F. Scudder. While at Baltimore the regiment sent out two detachments on special service, and an entire company was at one time at work among the secessionists of the eastern shore. The first expedition under Lieutenant Morris seized the steamer "Lady Washington," and the second under Captain Smith, captured the steamer "George Weens," and both prizes under considerable difficulty were taken to Washington. One company, at Denton, Carolina County, under command of Captain Lyon, arrested a number of secessionists and sent them to Fort McHenry. General Wool in special orders said: "During the three months term of service of the Thirty-seventh, the officers and men were at all times ready to do their duty in any position to which they might be called." In June, 1863, the regiment went to the war for the second time, and on the 1st of July they marched into Carlisle, being, it is said, the first union regiment to enter the city after the retreat of the Rebels, although the officers of the Twenty-second claim the honor for the men of their regiment; but where both did so well, the honors may be equally divided. Some of the members claim that the Thirty-seventh did more duty during the war than any other regiment in the National Guard.

FORTY-SEVENTH REGIMENT.—"Our Own," of Williamsburg. Notwithstanding the drain on Williamsburg for recruiting the Thirteenth and Twenty-eighth regiments, the newly formed Forty-seventh filled up its ranks rapidly. The Hon. Samuel T. Maddox, whose name was a tower of strength in Williamsburg, recruited a company, and the rush to enlist under him was astonishing. The regiment first left for the war in May, 1862, enlisting for three months. The officers were Col. I. V. Meserole, Lieut.-Col. George Sangster, Maj. Jeremiah Johnson, Surg. Dr. Cornelius H. Schaffs, Maj. J. E. Minor. During their time of service they did garrison duty at Fort McHenry, Baltimore, and though they never had an opportunity to distinguish themselves in the field, they manifested the greatest impatience to get into action. In June, 1863, the regiment went to the war again for thirty days. On their arrival at Baltimore they were ordered to Washington, where they encamped on Arlington Heights. Every night the regiment, in company with the Fourteenth Massachusetts, was sent out on picket duty; the lines extending along the road to Fairfax Court House. The regiment returned home June 25th, when a large number of the members re-enlisted in the Third Metropolitan Regiment.

SIXTY-NINTH REGIMENT.—When the apparition of civil war first started forth and appalled the people, the Sixty-ninth was the first of all foreign-born citizens to spring to the front. The Sixty-ninth was organized in 1851, under the command of Col. Charles S. Roe. Its subsequent commanders up to the commencement of the war, were Col. James B. Ryan and Michael Corcoran. A short time before the war broke out a stand of colors was presented to the regiment, and a sword of honor to Colonel Corcoran, as a testimonial of sympathy with a sentiment which made him refuse to parade an Irish regiment in honor of the reception in New York of the Prince of Wales. Mr. A. V. Stout presided on the occasion of the presentation. On the day after the presentation, the English depositors in Mr. Stout's bank (the Shoe and Leather) bustled up to the counter in one long continued current and withdrew every dollar that was in his keeping, to the amount of several hundred thousand dollars. The 23d of April, 1861, was a great day for the Irish citizens of New York. The Sixty-ninth—"an American regiment—all born in Ireland," departed for the scene of war with great *éclat*, setting the entire population of the lower wards of New York in a state of excitement bordering on madness. The regiment carried with them a beautiful banner, the gift of Mrs. Daly, the wife of the Hon. Charles P. Daly. The officers were Col. Michael Corcoran, Lieut.-

Col. Robert Nugent, Maj. James Bagley, Adjt. John McKeon, Chaplain Rev. Thomas Mooney, Surg. Dr. Kiernan. The regiment numbered 1000 muskets, but the rank and file and musicians numbered 1,300. Two thousand additional men could have been enlisted, but the orders from headquarters prevented Colonel Corcoran from mustering more than 1,000 muskets. As the regiment were marching down Broadway, they halted in front of the Astor House, and while there the heart of one of the recruits, a fine looking fellow, was besieged by the lamentations of his wife and children who were on the sidewalk. The poor fellow could not stand it, and rushed from the ranks. His comrades were disarming him in the street, when an elderly and very respectable looking gentleman, stepped out of the crowd of spectators, seized the abandoned musket and offered to take the vacant place. Upon inquiry it was ascertained that the gentleman who thus volunteered, was Mr. Michael Cooney, formerly of Albany, and one of the founders of the "Emmet Guard" of that city, and was the First Lieutenant of that company when they volunteered their services to the general government in 1847, to go to Mexico—the first company to do so in the Empire State. The offer, so prompt, and impulsive on the part of the old gentleman, elicited cheers from the crowd, but it was not accepted, doubtless on account of the age of him who made the patriotic offer. The regiment bore the hardships of the march without a single murmur or expression of dissatisfaction, and seemed determined to outdo their brethren in arms in their strict obedience to orders, and their readiness to serve their country in whatever duty they might be called upon to perform. On the 21st of May, Captain Thomas Francis Meagher, with 100 sons of the Irish sod, forming a Zouave company, started to join the regiment, and with the company also went 300 recruits to fill up the regiment. Among these gallant fellows was a member of the Pope's Irish Brigade, who had distinguished himself in the Army of the Pontiff, during the difficulties in Poland. His name was John Gleason. Gleason had been presented with a gold medal by Lamoriciere on the preceding 5th of October, for his gallant services at the battle of Ancona, and was promoted from the rank of sergeant to that of lieutenant. The latter distinction was accorded him for taking Monte Moratte, while in charge of a company of skirmishers. On the 23d of May, a detachment of the regiment stationed on the southern slope of Washington Heights, seized a train of cars, containing some 300 passengers, a portion of whom were retained as prisoners. On the 26th of May, the Mayor of Georgetown, in a letter to Colonel Corcoran, said: "I trust you are aware of our high appreciation of the valor and patriotism which have prompted the Sixty-ninth to repair here for the defence of our homes and lives, and our capital, for which we owe a debt of gratitude that can never be cancelled." "Nobly did the Sixty-ninth sustain its national character at the battle of Bull Run," said the Hon. Charles P Daly, "nobly did they stand up for the cause of their adopted country—for which Montgomery died, for the preservation of those blessings which Taylor, Smith, and Thornton, who signed the Declaration of Independence, meant to transmit to every Irishman who should make this country the land of his adoption." Although their term of service had expired, the members unanimously volunteered to serve throughout the battle, and were accordingly assigned the post of honor in the advance, when the grand army first moved forward. The most gallant charge of the day at Bull Run was made by the Sixty-ninth, the Seventy-ninth, and the Thirteenth New York State Militia regiments, who rushed upon one of the Rebel batteries, firing as they proceeded, and attacking it at the point of the bayonet. They were almost in possession of the Rebel guns, when a murderous volley raked their front and they were compelled to fall back. Colonel Corcoran, the life and soul of the regiment, who led them with solid front and steady steps to battle, and when the rout commenced which broke the lines of the regiment, remained with the flag, was captured, and became one of the chief victims of Southern retaliation and hate, being one of those afterwards selected to be hung, should our government decide on summary proceedings against the privateersmen. Dr. George W Bagley, of the Eleventh Virginia Regiment, says, "I saw George Burwell bring in Colonel Corcoran, his personal captive." At Bull Run fell the brave Capt. James Haggerty and Lieut. Edward Costello, beloved by all. The bravery of the officers of the regiment is indicated by the fact that five captaincies in the regular army were awarded to its members in honor of their gallant conduct on that occasion. Eighteen of the members died at Richmond, two of whom were wounded in the battle. After three months absence the regiment returned home, having added many a laurel to the crown of Ireland, and demonstrated that the power and responsibility of the bayonet, directed by the unflinching muscle of Irishmen, knowing no fear and fearing no danger, was the certain signal of victory and success. The Sixty-ninth did its duty faithfully and well. No better tribute can be awarded them, no richer guerdon offered, no brighter pearl bestowed. The first in love, the foremost in war, the last in a retreat from danger, the Irishman has made his name the wide world over. The men of the Sixty-ninth did but add another chapter to the glittering volumes of their heroic deeds. During their whole career, in the battle or out of it, on the field or in the trench, they forgot themselves, and thought only of their country. Fort Corcoran, built at Arlington Heights, will stand for ages as a monument of their persevering industry and patriotism. In the charge at Bull Run they threw off their coats and rushed into the fight without thinking of themselves. And so they came home ragged and half naked, wanting in everything but the courage and manliness which are essential features of their character. No one could look at their diminished ranks as they marched up Broadway, without saying to himself that such noble men were deserving of all the thanks that a nation could give, nor resist the suggestion of his good angel to bless old Ireland for such excellent citizens. On the 30th of May, 1862, the regiment again advanced to the defence of the nation, carrying with them the old Irish standard which was borne with so much valor at Bull Run, and wherever it was seen along the line of march it was honored by the people. Before their departure they were addressed by Father Mooney, who told them that "the best soldier was he that respected his God while he fought for his country." Colonel Corcoran being a prisoner at Richmond, the regiment was commanded by Maj. James Bagley. After performing faithfully all the service required of them to the perfect satisfaction of the Commanding General, the regiment returned home on the 27th of August. At four o'clock on that summer afternoon, the war worn veterans, with Corcoran at their head, marched up Broadway, amid the most intense excitement. Before his arrival home, the gallant Colonel had received as a mark of appreciation of his faithful services, a promotion to the rank of Brigadier-General. In response to the cordial reception he met with from the assembled crowds, he said that, "No inducement, however strong, not even the fee simple of Broadway, would restrain him from the battle-field." "Such a speech as that," said Mayor Opdyke, "deserves not only a brigade, but a division."

On the 22d of June, 1863, the regiment departed once more for the scene of action. It is a curious fact in connection with the regiment, militia though it be, that almost every officer in command had been subject to the vicissitudes of the field. The officers were Col. James Bagley, Lieut.-Col. James Cavanagh, Adjt. William Fogarty, Quartermaster James B. Tully. For the first week they were at Camp Ewen, McKim's mansion, Baltimore. The regiment witnessed every day heavy battalion and company drills under the personal supervision of Lieutenant-Colonel Cavanagh, who brought to the Sixty-ninth the experience of Manassas, Yorktown, the Seven Days, Antietam, Fredericksburg, and other bloody engagements, having been since 1861 Major of Colonel Nugent's Sixty-ninth volunteer regiment. Colonel Nugent went out with the old Sixty-ninth as Lieutenant-Colonel in 1861. During their entire term of service they were located in the city of Baltimore, and by the gallantry and soldierly bearing of its Colonel, officers and men, commended itself to General Schenck as set forth in the General's order directing their return home to help quell the riot in New York.

SEVENTY-FIRST REGIMENT.—In 1853, a battalion was organized, which was called the "American Rifles," comprising three companies. In 1855, three additional companies were added to the above and at an election of officers, Abram S. Vosburg was unanimously elected Colonel. The battalion then changed its name to the "American Guard," and was chartered as the Seventy-first Regiment, New York State Militia. It was this regiment that quelled the famous "Dead Rabbit" riot in 1857. Immediately after it was announced that the Seventy-first had volunteered in April, 1861, and that its tender was accepted by the government, the rush of recruits became tremendous, and more names were put upon the list than could by any possibility be enrolled in the companies. A week before, and scarcely a Corporal's guard of the regiment were ready to volunteer. On Saturday night, April 20th, the rolls were closed, with over 1,110 names registered and 200 applicants refused. On the 21st of April, the regiment left for the scene of action. The officers were—Col. Abram S. Vosburg, Lieut.-Col. Henry P. Martin, Maj. George A. Buckingham, Adjt. A. Hamilton Pride, Engineer E. A. Quintard, Quartermaster George W. Roosevelt, Surg. Charles McMillan, Asst. Surg. John E. A. Dodge, Chaplain Cornelius Carson, Paymaster Eugene Penguet, Serg.-Maj. Henry F Liebenau (now on the editorial staff of the New York *Star*); Quartermaster-Serg. Nicholas W Day (who later in the war became Colonel of the 131st Regiment, and acquitted himself with great distinction); Right Gen. Guide, S. E. Egbert; Left Gen. Guide, F. Shelby; Color Sergs. H. T. Searles and H. E. Smith. Soon after their departure a company of riflemen, called the "Parmenter Riflemen"—Company L, 19th N. Y. S. M., from Newburg, and accompanied by Gen. S. C. Parmenter, Col. William R. Brown, and Capt. E. Alsdorf, passed through New York, on their way to join the Seventy-first. The company was commanded by Captain Ellis, of New Windsor. The regiment went to Washington, and on its arrival there was quartered in the Inauguration Ball Room; thence they were ordered to the Navy Yard. This was the post of honor, being the most important place to defend against attack. The regiment was first under fire in the engagement at Acquia Creek, where they dismantled some of the enemy's guns, silenced one battery, besides disabling about thirty men. The conduct of Lieut. Thomas B. Prendergast was the subject of general commendation by the men under his command, and after his return home he was presented with a testimonial for his gallant conduct by Bryant's minstrels. The regiment had been from home but a few weeks when the national forces were called to sustain an almost irrreparable loss by the death of Colonel Vosburg, which was occasioned by over labor and exposure, which proved too much for his weak lungs. Colonel Vosburg was born in Kinderhook, Columbia County, in 1825. He was from one of the old Knickerbocker families. His grandfather took an active part in the Revolutionary War, and was among the first to throw off allegiance to the Crown. He was, in fact, a Whig, in face of the army of Kinderhook Tories. Colonel Vosburg, therefore, inherited patriotism from a worthy source, and his prompt response to the call of his country showed that he was not an unworthy descendant. No regiment had been given by New York, which, from the time it made its remarkable march from Annapolis to Washington, until the bloody day at Bull Run, that challenged more general admiration in all that constitutes good soldiers and brave men than the Seventy-first, under command of Col. Henry P Martin, who succeeded to the position made vacant by the death of Colonel Vosburg. Most notably did the regiment display the fruits of Colonel Vosburg's training at the battle of Bull Run. They fought like tigers, and were among the last to leave the field in good order. The regiment was one of the first in the engagement, as it was one of the last out of it. They lost more men in killed and wounded (seventy-five) than both the Rhode Island regiments together, upon whom Colonel Burnside, acting Brigadier-General, lavished the chief praise, although he alludes in his report to the bravery and steadiness manifested by Colonel Martin and his entire regiment. Among the brave men of the Seventy-first who fell at the battle of Bull Run were Captains Ellis and Hart, who fell while bravely leading their men into action. Captain Ellis was a son of Dr. Samuel C. Ellis, of New York, and was one of five brothers, all of whom participated in the battle. One brother, Capt. Augustus Van Horne Ellis, did all that human effort could do to preserve the lives of his men and bring them safely off the field. He afterwards became Colonel of the 124th Regiment—an Orange County regiment, at the head of which he participated with great distinction at Fredericksburg and Chancellorsville, and after a glorious career laid down his life at Gettysburg. Among the captured were Lieut. Edward B. Doherty and Capt. James Gillette, a son of the Rev. Dr. Gillette of New York. Lieutenant Doherty killed two horses under Colonel Barton, of Georgia, and finally killed the Colonel and captured his sword and sash. Lieutenant Doherty was captured on the 21st of July, but effected his escape on the 26th. Later in the war he was appointed Captain in the Sixteenth New York Cavalry Regiment, and commanded the company of that regiment to which Boston Corbett belonged, and which was instrumental in causing the death of Booth—the assassin of President Lincoln. While at Richmond, Captain Gillette was one of the prison secretaries, and he furnished the *Herald's* Fortress Monroe correspondent with a list of prisoners captured by the Rebel forces up to December 27, 1861, which was published in the New York *Herald* of January 6, 1862. Captain Gillette was one of four patriotic brothers, sons of the Rev. Dr. Gillette, all of whom served their country with great distinction throughout the war. Capt. James Gillette after his return home from captivity was appointed to a position on the Staff of General Geary, and was honorably mentioned for his bravery, especially at the battle of Chancellorsville. He died in November, 1880, and was characterized in an obituary notice as "a grand and noble man." In connection with this list of names referred to above the following strange and interesting developments occur. On the 29th of October, 1861, the New York *Herald* said in an account of the great expedition to Beaufort: "There is a painful rumor in circulation that a clerk of one of the men-of-war has been missing for three days, and is also suspected of having taken the signal book of the vessel with him. It is supposed that he took a boat and put off to Sewall's Point, and there joined the Rebels. If he has not already reached his destination, his capture will be certain."

On the 30th of October, 1861, the *Herald's* Washington corrrespondent wrote as follows: "The assertion in to-day's New York *Tribune*, 'upon good authority' that the private secretary of Commodore Dupont had absconded, carrying with him the maps and charts, and even the sealed orders of the Commodore, was pronounced at the Navy Department, in the presence of the Washington correspondent of that paper, to be totally and maliciously false."

On the 6th of January, 1862, when the *Herald* published the list of deserters and prisoners at Richmond, furnished by Captain Gillette, it said: "Among them will be found the name of Ernest Hale, commander's clerk, United States steamer "Pawnee." This is the individual who decamped with the signal books while Commodore Dupont's fleet rendezvoused in Hampton Roads."

On the 28th of May, 1862, the gallant heroes of Bull Run left for the war the second time, 820 strong. The officers were Col. Henry P. Martin, Lieut.-Col. Charles H. Smith, Adjt. A. H. Pride, Quartermaster George W. Roosevelt, Commissary Robert B. Roosevelt. On their arrival at Washington they were ordered to Tenallytown Creek. Their term of service expired on the 28th of August, but by special request of the Secretary of War, the regiment remained in the service two weeks longer. Just before their return home a deputation of the regiment waited upon the Secretary of War and informed him that all the men except eighty would re-enlist in the volunteer service. In June, 1863, the regiment was again called into service, and once more (June 17) they advanced to the front, under command of Col. Benjamin L. Trafford, formerly Captain of Company B. (Colonel Trafford died in December, 1883. At the time of his death he was editor of the *Democrat*, Red Bank, N. J.) The officers were Lieut.-Col. William J. Coles, Maj. David C. Muschutt, Adjt. John R. Livermore, Engineer Trumbull Smith, Surg. Dr. Edgar Birdsall, Quartermaster George W Roosevelt. The regiment saw hard work from the time they left New York, until their return home. They were in the extreme advance. They were driven gradually back before the advancing foe from Chambersburg to Harrisburg, a distance of nearly sixty miles. Most of their marches were made in the dead of night, accompanied by incessant rain and mud, followed by a cunning and indomitable enemy earnestly endeavoring to flank them. Once the Rebels nearly succeeded, and the regiment only escaped by marching "double quick" through fields of growing grain, the Rebels taking the road. As they entered Oyster Point, they thought they were at last to have some rest, but scarcely had they pitched their tents, when the Rebels commenced shelling them, and a sharp skirmish ensued. The post at the Point was occupied by four companies. Captain Schutt, of Company C, was in command, and Captain Mander, of Company B, about a mile from him. The men had not had their clothes off for fourteen days. Finally the troops commenced an active retreat again, so that they were on the constant move, never spending scarcely a dozen hours in the same place. The Seventy-first furnished a large number of officers for the volunteer service. The officers of the 131st Regiment were mostly from the Seventy-first. Among those whose services were especially conspicuous, and whose names received honorable mention, were Col. Peter J. Claassen, of the 132d Regiment; the gallant Capt. Henry W Hicks, Jr., of the 165th, a hero of Port Hudson; Lieut. James H. Sperling, of the Fifty-third, Regiment, who was presented with a sword by his friends of the Twenty-first ward, for his bravery at Bull Run; Lieut.-Col. Philip J. Parison, of the Fifty-seventh, killed at Antietam; William J. Burrowe, the hero of the affair at Lewinsville, who was appointed Aide-de-camp to General Smith; Lieut. Thomas B. Oakley, who was presented with a watch by his comrades of Company A, and was promoted to Major in the Seventy-first for his bravery at Bull Run.

SEVENTY-NINTH REGIMENT.—"Highland Guard." The Seventy-ninth was among the first to volunteer its services. The very fact of having assumed the name of one of old Scotia's noblest and bravest battalions, could not fail to stamp indelible fame and renown upon its escutcheon. After many vexatious delays the regiment departed for the front on the 2d of June, 1861. The officers were Col. James Cameron, a brother of Simon Cameron, Secretary of War in 1861 (who joined the regiment after its departure); Lieut.-Col. S. M. Elliott, commanding; Maj. David McLelland, Adjt. David Ireland (who later in the war was Colonel of the 137th Regiment, and died of disease in 1864); Surg. James Norval. At the battle of Bull Run, the most gallant charge of the day was made by the Seventy-ninth, Sixty-ninth and Thirteenth State Militia Regiments. Colonel Cameron gallantly led the Seventy-ninth to the charge; the brave Scotchmen were so eager for the fight, that they actually stripped off their shoes and coats and rushed upon the enemy. Colonel Cameron did not live to see the valiant deeds of those whom he commanded, for after discharging his revolver twice, and while in the act of shooting the third time, a ball from a muske penetrated his left breast, and he fell dead on the field, but the memory of their lost commander seemed only to add to their prowess, and under the lead of the brave Major McLelland, they rushed into the hottest of the fight and seemed determined to avenge his death. The Seventy-ninth was a three years regiment, and was known as the Seventy-ninth Volunteers.

—See Record of Seventy-ninth Volunteer Infantry.

EIGHTY-FOURTH REGIMENT.—In June, 1863, Governor Seymour organized and commissioned the Eighty-fourth as one of the regiments of the First Division. The officers were Col. Frederick A. Conkling, Lieut.-Col. Angus Cameron, Major Thomas Barclay, Adjt. James P. Raymond, Surgeon Jas. Norval. The regiment went to Baltimore, and while there Capt. William Atkinson's company constituted the provost-guard of the city. Company F, Capt. Alexander McLeod, were stationed in the jail, where 750 prisoners were confined. The guard was highly commended by the officers of the jail for their soldierly and gentlemanly conduct. The remainder of the regiment were in camp at the well-known grounds called Frisby's woods, about three miles from the city, except the command of Capt. William McKay, who had charge of the Light Street bridge. Lieutenant-Colonel Cameron and Major Barclay were alternately brigade officers of the day. Colonel Conkling made a very good soldier. The regiment returned home on the 3d of August, 1863, having been absent one month.

CAVALRY.

NEW YORK'S twenty-five regiments of cavalry had a conspicuous share in the hard fighting done by that branch of the service. Notwithstanding all the disadvantages and obstacles the three divisions of cavalry in the Army of the Potomac had to contend with, they proved during General Grant's campaign in 1864, to be the salvation of his army. In regard to what they did at Gettysburg General Custer said: "I challenge the annals of warfare to produce a more brilliant or successful charge than was made by the cavalry on the third day of the battle." Their effective work was proven on a hundred battle-fields, and the severity of their service is shown by the long list of losses, which were greater proportionately, than those of the infantry. A brief review of the regimental records will indicate the extent and variety of the service seen by the New York cavalrymen.

FIRST REGIMENT.—"Lincoln Cavalry." The regiment was organized in New York City, by Col. Andrew T. McReynolds, of Grand Rapids, Mich., formerly a captain in the regular army, who lost the use of an arm by a wound in a charge with Phil Kearny, in the taking of the city of Mexico, 1848. The commission for this regiment was issued to Col. Carl Schurz immediately after the attack on Fort Sumter, and as he was soon thereafter appointed Minister to Spain, the eight companies organized by Colonel Schurz were turned over to Colonel McReynolds.

It is remarkable how many of the wielders of the sabre, connected with the regiment, subsequently became distinguished by the use of their pens. Carl Schurz, Editor; Lieutenant-Colonel Battersby, who wrote "Bridle-Bits"; Joseph Pulitzer, Editor of the *World*; and Lemoyne Burleigh, Military Editor of the Brooklyn *Standard*.

In July, 1861, the regiment, 1,400 strong, left New York for the seat of war, being the first regiment of mounted men received into the service. From the time it left New York until its return, the history of the regiment was closely allied with the greatest engagements and victories of the war—their deeds of bravery were the theme of every tongue. Under such cavalry commanders as Stoneman, Pleasanton, Sheridan, Kilpatrick, Crook and Averill, they again and again distinguished themselves. The regiment was under fire during the war at least 300 times, in many instances fighting for six or eight days right along. At the battle of Ninevah, November 12, 1864, the brigade to which the regiment belonged made a terrific charge on the Rebels under Major-General Lomax, self-styled the "Savior of the Valley," completely routing them. This was considered one of the finest charges of that celebrated campaign. Col. Alonzo W Adams, who had succeeded Colonel McReynolds in command, led his regiment in person, capturing all the guns and battle-flags, and 200 prisoners. Seven hundred prisoners, two twelve-pound howitzers and 108 wagons, taken by Lee in the Gettysburg campaign, were recaptured by one hundred men of the regiment and one hundred of the Twelfth Pennsylvania at the battle of Greencastle, Pa. The detachment from the first was under command of Capt. Abram Jones. Captain Jones had entire command of the detachment, and captured more prisoners than he could guard.—The charge of the regiment at Capon Bridge, in October, 1862, was made under command of Capt. William H. Boyd, of Company C, who was subsequently promoted to Colonel of the Twenty-first Pennsylvania cavalry. In this charge Imboden's command was completely broken up. The brilliant charges at Piedmont and Lynchburg, were led by Maj. Timothy Quinn. The regiment opened the spring campaign of 1865, on the 1st and 2d of March, with two gallant charges in succession, under command of Lieut.-Col. Jenyns C. Battersby, and under the immediate direction of General Custer at Mount Crawford and Waynesboro. These charges were the opening of the ball in which Gen. Jubal Early's entire army was destroyed and driven in both charges some twenty miles, and everything seen was captured and left on the field for other regiments to gather up. The regiment claims to have captured more prisoners and property than any other cavalry regiment in the service—having captured over four hundred prisoners. At the engagement at Rood's Hill, Colonel Adams was complimented on the field by General Powell for his coolness and daring, and for the good discipline and efficiency of his regiment under a heavy fire. Colonel Adams went out as Lieutenant, and was promoted step by step till he reached the position of Colonel. At the battle of Sailor's Creek, the Sergeant-Major of the regiment, Oliver Lumphrey, lost his left leg. After Lumphrey was shot from his horse, his leg terribly shattered, he crawled to the side of a tree, and bracing himself against it, fired off the remaining shots in his pistol, crying out to his comrades,—"Go on, boys, don't stop for me, I can take care of myself." Thus it will be seen that few regiments have a more brilliant record than the First New York Cavalry. Major Joseph

Ketchum Stearns, one of the best officers of the regiment, died in February, 1866.

FIRST REGIMENT VETERAN CAVALRY.—This regiment was organized at Geneva in 1863. The Seventeenth Cavalry was consolidated with it. It went to the war under command of Col. John S. Platner. In 1864 the regiment participated with great credit in a number of engagements.

SECOND CAVALRY.—"Harris Light Cavalry." Secretary Stanton said: "No regiment in the United States service had done so much for the Government as the Harris Light Cavalry. To the Hon. Henry E. Davies, of Fishkill Landing, is the country indebted in a great measure for the organization of this regiment. In July, 1861, Judge Davies visited Washington for the purpose of ascertaining how his services could be made most effective in the way of hastening forward regiments from New York. He first called upon General Scott, who not only urged the immediate formation of a new cavalry regiment, but requested the Judge to name competent officers to command it. Judge Davies, accordingly recommended his nephew—J. Mansfield Davies, Judson Kilpatrick and Henry F. Davies, Jr., for important positions, and they were at once confirmed by the Secretary of War as Colonel, Lieutenant-Colonel and Major. Colonel Davies remained in command of the regiment until December, 1862, when he resigned, and was succeeded by Lieutenant-Colonel Kilpatrick. After a famous raid preceding the battle of Chancellorsville, which made the name of the United States Cavalry one of the proudest in the military service of the country, Colonel Kilpatrick was promoted to Brigadier-General, and Maj. Henry E. Davies (who became Lieutenant-Colonel after the resignation of his cousin) was promoted to Colonel. Colonel Davies commanded the regiment with great skill and bravery until September, 1863, when he, too, for meritorious services was promoted to Brigadier-General. The fourth Colonel of the regiment was Walter C. Hull—a brave and skilful officer, who was killed in action at Cedar Creek, in November, 1864. He was succeeded by Otto Harhaus, who resigned in September, 1864, when A. M. Randol became its sixth and last Colonel. Colonel Randol was promoted to Brevet Brigadier-General in 1865. Among the celebrated raids in which the Second participated, was that under Col. Ulric Dahlgren, known as the Richmond raid, when the regiment went inside the fortifications and approached within a mile and a half of the city. Maj. Edwin F. Cook, of the Second, was second in command of the expedition, and Capt.

J. F. B. Mitchell next. They were selected for their well-known and daring invincibility in desperate circumstances. Chaplain Edward R. Roe accompanied the regiment as volunteer aide to General Kilpatrick. Major Cook was captured and put in irons. Captain Mitchell cut his way through with the bulk of Colonel Dahlgren's party and joined the main command. Surg. S. F. Kingston was among the captured. During General Pope's campaign, Lieut. Robert Loudon captured the Confederate raider, Mosby, who at the time was General Stuart's Adjutant-General, and upon his person were found despatches showing the intentions of General Lee to fall upon Pope before he could be reinforced, and this information probably saved Pope's army from a great disaster.—Among the brave men of the regiment worthy of special mention were Sergs. Frank Miller and J. S. Calkin, to whom medals of honor were awarded by the Secretary of War, and Capt. Francis M. Plum, of whom it was said "no braver man ever drew a sword." Captain Plum (recently deceased) was a brother-in-law of Col. George L. Willard, of the 125th Regiment, and a son of the Hon. Elias Plum, of Troy.—This was the only regiment in the army that had as many as five Colonels promoted to Brigadier-Generals.

SECOND REGIMENT "MOUNTED RIFLES."—This regiment was organized at Buffalo, and went to the war under command of Col. John Fisk. It took part in a great number of battles and suffered especially in the battle in front of Petersburg.

THIRD CAVALRY.—"Van Allen Cavalry." Named in honor of its first Colonel, James H. Van Allen. When Colonel Van Allen resigned in April, 1862, he was succeeded by Col. Simon H. Mix. Colonel Van Allen was lost overboard in mid-ocean in July, 1886. Colonel Mix proved himself one of the best cavalry officers in the service, and commanded the regiment with distinguished credit until June, 1864, when he was killed in action at Petersburg. After the death of Colonel Mix the regiment returned to North Carolina, where they met with a warm reception from their old comrades. As they knew every by-path and lane as well as the veriest Secesh, and the Rebels knew it, too, the latter had to keep a much sharper lookout.—At one time during the war the regiment was within twelve miles of Richmond, and would have been there had it not been for a man named Bayle. (For explanation see Seventh Cavalry). Maj. G. W. Cole was appointed by General Butler Cavalry Inspector in his department, and later in the war became—Colonel of the Second United States Colored Cavalry. Many officers of the regiment were appointed to command the First United States Colored Cavalry Regiment.

Samuel C. Pierce, who was the last Lieutenant-Colonel of the regiment was several times captured by the enemy, but on each occasion effected his escape.

FOURTH CAVALRY.—The regiment was first commanded by Col. Christian Dickel, who was succeeded in 1862, by Col. Lewis P. di Cesnola. The Fourth served with credit under Fremont, Rosecrans, Sigel, Pope, Stoneman, etc., as the many flattering encomiums bestowed on it by their commanders testify. It went to the war with seven hundred men, and had added to it at various times about one thousand recruits, and numbered scarcely one hundred for active duty when discharged. The regiment opened the battle of Cross Keys, Va., and rendered itself conspicuous by its determined resistance to several charges made by the rebel forces—a resistance which was successful in saving Schirmer's battery from capture, besides inflicting severe chastisement on the enemy, and killing the Rebel General Ashby. Coöperating with the Second Michigan Cavalry, it made the only cavalry charge during the second battle of Bull Run, under the direction of Gen. John Buford. This was successful in checking the enemy's advance and saving many thousands from being captured. The Fourth participated in thirty-four battles and skirmishes, and its meritorious conduct in all of these was productive of many flattering tributes from the Generals under whom it served. Col. di Cesnola was captured and exchanged for Colonel Brown, of the Fifty-ninth Georgia Regiment. At the battle of Aldie, so gallant was the conduct of Colonel di Cesnola, that General Kilpatrick took off his sabre and presented it to the Colonel. At the third charge which the Colonel led in that battle, his horse was shot from under him, and he was captured. He is now manager of the Museum of Arts and Sciences in New York City.

FIFTH CAVALRY. —"First Ira Harris Guard." The regiment was raised by Col. Othneil de Forrest, immediately after the first battle of Bull Run, and went to the war nearly 1200 strong. It served under Custer and many others—all of whom made themselves remarkable as cavalry leaders in the history of the country. The first campaign of the regiment was down the Shenandoah Valley, after the defeat of Stonewall Jackson at Winchester, and at Harrisburg a portion of the regiment (Companies F, J, and E) charged upon Ashby's rebel cavalry and defeated them. This was the first cavalry charge of the war where sabres were used. When General

17

Banks fell back from Harrisburg, it brought up the rear of his army, and at Strasburg, when Jackson, coming through Front Royal, drove that General through the Valley, it was cut off, yet saved all his wagon train and Hampton's battery, and escorted them in safety into Maryland, by a circuitous march through the mountains. Afterwards, under General Hatch, in company with two other regiments, it captured Culpepper. At Orange Court House it distinguished itself, taking the place, after defeating the Seventh Virginia cavalry, and capturing forty-seven men and officers, including the commanding officer, Major Marshall. At Kelly's Ford it drove a large body of rebels from the woods, and then held the bridge all day against the attack of a part of Jackson's infantry. Afterwards it was selected by General Pope as his body-guard, and followed him to Bull Run. The regiment participated in the battles of Antietam, Gettysburg, Brandy Station, Wilderness, Spottsylvania, Petersburg, Winchester, Cedar Creek, besides forty-two lesser battles and 120 skirmishes. During General Kilpatrick's raid towards Richmond, when Col. Ulric Dahlgren was captured, Lieut. Theodore A. Boice, with twelve men, cut the track and destroyed the telegraph at Guinea Station. Lieut. Henry A. D. Merritt was also one of the heroes of that famous expedition, in which he was captured and suffered the hardships of a Rebel prison. The regiment returned home under command of Col. Amos H. White, with only 550 men out of 2500 that composed its original strength or afterwards joined it as recruits.

SIXTH CAVALRY.—" Second Ira Harris Guard."—The regiment left for the war in December, 1861, and went first to York, Pennsylvania, where it passed the winter in barracks, dismounted. In the spring of 1862, they were mounted, and one battalion sent to the Peninsula, the remainder of the regiment being first permanently employed in guarding Garnett's Ford. On General Burnside's evacuation of Fredericksburg, the Sixth formed part of his rear guard, which under their Colonel, Thomas C. Devin, ably performed the most arduous duty, for which Colonel Devin received merited acknowledgments from General Burnside. The regiment next took an active part in the Maryland campaign, being the first Union regiment to enter Frederick City, and doing good service at South Mountain and Antietam—the latter battle being opened by a squadron from the Sixth. For a brilliant affair at Levettsville the regiment was thanked in a special order from General Burnside. On the 30th of April, 1863, a spirited charge by 200 men upon the whole of Fitz Hugh Lee's brigade was a fit and stirring event for the opening of the great battle of Chancellorsville. It was in this charge that the regiment lost its commanding officer, Lieut-Col. Duncan McVicar. General Pleasanton said: "The heroism of the Sixth New York Cavalry in cutting its way to our line through treble the force of the enemy's cavalry, created the greatest admiration." At Beverly Ford the regiment took an active part. Colonel Devin commanding the division. At Aldie, Upperville, Middleburg, Gettysburg, Williamsport, Boonsboro, etc., the regiment did its full share of fighting. On the withdrawal of the Army of the Potomac from the Rapidan, October, 1863, the brigade to which the Sixth belonged acted as rear guard and performed arduous and important service. In 1865, Colonel Devin was promoted to Brigadier-General, and the regiment returned home under command of Col. Charles L. Fitzhugh, who, for meritorious services, was also promoted to Brevet Brigadier-General. It was affirmed in 1864 that the regiment had not lost a man by "gobbling" for over a year, having been on outpost duty during the whole time, while their loss in action was very small for the amount of duty performed, the Colonel knowing how to take the men into action, and how to bring them out.

In recognition of the gallantry of the regiment at the battle of Five Forks, where the men of the Sixth were the first to enter the Southern fortifications, General Sheridan presented the regiment with a flag, emblazoned with the words "Five Forks." At Cedar Creek the regiment led the charge over the bridge, and assisted in the capture of twenty-two field pieces. Out of the 1000 men who originally enlisted, but 200 answered to the roll-call at the final disbandment. Colonel Devin died in April, 1878.

SEVENTH CAVALRY. — "First Battalion Mounted Rifles." This regiment had the honor of first entering the enemy's works at Norfolk, in 1862. Within the short space of three weeks succeeding the occupation of Norfolk, the regiment captured Suffolk, and under command of Col. Charles C. Dodge (son of the Hon. William E. Dodge, of New York), explored the country for twenty miles around Norfolk, travelling 164 miles in four days—a march said to rival that of Havelock's in India. In the attack on Charles City Cross Road, Sergeant Wood, a brave and faithful officer, was mortally wounded. In October, 1864, Lieut. William W. Disosway, a son of Mr. Cornelius R. Disosway, a well-known lawyer of New York, was shot dead by a man named Patrick Boyle, one of the guard, Lieutenant Disosway, at the time, being ProvostM-arshal at Williamsburg. Boyle was tried by court-martial and sentenced to be hanged. The sentence was approved by General Butler, but was suspended by President Lincoln. Boyle, pending the suspension, escaped to the Rebels from Fort Magruder, and conveyed to them intelligence of the intended advance upon Richmond, thus causing the failure of that well planned expedition. At the battle of Darbytown Road, October 7, 1864, the regiment did bravely and suffered severely. Among the officers who especially distinguished themselves was Capt. John C. Oberteuffer, who was the hero of many an act of gallantry, and finally laid down his life in the engagement near Jones' Creek, Va., on the 21st of December, 1864.— Among the officers of the regiment was Lieut. Courtenay H. James —a nephew of the great English novelist.

EIGHTH CAVALRY.—This regiment was first commanded by Col. Samuel J. Crooks, who was succeeded by Col. Benjamin F. Davis, a splendid soldier, killed in action at Beverly Ford, June 9, 1863. It was in this engagement that the regiment suffered terribly, losing a large number of valuable officers besides Colonel Davis. A portion of the regiment in 1864 were at home on furlough, having re-enlisted. The men were from the vicinity of Rochester, and had achieved a reputation second to that of no regiment in Buford's old command. The Confederate General, John G. Walker, said: "A very meritorious and important movement was made by Colonel Davis of the Eighth New York Cavalry, at the time of the capture of Harper's Ferry, of which no mention has been made in either the Federal or Confederate official reports."

NINTH CAVALRY.—The regiment was raised mostly in Chautauqua County, except three fine companies from Wyoming, at a time when it was supposed the county had contributed all that could be mustered within its limits. But by the timely aid of the indefatigable Adjutant-General Thomas Hillhouse, seconded by Gen. Chester A. Arthur, the regiment was speedily raised and equipped for the field. The Colonel of the regiment was John Beardsley, a graduate of West Point, who had seen service in Florida and Mexico. Maj. George S. Nichols, who became Colonel of the regiment in 1865, was a member of the State Senate, and brought high abilities to bear upon his duties. The officers generally were well qualified for their positions, and the regiment was fortunate in the selection of them. Among the brilliant operations of the regiment will be remembered the reconnoissance in December, 1862, under General Stahl, by whose direction Maj. Charles McL. Knox, at the head of 200 men, charged through the principal streets of Berryville, Va., driving a superior force before them. The regiment next attacked the

Seventh Virginia Cavalry and routed them. Major Knox, who was discharged in 1864, for physical disability, was one of the most active and zealous cavalry officers in the service. Capt. Timothy Hanley, another brave and skilful officer, made a brilliant dash into Warrenton, at the head of his squadron and paid off an old score he had against the rebels. In March, 1865, Captain Hanley was promoted to Lieutenant-Colonel of the regiment. The Eighth claims the honor of having opened the battle of Gettysburg, and in the succeeding engagements at Hagerstown and Williamsport, July 6 and 7, 1863, and at Culpepper, in September, 1863, the regiment covered itself with glory. During the pursuit of Early, after the battle of Winchester, Colonel Nichols and the regiment rendered invaluable service. Of individual acts of gallantry, one of the most remarkable, perhaps, was made by Maj. William B. Martin. In front of General Buford's line were two belts of timber, extending from the main forest, the whole of which was occupied by the enemy in force, the line of skirmishers extending from one point to the other. Major Martin was ordered to sweep in the line of skirmishers. He did so by making one of the most brilliant dashes of the war. First sending a detachment commanded by Captain Hanley to clear one piece of the woods of the enemy's carbines, Major Martin with three companions dashed across the open space in the rear of the skirmishers, and drove the enemy out. In this engagement Capts. Campbell Dickson, and Conway W Ayres (who was killed in 1864), and Lieut. James B. Burrows (killed in 1864) acquitted themselves with great distinction. Among the brave men of this regiment may also be mentioned Privates Jeremiah Parke and George Reynolds, to whom were awarded medals of honor by the Secretary of War.

TENTH CAVALRY.—The regiment went to the war under command of Col. John C. Lemmon. It participated in twenty great engagements and in innumerable raids and skirmishes. In the great cavalry expedition under General Stoneman (Chancellorsville campaign) it took a prominent and honorable part. At Brandy Station the regiment fought with the greatest gallantry and repulsed the enemy in repeated charges, although losing heavily themselves. A short time before his death, Capt. Aaron T. Bliss said that in the action at Stoney Creek which occurred June 28, 1864, two days before his death, that his squadron consisted of sixty-eight men, and all but eight were killed or wounded before surrendering. Lieut.-Col. William Irvine was captured during the war and suffered terribly in the Rebel prisons; upon his return home he was appointed

Assistant Commissioner of Exchange. Lieutenant-Colonel Irvine was formerly a member of Congress from the Steuben district. Surg. Roger W Pease was promoted to Medical Director of the Cavalry Corps of the Army of the Potomac. Among the gallant men of the Tenth Cavalry, Charles Beach was conspicuous by his bravery. At the battle near Upperville, he had three horses shot under him, but escaped uninjured.

ELEVENTH CAVALRY—"Scott's 900." The regiment went to the war under command of Col. James B. Swain, with L. P. di Cesnola as Lieutenant-Colonel. Colonel Swain was discharged in 1864, and was succeeded by Col. John P Sherburne.—At the time of the Rebel cavalry raid into Poolsville, in April, 1863, Lieut. William Smith was supposed to have been captured, but was probably killed, as he has never since been heard of.—In a desperate fight at Fairfax Court House, June 27, 1863, a squadron, under command of Maj. S. Pierre Remington, encountered the Sixth Virginia Cavalry, and dashed at them with sabres. The Major made two charges and drove the enemy for three miles to a wood, and there encountered a superior force that checked him with the fire of carbines. The fight from beginning to end was fierce. Its termination, from the overwhelming disparity of numbers, was disastrous. Major Remington after having had his horse shot twice, cut his way out and made his escape with eighteen men. Capt. George A. Dagwell and Lieut. Augustus B. Hazleton were reported killed, but were fortunately spared and served with the regiment until its term of service expired. Lieut. D. von Weltzien was one of those captured, while acquitting himself heroically. Lieut. Col. di Cesnola resigned in June, 1862, and became Colonel of the 4th Cavalry.

TWELFTH CAVALRY.—The regiment went to the war in 1863, under command of Col. James W Savage. It participated in General Foster's raid to Tarboro, in July, 1863, where Capt. Cyrus Church was killed. It took part in resisting the Rebel attack on Newbern, and was engaged in the capture of Plymouth, where two companies of the regiment were captured, most of whom perished at Andersonville. Among those who survived was Lieut. Alonzo Cooper, a very gallant soldier, who has lately written a book on "In and Out of Rebel Prisons." The Twelfth was also engaged in the second attack on Newbern, and in numerous raids and skirmishes throughout the State. In March, 1865, the regiment led the advance of Schofield's column, which was moving to join General Sherman, and gained much credit for its fighting during the three days battles near Kinston, and subsequent skirmishes between that place and Goldsboro. Upon joining General Sherman the regiment was put into General Kilpatrick's division, and sent to guard the country about Tar River, where it was stationed until its return home in July, 1865. Among the officers of the regiment who were always conspicuous for gallantry and the welfare of their men, were Capt. John S Ellison, Capt. James L. Graham, Capt. Elam A. Mahon, Capt. J. W Van Valkenberg, Capt. John S. Loud, Maj. Rodney M. Taylor, Maj. Rowland R. West, Maj Floyd Clarkson, and Maj. J. Ward Gasper. Major Clarkson is now Commander of Post Lafayette, G. A. R.

THIRTEENTH CAVALRY.—First Seymour Light Cavalry It was first commanded by Col. Henry S. Gansevoort, who was soon promoted to Brevet Brigadier-General. The regiment first distinguished itself by the destruction of the Rebel pontoon bridges and train at Falling Waters,—a very daring exploit. It was in the brigade commanded by Col. C. R. Lowell; 400 of the men were from Rochester. The guerilla Mosby is said to have been wounded by Corporal Kane, of Company F.

FOURTEENTH CAVALRY.—This was a New York City regiment, and went to the war under command of Col. Thaddeus P Mott, a splendid officer, who had greatly distinguished himself as captain in the Third New York Independent Battery. The regiment participated with the Thirteenth Regiment in the destruction of the Rebel pontoon bridges and train at Falling Waters. The regiment took part in subduing the riot in New York, July, 1863, and General Wool complimented Colonel Mott and the officers for their gallant and efficient services. The Fourteenth next went to Louisiana, and acquitted itself gallantly in many engagements. Capt. John F. Porter was one of those brave men who endured the torments of a Southern prison. Colonel Mott was honorably discharged in 1864, and Abram Bassford was appointed his successor. From the long list of honored men who served as commissioned officers of the Fourteenth, the following names will be familiar to the surviving members— Lieut-Col. John W. Cropsey, Maj. John Ennis, Maj. James A. Duffy, Capt. Raymond H. Perry, Capt. W C. H. Andres, Capt. Charles E. Morton, Capt. Adolph Schmidt, and Lieut. Aaron Low, who was promoted to Captain in the Eighteenth Cavalry.

FIFTEENTH CAVALRY.—Nine companies of the regiment were from Syracuse. It was commanded by Col. Robert M. Richardson. The only commissioned officer killed in action was the brave Lieut.-

Col. Augustus I. Root, who was killed in April, 1865. The saltpetre works near Franklin, West Virginia, were destroyed by a scout under command of Lieutenant-Colonel Root. Colonel Richardson resigned in January, 1865, and the regiment returned home under command of Col. John J. Coppinger. Colonel Coppinger is a relative of the Hon. James G. Blaine. A feature of the regiment was that each company used the same kind and color of horses. The evolutions of Company C, under command of Cap. George M. Ellicott and Lieut. Hezekiah B. Ranny, could not be surpassed.

SIXTEENTH CAVALRY.—"Sprague's Light Cavalry." The regiment was organized at Plattsburg, and was first commanded by Col. H. M. Lazelle, who resigned in 1864, and was succeeded by Col. Nelson B. Sweitzer, who was in 1865 promoted to Brevet Brigadier-General. The regiment took a creditable part in putting down the draft riots in New York, in July, 1863, and was complimented by General Wool. In 1864, it participated in a severe engagement at Fairfax Station, Virginia, where the gallant Capt. James H. Fleming (the only commissioned officer lost during the war) was killed. In 1865 the regiment was consolidated with the Thirteenth New York Cavalry, and the consolidated force was known as the Third Provisional Cavalry Regiment.

SEVENTEENTH CAVALRY.—The regiment was never fully organized.

EIGHTEENTH CAVALRY.—"Corning Light Cavalry." The Eighteenth did not leave for the war until 1864. While in process of organization it rendered efficient service in quelling the riot in New York City. Most of the officers hailed from that City. They were Col. James J. Byrne, Lieut.-Col. John Tracey, Jr., Majs. Edward Byrne and John Ennis. Colonel Byrne had proved himself to be a gallant soldier while on the Staff of General Davidson during a raid from Baton Rouge to Pascagoula. At the battle of Sabine Cross Roads a squadron under command of Capt. William Davis had a warm position, fought bravely and lost heavily. Captain Davis proved himself a hero in every sense of the word.

NINETEENTH CAVALRY.—"First New York Dragoons." The Nineteenth was first commanded by Col. Alfred Gibbs, who was promoted in 1864 to Brigadier-General. His successor was Col. Thomas J. Thorp, who was also promoted to Brigadier-General in 1865. The regiment was organized at Portage, as the 130th New York Infantry. See Record of the 130th Infantry.

TWENTIETH CAVALRY.—"McClellan Cavalry." Col. Newton B. Lord, who commanded the Thirty-fifth New York Infantry in nine battles, was authorized by Governor Seymour to raise this regiment, which was largely made up from the Twenty-third, Twenty-fourth and Thirty-fifth Regiments. It went to the war 1,200 strong; the county of Jefferson, mainly, with a few adjoining counties assisting, had the honor of furnishing most of the men. Some six hundred were veterans. The Twentieth served in General Kautz's division with the Army of the James, during the siege of Richmond. It was afterwards merged into General McKenzie's independent brigade, and entered Lynchburg soon after the surrender of General Lee. Having been engaged in siege operations, the regiment has not so lengthy a record as those continuing with Sheridan through his valley campaigns.

TWENTY-FIRST CAVALRY.—The Twenty-first was commanded by Col. Wm. B. Tibbets, who was promoted to Brevet Brigadier-General in 1864. It was a Troy regiment, and was for a long time stationed in the defences of Washington. The regiment was engaged in several severe actions, and lost three commissioned officers during the war. Lieut.-Col. Charles Fitz Simons was wounded in the battle of Ashby's Gap. Capt. Henry E. Snow raised Company A, and was the first Captain appointed, and he was also the last field officer in command of the regiment, and possibly the last officer in the volunteer service of the State.

TWENTY-SECOND CAVALRY.—The first Colonel of the regiment was Samuel J. Crooks, who resigned in March, 1865, and was succeeded by Col. Horatio B. Reed. The regiment acquitted itself with distinction in the engagements at Kerneysville, White Oak Swamp, Va., and at Dinwiddie Court House.

TWENTY-THIRD CAVALRY.—This was known as "Mix's Battalion," composed of two companies.

TWENTY-FOURTH CAVALRY —Was organized at Auburn, and was commanded by Col. Walter C. Newberry, who was promoted for gallant conduct to Brevet Brigadier-General in 1865. In 1865 the regiment was consolidated with the Tenth New York Cavalry, and the consolidated force was known as the First Provisional Cavalry. The regiment took part in the following battles—Wilderness, Spottsylvania, Guinea Station, North Anna, Tolopotomoy, Bethesda Church, Coal Harbor, Petersburg. Cemetery Hill, Weldon Railroad, Ream's Station, Peebles' Farm, Vaughan Road, and Bellefield.

TWENTY-FIFTH CAVALRY.—" Sickles' Cavalry." The regiment never had any Colonel, but was commanded by Lieut.-Col. Aaron Seeley. Colonel Seeley was a very popular officer, and was for some time in command of a brigade. He was wounded at Woodstock. At the battle of Nineveh the regiment behaved splendidly. It formed part of Sheridan's famous cavalry force, and was with that gallant commander nearly all their term of service. It took part in fourteen great engagements and numerous skirmishes. The only commissioned officer killed in action was Lieut. Charles N. Howard.

TWENTY-SIXTH CAVALRY.—" First Frontier Cavalry." This regiment was organized at the very close of the war and was commanded by Col. Burr Porter.

ARTILLERY REGIMENTS AND BATTERIES.

HEAVY ARTILLERY.

SECOND HEAVY ARTILLERY. —(There was no First Regiment.) The regiment was organized at Utica, and was first commanded by Col. Milton Cogswell, formerly Colonel of the Forty-second "Tammany Regiment," who acquitted himself with great distinction in the engagement at Ball's Bluff, in 1861. Colonel Cogswell remained with the regiment until April, 1863, when he resigned and Joseph N. G. Whistler succeeded to the command. The regiment fought bravely at Bull Run, Spottsylvania, North Anna, Toloptomoy, Coal Harbor, Petersburg, Strawberry Plains, Deep Bottom and Ream's Station. It was entirely raised in Oneida County; thirty-four Indians of the Oneida tribe served in the regiment. Governor Morgan presented it with an elegant flag. Early in the war the regiment garrisoned Forts Ward, Worth and Blenker—the advanced line of defences on the Virginia side of the Potomac. At the time of the Rebel raid upon Manassas, August 29, 1862, it was the means of saving the remainder of General Taylor's New Jersey Brigade, by drawing the Rebel attention to them, holding them in check while the New Jersey troops made good their retreat. The regiment also covered the retreat of the Twelfth Pennsylvania Cavalry. Among the privates of the regiment whose bravery attracted the attention of their superiors were John J. Williamson, Charles A. Jones, George W. Lacy, and Edward Hanlon, who were promoted to Second Lieutenants, and Thomas Davis, who was awarded a medal of honor by the Secretary of War.

FOURTH HEAVY ARTILLERY.—No regiment had a more extensive reputation in the Army of the Potomac than the Fourth Heavy Artillery. Their duties throughout were numerous and difficult, there being no department or branch of service connected with the army but what the Fourth were duly represented. Their record is stainless, and their flag unfurled to the breeze the name of every engagement from the Wilderness to the Appomattox Court House. The regiment has its full share of noble names on the roll of our illustrious dead. After the surrender of Lee the regiment left the Second Corps and garrisoned nine forts, constituting the Third Battery of De Russey's division. Gen. Gustavus A. De Russey was the second Colonel of the regiment. The first was Col. Thomas D. Doubleday, who was discharged in March, 1863. Colonel De Russey was Colonel for only two months, when he was promoted to Brigadier-General, and was succeeded by Col. John C. Tidball, of the Second United States Artillery, another accomplished officer, who, for meritorious services, was promoted in 1865 to Brevet Brigadier-General.

Capt. William Arthur, a brother of the late President Arthur, was wounded at Coal Harbor. In 1863, a young Lieutenant of the Tenth Tennessee Regiment, came into the lines of the 4th, and joined Captain Arthur's company. His name was Low William Roscoe. Having had some difficulty with Captain Arthur, he took advantage of an opportunity unknown to others and shot him. The wound was not fatal. Roscoe was himself mortally wounded in front of Petersburg, and while on his death-bed, acknowledged having shot Arthur.

FIFTH HEAVY ARTILLERY.—This was a Brooklyn Regiment, although New York City and Lewis County furnished a large number of men. It was commanded by Col. Samuel Graham, a well-known citizen of Brooklyn, who held several public positions of prominence. It was the largest artillery regiment from the State, mustering 1800 officers and men, most of the officers having served a three months' campaign in the Fourteenth and Seventeenth Regiments. For the first two months the regiment was employed in manning the different fortifications in New York harbor, after which it was for two months in the defences of Fort Marshall, Baltimore. While lying at Baltimore, two companies were detached from the regiment, and under command of Maj. Henry B. McIlvaine, were sent to Harper's Ferry, and stationed on Maryland and Bolivar Heights. Here they were taken prisoners at the time of "Stonewall" Jackson's capture of Harper's Ferry. In the beginning of the year 1863, the regiment was sent to Harper's Ferry, but had only been there a short time when it was ordered back to Baltimore, where it was usefully employed for nearly a year. In April, 1864, it was again sent to Harper's Ferry, where it was engaged in artillery and infantry service. In this way it was occupied in guarding Maryland Heights, and assisted in building Forts Duncan and Sullivan—the companies of infantry doing exceedingly good service, which met with a merited recognition from commanding officers. In this neighborhood, the regiment remained until the 4th of July, on which day it was engaged with a heavy force of Early's men, who, 40,000 strong, made an attack on Harper's Ferry. On this occasion the regiment distinguished itself, but suffered a severe loss in killed and wounded. In the latter part of July, four companies—G, H, E, and F, were detached from the Second Battalion, and under command of Maj. Caspar Urban, joined the army of General Sheridan, and took part in all the great battles of the Valley. At the battles of Perryville, Winchester and Cedar Creek, these companies won distinction, but they suffered severely, for of the 700 men who composed the command of Major Urban, only 125 passed unharmed through the campaign. The other portion of the regiment, under command of Colonel Graham, were employed during this time at Pleasant Valley, pursuing guerillas, etc. On the 19th of November, 1863, Governor Seymour presented the regiment with a handsome silk regimental standard. In presenting the banner Governor Seymour said: "This day, when I took part in the celebration that was to consecrate yonder battle-field (Gettysburg), when I felt as an American citizen proud of my own country, and proud of the gallant services of her citizens, in every State, nevertheless my eye did involuntarily wander to that field where lies the glorious dead of our good and great State, and when I returned, to see marching before me your manly and sturdy columns, not knowing you belonged to New York, my heart did quicken and my pulse tingle to learn that you were acting under commissions issued by myself. Sergeant, I place these colors in your hands in the firm confidence that they will be borne through every field of triumph, of toil and of danger, in a way that will do honor to yourselves, to the great State which you represent, and the still greater country to which we all belong." On the 4th of March, 1864, the regiment's term of service expired and many of the men and officers returned home. But the regiment had been so largely reinforced during its stay at Baltimore, that it was still a strong organization, so strong indeed as to be counted a brigade. The regiment, though less distinguished than some others for the brilliancy of its achievements, rendered good service, and the efforts of its rank and file entitled them to the grateful remembrance of their fellow citizens. Colonel Graham died in May, 1884. Capt. Albert L. Munson was among the faithful and gallant officers of the regiment, and has an honorable record.

SIXTH HEAVY ARTILLERY.—This regiment was organized as the 135th New York Volunteer Infantry. On the 3d of October, 1862, it was changed to the Sixth Artillery, and joined the Army of the Potomac, participating in battles with the Second, Third, Fifth, and Sixth Corps of that army. On August 13, 1864, it was ordered to

Washington, D. C., for garrison duty, at which place it remained five weeks (this being the only garrison duty it ever did), when it was ordered to the army of the Shenandoah, General Sheridan commanding. It was here that it lost its beloved Colonel, J. Howard Kitching, who had been promoted to Brevet Brigadier-General. The regiment was commanded first by Col. William H. Morris, a splendid officer and charming gentleman, who in April, 1863, was promoted to Brigadier-General. He was succeeded by Colonel Kitching. After the latter's death, Col. George C. Kibbe was in command until June, 1865, when Stephen Baker became its last Colonel. When the regiment was mustered in (September 2, 1862), it numbered 1100 men. It returned home after three years hard service with 698 men, of which there were only about 250 of the original organization, the balance being one year men, who joined in 1864. Lieut. Charles P. Miller—a gallant soldier, died on the 19th of August, 1887, of pneumonia, at New London, and within one hour his wife died of the same disease. Lieut. Amos Cross was wounded, and has been for years an inmate of a Rhode Island Insane Asylum.

SEVENTH HEAVY ARTILLERY.—The regiment was organized at Albany in August, 1862, by Col. Lewis O. Morris. It was first known as the 113th Infantry, but was changed to the Seventh Heavy Artillery. It was stationed around Washington, until May, 1864, when it was assigned to the Second Army Corps. Its members participated in all the engagements from Spottsylvania to Petersburg, especially distinguishing themselves at Coal Harbor, where they were the first to enter the Rebel works and had the honor of capturing the Rebel colors. It was in this engagement that the State as well as the regiment was called to mourn the loss of Colonel Morris, a splendid soldier, and a member of one of the oldest families in the State. The regiment returned home with 316 men, out of about 1800 whose names had been enrolled, 300 having been discharged two months before. The remainder had been either killed or wounded. Capt. John S. McEwan is now Assistant Adjutant-General of the State.

EIGHTH HEAVY ARTILLERY.—Ten companies of this regiment were organized at Lockport, in August, 1862, as the 129th Infantry. It was changed in December, 1862, to the Eighth Heavy Artillery. The regiment was for a long time in Baltimore, garrisoning Forts Federal Hill, McHenry and Marshall. In May, 1864, it left Baltimore to join the Second Army Corps. On the 19th of May it fought its first battle at Spottsylvania, charging and driving the Rebels three successive times. At the battle of Coal Harbor, June 3, 1864, as the regiment was advancing across an open space, a masked battery opened upon it a withering fire. Col. Peter A. Porter led one charge of his regiment against the enemy in person and was killed within a few yards of the Rebel works. In connection with the fall of Colonel Porter, the following extract from his letter of 1863, declining the Republican nomination for Secretary of State, will be read with increased interest: "I left home," said Colonel Porter, "in command of a regiment composed mainly of the sons of friends and neighbors, in a measure committed to my care. I can hardly ask for my discharge, while theirs cannot be granted, and I have a strong desire, if alive, to carry back those whom the chances of time and war shall permit to be 'present,' and to 'account' in person for all." Colonel Porter was a son of the late P. R. Porter, of Niagara Falls, a conspicuous figure upon the frontier during the last war with Great Britain. In the battle of Coal Harbor the regiment lost twelve commissioned officers and two-thirds of its rank and file. Besides the battle of Coal Harbor, the regiment participated in nine great engagements, losing in all nineteen commissioned officers—a greater loss than was sustained by any other regiment from the State during the war. Among the brave men of the Eighth whose gallant services are worthy of special remembrance were Maj. Henry M. Starr, Maj. Samuel D. Ludden, Maj. James Low, Jr., and Maj. Erastus M. Spaulding, Lieut. Ashley P. Hawkins, Lieut. Edwin R. Loomis, Lieut. W W Stearns and Lieut. Marcus H. Chapelle; the latter lost an arm at Coal Harbor and is now in the New York Custom House. The Century Club of New York City presented medals to several of the privates for gallantry in battle, in rescuing the body of Colonel Porter from the field.

NINTH HEAVY ARTILLERY.—The Ninth New York Heavy Artillery was raised in Cayuga and Wayne counties, as the 138th Infantry, and went to Washington, 1,000 strong, under command of Col. Joseph Welling, of Lyons, N. Y.; William H. Seward, Jr., Lieutenant-Colonel; and Edwin P Taft, Major. The regiment was stationed in forts, in the defences of Washington, and two companies added, M and L. The latter was a new company recruited for the regiment, the former being a battery of Light Artillery, organized, I believe, in Western New York. The regiment was recruited to about 2,000 men, and was ordered to the Army of the Potomac, Sixth Corps, in the spring of 1864. Colonel Welling resigned and left the regiment after landing at Belle Plain, Va.; Lieutenant-Colonel Seward then took command. The first battle in which the regiment took part was at Coal Harbor, losing many officers and about 300 men. Part of the regiment was sent to Baltimore and were severely handled in the Monocacy fight; Major Taft lost a leg and was taken prisoner; Colonel Seward's horse was shot and fell upon his rider, breaking his ankle, and, of course, giving him a severe shock, but standing on his knees he cheered his men, and did much toward holding them against the superior numbers of the enemy, who were pressing from all sides. The regiment was afterwards commanded by Col. James W. Snyder (promoted from Major) and did good work in the Valley under Sheridan, losing heavily in officers and men. The regiment lay in works around Petersburg until the final assault, and were some of the first troops over the Rebel breastworks.

TENTH HEAVY ARTILLERY.—This regiment was formerly known as the First, Second and Fourth battalions, Black River Artillery. It was commanded by Col. Alexander Piper. It was raised principally in Jefferson County, and was originally 1,800 strong. They were for a long time in the defences of Washington, then with the Army of the Potomac in the battles before Petersburg, next with Sheridan at Cedar Creek, then back to the Army of the Potomac until the evacution of Richmond.

Eleventh and Twelfth Heavy Artillery Regiments were never fully organized.

THIRTEENTH HEAVY ARTILLERY.—The regiment was organized in New York City, and was commanded by Col. William A. Howard, formerly Colonel of the First Regiment (Marine) Light Artillery. Lieut. Johnston Livingston De Peyster raised the first flag over Richmond, when the city surrendered in 1865. The Third Battalion of the regiment under command of Maj. Robert W McLaughlin, consisting of Company I, Capt. Patrick A. O'Malley; Company K, Capt. Stewart J. Donnelly; Company L, Amya L. Fitch, and Company M, Capt. Edward C. Parkinson, altogether numbering 500 men, formed the celebrated Naval Brigade, Army of the James. This battalion consisted of sailors enlisted for service on the army light-draft iron-clad gunboats, which were built by Norman Wiard, to penetrate otherwise inaccessible places and meet the enemy most unexpectedly.

FOURTEENTH HEAVY ARTILLERY.—The regiment was raised in the neighborhood of Rochester, and was commanded by Col. Elisha G. Marshall, who in 1865 was promoted to Brevet Brigadier-General. The regiment participated bravely at Spottsylvania, and at Petersburg.

At Coal Harbor, the regiment again sustained fearful losses. Lieut. John H. Thompson was one of those captured, and suffered the torments of Rebel captivity until death put an end to his sufferings. Among the brave men of the regiment who escaped death and were especially esteemed by Company G, was Capt. Wm. A. Treadwell, to whom a sword was presented by his associates as a token of esteem for his soldierlike qualities. Private Hough of Company M, served the last watch on the morning of the day of the attack on Fort Steadman. On the same day an attack was made on Fort Haskell, and the bravery of Capt. Charles H. Houghton made him the hero of that affair. Mr. George L. Kirmer, in his article on "The Tragedy of the Crater," says: "The Fourteenth New York Heavy Artillery. serving as infantry, which led the assault, had but little over 300 duty men present. It had entered the campaign of the Wilderness 1,800 strong. The morning of the explosion the Colonel led the brigade and there was no other field officer present, the last Major having been killed in the charge of June. Only two of the Captains remained."

FIFTEENTH HEAVY ARTILLERY.—This was a New York City regiment, and was commanded by Colonel Louis Schirmer. It was a German regiment, and did its full share of fighting at the Wilderness. Spottsylvania, North Anna, Tolopotamoy, Bethesda Church, Petersburg, Chapel House and Hatcher's Run, and was conspicuous by its steadiness and bravery.

SIXTEENTH HEAVY ARTILLERY.—The Sixteenth was raised by Col. Joseph J. Morrison, and was the largest regiment in the United States or any other service. Colonel Morrison had previously distinguished himself as Captain of a light battery (Third Artillery), well known in North Carolina both by Union and Rebel troops as Morrison's battery. The Sixteenth participated in the siege of Petersburg, the many battles before Richmond, and the subjugation of Fort Fisher. In October, 1864, the regiment claimed the honor of having formed in line of battle closer to Richmond than any other regiment in the service had thus far done. The soldiers of the Sixteenth were often placed in positions of great hardship and danger of which no mention has been made in the official reports.

The Utica *Herald* said of General Butler's Dutch Gap Canal and of the assistance rendered by a portion of the Sixteenth:

"In the James River, about five miles below Richmond, was the peninsula known as Farrar's Island, in front of which the Confederates, who were making their final efforts for the lost cause, had totally obstructed the river with sunken ships and torpedoes. Above the Peninsula were the Howlett house batteries, which aided the great obstructions in preventing the national vessels from gaining a nearer approach to the Confederate works. With a view of outflanking the obstructions and the batteries, Gen. B. F. Butler ordered a cut to be made through the l ise of the peninsula. The position was exposed to the continuous fir of the Southerners, but when volunteers were called for from the Sixteenth New York Heavy Artillery to do the first turn of the work, eighty-seven men— four sergeants, seven corporals and seventy-six privates—promptly responded. They were to work seven and a half hours each day and were to receive eight cents for each hour's work. The detachment was put under the command of Capt. Thomas F. Sheppard, a well-known citizen of Penn Yan, and First Lieut. James M. Latimore, of this city, who had charge of the roll.

The construction was commenced August 10, not August 15, as it has been written, and the detachment worked until August 20, when other volunteers took its place. During the time several of the men were wounded and killed. They protected themselves by throwing up the dirt from the canal as far as possible, and lived in "gopher holes" along the river bank. The work was arduous and the pay small, but they performed their task with enthusiasm in the hope of the near overthrow of their enemies. Their zeal was poorly rewarded. Uncle Sam is supposed to be a good paymaster, but these eighty-seven men, through some mistake or oversight, never received pay for their extra labor.

While Captain Sheppard's detachment was at work upon the constructions one day, General Grant, entirely unattended, came over and stood upon the embankment. He talked with Lieutenant Latimore about the work and examined his roll of the men. While doing this a shell from Howlett's battery dropped into the ground a short distance behind him, but fortunately failed to explode. The great General by his words at the time showed his full appreciation of the voluntary duty of the men.

LIGHT ARTILLERY.

FIRST LIGHT ARTILLERY (Marine).—This regiment performed useful service under command of Col. Wm. A. Howard, late of the Revenue Service. It was organized on the principle of the Royal Marine Artillery. It was entirely the work of Colonel Howard, having been organized, recruited and drilled by him. The regiment served in gunboats, and worked their artillery on shore, or on board, as might be required, throwing the guns overboard and hauling them to the land, or the reverse when wanted. It was in the department of North Carolina, where it blockaded the ports for a long time, besides participating in several battles under General Burnside. The headquarters of Colonel Howard were at Newbern, but the regiment was at Roanoke Island, of which Colonel Howard was Governor. It was disbanded in March, 1863, and Colonel Howard was appointed Colonel of the Thirteenth Heavy Artillery.

FIRST LIGHT ARTILLERY.—The regiment was first commanded by Col. Guilford D. Bailey, who was killed at Fair Oaks on the 31st of May, 1862. General Casey, in his Report of that battle, says: "I cannot forbear mention of the severe misfortune sustained by the division and the service in the loss of Colonel Bailey, my Chief of Artillery, who fell in the attempt to spike the pieces in my redoubt, which were necessarily abandoned." Battery H had its Captain, Joseph Spratt (who was in 1863, promoted to Lieutenant-Colonel of the Tenth New York Artillery), and Lieut. John H. Howell, and many privates wounded. At the commencement of the engagement, Batteries A and H, commanded by Lieut. George P. Hart (later in the war Major of the First U. S. Colored Regiment, of the District of Columbia), and Captain Spratt respectively, did great execution, till the enemy was right upon them, when, what was left of them were obliged to withdraw, taking with them what they could of their killed and wounded, but leaving several of their guns in the hands of the enemy. At the battle of Williamsburg (preceding Fair Oaks), Col. Charles S. Wainwright, who succeeded Colonel Bailey in command, spoke in terms of great praise of Capt. Thomas W Osborne, Sergeants Ham and Doran, Privates Barry and Conway, of Company H, and Privates Shoemaker and Westcott, of Company D. At the time of the rebel raid upon Manassas, 1862, the Rebels fell upon the regiment by surprise, the officer in command supposing the rebel force to be our cavalry, until too late, and eight of our guns were captured. This was not done, however, until after a most sanguinary resistance. During the artillery duel at Chancellorsville, on the afternoon of May 2, Battery L sustained the heaviest losses. There were excellent artillerists with the battery, who punished the rebels severely. Colonel Wainwright was in 1864 promoted to Brevet Brigadier-General.

THIRD LIGHT ARTILLERY.—The regiment entered the service in 1861 as the Nineteenth Infantry, and served as such until 1863, when the two years' men were discharged and additional recruits forwarded, sufficient to reorganize as the Third New York Heavy Artillery, but soon their arms were changed to that of Light Artillery, and as such served with distinction in the Army of the Ohio, under Schofield, being attached to the Twenty-third Corps. The various batteries saw service under Generals Foster, Hunter, Peck, Sheridan and Schofield, and their banners bear the following inscriptions: Fort Macon, Washington, Hawk's Mills, Kinston, Whitehall, Goldsboro, Newbern. The regiment was for some time at Hatteras Inlet—a position worse than condemning them to the galleys, but the officers and men bore their privations with manly, soldierlike fortitude. Capt. John H. Howell, of Battery M, formerly of the First Artillery, as efficient an officer as he is a brave, accomplished gentleman, commanded the post for some time, and contracted a disease which greatly injured his constitution. He was afterwards appointed Chief of Ordnance on the Staff of General Nagle, at Hilton Head. Captain Howell was in New York during the riots of 1863, and rendered such valuable service that he was specially mentioned in official reports for his gallant conduct. There are few among the surviving members who do not remember the siege of Fort Macon. The only man killed on our side during the bombardment is said to have been William Dart, of Company I, from Canastoga. Battery Flagler was admirably manned by a portion of Battery I, Capt. John H. Ammon and Lieut. George W Thomas, and Battery G, Capt. William A. Kelsey. During the siege of Washington, the guns were splendidly served by Capt. William J. Riggs. Lieut. William F. Field and Lieut. John O'Niel, of Battery H. The latter died of disease contracted in the service in 1864. Lieutenant O'Niel's Battery H engaged the enemy for three-quarters of an hour on the main street, until every man, except one, was shot from his post. He then, with the assistance of the remaining man, Sergeant King, and some volunteers from an infantry regiment, dragged the pieces to a place of safety. Lieut. Paul Birchmyer, of Battery H, with a detachment manned the batteries at the time of the attack upon the fortifications around Charleston, S. C. Col. James H. Ledlie, who was promoted to Brigadier-General in 1862, was honorably mentioned for the skilful manner in which he operated his pieces at the battle of Kinston. A medal was presented to Capt. Joseph J. Morrison by the officers and men of Battery B. Around the margin of the medal are inscribed the names of Newbern, Washington, Plymouth, Weldon, Kinston, Whitehall, Goldsboro and Charleston—battle-fields where he led the battery. Captain Morrison resigned in May, 1863, and was appointed Colonel of the Sixteenth Heavy Artillery, and Capt. John H. Ammon, of Battery I, was appointed Lieutenant-

Colonel. The regiment went to the war under command of Col. John S. Clark, who was promoted to Brigadier-General, in November, 1861. The Lieutenant-Colonel of the regiment was Clarence A. Seward, a nephew of the Hon. William H. Seward, and now one of the most eminent lawyers of New York. All the commissioned officers lost by the regiment during the war died of disease, except Lieut. Edward A. Wildt, who was killed in action at Honey Hill, S. C., November, 1864.

INDEPENDENT BATTERIES.

FIRST BATTERY.—It was first commanded by Capt. Terence J. Kennedy, who was in 1862 promoted to Major of the Third Artillery. He was succeeded by Capt. Andrew Cowan. Major Kennedy died in October, 1863. He claimed to have been the first man in the State to enroll himself in defence of the Union. The names of thirty battles are inserted on the colors of the battery. On every field the battery fought well and nobly; but the grandest example of their courage and discipline was "double canister at ten yards," on Cemetery Ridge, Gettysburg. The last canister fired, they hastily dragged the guns below the crest for shelter, but there was no enemy left, able to follow or seize them.

SECOND BATTERY.—Capt. Charles Bookwood resigned early in the war, and was succeeded by Capt. Louis Schirmer.—The battery fought splendidly at Gettysburg, where Lieut. Theodore Blume was killed. This was the only battery that fired a gun with Hancock's brigade, at the battle of Williamsburg. It was organized at Auburn and took part in nineteen battles.

THIRD BATTERY.—This battery was known as Mott's battery, its captain being Thaddeus P. Mott, a son of the eminent physician and surgeon—the late Dr. Valentine Mott. Captain Mott served his country faithfully on the upper Potomac, in the early part of the war; also in the affair at Lewinsville, Va., in September, 1862, when his battery confronted the famous Washington Artillery, causing them to beat a hasty retreat. In the Seven Days' battles, on the Peninsula, the battery, under the personal command of Captain Mott, fought the enemy for five consecutive hours, defeating the rebels at every point, but with a fearful loss to his men. All the officers attached to the battery were promoted from the ranks. Lieut. Robert B. Ballestier was one of the heroes of the first battle of Bull Run. Lieut. Leon Rheims was honorably mentioned in an account of the affair at Lewinsville, where the battery fired 954 shots. Captain Mott resigned in July, 1862, and was appointed Colonel of the Fourteenth New York Cavalry. He was succeeded in command of the battery by Capt. William A. Harn.

FOURTH BATTERY.—Capt. James E. Smith. The battery rendered splendid service at Gettysburg. The enemy's movements in that battle indicated their purpose to seize Round Top Hill, and this in their possession, General Longstreet would have had easy work in cutting up our left wing. To prevent this, General Sickles directed General Ward's brigade and Smith's battery, as the Fourth was called, to secure that vital position. The battery was disbanded towards the close of the year 1863. In 1887 Captain Smith was chief of the Certificate Division of the Pension Office.

SIXTH BATTERY.—Lieut. Washington A. Roebling subsequently became famous as the builder of the Brooklyn Bridge.

SEVENTH BATTERY.—Capt. Peter C. Regan. The battery was one of the finest in the service, and participated in most of the battles fought by General McClellan and all the other commanders of the Army of the Potomac. It was organized at Newburg. In the attack on Fort Harrison, they turned the guns on the enemy. The officers who returned home with the battery, were besides Captain Regan, Lieuts. Martin V McIntyre, John S. Bennett, John B. Brosero and Abram A. Smith.

EIGHTH BATTERY.—Capt. Peter Morton. This was a Newburg battery, and served creditably for three years.

ELEVENTH BATTERY.—Capt. George W Davey. It was organized at Albany and took an honorable part in the battles of Second Bull Run, Fredericksburg, Chancellorsville, Gettysburg, Mine Run, North Anna, Tolopotomoy, Coal Harbor, Petersburg, Deep Bottom.

THIRTEENTH BATTERY.—The battery was commanded by Capt. Henry Bundy; it served with the Army of the Potomac until April, 1862; when it was ordered to the Mountain Department under General Fremont. It afterwards served under General Pope in his campaign in Virginia, and suffered severely in men.—When General Pope was relieved, it joined the Army of the Potomac, with which it served until ordered to the Department of the Cumberland, in September, 1863. It formed part of the forces that drove the enemy from

Lookout Valley. It took part in the battle of Mission Ridge, and subsequently accompanied the forces sent to the relief of Knoxville. The men re-enlisted at Bridgeport, Alabama, January 1, 1864. The battery took part in every engagement with the Twentieth Army Corps in the campaign from Chattanooga to Atlanta, and lost so heavily in men that it had to be twice filled by details of infantry. After the fall of Atlanta, all the detailed men were ordered to rejoin their regiments, which reduced the effective force of the battery to eighty-six men, and it was then ordered to garrison duty. On their tattered battle-flag were inscribed the following battles in which they had been engaged: Cross Keys, Freeman's Ford, White Sulphur Springs, Waterloo Bridge, Second Bull Run, Chancellorsville, Gettysburg, Mission Ridge, Mill Creek, Resaca, New Hope Church, Pine Knob, Muddy Creek, Nose Creek, Culp's Farm, Kenesaw, Peach Tree Creek, Atlanta, Nashville. A sword was presented to Capt. William Wheeler by his associates and men of the battery, as a token of their admiration for him, but the brave soldier did not live long to use it, for he fell in action near Marietta, Ga., on the 22d of June, 1864.

FOURTEENTH BATTERY.—Capt. James McKay Rorty. The Fourteenth and Fifteenth Batteries originally formed the Second New York Artillery. The battalion was organized in New York City in December, 1861, and its designation changed to the Fourteenth and Fifteenth Batteries in October, 1862. It was transferred to Companies B and G, First New York Artillery, in September, 1863.

FIFTEENTH BATTERY.—Capt. Patrick Hart. This old battery went to the war with the famous Irish Brigade, but was soon separated from the brigade and assigned to the Fifth Army Corps, and was known as the fighting battery of that corps. It took part in nearly all the battles of the Army of the Potomac, and returned home in July, 1865, with but forty-eight of its original number.

NINETEENTH BATTERY.—Capt. Edward W. Rogers. The battery did its full share of hard fighting, and acquitted itself honorably in the battles of Suffolk, Spottsylvania, North Anna, Coal Harbor, Weldon Railroad, Petersburg and Hatcher's Run.

TWENTIETH BATTERY.—Capt. B. Franklin Ryer. The battery was quartered in the harbor of New York, doing garrison duty on Governor's Island. Its principal active service was in quelling the riot in New York.

TWENTY-THIRD BATTERY.—Capt. Samuel Kittinger. The battery was formerly known as Company A, "Rocket Battalion." General Peck complimented the battery for its gallant behavior in the engagement near Greenville, N. C. Capt. Alfred Ransom and Lieut. Thomas Low were among the gallant men of the battery.

TWENTY-FOURTH BATTERY.—Capt. A. Lester Cady. Captain Cady with a squad of his men made a raid to Lake Phelps, N. C., and did some valuable service.

TWENTY-SEVENTH BATTERY.—Capt. John B. Eaton. The battery acquitted itself with special distinction at the battle of Petersburg. It was from Buffalo.

TWENTY-EIGHTH BATTERY.—Capt. Josiah C. Hannum. The battery was quartered in the harbor of New York, doing garrison duty at Fort Schuyler. Their principal active service was in subduing the riot in New York in July, 1863.

ENGINEER REGIMENTS.

FIRST ENGINEER REGIMENT.—"Serrell's Engineers." The regiment was organized in New York City, and was known as "Serrell's Engineers." Col. Edward W. Serrell commanded the regiment all through the war, or until February, 1865, when he was honorably discharged, and James F. Hall succeeded to the command. Colonel Hall rose to the rank of Brevet Brigadier-General, and died in January, 1884.

The regiment was for some time in the Department of the South, and its flag was the first to float over Fort Pulaski. At Bermuda Hundred the regiment rendered valuable service, and also in the siege of Petersburg. Among the commissioned officers whose names deserve remembrance for gallantry and devotion, were Capt. Charles B. Parsons, Capt. Richard W. Coe, Capt. Thomas B. Brooks, Capt. Charles P. McKenna, Capt. John L. Suess, Maj. Frederick E. Graef, Capt. Henry M. Dalrymple, and Capt. Samuel C. Eaton.

FIFTEENTH ENGINEER REGIMENT.—This was a New York City regiment, and was first commanded by Col. John McLeod Murphy, who resigned in 1862, and was succeeded by Col. Clinton G. Colgate. (Colonel Colgate died in November, 1886.) It was largely through the skill and sleepless energy of Lieut. Calvert S. Webster, that the Chickahominy was spanned by those half-dozen bridges over which the army passed on their way to Richmond in 1862. Eugene Webster, the elder brother of Lieutenant Webster, took part in the same battles with his brother, but on the opposite side; Eugene being on the staff of the Confederate General Lee. Lieutenant Webster died at New Haven in 1862, of disease contracted in the service of his country. He was a son of William G. Webster of New Haven, and a great-grandson, through his mother, who was a Custis, of Martha Washington.

Upon the return home of the regiment it was re-organized, and again towards the close of the war went to the front under command of Col. Wesley Brainerd, with William A. Ketchum as Lieutenant-Colonel. Colonel Brainerd had formerly been Major in the Fiftieth Engineer Regiment.

FIFTIETH ENGINEER REGIMENT.—"Stuart's Engineers." The regiment was first commanded by Col. Charles B. Stuart, who resigned in June, 1863, and was succeeded by Col. Wm. H. Pettes.

The largest pontoon bridge ever built in this country was built by Capt. Porteus C. Gilbert. It extended across the Chickahominy, and was laid on the occasion of General McClellan's withdrawing his troops from Harrison's Landing. The regiment also laid the pontoon bridge at Fredericksburg (Burnside's campaign), in the laying of which Capt. Augustus S. Perkins lost his life. The duties devolving upon the regiment were severe in the extreme, and hundreds who survived the war were broken in health by the exacting nature of the work they were obliged to perform. The following are a few of the commissioned officers whose names adorn the history of this famous regiment: Lieut.-Col. Ira Spaulding, Maj. James H. McDonald, Maj. William W Folwell, Maj. George W. Ford, Maj. Frederick E. Embick, Maj. Edmond O. Beers, Capt. Michael H. McGrath, Capt. Martin Van Brocklin, Maj. Wesley Brainerd, Lieut. Edward C. James, Capt. Mahlom B. Folwell, and Lieut. A. Barton Hough. Major Brainerd was promoted to Colonel of the Fifteenth Engineers; Lieutenant James was promoted to Major in the Sixtieth Volunteer Infantry.

VOLUNTEER INFANTRY REGIMENTS.

FIRST REGIMENT.—" National Guard." The regiment was organized in New York City for two years service. It went to the war in May, 1861, under command of Col. William H. Allen. A short time after leaving home, Col. J. Fred Pierson succeeded Colonel Allen in command of the regiment. In the battles on the Peninsula under General McClellan, nine out of ten of the Color-Guard were shot, and the regiment by its gallantry, steadiness, and endurance displayed its worthiness to bear the name of the First Regiment from the State of New York. Lieut.-Col. Garrett Dyckman was the person to whom was awarded the gold snuff box, bequeathed by General Jackson to the bravest man in the State of New York.

SECOND REGIMENT.—"Troy Regiment." This was a two years regiment, and was among the first in Hooker's fighting division. It went to the war under command of Col. Joseph B. Carr, who was soon after promoted to Brigadier-General, and his subsequent career proved the wisdom of his promotion. He was succeeded in command by Col. Sidney W. Park, who had a leg shot away in a brilliant charge at Chancellorsville. The reception of the regiment upon its return home was the greatest gala-day ever known in Troy.

THIRD REGIMENT.—Organized at Albany. Colors presented by Bowen, Holmes & Co. The regiment went to the war under command of Col. Frederick Townsend. Colonel Townsend, after leading the regiment to the seat of war, resigned in June, 1861, and was appointed Major in the regular army, and subsequently participated with distinguished credit in the battles of Pea Ridge and Stone River. Colonel Townsend was succeeded in command by Col. Samuel M. Alford, and in June, 1864, John E. Mulford became the third Colonel. The latter was in 1865 promoted to Brevet Brigadier-General. Colonel Mulford subsequently became famous as Commissioner for the exchange of prisoners. Company A was the first company raised on Long Island, and was composed of Williamsburg firemen. Next to the Fifth Infantry, the Third furnished a larger number of officers for the army than any other regiment from the State. When its term of service expired, only two officers were in the regiment holding original commissions, the most of the remainder having been promoted from the ranks. General Dix, in complimentary orders, said: "In discipline, courage, and in a faithful discharge of their duties, the Major General Commanding ventures to say they are not surpassed by any other regiment in the service." The regiment took part in the battle of Big Bethel,—the first battle in which New York troops were engaged. During the siege of Suffolk it bravely defended South Quay battery. Among the honored dead of the Third was Capt. Stephen W Fullerton, of Newburg, a nephew of Judge Fullerton. Captain Fullerton was a Member of Assembly from Orange County, when the war broke out, and is said to have raised the first company of volunteers organized in the State.

FOURTH REGIMENT.—"Scott Life Guard." Every officer in the Fourth with the exception of Lieut. John H. Fullerton (an uncle of Captain Fullerton, of the Third Regiment) served in the Mexican War. The regiment was first mustered into the service of the State April 22, 1861. Immediately after the first battle of Bull Run, they were placed on duty guarding the line of railroad from Baltimore to Havre de Grace, a duty very harassing and arduous, as the pickets of the regiment covered a distance of about fifty miles, and constant attempts were made to burn the bridges, etc., on the route. In April, 1862, they were moved to Fort McHenry, Baltimore, and from there to Suffolk, Va., then the outpost of our army in that department. After the second battle of Bull Run they were ordered to the defences of Washington, then threatened by the enemy, and were attached to McClellan's army. The first battle of the regiment was Antietam, where General Hancock is said to have fairly danced up and down in his saddle for joy to see the regiment so long in position under the destructive fire the enemy were pouring into their ranks. They suffered fearfully, losing some two hundred men, one-third of those engaged. They also suffered severely at Fredericksburg. The regiment went to the war under command of Col. Alfred W. Taylor, who was succeeded in July, 1862, by Col. John D. McGregor.

FIFTH REGIMENT.—"Duryea's Zouaves." During the war 2,164 men were recruited and assigned to this regiment. In 1865, seven hundred men returned home, of whom about one hundred were recruited in 1861. The Fifth was attached to the First Brigade, Second Division, Fifth Army Corps, and wore for its distinctive mark the "white cross." At the battle of Gaines Mills when the Regulars, with whom the Fifth was brigaded, were forced to retire in confusion, the regiment advanced to the position and repulsed the onset in such splendid style as to draw down cheers of admiration from all who witnessed it, and then held the ground for four terrible hours against immense odds, and only abandoned it finally during the night, when the whole army retreated behind the Chickahominy. At the second battle of Bull Run, the regiment lost in fifteen minutes, out of some 580 men, 110 killed and 200 wounded. Few, if any regiments, lost more men in a single engagement and in a shorter space of time. The regiment was commanded during the war by six Colonels, three of whom were promoted to Generals. Fishkill was represented in this regiment by Maj. J. Mansfield Davies and Capt. Henry E. Davies, Jr., the former a nephew and the latter a son of the Hon. Henry E. Davies. In August, 1861, both of these gallant officers resigned, and Maj. J. Mansfield Davies was promoted to Colonel of the Second Cavalry Regiment, and Capt. Henry E. Davies, Jr., to Lieutenant-Colonel. Upon the resignation of his cousin, J. Mansfield Davies, in December, Lieutenant-Colonel Davies succeeded to the command of the regiment. From the very commencement of his military career as Captain in the Fifth, Henry E. Davies, Jr. rose steadily and rapidly by his devotion to duty and gallantry in action. From Colonel of the Second Cavalry, he was promoted, on the 16th of September, 1863, to Brigadier-General, and finally for his bravery and gallantry in charging on the 6th of April, 1865, at Sailor's Creek, the enemy in breastworks, and capturing the same, with three guns, two Generals and a large number of prisoners, he was promoted to a full Major-General. Capt. Gouverneur Carr was promoted to Major of the 165th. He went to the war from the editorial rooms of the New York *Times*, as did also another gallant soldier, Charles G. Halpine, although the latter was not a member of the Fifth.

SIXTH REGIMENT.—"Wilson's Zouaves." Col. William Wilson sent to the Mayor of New York a Secession flag, which was the first Secession flag raised in Florida, and the one under which the State seceded.

SEVENTH REGIMENT.—"Steuben Regiment." The Seventh was in French's Division of Sumner's Corps, a division that gained from the veteran General Sumner, when examined before the Committee on the Conduct of the War, the credit of "never turning their backs upon the enemy." The Seventh participated in eight great battles, and lost during its term of service fourteen officers killed and fifteen wounded, besides 180 enlisted men killed and 450 wounded. The first great battle in which the regiment was engaged was Fredericksburg, in December, 186., and lost in that engagement nine commissioned officers, more than any other regiment from the State. The regiment went to the war under command of Col. George Von Schack, a young Prussian officer. When Sumter was attacked he was beaming in the favor of the Court of Berlin, but at once decided to cast his lot with America and immediately started for New York and joined the Seventh. He was promoted many times until he reached the rank of Colonel, and was subsequently breveted by the President and confirmed by the Senate as Brigadier-General, for gallant and meritorious services. There were two regiments known as the Seventh Infantry. The first was organized in 1861, and when its term of service expired was reorganized and again went to the war in 1863, with Colonel Von Schack as its Colonel. During the two years term of service the regiment suffered severely, especially at Antietam and Fredericksburg. At Fredericksburg nine commissioned officers were killed outright.

EIGHTH REGIMENT.—"First German Rifles." Colors were presented by Mrs. Belmont. The regiment went to the field under the command of Col. Louis Blenker, who was soon after promoted to Brigadier-General, and died in October, 1863. He was succeeded by Col. Felix Prince Salm-Salm. At the battle of Cross Keys the regiment advanced gallantly under a heavy fire, but being so long unsupported and largely outnumbered, it was badly cut up, losing not less than three hundred men—more than half its strength. The regiment suffered severely by the loss of "missing" commissioned officers—no less than seven having disappeared and have not since been heard of. Colonel Salm-Salm was a cousin of the King of Prussia. After the war he went to Mexico, and devoted himself to saving the life of Maximilian. He was killed at the battle of Gravelotte.

NINTH REGIMENT.—"Hawkins Zouaves." This was a two years regiment, and was commanded by Col. Rush C. Hawkins, with George F. Betts as Lieutenant-Colonel. The regiment fought well at the battles of Camden and South Mountain. At Antietam the regiment lost nearly half their men—ninety-five being killed outright. John G. Curtin, of Company D, having lost his arm at South Mountain, the officers and men of his company raised the sum of five hundred dollars to enable him to start in business. This shows of what material the regiment was composed. In the same battle Private John Van Deusen had his right arm shot off. In 1884 Van Deusen was the janitor of the Gramercy Park flats, who was assaulted by thieves and badly injured. Henry Gunther, who followed the flag of the regiment in many a battle was in 1887 one of the Aldermen of New York City. Lieut.-Col. Edward A. Kimball was the officer shot dead by General Corcoran. Colonel Kimball claimed the honor of having hauled down the Mexican flag at the storming of Chapultepec and planting the Stars and Stripes in its place; but this distinction was also claimed by Colonel Inness of the Thirty-sixth Regiment. Captain John W. Jacobus and Henry C. Perley were brave and faithful officers, and have, since the war, been conspicuous in the public affairs of New York City.

TENTH REGIMENT.—"National Zouaves." The Tenth will always occupy an honorable place in the history of the Rebellion, for it had its full share of sacrifices and was composed of a gallant body of officers and privates, who served their country faithfully and bravely through twenty-one great battles, and all the hardships incident to a soldier's life.

The Tenth may date its origin from the time of the first meeting held to organize troops to defend the Government, should the occasion require.—This meeting, previously referred to in this volume, was held at the Mercer House, and among those present was Mr. Frank J. White and Mr. Charles H. Ludwig. These gentlemen and others, were instrumental in initiating a movement which resulted in the organization of the Tenth Regiment. Mr. White became a captain in the regiment, and Mr. Ludwig enlisted as a private. The former remained with the regiment but a short time, and subsequently became famous by the capture of Lexington, Mo. Mr. Ludwig served all through the war and by his courage and meritorious conduct won the esteem and admiration of his superior officers. He is now at the head of one of the leading printing houses of New York City.

The regiment went to the war under command of Col. W. W. McChesney, who was soon succeeded by Col. John E. Bendix, and it is not wonderful that under such a leader the regiment soon attained a degree of proficiency that enabled it to secure a most honorable record.

The first great battle in which the Tenth was engaged was Gaines Mills, a battle in which it suffered severely, but nearly every officer and private proved himself a hero. Captains Salmon Winchester, James Henry Briggs, and George F. Hopper were always in the front encouraging their men to brave and gallant efforts, and their example was emulated by nearly all the officers, of whom a large number were promoted for their conspicuous courage on this occasion.

They were Lieuts. Alfred Chamberlain, Charles Hill, Charles D. Stocking, Harvey V Russell, Norwood A. Halsey, Gabriel Cunningham, Serg. Josiah Hedden, who was killed at the Second battle of Bull Run, Serg. Charles W Cowtan, who continued through out the war to prove himself an admirable officer and accomplished gentleman, and Serg. James M. Smith. Capt. Oscar F. Angell was captured. He was finally exchanged, and was killed in action May, 1864. Lieut. John A. Brady commanded his company with such skill and bravery as to receive the commendations of his commanding officer. Brady died in July, 1871. At Malvern Hill, the Tenth was the last regiment to leave the field. At the Second battle of Bull Run the regiment lost about one hundred and fifty men in killed and wounded. General Warren said of the conduct of the regiment in this battle, "Braver men than those of the Tenth, who fought and fell, could not be found." Color-bearer H. Alexander was badly wounded in three different parts of the body, but he still clung to the colors and would not allow them to be taken from him. As he was being lifted up the steps of the hospital, he became insensible, and an effort was made to take the flag from him, but his clutch was like a grasp of iron; his hands seemed glued with his own blood to the Stars and Stripes. "Brave and noble fellow!" burst involuntarily from Surgeons and bystanders. The next great battle in which the Tenth participated was Fredericksburg and the storming of Marye's Heights, and General French said of the conduct of the regiment; "The Tenth was magnificent. No troops ever stood fire better or longer than they." Colonel Bendix was wounded, after which Capt. George F. Hopper, an admirable officer, took command. Later in the war Capt. Hopper was promoted to Lieutenant-Colonel. Of the twelve commissioned officers who went into the battle, only three escaped unhurt; Capts. Joseph Newburg, George F. Tait, Alfred Chamberlain and Gabriel Cunningham being among the severely injured. When the regiment was about to leave for home, at the expiration of its term of service, General French issued an order in which he said, "The General commanding division deems it his duty to express to Colonel Bendix, his officers and men, the high position they attained for the regiment in the soldierly characteristics of bravery, discipline and a military tone and bearing not excelled in the army." In May, 1863, the original members were mustered out, and the three years recruits, consolidated into battalions of six companies, which was retained in service as such until the close of the war. All through General Grant's Virginia campaign the regiment acquitted itself with the same heroism that had marked its earlier record. In the Wilderness battles the regiment was commanded by

Capt. George M. Dewey, and on the sixth of May, about one hundred men were killed and wounded in the engagements at Petersburg. General Egan testified to the valuable services rendered by the Tenth. At Coal Harbor, among the gallant soldiers of the regiment who fell in defence of their country were Serg. George P Chase and Corp. George W Reynolds.

Lieuts. George Hackett, and Frank M. Clark, Privates Joseph W Kay, George W Bell and William H. Reese were among the wounded in the Wilderness battles. Private George Wells, of Company F, a very brave soldier, was mortally wounded. In addition to those who have been alluded to for gallant and meritorious conduct, the following names are justly entitled to a place on the Roll of Honor: Lieuts. Henry V Martin, Putnam Field, W. H. H. Wilcox, James M. Smith, James Whitelow, John H. Murray, Thomas D. Mosscrop, Capt. Robert A. Dimmock, Sergs. Edward Harrison, William Early, William McNulty, Private Christopher Farrell, and Private Charles Lederer. Lederer shot the rebel who would otherwise have killed Lieutenant-Colonel Marshall. Capt. William F. Beers died in 1872. At the time of his death he was connected with the New York *Tribune*.

ELEVENTH REGIMENT.—" First Fire Zouaves." Presented with a magnificent banner by the late Mrs. Astor. This was the regiment commanded originally by Col. Eimer E. Ellsworth, who was assassinated by Thomas Jackson, at the Marshall House, Alexandria, Va., in April, 1861, while attempting to take from the roof of Jackson's house a secession flag. The regiment was composed of 1,100 men from the New York Fire Department. After the death of Ellsworth, Lieut.-Col. Noah L. Farnham took command of the regiment. At the first battle of Bull Run the Eleventh fought like tigers and were badly cut up. General Heintzleman testified to their bravery. It is said that the Black Horse Cavalry, of Virginia, made an attack upon the rear of our army, and that the Zouaves turned, fired and killed a great number of them. A short time before the term of the regiment expired Charles McK. Leoser was appointed Colonel of the regiment.—Lieut.-Col. John A. Creiger was a great-great-grandson of John A. Creiger, the first commissioned officer on Manhattan Island. The commission was issued to him by Governor Stuyvesant in 1659.

TWELFTH REGIMENT.—The Twelfth went to the war under command of Col. Ezra L. Walrath, who remained with the regiment but a short time, when Col. Henry A. Weeks succeeded him in command. In the battles on the Peninsula the regiment fought splendidly. At Groveton, Colonel Weeks commanded a brigade and was badly wounded. At Malvern Hill Maj. Henry A. Barnum, while leading the regiment in an attack was shot through the body and left for dead on the field. The Major had previously distinguished himself before Yorktown upon the occasion of a Rebel sortie, holding the outposts with less than half as many men as were in the enemy's ranks, and driving them back with great loss. When the two years term of the regiment expired he was mustered out of the service. He soon after, however, reëntered the service and raised the 149th Regiment, of which he was elected Colonel, and finally was promoted to Brigadier-General. General Barnum said of his old regiment—the Twelfth—" General Richardson sent special thanks to the Twelfth for saving the left wing of the army at one time during the Peninsula battles." At the second battle of Bull Run the Twelfth formed part of General Butterfield's brigade. The regiment marched twenty-one days without change of clothing, and went into the battle in this fatigued condition. At Fredericksburg the Twelfth was again conspicuous for its gallantry, and lost many valuable officers. When the regiment was mustered out scarcely a vestige of its original element remained. Lieut. Silas Titus—a gallant soldier, was promoted to Colonel of the 122d Regiment."

THIRTEENTH REGIMENT.—The first Colonel of the regiment was Isaac F. Quimby, who resigned early in 1861. He was succeeded by Col. John Pickell, and he in his turn by Col. Elisha G. Marshall. The regiment was with the Army of the Potomac, and in the battles on the Peninsula it bore an honorable part. At the battle of Chickahominy, Maj. George Hyland, Jr., commanded Companies B and D, with great skill and bravery. At Gaines Mills, the regiment captured the flags of the Fifth and Seventh Tennessee Regiments. At the second battle of Bull Run the Thirteenth lost over two hundred men out of five hundred taken into the fight. Two or three times the flags of the regiment went down, but there were strong and faithful hands ready each time to lift them up, and they were not dishonored, though they were sadly riddled and torn by the deadly storm of bullets hurled at their defenders. The Thirteenth furnished many valuable officers for other regiments, including Captain Robert F. Taylor, who was promoted to Colonel of the Thirty-third Regiment, and Capt. Horace Boughton to Lieutenant-Colonel of the 143d.

FOURTEENTH REGIMENT.—The regiment was organized at

Albany, and went to the war for two years under command of Col. James McQuade. General Fitz John Porter said: "At the battle of Gaines Mills, Colonel McQuade, with his regiment, against orders, and, at the risk of defeat and disaster, and yielding to impulse, gallantly dashed forward and repulsed an attacking party." "Colonel McQuade," said General Porter, "was the only regimental commander in Griffin's brigade, who escaped death during the Seven Days battles, and he only by a miracle, for he was constantly exposed." For ten days previous to the battle of Chancellorsville, Colonel McQuade had been ill, but when the battle began he was taken in an ambulance to the field where he mounted his horse and commanded his troops throughout the fight. The battle over, he fell from his horse exhausted, and was confined to his bed for two weeks. He returned to Utica with his regiment in 1863. President Johnson promoted the Colonel to Brevet Brigadier-General. The Colonel died in March, 1885. The regiment went to war with 776 men, and returned home with 439. It lost 325 in killed and wounded.

SIXTEENTH REGIMENT.—The Sixteenth went to war under command of Col. Thomas A. Davies—a brother of the late Hon. Henry E. Davies. It was composed largely of St. Lawrence County men. When Colonel Davies was placed in command of a brigade, Adjt. Joseph Howland, son of the late Samuel Howland, succeeded to the command of the regiment. It was a movement on the part of the Sixteenth that brought on the battle of West Point in 1862. In the seven days fighting on the Peninsula the regiment lost 228 men. They wore straw hats and were conspicuous targets for the enemy. At Gaines Mills, both Colonel Howland and Lieut.-Col. Samuel Marsh were severely wounded. Colonel Marsh expired after enduring terrible agony on the following 4th of July. General Bartlett said: "To Colonel Howland I am indebted for maintaining the extreme right of my line at Gaines Mills, and nobly leading his regiment to the charge and retaking two guns from the enemy;— whatever of noble, moral, physical, and manly courage has ever been given by God to man, has fallen to his lot." Colonel Howland died at Fishkill, April, 1880.

At the battle of Chancellorsville, one company of the regiment took up the field in the attack on Salem Heights forty-six men, twenty-five of whom were left dead and wounded after one charge, and of the remainder who escaped, there was hardly one whose garments were not torn by the whistling bullets. Six officers of the regiment were promoted from merit alone to higher positions.

They were Thomas A. Davies to Brigadier-General, Captain John L. Stetson to Lieutenant-Colonel of the Fifty-ninth Regiment, Captain N. Martin Curtis (who subsequently became a hero of Fort Fisher), to Lieutenant-Colonel of the 142d; Lieut. Frederick F. Wead to Lieutenant-Colonel of the Ninety-eighth New York, and Lieut. Robert P Wilson to Captain and Assistant Adjutant-General.

SEVENTEENTH REGIMENT.—"Westchester Chasseurs." The regiment was commanded by Col. H. S. Lansing, with Thomas F. Morris as Lieutenant-Colonel. When Lieutenant-Colonel Morris resigned in 1862, Nelson B. Bartram became his successor. The Seventeenth subsequently became the first veteran regiment to return to the war in October, 1863. The Seventeenth and a Massachusetts regiment constituted the entire infantry force under General Stoneman on the Peninsula when he made that hasty, timely and terrible march. At Hanover Court House the Seventeenth took one of the enemy's guns. General Butterfield spoke of the splendid advance of the brigade, led by the Seventeenth and Forty-fourth New York at the battle of Groveton. At the battle of Bull Run no less than four color-bearers lost their lives in its defence, and the flag being saved, and rigged to a new staff, was returned to the Common Council of New York, as a proof of the valor of the regiment. The regiment lost over 200 men at Bull Run, out of 550 who went into the battle.

Lieutenant-Colonel Nelson B. Bartram subsequently commanded the Twenty-sixth United States Colored Regiment. He died in 1886.

The regiment returned home at the expiration of its term of service, and having been reorganized returned to the seat of war under command of Col. William T. C. Grower, a very gallant soldier, who had been Major in the old regiment. Colonel Grower was mortally wounded in the engagement at Jonesboro, Ga. The regiment accompanied General Sherman's army to North Carolina, and took part in the engagement at Averysboro. Among the commissioned officers who were always conspicuous for their gallantry, were Major Alexander S. Marshall, Lieut.-Col. Edward Jardine, Lieut. G. A. C. Barnett, Capt. James B. Horner, Capt. Augustus B. Sage, and Capt. Hiram Wilde. Private J. L. Sayles was in 1886 commander of the Grand Army of the Republic, State of New York.

EIGHTEENTH REGIMENT.—"New York State Rifles." The Eighteenth went to the war under command of Col. William A. Jackson, who died at Washington in November, 1861. He was succeeded by

Col. Wm. H. Young, who resigned in 1862, when George R. Meyers became its third and last Colonel. Colonel Young was personally complimented for his cool and daring courage and the valor of his regiment at the battle of West Point. At the battle of Gaines Mills the regiment lost 180 in killed, wounded and missing. For its steadiness under fire at the battle of South Mountain the regiment received honorable mention in the official reports. A large number of the fallen heroes of the regiment were from Fishkill, on the Hudson. Among them were Privates John Delany, William J. Hadden, John M. Pyres, William Cherry, William H. Williams, James Moore, Alonzo Brundage, Corporal Wm. H. Astin and David Ticehurst.

NINETEENTH REGIMENT.—This was the Third Heavy Artillery Regiment. See Third Artillery.

TWENTIETH REGIMENT.—"Turner Rifles." Flag presented by Mrs. Charles Edward Strong. This was Col. Max Webber's splendid German regiment. Testimonials from the brigade and division commanders testify to the conspicuous bravery of the officers of the regiment. Nearly all the men had been engaged in the revolution of 1845, in the Fatherland, and were exiles from home.

At Antietam the regiment suffered terribly, losing no less than seven commissioned officers.

Colonel Webber was promoted to Brigadier-General in 1862, and Francis Weiss succeeded to the command. He commanded the regiment for only two months, when Ernest Von Vegesack was appointed Colonel. Although the term of the regiment expired on the 3d of May, 1863, the men, with the exception of 100, refused to leave their brigade until the battle of Chancellorsville was fought. The remnant of the regiment, numbering 449 men, went into the action, and by their devoted gallantry atoned for the disgrace cast upon them by their comrades. Only 240 of them returned to camp; the rest fell under the enemy's bullets.

TWENTY-FIRST REGIMENT.—The regiment was commanded by Col. William F Rogers, and Adrian R. Root as Lieutenant-Colonel. Colonel Root was in 1862 promoted to the Colonelcy of the Ninety-fourth Regiment and subsequently rose to the rank of Brevet Brigadier-General. At the second battle of Bull Run the regiment was conspicuous for its bravery.

TWENTY-SECOND REGIMENT.—Col. Walter Phelps, Jr. The regiment is said to have lost more men at the second battle of Bull Run than any other regiment. They entered the field with twenty-six officers and 600 men, and came off with two officers and 220 men—the proportion of officers killed and wounded being greater up to that time, than of any other corps since the war commenced. Ten commissioned officers were killed or mortally wounded.

At the battle of Chickahominy the regiment did its share of fighting. At Antietam the regiment was again engaged, and General Doubleday in his Report of the battle of South Mountain alludes in terms of great praise to the gallantry of Capt. Jacob L. Yates, who was at the time in command of the regiment. Capt. Oliver D. Peabody who enlisted as a private, first smelt powder at Plattsburg, when the British appeared at that place in 1813.

TWENTY-THIRD REGIMENT.—General Doubleday in his Report of the battle of South Mountain refers in complimentary terms to the steadiness and gallantry of the regiment and to the brave and skilful manner in which it was led by Col. Henry C. Hoffman.

TWENTY-FOURTH REGIMENT.—"First Oswego Regiment." The regiment went to the war under command of Col. Timothy Sullivan. During the battle of South Mountain, General McClellan unexpectedly rode up, and halting in front of the Twenty-fourth, exclaimed: "Boys, you have driven the enemy from these hills, and now you must follow them up." After this the regiment fought with undaunted courage.

At the second battle of Bull Run, the regiment fought splendidly and suffered terribly, as will be realized from the fact that it lost no less than six commissioned officers. Colonel Sullivan resigned in January, 1863, and was succeeded by Col. Samuel R. Beardsley.

TWENTY-FIFTH REGIMENT.—"Union Rangers." The Twenty-fifth Regiment opened the battle of Hanover Court House, where it lost many valuable officers. At the battle of Gaines Mills, the regiment, led by Lieut.-Col. Charles A. Johnson, twice repulsed the enemy from its immediate front, but after a hard fight at close quarters with greatly superior numbers they were compelled to give up the position.

TWENTY-SIXTH REGIMENT.—The first Colonel of the regiment was William H. Christian, who was succeeded in 1862 by Col. Richard H. Richardson. The regiment took part in the battles of Second Bull Run and Fredericksburg, and most of its losses occurred in those two battles.

TWENTY-SEVENTH REGIMENT.—The Twenty-seventh went to the war under command of Col. Henry W. Slocum, who was soon promoted to Brigadier-General. His successor was Col. Joseph J. Bartlett, who, in 1862 was also promoted to Brigadier-General—the Twenty-seventh can thus be proud of having furnished the army with two of its most distinguished generals. When Colonel Bartlett was promoted, Col. Alexander D. Adams became the third Colonel of the regiment. The promotions from the ranks within the regiment during the war were upwards of ninety, and outside of the regiment were double. Capt. Hiram C. Rogers won a brigadier's star on the Staff of General Slocum and proved himself worthy of the promotion. It was Lieutenant H. McMahon who carried the flag of the Twenty-seventh at Crampton's Gap in 1862 and was severely wounded. The Twenty-first cavalry regiment was made up largely from the Twenty-seventh. A daughter of General Slocum was adopted by the regiment, and twenty-five years later (1887) Miss Slocum entertained the surviving members of the regiment at her father's residence in Brooklyn. In Capt. George G. Wanzer's company was a private, who subsequently became distinguished as an author—Albion W Tourgee, who was wounded and taken prisoner at the first battle of Bull Run. The regiment was mentioned in the brigade commander's reports of the battle of Bull Run as one of the few commands that re-formed, and went into the battle after being broken. At the battle of West Point the regiment went ashore in the face of the enemy in row-boats, advanced on the open plain, and guarded the disembarkation of troops, stores and cannon. At the battle of Gaines Mills, under the lead of Lieutenant-Colonel Adams, the regiment charged through a tremendous fire with a shout, and without firing so much as a single shot till the ground was cleared. Colonel Bartlett commanded a brigade, and led in person each of his four regiments to the charge separately, and was promoted to Brigadier-General for his gallantry in this action. During the Seven Days battles the regiment was under fire every day. Maj. Curtiss C. Gardiner, a gallant officer, was severely wounded at Gaines Mills. At Fredericksburg, the Twenty-seventh was the first regiment to cross the Rappahannock in the Left Grand Division, and drove the enemy's skirmishers back from the river.

TWENTY-EIGHTH REGIMENT.—The Twenty-eighth bore the brunt of the battle of Cedar Mountain, where Col. Dudley Donnelly was mortally wounded.

The regiment opposed an entire Rebel brigade under command of General Winder. They were surrounded on all sides, and nearly all who kept their places in line of battle were either killed, wounded or taken prisoners. After the loss of Colonel Donnelly, Edwin F. Brown succeeded to the Colonelcy of the regiment.

TWENTY-NINTH REGIMENT.—"German Regiment." The regiment returned home with only 356 men. Their colors showed the fierce storm of iron hail they had endured in nearly all the great engagements of the Army of the Potomac. At Chancellorsville the Twenty-ninth belonged to a brigade to which was due the credit of saving our trains and ammunition from capture. Col. Adolph Von Steinwehr was promoted to Brigadier-General, and his record is brilliant. General Von Steinwehr said of the conduct of the regiment at Chancellorsville, "You, together with the other regiments of my brigade bravely defended your position, when all around lay in confusion."

THIRTIETH REGIMENT.—The Thirtieth was composed of companies from Saratoga Springs, Greenfield, Troy, Lansingburg, Albany, Schenectady and Poughkeepsie. The regiment went to the war under command of Col. Edward Frisby, who was killed at the second battle of Bull Run. In this battle the regiment was exposed to a terrible fire and suffered severely. Corporal Lawrence behaved with extraordinary gallantry until shot down. He was succeeded by five other standard bearers, each of whom, one after another, shared the same fate. After the death of Colonel Frisby, Col. William M. Searing assumed command of the regiment. From among the officers of the Thirtieth who deserve to rank among the heroes of the war were Lieut. Richard C. Bentley, who was promoted to Lieutenant-Colonel of the Sixty-third; Lieut. Walter Cutting to Captain and Aide-de-camp; Lieut. Charles E. Russ to Captain; Lieut. Alonzo Alden to Major of the 169th, and subsequently promoted to Brevet Brigadier-General; Capt. Robert B. Everett, Lieut. Philip Keeler and Lieut. Robert G. Noxon, who were transferred to the Seventy-sixth, and all three were killed at Gettysburg. Lieut. Michael Long was also transferred to the Seventy-sixth, and was the only one of the four that survived the battle of Gettysburg.

THIRTY-FIRST REGIMENT.—"Montezuma Regiment." This was a New York City regiment, and its first commander was Col. Calvin E. Pratt, who was, in 1862, promoted to Brigadier-General. His successor in command of the regiment was Col. Frank Jones. At the battle of West Point the regiment succeeded in resisting, unaided, the attack of four regiments for upwards of three hours. Out of nineteen officers four were killed and five wounded. In the storming of Marye's Heights (Chancellorsville), the regiment, led by the gallant Lieut. Col. Leopold C. Newman, was the first in the enemy's works, riddled in the passage thither by a whole charge of grapeshot, and at a cost of many brave soldiers and officers. Colonel Pratt commanded a brigade, which had the honor to open the battle on the 2d of May.

In 1864, Lieut. William Tracy was commissioned Captain in the Twenty-sixth United States Colored Regiment. He died in December, 1886.

Surg. Frank H. Hamilton died in August, 1886; George Herman of Company F received in 1887 a pension amounting to $11,000.

THIRTY-SECOND REGIMENT.—"First California Regiment." The first battle in which the regiment was engaged was the battle of West Point, where it sustained a severe loss, both of officers and men. The regiment under command of Col. Francis E. Pinto, claim the credit of being the first of Burnside's army to cross over to Fredericksburg and plant our standard on the soil. It was also conspicuous for its gallantry at the battle of South Mountain. When the regiment was about to leave for home General Sedgwick issued a special order complimenting it on its honorable record.

THIRTY-THIRD REGIMENT.—The following is an extract from a speech of General McClellan to the regiment, which, with the Seventh Maine, made the brilliant charge under General Hancock at the battle of Williamsburg: "On that little hill you saved our army from a disgraceful defeat. Bear upon your colors the inscription 'Williamsburg' as a token of your bravery, and as the highest honor I can confer upon you."

The Thirty-third and the Seventy-seventh New York drove the enemy out of the village of Mechanicsville. General Davidson said in his Report of the battle of Gaines Mills: "The Thirty-third had the honor of repulsing the enemy most handsomely." At the battle of Fredericksburg the regiment again fought bravely. John S. Heavem was the first man wounded in Franklin's command.

In the charge on Marye's Heights (Chancellorsville) on the 3d of May, 1863, the Thirty-third constituted the right of the charging column. Steadily the men pressed forward under a heavy shower of canister, dashed over the Cemetery Heights, then down the ravine at the left; through underbrush and obstructions of every kind, and up the steep sides of Marye's Heights to the very mouth of the Rebel cannon which were belching forth their iron hail. The regiment was the first to reach the ramparts. It was commanded by Col. Robert F. Taylor, Lieut.-Col. Joseph W Corning, and Maj. John S. Platner, all of whom proved themselves worthy of their positions. Several of the officers of the Thirty-third acquitted themselves honorably after promotion to higher positions, among whom were Capt. George M. Guion, who became Colonel of the 148th Regiment, Capt. Theodore B. Hamilton, promoted to Lieutenant-Colonel of the Sixty-second, and Lieut. Wm. H. Long, promoted to Captain and Assistant Adjutant-General.

THIRTY-FOURTH REGIMENT.—At the battle of Fair Oaks the regiment formed part of Gorman's brigade of Sedgwick's division. The Rebels charged upon our column, and the main strength of the charge fell upon the Thirty-fourth. Nobly did they sustain the reputation of their State. Firm as a rock stood they against the advancing enemy. At the battle of Antietam the regiment maintained their well-earned laurels, but lost heavily in officers and men. William LaDew was the first Colonel of the regiment, and when he resigned James A. Suiter was appointed his successor. Colonel Suiter also resigned in 1863, when Byron Laflin became the last Colonel of the regiment. After the battle of Fair Oaks General Gorman wrote a letter to Governor Morgan eulogizing the bravery of the Thirty-fourth.

THIRTY-FIFTH REGIMENT.—"Jefferson County Regiment." The regiment went to the war under command of Col. William C. Brown, who remained with it but a short time, when he resigned, in 1863, and Newton B. Lord was appointed Colonel. Colonel Lord resigned and John G. Todd was placed in command. At the battle of Antietam the regiment behaved with more than ordinary gallantry, and here it lost the only commissioned officer killed during the war, Capt. John R. Barnett, who fell mortally wounded while in the display of the highest military skill and courage. In this battle the regiment captured the flag of the Seventh Texas Regiment. Fredericksburg was the last battle in which the regiment was engaged. On leaving the army for home General Patrick shook hands with each man as an earnest of the feeling with which he bade them good-by.

THIRTY-SIXTH REGIMENT.—"Washington Volunteers." This was a New York City regiment and went to the seat of war under command of Col. Charles H. Innes. Not less than ten of the officers served in the Crimean and Indian wars. The Adjutant-General of the State of Massachusetts said: "The Tenth Massachusetts and the Thirty-sixth New York almost annihilated an entire Rebel brigade at the battle of Malvern Hill. In the attack upon Marye's Heights (Chancellorsville) May 3d, 1863, Capt. J. Townsend Daniel (as appears in special orders from the War Department) led the right company of the Thirty-sixth, which was the first to plant its colors on the heights. At one time the column faltered, but was handsomely rallied by Lieut.-Col. James J. Walsh, and Maj. Elihu J. Faxon, who was one of the first men killed.

THIRTY-SEVENTH REGIMENT.—"Irish Rifles." General McDowell in his Report of the battle of Bull Run said: "The Thirty-seventh New York kept possession of Fairfax Station for twelve hours after the retreat, and brought away all the ordnance and quartermaster stores, and then retired in good order along the line of the railway. The Thirty-seventh, with the Thirty-ninth and Fortieth, are said to have borne the brunt of the battle of Williamsburg. At Fair Oaks General Kearny led a charge of the regiment, and in his report said, "The services of the Thirty-seventh were invaluable." General Berry in his Report of the battle of Fredericksburg said: "The Thirty-seventh contributed largely in repulsing the enemy. It has won laurels in this fight, which added to its very many ones, makes the organization one of the most noted in the volunteer service." General Sickles complimented the regiment on its behavior at the battle of Chancellorsville. Col. John H. McCunn was but a short time in command of the regiment. He was succeeded by one every way worthy to command so gallant an organization, Col. S. B. Hayman.

Of those who rose to higher positions through force of merit, may be mentioned Maj. Patrick H. Jones, who became Colonel of the 154th Regiment and subsequently rose to the rank of Brigadier-General, and Lieut. Wilson Barstow, promoted to Captain and Aide-de-camp. Maj. Wm. De Lacy was another gallant soldier, as was also Lieut.-Col. Gilbert Riordan.

THIRTY-EIGHTH REGIMENT.— "Second Regiment Scott Life Guard." The Thirty-eighth participated in the first battle of Bull Run, and Lieut.-Col. Addison Farnesworth, U. S. A., said: "During all my experience in former campaigns and presence on many a battle-field, I never witnessed greater bravery or more soldierly requisites than were displayed by the Thirty-eighth at Bull Run."

General Birney, in his Report of the battle of Williamsburg said: "The Thirty-eighth preserved well the high reputation it gained for gallantry at Bull Run, and, although in that engagement, and in this, it has lost fifteen officers and one-third of its members, it is still ready to devote the remainder to the flag." General Kearny said, "To Colonel Ward fell the good fortune to lead the most important charge of the day at Williamsburg." The charge is said to have divided the fortunes of the day in our favor. In a letter to Governor Morgan, General Kearny said, "New York will always hold her place while she has such sons to represent her."

General Sickles said of the services of the Thirty-seventh and Thirty-eighth Regiments at Chancellorsville, "Wherever valor and fidelity are passports to honor and hospitality, these twin regiments, on whose colors the shamrock and the stars are blended, will be heartily welcome."

In both the battles of Bull Run and Williamsburg the Thirty-eighth was opposed by the Fifteenth Louisiana Regiment. Cols. J. H. Hobart Ward and Regis de Trobriand were promoted to the rank of Brigadier-Generals. Maj. Augustus Funk, a gallant officer, was promoted to the Colonelcy of the Thirty-ninth Regiment; Lieut.-Col. Addison Farnesworth to Colonel of the Seventy-ninth, and Capt. John M. Cooney to Assistant Adjutant-General.

THIRTY-NINTH REGIMENT.—"Garibaldi Guards." The Thirty-ninth fought gallantly at First Bull Run, Cross Keys, Gettysburg, North Anna, Bristoe Station, Po River, Mine Run, Spottsylvania, Wilderness, Tolopotomoy, Coal Harbor, Petersburg, Strawberry Plains, Ream's Station and Deep Bottom. The regiment was organized chiefly through the exertions of Mr. Charles B. Norton, who was appointed Quartermaster, and later in the war, upon the recommendation of General McClellan, he was promoted to Brigade Quartermaster. A flag was presented to the regiment by a daughter of General Avezzana. This was the tri-colored standard which the patriot Garibaldi bore in triumph through the campaign of 1848-49, and with his own hands planted on the battlements of one of the castles of the Eternal City—a triumphant emblem of liberty and power.

FORTIETH REGIMENT.—"Mozart Regiment." The Fortieth took part in twenty-one great battles and lost twelve commissioned officers. The Fortieth, with the Thirty-seventh and Thirty-eighth bore the brunt of the battle of Williamsburg. General Kearny said: "The conduct of the regiment at the battle of Savage's Station was magnificent."

General Birney, in his Report of the battle of Chantilly said: "The

Fortieth moved across the corn-field, down the ravine, and up the opposite slope, with the greatest gallantry and determination, and almost immediately broke the Rebel lines and put them to flight."

In 1886, there were but ninety of the veterans of the regiment living. Colonel Edward Riley, who took the regiment to the front in 1861, and Col. Madison M. Cannon, who headed the little band of survivors on their march home, were still among the living. Col. Thomas W Egan, who rose to the rank of Brigadier-General, died in February, 1887.

FORTY-FIRST REGIMENT.—"De Kalb Regiment." The regiment was commanded by Col. Leopold Von Gilsa. At the second battle of Bull Run it lost the only commissioned officer in the war—Lieut. Richard Kurz. Lieut.-Col. Emil Dnyseng resigned in 1861, and became Major of the Fifteenth Heavy Artillery, and was mortally wounded in one of the last engagements of the war. Colors were presented to the regiment by a daughter of Mr. R. A. Witthaus. The regiment was composed entirely of Germans, of whom about six hundred had been in the Prussian army in 1848-51. Twenty-three of its thirty-three officers were veterans tried by fire.

FORTY-SECOND REGIMENT.—"Tammany Jackson Guard." When Fort Sumter was attacked, Tammany Hall took immediate action in placing itself on the side of the Union, and at its own expense recruited, equipped, and sent the Forty-second to the field— a regiment whose record on many a bloody field is unsurpassed by any other that fought under the Stars and Stripes. Col. Wm. D. Kennedy was the Grand Sachem when he received his commission as commander of the regiment. Over seven thousand men fought under the regimental banner, and less than five hundred returned home. Of the original 1200 only 250 returned. Colonel Kennedy, like Vosburg and Ellsworth, did not live to command the regiment in battle, for he died of disease in July, 1861. At the battle of Ball's Bluff the regiment first saw service. When General Baker fell, Colonel Cogswell (who had succeeded Colonel Kennedy), took command of a brigade. Colonel Cogswell ordered his brigade to cut their way through to Edwards Ferry. In the beginning of the engagement Capt. Timothy O'Meara placed by the side of the star spangled banner the green flag of his native isle. The twin emblems seemed to inspire the men with redoubled energy and intrepidity, and they charged upon the enemy with terrible effect. Nor did they give way till all hopes were dead. Colonel Cogswell and Captain O'Meara were captured, and shared the horrors of rebel captivity. At the battle of Antietam the regiment lost 180 killed, wounded and missing out of 280 who went into the battle. At Gettysburg Lieut.-Col. William A. Lynch, seeing the color-sergeant shot down, and the men wavering under a terrible fire, sprung from his horse, tore the standard from the hands of the patriotic and dying sergeant, and bearing it at the head of his command, restored the temporary flagging hopes of the regiment. This brave man died in August, 1887.

FORTY-THIRD REGIMENT.—"Albany and Yates Rifles." The first Colonel of the regiment was Francis L. Vinton, who was, in 1863, promoted to Brigadier-General. He was succeeded by Col. Benjamin F. Baker, who remained with the regiment until February, 1864, when he resigned. Five gallant officers served as Lieutenant Colonels: Charles H. Pierson, Volkert van Patten, Charles A. Milliken, John Wilson and James D. Visscher. Wilson died of wounds received at the battle of the Wilderness, and Visscher was killed in action July 12, 1864. During General McClellan's Peninsula campaign the Forty-third held the extreme right on the Chickahominy and its steady valor contributed greatly to General Porter's success in withdrawing from his position to the new base on the James River. After the battles of the Wilderness in May, 1864, the Forty-third was a mere wreck of the splendid regiment that went into action on the 6th of that month. Its three field officers were dead or dying, and the regiment caught in the bloody surge of the night of the 6th was almost no more. Lieutenant-Colonel Wilson lived but a few hours after being wounded, Capt. William Wallace was instantly killed, and Maj. John Fryer lived about two weeks after receiving his mortal wound. He was one of the youngest officers of the Sixth Corps, only twenty-one years of age. The color-guard and colors of the regiment were captured, and Sergeant Hackett, the brave standard bearer, was sent to Andersonville. Thoughtfully had he in the darkness stripped the flag from the staff and wrapped it around his body. He kept those colors concealed about him, and soon after died in his loathsome confinement. He was buried with the flag he had borne aloft still hidden beneath his uniform. The regiment was now reduced to seven commissioned officers and ninety-two men. Lieutenant-Colonel Visscher now assumed command of the glorious remnant, but the bullets of the enemy on the 12th of July, in the Shenandoah Valley, removed him from a position that he would have doubtless continued to hold with honor to himself and the welfare of his men. Colonel Upton said of the battle of Spottsylvania: "Captain Burham, of the Forty-third New York, had two colors in his hands when he was killed in coming back from the second line." This is evidently a mistake, as there was no officer of that name connected with the regiment, and the statement probably refers to Captain David Burhans, who, however, was not killed, but remained with the regiment for a year longer and was discharged in June, 1865. At the battles of Chancellorsville and Gettysburg the Forty-third exhibited the highest degree of courage and suffered severely. Mr. Simeon Draper presented a flag to the regiment.

FORTY-FOURTH REGIMENT.—"People's Ellsworth Regiment." At the battle of Malvern Hill the regiment in the most critical movement in the fortunes of the day, were ordered to charge bayonets upon the enemy, which it most gallantly performed under a sharp fire, repulsing the enemy and capturing a stand of colors, but of the 225 men with which the charge was made, 100 were killed or wounded. This charge turned the fortunes of the day and gave victory to our arms. Gen. Fitz John Porter said: "Col. James C. Rice drove a portion of the enemy from the field, taking a flag, bearing the inscription "Seven Pines." During the battle Colonel Rice halted his men four times under the fire of the enemy, and when he had arranged them to his satisfaction, he ordered the famous bayonet charge on a brigade of Confederates, and took more prisoners than he brought men of his own alive out of the engagement. Colonel Rice said of the battle: "History will record the engagement as one of the most severe and brilliant contests of the war." Corporal Chandler of Company F, the Color-Sergeant, was wounded. The flag was then seized by Corporal Young, and no sooner had he raised it than he was shot. Young Chandler, who had been wounded in the leg and arm, with his wounds bleeding, crept to the staff, and with great effort raised it the third time. In a moment he was again shot in the breast and soon after expired. His last words were, "I regret that I have only one life to give to my country." General Butterfield spoke of the splendid advance of the brigade, led by the Forty-fourth and Seventeenth New York at the battle of Groveton. On the thirtieth of May, 1863, the Forty-fourth led the advance of the army to Chancellorsville, and in that battle, as well as at Gettysburg and the Wilderness, the Forty-fourth retained the honors won at Malvern Hill. In August, 1863, Colonel Rice was promoted to Brigadier-General, in which position this splendid Christian soldier displayed all the qualities that make up a skilful and courageous military leader, and, after being mortally wounded, his last words were "Turn me over, that I may die with my face to the enemy." Lieut. Charles E. Pease was in 1863 promoted to a position on the Staff of General Meade. He was the officer who carried the letter to

General Grant, which proved to contain an offer of capitulation from General Lee, and Lieutenant Pease was the first officer to announce the glad tidings to the Army of the Potomac. He died in 1886.

FORTY-FIFTH REGIMENT.—"Fifth German Rifles," Col. George Van Arnsburg. The battle of Cross Keys was the first important engagement in which the regiment participated. At Chancellorsville the regiment suffered severely and lost many gallant officers. At the battle of Resaca the Forty-fifth in a most gallant manner saved the Fifth Indiana Battery from capture.

FORTY-SIXTH REGIMENT.—"Fremont Regiment." The Forty-sixth has a fine record, having participated with great gallantry at Hilton Head, Bull Run, Chantilly, South Mountain, Antietam, Fredericksburg, Siege of Vicksburg, Jackson, Weldon Railroad, Blue Springs, Campbell Station, Knoxville, Petersburg, Poplar Spring Church, Ream's Station and Coal Harbor. At Chantilly the regiment formed part of General Stevens' brigade, which received the first volley from Rebel muskets. The regiment with fixed bayonets charged through the woods, and drove the Rebels before them with great slaughter. The regiment went to the war under command of Col. Rudolph Rosa, with Germain Metternich, Lieutenant-Colonel. Colonel Metternich was accidentally killed in 1862.

FORTY-SEVENTH REGIMENT.—The regiment was first commanded by Col. Henry Moore, who was succeeded by Col. James L. Frazer, and finally, by Col. Christopher R. McDonald. The services of the regiment were specially invaluable at the battle of Olustee, Fla., February 20, 1864, where it lost several of its best officers. Sergeant Cox was wounded in the breast; the Colonel ordered another sergeant to take the colors; Sergeant Cox again seized the flag, advanced twenty-five paces to the front, waved them in front of the foe, and fell with a bullet in his leg. A color corporal took the colors and was killed. All the other color-bearers but one, successively met their death in defence of the regimental banner. After this battle the regiment returned North, joined the Army of the Potomac, and participated in General Grant's campaign. At the battle of the Wilderness the regiment behaved nobly, as it did also in the assault on Fort Fisher in 1865. The long list of officers of the Forty-seventh, whose names are worthy of special remembrance, includes Lieut.-Col. Alfred B. Nicholson, who died in February, 1884. Maj. Frank A. Butts, Capts. Frederick A. Sawyer, Eugene Douglass,

George B. Kirby. Charles W. Gallear, Lieuts. Hugh S. Sanford, Joseph J. Humphreys, William S. Warren, Majs. Edward Eddy, Jr., Hiram Pulver and John G. Borden. Major Frank A. Butts, a splendid officer, took command of the regiment after the wounding of Colonel McDonald at the battle of Olustee, and brought it off the field. Colonel McDonald died in October, 1874.

FORTY-EIGHTH REGIMENT.—"Continental Guard." The Forty-eighth was largely composed of Brooklyn men. Few regiments have a more brilliant record, and few suffered more severely. No less than eighteen of its commissioned officers were killed or mortally wounded during its term of service. The regiment went to the field under command of Col. James H. Perry, who died of disease at Fort Pulaski, June 18, 1862. Col. Wm. H. Barton succeeded Colonel Perry in command of the regiment, and held the position until December, 1864, when he resigned, and William B. Coan became the third and last Colonel of the regiment, The Forty-eighth was for a long time in the department of the South, and acquitted itself with great gallantry at Fort Wagner as is evinced by the fact that five of its commissioned officers were killed in that sanguinary engagement. The regiment was also engaged in the battle of Olustee, Fla. After the latter engagement the Forty-eighth, with the Forty-seventh, returned North and took part in General Grant's Virginia campaign. At Fort Fisher, Capt. James W Dunn was wounded inside the fort after dark, and for lack of proper attention he died from hemorrhage: Colonel Coan was wounded in the head—a severe flesh wound, while getting his men into position, before the charge began. The following are a few of the gallant heroes of the Forty-eighth, whose names should stand conspicuous on the Roll of Honor: Major Nere A. Elfwing, Lieut. B. R. Corwin, Lieut. Benjamin Seaward, Capt. Van Rensselaer K. Hilliard, Capt. Edward Downer, Capt. Henry T. Garaghan, Capt. Albert F Miller, Capt. Elbridge J. Hutchinson, Lieut. Christopher Hale, Lieut. Albert F. Howland, Lieut. Roger Edwards, Lieut. Henry W. Robinson and Capt. Adon Lippencott.

FORTY-NINTH REGIMENT.—Flag presented to the regiment by Mrs. Egbert L. Viele. The Forty-ninth has a splendid record. The regiment was engaged in twenty-two great battles and lost like the Forty-eighth, eighteen commmissioned officers. The first Colonel of the regiment was Daniel D. Bidwell—an admirable officer, who was, in 1864, promoted to Brigadier-General. The regiment was composed largely of men from Buffalo. The Forty-ninth was with the Army of the Potomac and suffered terribly in the battles of the Wilderness and Spottsylvania. In the charge on Marye's Heights, May 3, 1863, the regiment with the Thirty-third and Seventy-seventh bore the brunt of the assault.

Capt. Julius C. Borcherdt says of the part taken by the regiment: "At the battle of the Wilderness on the 6th of May, 1864, battle opened at four A. M., heavy musketry until five; then a battery opened upon us in our immediate front, doing terrible execution with their shell and solid shot, they could not have had a better range. At six A. M. a ten pound solid shot first passed through a large oak tree, then striking Capt. John F. E. Plogsted, who was sitting on the ground leaning against a large tree immediately in front and right of company, taking off his left leg and shattering his right leg and arm, then passing through under my company, throwing Private John Weismantel some six feet into the air, and finally bringing up at my left against Orderly Serg. Gus Meyers, rolling him several feet but not injuring him. Weismantel was killed by the concussion; not a wound or drop of blood showed. I had Captain Plogsted removed to the rear at once. It will be hard to forget the death-look on his face when he gave me his last message for his wife: he died at 6.30 A. M. Immediately after removing the Captain, a shell burst in front of my company, a piece perforating the rim of my hat and part of it wounding Private Joe Klein in the hand and arm. The loss was proving so great to our regiment from this cannonading, that Colonel Bidwell ordered the regiment to double-quick to the front about one hundred yards to get out of their line of fire. The way they piled in the shot and shell while we were advancing! A perfect hail of canister greeted us, killing Capt. Charles H. Hickmott, Lieut. Henry C. Valentine, and a large number of men. As the words "Halt! lie down!" were given, a shell burst within ten feet of my company, one piece passing through a file of my men a foot to the left of me, throwing their blood and flesh all over me, also wounding Ed. Borcherdt; a large piece passing to my immediate right, killing Lieut. Reuben M. Preston, tearing off his entire face. Poor fellow! he was one of our noblest young men in the service! So young and so full of hope! What a shock it will be for his young bride! But God is just.

"Our loss is very heavy in killed and wounded to-day, especially in officers. We have now only three Captains and seven Lieutenants left. No direct charge was made upon us. But we were annoyed by their sharpshooters and occasional shelling until four P. M., when orders came to return to a rear line some two hundred yards—

some light earthworks which had been thrown up by the Third Heavy Artillery. Heavy firing to our left, where General Hancock must be having a hard struggle with the Johnnies, and our noble Vermont Brigade is no doubt having its share of hard knocks.

"At six P. M., the rebels charged in heavy columns on our whole front, making charge after charge. We held them until seven o'clock, when our extreme right gave way, which was held by new troops of our First Division. Our old brigade held him in check until we received a front, flank and even rear fire, which made it decidedly uncomfortable for us; still we held on, jumping from one side of the rifle-pit to the other, until General Sedgwick appeared along about eight P. M., and ordered Colonel Bidwell to clear the plank road and woods in the rear. Colonel Bidwell gave the order, and with a yell the boys charged and cleared the woods, capturing quite a number of prisoners. I was on the extreme left of the column, when, in the darkness and dense jungle of underbrush, I was separated from my command and fell into rebel hands. At that moment a portion of the Ninety-fifth Pennsylvania, in running to the rear, the rebels mistook for a charging column, and gave way. I placed myself at the head of them, and made for our lines. Came near being lost in the wilderness. I rejoined my command at three A. M."

FIFTY-FIRST REGIMENT.—"Shepard Rifles." The Fifty-first had a brilliant and more than ordinarily varied career. They fought and conquered on three sides of the grand square embraced by our lines—on the Atlantic, along the Border States and on the Mississippi. At the battle of Roanoke Island, Capt. David F. Wright, Company A (color company), planted the American flag upon the ramparts of the Rebel fort in advance of any other regiment. Lieuts. Palin H. Sims and James J. Johnston took possession of the guns of the fort. At Antietam, in the short space of five minutes the regiment lost ninety-five men. At Fredericksburg, they were in Sumner's corps and lost six color-bearers and eighty men, and their regimental flag was the last to leave the field. The flag of the Fifty-first was the first to wave over the capitol at Jackson, Miss. Only 200 men returned home out of 1200 with which they originally left New York. Before the departure of the regiment for the war, Col. Elliott F. Shepard, of Governor Morgan's Staff, presented it, in a very eloquent address, with an elegant banner. Col. Edward Ferrero first commanded the regiment, and in 1862 he was promoted to Brigadier-General. Col. Robert B. Potter was also promoted to Brigadier-General in 1863. Colonel Potter was president of the

Vallandigham Court Martial. Col. Charles W. Le Gendre was honorably discharged in 1864. The last Colonel was John G. Wright, who was promoted from Major. Major Wright was captured at the battle of Poplar Springs Church. He had been through thirty-five battles, and all his comrades testify to his courage and devotion. At the battles of South Mountain, Newbern, Wilderness, Petersburg, as well as Antietam, and Fredericksburg, the regiment was unsurpassed for its bravery and good conduct. At the battle of Fredericksburg, Hancock's division had fallen back, entirely exposing his right flank. Sustaining his position with two additional brigades, he deputed the work of carrying the heights to General Ferrero. At his command the Fifty-first charged up the slope, through a shower of musket balls, drove the enemy back in confusion from the rifle pits to the shelter of the earthworks and became masters of the position. The regiment lost six color-bearers, and their flag was the last to leave the field.

Among the commissioned officers of the regiment whose names will be remembered by the surviving veterans were Lieut. Col. Theodore B. Marsh, Lieut.-Col. R. C. Mitchell, Capt. Clifford Coddington, Capt. Henry W. Francis, Capt. Henry H. Holbrook, Capt. Chas. W. Walton, Capt. George A. Tuttle, Adjt. Abram W McKee, Lieut. Leonard S. Schoonmaker and Maj. George W. Whitman.

Lieut. Gilbert H. McKibbin was promoted for gallantry and meritorious conduct to Captain and Assistant Adjutant-General.

FIFTY-SECOND REGIMENT.—"German Rangers or Sigel Rifles." The Fifty-second has a splendid record. It was in twenty-two great battles and its losses were terrible. Thirty-five men and five officers were all that remained of the regiment upon its return home after its three years of gallant service. The regiment returned home under command of Maj. Henry P. Ritzius.

FIFTY-FOURTH REGIMENT.—This was a noble regiment, and its officers were generally well selected and worthy of their positions. Col. Eugene A. Kozlay was an admirable officer, as was also Lieut.-Col. Charles Ashby, a nephew of the Rebel General Ashby, killed in 1862. Lieutenant-Colonel Ashby resigned in 1863, and in 1864 Bankson T. Morgan was promoted to the position. At the second battle of Bull Run the regiment lost 187 men and two commissioned officers.

FIFTY-FIFTH REGIMENT.—"Lafayette Guard." Col. Regis de Trobriand. At the battle of Fair Oaks, the regiment saved from imminent capture eight pieces of artillery after a most brilliant charge, in which it drove the enemy back to the woods at the point of the bayonet. All this at the sacrifice of nearly one quarter of the numbers of men engaged. The regiment was consolidated with the Thirty-eighth Regiment in 1862, and its honors became blended with that gallant regiment. General Keyes said,—" The Fifty-fifth at Fair Oaks vindicated its claim to the proud title of 'Guard Lafayette,'" and General Nagle said: "The regiment fought most gallantly."

FIFTY-SIXTH REGIMENT.—The Fifty-sixth took part in fourteen battles and many skirmishes. At the battle of Fair Oaks, it went into action 500 strong, and lost in killed and wounded nearly half their number. General Nagle said: "The Fifty-sixth and the 100th were the first to advance upon Williamsburg, and when ordered by General McClellan to support General Hancock the enemy gave up the contest." The regiment was originally commanded by Col. Charles H. Van Wyck, who was promoted, in 1865, to Brevet Brigadier-General.

Lieut-Col. John J. Wheeler resigned in 1864, and was succeeded by Rockwell Tyler.

FIFTY-SEVENTH REGIMENT.—"National Guard Rifles." The Fifty-seventh was first commanded by Col. Samuel K. Zook,—who was the very personification of gallantry. Colonel Zook was promoted to Brigadier-General in May, 1863, and was killed on the second day of the battle of Gettysburg. At the battle of Antietam the regiment was commanded by Lieut.-Col. Alfred B. Chapman. In this engagement three of the fourteen commissioned officers were killed and six wounded. The regiment left the field with only six officers and 180 men—less than half the number who left home the year before. But the regiment made their foes suffer more than an equal proportion: in one charge the Fifty-seventh took more prisoners than the regiment numbered, and captured the colors of the Twelfth Alabama Regiment. At Fredericksburg the regiment fought bravely and again suffered severely. In the battle of the Wilderness, Lieutenant-Colonel Chapman was killed while encouraging his men in the midst of the conflict. The Fifty-seventh returned home under the command of Col. James W. Britt, who is now an officer in the New York Custom House. The regiment was engaged in twenty-three important battles.

FIFTY-NINTH REGIMENT.—Colors presented by Hon. A. C. Kingsland. The Fifty-ninth has a brilliant record, having participated in twenty-three great battles in which it lost fourteen commissioned officers. It was originally commanded by Col. Wm. Linn Tidball and Philip J. Joachimsen, as Lieutenant-Colonel. Colonel Tidball resigned in January, 1863. In 1864 Wm. A. Olmsted was appointed to the position. Colonel Olmsted was a very popular officer, and at the close of the war was promoted to Brevet Brigadier-General. At the battle of Antietam the regiment held their position in front of the line of battle until flanked on both sides by the enemy, and ordered from the field by General Sumner in person. They went into the fight with 400 men and twenty-four officers, and came out with twelve officers and 146 men.

SIXTIETH REGIMENT.—"St. Lawrence Regiment." Colonel George S. Greene was promoted to Brigadier-General in April, 1862, and his successor, Col. Wm. B. Goodrich, was mortally wounded at the battle of Antietam, while in the display of great valor. At Gettysburg the regiment fought bravely, where it was called to part with many valuable officers. The regiment went to the war under command of Col. William B. Hayward, who resigned in 1862.

SIXTY-FIRST REGIMENT.—"Clinton Guard." The Sixty-first was a New York City regiment. Its first Colonel was Francis C. Barlow, who was promoted to Brigadier-General in 1862. At the battle of Fair Oaks, the Sixty-first was the only regiment of its brigade that did not break and run at some time or other. General Howard said that "he did not believe there were any braver men in the world." The Sixty-first entered the field of Antietam under command of Colonel Barlow. Colonel Barlow was severely wounded and his life despaired of by all except his faithful wife, to whom he was married on the same evening that he went to the war. Mrs. Barlow was a daughter of Mr. Francis George Shaw, of Staten Island, and a sister of Col. Robert G. Shaw, who was killed at Fort Wagner, while in command of the Fifty-fourth Massachusetts Regiment—the first colored regiment raised in the Northern States. General Caldwell, in his report of the battle of Antietam, says: "Whatever praise is due to the most distinguished bravery, the utmost coolness and quickness of perception, the greatest promptitude and skill in handling troops under fire, is justly due to Colonel Barlow." While lying in the hospital Colonel Barlow received his commission as Brigadier-General, and he was succeeded in command of the regiment by Col. Nelson A. Miles, than whom the service possessed no more efficient officer. General Doubleday, in his narrative of Chancellorsville, "Campaigns of the Civil War," says, "Colonel Miles was shot through the body, while encouraging his men to defend the position." This "shot through the body" did not prove fatal, for the Colonel was promoted to Brigadier-General one year after the battle referred to by General Doubleday. The regiment participated with honor in twenty-four battles. At Fair Oaks the regiment suffered terribly. The long list of killed or mortally wounded includes officers whom the State could not afford to lose. At Gettysburg General Barlow was again wounded and fell into the hands of the enemy. So well satisfied was Gen. Jubal Early that Barlow would die, that he said to him, "You will never live to fight again," to which General Barlow replied, "I will live to fight you yet, General," and the prophecy was fulfilled at the battle of Spottsylvania, in 1864, where Barlow, having in the meantime been promoted to Major-General, in a brilliant manner snatched from Early's corps an entire division. By his capture of Maj. Gen. Edward Johnson and 5,000 men at Spottsylvania Court House, he won his brevet, and his conduct during the closing campaign of the war was such that Generals Grant and Meade selected him for the only full vacant Major-Generalship. General Barlow is also a brother-in-law of George Wm. Curtis, who married another daughter of Mr. Shaw.

Among the officers who survived the war, and whose records entitled them to grateful remembrance, were, Col. George W. Scott (a very popular officer), who was promoted to Brevet Brigadier General, Lieut.-Col. Oscar K. Broady, Capt. Theodore W. Greig, Maj. George W. Schaffer, Lieut.-Col. Richard A. Brown, Capt. Willard Keech, Capt. Thomas Welsh, Lieut. Rufus L. Rundell and Lieut. Wm. H. French, Jr.

SIXTY-SECOND REGIMENT.—"Anderson Zouaves." The regiment bore an honorable part in nineteen of the principal battles of the Army of the Potomac. After the terrible battle of Williamsburg, General Kearny, being anxious to know whether or not the Rebel forts were deserted, the Sixty-second pushed up and took the fort next on the left, and planted thereon the Stars and Stripes. This gallant act was performed by Abram T. Perine, color-sergeant of Company C. The gallantry with which the regiment moved up to receive the enemy's fire in the assault upon Marye's Heights in May, 1863 (Chancellorsville) ; and in about as many seconds, lost, in killed and wounded, sixty-four officers and men, "was," said General Wheaton, "worthy of especial praise and notice." On many occasions the gallantry of the regiment called forth the commendations of their commanders. General Wheaton was unreserved in his commendations of Lieut. Edward H. Morris. By his skill and good judgment the advance of the enemy s masses was delayed, and time given to move off the brigade Had a less discreet officer been in command, the whole brigade would have been captured ; as it was, the brave Lieutenant was himself made a prisoner. Col. John L. Riker was killed at Fair Oaks, and his last words were "Boys, we're surrounded—give them cold steel." In view of the number of battles in which the Sixty-second was engaged, its loss in commissioned officers was remarkably small—only two being killed during the war : Colonel Riker and Maj. Wilson Hubbel. The latter was killed outright at Coal Harbor on the 3d of June, 1864. Of those who returned home and whose names are associated with the valor of the regiment there were among many others, Lieut.-Col. Theodore B. Hamilton, Col. David J. Nevin, Capt. William Ackerman, Capt. Frederick Hanson, Capt. George H. Eddy, Capt. William H. Baker and Capt. William F. Davies. Capt. Jacob Duryee, who recruited and reorganized Company H, died in June, 1889. His grandfather fought in the War of 1812.

SIXTY-THIRD REGIMENT.—This was a New York City regiment and has also a splendid record. It was actively engaged in twenty-four great battles and lost fourteen commissioned officers. The regiment was especially conspicuous for deeds of bravery at the battle of Antietam. The colors were shot down sixteen times, and on each occasion a man was ready to spring forward and place the colors in front. Fifteen of those gallant men were more or less severely wounded. In Company G all the commissioned officers and non-commissioned officers, except two corporals, were either killed or wounded. Col. James D. Brady arose step by step from private to colonel.

SIXTY-FOURTH REGIMENT.—"Cattaraugus Regiment." No regiment from the State has a more enviable record than the Sixty-fourth; few participated in a greater number of battles or lost a larger percentage of its men and officers. The regiment was engaged in nearly all the great engagements of the Army of the Potomac, from Yorktown to Ream's Station. At the battle of Antietam, the regiment captured two stands of colors and several hundred prisoners. The Sixty-fourth fought with the remnant of the Sixty-first, in Caldwell's brigade of Sedgwick's division. The following officers remained with the regiment during its term of service and are entitled to remembrance for their valor and devotion to the service for which they had enlisted: Maj. Lemen W Bradley, Capt. Orvel H. Willard, Capt. Lewis H. Fassett, Capt. Richard F. Lincoln, Capt. Horatio T. Hunt, Capt. William W Roller, Capt. John A. Manley, Lieut. Austin B. Rumsey, Lieut. Addison Pierce, Lieut. Wm. C. Bockoven, Lieut. Wm. W Russell, Lieut. Edw. T. McCutchem, Lieut. Albin C. Blackmore.

The regiment returned home under command of Col. William Glenny—an admirable soldier, who, in 1865, was promoted to Brevet Brigadier-General.

SIXTY-FIFTH REGIMENT. "First United States Chasseurs." On every battle-field fought by the Army of the Potomac, there lie the dead of the Sixty-fifth, while a goodly portion sacrificed their lives in the Shenandoah Valley. The regiment went to the war under command of Col. John Cochrane, who was promoted to Brigadier-General in July, 1862. He was succeeded by Col. Alexander Shaler, who, in May, 1863, was also promoted to Brigadier-General. Joseph H. Hamblin succeeded Colonel Shaler in command of the regiment, and, in 1864, he, too, was promoted to Brigadier-General. Three Brigadier-Generals were thus contributed to the army by the Sixty-fifth Regiment. Colonel Hamblin is said to have been the handsomest officer in the Army of the Potomac. At the battle of Malvern Hill, when it seemed almost the fashion to fall back, the Sixty-fifth was one of the few regiments that not only held its ground, but delivered such a fire that the Rebel officers pronounced it equal to "hell." At the battle of Fair Oaks, Colonel Cochrane handled his regiment admirably and displayed great skill and bravery. General Keyes said, " The Sixty-fifth fought bravely and captured the colors of the Twenty-third North Carolina Regiment,—the first battle-flag captured during the campaign." The correctness of this statement will be disputed, for Lieut. John N. Coyne, of the Seventieth New York Regiment, was awarded a medal for capturing a battle flag at the battle of Williamsburg, which was previous to the battle of Fair Oaks. At Fredericksburg, Colonel Shaler was selected for his bravery to lead a brigade under General Sedgwick, and the distinguished services rendered by the Colonel on that occasion resulted in his promotion to Brigadier-General. At the battle of the "Opequan," Colonel Hamblin had charge of a brigade, and Capt. Henry C. Fisk (who in 1865 was promoted to Colonel) commanded the regiment. Colonel Hamblin was always where bullets flew the thickest, and had his horse shot from under him; still he continued undaunted to cheer his men on. The officers of the regiment were all conspicuous for their bravery. At the battle of Cedar Creek,

October 19, 1864, the regiment lost its Lieutenant-Colonel, Thomas J. Higginbotham—a very valuable officer, who was killed outright while leading his men against the foe. At Cedar Creek, Capt. John J. Wilber, and Capt. Charles H. Woodman were especially conspicuous for their gallantry; they were as usual self-possessed, brave and cool. The latter had a horse shot from under him.

Few regiments were better officered than the Sixty-fifth, and the following, who were mustered out on expiration of term of service, will be remembered by the surviving veterans of the regiment: Capt. B. B. Miller, Capt. Henry C. Ellis, Capt. Ivan Tailof, Capt. George A. Bernard, Capt. Andrew S. Bushee, Capt. Samuel Truesdell, Capt. E. E. Cozens, Lieut. W. J. Morton, Lieut. M. A. Stearns, Lieut. W. R. Hedden, Lieut. W R. Roome, Lieut. W H. Welsh, Lieut. A. J. Verplank, Lieut. W O. Macay, Lieut. Charles Crowell, Lieut. A. J. Sizer, Lieut. W. G. Ford, Lieut. Henry R. Hentstein.

Besides these should also be remembered Capt. Edward H. Little, who was promoted to Major of the 127th Regiment; Capt. Wm. Gurney, promoted to Colonel of the 127th; and Lieut. LeRoy Crockett, promoted to Major of the Seventy-second Ohio; Lieut.-Col. David J. Miller, Maj. Edmund K. Russell, Capt. F. J. Volks, Capt. Michael Divine, Capt. J. C. Ball, and Capt. Thomas J. Hassett were all heroes and did their part towards sustaining the reputation of the "First United States Chasseurs."

SIXTY-SIXTH REGIMENT.—The Sixty-sixth was another splendid regiment, of which the city and State might well be proud. The regiment participated in twenty-three great battles; 400 out of 900 men were lost in action during the war, and many others died from wounds or illness. Out of the remainder (150) 133 re-enlisted at the expiration of their term of service. On the 10th of March, 1862, they took up the line of march for Manassas (the Rebel stronghold). At night, after a fatiguing march of eighteen miles through the woods, in single, sometimes double files, over hills so steep they had to assist their ascent by grasping the bushes, and fording numerous streams, and in a drenching rain, they bivouacked near Bull Run. Col. Orlando W. Morris led his regiment with unsurpassed coolness and bravery at the battle of Chancellorsville, where he was wounded; and at Gettysburg he was again wounded. Colonel Morris in his Report of the battle of Chancellorsville said,—"Of the conduct of the officers and men of the Sixty-sixth I cannot speak in too high terms. It was all that could be expected of the bravest." Colonel Morris, while bravely bearing the colors of his regiment in the midst of the conflict at the battle of Coal Harbor, was killed—leaving the reputation of a high-minded Christian soldier. Colonel Morris was presented with an elegant sword at the Sanitary Fair, in New York, in 1864, by his fellow citizens, in recognition of his gallant conduct. This sword is now in possession of his brother, Mr. Charles S. Morris, of Elizabeth, New Jersey. The desperate bravery of the Sixty-sixth at Fredericksburg, in December, 1862, is proved by the fact that almost the entire regiment lay dead on the field.

Lieut. Adolphus Nelson, a gallant officer and a son of Judge Nelson of Westchester County, was killed by a mob on Staten Island in June, 1863.

SIXTY-SEVENTH REGIMENT.—"First Long Island Regiment." The regiment went to the war under command of Col. Julius W Adams. Colonel Adams resigned in 1862, and was succeeded by Col. Nelson Cross. Colonel Adams said, "This was the first regiment in the State to offer its services for the war." General Nagle said of the regiment at the battle of Fair Oaks: "Occupying the most advanced position, my brigade made the most desperate, bloody and obstinate fight of the day. The key point of the battle was held by the Sixty-seventh New York, and they held it against great odds until the arrival of reinforcements." The Prince de Joinville said, "Had the Sixty-seventh given way the army would have been destroyed." Serg.-Maj. Martin did his duty nobly, rallying the regiment around their standard, and leading them forward when nearly every officer was killed or wounded. His services were noticed by his commanding officer, who promoted him on the field. Among the wounded was Capt. Augustus Belknap, Jr. At the storming of Marye's Heights (Chancellorsville) the Sixty-seventh was in the advance, and the record of services rendered on other important occasions by its gallant Colonel, Nelson Cross, was in keeping with the reckless energy shown on these bloody heights. The regiment was in seventeen battles and was reduced in numbers during its two and a half years' service, from nearly 1000 to less than 400, of which remnant nearly two thirds re-enlisted for three years. The Sixty-seventh is the regiment in which the famous Miles O'Reilly served as Sergeant in Company C. Captain Belknap died in June, 1889.

SIXTY-EIGHTH REGIMENT.—" Cameron Rifles." This was a German regiment, and was first commanded by Col. Robert J. Betje, and afterwards by Col. Felix Salm-Salm, a foreign officer who rendered good service to the Union cause. The regiment took part in many of the great battles, and suffered severely, especially at Chancellorsville, Gettysburg and White Sulphur Springs. Colonel Salm-Saim was killed in the battle of Gravelotte.

SIXTY-NINTH REGIMENT.—"First Regiment, Irish Brigade." The regiment lost at the battle of Fair Oaks the day on which it won its first laurels, and in the succeeding battle of Malvern Hill, 410 brave fellows. At the battle of Fredericksburg two companies of the Sixty-ninth were detailed to capture a house filled with Rebel sharpshooters, on the right of the stone-wall. Under the lead of Capt. James Saunders, to the work they rushed impetuously, dwindling and melting away before the enemy's sure and destructive fusillade, as they advanced, driving the Rebels out, but at the cost of two-thirds of the two companies of heroes who had thus honored the country and the army. The Sixty-ninth took part in twenty-three great battles.

The following are among the officers who were identified with the Sixty-ninth and passed into civil life with honorable war records:

Col. Robert Nugent, promoted to Brevet Brigadier-General in 1865, Lieut.-Col. James Kelly, Lieut.-Col. James J. Smith, Maj. Richard Moroney, Capt. Edward F. O'Connor, Maj. James Cavanagh, Maj. John D. Mulhall, Lieut. Charles J. Clark, Capt. Robert H. Milliken, Capt. Maurice W. Wall, Capt. Michael H. Murphy, Lieut.-Col. James E. McGee, Lieut. Dennis F Sullivan and Lieut. James G. Smith.

SEVENTIETH REGIMENT.—"First Excelsior Brigade."—The regiment went to the war under command of Col. Daniel E. Sickles, who, in September, 1861, was promoted to Brigadier-General, and was succeeded by Col. William Dwight, who was also promoted to Brigadier-General. At the battle of Williamsburg, the first Rebel regiment that confronted the Seventieth took it for one of its own side, and the commanding officer, dictated by his assistant, demanded Colonel Dwight to show his colors, at the same time the Rebel flag was displayed by the Rebel color-bearer. Then our standard was raised, and the Stars and Stripes waved in defiance of the ensign of the enemy. No sooner had the good old flag been espied than a volley was discharged at our men; but it passed over their heads. The fire was returned with good effect. It was here that the gallant Captain O'Rielly fell dead as he gave the order, "Boys, follow me. Forward, March!" Captain O'Rielly was the first officer from the Genesee Valley, at least from the city of Rochester, who fell in the war. He was a son of the late Henry O'Rielly, of telegraph fame. After the battle Lieutenant-Colonel Farnum, in a letter to Mayor Opdyke of New York, said: "Under the precious rags which were once so proudly borne more men have fallen in a single fight than ever fell under any other flag in the army of the United States since the war commenced. The regiment went into the field with 600 privates and twenty-seven officers, and more than half of the privates were killed or wounded, as were also twenty-three of the twenty-seven officers." As this broken but unconquered band marched by General Heintzleman, to the rear, the General and his Staff uncovered their heads. "Soldiers," said General Heintzleman, "when you took the name of the First Excelsior, you had done nothing to deserve it, now you have won it."

Surg. Harvey E. Brown died in August, 1889. He rendered notable service in 1861. Surgeon Brown was a graduate of the University of New York, and was a son of that gallant soldier, Col. Harvey Brown of the Fifth United States Artillery, who, as Commander of United States troops, rendered invaluable assistance in quelling the disturbances in New York City at the time of the riot in 1863.

SEVENTY-FIRST REGIMENT.—"Second Excelsior Brigade." The regiment was commanded by Col. George B. Hall. At the battle of Fair Oaks, General Sickles rode along the front of his men, and gave orders for the regiment to "charge bayonets." Col. George B. Hall gallantly led the charge, one of the most brilliant made in any battle; not a man shirked or straggled from the ranks. The regiment arrived just in time to assist General Brooks' brigade, then hard pressed, and doubtless saved his troops from disaster. The regiment also bore an honorable part in the battle of Bristoe Station, where it again suffered severely.

SEVENTY-SECOND REGIMENT.—"Third Excelsior Brigade." General Hooker, in his Report of the battle of Malvern Hill, says: "I especially invite attention to the brilliant conduct of Colonel Nelson Taylor's regiment, (Seventy-second N. Y.). The loss sustained by the regiment is the truest index of its services." Colonel Taylor was promoted to Brigadier-General in September, 1862, and his successor, the brave and lamented Col. William O. Stevens, was killed at the battle of Chancellorsville. After the death of Colonel Stevens, Col. John S. Austin assumed command of the regiment and John Leonard was appointed Lieutenant-Colonel. Many promotions were made from the Seventy-second to positions in other regiments. Capt. Robert T. Johnson was promoted to Major of the 144th, and

Lieut. Thomas W G. Fry rose to the rank of Captain and Commissary of Subsistence.

SEVENTY-THIRD REGIMENT.—"Fourth Excelsior Brigade." To General Heintzleman's corps belonged the honor of being the first to enter the abandoned works of the enemy at Yorktown, and to Col. William R. Brewster of the Seventy-third was due the credit of raising the first flag over the evacuated town. General Sickles said, "Nothing could resist the impetuous rush of the regiment at the battle of Fair Oaks." General McClellan said, "I well remember the gallantry of the Seventy-third at Williamsburg, Fair Oaks and during the Seven Days battles."

Colonel Brewster rose from a sick bed to command the Excelsior Brigade at the battle of Mine Run, November 27, 1863, and by his presence inspired his men to the utmost enthusiasm. Among the brave men of the Seventy-third, Maj. Michael W Burns is deserving of especial remembrance. He was promoted from a Captaincy in his regiment after the Seven Days battles, where he was taken prisoner by the Rebels and subsequently exchanged. He was complimented for his bravery by General Hooker and every field officer in his brigade. At the battle of Gettysburg, the regiment was magnificently handled by Major Burns. He was presented with a sword, sash and belt by the citizens of the Fifth Ward, New York, as a testimonial of their appreciation of his gallantry in the field. In 1863, Major Burns was promoted to Lieutenant-Colonel of his regiment, and in 1865, to Brevet Colonel. Colonel Burns died in December, 1883. At the battle of Williamsburg, Lieutenant-Colonel Lewis Benedict, Jr., was last seen, standing up to his full height, and waving his men forward with his pistol. He was heard to shout: "Fight, men, fight to the last." Benedict, or "Poor Old Pop," as he was called, was captured in this battle. The regiment lost in action seven hundred officers and men, of whom all but forty-six were killed or wounded. It captured during the war five Rebel colors, five pieces of artillery, and never lost any. The regiment was in twenty-three great battles and lost nineteen commissioned officers. The regiment also lost heavily at Chancellorsville, and it is claimed by many that Stonewall Jackson was mortally wounded by the bullets of the Seventy-third; but of this there is much doubt. Colonel Brewster was promoted to Brevet Brigadier-General in 1864.

SEVENTY-FOURTH REGIMENT.—"Fifth Excelsior Regiment." The regiment went to the war under command of Col. Charles K.

Graham, who was promoted to Brigadier-General in 1863. (General Graham died in May, 1889.) Colonel Graham was succeeded by Col. Thomas Holt, whose name appears in the Official Records at Washington, as having been "missing" since November 30, 1863. Ten commissioned officers were lost by the regiment during its term of service. Among the gallant men who returned home with the regiment were, Lieut. Colonel Wm. H. Lounsbury, Maj. Lovell Purdy, Jr., Capt. Francis E. Tyler, Capt. Wm. Conway, Capt. Victor Hurlaux, Maj. George H. Quarterman, Maj. Henry M. Alles, Lieut. Charles W. Squier, Capt. Frederick E. Garnett. Captain Garnett has recently written an admirable article on the battles of the Wilderness.

It was on the evidence of Private Thomas Wallsch—who suffered fearfully at Andersonville that Wirz—the keeper, was convicted and hung. Mr. Wallsch, who died recently, was a man of high intellectual attainments, and for some time after the close of the war held a position in the Post office Department at Washington.

SEVENTY-FIFTH REGIMENT.—The regiment was engaged in the battles of Cotten, Bisland, Port Hudson and Winchester. On the occasion of a review of the regiment at New Orleans, General Butler declared it to be "one of the finest he had ever seen." At the battle of Winchester, Lieut.-Col. Willoughby Babcock was wounded, taken prisoner, and soon after died. The regiment behaved splendidly at Port Hudson. The Seventy-fifth furnished many officers for other regiments, including Capt. Clinton McDougall, to Colonel of the 111th Regiment; Capt. James H. Hinman to Major of the 111th; Capt. Luther Goodrich to Colonel of the Eighty-eighth United States Colored Troops; Lieut. Charles W. Drew, to Colonel of the Seventy-sixth United States Colored Troops; and Lieut. Augustus W. Benedict to Major of the Seventy-sixth United States Colored Troops. Lieut.-Col. Robert P. York was an admirable officer, as were also Maj. Benjamin F. Thurber, Capt. Frank Silsby, Capt. Anson Tuller, Capt. Arba M. Seymour, Lieut. William H. Sayre, Lieut. Isaac Stark, Lieut. Frederick Cossum, Lieut. William H. Root, Lieut. Roselle B. Roe, Capt. George B. McFarlan, Capt. William M. Hosmer, Capt. Charles H. Cox, Capt. Lester D. Wilson and Lieut. Charles W. Wolcott.

SEVENTY-SIXTH REGIMENT.—"Cortland County Regiment." The Seventy-sixth has a brilliant record, and lost in battle some of the best officers the State could furnish. In the terrible slaughter of the 28th of August, 1862, near Gainsville, where the whole regiment seemed to be mowed down, the color-bearer, and with him the colors, was brought to the ground. Color-Bearer Charles E. Stamp, immediately rushed forward and rescued the colors amid a storm of bullets, and bore them through the rest of the fight. The Colonel at once promoted him to the rank of Color-Sergeant for his gallantry. At South Mountain, Stamp advanced a short distance ahead of his regiment, and driving his flag staff down into the earth, he cried: "There, come up to that." But he was too good a mark, and he was killed by a bullet piercing his forehead. At Second Bull Run and at Gettysburg the Seventy-sixth bore a conspicuous part and covered itself with glory. The regiment had three Colonels, viz.: Nelson W. Green, William P. Wainwright, and Charles E. Livingstone.

SEVENTY-SEVENTH REGIMENT.—"Bemis Heights Regiment." The regiment took the most prominent part in the battle of Mechanicsville, and was encouraged in their charge upon the Rebels by their gallant Colonel, James B. McKean. A Rebel guidon was captured by the regiment, bearing the inscription, "Victory or Death." The Seventy-seventh were engaged in twenty great battles, and at the battles of Fredericksburg and Spottsylvania Court House, behaved with the greatest bravery and suffered severely. In the charge on Marye's Heights, May 3, 1863, the regiment did nobly, and with the Thirty-third and the Forty-ninth bore the brunt of the assault.

SEVENTY-EIGHTH REGIMENT.—"Cameron Highlanders." In 1864, the regiment was consolidated with the 102d Regiment. It went to the war under command of Col. Daniel Ullman, who was in 1863 promoted to Brigadier-General. In 1864, Col. Herbert Hammerstein was appointed to the command of the regiment, and Harvey S. Chatfield, Lieutenant-Colonel. At the battles of South Mountain and Antietam the regiment fought bravely and also at Chancellorsville. At Chancellorsville, George Washington Monks received a bullet in his brain which he carried for twenty-three years, until January, 1886, when he died. Seven days is the longest time any one else was ever known to survive such a wound. Lieutenant-Colonel Chatfield, now a member of the bar of New York City, was a gallant soldier, as was also Adj. Henry P. Herring.

SEVENTY-NINTH REGIMENT.—" Highlanders" Seventy-ninth State Militia.) When the regiment went into Virginia at the commencement of the war it laid aside the "Kilts" together with the plaid trowsers and donned the ordinary blue. This was the first three years regiment to return home from the war. At the battle of Chantilly Gen. Isaac I. Stevens (formerly Colonel of the regiment), seizing the colors of the Seventy-ninth, exclaimed: "We are all Highlanders; follow, Highlanders; forward, my brave Highlanders." The Highlanders did follow their Scottish Chief, but while sweeping forward a ball struck him in the right temple, killing him instantly,—the very manner of death he had craved when discussing with his brother officers, the day before, the probabilities of his own fall. One hour afterwards, when taken up, his hand was still clinched around the flag-staff. A moment after General Stevens seized the colors, his son, Capt. Hazard Stevens, fell wounded, and cried to his father that he was hurt. With but a glance back, that Roman father said: "I can't attend to you now, Hazard; Corporal Thompson, see to my son." An official order was read to the regiment, complimenting them for their bravery at South Mountain and Antietam. At the first battle of Bull Run, the most important charge of the day was made by the Seventy-ninth and Sixty-ninth New York Regiments, but its brave Colonel, James Cameron, did not live to see the valiant deeds of those whom he commanded, for while in the act of cheering on his men, he fell a martyr on the field. Instead of becoming disheartened, these descendants of Wallace and of Bruce pushed on, encouraged by the brave Maj. David McLelland, and Adjt. David Ireland, in their charge upon the enemy. "Chantilly, Coosaw, both Bull Runs, Port Royal, and Blue Springs, Jackson and Knoxville, in their turn, have seen their Highland Flings." Among the individual acts of heroism, was that of Capt. Francis W. Judge, of Company K, who, when the battle-flag of a Georgia regiment was raised upon the parapet of Fort Sanders, rushed out amid the bullets, and tearing it down, carried it through the embrasures, a prize to his comrades. The Seventy-ninth was engaged in sixteen battles, and it is remarkable that its loss in commissioned officers should have been so small and unusually light; only two were killed in battle. Among the survivors of the war, whose military records have received honorable mention, were Maj. Andrew D. Baird, Capt. Alexander L. Baird. Col. David Morrison, Maj. William Simpson, Capt. Wm. S. Montgomery, Capt. Joseph Laing, Capt. Samuel T. Wallace, Capt. Wm. C. Clark, Capt. John Glendinning, Capt. Robert Armon, Capt. John Windsor, Capt. Robert Gair. Lieut. James Gilmore, Lieut. George D. Martin, Lieut. George Harrison, Lieut. James Donaldson, Lieut. John S. Dingwall, Lieut. George H. Ladley, Lieut. John Whyte, Lieut. Charles Watson, Lieut. Thomas Hamilton, Lieut. James McGiffin, Lieut. Henry Hutchinson and Lieut. Charles Riley.

Major Andrew D. Baird is now one of Brooklyn's most influential citizens.

EIGHTIETH REGIMENT.—(Twentieth State Militia.) At the second battle of Bull Run the regiment lost three valuable officers, by the fall of Col. George W Pratt, Capt. Peletiah Ward, and Lieut. John B. Horner. The regiment was at close quarters with the enemy in a piece of woods, and while thus engaged, Captain Ward was wounded in the arm by a sword. Nothing daunted, however, he seized the colors of the regiment, which had been shot down, and while in the act of cheering on his men to renewed efforts he was shot in the thigh. He was then taken from the field, but not before he had sustained the third wound, which proved mortal. He was a man of unbounded generosity and true nobility, and at the time of his enlistment, he was pastor of the Ellenville Methodist Episcopal Church. The day before the battle of Gettysburg, the regiment was ordered to join the First Corps, and after the battle, but a fragment of its number remained; eighteen of the twenty-eight officers who went into the battle were killed or wounded, with 160 privates killed and wounded, out of 280 who entered the fight. The regiment returned home in 1864, with only 342 men out of 1300 that had been connected with it. The regiment was organized at Kingston. Colonel Pratt was succeeded by Col. Theodore B. Gates, and a more worthy successor could not have been found. Colonel Gates led the van in every onslaught, encouraging his troops by his noble daring, and constantly watching over the comfort and welfare of his men while in hospital and camp. At Gettysburg, on the third day, the regiment made a brilliant and successful charge under the lead of its brave Colonel. General Doubleday said in "The Campaigns of the Civil War,"—"The skill and energy of Colonel Gates were of great service to me during the battle." When Colonel Gates was promoted to the command of a brigade, Jacob B. Hardenbergh succeeded to the command of the regiment. Among those who returned home with honorable records were Maj. Walter A. Van Rensselaer, Capt. Wm. H. Cunningham, Lieut. Andrew S. Schutt, Lieut. Abram Merritt, Lieut. Edward A. Ross, Lieut. Wm. S. Freligh, Lieut. George B. Walcott, Lieut. Francis D. Devail, Lieut.-Col. John McEntee, Maj. John R. Leslie, Capt. Elson M. Misner, Capt. Daniel McMahon. General Gates is now a member of the bar of New York City.

EIGHTY-FIRST REGIMENT.—"Second Oswego Regiment." The regiment returned home in March, 1864, with only 370 men out of 1050 who went to war two years before. Its gallant Colonel,

Jacob J. DeForest, was with the regiment from its formation to September 1, 1864. He enrolled the first and last man, and was desperately wounded at the battle of Fair Oaks, where the regiment behaved with especial gallantry and lost 130 men. Twelve commissioned officers were killed or mortally wounded. At Chapin's Farm the Color-Sergeant of the regiment is said to have planted the first Union flag on the parapet of the Rebel fort. The Eighty-first was the first regiment to gain the Rebel works and succeeded in carrying the redoubts. It lost in this engagement probably more men than any other regiment in its division, and captured twelve of the sixteen pieces of artillery. The Eighty-first furnished many officers for other regiments, including Lieut. Peter French, who was promoted to Major in the Forty-sixth Regiment, Capt. Augustus G. Bennett, Lieut. Richard H. Willoughby, Lieut. Edgar Abeel, Lieut. Henry Sharp and Lieut. Brantley G. Read, were promoted to positions in the Twenty-first United States Colored Regiment.

The following were mustered out with honorable records on the expiration of their term of service: Lieut.-Col. John B. Raulston, Maj. David B. White, Capt. Rudolphus D. S. Tyler, Capt. Martin J. DeForest, Capt. Hugh Anderson, Capt. E. A. Stimson, Lieut. Edward A. Cook, Lieut. George C. Smith, Lieut. Julius H. Clark and Lieut. Maurice P Tidd.

EIGHTY-SECOND REGIMENT.—(Second State Militia.) The regiment went to the war under command of Col. George W. B. Tompkins, who resigned in May, 1862. The regiment behaved with such conspicuous bravery at the battle of Fair Oaks that General Gorman addressed a letter to Governor Morgan eulogistic of the officers and men. At the battle of Gettysburg, of 246 men who went into battle only sixty came out alive. Lieut.-Col. James Huston was killed at the head of his regiment while gallantly urging his men to stand against the desperate assaults of Ewell's Corps. Serg. Hugh Carey captured the flag of the Seventh Virginia Regiment. He was twice wounded at Gettysburg. Carey was a brother of stenographer Carey of the Supreme Court, and died in March, 1886. Lieut.-Col. J. H. Wilcox died in June, 1887. At the close of the war he was brevetted Brigadier-General for gallant conduct in the field.

Ten commissioned officers of the regiment were killed or mortally wounded during its term of service.

EIGHTY-THIRD REGIMENT.—(Ninth State Militia.) The number of this regiment was significant, and was hated by the Rebels, when they remembered the obstinate fighting spirit of the Ninth Militia, the Ninth Volunteers, the Ninth New Jerseys, the Ninth Pennsylvanias and any number of other Ninths, too numerous to mention. On many a bloody field in Virginia have the soldiers of the glorious Ninth fallen, and in many a Rebel dungeon have they spent their last hours. The regiment went to the war 1100 strong, and not more than 100 rank and file and twenty officers returned home. The regiment was among the first to open the battle of Antietam. At a period of great emergency General Hooker called on General Ricketts for his best brigade, and Ricketts sent forward Hartsuff's brigade, to which the Ninth belonged. In this battle the regiment lost nineteen killed and one hundred wounded. The regiment may claim the honor of also opening the battle of Fredericksburg. Just before sunrise, on the 13th of December, Franklin moved his corps, and skirmishing at once commenced. The regiment was ordered to charge and take a Rebel battery at the point of the bayonet, which was giving much annoyance. Under command of Capt. John Hendrickson, the regiment obeyed the order with alacrity, and appeared to melt away before the leaden storm that was poured upon them. Bravely did the boys stand up to the work, although after a fierce struggle they were obliged to fall back. The regiment lost 132 men and seven officers out of 300 men and eleven officers who went into the battle. At the battle of Gettysburg, every man in the regiment but twenty was either killed or wounded.

The first Colonel of the regiment was John W. Stiles. Colonel Stiles resigned in 1863, and died in 1885. He was succeeded by Capt. John Hendrickson. Colonel Hendrickson was a brave officer, but having been wounded in action, was compelled to resign in August, 1863. He was succeeded by Col. Joseph A. Moesch, another gallant soldier, who was killed in the battles of the Wilderness. Some of the bravest men of the regiment were in the ranks, and many of them received severe wounds which prevented all hope of military promotion. Among such men of the Eighty-third was Private A. G. Iffla—now in the New York Custom House—who was so severely wounded at the battle of Antietam, that a leg had to be amputated, and he was obliged to remain ten days on the field before he could be moved, so severe were his sufferings. Iffla was probably the shortest man in the army, being almost liliputian by the side of Lieut.-Col. M. N. Curtis of the 142d Regiment, who was the tallest man in the Army of the Potomac. The Eighty-third participated in eighteen battles and lost in killed and wounded, and those who died of wounds, 684 in all.

EIGHTY-FOURTH REGIMENT.—"Fourteenth State Militia." No regulars that ever served on any field won more imperishable honor than this regiment of militia from the city of Brooklyn. On the 16th of May, the ladies of Brooklyn presented the regiment with a beautiful flag. The Rev. Joseph S. Inskip, Chaplain of the regiment, in returning thanks for the presentation, said : "If ever that flag shall be laid low, the Fourteenth Regiment shall be buried with it, and that, too, with a Chaplain, so help me God." At the battle of Bull Run, the regiment suffered lamentably. Col. Alfred M. Wood was captured, and became one of those selected to be hung should our Government decide on summary proceedings against the privateersmen. Colonel Wood, while in captivity, manifested by every word and act his undying devotion to the flag, and they found although they had captured Brooklyn's "Wood," it would not burn except with patriotic fire. At South Mountain, the regiment, which first drew the Rebel fire on the right in Keyes's division fought splendidly. The regiment attacked the Fourteenth Virginia Regiment, into which they poured such an effective fire, that after the battle, Colonel Strong and 150 of his men lay dead on the field. At Antietam, the regiment, in Doubleday's division fought in the most gallant manner and suffered severely. What scenes of carnage had that handful of patriots lived through ! Always in front, fearless and unflinching, they stood where the havoc of war raged the wildest, and pressed on through fire and sword into the enemy's line and works, thus showing that "the spirit of liberty which inspired the Long Island forefathers had not died out, but remained in the hearts of their sons."

Surg. James M. Farley, who died recently, was the surgeon who amputated the leg of the Rebel General Ewell.

General Doubleday, in his narrative of the first day's battle of Gettysburg, in the "Campaigns of the Civil War," says:—"The two regiments posted by Reynolds, the Fourteenth Brooklyn and Ninety-fifth New York, finding their support gone on the right, while Archer's Rebel brigade was advancing to envelop their left, fell back leisurely under Col. Edward B. Fowler of the Fourteenth Brooklyn, who assumed command of both, as the ranking officer present." "Fortunately, Fowler's two regiments came on to join Dawes, who went forward with great spirit, but was altogether too weak to assail such a force. The Rebels made a fierce and obstinate resistance, but while Fowler confronted them above, Dawes brought a gun to enfilade their position, and formed his men across the cut, by Fowler's order, to fire through it. The Rebels could not resist this, the greater number gave themselves up as prisoners and the others escaped." Colonel Fowler can accordingly be regarded as one of the chief heroes of the first day's battle of Gettysburg.

James B. Tomsey, one of the most gallant fighters of the regiment died recently, having been since the war a clerk in the Brooklyn Post Office.

EIGHTY-FIFTH REGIMENT.—In April, 1864, the Rebels made a most determined attack upon Fort Gray, and in no less than three several assaults, they were repulsed in the most gallant manner by Capt. John A. Brown, of the Eighty-fifth, commanding the fort. Col. Enrico Fardello was promoted to Brevet Brigadier-General in 1865. Col. Jonathan S. Belknap, in command at Fort Anderson, wrote to the commanding naval officer as follows: When on the 14th of March, General Pettigrew, with eighteen pieces of artillery and more than 3000 men, made his furious assault on Fort Anderson, garrisoned by 300 men of my command, the capture or destruction of the brave little band seemed inevitable. But the gunboats came promptly to the rescue. Your well directed fire drove the enemy from the field, covered the landing of the Eighty-fifth New York, sent to the relief of the garrison, and the repulse of the Rebel army was complete.

Lieut.-Col. Abijah J. Wellman died June, 1888. He entered the service as Major, and was severely wounded at Fair Oaks, from the effects of which he suffered during the rest of his life.

Capt. John Raines served until July, 1863, when he resigned, having performed his duties faithfully and bravely. He is now a member of the Republican State Committee.

EIGHTY-SIXTH REGIMENT.—"Steuben Rangers." The Eighty-sixth was engaged in the second battle of Bull Run, Fredericksburg, Chancellorsville, Gettysburg, Mine Run, Wilderness, Spottsylvania, North Anna, Tolopotomoy, Coal Harbor, Petersburg, Deep Bottom and Boydton Road.

Thirteen commissioned officers were killed or mortally wounded, which indicates how great must have been the loss among the rank and file. The first Colonel of the regiment was Benjamin P. Bailey, who resigned in 1863, and was succeeded by Col. Benjamin Higgins.

EIGHTY-SEVENTH REGIMENT.—At the battle of Oak Grove, the colors of the regiment were completely riddled with bullets, but Color-Bearer R. H. Ryder never for a moment left his exposed position. The regiment, 250 strong, under command of Lieut.-Col. Richard A. Bachia, filed across the field opposite the redoubts, to the support of the Twentieth Indiana, who were advancing through the thicket. After passing through a piece of woods to the left, the enemy made an advance from the woods on the right, and were supported by pickets posted in two houses a short distance off, and two small rifle pits in close proximity. A line of skirmishers was thrown out, when the regiment advanced in line of battle, taking possession of the houses and rifle pits, which they held during the day, and at night fell back to their original position. The regiment was commanded by Col. Stephen A. Dodge. General Nagle alluded in complimentary terms to the conduct of the regiment at the battle of Fair Oaks. The only commissioned officer killed in battle was Capt. Matthew W. Jackson, who fell at the second battle of Bull Run.

It was at the battle of Bull Run that Corporal James Tanner, now Commissioner of Pensions at Washington, was terribly wounded.

Private Charles A. Orr became in 1886, Senior Vice-Commander of the Grand Army of the Republic, State of New York.

EIGHTY-EIGHTH REGIMENT.—When the Irish brigade was organized, Patrick K. Horgan raised a company at his own expense, which became Company D. Horgan was severely wounded in the foot at Savage's Station, but refused to leave the field.

Company D was cut to pieces at Antietam. Captain Horgan was again severely wounded at Fredericksburg, and was mentioned in General Orders by General Hancock for bravery. His injuries now forced his retirement. He died in December, 1886.

At the battle of Malvern Hill the regiment was so infuriated by the slaughter of their brave companions-in-arms, that under the lead of the brave Maj. James Quinlan, they made a desperate assault on the enemy with the bayonet, and were only prevented from rushing on the batteries of the wily enemy by the loud command of their officers. The regiment took a most honorable part in the battles of Antietam, Fredericksburg, the Wilderness, and Petersburg. At the latter battle Col. Patrick Kelly was killed. The regiment lost eighteen commissioned officers, among whom were two sons of the late Thomas Addis Emmett. Capt. William J. Nagle was the oldest of five brothers who enlisted in defence of the Union.

EIGHTY-NINTH REGIMENT.—The regiment was commanded by Col. Harrison S. Fairchild, who was promoted in 1865, to Brevet Brigadier-General.

At South Mountain the Eighty-ninth resisted, at the point of the bayonet, the charge of the enemy, in a most gallant style. The regiment made itself historic by the famous crossing in small boats at Fredericksburg, in December, 1862.

At Fair Oaks, Antietam and Petersburg the regiment fought bravely and suffered severely.

Lieut. Frank S. Smith was always at the post of duty, and proved himself a gallant soldier. He is now a member of the Republican State Committee.

NINETIETH REGIMENT.—The regiment was stationed for a long time at Key West. During the first six months after its arrival, it was reduced by disease from 900 to less than 700.

Lieut.-Col. Louis W Tinelli, Capt. Jeremiah Simpson, Lieuts. Henry F. Blackwell, John T. Sheppard and Andrew S. Onderdonk were among those who shared the fortunes of the Ninetieth.

The Ninetieth participated with great credit in the battle of Cedar Creek, October 19, 1864. The regiment was commanded by Maj. John C. Smart, who had just given the order to fall back when he was shot dead.

General McMillan, in his Report, refers to the gallantry of the Ninetieth at Cedar Creek. Adair Creek was the last battle in which the regiment was engaged.

NINETY-FIRST REGIMENT.—"McClellan Chasseurs." The regiment was organized in December, 1861, and returned to Albany in July, 1864, with only 364 men. It was then reorganized and left for the field with 1600 men.

Port Hudson was the principal battle in which the regiment was engaged, and it was in this battle that its losses were chiefly incurred.

Col. Jonathan Tarbell was promoted in 1865, to Brevet Brigadier-General. In 1864, Capt. Edward A. Selkirk was promoted to Major of the Second Heavy Artillery Regiment; and Capt. George W Schaffer to Major of the Sixty-first Regiment. Alfred Wagstaff, Jr., was Major of the regiment, and William J. Denslow, Lieutenant-Colonel.

NINETY-SECOND REGIMENT.—The Ninety-second was organized at Potsdam. At the battle of Fair Oaks the regiment made a very brilliant charge, and thereby saved Regan's battery. In this battle the regiment was badly cut up. Col. Lewis C Hunt was among the wounded, and in 1862 he was promoted to Brigadier-General. Capt. Cyrus O. Hubbell and Lieuts. Giles F Ward, James O'Neil and Morris C. Foote were among the gallant officers of the regiment. Captain Hubbell was in 1887 an Alderman of New York City. General Heintzleman said: "The Ninety-second and the 100th New

York regiments made a charge on the enemy at Fair Oaks that would have honored veteran troops."

NINETY-THIRD REGIMENT.—"Morgan Rifles." Capt. Walter W. Bramen is entitled to great credit for his coolness during the bombardment at night on the James River. He was officer of the night, and had many prisoners in the guard-house, and notwithstanding the whole guard had to move to a safer place, he did not lose a man. The regiment for a long time filled the responsible post of headquarters and provost guard to the Army of the Potomac, and during this service they seized and turned over to the authorities at Washington over 20,000 prisoners.

The Ninety-third participated gallantly in fifteen great battles—Yorktown was the first; Boydton Road the last. The Ninety-third was commanded by Col. John S. Crocker, with Benjamin C. Butler Lieutenant-Colonel.

Capt. Charles A. Quinn, a gallant officer, died recently.

NINETY-FOURTH REGIMENT.—"Bell Jefferson Rifles." The Ninety-fourth took part in twenty-four engagements, and its tattered colors evinced their severity. It contained over 3,000 men during its term of service, and returned home with only 579. Col. Adrian R. Root was twice brevetted for faithful and meritorious services. The first great battle in which the Ninety-fourth was engaged was Cedar Mountain, where it lost many valuable officers and gallant men. The first Colonel of the regiment was Henry K. Viele, who resigned in 1862 and was succeeded by Colonel Root. Colonel Root in 1865 was promoted to Brevet Brigadier-General, a distinction most worthily earned. Capt. Walter T. Chester claimed to have been the last man mustered out of the United States Service, but Private Charles W. Hooper of the First New York Engineers claims the same distinction.

Maj. John McMahon was promoted to the Colonelcy of the 188th Regiment, and Capt. Isaac Doolittle to Lieutenant-Colonel of the same.

Capt. Byron Parsons, Adjt. Chas. E. Hulbert, Lieut. Alba A. Johnson, Lieut. J. J. Shedd, Lieut. Henry Swan and Lieut. Charles W. Sloat, were all valuable officers and gallant soldiers.

NINETY-FIFTH REGIMENT.—"Warren Rifles." The regiment suffered more severely than the average at the battle of South Mountain, as it was in the advance and hotly engaged. The Ninety-fifth went into the fight under command of Maj. Edward Pye, with 258 men; after the battle it could muster but 153. Major Pye was promoted to Colonel, and died in 1864, of wounds received in action. The Rebel General Garland was killed at South Mountain by the bullets of the Ninety-fifth. Colonel Pye was mortally wounded at Coal Harbor.

At Gettysburg the Ninety-fifth and the Fourteenth Brooklyn captured General Archer and his brigade. The first Colonel of the Ninety-fifth was George H. Biddle, who resigned in 1863. Major Pye was appointed his successor. Lieut.-Col. James Creney, Capts Wm. L. Sherwood, Reuben Biggs, Abram S. Gurnee, George H. Everett, Henry M. Jennings, Archibald McC. Bush and Edward A. Cowdry and Lieutenants Hiram Osborne, Wm. O. Chapman, John M. Armstrong and Wm. F. Ingmire are all honorably identified with the gallant achievements of the regiment. Capt. Samuel C. Timpson—a splendid officer, was captured in the Wilderness battle and died in a rebel prison.

NINETY-SIXTH REGIMENT.—The regiment participated in thirty great battles, as large if not a larger number than has been credited by the War Department to any other regiment from the State. Col. Charles O. Gray was killed at Kinston, N. C., in 1862. He was succeeded by Col. Edgar M. Cullen. In 1886 Colonel Cullen was Judge of the Supreme Court, Second Judicial District. Colonel Cullen resigned in 1865, when Stephen Moffitt became the last Colonel of the regiment.

There was a generous rivalry between the color-bearers of the Ninety-sixth and the Eighth Connecticut, as to which was the first to plant their colors on Battery Harrison. So nearly equal were they, however, that it is difficult to say which was in the advance.

NINETY-SEVENTH.—"Conkling Rifles." At the second battle of Bull Run, the regiment was in General Duryea's brigade, and was in the advance, subject to the hottest of the fire throughout the day. They received great praise for their steadiness and coolness under the galling fire of the enemy.

The regiment participated in sixteen great battles. Its first Colonel was Charles Wheelock, who was promoted to Brevet Brigadier-General in 1864, and died in 1865. He was succeeded by Col. John P. Spofford. Capt. Samuel M. Ferguson died in March, 1886.

Surg. George S. Little is now Superintendent of the Brooklyn E. D. Hospital.

NINETY-EIGHTH REGIMENT.—The first battle in which the regiment was engaged was Fair Oaks. Col. William Dutton, who died in 1862, graduated at West Point in the same class with General McClellan. The regiment was next commanded by Col. Charles Durkee who resigned in 1863 and was succeeded by Frederick F. Wead—a fine soldier, who was killed at Coal Harbor in 1864. The regiment lost eight commissioned officers during its term of service.

NINETY-NINTH REGIMENT.—"Union Coast Guard." As a coast guard it participated in the battle of Big Bethel, besides, in detachments, operating frequently against the rebels on Craney Island, Sewell's Point and New Market Bridge, Va. In August, 1861, it was re-organized into an infantry regiment. In June, 1864, the organization was again formed into a veteran battalion. It participated in the battles at Cherry Stone Creek, Harrison Junction, and Kinston. It was identified with a great number of fights, both in Virginia and North Carolina. Strong detachments of the regiment shared in the glory of the Burnside expedition in the establishment of the First Union foothold in the state of North Carolina, beginning with Fort Mercer, Cape Hatteras, and Roanoke Island. In the action at Franklin, Va., Capt. James H. Hart, a most gallant officer, was killed, and was the only commissioned officer lost in battle.

ONE HUNDREDTH REGIMENT.—General Heintzleman said "the One Hundredth made a charge on the enemy at Williamsburg that would have honored veteran troops." At the battle of Fair Oaks, Capt. John W. Wilkeson lost his life from his over-anxious and ever-conscientious desire to maintain honorable control of his company and bring it in order off the field. Every other company in the regiment had broken. He made his men "face about," "fire," and "retreat," "halt," "load," "face again, and "fire," and retreat" again. His military place in this manœuvre was in front of his men when they retreated, and in the rear of them when they faced about to fire. Too brave and too proud to require a courage from common soldiers of which he did not set the example as an officer, he marched on their flank, and in the rear of them while retreating. In this conspicuous place of danger, a bullet through his breast killed the last officer of the regiment that was left on the field, and ended the regiment's part in that great battle. Col. James M. Brown was also killed in this action. The regiment took a gallant part at the battle near Deep Bottom, Drury's Bluff, and Morris Island, South Carolina, in each of which many valuable officers were killed, and the regiment suffered severely in the loss of privates. During the closing operations around Petersburg, General Grant rode up to General Terry and said; "What does this mean?" Why are not those lines connected? They will sweep right in here and turn you right and left. What troops have you here? "The One Hundredth New York," said General Terry. "Colonel Dandy's Regiment? send him here," said Grant. Now Dandy (George B.), was a West Pointer, and a "whooper." He rode up and saluted, as General Grant said,—"I want you to take your regiment down, and connect those lines in that ravine. Colonel Dandy saluted again, with "certainly, sir;" and then formed his regiment as if he was going out on dress parade, colors in the centre, and swung down into the ravine under fire of the battery, and when the work was over rode back, with another salute,—"The lines are connected, sir." "How many men did you lose?" asked Grant. "None, sir," said Dandy. "I thought so, replied General Grant. Colonel Dandy was promoted to Brevet Brigadier-General in 1865.

ONE HUNDRED FIRST REGIMENT.—The regiment participated with great bravery in the battle of Chantilly. Col. George F. Chester was especially distinguished for his skill and courage. At the battle of Malvern Hill, two companies supported Randolph's Rhode Island Battery. The balls flew around them thick and fast, but strange to say, only a few men were killed and wounded. Lieut. William M. Smith was conspicuous by his bravery and gallant bearing. The regiment having been greatly reduced, it was consolidated with the Thirty-seventh New York Volunteers, in December, 1862. Maj. Samuel L. Mitchell, Jr., a gallant soldier, was a son of the late Samuel L. Mitchell, one of New York's most estimable citizens.

ONE HUNDRED SECOND REGIMENT.—At Cedar Mountain, the regiment, commanded by Col. T. B. Van Buren, suffered severely. Capt. Julius Spring, one of the bravest and most ardent spirits of the war, fell while cheering on his men. The dead of the 102d were buried as they fell, in Virginia, Maryland, Pennsylvania, Tennessee, Georgia, North and South Carolina. Their division commander, Maj. Gen. John W. Geary, complimented them as follows: "It may safely be asserted that no organization in the army has a prouder record or has passed through more arduous, varied and bloody campaigns." The 102d was the only regiment from New York City that was with General Sherman all through his grand march. The regiment belonged to the famous White Star Division, which led the assault on Lookout Mountain. The regiment acted as the advance guard of skirmishers and was the first to dash across the crest in the attack. It was here that the gallant Maj. Gilbert M. Elliott was killed. At the battle of Antietam the ground on which the 102d was ordered to form was broken by a huge rock and an intervening fence, which rendered their movements in the face of a galling fire from the enemy exceedingly difficult. Determined that the brave little band should not yield under any circumstances, the officers stepped from the ranks and led the way. Capt. M. E. Cornell scaled the fence not thirty feet from the enemy's sharpshooters, and called to his comrades to follow him, which they did, and with a wild cheer, but alas! he was marked for destruction, and his comrades rushed over his dead body and drove the enemy more than a mile from their position. Colonel Van Buren resigned in 1862. He was succeeded by Col. James C. Lane, who was honorably discharged in 1864, when Herbert Hammerstein became Colonel of the regiment. Colonel Lane was a very popular officer and was presented by the regiment with a medal of honor, on which was inscribed "He was our leader, God bless him!" The Colonel died August, 1889. Colonel Hammerstein retained the position until January, 1865, when Lieut. Col. Harvey S Chatfield, of the Seventy-eighth regiment, a very gallant soldier, became the fourth and last Colonel of the regiment. Colonel Chatfield is now a well-known member of the New York Bar. In the long list of officers of the 102d, whose valor and devotion to the cause entitle them to remembrance, will be found the names of Lieut.-Col. Oscar J. Spaulding, Maj. R. H. Wilbur, Captain Barent Van Buren, William H. Griffin, Robert B. Hathaway, Henry M. Maguire, Eugene Schilling, Theodore D. Cornell, Isaac Van Steenberg, John R. Elliott, Capt. Daniel M. Elmore (who died in November, 1886), Capt. William H. Batchelder, and Lieuts. Charles Mooney, William Wright, Irvine Carman, Frederick Weber, Phineas C. Kingsland, Cuyler Garrett, and Edwin G. Davies.

ONE HUNDRED THIRD REGIMENT.—At the battle of Antietam the regiment, under command of Maj. Benjamin Ringold, supported the Ninth New York Regiment. Of the 187 men who took part in the charge on the stone bridge, twenty-seven were killed, seventy-five wounded, and twenty-nine were missing. Four successive color-sergeants were killed; also Capt. Henry A. Sand and Capt. William Brandt, who raised the colors again after the sergeants were killed. Col. F. W. Egloffstein was wounded and compelled to resign. Major Ringold was appointed his successor, and was mortally wounded at the battle of Chancellorsville. William Heine, engineer on the Staff of General Dix, was the next colonel of the regiment.

ONE HUNDRED FOURTH REGIMENT.—"Wadsworth Guard." The 104th bore an honorable part in the battle of Cedar Mountain, Second Bull Run, South Mountain, Mine Run, Wilderness, Fredericksburg, Antietam, Chantilly, Chancellorsville, Gettysburg, North Anna, Spottsylvania, Bethesda Church, Weldon Railroad, Petersburg. At the Second Bull Run the regiment was commanded in an admirable manner by Maj. Lewis C. Skinner. Lieut. John P Rudd was the first man of the regiment killed.

ONE HUNDRED FIFTH REGIMENT.—The regiment took an honorable part in the battle of Antietam, where it lost its Lieutenant-Colonel, Howard Carroll. James M. Fuller was the first Colonel; he resigned in 1862, and John W Shedd became his successor.

ONE HUNDRED SIXTH REGIMENT.—At Sailor's Creek, April 6, 1865, the 106th (through Brevet Lieut.-Col. Hiram W Day), received the flag of truce surrendering Lieut.-Gen. Ewell and his troops, (surrender of General Lee, April 9). The defence of the bridge at Fairmount, Va., in April, 1865, by a detachment of the 106th under Col. Edward C. James, was one of the most brilliant of the war. Fearing the destruction of the magnificent trestle work over the Monongahela river at that point by the Rebels, Company F, Capt. Martin J. Chamberlain (who was killed in 1864), and Company D, Capt. Alvah W Briggs (who was promoted to Brevet Colonel in 1865), were despatched to protect it. Seven times did the Rebels charge our men, and although thirty to one, they were seven times repulsed. At length, after three hours' fighting, the Rebels, with an overwhelming sweep, rode over our little braves, taking them all. No sooner was the capture complete than the Rebels gave the boys three cheers for their gallant defence. The regiment took part in twenty-two great battles, and returned home with only 400 men.

A beautiful flag was presented to the regiment in 1864 by the ladies of St. Lawrence and Franklin Counties as a token of their bravery and devotion. Col. Andrew N. McDonald died in January, 1885, from the effects of an overdose of morphine. He had been one of the youngest Colonels in the Army.

The 106th participated with honor in the battles of Fairmount, Martinsburg, Wapping Heights, Wilderness, Spottsylvania, Coal Harbor, Petersburg, Monocacy, Opequan, Fisher's Hill, Cedar Creek. Lieut.-Col. Alvah W Briggs, Maj. Edward M. Payne, Captains Horace L. Aldridge, Charles Snyder, Thomas Shaw, Joseph C. Robinson, and Lieut. Robert H. Cox and Sergt. Donald Grant are all entitled to recognition for soldierly and meritorious conduct.

ONE HUNDRED SEVENTH REGIMENT.—It is worthy of note that the first regiment organized and sent to the war under the new call from the President for 300,000 volunteers, was the 107th, raised by two patriotic representatives in the Legislature,—Robert Van Valkenburg, who became Colonel, and Alexander S. Diven, who, after Colonel Van Valkenburg's resignation, succeeded to the command and was promoted to Brevet Brigadier-General a few months later. The regiment fought bravely at Chancellorsville and at the battle of Dallas, Ga. Lieut.-Col. William F. Fox, a gallant officer of the 107th, has, since the close of the war, rendered the country a service by the compilation of an invaluable work entitled "The Chances of being Killed in Battle." Colonel Fox is now a resident of Albany.

ONE HUNDRED EIGHTH REGIMENT.—The first flag presented to the regiment was by Gen. Chester A. Arthur. This beautiful banner was badly shattered at the battle of Antietam—the first battle in which the regiment was engaged. It came out of that fight with its centre rent and pierced by sixty-nine bullets. In addition to this flag, the regiment received from Governor Morgan one of the prize banners pledged to the four regiments respectively, to be organized under the call of July 12, 1862, the 102d being the second organized under that call. The third flag was presented by the ladies of Brighton, Monroe County. At Antietam the regiment was actively engaged from 8 A. M. until 4.30 P. M. on the front line, and in an open field near the centre of the line. The regiment lost 169 out of 600 in this battle. At Fredericksburg fifty-three were lost out of above 340 engaged. Col. Oliver H. Palmer was promoted to Brevet Brigadier-General for faithful and meritorious services. The Colonel died in 1884. In the fight at Morton's Ford, Va., in 1864, the regiment advanced rapidly, and without firing a shot, to a stone wall occupied by the enemy, when they delivered a volley, and with shouts leaped the wall, and were soon in possession of an important position which virtually closed the contest.

ONE HUNDRED NINTH REGIMENT.—The regiment went to the war under command of Col. Benjamin F. Tracy (now Secretary of the Navy). Colonel Tracy resigned in 1864 and was succeeded by Col. Isaac S. Catlin, who was promoted for skill and bravery in many desperate battles, to Brevet Brigadier-General. The 109th participated in the battles of the Wilderness, Spottsylvania, Coal Harbor, Petersburg, Weldon Railroad, Ream's Station, Poplar Spring Church and Hatcher's Run.

Maj. George W. Dunn, who has since the war been conspicuous in public affairs, was a gallant officer and acquitted himself with honorable distinction. He is now a member of the Republican State Committee.

ONE HUNDRED TENTH REGIMENT.—The regiment was organized at Oswego, and went to the front under command of Col. Clinton H. Sage. Colonel Sage resigned in 1863, and Col. DeWitt C Littlejohn became his successor. Colonel Littlejohn commanded the regiment but a short time, when Charles Hamilton was appointed Colonel of the regiment. The regiment was engaged in the battles of Bisland and Port Hudson. Capt. James Doyle, one of the bravest of the brave, lost his left arm at Port Hudson.

ONE HUNDRED ELEVENTH REGIMENT.—The regiment was organized at Auburn, from companies recruited in Cayuga and Wayne counties. It was mustered into the service August 20, 1862, and left the city the following day for Harper's Ferry, Va., where, after joining that ill-fated garrison, it was included in its surrender shortly afterwards. The men were released on parole, but were not declared exchanged until December, 1862, when they entered the field again, and went into winter quarters at Centreville, remaining there several months in a brigade commanded by Gen. Alexander Hayes. The first Colonel of the regiment was Jesse Seguin, who resigned in January, 1863, when Clinton D. McDougall became his successor. Colonel McDougall was an admirable officer, and for gallant and meritorious services was promoted in 1865 to the rank of Brevet Brigadier-General. On June 25, 1863, General Hayes' brigade joined the Second Corps, which was marching by on its way to Gettysburg. The regiment left two companies on guard at Accotink Bridge, with the remaining eight companies numbering 300 men. It was engaged at Gettysburg on the second day of the battle in the brilliant and successful charge of Willard's brigade, losing there 58 killed, 177 wounded, and 14 missing. Total 249. The *National Tribune* said of the battle of Gettysburg, "the 111th lost twenty-two per cent. of its number engaged—killed and mortally wounded. That is nearly one man in every four that it took into action. This was a very startling loss, and half as many again, in proportion, as the Light Brigade lost in its famous charge at Balaklava. Of the wounded 30 died, making 88 killed in the battle. From Gettysburg until the end the regiment fought under Hancock. At the battle of the Wilderness the regiment fought splendidly, and lost 42 men killed, 119 wounded, and 17 missing, total 178—half of its effective force. The regiment bore a most honorable part in twenty-two great battles. Seventeen hundred men were connected with the 111th, during its term of service, of whom 778 were killed and wounded—74 of which died in Rebel prisons. The dead of the regiment number the largest, with the exception of the Sixty-ninth New York, of any regiment from the State. Total dead of the Sixty-ninth, was 401; of the 111th, 400.

On the 30th of October, 1864, during the siege of Petersburg, 86 of the members were captured and sent first to Libby Prison; afterwards to Salisbury Prison, N. C. When the prisoners were released in March, 1865, in consequence of Sherman's march to the sea, only 40 of the 86 were living, the remainder having succumbed to the horrors attending their confinement; and of the remaining 40, several died shortly after leaving the prison. In this little band of suffering martyrs was Mr. Robert L. Drummond, a gentleman who has since attained honorable distinction in civil life. Mr. Drummond graduated at the Albany Law School, and since the close of the war has for nine years been District Attorney for Cayuga County.

Nearly all the officers have honorable records, and several were promoted to higher positions in other regiments. The survivors doubtless remember the bravery, skill and devotion manifested by the following named officers: Lieut.-Col. Lewis W Husk, Maj. Sidney Mead, Maj. James H. Hinman, Maj. Joseph W Corning, Lieut.-Col. Isaac M. Lusk, Capts. Ira Jones, Sebastian D. Holmes, John A. Laing, Marcus W Murdock, Samuel C. Bradley, Lafayette Mumford, Philip Lape; Lients. John J. Brinckerhoff, George Parker, Charles A. Farnum, George W. Moore, Andrew P. Camp, Stephen A. Pyatt, Arthur W Marshall, and many others. Capt. Robert C. Perry died in 1881. Lieut. Edwin K. Burnham, another gallant officer of the 111th, is now superintendent of public buildings at Albany.

ONE HUNDRED TWELFTH REGIMENT.—The regiment served with great credit in the siege of Suffolk, in 1862-63, in the siege of Charleston, under Gilmore, and in the Florida campaign. It was afterwards transferred to General Butler's department, Fortress Monroe, and participated in the attack upon Richmond, via the James River. Col. Jeremiah C. Drake was mortally wounded at Coal Harbor in 1864. Early in the war he was Captain in the Forty-Ninth New York. Col. John F. Smith died of wounds received while bravely leading his regiment in the assault on Fort Fisher. He was a thorough soldier and polished gentleman. After the death of Colonel Smith, Ephraim A. Ludwick became Colonel of the regiment. The 112th lost twelve commissioned officers during the war.

ONE HUNDRED THIRTEENTH REGIMENT.—This was the Seventh Heavy Artillery.

ONE HUNDRED FOURTEENTH REGIMENT.—The regiment maintained their ground manfully and repulsed the enemy most handsomely at the battle of Pleasant Hill, La. The regiment also fought bravely at Bisland and Port Hudson, where Col. Elisha B. Smith was mortally wounded. Eight other commissioned officers were lost by the regiment during its term of service. Col. Samuel R. Per Lee succeeded Colonel Smith in command. At Sabine Cross Roads, Lieut.-Col. Henry B. Morse was wounded.

At Port Hudson the regiment fought splendidly and suffered severely. A valuable article on the siege of Port Hudson has recently been written and published by Capt. James F. Fitts. Captain Fitts in his narrative, says: "A detachment of the regiment was at one time on duty at sea, 500 miles from the Florida coast in British and Spanish waters. This was the most distant point from the territorial limits of the United States during the war." The history of the war cannot furnish instances of greater gallantry than was displayed by the 114th at the battle of Winchester. The regiment was subjected to as heavy a fire as ever a regiment received; but nobly did they maintain their position, losing in killed and wounded two thirds of their number.

At Cedar Creek the conduct of the regiment was magnificent, and General McMullen alluded to its conduct in complimentary terms. The regiment fought in the fog and misty daylight, as though determined to die to a man rather than yield an inch. The regiment was detailed to act as guard to the Nineteenth Corps train, and did their work bravely, taking it off the ground and out of the enemy's reach, but not without a severe loss in killed and wounded.

The whole number of men enlisted in the regiment was 1113; of this number 174 died of disease; 250 were discharged in hospital, and 431, more than one third of the whole strength were killed or wounded in action. At Fisher's Hill the regiment suffered fearfully, losing 123 out of 250, who went into the action. Company G was largely composed of students from Madison University. Colonel Per Lee was wounded at Winchester, and his gallantry and admirable qualities as a commanding officer were recognized by promotion to Brevet Brigadier-General. Surg. Harris H. Beecher served faithfully during the war, and died in July, 1889.

ONE HUNDRED FIFTEENTH REGIMENT.—At the battle of Olustee, Florida, nearly all the color-guard were shot down. The regiment suffered fearfully—the desperate assaults on the Union right failed to drive in the brave 115th. General Hatch, in general orders, made known to his command the successful accomplishment of a daring and difficult expedition by a detachment of twenty-five men of the 115th sent out from Pilatka. One thousand four hundred and ninety-three men were raised for this regiment. They had seven officers killed and eighteen wounded. Took part in sixteen battles.

The regiment was organized at Fonda, and was commanded by Col. Simon Sammon, who resigned in November, 1864. Nathan J. Johnson was promoted to Brevet Colonel in March, 1865. Lieut.-Col. George S. Batchelor, now Assistant Secretary of the Treasury, resigned in 1863, and was succeeded by Ezra L. Walrath, formerly Colonel of the Twelfth Regiment.

ONE HUNDRED SIXTEENTH REGIMENT.—The 116th did the real fighting at the battle of Plains Store, and the regiment was complimented on the battle-field by General Augur. At Port Hudson the regiment bore a glorious part and suffered severely, losing among others its gallant Colonel, Edward P. Chapin. Col. George M. Love succeeded Colonel Chapin in command of the regiment, and in recognition of his valuable services he was promoted to Brevet Brigadier-General in 1865. Colonel Love is said to have captured the first Confederate flag captured at the battle of Cedar Creek. Colonel Love died in April, 1887. Adj. John B. Weber was, in 1887, a member of Congress.

ONE HUNDRED SEVENTEENTH REGIMENT.—The 117th was from Rome. The first Colonel of the regiment was William R. Pease, who resigned in October, 1863; the next Colonel was Alvin White, who resigned in July, 1864, when Rufus Daggett succeeded to the command, and in 1865 Colonel Daggett was promoted to Brevet Brigadier-General. At Coal Harbor, Petersburg and Drury's Bluff, the regiment fought splendidly and suffered greatly. The regiment belonged to the first brigade of the second division of the Tenth Corps. The brigade was the first to storm and take Fort Fisher, during which every officer and man covered himself with glory, and saw the colors first planted on the parapet of the fort. Colonel Daggett was honorably mentioned in the official report of General Ames. Surg. James A. Morris was blown up at Fort Fisher, and his body had to be dug out of the sand which covered him, but he was not seriously injured.

ONE HUNDRED EIGHTEENTH REGIMENT.—Among the officers and in the ranks of this regiment were some of the most prominent young men of the Sixteenth Senatorial District. The regiment went to the war with 1040 men, under command of Col. Samuel T. Richards, who resigned in 1863, and was succeeded by Col. Oliver Keese, Jr., who resigned in 1864, and was succeeded by Col. George F. Nichols. The ravages of war fearfully reduced their numbers, and few regiments saw such losses as the 118th. It was selected to be armed with "Spencer's Repeating Rifles" and always formed the skirmishers, covering the advance of the Third Division, Twenty-fourth Corps. It formed a portion of the skirmishers of the Third division when Richmond was finally occupied in 1865, and was the first organized Federal infantry in that city. It wears by order on its colors the names of twelve great battles.

ONE HUNDRED NINETEENTH REGIMENT.—The aggregate number of officers who served with the 119th was sixty-nine, and privates, 981. The regiment returned home with 306 officers and men, and had received only eight recruits. They were in General Geary's division (White Star),—Twentieth Corps, army of Georgia. Col. Elias Peisener was killed at Chancellorsville, cheering his men at the moment he fell, and notwithstanding the loss of its beloved Colonel and one-third of its whole rank and file, the regiment returned from the field in good order, preserving their banners and accoutrements amid the disorder and flight of the residue of the corps. At Gettysburg the regiment was admirably commanded by Col. John T. Lockman. In the successful charge on the Rebel front at Resaca, the regiment lost its brave Lieutenant Colonel, Edward P. Lloyd. No regiment was more frequently under fire or employed in more difficult or important enterprises than the 119th. Colonel Lockman is now a member of the New York Bar. Maj. Benjamin A. Willis—a most estimable man and gallant soldier, died in October, 1886. Maj. Harvey Baldwin, Capt. James P Batterson, Capt. Charles S. Caswell, Capt. Francis A. O. Gartner, Capt. Charles Becker, Capt. Louis Leubuscher, Capt. Francis Peisener, were all brave and gallant soldiers.

ONE HUNDRED TWENTIETH REGIMENT.—The regiment belonged to the famous Sickles brigade, and was raised at Kingston. It participated in thirteen great battles and the surrender of Lee's army. During the battle of Gettysburg on the 2d of July, the regiment rallied three several times around their colors, being every time repulsed by the superior numbers of the enemy. Very few regiments can be rallied the second time. Col. George H. Sharp (lately Surveyor of the Port of New York) paroled Lee's army. He had been promoted to Brevet Brigadier-General in 1864. The regiment lost thirteen commissioned officers in battle. Lieut.-Col. John R. Tappan was mustered out on expiration of term of service, when Cornelius D. Westbrook became Lieutenant-Colonel. He was finally succeeded by Lieut.-Col. Abram L. Lockwood, who rose to the rank of Brevet-Colonel in 1865, and Maj. Walter P. Scott to Brevet-Lieutenant-Colonel. Capt. Alonzo R. Cole, Lieut. James H. Lockwood and Lieut. Marquis M. Drake were among the surviving heroes of the 120th.

ONE HUNDRED TWENTY-FIRST REGIMENT.—Few regiments suffered more severely or have a more brilliant record than the 121st. At Fredericksburg, Gettysburg, Salem Heights, Spottsylvania, Wilderness, Coal Harbor, Fisher's Hill and Petersburg, the regiment nobly sustained the honor of the Empire State. There could be no better evidence of the gallantry of the regiment than the fact that fourteen commissioned officers were killed or mortally wounded during the war. Col. Richard Franchot was the first Colonel; he resigned in 1862, when Emory Upton was placed in command of the regiment. Colonel Upton was at the time only twenty-two years of age. In 1864 he was promoted to Brigadier-General, and in that position won for himself a most enviable reputation. Colonel Upton died recently. At the battle of Opequan, General Upton was wounded while carrying forward the colors of the regiment in the final charge. At the battle of Rappahannock Station the 121st came up in splendid style and deserves as much credit for gallantry as any regiment engaged. At the battle of the Wilderness, Lieut.-Col. Egbert Olcott was shot in the head, thrown from his horse, and abandoned to his fate. He, recovered, however, and was promoted to Brevet Colonel of the regiment in 1864.

Among the officers of the 121st, who shared the fortunes of the regiment during nearly its entire term of service were Lieut. Henry Upton, Lieuts. Thomas C. Adams, Delos M. Kenyon, G. W. Quackenbush, Maj. Henry M. Galpin, Capt. Marcus R. Casler, Daniel D. Jackson, Maj. John S. Kidder, Maj. James W Cronkite, Capts. A. M. Tyler, Lansing B. Paine, James W Johnston, Hiram C. Van Scoy and Thomas J. Hassett.

One of the most costly sacrifices the regiment sustained during the war was in the fall of Capt. Charles A. Butts on the 10th of May, 1864, at the battle of the Wilderness. At the time of the second call of the President for troops Captain Butts was a member of the graduating class of Hamilton College. He however left college and joined the regiment as a private. His gallantry soon attracted the attention of his superior officers and he was promoted gradually to the rank of Captain. After receiving his mortal wound his comrades endeavored to remove him from the field, but he implored them to leave him to his fate, fearful that they would be captured. Sadly they were compelled to do so, and the next day the battle-ground was burned over, and no trace of his remains have ever been found.

ONE HUNDRED TWENTY-SECOND REGIMENT.—The regiment was from Syracuse, and was commanded by Col. Silas Titus, who remained with the regiment until January, 1865, when he was honorably discharged. All the brigade and division commanders testified to the superior gallantry of the regiment on many of the great battle-fields, such as Chancellorsville, Gettysburg, Rappahannock Station, Wilderness, Spottsylvania and Cedar Creek. At Chancellorsville on the morning of May 3, General Shaler's brigade was ordered to regain a line of rifle pits, from which Green's brigade had fallen back the night before. The 122d took the lead, and troops never loaded and fired with greater precision and rapidity. The rifle pits were taken. Many valuable officers were killed outright, including the brave Lieut.-Col. Augustus W Dwight, who fell in action near Petersburg, March 25, 1865. Lieut. Theodore L. Poole lost his arm while bravely defending the flag. Among those who served their time with the regiment and were honorably discharged were Maj. Joshua B. Davis, Captains Morris H. Church, Lucius A. Dillingham, John M. Dwight, George W Platt, Davis Cossitt, Frank Lester, Edward P. Luther, Francis Colahan, Andrew J. Smith and Lieuts. Otto W Parrison, George H. Gilbert, Charles W. Ostrander and Adolph Wilman.

ONE HUNDRED TWENTY-THIRD REGIMENT.—It was in the action at Dallas, Ga., that Col. Archibald L. McDougall received his fatal wound, after proving himself a true and gallant officer, previous to which the regiment lost its Lieutenant-Colonel, Franklin Norton, at the battle of Chancellorsville. James C. Rogers succeeded Colonel McDougall in command of the regiment, and in 1865, he was promoted to Brevet Brigadier-General. The regiment was organized at Salem, and fought bravely at Peach Tree Creek where it lost heavily.

ONE HUNDRED TWENTY-FOURTH REGIMENT.—The 124th was from Goshen, and after three years hard service returned home with

333 men, out of 1300 men who had been connected with the organization. Two hundred and twenty-five of the men who took the field with the regiment, passed with it through all the battles of the Army of the Potomac, and returned home with the organization. Only three of the original officers retained command at the close of the service. Its first Colonel was A. Van Horn Ellis, who was killed at Gettysburg. The second Colonel of the regiment was Francis M. Cummins. Colonel Cummins died in March, 1884. Major Henry S. Murray, a gallant soldier, was captured, and was for some time confined in Libby Prison. The regiment was known as the "Orange Blossoms." The survivors of the 124th were the first in the State to erect a monument at Gettysburg to the memory of their fallen comrades. Colonel Ellis's heroic efforts to redeem the fortunes of the day at the battle of Chancellorsville, were the subject of universal admiration.

ONE HUNDRED TWENTY-FIFTH REGIMENT.—The regiment was organized at Troy, and was commanded by Col. George L. Willard, a son-in-law of the late Elias Plum, Esq., of that city. Colonel Willard was Major in the Nineteenth United States Infantry, an accomplished soldier, who had been in the service fourteen years, and who, after participating with honor in many of the severest battles of the war, finally met a soldier's death on the field of Gettysburg. The Lieutenant-Colonel of the regiment, Aaron B. Myers, was mortally wounded in the Wilderness, and twelve other commissioned officers fell in the many bloody battles in which the 125th was engaged. The 125th and 126th claim the honor of first crossing the river when the Army of the Potomac moved in February, 1864. Col. Levin Crandell was Colonel Willard's successor, and Joseph Hyde succeeded Lieutenant-Colonel Myers.

ONE HUNDRED TWENTY-SIXTH REGIMENT.—The 126th was organized at Geneva, and bears upon its colors the names of thirteen great battles. Col. Eliakim Sherrill was killed at Gettysburg, and Lieut.-Col. William H. Baird was killed while charging on the enemy's works at Petersburg. That the regiment did its part honorably and suffered severely, is evident from the fact that sixteen commissioned officers were killed or mortally wounded in action. Col. James M. Bull succeeded Colonel Sherrill in command of the regiment, and in April, 1864, he resigned, and after that time the regiment had no Colonel or Lieutenant-Colonel, except during the two months preceding the death of Lieutenant-Colonel Baird.

ONE HUNDRED TWENTY-SEVENTH REGIMENT.—The regiment went to the war about one thousand strong, with its full complement of officers, and returned with twenty-five officers and 530 men. The regiment arrived at Charleston, S. C., a few days after its evacuation, and was detailed by order of General Sherman for permanent city garrison, on account of its good character, and Col. William Gurney was appointed permanent post commander. A large part of the regiment was from Long Island, the remainder from New York City. The 127th took a very prominent part in the battle of Honey Hill, S. C., in November, 1864, and in the following month at Devereaux Neck, S. C. The Lieutenant-Colonel of the regiment was Stewart L. Woodford, who, in March, 1865, was promoted to Colonel at the 103d United States Colored Troops, and at the close of the war to Brigadier-General. Colonel Gurney was also promoted in 1865 to Brevet Brigadier-General. The only commissioned officer lost by the regiment during the war was Capt. Cornelius A. Cooper, who died of disease in 1862.

ONE HUNDRED TWENTY-EIGHTH REGIMENT.—The first effort to raise a regiment in Columbia County was made on the 23d of July, 1862, in a call to form Company A. The company soon filled its ranks, and others soon followed in quick succession. Dutchess, the sister county of Columbia, contributed Companies B, C, D, F, H and I. The efforts of the public men of Dutchess County were constant in helping to form the regiment, and none were more unremitting in their labors than the late Hon. William Kelly, of Rhinebeck. Companies F and H were from Fishkill, about one hundred men from that town enlisting as privates at the time of the organization of the companies. The following are the commissioned and non-commissioned officers of the regiment who were residents of Fishkill Landing and Matteawan: Quartermaster Alexander Annan, (died recently); Commissary Sergeant E. Augustus Brett; Ordinance Sergeant John Matthews; Corporal Washington J. Montfort, of Company D; Lieutenant, Henry H. Sincerbox, of Company H; Orderly Sergeant Columbus S. Keys, Company H; Sergeant Benjamin F. Benson, Company H; Sergeant Garret F. Dillon, Company H; Corporal A. B. Mase, Company H; Corporal Charles H. Weller, Company H; Company F, Capt. Arthur DeWint; First Lieutenant J. J. Williamson; Second Lieutenant C. R. Anderson; Orderly Sergeant Henry Rothery; Second Sergeant Charles Van Tine; Third Sergeant David Warren; Fourth Sergeant David C. Van Amburgh; Fifth Sergeant Francis H. Brett; Corporals Augustus M. Myers; Second, Joseph Seymour; Third, Samuel Speeding; Fourth, Lewis Pearsall;

Fifth, Augustus H. Terry; Sixth, Jeremiah Boice; Seventh, William Bailey; Eighth, Robert Pickles.

The Colonel of the regiment was David S. Cowles, a lawyer of the city of Hudson, and a brother of Judge E. P. Cowles. The Lieutenant-Colonel was James Smith, and the Chaplain Rev. John Parker, of the Methodist Episcopal Church. On the 31st of August, the regimental flags were presented to the regiment in the presence of 4000 spectators. Colonel Cowles, in response to the presentation speech, announced the firm purpose of the regiment, that the flags should never be returned dishonored, and concluded as follows: " And should it be the destiny of some of us to fall, you may truthfully write upon the marble that shall mark the resting place of each,

> " He lived as mothers wish their sons to live,
> And died as fathers wish their sons to die."

On the 5th of September, the regiment left for the seat of war. After marching and countermarching, performing garrison duty in various places, it finally embarked for Louisiana, and in April, 1863, the regiment was complimented by General Sherman for the success of its first achievement—the capture of a large quantity of property at Gainesville. As one after another we have seen the regiments of the Empire State when brought to the stern crisis of battle, meet undismayed the dread encounter, and by their steady heroism add glory after glory to their flag, so at the great battle of Port Hudson on the 27th of May, 1863, came the splendid 128th, and no more desperate fighting ever took place than that of the division of General Sherman to which the 128th belonged. The division moved steadily forward under the most murderous fire of shot, shell, grape, canister and musketry. Colonel Cowles was on foot, and gallantly led his columns to a charge on the fortifications. His comrades were struggling hand to hand with the enemy, and he was eager to share with them the fortunes of the day. Placing himself conspicuously in front, with a clear voice heard above the tumult, he was encouraging and leading his men to the assault, when within a few rods of a gateway which formed the entrance to the rebel works, two balls struck him, one entering his breast and passing through his body. " Boys, have I not done my duty? Tell my mother I died with my face to the enemy. Christ Jesus, receive my spirit," were the last words of Colonel Cowles. Upon the fall of Colonel Cowles the command of the regiment devolved upon Capt. Francis S. Keese, of Dutchess County, whose bravery at this critical point was only equalled by his coolness and self-reliance. It was during this assault that Orderly Serg. Charles L. Van Slyck, of Kinderhook, was killed. He fell by a shot that took away both legs at the knee, but notwithstanding the near approach of death, this brave officer continued to fire at the enemy until another shot hit him in the breast and terminated his life. John Hughes of Mattewan was instantly killed by being shot in the head while advancing on the enemy. Lewis Pearsall of Matteawan was also among the brave men mortally wounded. On the 14th of June, the second assault on Port Hudson, in which the Union forces were repulsed, was made. In this assault the 128th lost but one man killed—Robert P. Churchill, of Company C, from Rhinebeck. Capt. George W Van Slyck, Capt. Arthur DeWint, Adjt. J. P. Wilkinson and nineteen men were wounded. After the repulse, a general order was issued by the commanding general, summoning the bold men of the corps to organize a storming party of 1000 men to vindicate the flag of the Union and the memory of its defenders who had fallen. The 128th responded to the call, and a large number of the members volunteered. They were placed under command of Captain Keese, who distinguished himself so greatly in the assault of May 14. These brave men took part in many assaults and participated in many bloody repulses.

After the fall of Port Hudson on the 9th of July, 1863, the regiment was ordered to proceed to Baton Rouge, under command of General Arnold, and after the most fatiguing march ever made by the regiment, reached that city on the 22d. At Baton Rouge, Capt. Arthur De Wint, who was badly wounded at Port Hudson while displaying the utmost heroism and gallantry, resigned his position and returned home. Just before the battle of Port Hudson, he wrote to his sister: " I shall take no other mode of promotion than that which lies in the path of duty and bravery." Captain De Wint is a descendant of President John Adams, and it is said that his father, when asked early in the war by Chaplain Parker if he had any message to send to his son, said: " Tell him to stand up to the scratch, and thrash the rascals." The 128th next took part in the ill-fated Red River expedition, which resulted in nothing but loss of men, except to show how, under fatigue and disaster, the American soldier can sustain his devotion to the National unity. The battle of Cane River was one of the battles resulting from this expedition, and the 128th was the first to cross the river and plant a flag upon the hill. The regiment, led by Lieut.-Col. James Smith, also made a brilliant charge on the enemy during the engagement, routing them and taking many prisoners. In July, the regiment sailed under sealed orders for Washington, when it joined the Nineteenth Army Corps, in General Sheridan's division.

In the successful engagements in the Shenandoah Valley, the 128th was assigned the honor of leading a charge upon a strong Rebel position near Strasburg. In the succeeding engagement at Winchester, Major Keese and four other officers, and sixty men were killed or wounded. During the three engagements of Winchester, Fisher's Creek and Cedar Creek, the regiment lost 200 in killed, wounded and missing. General Emory says in his Report of the battle of Fisher's Creek: "To strengthen and shorten our lines it became necessary to drive in the enemy s skirmishers and occupy their lines. This was handsomely done by the 128th, Lieut.-Col. James P. Foster commanding, supported by the 176th New York." At the battle of Cedar Creek, Capt. Robert F Wilkinson, on General Emory's Staff, was severely wounded, and six privates were killed. After these battles the regiment was engaged in garrison duty at Winchester, Newbern and Savannah—its last march from Savannah to Augusta, a distance of 130 miles, was accomplished in six days. At Augusta, the regiment was mustered out of the service, and returned home with only 400 men of the original 960, and 173 recruits. The first loss sustained by the regiment was in the death of Surg. Daniel P. Van Vleek, of Kinderhook, who died on board United States steam Transport, September 21, 1862. The second loss was in the death of Lieut. F. W. Sterling, who also died at sea, December 6, 1862. Twenty-four privates died in the Rebel prison at Salisbury. Among them were J. Powles and J. Wilhelm, of Fishkill; also private John Hague, a son of Rev. J. B. Hague, of Hudson. Among the brave men of the regiment who became martyrs to the war, the name of Capt. Edward Gifford, of Hudson, Company A, must not be forgotten. During the siege of Port Hudson he was captured, and after an imprisonment of thirty-nine days, effected his escape in the most daring and remarkable manner. But his sufferings resulted in his death, which deprived the regiment of a faithful, efficient officer. While in Louisiana, many members of the regiment were transferred to the Corps d'Afrique, organized by General Banks. Few companies of any regiment can boast of a larger number of promotions for gallant and meritorious services than Companies F and H. The reception given to these two companies by the citizens of Fishkill, upon their return home, will long be remembered. The "Denning Guard" turned out with full ranks, and presented a fine appearance; also the veterans, firemen, citizens, etc. Flags and floral decorations were numerous, and the whole population turned out to give the brave defenders of the Union a cordial and grateful reception, which was closed by an eloquent and touching address by the Rev. Joseph Kimball, of the Reformed Dutch Church.

ONE HUNDRED TWENTY-NINTH REGIMENT.—See Eighth Heavy Artillery.

ONE HUNDRED THIRTIETH REGIMENT.—See Nineteenth Cavalry.

ONE HUNDRED THIRTY-FIRST REGIMENT.—This regiment was raised from among the Metropolitan Police, and was the first regiment of the Metropolitan brigade. It went to the war under command of Col. Charles S. Trumbull, and most of the officers hailed from the Seventh regiment. It went with the Banks expedition to Louisiana, and became attached to the famous Nineteenth army corps. The regiment participated most honorably in the Port Hudson campaign, where it suffered severely. In 1864, it left the Department of the Gulf and joined General Butler at Bermuda Hundred, Va., and shortly after joined General Sheridan in the Shenandoah Valley, and participated in his gallant achievements, losing very heavily at the battle of Opequan, September, 1864. After this it went to North Carolina, and became attached to the Tenth army corps, and then to General Sherman's army. In May, 1865, it went to Augusta, Ga., and in June, arrived at Savannah, and was there mustered out of the service. The regiment travelled over ten thousand miles by land and water during its term of service. It was known as the fighting regiment, and participated in the battles of Irish Bend, Vermilion Bayou, Port Hudson, Cox's Plantation, Opequan, Fisher's Hill, Cedar Creek. The regiment returned home with only 240 men out of 1000 with which it went to the war. General Sheridan attributed our victory at Winchester, September, 1864, to the heroism displayed by the 131st. Colonel Trumbull resigned in 1863, and Nicholas W. Day became his successor.

ONE HUNDRED THIRTY-SECOND REGIMENT.—" Second Empire Brigade." This was a New York City regiment, and was commanded by Col. Peter J. Claassen. The only commissioned officer killed was Lieut. Arnold Zenette, who fell in action at Batchelor's Creek, N. C., in 1864. In this battle the enemy charged three successive times and as often were handsomely repulsed by the brave boys of Companies D, E, and G, who were defending the bridge on the Neuse River. The enemy were finally reinforced, and after four hours of hard fighting the little garrison was forced to retire from its defence. Had not eleven men of the regiment, under Lieut. Abram P. Harring, kept back the rebel army until the rest of the regiment came up. Newbern would have been captured. Colonel Claassen comprehended the nature of the rebel attack from the first. The regiment went to the field with 900 men and returned home with 304 men and officers. During its three years term of service it was almost continually on outpost duty. Capt. Abraham Dowdney died in 1886; at the time of his death he was a member of Congress. There was a part of a company composed of Indians in the regiment, and of the number the First Lieutenant and First Sergeant were full-blooded redskins. They made good soldiers, and all lived to get home but one, who was captured and died at Andersonville. Up to September, 1863, there had been more promotions from the ranks in the 132d, than any other regiment from the State.

ONE HUNDRED THIRTY-THIRD REGIMENT.—"Second Regiment Metropolitan Guard." The record of the 133d is a brilliant one. They were especially commended by Gen. Halbert E. Paine for gallantry in the assault on Port Hudson, June 14th, 1863, and also by Admiral Porter, for assistance in building a dam on Red River, to enable the iron-clad fleet to pass the rapids in May, 1864.

The regiment was admirably commanded by Col. Leonard D. H. Currie, and Lieut.-Col. Anthony J. Allaire, now a popular officer of the Metropolitan Police. Capts. N. W. Meserole, John Silvey, George H. Simpson, John H. Greer and Lieuts. S. L. Davids, George W La Roza, and J. H. Cartwright were gallant officers, and shared the honors of the regiment.

ONE HUNDRED THIRTY-FOURTH REGIMENT.—The 134th was from Schoharie County, and fought bravely at Gettysburg, Dug Gap, and in the siege of Savannah. Col. Charles R. Coster, who died recently, was one of the best officers in the service; Capt. Austin A. Yates was another splendid soldier. He enlisted as a private, and by merit alone rose to the rank of Major. In 1885 he was nominated for State Senator.

ONE HUNDRED THIRTY-FIFTH REGIMENT.—See Sixth Heavy Artillery.

ONE HUNDRED THIRTY-SIXTH REGIMENT.—The regiment was from Portage, and was commanded by Col. James Wood, Jr., who was promoted to Brevet Brigadier-General in 1865. The 136th fought bravely at the battle of Chattanooga. Lieut.-Cols. Lester B. Faulkner and Henry L. Arnold were brave and valuable officers.

ONE HUNDRED THIRTY-SEVENTH REGIMENT.—This was one of the four regiments in General Geary's (White Star) division, that formed the front line in the assault upon Lookout Mountain. The regiment suffered severely at Gettysburg and Chattanooga. Col. David Ireland died of disease at Atlanta, Ga., in 1864.

ONE HUNDRED THIRTY-EIGHTH REGIMENT.—See Ninth Heavy Artillery.

ONE HUNDRED THIRTY-NINTH REGIMENT.— The City of Brooklyn may well feel proud of this organization. It was originally commanded by Col. Anthony Conk, who resigned in 1863, and was succeeded by Col. Samuel H. Roberts. The 139th went to the war with 1000 men, to which 250 recruits were added, and returned home with only 340. It was in the Army of the James nearly its entire term of service, and was the third regiment to enter Richmond when that city capitulated. At one time during the war, the regiment marched sixty-one miles in fifty-four hours and captured the rebel garrison at Charles City Cross Roads. Lieut.-Col. Edgar Perry and Capt. S. Clark Beecher, were killed at the battle of Coal Harbor. Lieutenant-Colonel Perry was a son of the late Eli Perry, of Orange County, and nephew of the Hon. William E. Hasbrook, of Newburg, and of Col. John H. Perry, of the Forty-eighth New York, who was killed at Fort Pulaski. He was a brave and promising young officer, and at the time of his death was in command of the regiment. Colonel Roberts signalized himself at the head of his regiment on many a hard fought battle-field. At Petersburg he was chosen on account of his daring and coolness to lead the forlorn hope, and the valor of his command could not be surpassed. Colonel Roberts was promoted to Brevet Brigadier-General, and died in July, 1885.

ONE HUNDRED FORTIETH REGIMENT.—The regiment was known as the "Rochester Racehorses." It participated in nearly all the great engagements of the Army of the Potomac, from Fredericksburg to the close of the war. It suffered severely at Gettysburg, where fell Col. Patrick H. O'Rorke. Rochester may be proud of the record of her 140th. It was in the Third Brigade of Sykes division, Fifth Corps. Few men made a more brilliant record than Colonel O'Rorke. He was mounted on a rock, cheering on his men at Little Round Top, when a bullet struck him. He had been graduated at the head of his class at West Point, in 1861, and was only twenty-five years of age when he was killed. His devoted wife, to whom he had been married but a short time, soon after his death retired to a convent, where she has ever since remained.

At the battle of Poplar Spring Church, Lieut.-Col. Elwell S. Otis commanded a brigade with the greatest skill and bravery. Colonel Otis was wounded in this engagement and was soon after promoted to Brevet-Colonel of the regiment.

See record of the 146th for further information about the 140th at Gettysburg.

ONE HUNDRED FORTY-FIRST REGIMENT.—The 141st was raised at Elmira, and was first commanded by Col. Samuel G. Hathaway. Colonel Hathaway resigned in February, 1863, and John W Divinny was appointed his successor. On the 1st of June, 1863, Colonel Divinny also resigned and Wm. K. Logie became the third colonel, and one year later Colonel Logie was killed while gallantly leading and encouraging his men at the battle of Peach Tree Creek, Ga.

At the battle of Resaca, the regiment fought bravely and suffered severely. Lieut.-Col. James C. Beecher committed suicide in 1886. He was early in the war chaplain of the Sixty-seventh Regiment.

ONE HUNDRED FORTY-SECOND REGIMENT.—The regiment belonged to the brigade that was the first to storm and take Fort Fisher, in 1865, during which its unflinching bravery deserves lasting remembrance. Col. Martin N. Curtis, the tallest man in the Army of the Potomac, and now a member of the New York Legislature, was the first to gain a foothold within the Rebel parapet. The Colonel was promoted to Brigadier-General in 1865. Lieut.-Col. Albert M. Barney was honorably mentioned in General Ames' report of the assault. Colonel Barney was promoted to Brigadier-General, and died in August, 1886.

At the battle of Chapin's Farm, the regiment went into action five hundred strong and lost one hundred men in less than thirty minutes.

Capts. David A. Nevin, William Dodge, Franklin F. Brown, Jonathan Houghton, Dan. S. Griffin, Wm. Wheeler, Wm. D. Brennan, Birney B. Keeler, Hiram A. Winslow, William H. Walling and Amos Wells were among the gallant soldiers of the 142d. Surgeon Hans Powell died in January, 1885.

ONE HUNDRED FORTY-THIRD REGIMENT.—The regiment was from Monticello, and went to the war under command of Col. David P DeWitt. Soon after the war commenced Colonel DeWitt left a luxurious home at Middletown, and was appointed Major of the Second Maryland Regiment. After holding this position for a short time he became Colonel of the Third Maryland. The Third was soon reduced to a mere skeleton, and the Colonel was relieved from the command and commissioned Colonel of the 143d New York. Upon taking the field it was assigned to the defences of Washington, where it remained until April, 1863, when it was transferred to the department of Virginia. It took part in the siege of Suffolk and the operations against Richmond. After the battle of Gettysburg it was transferred to the Army of the Potomac, and in the following September was sent with General Hooker to the Army of the Cumberland, in which it served during the Chattanooga and Knoxville campaigns. After that it formed part of General Sherman's command, and participated in all of the battles and campaigns in which the Twentieth Corps were engaged, from Chattanooga to Raleigh. The regiment never took a step backward and was highly complimented for its bravery and efficiency. The regiment returned home under command of Col. Horace Houghton, who was promoted in 1865 to Brevet Brigadier-General.

Near the close of the war, on the 6th of March, 1865, in the action at Natural Bridge, Florida, fell Lieut. Edward Carrington, at the time of his death on the Staff of General Newton, a splendid soldier, and a man possessed of an unusually brilliant and solid mind. After the battle of Kenesaw Mountain, Lieutenant Carrington was the only member of General Newton's Staff who remained uninjured. He was a graduate of Yale College and studied law in the office of Messrs. Bowdoin, Laroque & Barlow.

ONE HUNDRED FORTY-FOURTH REGIMENT.—The 144th was raised in twenty days in Delaware County, and when it left Delhi numbered 956 men. In the fall of 1864 it was reduced to between three and four hundred. It was then filled up to one thousand men by one year recruits from the same county. From Delhi the regiment proceeded at once to the defences of the capital at Upton Hill, Cloud's Mills and Vienna. In the spring of 1863 they were sent to Suffolk, and remained there during Longstreet's siege of that place. In May the regiment was placed in General Gordon's command at West Point, Va., and participated in Keyes's demonstration against Richmond. In July they joined the Army of the Potomac. In the fall and winter of 1863 the regiment was engaged at Folly Island and Morris Island, and formed a part of Gilmore's force during the bombardment of Sumter and Charleston. It was also engaged at Seabrook and John's Island. In February the regiment went to Florida, where it was engaged chiefly in raiding. It returned to Hilton Head in June, 1864, and was with Foster in his co-operative movements with Sherman. At Honey Hill, Devereaux Neck and Coosawatchie it was engaged under Porter, while Sherman flanked Charleston. Col. William J. Slidell was a nephew of the famous John Slidell, Rebel envoy to European courts. The first Colonel of the regiment was Robert S. Hughston, the next was David E. Gregory, the third was Slidell, and the last was James Lewis. Lieut.-Col. Calvin A. Rice and Maj. William Plaskett were among the valuable officers. The only commissioned officer killed in action was Lieut. James W. Mack, killed at Honey Hill.

ONE HUNDRED FORTY-FIFTH REGIMENT.—Chancellorsville was the principal engagement in which the regiment took part. The regiment never had a Colonel. It was disbanded in December, 1863, and the members transferred to other regiments. The only commissioned officer killed in action was Lieut. Wm. H. Poole, killed at Chancellorsville.

ONE HUNDRED FORTY-SIXTH REGIMENT.—The regiment was from Oneida County, and was known as the "Fifth Oneida." The first Colonel of the regiment was Kenner Garrard, who, as Captain in the Fifth United States Cavalry, was made a prisoner of war by the disgraceful surrender of General Twiggs, in Texas in 1860. The 146th were in the Third Brigade of Sykes' division of the Fifth Corps. Its first battle was Fredericksburg, in 1862. At Chancellorsville the regiment suffered heavily on the first day's fight and acquitted itself with honor. At Gettysburg, the brigade made a charge in support of the flying columns of the Third Corps, which had met with a temporary reverse. Subsequently the brigade, consisting of the 140th and 146th charged up and obtained possession of the famous Round Top, but at a severe loss in officers and men. It was here that Colonel O'Rorke of the 140th was killed. Colonel Garrard was made Brigadier-General for gallant conduct at Gettysburg. At the battle of the Wilderness, the 140th and 146th made the first charge of the day, both regiments losing terribly. The 146th suffered almost total annihilation, for out of nearly 600 muskets, the loss was some 400 in killed, wounded and missing. Among the killed was Col. David T. Jenkins. Colonel Jenkins was considered one of the best engineer officers in the Army of the Potomac, who were not graduates of West Point. Colonel Garrard, after his promotion, made for himself a high reputation in the West as a cavalry officer and it was he who held Cumberland Gap so long against the attacks of the enemy. The gallant officers of the 146th, whose services entitle them to grateful remembrance were, among many others: Capts. Benjamin F Wright, Henry E. Jones, Wm. A. Walker, Henry Loomis, Levi H. York, Robert P. Warren, H. W. S. Swett, Lawrence Fitzpatrick, Alonzo J. King, Charles K. Dutton, Lieut.-Col. James

Grindlay, Maj. Isaac P. Powell and Maj. Peter Claesgent. The regiment returned home with twenty-eight officers and 250 men—120 were killed in action.

ONE HUNDRED FORTY-SEVENTH REGIMENT.—The regiment was from Oswego and has a brilliant record. It went to the war under command of Col. Andrew S. Warner. Colonel Warner resigned in February, 1863. John G. Butler was the next Colonel; he remained in command until November, 1863, when Francis C. Miller was appointed to the position. The regiment participated with great gallantry in twelve of the leading engagements of the Army of the Potomac. On the first day of the battle of Gettysburg, Maj. George Harney not receiving the order to retire which was sent to the regiment, held it to its position, until, having lost half its members, the order to retire was repeated. Lieut. Joel A. Baker died in January, 1885. At the time of his death he was Chief of Police of Oswego.

The regiment lost eleven commissioned officers.

ONE HUNDRED FORTY-EIGHTH REGIMENT.—The 148th was from Geneva, and went to the front under command of Col. William Johnson, who resigned in October, 1863, and Col. George M. Guion became his successor. In October, 1864, Colonel Guion resigned, and Col. John B. Murray became his successor. Colonel Murray was an admirable officer and rose to the rank of Brevet Brigadier-General. The regiment fought bravely at Fair Oaks in 1864 (where Captain Gage was killed while displaying conspicuous gallantry), Coal Harbor, Rice's Station and in the operations around Petersburg. Mr. Conrad Bancroft enlisted as a private. He was a single man, and invested all his bounty and seven hundred dollars additional in the town bonds for a war fund, and made a will by which, in case he did not return, all his property was to be distributed among the widows and orphan children of Canandaigua. The following are the names of a few of the commissioned officers of the 148th, whose honorable records deserve remembrance: Lieut.-Col. Fred L. Manning, Maj. John Cooley, Capt. John R. McNaughton, Capt. Henry R. Murray, Capt. Henry Parsons, Capt. Edward Cole, Capt. Cortland Van Rensselaer, Lieuts. Erastus H. Lewis, Jay W. Neighbor, Harvey S. McLeod, Richard Edwards, Capt. Nicholas R. Johnston, Capt. Hiram H. Hewitt and Capt. Edgar A. Griswold. Corporal E. Van Winkle, Privates Henry S. Welles and George A. Buchanan were heroes of special acts of gallantry and recipients of medals of honor from the War Department.

ONE HUNDRED FORTY-NINTH REGIMENT. —The 149th was from Syracuse, and the regiment can boast of having been commanded by one of the bravest and most successful soldiers furnished by the State—Col. Henry A. Barnum. The Colonel was wounded at Malvern Hill and again at Lookout Mountain, and for gallant and meritorious services was promoted, in 1865, to Brigadier-General. The 149th was one of the two New York regiments in Geary's division that formed the front line in the assault upon Lookout Mountain, and four of the ten stand of colors captured in the battle of Chattanooga, were taken by the 149th.

During the military operations following the battle of Chickamauga, including the famous "battle above the clouds" on Lookout Mountain and the hot fight at Missionary Ridge, Colonel Barnum's regiment, the 149th New York, captured five Rebel flags out of a total of eleven taken in action at Chattanooga. Its commander, who still carried an open bullet-hole through his body from the wound received at Malvern Hill, was shot through the sword arm under the towering crest of Lookout Mountain. Gen. George A. Thomas' attention was directed to the 149th by reason of these facts, and having assured himself of Colonel Barnum's great personal bravery in the battles at Chattanooga, he, by a special order, conferred upon Colonel Barnum the highest honor in his power by selecting him to carry the captured flags to Washington and deliver them to the Adjutant-General.

Colonel Barnum fulfilled this distinguished duty, displaying the flags at the great Sanitary Fair in Cincinnati, at a similar fair at his then home in Syracuse, and before the Legislative Assembly of this State at Albany. A resolution of thanks to Colonel Barnum was passed by the Assembly, January 5, 1864. En route from Albany a fearful abscess developed in the unhealed body wound of the Colonel, and at New York Dr. Lewis A. Sayre operated on the wound and passed an oakum rope through the track of the bullet, from front to rear through the left ilium.

Delaying in New York only two days, Colonel Barnum proceeded to Washington, but was there confined to his hotel for some weeks by the painful and prostrating condition of his wounds. As soon as able to ride to the War Department, Colonel Barnum sent a note to the Adjutant-General of the army, notifying him that he was there to turn over the flags to the Government in pursuance of his orders from General Thomas. A brief note directing him to deliver the flags to the officer in charge of trophies at the War Department was the only recognition the gallant officer received from his government. He obeyed these orders to the letter. Others had come to Washington on like errands and had been honored by promotion, medals and special mention in the halls of Congress. For Colonel Barnum, sick and suffering as he was, was reserved the indignity of being treated, not as a gallant soldier who had well nigh lost his life in his country's service, but as a simple messenger detailed to carry property from point to point.

The young officer's pride forbade his soliciting other recognition; his soldierly instinct made complaint impossible. Waiting but a few days longer, to nurse his strength, he returned to his command. His personal courage in future battles gained for him the rank of Brigadier-General, but not until twenty-five years later did he receive the medal so dear to every soldier's heart.

In the list of officers who remained with the regiment during nearly its entire term of service and acquitted themselves with honorable distinction were Maj. Abel G. Cook, Maj. Henry N. Burhans, Lieut.-Col. Nicholas Grumbach, Capts. Eben G. Townsend, and James E. Doran, Lieuts. Orson Coville, George G. Truair, Matthew H. Westcott, Walter M. Dallman and Alexander McKinstry.

ONE HUNDRED AND FIFTIETH REGIMENT.—This splendid Dutchess County regiment knows what fighting is, and never had to show the Rebels their backs, and it knows how to "forage liberally" on the enemy's country, as South Carolina too well knows. The regiment was organized by Col. John H. Ketcham, at Poughkeepsie, and was commanded by him until the fall of Atlanta, and for a short time at the siege of Savannah, where he was severely wounded. While suffering from his wound, he was breveted Brigadier-General, but failing to gain health and strength for the field, he tendered his resignation, believing that officers holding rank and drawing pay should be with their commands. Being the idol of his regiment, his retirement was a source of regret to all who had been under his command. Colonel Ketcham is now a Representative in Congress— his record is an honorable one both in a military and civil sense. He has served his State in many official capacities—first as supervisor of his native town (Dover), next as Member of Assembly, next in the State Senate, five times a member of Congress, a delegate to the National Republican Convention, and Commissioner of the District of Columbia. The 150th Regiment, which he commanded, had about 1300 men on its rolls from first to last, and returned home in 1865 with fearfully thinned ranks. The regiment first did guard duty in the city of Baltimore, when it went to Gettysburg, and took part in that great battle. In September, 1863, the regiment went west and served in the Second Brigade, First Division, Twentieth

Corps, and followed the fortunes of General Sherman; and has been especially mentioned for its bravery in a speech by General Sherman and in a letter by General Slocum. Few names will shine brighter in the history of the 150th Regiment than that of Capt. John S. Scofield, of Glenham, who after serving most honorably at Gettysburg, in Sherman's march to the sea, and siege of Atlanta, returned home when the regiment was mustered out, but has since gone to an honored grave, having died December 11, 1876, and his body was interred in Fishkill Rural Cemetery. The regiment came home under command of Alfred B. Smith, of Poughkeepsie, who went out as Major, and rose to the position of Colonel through a steady attention to duty and the constant exhibition of those qualities of head and heart that constitute the true soldier. Colonel Smith was promoted to Brevet Brigadier-General in 1865. Fishkill contributed thirty-four brave fellows to the regiment at the time it was organized.

The officers of the 150th were all admirably well qualified for their positions, and some of those who survived the dangers of the war now occupy exalted positions in civil life; among them Maj. Henry A. Gildersleeve, who is one of the Judges of the Court of General Sessions, in New York City; Lieut.-Col. Charles G. Bartlett was a brave and valuable officer, as were also Capt. Benjamin S. Broas, Lieut. Wade H. Steenburgh, Capt. Obed Wheeler, Capt. S. V. R. Cruger, who was supposed to have been mortally wounded at the battle of Resaca, and Lieut. Cyrus S. Roberts and Perry W. Chapman.

ONE HUNDRED FIFTY-FIRST REGIMENT.—The 151st was organized at Lockport, and went to the war under command of Col. William Emerson. Colonel Emerson remained with the regiment until December, 1864, when he was honorably discharged. There were three Lieutenant-Colonels connected with the regiment during its term of service: Lieut.-Col. Erwin A. Bowen was honorably discharged February 26, 1864; Thomas M. Fay honorably discharged November 5, 1864; and in 1865 Lieut.-Col. Charles Bogardus was promoted to Brevet-Colonel. The regiment did its share of the fighting at Wapping Heights, Wilderness, Spottsylvania, Coal-Harbor, Petersburg, Monocacy, Opequan, Fisher's Hill and Cedar Creek. Four commissioned officers were killed in action.

ONE HUNDRED FIFTY-SECOND REGIMENT.—In 1863, the regiment served under General Peck at Suffolk, and General Keyes on the Peninsula. Being at Washington, en-route for the Army of the Potomac when the riots occurred in New York City, it was ordered there, where it remained until October, when it proceeded to the Army of the Potomac, and joined the First Brigade, Second Division, Second Corps. The regiment took part in all the succeeding engagements of that army and the series of movements which ended in the surrender of General Lee. The regiment met with heavy losses, and returned home with only 256 men.

The regiment was organized at Mohawk. Leonard Boyer was Colonel of the regiment until January, 1863, when he resigned. Col. Alonzo Ferguson then took command. In November, 1863, Colonel Ferguson was honorably discharged.

ONE HUNDRED FIFTY-THIRD REGIMENT.—The regiment did its share in making history and putting down the Rebellion. It was first stationed at Alexandria, Va., as provost guard, after which it occupied Washington, doing the same duty there. It was subsequently transferred to the Gulf Department, and participated in the Red River campaign, losing heavily in the battles of Sabine Cross Roads, Pleasant Hill, Cane River Crossing and Mansura. The regiment was commended by the Commanding General for distinguished bravery in these battles. In 1864 the 153d came back to Washington to defend it from an expected attack by Early, becoming part and parcel of Sheridan's army—First Brigade, First Division, Nineteenth Corps. It took part in the battles of Winchester, Fisher's Hill, Cedar Creek and many skirmishes. After the surrender of Lee it moved to Savannah, where the regiment, by the gentlemanly conduct of its officers and men, won the esteem and respect of the citizens. Col. Edwin P. Davis was brevetted Brigadier-General for meritorious service. The first Colonel of the regiment was Duncan McMartin, who resigned in April, 1863, when Colonel Davis succeeded to the position. There were four Lieutenant-Colonels connected with the 153d, viz: Thomas Armstrong, William H. Printup, Alexander Strain and George H. McLaughlin. The regiment was organized at Fonda.

ONE HUNDRED FIFTY-FOURTH REGIMENT.—The regiment was organized at Jamestown, and went to the war under command of Col. Patrick H. Jones, who, in 1865, was promoted to Brigadier-General. At the battle of Chancellorsville, the regiment belonged to a brigade in General Howard's Eleventh Corps, commanded by Colonel Bushbeck—the only brigade in the corps that fought bravely. It fought with great courage until an attempt to longer hold its position would have been madness, and it then stubbornly withdrew. To this brigade is the credit due of saving from capture the trains and artillery of the corps. The boats which had been secreted in

Marsh Run, which empties into the Rappahannock, were manned by the 154th New York and Seventy-third Pennsylvania regiments, who pushed fearlessly across the river and took possession of the opposite bank.

ONE HUNDRED FIFTY-FIFTH REGIMENT.—The regiment was greatly indebted to the venerable and wealthy Bishop Tinson for his generosity in aiding in its formation. It went to the war under command of Col. William McEvilly, and it would have been hard to find a better man for the position—his appearance alone commanded respect. The 155th followed the flag of the famous Irish Brigade throughout its services, and on many battle-fields contributed to its fame. Lieut.-Col. Hugh C. Flood was wounded at Spottsylvania, from the effects of which he finally died. Capt. John Byrnes was taken prisoner at Ream's Station. Out of its original number of 700 strong, its losses were 6 officers killed, 10 wounded and 9 taken prisoners, 42 men were killed, 256 wounded and 67 missing. The 155th furnished several valuable officers for other regiments. Lieut.-Col. James P. McMahon was promoted to Colonel of the 164th, and was killed at Coal Harbor. Lieut. John Tracy, Jr., promoted to Major of the Eighteenth Cavalry; Second Lieut. James S. Van Cortlandt to First Lieutenant in the 22d Cavalry regiment.

ONE HUNDRED FIFTY-SIXTH REGIMENT.—It was in the Gulf Department for two years—Gen. N. P. Banks, commander. It made a march after the Bisland fight to Alexandria, La., and subsequently was in the fight at Port Hudson and the capture of that place, where on the 14th of June, 1863, Lieut.-Col. Thomas Fowler, of Kingston, who was leading the regiment in a charge, had both legs shot off and died soon after. Here, also, and for some time previous, Companies A, G, and D acted as Banks' Headquarters Guard. They retained this honorable position until the surrender of Port Hudson, and General Banks returned to New Orleans. Afterwards the regiment was present in clearing out obstructions from the Red River, and at Morganza Bend the "boys" had a chance to try their metal with the Rebels. This was in 1864, and during the same year it came north and was at the battle of Opequan Creek near Winchester; then went up the valley with Sheridan to Cedar Creek, where it took part in that battle. The regiment was also in the fight at Fisher's Hill, after which it was sent to Savannah, Ga., and did duty in different parts of that State. The regiment never lost its colors, but brought them back after three years' service, bloodstained, riddled and torn.

At the battle of Cedar Creek the colors of the regiment were borne by Corporals of the Color Guard, the National flag by Daniel T. Ronk, the State colors by C. T. Green. Corporal Green fell with the colors. Serg. Frank Decker, of Company E, immediately raised them from the ground, and with them in one hand, and a musket in the other floated them defiantly over the heads, as it were, of the enemy; but soon he also fell severely wounded; Capt. Alfred Cooley (having succeeded the brave Capt. James J. Hoyt in command of the regiment) being near by when Decker fell, stripped the colors from the staff. The Rebels now came up and demanded his surrender, but the captain managed to escape and thereby saved the colors. Col. Jacob Sharpe commanded a brigade with great skill and bravery at the battle of Winchester, where he was wounded. At the battle of Opequan, Lieut.-Col. Alfred Neafie commanded the regiment, and showed himself to be an officer of the best military qualities.

The 156th was a New York City regiment. It was first commanded by Col. Erastus Cooke, who resigned in March, 1863, and immediately thereupon Col. Jacob Sharpe was placed at the head of the regiment.

ONE HUNDRED FIFTY-SEVENTH REGIMENT.—This regiment was organized at Hamilton, September, 1862, and participated with distinguished credit in eight important engagements. It was alluded to in terms of the highest praise for its gallantry at the battle of Gettysburg, where it suffered terribly. Lieut.-Col. Geo. W. Arrowsmith, whose bravery was unsurpassed, was among the killed on the first day of the battle. The regiment lost seven commissioned officers killed or mortally wounded. Col. Philip P. Brown, Jr., commanded the regiment with distinguished credit. Capts. Lafayette McWilliams, E. Charlier, George L. Warren, Garret S. Van Hoesen and Lieuts. James A. Coffin and R. Walworth Bourne, were among the gallant men whose names were identified with the valor of the regiment.

ONE HUNDRED FIFTY-EIGHTH REGIMENT.—"First Empire Regiment." This was a Brooklyn regiment. It went to the war under command of Col. James Jourdan, who was promoted to Brevet Brigadier-General, and was succeeded by Col. W H. McNary, who, in 1865, was also promoted to Brevet Brigadier-General. The regiment was complimented in General Orders by General Peck, for its gallant conduct on the occasion of a successful expedition to Bear Island, in 1862, by which very extensive salt manufacturing works were destroyed. At Norfolk the 158th was attached to the provost guard. The regiment went to the relief of General Foster, when he was beleagured at Washington, N. C. The regiment made several brilliant raids into North Carolina. Subsequently Lieutenant Colonel McNary, who is said to be as brave a man as ever lived, and led his regiment wherever it went, was appointed Military Governor of Beaufort. In 1864, the regiment, under command of Colonel Jourdan made a dash into Jones and Onslow counties, N. C. This was one of the most brilliant raids that had occurred, and reflected great credit upon Colonel Jourdan and his gallant regiment. At Fort Gregg, Va., in April, 1865, the regiment lost the only commissioned officer killed in action, by the fall of Lieut. Edward Reilly. The 158th returned home with 350 men out of about 700 that went to the war in 1862. General Butler telegraphed to General Grant: "The 158th is with the Army of the James, and won its colors handsomely at Battery Harrison. Four of the enlisted men of the regiment were awarded medals of honor by the Secretary of War—they were Serg. Wm. Laing, Serg. James Howard, Private John Schilling and Private G. M. Grub.

ONE HUNDRED FIFTY-NINTH REGIMENT.—The first battle in which the regiment was engaged was "Irish Bend," La., April 14, 1863, where it fought bravely and lost many of its best officers. Col. Edward L. Molineaux was severely wounded. After recovering from the effects of his wound he was appointed Inspector-General of the Nineteenth Corps, and in 1864 was promoted to Brevet Brigadier-General. The regiment participated with credit in the siege of Port Hudson. After the battle the regiment returned North and at the battle of Cedar Creek, Va., October, 1864, it received honorable mention for its gallantry.

ONE HUNDRED SIXTIETH REGIMENT.—The regiment bore an honorable part in the battles of "Cotton," Plain's Store, Cox's Plantation, Bisland, Port Hudson, Pleasant Hill, Cedar Creek, and Winchester. The regiment went to the war under command of Col. Charles C. Dwight, who later in the war was appointed by General Banks Judge of the Provost Court of the Department of the Gulf. The 160th was for sometime on provost guard duty at Opelousas. Company F. Captain Josiah P. Jewett, was on board the steamer "Diana" and acted with great bravery in the battle between the vessel and Rebel batteries near Brashear City, La. Captain Jewett died in May 1863, of wounds received in action.

At the battle of Winchester Lieut.-Col. John B. Van Petten

received a bullet through his thigh, but refused to give up command of his regiment until the fighting was over. As he led off at the head of it, General Emory said to him "Colonel, you are going into a hot fire, you had better dismount."—"Cannot walk, sir." replied the Colonel pointing to his bandaged thigh. In April, 1865, Colonel Van Petten was promoted to Colonel of the 193d regiment.

ONE HUNDRED SIXTY-FIRST REGIMENT.—"Plain's Store," Port Hudson and Cox's Plantation were the principal engagements in which the 161st took part. In September 1864, the regiment formed part of the expedition to Texas, and were on board the gunboats. The first Colonel was Gabriel T. Harrower, who resigned after being with the regiment about a year. The official records represent that Lieut. John Jay has been missing since December 31, 1862.

ONE HUNDRED SIXTY-SECOND REGIMENT.—"Third Metropolitan Guard." This was a New York City regiment and went to the front under command of Col. Lewis Benedict, who was killed at the battle of Pleasant Hill, La., while bravely leading a charge. The regiment fought bravely at Bisland and Port Hudson. After the death of Colonel Benedict, Justus W. Blanchard was appointed to the command, and in 1865 he was promoted for gallantry to Brevet Brigadier-General.

ONE HUNDRED SIXTY-THIRD REGIMENT.—"Third Empire Regiment." The regiment behaved most gallantly at the battle of Fredericksburg, where it lost 150 men, killed, wounded, and missing. Lieut. William Davis, Serg.-Maj. Richard F. Tighe, Color Serg. Earnest Funk and Orderly Serg. Charles R. Near, were promoted on the field for bravery exhibited in the face of the enemy. At Fredericksburg the 163d had to mourn the loss of many a brave officer and efficient private. After the battle the regiment was consolidated with the Seventy-third New York. General Whipple, in announcing the order of the War Department for the consolidation said: "The General Commanding desires to assure the officers and men of the gallant 163d Regiment, that his separation from them is a most painful one. By uniform good conduct in camp, and on the march, and especially by bravery in battle, the regiment has won the approbation and confidence of all, and although it goes to add lustre to another organization, it has given renown to the colors and to the men of the 163d New York."

ONE HUNDRED SIXTY-FOURTH REGIMENT.—The regiment was often called the "Buffalo Tigers." It was almost entirely raised by the exertions of Col. John E. McMahon—a graduate of Fordham College, and afterwards Private Secretary to Governor Seymour. Colonel McMahon was one of three brothers, all of whom became colonels in our army. Colonel McMahon was with his regiment but a short time, for in March, 1863, he died of disease contracted while in the discharge of his duties. He was succeeded by his brother James P. McMahon, who was promoted to the position from Lieut.-Col. of the 155th. As captain in the Sixty-ninth regiment, James P. McMahon led the regiment in the memorable charge at Fair Oaks. At the battle of Coal Harbor, in 1864, Colonel McMahon fell dead at the head of his regiment. The only surviving brother is Gen. Martin T. McMahon, United States Marshal for the district of New York. The regiment took part in the siege of Suffolk, and was sent out on many daring expeditions—one was to cut Mosby off in his retreat to Aldie. The regiment returned home under command of Col. William DeLacy, who was severely wounded while charging on the enemy at Spottsvylvania Court House. The regiment lost eighteen officers killed and nine wounded; of the former number nine were wounded at the battle of Coal Harbor, and afterwards died of their wounds. Upwards of seven hundred of the file were killed or wounded. Colonel DeLacy had served with great gallantry as Major of the Thirty-seventh Regiment, from which position he was promoted to Lieutenant-Colonel of the 164th. He was wounded several times and returned after each hospital discharge to do battle for the flag. The Colonel rose to the rank of Brevet Brigadier-General. He is now engaged in the printing business in New York City. General Humphreys, in his narrative of the battle of Coal Harbor—"Campaigns of the Civil War," says: "Colonel McMahon, 164th New York, forming the left of McKeon's brigade, but separated from it by the swamps, gained the breastworks, with a portion of his regiment, and whilst alongside of his colors, cheering on his men, fell with many wounds, dying in the enemy's hands, they capturing his colors and the men with them." Maj. John Beattie died in March, 1885. At the battle of Ream's Station Major Beattie was promoted on the field for gallantry, from the position of Adjutant to that of Major. He was wounded three times during the war, and was taken prisoner at the battle of Coal Harbor, and for nine months suffered the miseries of Rebel prisons.

ONE HUNDRED SIXTY-FIFTH REGIMENT.—The 165th was organized on Staten Island and went to the war under command of Lieut.-

Col. Abel Smith, Jr., who was mortally wounded at Port Hudson. Among the officers who were especially active in organizing the regiment were Capt. Henry W. Hicks, Jr., Capt. Gould H. Thorpe and Capt. W. W. Stephenson.

The regiment fought bravely at Port Hudson, where it lost many valuable officers and gallant men.

Adj. Nathan S. Putnam—a fine soldier, and who was badly wounded at Port Hudson, died in January, 1886.

ONE HUNDRED SIXTY-SIXTH AND ONE HUNDRED SIXTY-SEVENTH REGIMENTS.—Failed to complete their organizations.

ONE HUNDRED SIXTY-EIGHTH REGIMENT.—The regiment was from Newburg. It was sometimes classed as the Nineteenth State Militia, but the official records do not recognize it as such. It was a nine months regiment, and was under command of Col. William R. Brown. The 168th acquitted itself with great credit on the occasion of a raid into King Williams County, Va. Lieut.-Col. James Low, Jr., resigned in 1863.

ONE HUNDRED SIXTY-NINTH REGIMENT.—This was a Troy regiment, although partly organized in New York City. It was composed of some of the best blood the State sent to the field. It went to the war under command of Col. Clarence Buell, upon whom descended the star that was to have descended upon Col. George L. Willard, of the 125th, who was killed at Gettysburg. During the siege of Suffolk and in the fighting on the Edenton Road, N. C., in April, 1863, the regiment behaved most gallantly. So much so, that the Brigade-Commander issued a special order exceedingly complimentary to the regiment. During the siege of Suffolk, Colonel Buell was wounded and incapacitated for further service. He was succeeded by Lieut.-Col. John McConihe, who was one of the wounded heroes of the battle of Shiloh, in 1862. As an evidence of the appreciation with which his gallantry was regarded by the citizens of Troy, he was presented with a sword, on which is the inscription, "Come on, boys! Shiloh, April 7, 1862." Presented by the citizens of Troy as a token of their esteem and of their high appreciation of his gallantry and military bearing throughout the campaign in Missouri, in 1861; on the bloody field of Shiloh, where he was severely wounded, in the action on the Edenton Road, N. C., and at the siege of Charleston. At the battle of Coal Harbor, this brave officer was killed while in the continuance of the same soldierly skill and bravery that had marked his previous career. When McConihe fell, Maj. Alonzo Alden became the third colonel of the regiment, and for gallant and meritorious services he was promoted to Brevet Brigadier-General in 1865. The regiment suffered terribly at Coal Harbor. It was engaged in all the operations on the line in front of Petersburg and Richmond from June 18, to December 7. Many and severe were the fights it fought and heavy the loss it sustained, until its rank and file were so reduced that the entire number for duty at one time was only eighty-nine men. In the assault on Fort Fisher the regiment fought gallantly and lost heavily. It suffered a loss of eighty-one men by the explosion of the magazine in the fort the morning after the capture. Colonel Alden was badly injured by the explosion. After Fort Fisher the regiment was engaged in the operations against Fort Anderson and Wilmington, and was the first to enter the latter city. It marched with Sherman after Joe Johnston, and entered Raleigh with the advance of our troops, where it remained as a garrison until it was mustered out. In all its fights the regiment never showed a disposition to flinch, and officers and men behaved in the most gallant and praiseworthy manner, earning for themselves laurels which never fade.

Among the brave men of the regiment who belonged to a class of soldiers the fewer of whom we lost the better it was for the cause of the Union, may be mentioned Capt. Joseph H. Allen, who rose to the position of Major and subsequently Brevet Lieutenant-Colonel, Capt. Bernard N. Smith, Capt. Warren B. Coleman and private William H. Merriam, who was promoted for gallantry in another regiment. Merriam was long and creditably connected with the press and was at one time editor of the late Troy *Daily Budget*.

In the assault on Fort Fisher, in 1865, the regiment lost 139 men—a larger loss than was sustained by any other regiment. General Ames in his report of the attack, says Lieut.-Col. James A. Colvin behaved in the most gallant manner, and rendered great service in collecting and organizing the troops which had become separated from their commands, and in leading them to positions where important advantages were gained.

ONE HUNDRED SEVENTIETH REGIMENT.—The regiment was organized on Staten Island and went to the war under command of Col. Peter McDermott. Colonel McDermott was with the regiment but a short time when he resigned and Col. James P. McIvor succeeded to the vacant position. Colonel McIvor was a very superior officer, and his gallantry was rewarded by promotion to the rank of Brevet Brigadier-General. The 170th took part in eleven sanguinary engagements and thirteen of its officers were killed in action. Capt. George S. Turner was captured and died of ill treatment at

Salisbury prison. Adjt. Patrick R. Dunne, Lieut. James Freelan and Lieut. Patrick Quigley were captured at Ream's Station. Lieut. Michael K. Reily was another gallant soldier, captured and confined in the Charleston jail, from which he finally effected his escape. General Egan wrote to the Adjutant-General and commended in the highest terms of praise the conduct of the regiment in the operations around Petersburg.

ONE HUNDRED SEVENTY-FIRST AND ONE HUNDRED SEVENTY-SECOND REGIMENTS.—Were never organized.

ONE HUNDRED SEVENTY-THIRD REGIMENT.—"Fourth National Guard." The 173d was raised principally in Brooklyn, under the auspices of the police commissioners. It first went to Louisiana and participated in Banks' Red River expedition, and also in the assaults upon Port Hudson, where it suffered severely. When General Grant assumed command of the Army of the Potomac, the regiment came North, and joined General Sheridan's command in the Shenandoah Valley, where it took part in the engagements of Fisher's Hill, Winchester and Cedar Creek, in each of which the regiment fought with great gallantry. After the surrender of General Lee they went to Savannah, from which place it returned home under command of Col. Louis M. Peck. In 1864 the city of Brooklyn presented the regiment with a new stand of colors—the banner bearing upon its folds the names of the battles in which the regiment had up to that time participated.

The following named non-commissioned officers, members of the color-guard, were severely wounded while carrying the old colors; Sergs. J. Cary and G. Kendrick; Corps. William Eckles, Patrick Kelly, John W King, Edward Clifton and J. Gregory.

The regiment went to war under command of Col. Charles B. Morton and William N. Green, Jr., as Lieutenant-Colonel. Colonel Morton resigned in March, 1863, and was succeeded by Colonel Peck. Lieutenant-Colonel Green was mortally wounded at Port Hudson, and M. T. Holbrook, formerly connected with the police, became Lieutenant-Colonel of the regiment.

ONE HUNDRED SEVENTY-FOURTH REGIMENT.—"Fifth National Guards." The regiment fought bravely at Plain's Store, Port Hudson, and Cox's Plantation. At Port Hudson it was badly cut up. They took three guns from the enemy but could not hold them and were obliged to leave them. On the 13th of July, 1863, the regiment met with the only loss it sustained during the war among its commissioned officers, by the fall of the brave Lieutenant De Van Postly, who fell in the engagement near Donaldsonville.

Col. Theodore W. Parmele resigned in July, 1863, and was succeeded by Col. B. F. Gatt.

ONE HUNDRED SEVENTY-FIFTH REGIMENT.—This regiment was commanded by the gallant Col. Michael K. Bryan, who fell while bravely encouraging his men in the action before Port Hudson, June 14, 1863. The regiment afterwards took part in the expedition to Texas. In the engagement at Vermilion Bayou, the Rebels in the abatis fought bravely, and our forces fell back about twenty feet, when Serg. Charles W Kennedy, of Company I, advancing to the front, waved his musket and impulsively shouted, "Let's try it, boys, again, we'll have it this time, follow me," and the gallant fellow bounded forward, the rest following with a yell, when the ditch, obstructions and guns were passed in a moment, and the next instant the abatis was taken. Lieut.-Col. John A. Foster was promoted to Brevet Brigadier-General in recognition of his valuable services during the war.

ONE HUNDRED SEVENTY-SIXTH REGIMENT.—"Ironsides." The 176th was organized in New York City and Hamilton County, and went to the war under command of Col. Charles C. Nott, now one of the judges of the Court of Claims. A. J. H. Duganne was Lieutenant-Colonel, Morgan Morgans, Jr., Major, David Drake, Adjutant, Matthew C. Kempsey, Chaplain. This was one of the last regiments organized and one of the last that remained in the service. It was organized under the direction of the Young Men's Christian Association of New York City. The regiment participated in Banks' Red River expedition, and took an active part in the defence of New Orleans against General Taylor's grand advance during the Port Hudson campaign. The battle of Lafourche Crossing was fought by the 176th under command of Major Morgans, and no battle was fought more gloriously or victoriously for the Union cause. Morgans commanded from the top of a sugar hogshead in lieu of a horse, and won the admiration and confidence of his men. About the time of the fight at Lafourche, a portion of the regiment was engaged in a disastrous fight at Brashear City, where no one was in command, and "where everybody except the enemy was captured." But this unfortunate affair was not owing to any lack of bravery on the part of the members of the 175th. In fact they resisted the foe with all the courage that could have been expected of brave and gallant men.

Colonel Nott, Capts. William P. Coe, Samuel E. Thomason, Lieuts. Phoebus W Lyon, John F. Kimball, David G. Wellington, Charles P Sherman, Louis W. Stevenson and David G. Gillette were among the captured. Lieutenant Kimball died in prison and Capt. John S. Cutter after exhibiting the greatest heroism was shot through the heart.

In July, 1864, the regiment accompanied the Nineteenth Corps to Maryland, and arrived in time to assist in repelling Jubal Early's invasion. It afterwards served under General Sheridan, throughout his brilliant campaign in the Shenandoah Valley and gained honorable mention for its conduct in each of his three great victories. In the assault on Fort Fisher the regiment captured four guns in the enemy's works. General Emory in his report of that battle, says: "To strengthen and shorten our lines, it became necessary to drive in the enemy's skirmishers and occupy their lines. This was handsomely done by the 128th New York, supported by the 176th."

Lieut.-Col. A. J. H. Duganne died October, 1884. Maj. George Haven Putnam is now a member of the firm of George P. Putnam's Sons, the well-known publishing house in New York City. Adjutant Drake died in August, 1879. He was a son of the Hon. Elias G. Drake of New York.

ONE HUNDRED SEVENTY-SEVENTH REGIMENT.—This regiment was organized at Albany for nine months service. It went to the field under command of Col. Ira W. Ainsworth, with David M. Woodhall as Lieutenant-Colonel,—both brave and skilful officers. The regiment performed its part gallantly in the assault upon Port Hudson, and had its full share of noble sacrifices. Lieutenant-Colonel Woodhall died in July, 1885. At the time of his death he was Brigadier-General of the Ninth Brigade, State Militia.

ONE HUNDRED SEVENTY-NINTH REGIMENT.—The 179th was organized at Elmira towards the close of the war. It fought splendidly in the engagements before Petersburg.—Weldon Railroad, Poplar Spring Church, and Hatcher's Run. The regiment was ably commanded by Col. William M. Gregg. Its Lieut.-Col., Franklin B. Doty, was mortally wounded, April 5, 1865.

ONE HUNDRED EIGHTIETH AND ONE HUNDRED EIGHTY-FIRST REGIMENTS.—Were never organized.

ONE HUNDRED EIGHTY-SECOND REGIMENT.—Sixty-ninth National Guard Artillery. The nucleus of this regiment was the old Sixty-ninth State Militia, which participated in the first battle of Bull Run. After that fatal disaster, in which it fought so gallantly, it returned home, and when the Corcoran Legion was organized, more than half of the officers and men joined it. Difficulties arising at the time prevented the entire regiment from enlisting in it. It was recruited to the full complement of men, and marched with the brigade when it left New York. The regiment was commanded by Col. Matthew Murphy, who died in 1865, of wounds received in action. The regiment participated in the siege of Suffolk, and fought bravely at Coal Harbor. By order of General Meade nineteen battles were inscribed on the regimental banners. These battles tell of frightful sacrifices in officers and men. At the battle of Ream's Station the regiment suffered terribly. Out of the eight hundred strong with which it left home there only remained 170 upon its return.

Among the veterans of this gallant regiment whose honorable records are identified with its history were Capt. Michael Kelly, Capt. Thomas M. Canton, Lieuts. Edward Kelly, Patrick Snee, Christopher J. Bell, Matthew J. Barny, Richard McGee and Maj. Robert Haggart, and Lieut.-Col. John Coonan.

ONE HUNDRED EIGHTY-THIRD REGIMENT.—Regiment was never organized.

ONE HUNDRED EIGHTY-FOURTH REGIMENT.—The 184th was organized at Oswego in August, 1864, to serve one year. It was commanded by Col. Wardwell G. Robinson and Lieut.-Col. William P. McKinley. The regiment fought bravely at the battle of Cedar Creek, October 19, 1864.

ONE HUNDRED EIGHTY-FIFTH REGIMENT.—On the 23d of August, 1864, a public meeting was held at the City Hall, Syracuse, and a committee of leading citizens was formed for the purpose of organizing a regiment. The muster of the regiment took place September 22, 1864, and on the following day the command left for the Army of the Potomac. The regiment immediately entered into active service before Petersburg. The first death in the regiment was that of A. B. Neal, who died in camp, October 24, 1864. October 26, the regiment arrived at the South Side Railroad, where an attack was made by General Hancock's forces upon the enemy. The regiment sustained no loss here. On December 5th the regiment was instrumental in destroying the Weldon Railroad, and after that frequent raids were made into the enemy's line. The regiment was in the second battle of Hatcher's Run. On the 5th of March the advance upon Fort Steadman was made. Attacks were also made on Petersburg, the Quaker Road, where Col. Gustavus Sniper saved the day for General Chamberlain, and the victory was gained, but 225 men were killed and many wounded. During the engagement Colonel Sniper grasped the colors, after the death of the bearer, and led the victorious charge. The regiment repelled the attack made by the enemy on Fort Steadman; they were in the great battle of Five Forks and were in the last skirmish at Appomattox.

The regiment went to the war under command of Col. Edwin S. Jenney, who was honorably discharged in February, 1865. In 1885 Colonel Jenney was city attorney of Syracuse. Col. Gustavus Sniper succeeded Colonel Jenney in command of the regiment. In the battle of March 29, 1865 (Petersburg), Colonel Sniper led the regiment personally in a brilliant and successful charge, carrying the regimental colors after three color-bearers had been shot down. The conduct of the officers and men was of the most admirable character and they were all entitled to the greatest credit. Among those who returned home with the regiment were Lieuts. Lewis S. Edgar, Stephen S. Jordan, Wm. A. Brooks, Jacob M. Doran and F. Augustus Schermerhorn. The latter is now one of the trustees of Columbia College. The 185th went to the war with 923 men, including officers, and returned with twenty-two officers and 544 enlisted men. They returned with a most brilliant record.

ONE HUNDRED EIGHTY-SIXTH REGIMENT.—The regiment was raised principally in Jefferson County, and was officered in part by those who had seen two years service in the old Thirty-fifth New York Volunteers. It went to the war under command of Col. Bradley Winslow, who, in 1865, was promoted for meritorious services to Brevet Brigadier-General. Although but about eight months in the service, it participated in several hard fought battles. In the battle of April 2, 1865, before Petersburg, the regiment was among the first to enter the Rebel fortifications, and was highly complimented by its brigade and division commanders for the gallantry shown in the charge on Fort Mahone. In this charge Colonel Winslow was wounded while leading his men.

ONE HUNDRED EIGHTY-SEVENTH REGIMENT.—The regiment was organized at Buffalo, and went to the war in October, 1864, under command of Col. Daniel Myers. The regiment has an honorable record in connection with the battle of Hatcher's Run.

ONE HUNDRED EIGHTY-EIGHTH REGIMENT.—The 188th was organized at Dunkirk, and went to the front near the close of the war under command of Col. John McMahon. Like the 187th, it fought well at the battle at Hatcher's Run.

ONE HUNDRED EIGHTY-NINTH REGIMENT.—The 189th was organized at Elmira, and was commanded by Col. Allen L. Burr. The regiment joined the Fifth Army Corps just previous to the battle of Hatcher's Run. Then, and afterwards, during the active campaign, Colonel Burr, though a good and highly valued officer, was unfortunately sick, and the command of the regiment in every fight devolved upon Lieut.-Col. Joseph G. Townsend. The regiment fought bravely at Petersburg, where on the 11th of January, 1865, Capt. Burrage Rice, a most capable and popular officer, was deliberately murdered after surrender. Previous to the return home of the regiment, General Gregory, to whose brigade it had been attached, made a very touching and forcible speech eulogistic of its good conduct.

ONE HUNDRED NINETIETH AND ONE HUNDRED NINETY-FIRST REGIMENTS.—Only a battalion for these regiments was raised.

ONE HUNDRED NINETY-SECOND REGIMENT.—The 192d was not organized until one month before the surrender of Lee. Nathan G. Axtell was the Colonel. He was formerly Chaplain of the Thirtieth Regiment, and was called the "fighting Chaplain." He was a good officer and a perfect gentleman. Capt. Stephen H. Bogardus, Jr., was presented with a sword by the members of his company as a testimonial of their admiration for him as a soldier and a friend.

ONE HUNDRED NINETY-THIRD REGIMENT.—The 193d was organized at Auburn in April, 1865. Col. J. B. Van Petten was in command. He had won a good record as Lieutenant-Colonel of the 160th Regiment, and was finally promoted to Brevet Brigadier-General.

APPENDIX III.

OUR HONORED DEAD.

COMMISSIONED OFFICERS OF THE VOLUNTEER REGIMENTS FROM THE STATE OF NEW YORK WHO WERE KILLED, DIED FROM THE EFFECTS OF WOUNDS RECEIVED OR DISEASE CONTRACTED IN DEFENCE OF THE GOVERNMENT DURING THE WAR OF THE REBELLION.

"Rest, dear Saints!
Rest within the bosom of that earth,
Thou did so much to make
A more worthy residence for thy fellow men."

REV. HENRY W. BELLOWS.

NAME.	RANK.	REGIMENT.	DIED OF WOUNDS.	KILLED.	BATTLE.
ATWOOD, JAMES L.	Lieut.	2d Mt. R.		June 26, '64	Petersburg, Va.
Ayres, Conway W.	Capt.	9th Cav.		Sep. 19, '64	
Alford, Charles B.	Lieut.	19th Cav.		Aug. 20, '64	Smithfield.
Ames, Albert N.	Lieut.	L. Art.		Sep. 26, '64	Near Petersburg.
Arndt, Albert	Major	L. Art.	Sep. 18, '62		
Angell, Oscar F.	Capt.	10th Inf.		Mar. 10, '64	Po. River, Va.
Alden, Henry H.	Capt.	42d Inf.		Oct. 21, '61	Ball's Bluff.
Arnold, Henry	Capt.	47th Inf.		Feb. 20, '64	
Allen, George D.	Lieut.	51st Inf.		Mar. 14, '62	Newbern.
Antonieski, Edward	Capt.	58th Inf.	July 25, '63		
Angell, M. C.	Capt.	61st Inf.	Sep. 17, '62		Antietam.
Alton, Pulaski V.	Lieut.	64th Inf.		May 12, '64	Spottsylvania.
Andrews, Robert D.	Lieut.	74th Inf.		Aug. 27, '62	Bristoe Station.
Anderson, Rudolf N.	Lieut.	74th Inf.	Nov. 20, '62		Bristoe Station.
Avery, William E.	Lieut.	75th Inf.		May 27, '63	Port Hudson, La.
Angle, William W.	Capt.	86th Inf.		May 3, '63	Chancellorsville.
Anderson, Hiram J.	Lt.-Col.	92d Inf.		June 1, '64	Coal Harbor.
Andrews, Andrew J.	Lieut.	104th Inf.	Jan. 26, '63		
Antiet, Carl V.	Lieut.	108th Inf.		July 3, '63	Gettysburg.
Arnold, Thos. S.	Capt.	121st Inf.	May 18, '63		Salem Chapel, Va.
Abreetz, Charles A.	Lieut.	134th Inf.		Dec. 13, '64	Siege of Savannah.
Alexander, Jr., Wm. H.	Lieut.	139th Inf.		Oct. 29, '64	Fair Oaks.
Adams, Oscar M.	Lieut.	148th Inf.	June 19, '64		
Arrowsmith, George W.	Lt.-Col.	157th Inf.		July 1, '63	Gettysburg.

NAME.	RANK.	REGIMENT.	DIED OF WOUNDS.	KILLED.	BATTLE.
Adams, George A.	Capt.	157th Inf.	July 25, '63		Gettysburg.
Abraham, Joseph S.	Lieut.	164th Inf.		June 3, '64	Coal Harbor.
BRETT, ROBERT H.	Capt.	1st Vet. Cav.		May 30, '64	Newtown, Va.
Bedell, John V	Lieut.	2d Mt. R.	July 18, '64		Petersburg, Va.
Baker, August	Capt.	5th Cav.	Sep. 18, '63		Kelly's Ford.
Bliss, Aaron T.	Capt.	10th Cav.		June 30, '64	Ream's Station, Va.
Boyd, Horatio H.	Lieut.	10th Cav.		June 19, '63	Middleburg, Va.
Beardsley, Bronson	Lieut.	10th Cav.	June 23, '63		Middleburg, Va.
Burch, Calvin	Capt.	24th Cav.		June 18, '64	
Berry, William A.	Capt.	2d H. Art.		June 18, '64	Near Petersburg.
Burghardt, Charles H.	Lieut.	4th H. Art.	Apl. 17, '65		
Bell, Robert H.	Capt.	7th H. Art.	June 19, '64		
Barclay, Michael H.	Lieut.	7th H. Art.	July 6, '64		
Bates, William W.	Lt.-Col.	8th H. Art.	June 25, '64		
Blake, Edwin L.	Major	8th H. Art.	June 19, '64		Petersburg.
Brown, Fayette S.	Lieut.	8th H. Art.		June 3, '64	Coal Harbor.
Bentley, Elisha	Lieut.	14th H. Art.		June 3, '64	Coal Harbor.
Braunstein, Franz	Lieut.	15th H. Art.	June 15, '64		
Bailey, Guilford D.	Col.	1st Lt. Art.		May 31, '62	Fair Oaks, Va.
Brower, Henry D.	Lieut.	Lt. Art.		Aug. 25, '64	Ream's Station.
Blume, Theodore	Lieut.			July 1, '63	Gettysburg.
Brooks, J. Howard	Lieut.	1st Engrs.	Aug. 5, '64		Petersburg.
Becker, Edward H.	Capt.	7th Inf.		Dec. 13, '62	Fredericksburg.
Bottcher, Max	Capt.	7th Inf.		Dec. 13, '62	Fredericksburg.
Bartels, Erichs	Lieut.	7th Inf.		Mar. 31, '65	Nr Boydtown r'd, Va
Burton, Henry C.	Lieut.	12th Inf.		June 27, '62	
Barnard, Alanson M.	Lieut.	16th Inf.		June 27, '62	Gaines Mills, Va.
Blauvelt, Isaac D.	Capt.	17th Inf.		Aug. 30, '62	2d Bull Run.
Barnett, William G.	Capt.	17th Inf.		Mar. 16, '65	Averysboro, N. C.
Barry, George	Capt.	18th Inf.		June 27, '62	Gaines Mills, Va.
Beaumont, Carlisle D.	Lieut.	22d Inf.		Aug. 29, '62	2d Bull Run.
Beattee, William T.	Lieut.	22d Inf.		Aug. 30, '62	2d Bull Run.
Barney, Andrew J.	Major	24th Inf.		Aug. 30, '62	2d Bull Run.
Buckley, John P.	Capt.	24th Inf.		Aug. 30, '62	2d Bull Run.
Brown, James A.	Lieut.	24th Inf.	Sep. 21, '62		2d Bull Run.
Bacon, William K.	Lieut.	26th Inf.	Dec. 15, '62		Fredericksburg.
Bode, Bernard	Capt.	29th Inf.		May 2, '63	Chancellorsville.
Babcock, Horatio G.	Lieut.	31st Inf.	May 9, '62		
Brown, Sylvester H.	Capt.	32d Inf.		May 7, '62	West Point.
Brown, Josiah	Lieut.	32d Inf.		Sep. 14, '62	South Mountain.
Brown, George W	Lieut.	33d Inf.	May 21, '62		Williamsburg.
Brown, Charles L.	Major	34th Inf.	July 3, '62		
Barnett, Jas. R.	Capt.	35th Inf.		Sep. 18, '62	Antietam.
Brown, Edmond W.	Lieut.	37th Inf.	May 22, '62		Williamsburg.
Bruen, David R.	Lieut.	39th Inf.		Nov. 24, '64	Near Petersburg.
Bailey, Theodore S.	Lieut.	43d Inf.		May 5, '64	Wilderness.
Bisky, Louis	Capt.	45th Inf.		May 2, '63	Chancellorsville.
Bunker, Charles H.	Lieut.	51st Inf.		Aug. 13, '64	Petersburg.
Butler, Frank	Lieut.	51st Inf.	Sep. 30, '64		
Burke, John	Lieut.	52d Inf.		Mar. 31, '65	Hatcher's Run.
Beer, Adolph	Lieut.	54th Inf.		Aug. 30, '62	2d Bull Run.
Braun, Frederick	Capt.	58th Inf.		May 2, '63	Chancellorsville.
Brooks, Arthur L.	Capt.	61st Inf.		June 1, '62	
Boyle, Peter T.	Capt.	63d Inf.		May 5, '64	Wilderness.
Babcock, Willis G.	Lieut.	64th Inf.		July 2, '63	Gettysburg.
Byron, William	Lieut.	65th Inf.	Apl. 2, '65		
Bull, James H.	Lt.-Col.	66th Inf.		Dec. 11, '62	Fredericksburg.
Bulis, James E.	Lieut.	66th Inf.		June 17, '64	
Blake, John J.	Capt.	69th Inf.	June 8, '64		
Birmingham, Andrew	Lieut.	69th Inf.	Dec. 17, '62		Fredericksburg.
Buckley, Patrick	Lieut.	69th Inf.		Sep. 17, '62	Antietam.
Brunn, Jacob	Capt.	70th Inf.		May 5, '62	Williamsburg.
Bugbee, William H.	Capt.	70th Inf.		May 5, '62	Williamsburg.
Barrett, Patrick	Capt.	72d Inf.		May 6, '62	Williamsburg.

NAME.	RANK.	REGIMENT.	DIED OF WOUNDS.	KILLED.	BATTLE.
Bliss, Harman W.	Capt.	72d Inf.	June 6, '63		Chancellorsville.
Brooks, Wm. C.	Lieut.	72d Inf.	May 3, '63		Chancellorsville.
Beach, Benjamin	Lieut.	73d Inf.		May 5, '62	Williamsburg.
Babcock, Willoughby	Lt.-Col.	75th Inf.	Oct. 6, '64		
Bartholomew, N. G.	Capt.	76th Inf.		May 5, '64	Wilderness.
Belding, John M.	Lieut.	77th Inf.	Oct. 27, '64		
Brown, David	Capt.	79th Inf.		July 21, '61	Bull Run.
Baldwin, Ambrose N.	Capt.	80th Inf.		July 3, '63	Gettysburg.
Brankstone, Geo. W.	Lieut.	80th Inf.		July 1, '63	Gettysburg.
Ballard, Willard W.	Capt.	81st Inf.		June 3, '64	Coal Harbor.
Burke, John W	Lieut.	81st Inf.		June 2, '64	Coal Harbor.
Bloomfield, James H.	Lieut.	84th Inf.	May 24, '63		
Bailey, Stephen A.	Lieut.	86th Inf.	Apl. 8, '65		
Byrnes, James E.	Lieut.	88th Inf.		June 3, '64	
Burt, Albert C.	Lieut.	89th Inf.		Oct. 27, '64	Fair Oaks.
Bailey, John	Capt.	93d Inf.		May 5, '64	Wilderness.
Barnes, Dennis E.	Capt.	93d Inf.		May 6, '64	Wilderness.
Burn, Beujamin B.	Capt.	95th Inf.	May 6, '64		
Benedict, Walter H.	Capt.	96th Inf.		May 16, '64	
Brown, James M.	Col.	100th Inf.		May 31, '62	Fair Oaks.
Brown, Cyrus	Lieut.	100th Inf.	Aug. 13, '63		
Bacon, Francis	Lieut.	102d Inf.		May 3, '63	Chancellorsville.
Buckley, Chas. C.	Lieut.	105th Inf.		Sept. 17, '62	Antietam.
Bayne, Jas. H.	Lieut.	106th Inf.		June 1, '64	Coal Harbor.
Blackman, Aaron B.	Lieut.	106th Inf.		June 1, '64	Coal Harbor.
Barton, Daniel W.	Lieut.	109th Inf.		May 12, '64	Spottsylvania.
Belding, Silas W.	Lieut.	111th Inf.		Apl. 2, '65	Sutherl'd St'n, Va.
Breed, Edwin E.	Lieut.	114th Inf.		Sep. 19, '64	Ocoquan, Va.
Burch, Isaac	Lieut.	114th Inf.	Oct. 21, '64		Cedar Creek, Va.
Bowsky, Charles	Lieut.	116th Inf.	June 5, '63		
Brigham, Geo. W.	Capt.	117th Inf.	May 17, '64		
Barker, Ayers G.	Capt.	120th Inf.		July 2, '63	Gettysburg.
Burhans, John R.	Lieut.	120th Inf.		July 2, '63	Gettysburg.
Butts, Charles A.	Capt.	121st Inf.		May 10, '64	
Burrell, Jonathan	Capt.	121st Inf.	Oct. 26, '64		
Brower, Jabez M.	Major	122d Inf.		Oct. 19, '64	
Brown, Milnor	Lieut.	124th Inf.		July 2, '63	Gettysburg.
Birdsall, Jonathan	Lieut.	124th Inf.		Oct. 22, '64	Petersburg.
Barnes, Edward N.	Lieut.	125th Inf.	June 27, '64		
Bryan, George A.	Lieut.	125th Inf.		June 16, '64	
Baird, Wm. H.	Lt.-Col.	126th Inf.		June 16, '64	Petersburg.
Brown, Jr., Morris	Capt.	126th Inf.		June 22, '64	Petersburg.
Benjamin, Nathan J.	Lieut.	131st Inf.		July 14, '63	Port Hudson.
Beecher, S. Clark	Capt.	139th Inf.		June 2, '64	Coal Harbor.
Baur, Frederick	Lieut.	140th Inf.		May 3, '64	
Barber, Alfred E.	Lieut.	141st Inf.		May 15, '64	Resaca, Ga.
Brickingham, Chas. L.	Lieut.	146th Inf.		Sept. 2, '64	Near Weldon R. R.
Brown, James	Lieut.	147th Inf.	July 4, '64		
Bristol, Lansing	Lieut.	147th Inf.		Feb. 6, '65	Hatcher's Run, Va.
Breed, Benjamin F.	Lieut.	149th Inf.		May 3, '63	Chancellorsville.
Billings, Cornelius C.	Capt.	151st Inf.		May 6, '84	Wilderness.
Backus, Jason K.	Capt.	157th Inf.		July 1, '63	Gettysburg.
Benedict, Lewis	Col.	162d Inf.		Apl. 9, '64	
Bogart, James H.	Major	162d Inf.		June 14, '63	
Brocklow, Theodore F.	Capt.	163d Inf.		Dec. 13, '62	Fredericksburg.
Byrne, John J.	Lieut.	163d Inf.		Dec. 13, '62	Fredericksburg.
Behers, Frederick W.	Lieut.	163d Inf.		Dec. 13, '62	Fredericksburg.
Boyle, Robert	Lieut.	164th Inf.	July 29, '64		
Birdsall, Walter S.	Lieut.	169th Inf.		May 16, '64	Walthall, Va.
Bryan, Michael K.	Col.	175th Inf.		June 14, '63	Port Hudson.
Barton, John	Major	179th Inf.	July 31, '64		Petersburg.
Blachford, Daniel	Capt.	179th Inf.		June 17, '64	Petersburg.
Bowker, James B.	Lieut.	179th Inf.	Oct. 27, '64		
Butler, William	Major	182d Inf.	Aug. 16, '64		

NAME.	RANK.	REGIMENT.	DIED OF WOUNDS.	KILLED.	BATTLE.
Butler, Edward K.	Capt.	182d Inf.		June 3, '64	Coal Harbor.
Bauder, E. F.	Lieut.	185th Inf.	Apl. 15, '65		
Conway, Joseph E.	Capt.	1st Vet. Cav.		July 25, '64	Martinsburg, Va.
Compton, Frederick	Lieut.	2d Vet. Cav.		Aug. 29, '62	2d Bull Run.
Carter, Chas. F.	Capt.	2d Vet. Cav.	July 13, '64		
Crozier, Robert	Lieut.	6th Cav.		May 7, '63	Nr. West Point, Va.
Carrell, John	Lieut.	6th Cav.	Jan. 18, '65		
Cutler, Henry C.	Lieut.	8th Cav.		June 9, '63	Beverly Ford, Va.
Church, Cyrus	Capt.	12th Cav.		July 20, '63	Tarboro, N. C.
Cone, Chas. H.	Lieut.	21st Cav.		July 19, '64	Ashby's Ford, Va.
Clapp, A. G.	Lieut.	8th H. Art.	Nov. 21, '64		
Caldwell, Joseph S.	Lieut.	8th H. Art.		June 3, '64	Coal Harbor, Va.
Chase, Arthur L.	Lieut.	8th H. Art.		June 3, '64	Coal Harbor, Va.
Campbell, Oliver M.	Lieut.	8th H. Art.		June 3, '64	Coal Harbor, Va.
Carpenter, Orrin B	Lieut.	9th H. Art.		Oct. 19, '64	
Chapman, Henry K.	Lieut.	4th Inf.	Sep. 17, '62		Antietam.
Cartwright, Thos. W	Capt.	5th Inf.	Dec. 26, '62		
Cooper, E. C.	Lieut.	9th Inf.		Sep. 17, '62	Antietam.
Cornell, Henry	Lieut.	11th Inf.		Sep. 18, '62	McCloud's Mills, Va.
Cadwell, Miles P. S.	Capt.	22d Inf.		Aug. 30, '62	2d Bull Run.
Clute, Hiram	Lieut.	22d Inf.	Sep. 28, '62		
Cushing, Charles	Lieut.	22d Inf.		Sep. 17, '62	Antietam.
Corse, Henry B.	Lieut.	24th Inf.		Aug. 30, '62	2d Bull Run.
Cassleman, Montgomery	Capt.	26th Inf.		Aug. 30, '62	2d Bull Run.
Church, Moses	Lieut.	33d Inf.	June 28, '62		
Clark, Thomas	Lieut.	40th Inf.		July 29, '64	
Carter, John B.	Lieut.	43d Inf.		Sep. 19, '64	Winchester.
Caesar, Herman	Capt.	52d Inf.	May 2, '63		
Chapman, Alford B.	Lt.-Col.	57th Inf.		May 5, '64	Wilderness, Va.
Collins, Wm. A.	Capt.	61st Inf.		May 8, '64	
Coultis, Wm. Henry	Lieut.	61st Inf.	June 23, '62		
Carroll, Edward B	Capt.	63d Inf.		Apl. 2, '65	
Crissy, Frederick M.	Lieut.	66th Inf.		Sep. 17, '62	Antietam.
Cooper, T. Colden	Capt.	67th Inf.		May 6, '64	Wilderness.
Conway, John	Lieut.	69th Inf.		Dec. 12, '62	Fredericksburg
Chamberlain, Henry	Lieut.	70th Inf.		May 5, —	Williamsburg.
Chester, Wm. H.	Capt.	74th Inf.		July 3, '63	Gettysburg.
Crandall, Chauncey D.	Lieut.	76th Inf.		Dec. 13, '62	Fredericksburg.
Carpenter, Wm. B.	Capt.	77th Inf.		May 10, '64	Spottsylvania.
Courter, Chas. A.	Lieut.	78th Inf.		May 3, '63	Chancellorsville
Cameron, James	Col.	79th Inf.		July 21, '61	Bull Run.
Corbin, Joseph S.	Capt.	80th Inf.		July 1, '63	Gettysburg.
Copeland, Amos M.	Lieut.	81st Inf.	Jan. 10, '65		
Cranston, John	Lieut.	82d Inf.	July 27, '63		
Conally, John M K.	Capt.	83d Inf.		May 12, '64	Spottsylvania.
Clark, Chas. A.	Lieut.	83d Inf.		July 1, '63	Gettysburg.
Chapin, Nelson	Capt.	85th Inf.		Apl. 20, '64	Plymouth, N. C.
Chapin, Barna I.	Lt.-Col.	86th Inf.		May 3, '63	Chancellorsville
Cherry, James	Lieut.	86th Inf.	May 10, '64		
Clooney, Patrick F.	Capt.	88th Inf.		Sep. 17, '62	Antietam.
Cray, James L.	Capt.	96th Inf.	June 10, '64		Coal Harbor.
Cady, Rush P.	Lieut.	97th Inf.	July 24, '63		Gettysburg.
Cornell, M. E.	Capt.	102d Inf.		Sep. 17, '62	Antietam.
Cavanaugh, Arthur	Capt.	102d Inf.	Oct. 28, '62		
Carroll, Howard	Lt.-Col.	105th Inf.	Sep. 29, '62		
Chamberlain, Martin J.	Capt.	106th Inf.	July 22, '64		Monocacy, Md.
Card, Dayton T.	Lieut.	108th Inf.		July 3, '63	Gettysburg.
Carpenter, Elial F.	Lt.-Col.	112th Inf.	May 18, '64		
Chapin, Edward P.	Col.	116th Inf.		May 27, '63	Port Hudson.
Casselmain, Wm. C.	Lieut.	117th Inf.		May 15, '64	Drury's Bluff.
Chamberlain, James	Capt.	120th Inf.		Oct. 27, '64	
Creighton, Michael E.	Lieut.	120th Inf.		July 2, '63	Gettysburg.
Carle, Jason	Lieut.	120th Inf.		July 2, '63	Gettysburg.
Corbett, John C.	Lieut.	123d Inf.		May 3, '63	Chancellorsville.

NAME.	RANK.	REGIMENT.	DIED OF WOUNDS.	KILLED.	BATTLE.
Cromwell, James	Major	124th Inf.		July 2, '63	Gettysburg.
Crist, David	Capt.	124th Inf.		May 30, '64	
Cormick, Edward J.	Capt.	124th Inf.		Apl. 1, '65	Petersburg.
Clapp, E. S. P.	Lieut.	125th Inf.	June 5, '64		
Coleman, Isaac De Witt	Lieut.	125th Inf.		June 16, '64	Petersburg.
Cleminshaw, Chas. E.	Lieut.	125th Inf.		May 12, '64	Spottsylvania.
Clapp, Alfred R.	Lieut.	126th Inf.		Sep. 15, '62	Harper's Ferry.
Cowles, David S.	Col.	128th Inf.		May 27, '63	Port Hudson.
Carrington, Edward	Lieut.	143d Inf.		Mar. 6, '65	Natural Bridge, Fla.
Curran, Henry H.	Major	146th Inf.		May 5, '64	Wilderness.
Chalmers, Hugh	Lieut.	146th Inf.	June 9, '64		
Coan, Arthur V.	Lieut.	146th Inf.	Sep. 30, '64		Near Weldon R. R.
Crosby, Allanson	Capt.	154th Inf.	July 9, '64		
Cronin, Philip	Lieut.	155th Inf.	Oct. 6, '64		
Cotton, Charles R.	Capt.	160th Inf.		Apl. 9, '64	Pleasant Hill, La.
Carville, C. R.	Lieut.	165th Inf.		May 27, '63	Port Hudson.
Crippen, Norman J.	Lieut.	169th Inf.		Aug. 13, '64	Dutch Gap, Va.
Cipperly, Samuel L.	Lieut.	169th Inf.		June 16, '65	Fort Fisher, N. C.
Corneery, John	Capt.	170th Inf.	Sep. 9, '64		
Cochen, Henry	Capt.	173d Inf.		June 14, '63	Port Hudson.
Cutter, John S.	Capt.	176th Inf.		June 23, '63	Brashear City, La.
Clark, Hiram	Lieut.	185th Inf.		Apl. 9, '65	
DECKER, JAMES N.	Lieut.	2d Cav.		Apl. 17, '62	Near Falmouth, Va.
Dunn, Melville S.	Lieut.	2d Vet. Cav.		Apl. 4, '64	
De Long, James B. N.	Lieut.	2d Mt. Rifles		June 18, '64	Petersburg.
Dwyre, Philip	Lieut.	5th Cav.	May 27, '62		Front Royal, Va.
Dye, Elam S.	Lieut.	5th Cav.		June 30, '63	Hanover, Pa.
Davis, Benjamin F.	Col.	8th Cav.		June 9, '63	Beverly Ford, Va.
Doran, James E.	Major	24th Cav.	Apl. 15, '65		
Dawson, Geo. S.	Capt.	2d H. Art.	Dec. 6, '64		
Duysing, Emil	Major	15th H. Art.	May 27, '65		
De Mott, Charles	Lieut.	1st L. Art.		June 3, '64	Bethesda Church.
Davis, Henry W.	Capt.	1st L. Art.	May 26, '64		Jericho Ford.
Downs, John S.	Capt.	4th Inf.		Sep. 17, '62	Antietam.
Du Four, Faber	Capt.	7th Inf.		Dec. 13, '62	Fredericksburg.
Divver, Daniel	Lieut.	11th Inf.		July 21, '61	Bull Run.
Demarest, James H.	Capt.	17th Inf.		Aug. 30, '62	2d Bull Run.
Davis, Thomas	Capt.	26th Inf.		Aug. 30, '62	2d Bull Run.
Donnelly, Dudley	Col.	28th Inf.	Aug. 15, '62		Cedar Mountain.
Dargen, Francis	Lieut.	30th Inf.		Aug. 30, '62	2d Bull Run.
De Witt, Calvin S.	Capt.	38th Inf.		May 12, '62	
Dwyer, Samuel C.	Capt.	38th Inf.	May 19, '62		Williamsburg.
Dexter, Samuel	Lieut.	42d Inf.		Sep. 17, '62	Antietam.
Dempsey, John M.	Lieut.	43d Inf.	May 6, '65		
Dunham, Eugene L.	Lieut.	44th Inf.		July 2, '63	Gettysburg.
Dessauer, Francis A.	Capt.	45th Inf.		May 2, '63	Chancellorsville.
D'Arcy, Wm. E.	Capt.	48th Inf.		Aug. 14, '64	Deep Bottom.
Dunn, James W.	Capt.	48th Inf.		Jan. 15, '65	Fort Fisher.
Darbey, Henry H.	Capt.	64th Inf.	Apl. 11, '65		Farmville, Va.
Dodge, John P.	Capt.	66th Inf.		Dec. 15, '62	Fredericksburg.
Duffy, Felix	Capt.	69th Inf.		Sep. 17, '62	Antietam.
Doyle, Stephen M.	Capt.	72d Inf.		July 18, '62	Malvern Hill.
Donald, Alfred A.	Capt.	73d Inf.		Aug. 27, '62	
Dennen, Thomas	Lieut.	73d Inf.		May 2, '63	Chancellorsville.
Dennen, George	Lieut.	73d Inf.		July 2, '63	Gettysburg.
Dussuet, Charles	Lieut.	74th Inf.		May 10, '64	Spottsylvania.
Dennison, Ansel	Lieut.	77th Inf.	Feb. 28, '63		
Dolbier, Samuel	Lieut.	81st Inf.		Sep. 29, '64	Chapin's Farm.
Delaney, James J.	Capt.	82d Inf.		June 29, '62	
Davey, George R.	Capt.	84th Inf.		Aug. 29, '62	2d Bull Run.
Danford, Charles H.	Lieut.	93d Inf.		Apl. 7, '65	
Drescher, William C.	Lieut.	97th Inf.		May 6, '64	Wilderness.
Delormi, Louis	Lieut.	97th Inf.		Sep. 17, '62	Antietam.
Dandy, James H.	Major	100th Inf.		Apl. 2, '65	

NAME.	RANK.	REGIMENT.	DIED OF WOUNDS.	KILLED.	BATTLE.
Dutton, William F.	Lieut.	108th Inf.	July 19, '64		
Drake, John H.	Lieut.	111th Inf.		July 3, '63	Gettysburg.
Drake, Jeremiah C.	Col.	112th Inf.	June 2, '64		
Dann, Isaac H.	Lieut.	117th Inf.	June 4, '64		Coal Harbor.
Dedrick, William H.	Lieut.	120th Inf.		Sep. 20, '64	
Douw, John D. P.	Capt.	121st Inf.	Nov. 11, '64		
Doubleday, U. F.	Lieut.	121st Inf.		May 3, '63	Chancellorsville.
Duroe, Horatio N.	Lieut.	121st Inf.		Mar. 25, '65	Fort Fisher.
Dwight, Augustus W.	Lt.-Col.	122d Inf.		Mar. 25, '65	Petersburg.
Daicy, John H.	Lt.-Col.	123d Inf.	July 22, '64		P'ch Tree Cr'k, Ga.
De Valier, George B.	Lt.-Col.	133d Inf.	Apl. 26, '63		
Denton, B. F.	Lt.-Col.	133d Inf.		June 14, '63	Port Hudson.
Davis, Joseph A.	Lt.-Col.	149th Inf.		May 3, '63	Chancellorsville.
Dumphey, Richard B.	Lt.-Col.	155th Inf.	June 4, '64		
Dwight, Albert J.	Lt.-Col.	155th Inf.		June 22, '64	Petersburg.
Draper, Gilbert A.	Lt.-Col.	159th Inf.		Apl. 14, '63	
Dexter, S. N.	Capt.	160th Inf.		Sep. 19, '64	Nr. Winchester, Va.
Donnelly, John B.	Major	170th Inf.		Aug. 25, '64	Ream s Station.
Doty, Franklin B.	Lt.-Col.	179th Inf.	Apl. 5, '65		Petersburg.
EFNER, BENJAMIN C.	Lieut.	8th Cav.	June 11. '63		Beverly Ford, Va.
Evans, Charles S.	Lieut.	7th H. Art.	June 5, '64		Coal Harbor.
Ellis, James U.	Lieut.	9th H. Art.	July 9, '64		
Elmeier, Herman	Lieut.	7th Inf.	Apl. 10, '65		
Esselstyn, Richard	Lieut.	25th Inf.	May 31, '62		Hanover C. H.
Evry, Chas. C.	Lieut.	47th Inf.		Feb. 20, '64	Olustee, Fla.
Edwards, Robt. S.	Lieut.	48th Inf.		July 18, '63	Fort Wagner.
Ellis, William	Major	49th Inf.	Aug. 3, '64		
Ellis, Harrison F.	Lieut.	72d Inf.		May 3, '63	Chancellorsville.
Everett, Robert B.	Capt.	76th Inf.		July 1, '63	Gettysburg.
Ellsworth, Daniel S.	Capt.	86th Inf.		May 3, '63	Chancellorsville.
England, Theophilus L.	Lt.-Col.	89th Inf.		June 18, '64	Near Petersburg.
Eldridge, Norman F.	Lieut.	93d Inf.		May 6, '64	Wilderness.
Elliott, Gilbert M.	Major	102d Inf.		Nov. 24, '64	Lookout Mountain.
Evans, Robert	Lieut.	108th Inf.		July 2, '63	Gettysburg.
Edmons, Geo. W.	Lieut.	112th Inf.		Oct. 27, '64	
Ellis, A. Van Horn	Col.	124th Inf.		July 2, '63	Gettysburg.
Elliott, James M.	Capt.	142d Inf.		Jan. 15, '65	Fort Fisher, Va.
Eagan, Michael J.	Lieut.	170th Inf.		June 16, '64	
FOOTE, BENJAMIN F.	Capt.	8th Cav.		June 9, '63	Beverly Ford.
Follett, Charles D.	Capt.	8th Cav.	June 4, '63		
Fleming, James H.	Capt.	16th Cav.		Aug. 8, '64	Fairfax Station.
Flannagan, Ichabod P.	Lieut.	4th H. Art.		Aug. 25, '64	Ream's Station.
Fountain, Elias	Lieut.	6th H. Art.	Oct. 19, '64		
Farnham, Noah L.	Lt.-Col.	11th Inf.	Aug. 14, '61		Bull Run.
Fisher, Edward M.	Lieut.	12th Inf.		June 27, '62	Chickahominy, Va.
Frick, Adolph	Lieut.	20th Inf.	Sep. 17, '62		Antietam.
Ferguson, Archibald H.	Capt.	25th Inf.	June 28, '62		
Fisk, George E.	Lieut.	25th Inf.		May 27, '62	Hanover C. H.
Fairman, Washington B.	Lieut.	25th Inf.	June 30, '62		Gaines Mill.
Frisby, Edward	Col.	30th Inf.		Aug. 30, '62	2d Bull Run.
Faxon, Elihu J.	Major	36th Inf.		May 3, '63	Chancellorsville.
Fennon, William J.	Lieut.	37th Inf.		May 31, '62	Seven Pines.
Fryer, John	Major	43d Inf.	May 12, '64		
Farrell, James	Capt.	48th Inf.		July 18, '63	Fort Wagner, S. C.
Fox, Charles E.	Lieut.	48th Inf.	Aug. 11, '63		Fort Wagner.
Fee, John A.	Capt.	48th Inf.	July 15, '64		Near Petersburg.
Fowler, Andrew L.	Lieut.	51st Inf.		Sep. 17, '62	Antietam.
Folger, Henry H	Lieut.	57th Inf.		Sep. 17, '62	Antietam.
Florentine, Abraham	Capt.	59th Inf.	Oct. 19, '62		Antietam.
Fuller, Henry V.	Capt.	64th Inf.		July 2, '63	Gettysburg.
Fisk, George R.	Lieut.	64th Inf.		May 12, '64	Spottsylvania.
Friederich, Otto	Capt.	68th Inf.	July 2, '63		Gettysburg.
Foss, Charles A.	Lieut.	72d Inf.	July 7, '63		Gettysburg.

NAME.	RANK.	REGIMENT.	DIED OF WOUNDS.	KILLED.	BATTLE.
Fish, Elias A.	Capt.	81st Inf.	Oct. 2, '64		
Ferris, Thaddeus C.	Lieut.	90th Inf.		Oct. 19, '64	Cedar Creek, Va.
Fish, Henry H.	Major	94th Inf.		Apl. 1, '65	
French, George	Capt.	94th Inf.		Apl. 1, '65	
Faville, Dwight S.	Lieut.	97th Inf.		Aug. 31, '62	2d Bull Run.
French, James H.	Lieut.	100th Inf.	May 22, '64		
Force, George B.	Major	108th Inf.		Sep. 17, '62	Antietam.
Francisco, Francis H.	Lieut.	115th Inf.		Aug. 16, '64	Deep Bottom, Va.
Frost, Emil	Lieut.	119th Inf.		July 2, '63	Gettysburg.
Freelewick, Frederick	Lieut.	120th Inf.		July 2, '63	Gettysburg.
Fish, John D.	Capt.	121st Inf.		May 12, '64	Spottsylvania
Ford, Frederick E.	Lieut.	121st Inf.		May 3, '63	Chancellorsville.
Finnegan, James	Capt.	124th Inf.	Oct. 28, '64		
Forrest, Edwin	Capt.	131th Inf.	May 20, '64		Dug Gap, Ga.
Froeligh, Peter D.	Lieut.	146th Inf.		May 5, '64	Wilderness.
Freer, John T.	Lieut.	156th Inf.		Apl. 13, '63	Bisland, La.
Frank, Harrison	Capt.	157th Inf.		July 2, '63	Gettysburg.
Fitch, Lewis E.	Lieut.	161st Inf.		Apl. 8, '64	Sabine Cross Roads.
Finley, Madison K.	Lieut.	162d Inf.	Apl. 21, '64		
Fitzmaurice, John S.	Lieut.	170th Inf.		May 18, '64	
Farwell, Allen T.	Capt.	179th Inf.		July 30, '64	
GALL, ALEXANDER	Lieut.	5th Cav.		June 30, '63	Hanover, Pa.
Greenleaf, Chas. H.	Lieut.	5th Cav.	Aug. 26, '64		
Goodrich, Asa L.	Capt.	8th Cav.		Apl. 3, '65	
Glennon, Patrick R.	Lieut.	22d Cav.		June 22, '64	Dinwiddie C. H., Va
Gibbons, Austin	Lieut.	24th Cav.	Nov. 18, '64		
Gardner, Alexander	Capt.	8th H. Art.		June 3, '64	Coal Harbor.
Gladden, G.	Lieut.	8th H. Art.		June 3, '64	Coal Harbor.
Glass, Robert	Lieut.	8th H. Art.	July 15, '64		
Gregory, Truman	Capt.	9th H. Art.	June 23, '64		
Gordon, John S.	Capt.	13th H. Art.		Oct. 7, '64	Swift Creek, N. C.
Gossin, Andrew	Lieut.	14th H. Art.		Dec. 1, '64	Petersburg.
Gadsden, Chas. A.	Lieut.	9th Inf.		Apl. 19, '62	Camden.
Goetling, William	Lieut.	13th Inf.		Aug. 30, '62	2d Bull Run.
Griffith, Geo. W.	Lieut.	14th Inf.		July 1, '62	
Grower, Wm. T. C.	Col.	17th Inf.	Sep. 3, '64		Jonesboro, Ga.
Gerety, Michael	Capt.	42d Inf.		Oct. 21, '61	Ball's Bluff.
Gillies, James	Lieut.	42d Inf.		Oct. 21, '61	Ball's Bluff.
Gilfillan, Wm. H.	Capt.	43d Inf.		July 3, '63	Gettysburg.
Grassan, Henry	Lieut.	45th Inf.	June 21, '62		
Grotowsky, Wilhelm	Lieut.	46th Inf.	June 2, '62		
Green, James M.	Lt.-Col.	48th Inf.		July 18, '63	Fort Wagner, S. C.
Goodrich, Wm. B.	Col.	60th Inf.		Sep. 17, '62	Antietam.
Garland, Franklin K.	Lieut.	61st Inf.	July 4, '63		Gettysburg.
Gibbs, Thomas O.	Lieut.	67th Inf.		May 12, '64	Spottsylvania.
Grecheneck, George	Capt.	72d Inf.	May 17, '62		Williamsburg.
Glass, John J.	Lieut.	73d Inf.		May 5, '62	Williamsburg.
Grover, Andrew J.	Major	76th Inf.		July 1, '63	Gettysburg.
Guyer, Frederick	Capt.	83d Inf.		May 6, '64	Wilderness.
Grunan, Isaiah	Lieut.	84th Inf.	Sep. 9, '62		
Gray, Robert Listen	Lieut.	93d Inf.		May 5, '64	Wilderness.
Gray, Charles O.	Col.	96th Inf.		Dec 14, '62	Kinston, N. C.
Gorman, John	Capt.	109th Inf.		May 31, '63	Near Hanovertown.
Griswold, N. J.	Lieut.	109th Inf.		July 30, '64	Petersburg.
Granger, Erastus M.	Lieut.	111th Inf.		July 3, '63	Gettysburg.
Gowdy, Henry	Lieut.	124th Inf.	May 11, '63		Chancellorsville.
Green, Eglow L.	Lieut.	125th Inf.	June 17, '64		
Gregg, Joseph H.	Capt.	137th Inf.	July 3, '63		Gettysburg.
Gaylord, Sidney C.	Lieut.	147th Inf.		June 18, '64	
Gage, E. Darwin	Capt.	148th Inf.		Oct. 27, '64	Fair Oaks, Va.
Gridley, Henry	Lieut.	150th Inf.		June 22, '64	Culp's Farm, Ga.
Goodspeed, Benjamin	Capt.	151st Inf.		June 3, '64	Coal Harbor.
Griffin, John W.	Lieut.	170th Inf.		May 24, '64	North Anna River.
Green, Jr., Wm. N.	Lt.-Col.	173d Inf.	May 14, '64		

THE HONORS OF THE EMPIRE STATE

NAME.	RANK.	REGIMENT.	DIED OF WOUNDS.	KILLED.	BATTLE.
Hidden, Henry B.	Lieut.	1st Cav.		Mar. 9, '62	Sangster Station.
Hull, Walter C.	Col.	2d Cav.		Nov. 12, '64	Cedar Creek, Va.
Hall, Thomas	Lieut.	2d Vet.Cav.	Apl. 14, '64		
Hart, William	Capt.	4th Cav.		Sep. 16, '63	Raccoon Ford.
Hannas, Diodate C.	Capt.	6th Cav.	Sep. 10, '62		
Hawes, Edward S.	Lieut.	10th Cav.		June 19, '63	Middleburg, Va.
Halleck, Franklin B.	Capt.	11th Cav.	May 17, '64		New River, La.
Hubbard, Henry A.	Capt.	12th Cav.	Apl. 7, '65		
Hammond, Alvaro	Lieut.	18th Cav.		Apl. 8, '64	Sabine C'ss R'ds Lt
Holcomb, Nelson B.	Lieut.	21st Cav.	Dec. 6, '64		
Howard, Charles N.	Lieut.	25th Cav.		June 21, '64	
Hooker, Henry C.	Capt.	2d H. Art.		Aug. 14, '64	
Howard, Frederick H.	Lieut.	2d H. Art.	Aug. 16, '64		
Hamel, David	Lieut.	6th H. Art.	May 27, 64		
Hawkins, William J.	Capt.	8th H. Art.		June 23, '64	
Hoyt, George A.	Capt.	8th H. Art.		July 5, '64	Petersburg.
Hard, Wallace B.	Lieut.	8th H. Art.		June 3, '64	Coal Harbor.
Howard, Orson	Capt.	9th H. Art.		Oct. 19, '64	Cedar Creek, Va.
Hedges, Job C.	Major	14th H. Art.		June 17, '64	Petersburg.
Hartley, Ezra T.	Lieut.	14th H. Art.		July 3, '64	Petersburg.
Henchen, Francis	Lieut.	L. Art.		July 27, 64	
Hager, George O.	Capt.	5th Inf.		Aug. 30, '62	
Heringer, Oscar V.	Capt.	7th Inf.	Jan. 30, '63		Fredericksburg.
Husler, Charles	Capt.	7th Inf.	Feb. 26, '63		Antietam.
Hedden, Josiah	Lieut.	10th Inf.		Aug. 30, '62	2d Bull Run.
Hoagland, Wm. H.	Capt.	12th Inf.		Dec. 13, '62	Fredericksburg.
Harrer, Frederick	Capt.	14th Inf.	July 13, '62		Gaines Mills, Va.
Horsfall, William	Capt.	18th Inf.		Sep. 14, '62	Crampton's Gap, V
Hubbard, Daniel C.	Lieut.	24th Inf.	Aug. 30, '62		2d Bull Run.
Halpin, Charles	Lieut.	25th Inf.		May 27, '62	Hanover C. H.
Holliday, Harrison	Capt.	30th Inf.	Sep. 17, '62		Antietam.
Heiss, August	Capt.	31st Inf.		May 7, 62	West Point.
Hill, Clarence E.	Lieut.	34th Inf.		Sep. 17, '62	Antietam.
Hays, Patrick H.	Lieut.	37th Inf.		May 5, '62	Williamsburg.
Horn, John	Capt.	40th Inf.		Dec. 13, '62	Fredericksburg.
Hoestriech, George	Capt.	46th Inf.	Aug. 29, '62		2d Bull Run.
Hunting, Edward F.	Lieut.	47th Inf.		Feb. 20, '64	
Hurst, Frederick	Capt.	48th Inf.	July 31, '63		Charleston, S. C.
Holt, Erastus D.	Lt.-Col.	49th Inf.	Apl. 7, '65		
Hickmott, Charles H.	Capt.	49th Inf.	May 6, '64		
Heacock, Reuben B.	Capt.	49th Inf.		May 18, '64	
Haas, Herman	Lieut.	49th Inf.		May 12, '64	
Haberkorn, Emil	Lieut.	54th Inf.		Aug. 30, '62	2d Bull Run.
Highbee, Henry H.	Lieut.	57th Inf.		Sep. 17, '62	Antietam.
Hubbell, Wilson	Major	62d Inf.		June 3, '64	Coal Harbor, Va.
Hewitt, Leroy S.	Lieut.	64th Inf.		July 8, '62	Savage's Station.
Higginbotham, Thos. J.	Lt.-Col.	65th Inf.		Oct. 19, '64	
Hoga, Adalbert	Lieut.	68th Inf.	May 2, '63		Chancellorsville.
Hurley, John	Surgeon	69th Inf.		Apl. 15, '63	
Hagner, Herrick	Lieut.	70th Inf.		May 5, '62	Williamsburg.
Hydorn, Charles H.	Lieut.	72d Inf.		May 3, '63	Chancellorsville.
Herbert, Wm. L.	Lieut.	73d Inf.		July 2, '63	Gettysburg.
Harrison, Edward A.	Capt.	74th Inf.		Aug. 27, '62	Bristoe Station.
Hutchinson, Luther T.	Lieut.	75th Inf.		June 14, '63	Port Hudson, La.
Horner, John R.	Lieut.	80th Inf.		Aug. 30, '62	2d Bull Run.
Huston, James	Lt.-Col.	82d Inf.		July 2, '63	Gettysburg.
Hoyt, Jonah C.	Capt.	82d Inf.		July 2, '63	
Hawley, Harvey P.	Lieut.	82d Inf.		May 31, '62	
Hirt, Felix	Lieut.	83d Inf.		Dec. 13, '62	Fredericksburg.
Horgan, William	Major	88th Inf.		Dec. 13, '62	Fredericksburg.
Hackett, Francis J.	Lieut.	88th Inf.		July 1, '62	Malvern Hill.
Hallock, John	Capt.	96th Inf.		June 3, '64	Coal Harbor, Va.
Hart, James H.	Capt.	99th Inf.		June 16, '63	Franklin, Va.
Haddock, Herbert H.	Lieut.	100th Inf.		July 18, '63	
Hoyt, Agor H.	Lieut.	100th Inf.	May 16, '64		Drury's Bluff, Va.

NAME.	RANK.	REGIMENT.	DIED OF WOUNDS.	KILLED.	BATTLE.
Hooker, Alfred J.	Capt.	106th Inf.		July 9, '64	Monocacy, Md.
Hathaway, Gilbert W.	Lieut.	106th Inf.		May 9, '64	Spottsylvania.
Hill, John D.	Lieut.	107th Inf.		May 25, '64	Dallas, Ga.
Holmes, Robert E.	Lieut.	108th Inf.		Sep. 17, '62	Antietam.
Hill, Horace G.	Lieut.	111th Inf.		May 5, '64	Wilderness.
Hull, Henry	Lieut.	112th Inf.	July 3, '64		
Hunt, Wm. J.	Capt.	117th Inf.	July 29, '64		
Hollister, Lansing	Capt.	120th Inf.		July 2, '63	Gettysburg.
Howland, T. C.	Capt.	121st Inf.		Apl. 6, '65	Sailor's Creek, Va.
Hoyt, Henry H.	Lieut.	122d Inf.		June 21, '64	Petersburg.
Herendeen, Orin J.	Capt.	126th Inf.		July 3, '63	Gettysburg.
Hunton, Jr., Abraham	Lieut.	126th Inf.	June 7, '64		
Holmes, Rufus R.	Lieut.	126th Inf.		July 4, '63	Gettysburg.
Hallett, Henry W.	Lieut.	137th Inf.		July 2, '63	Gettysburg.
Hordenbough, R. M. J.	Lieut.	143d Inf.	Mar. 16, '65		
Hamlin, Franklin N.	Lieut.	147th Inf.	Jan. 25, '64		
Hulsen, Washington W.	Capt.	152d Inf.		May 5, '64	
Hart, Thomas	Capt.	155th Inf.	June 25, '64		
Hunt, Major L.	Lieut.	157th Inf.		May 2, '63	Chancellorsville.
Henery, J. F.	Lieut.	157th Inf.	July 24, '63		Gettysburg.
Hart, Robert McD.	Major	159th Inf.		Oct. 19, '64	Cedar Creek, Va.
Haws, William C.	Lieut.	162d Inf.	Apl. 29, '64		
Hickey, Thomas	Capt.	164th Inf.		June 3, '64	Coal Harbor.
Hughes, John H.	Lieut.	169th Inf.	Sep. 6, '63		
INGRAHAM, AARON H.	Lieut.	48th Inf.		June 1, '64	Coal Harbor.
Ince, George H.	Capt.	66th Inf.		July 2, '63	Gettysburg.
JONES, D. K. SMITH	Capt.	4th H. Art.		June 17, '64	
Jones, Edward	Major	6th H. Art.	Oct. 30, '64		
Johnson, William H.	Lieut.	L. Art.	Nov. 2, '64		
Jacobi, Frederick	Lieut.	7th Inf.		Dec. 13, '62	Fredericksburg.
Jennings, Charles E.	Capt.	20th Inf.	Oct. 1, '62		
Jewsbury, John	Lieut.	31st Inf.		May 3, '63	
Jordan, Albert	Lieut.	39th Inf.	June 15, '62		Cross Keys.
Johnson, Wm. H. H.	Lieut.	40th Inf.		July 2, '63	Gettysburg.
Johnson, Seth F.	Capt.	44th Inf.		May 5, '64	Wilderness.
Johnson, Geo. W.	Lt.-Col.	49th Inf.	July 27, '64		
Johnson, David R.	Capt.	51st Inf.	May 19, '62		
Jenkins, Daniel E.	Capt.	51st Inf.		May 6, '64	Wilderness.
Jennings, Gould J.	Capt.	59th Inf.	Oct. 25, '62		Antietam.
Jackson, Edward	Lieut.	82d Inf.	June 3, '64		
Jackson, Mathew M.	Capt.	87th Inf.		Aug. 29, '62	2d Bull Run.
Joyce, John O'C.	Capt.	88th Inf.		Sep. 17, '62	Antietam.
Judd, Seymour L.	Capt.	89th Inf.	Aug. 27, '64		Near Petersburg.
Johnson, John G.	Lieut.	96th Inf.	June -, '64		Coal Harbor.
Jones, Richard	Capt.	97th Inf.	Sep. 5, '62		2d Bull Run.
Johnston, Thomas	Lieut.	104th Inf.	July 8, '63		Gettysburg.
Jones, E. C.	Lieut.	109th Inf.	June 17, '64		Petersburg.
Jones, David	Lieut.	116th Inf.	June 2, '63		Port Hudson.
Jackson, William A.	Capt.	124th Inf.		June 18, '64	Petersburg.
Jones, Edward P.	Capt.	125th Inf.		May 12, '64	Spottsylvania.
Johnson, Jr., Wm. P.	Capt.	142d Inf.		July 30, '64	Petersburg, Va.
Jenkins, David T.	Col.	146th Inf.		May 5, '64	Wilderness.
Jackson, Caleb G.	Lieut.	148th Inf.		Apl. 6, '65	Rice's Station, Va.
Jewett, Josiah P.	Capt.	160th Inf.	May 10, '63		
Johnson, Frank T.	Capt.	162d Inf.	Apl. 9, '64		
KNEMM, FRANCIS	Lieut.	2d H. Art.		May 19, '64	At the Pines, Va.
Kitching, J. Howard	Col.	6th H. Art.	Jan. 10, '65		
Kennedy, James	Capt.	7th H. Art.	Sep. 10, '64		
Kieffer, Luther	Capt.	14th H. Art.		June 2, '64	Coal Harbor.
Klein, Charles E.	Lieut.	31st Inf.	May 9, '62		
Kurz, Richard	Lieut.	41st Inf.		Aug. 30, '62	2d Bull Run.
Knickerbocker, Hugh B.	Capt.	43d Inf.		May 3, '63	Chancellorsville.

NAME.	RANK.	REGIMENT.	DIED OF WOUNDS.	KILLED.	BATTLE.
Koonz, George H.	Lieut.	43d Inf.		May 3, '63	Chancellorsville.
Keenan, James N.	Lieut.	48th Inf.	Feb. 20, '64		Olustee, Fla.
Klingenberg, Max	Lieut.	52d Inf.		Mar. 31, '65	Weldon Railroad.
Kirk, William A.	Major	57th Inf.	June 20, '64		Petersburg.
Kavanagh, John	Capt.	63d Inf.		Sep. 17, '62	Antietam.
Kendall, Ezra W.	Lieut.	64th Inf.		June 1, '62	Fair Oaks.
Koenig, Paul	Capt.	68th Inf.		Aug. 31, '63	Wh. Sulph. Spring
Kelly, Richard A.	Capt.	69th Inf.		May 12, '64	Spottsylvania.
Kelly, Patrick J.	Lieut.	69th Inf.		Sep. 17, '62	Antietam.
King, Richard P.	Lieut.	69th Inf.	May 26, '64		
Kibburn, Wm. W.	Lieut.	70th Inf.		May 5, '62	Williamsburg.
Keeler, Philip	Lieut.	76th Inf.	July 1, '63		Gettysburg.
Kingman, Lyman M.	Capt.	81st Inf.		May 31, '62	Fair Oaks.
Kelly, John	Lieut.	82d Inf.		May 6, '64	Wilderness.
Keating, Michael	Lieut.	82d Inf.		June 5, '64	
Kelly, Patrick	Col.	88th Inf.		June 16, '64	Petersburg.
King, Timothy	Lieut.	88th Inf.		June 1, '62	Fair Oaks.
Kelley, John E.	Major	96th Inf.		May 29, '62	
Koch, John	Lieut.	97th Inf.		June 5, '64	
Kellogg, Samuel S.	Lieut.	100th Inf.		May 31, '62	Fair Oaks.
Kelly, John	Capt.	104th Inf.		Sep. 17, '62	Antietam.
Kingston, John	Lieut.	106th Inf.		July 9, '64	Monocacy, Md.
Knox, John F.	Capt.	107th Inf.	May 29, '64		Dallas, Ga.
Kinleyside, John S.	Lieut.	108th Inf.		June 3, '64	Coal Harbor.
Knowlton, Daniel C.	Capt.	114th Inf.		Oct. 19, '64	Cedar Creek.
Ketchum, Edward H.	Lieut.	120th Inf.		July 3, '63	Gettysburg.
Klein, Charles P.	Lieut.	140th Inf.	July 2, '63		Gettysburg.
Klock, Jacob C.	Capt.	153d Inf.	Oct. 15, '64		Winchester, Va.
Keeley, James H.	Capt.	170th Inf.		Aug. 25, '64	
Kelly, Martin	Lieut.	182d Inf.	May 26, '64		
LAYTON, DANIEL	Lieut.	22d Cav.	June 14, '64		W. Oak Swamp, V
Lee, Michael J.	Lieut.	4th H. Art.	June 9, '64		
Low, Thomas	Capt.	8th H. Art.	Apl. 25, '65		
Lewis, Wilber F.	Capt.	5th Inf.		Aug. 30, '62	
Loetze, Hugo	Lieut.	7th Inf.		Sep. 17, '62	Antietam.
Lange, Stephen	Lieut.	7th Inf.	July 1, '62		Malvern Hill.
Lema, Albert S.	Lieut.	13th Inf.	June 27, '62		Gaines Mills.
Lloyd, Edward H.	Lieut.	14th Inf.		July 1, '62	Malvern Hill.
Lorenz, G. Adolph	Lieut.	20th Inf.		Sep. 17, '62	Antietam.
Lohman, Christian	Lieut.	20th Inf.	Oct. 9, '62		Antietam.
Lendrum, Duncan	Lieut.	22d Inf.		Aug. 30, '62	2d Bull Run.
Leonard, Hugh	Lieut.	26th Inf.		Aug. 30, '62	2d Bull Run.
Leipe, B'r'n Von Zeidlitz	Lieut.	29th Inf.	Sep. 7, '62		
Lamon, George F.	Lt.-Col.	32d Inf.	Nov. 10, '62		
Lennon, Patrick H.	Capt.	42d Inf.		May 12, '64	
Lodge, Douglas	Capt.	43d Inf.		May 4, '63	Chancellorsville.
Larahee, Lucius S.	Capt.	44th Inf.		July 2, '63	Gettysburg.
Leonhard, Charles	Capt.	45th Inf.		May 2, '63	Chancellorsville.
Lunkenbein, Peter	Lieut.	46th Inf.	Apl. 24, '62		
Lent, Louis F.	Capt.	48th Inf.		July 10, '63	Morris Island, S. C
Lambert, Jr., David	Lieut.	49th Inf.		July 12, '64	
Laty, Charles	Lieut.	52d Inf.		Dec. 13, '62	Fredericksburg.
Lynch, John C.	Capt.	63d Inf.		May 3, '63	Chancellorsville.
Lydon, Patrick W.	Lieut.	63d Inf.		Sep. 17, '62	Antietam.
Lynch, George	Lieut.	63d Inf.	Sep. 18, '62		Antietam.
Lewis, Alfred H.	Lieut.	64th Inf.		July 2, '63	Gettysburg.
Laurier, Theodore	Lieut.	71st Inf.	June 3, '62		Fair Oaks.
Lowentrout, Jno. L.	Lieut.	71st Inf.		Aug. 27, '62	Bristoe Station.
Le Fort, George	Capt.	73d Inf.		May 20, '64	
Leonard, Benedict A.	Lieut.	73d Inf.		May 12, '64	Spottsylvania.
Lewis, Henry H.	Lieut.	73d Inf.		Aug. 27, '62	Bristoe Station.
Lennon, Martin	Capt.	77th Inf.	Nov. 1, '64		
Layton, Thomas	Lieut.	83d Inf.		Dec. 13, '62	Fredericksburg.
Little, Stephen B.	Lieut.	96th Inf.		June 3, '64	Coal Harbor.

IN THE WAR OF THE REBELLION.

NAME.	RANK.	REGIMENT.	DIED OF WOUNDS.	KILLED.	BATTLE.
Linnabaer, T. J.	Lieut.	116th Inf.		June 14, '63	Port Hudson.
Lloyd, Edward F.	Lt.-Col.	119th Inf.		May 15, '64	Resaca, Ga.
Lockwood, John J.	Lieut.	120th Inf.		May 5, '64	Wilderness.
Lincoln, Spencer F.	Lieut.	126th Inf.	July 18, '64		
Logie, William K.	Col.	141st Inf.		July 20, '64	Peach Tree Cr'k, Ga.
Lindsay, David J.	Capt.	149th Inf.		July 20, '64	Peach Tree Cr'k, Ga.
Larkin, Christopher	Lieut.	156th Inf.		Oct. 19, '64	Cedar Creek, Va.
Lower, Randall D.	Lieut.	157th Inf.		July 1, '63	Gettysburg.
Lathrop, Robert D.	Lieut.	159th Inf.		Apl. 14, '63	
Lockwood, Byron L.	Lieut.	159th Inf.		Apl. 14, '63	
Lynch, Jeremiah	Capt.	170th Inf.	June 7, '64		
Logue, Patrick	Lieut.	170th Inf.		May 24, '64	Spottsylvania.
Lee, Henry R.	Capt.	173d Inf.	May 5, '64		Cane River.
MORGAN, WM. L.	Capt.	1st. V. Cav.		Feb. 20, '64	Upperville, Va.
Martenson, Augustus ?.	Lieut.	2d Cav.		June 17, '63	
Morse, Eli	Capt.	2d M. Rifles	Apl. 1, '65		Dinwiddie C. H., Va.
Morrison, Jeremiah R.	Lieut.	2d M. Rifles	June 6, '64		
Mix, Simon H.	Col.	3d Cav.		June 15, '64	Petersburg.
Mayes, John	Lieut.	3d Cav.		May 7, '64	Stony Creek, Va.
Mann, Nehemiah H.	Capt.	4th Cav.		Aug. 16, '64	Chester Gap, Va.
McGuinn, Luke	Capt.	5th Cav.		May 5, '64	Wilderness, Va.
McVicar, Duncan	Lt.-Col.	6th Cav.		Apl. 30, '63	Spottsylvania C. H.
Main, John G.	Lieut.	6th Cav.		Oct. 19, '64	Nr. Strausburg, Va.
McNair, James	Capt.	8th Cav.		June 23, '64	
Mitchell, Wm. H.	Capt.	21st Cav.		May 15, '64	New Market, Va.
McKeel, James M.	Capt.	4th H. Art.		Aug. 25, '64	Ream's Station.
Morris, Lewis O.	Col.	7th H. Art.		June 4, '64	
Morris, John A.	Capt.	7th H. Art.		May 19, '64	Spottsylvania.
Maguire, Charles	Capt.	7th H. Art.	July 4, '64		
McCulloch, Charles	Capt.	7th H. Art.		May 19, '64	Spottsylvania.
McClure, Thos. J.	Lieut.	7th H. Art.		June 3, '64	Coal Harbor.
McGinnis, James	Capt.	8th H. Art.		Aug. 25, '64	Ream's Station.
Miller, Wm. C.	Lieut.	15th H. Art.		May 6, '64	Wilderness.
Mueller, Robert	Lieut.	15th H. Art.	Aug. 23, '64		
Murphy, Lawrence	Capt.	5th Inf.		June 2, '64	
Montgomery, Chas. S.	Capt.	5th Inf.		Feb. 6, '65	Hatcher's Run.
Morrell, Francis A.	Lieut.	10th Inf.	Feb. 4, '63		Fredericksburg.
Monk, Wm. H.	Lieut.	10th Inf.	May 28, '64		
Marsh, Samuel	Lt.-Col.	16th Inf.	July 4, '62		Gaines Mills, Va.
McFadden, John	Lieut.	16th Inf.	Aug. 8, '62		Gaines Mills, Va.
Merkle, Robert	Capt.	20th Inf.	Sep. 26, '62		Antietam.
McCoy, Robert E.	Capt.	22d Inf.		Aug. 29, '62	2d Bull Run.
Milliman, Henry S.	Capt.	22d Inf.	Sep. 10, '62		2d Bull Run.
McMahon, Michael	Capt.	25th Inf.		May 27, '62	Hanover C. H.
Morse, William	Lieut.	30th Inf.		Aug. 30, '62	2d Bull Run.
Mallon, James E.	Col.	42d Inf.		Oct. 14, '63	Bristoe Station.
McPherson, Charles	Capt.	42d Inf.		Sep. 17, '62	Antietam.
Mentzel, Herman	Lieut.	46th Inf.		Jan. 22, '64	
Markscheffel, Theodore	Lieut.	46th Inf.		June 12, '64	Coal Harbor.
Moser, Samuel H.	Capt.	48th Inf.		May 16, '64	Palmer Creek.
Moody, Miller	Capt.	59th Inf.	Nov. 7, '62		Antietam.
Masset, W. Carey	Lt.-Col.	61st Inf.		June 1, '62	Fair Oaks.
Morrison, Thos. G.	Capt.	61st Inf.	May 8, '64		
McIntyre, William	Lieut.	61st Inf.		June 1, '62	Fair Oaks.
Malcolm, William	Lieut.	61st Inf.		Apl. 6, '65	
Macky, James E.	Lieut.	63d Inf.	Sep. 17, '62		Antietam.
McDonald, Miles	Lieut.	63d Inf.		June 17, '64	Petersburg.
McConnell, Henry	Lieut.	63d Inf.		Sep. 17, '62	Antietam.
Messervey, James J.	Capt.	64th Inf.		Aug. 17, '64	Deep Bottom, Va.
Morris, Orlando W.	Col.	66th Inf.		June 3, '64	Coal Harbor.
Munn, Elijah F.	Capt.	66th Inf.		July 2, '63	Gettysburg.
Mitchell, John	Capt.	70th Inf.		May 5, '62	Williamsburg.
Murphy, Terance	Lieut.	71st Inf.		Aug. 27, '62	Bristoe Station.
McDonough, Henry J.	Capt.	72d Inf.		Nov. 27, '63	Locust Grove, Va.

NAME.	RANK.	REGIMENT.	DIED OF WOUNDS.	KILLED.	BATTLE.
Marksman, James	Lieut.	73d Inf.		July 3, '63	Gettysburg.
McAllister, John	Lieut.	73d Inf.		Aug. 27, '62	Bristoe Station.
McCune, Alexander M.	Capt.	74th Inf.		June 7, '64	
Mitchell, Peter M. J.	Capt.	78th Inf.		Sep. 17, '62	Antietam.
McAmbly, John	Major	81st Inf.		May 31, '62	Fair Oaks.
Martin, James	Capt.	81st Inf.		June 3, '64	Coal Harbor.
McDonald, John H.	Lieut.	82d Inf.		July 3, '63	Gettysburg.
Moesch, Jos. A.	Col.	83d Inf.		May 6, '64	Wilderness.
Mallory, George	Capt.	84th Inf.		Aug. 29, '62	2d Bull Run.
Myers, David	Capt.	84th Inf.	Sep. 25, '62		
Murphy, Thomas	Lieut.	88th Inf.		Dec. 13, '62	Fredericksburg.
McClelland, Wm.	Lieut.	88th Inf.		July 2, '62	Gettysburg.
McCarthy, Daniel	Lieut.	88th Inf.		Dec. 13, '62	Fredericksburg.
Morren, Wm. J.	Lieut.	97th Inf.		July 1, '63	Gettysburg.
Mead, John	Capt.	102d Inf.		July 3, '63	Gettysburg.
Mount, Geo. F.	Lieut.	112th Inf.		Aug. 25, '64	
McKittrick, Wm. H.	Capt.	115th Inf.		Sep. 29, '64	Chapin's Farm, Va
Morton, John T.	Lieut.	121st Inf.		Apl. 6, '65	Sailor's Creek.
McDougall, Archibald L.	Col.	123d Inf.	June 23, '64		Dallas, Ga.
Myers, Aaron B.	Lt.-Col.	125th Inf.	May 8, '64		Wilderness.
Miller, Merritt B.	Lieut.	125th Inf.	June 26, '64		
Munson, Ira	Capt.	126th Inf.	May 14, '64		
McDonald, Jno. A.	Lieut.	126th Inf.		June 16, '64	Petersburg.
Middleton, Benjamin F.	Lieut.	139th Inf.		Sep. 29, '64	Chapin's Farm. Va
Mack, James W.	Lieut.	144th Inf.		Nov. 30, '64	Harry Hills, S. C.
Mace, Guilford D.	Lieut.	147th Inf.		July 1, '63	Gettysburg.
McAssy, Daniel	Lieut.	147th Inf.		July 1, '63	Gettysburg.
Musson, Willard A.	Capt.	152d Inf.		Oct. 27, '64	
Manly, John W.	Lieut.	159th Inf.		Apl. 14, '63	
McDonough, Nicholas	Lieut.	160th Inf.	May 18, '64		Pleasant Hill, La.
Maxson, B. Frank	Lieut.	160th Inf.		Sep. 19, '64	Cedar Creek, Va.
McMahon, Jas. P.	Col.	164th Inf.		June 3, '64	Coal Harbor.
Maroney, William	Capt.	164th Inf.	June 20, '64		
McCaffry, Edward	Lieut.	164th Inf.	June 4, '64		
McTavish, Hugh G.	Lieut.	164th Inf.	Mar. 12, '65		
McConihe, John	Col.	169th Inf.		June 1, '64	Coal Harbor.
McCarty, Patrick	Capt.	170th Inf.		May 24, '64	
Merrimann, H. N.	Capt.	177th Inf.	July 14, '63		
Murphy, Mathew	Col.	182d Inf.	Apl. 16, '65		
Minier, Daniel	Lieut.	185th Inf.		Mar. 29, '65	
NUMAN, JOHN F.	Lieut.	2d M. Rifles		Dec. 9, '64	Hatcher's Run.
Norris, William T.	Lieut.	22d Inf.		Aug. 30, '62	2d Bull Run.
Noxon, Robert G.	Lieut.	76th Inf.	Sep. -, '63		Gettysburg.
Newmann, August	Lieut.	103d Inf.	May 12, '63		
Norton, Franklin	Lt.-Col.	123d Inf.	May 12, '63		Chancellorsville.
Nichols, Isaac	Capt.	124th Inf.		July 2, '63	Gettysburg.
Noyes, Samuel C.	Lieut.	154th Inf.		May 2, '63	Chancellorsville.
Nolan, John	Lieut.	155th Inf.	June 25, '64		
Neville, John	Lieut.	162d Inf.	July 17, '63		
Nugent, John H.	Capt.	182d Inf.		June 3, '64	Coal Harbor.
O'KEEFE, JOSEPH O.	Major	2d Cav.	Apl. 6, '65		
Oberteuffer, John C.	Capt.	7th Cav.		Dec. 21, '64	Nr Jones' Creek, Va
Ordner, John	Capt.	10th Cav.		June 2, '64	St. Mary's Ch., Va.
O'Brien, Michael	Capt.	2d H. Art.		June 6, '64	Coal Harbor.
Orr, William E.	Lieut.	7th H. Art.	June 2, '64		
Oldswager, John	Lieut.	9th H. Art.		Oct. 19, '64	
O'Donohue, William	Capt.	Light Art.		May 3, '63	Chancellorsville.
Osborne, George	Lieut.	5th Inf.		Aug. 18, '64	Weldon R. R., Va.
O'Leary, Jeremiah	Lieut.	37th Inf.		May 5, '62	Williamsburg.
O'Keefe, Thomas J.	Lieut.	39th Inf.		May 12, '64	Spottsylvania, Va.
Ohmes, Henry W.	Capt.	46th Inf.		June 18, '64	Petersburg.
O Brien, Jeremiah	Lieut.	48th Inf.		July 30, '64	Petersburg.
Owens, James A.	Lieut.	61st Inf.		June 1, '64	

IN THE WAR OF THE REBELLION.

NAME.	RANK.	REGIMENT.	DIED OF WOUNDS.	KILLED.	BATTLE.
O'Neil, Bernard S.	Capt.	69th Inf.		June 16, '64	
O'Rielly, Henry Brooks	Capt.	70th Inf.		May 5, '62	Williamsburg.
Oakley, Sumner	Capt.	77th Inf.	Mar. 25, '65		
O'Donoghue, Joseph	Capt.	88th Inf.	July 3, '62		Malvern Hill.
O'Driscoll, Robert J.	Lieut.	88th Inf.	Oct. 27, '64		
Osborn, Charles W.	Lieut.	95th Inf.		May 6, '64	Wilderness, Va.
Olney, Stephen S.	Lieut.	115th Inf.		Jan. 15, '65	Fort Fisher.
O'Wily, Henry	Capt.	123d Inf.		July 20, '64	P'ch Tree Creek, Ga
Owen, Henry B.	Capt.	126th Inf.		May 12, '64	
Owen, George C.	Lieut.	137th Inf.		Nov. 24, '63	Lookout Mountain.
O'Rorke, Patrick	Col.	140th Inf.		July 2, '63	Gettysburg.
O'Connell, Michael	Lieut.	155th Inf.		Aug. 25, '64	Ream's Station.
Oakley, Stephen C.	Lieut.	162d Inf.	May 28, '63		
O'Sullivan, James A.	Lieut.	164th Inf.		May 18, '64	Spottsylvania.
PRENDERGRAST, R. G.	Capt.	1st Cav.		Nov. 12, '64	Nineveh, Va.
Phillips, William W.	Lieut.	6th Cav.	June 11, '63		
Paige, W. W.	Capt.	10th Cav.		June 22, '64	
Pittman, August	Lieut.	12th Cav.		Mar. 8, '65	Wise's Ford, N. C.
Pitchler, Peter	Lieut.	2d H. Art.	Apl. 5, '65		
Platt, Horton R.	Lieut.	6th H. Art.	May 21, '64		
Porter, Peter A.	Col.	8th H. Art.		June 3, '64	Coal Harbor.
Porsch, Robert	Lieut.	15th H. Art.	Sep. 25, '64		
Perkins, Aug. S.	Capt.	50th Eng.		Dec. 11, '62	Fredericksburg.
Perkins S. Lee	Capt.	2d Inf.	Aug. 31, '62		
Partridge, Wm. T.	Capt.	5th Inf.		June 27, '62	Gaines Mills.
Pabst, Jacob	Lieut.	20th Inf.		Sep. 17, '62	Antietam.
Piersons, Chas. B.	Lieut.	22d Inf.	Sep. 17, '62		Bull Run.
Pawling, Teneyck G.	Lieut.	24th Inf.		Aug. 30, '62	2d Bull Run.
Park, Asa	Lieut.	27th Inf.		July 21, '61	1st Bull Run.
Pross, Frederick	Lieut.	31st Inf.		May 7, '62	West Point.
Paush, Theodore	Lieut.	39th Inf.		July 2, '62	Gettysburg.
Peel, Washington	Lieut.	40th Inf.		Sep. 20, '64	Near Petersburg.
Paxson, James O.	Capt.	48th Inf.	July 31, '63		Fort Wagner.
Plogsted, John F. E.	Capt.	49th Inf.	May 6, '64		Wilderness.
Preston, Reuben M.	Lieut.	49th Inf.		May 6, '64	Wilderness.
Pfantz, Albert	Lieut.	52d Inf.	June 1, '62		
Parison, Philip J.	Lt.-Col.	57th Inf.		Sep. 17, '62	Antietam.
Pon, Paul M.	Lieut.	57th Inf.		Dec. 12, '62	Fredericksburg.
Pohlman, Wm. H.	Lieut.	59th Inf.	July 21, '63		
Plumb, Isaac	Capt.	61st Inf.	June 11, '64		
Parker, Frederick	Lieut.	64th Inf.	Dec. 18, '62		Fredericksburg.
Price, Benjamin	Capt.	70th Inf.		July 23, '63	
Palmer, J. L.	Lieut.	71st Inf.		June 15, '62	Fair Oaks.
Purtell, Michael D.	Capt.	73d Inf.		May 10, '64	Spottsylvania.
Phelan, John	Capt.	73d Inf.		May 12, '64	Spottsylvania.
Preston, Chas. S.	Lieut.	74th Inf.		July 23, '62	Wapping Heights.
Phenis, Barnard	Lieut.	76th Inf.	Aug. 18, '64		Near Petersburg.
Peirce, Stephen H.	Lieut.	77th Inf.		Mar. 25, '65	
Peterson, Peirson B.	Lieut.	78th Inf.	Oct. 27, '62		Antietam.
Pratt, Geo. W.	Col.	80th Inf.	Sep. 11, '62		2d Bull Run.
Porter, Lewis B.	Capt.	81st Inf.	Nov. 15, '64		
Phinney, John	Capt.	86th Inf.	Aug. 10, '64		
Pye, Edward	Col.	95th Inf.	June 12, '64		
Phelps, A. B.	Lieut.	98th Inf.		May 16, '64	Drury's Bluff.
Peach, James L.	Capt.	106th Inf.		Oct. 11, '63	Culpepper, Va.
Parker, Samuel	Capt.	106th Inf.	Oct. 3, '64		Fisher's Hill, Va.
Proseus, Augustus W	Lieut.	111th Inf.		July 3, '63	Gettysburg.
Palmeter, John G.	Capt.	112th Inf.	Aug. 1, '64		
Pierce, Gordon L.	Lieut.	112th Inf.		June 1, '64	
Pruyn, Charles E.	Major	118th Inf.		June 15, '64	
Peisener, Elias	Col.	119th Inf.		May 2, '63	Chancellorsville.
Peirce, Silas E.	Lieut.	121st Inf.	May 13, '64		
Plumb, Wm. H.	Capt.	125th Inf.	Oct. 15, '63		
Palmer, Henry I.	Lieut.	134th Inf.		July 1, '63	Gettysburg.

25

NAME.	RANK.	REGIMENT.	DIED OF WOUNDS.	KILLED.	BATTLE.
Perry, Edgar	Lt.-Col.	139th Inf.		June 3, '64	Coal Harbor.
Poole, Wm. H.	Lieut.	145th Inf.		May 3, '63	Chancellorsville.
Pelouze, Edward	Capt.	155th Inf.		Aug. 25, '64	
Purdy, David	Capt.	155th Inf.	Feb. 22, '65		
Pluuket, Wm. R.	Lieut.	159th Inf.	Apl. 17, '63		
Price, Charles P.	Lieut.	159th Inf.	Apl. 17, '63		
Power, G. A.	Major	173d Inf.	July 9, '63		
Podger, Samuel H.	Lieut.	173d Inf.	June 26, '63		Port Hudson.
Postley, De Van	Lieut.	174th Inf.	July 13, '63		nr. D'n'lds'nville.
Phillips, Augustus	Lieut.	184th Inf.		Oct. 19, '64	Cedar Creek, Va
QUIRK, THOMAS W.	Capt.	83d Inf.		July 1, '63	Gettysburg.
Quay, John	Capt.	125th Inf.		Apl. 2, '65	
REEVES, JAMES E.	Lieut.	8th Cav.	June 12, '63		
Rulison, William H.	Surgeon	9th Cav.		Aug. 29, '64	
Robb, William J.	Lieut.	10th Cav.		June 9, '63	Brandy Station.
Root, Augustus I.	Lt.-Col.	15th Cav.	Apl. 8, '65		
Roff, William H.	Lieut.	2d H. Art.	July 3, '64		
Rasbery, William J.	Lieut.	6th H. Art.		Oct. 19, '64	Cedar Creek, Va
Read, John B.	Lieut.	7th H. Art.		June 3, '64	Coal Harbor.
Rector, Jr., George W.	Lieut.	8th H. Art.	Oct. 29, '64		Hatcher's Run, '
Rieman, Adolph	Lieut.	15th H. Art.	Feb 8, '65.	Feb. 8, '65	
Reed, James	Lieut.	17th Inf.		Aug. 30, '62	2d Bull Run.
Rogers, Theodore C.	Capt.	18th Inf.		June 27, '62	Gaines Mills, Vn.
Russell, John H.	Lieut.	18th Inf.	July 28, '62		Gaines Mills, Va.
Roth, Louis	Lieut.	20th Inf.	Sep. 18, '62		Antietam.
Rice, Philip	Lieut.	30th Inf.		Aug. 29, '62	2d Bull Run.
Rossiter, Charles D.	Lieut.	33d Inf.	May 4, '63		Fredericksburg.
Rich, Theodore F.	Capt.	39th Inf.		Aug. 25, '64	Ream's Station.
Reynolds, Edward	Capt.	59th Inf.	Dec. 24, '62		Fredericksburg.
Roosa, Stephen C.	Lieut.	59th Inf.	Sep. 20, '62		Antietam.
Riker, John L.	Col.	62d Inf.		May 31, '62	Fair Oaks.
Rysdyk, George F.	Lieut.	67th Inf.		May 31, '62	Fair Oaks.
Reynolds, Thomas	Lieut.	69th Inf.		July 1, '62	Malvern Hill.
Rugg, Orrin P.	Capt.	77th Inf.		May 12, '64	Spottsylvania.
Rix, Daniel C.	Capt.	81st Inf.		Sep. 29, '64	Nr Fortress Mun
Reynolds, Charles M.	Lieut.	83d Inf.		May 8, '64	
Rae, William C.	Lieut.	84th Inf.		May 10, '64	
Ryder, Patrick	Capt.	88th Inf.		May 5, '64	Wilderness.
Rogers, Lyman A.	Capt.	98th Inf.	July 10, '64		Coal Harbor.
Ransom, Charles M.	Lieut.	98th Inf.	July 14, '64		Coal Harbor.
Richardson, William	Capt.	100th Inf.	June 27, '64		Deep Bottom, Va
Runckle, Charles H.	Lieut.	100th Inf.		July 18, '63	Morris Island, S.
Ringold, Benjamin	Col.	103d Inf.	May 3, '63		Chancellorsville.
Rudd, John P.	Lieut.	104th Inf.		Aug. 30, '62	2d Bull Run.
Rutter, Nathaniel E.	Capt.	107th Inf.		May 1, '63	Chancellorsville.
Randall, Valorus	Lieut.	110th Inf.		June 14, '63	Port Hudson.
Reynolds, Michael	Lieut.	118th Inf.		June 2, '64	Coal Harbor.
Ryan, George	Col.	140th Inf.		May 8, '64	
Ransom, John D.	Capt.	142d Inf.	Nov. 10, '64		
Ratcliff, Wm. M.	Lieut.	143d Inf.		July 20, '64	P'ch Tree Creek,
Randall, Charles B.	Lt.-Col.	149th Inf.		July 20, '64	P'ch Tree Creek,
Reilly, Edward	Lieut.	158th Inf.		Apl. 2, '65	Fort Gregg, Va.
Richmond, Duncan	Capt.	150th Inf.	Oct. 19, '64		
Reddy, James M.	Lieut.	164th Inf.		June 3, '64	Coal Harbor.
Ryan, Michael	Lieut.	169th Inf.		Jan. 15, '65	Fort Fisher.
Redmond, Michael W.	Lieut.	182d Inf.		Jan. 22, '64	
Rice, Burrage	Capt.	189th Inf.		Jan. 11, '65	Petersburg.
SAVACOAL, EDWIN F.	Capt.	1st Cav.	June 3, '65		Sailor's Run, Va
Sullivan, Jerry A.	Major	1st V. Cav.		May 10, '64	Cabletown, Va.
Smith, Herman E.	Lieut.	3d Cav.		Oct. 7, '64	
Saunders, F. J.	Lieut.	6th Cav.	Dec. 15, '64		Winchester, Va.
Sayles, James A.	Capt.	8th Cav.		June 23, '64	Nottaway C. H.,

IN THE WAR OF THE REBELLION.

NAME.	RANK.	REGIMENT.	DIED OF WOUNDS.	KILLED.	BATTLE.
Sackett, William	Col.	9th Cav.	June 10, '64		Trevellean St'n, Va.
Schlick, Theodore	Major	22d Cav.		Aug. 25, '64	Kearneysville, Va.
Simons, Geo. W.	Capt.	24th Cav.	Sep. 4, '64		
Springsteed, Edward A.	Major	7th H. Art.		Aug. 25 '64	Ream's Station.
Stone, David H.	Lieut.	9th H. Art.		Jan. 14, '64	Petersburg.
Schamberger, Leander	Major	15th H. Art.	May 27, '64		
Stoeckner, Francis	Capt.	15th H. Art.		June 22, '64	
Southard, Henry D.	Capt.	1st Eng.	June 3, '64		Bermuda Hundred.
Sovereign, Frederick W.	Lieut.	5th Inf.		Aug. 30, '62	Manassas Plains.
Sievoight, Carl	Lieut.	7th Inf.		Dec. 13, '62	Fredericksburg.
Sick, Emil	Lieut.	7th Inf.		Oct. 27, '64	Fort Sedgwick, Va.
Savage, Charles H.	Capt.	13th Inf.		Aug. 30, '62	2d Bull Run.
Skillen, Charles H.	Lt.-Col.	14th Inf.		June 27, '62	Gaines Mills, Va.
Sprout, Charles P.	Lieut.	28th Inf.		Aug. 9, '62	Cedar Mountain.
Sullivan, Wm. O.	Capt.	40th Inf.		Dec. 13, '62	Fredericksburg.
Stephens, Wm. R.	Lieut.	40th Inf.		Dec. 13, '62	Fredericksburg.
Shuter, James	Lieut.	40th Inf.		June 16, '64	Petersburg.
Sehrt, Ferdinand	Lieut.	46th Inf.		June 16, '62	
Shenk, Otto	Surgeon	46th Inf.	Aug. 21, '64		
Scott, James	Capt.	47th Inf.		Feb. 11, '65	Fort Fisher.
Smith, John A.	Lieut.	47th Inf.		May 7, '64	
Schlondorf, Geo. L.	Lieut.	47th Inf.		May 7, '64	
Swartwout, Samuel M.	Major	48th Inf.		July 30, '64	Near Petersburg.
Sears, Henry H.	Lieut.	48th Inf.	Aug. 16, '64		Deep Bottom, Va.
Sims, Samuel H.	Capt.	51st Inf.		July 30, '64	Petersburg, Va.
Sringweiler, Chas. F.	Lieut.	51st Inf.		Sep. 14, '62	South Mountain.
Scherrer, William	Capt.	52d Inf.	May 26, '64		
Schreiber, Paul	Lieut.	52d Inf.		Mar. 31, '65	Hatcher's Run.
Stoldt, Gustave	Capt.	58th Inf.	July 20, '63		
Stetson, John L.	Lt.-Col.	59th Inf.		Sep. 17, '62	Antietam.
Smurr, William H.	Lieut.	59th Inf.		Sep. 17, '62	Antietam.
Seymour, Hannibal	Lieut.	59th Inf.	Dec. 12, '62		Fredericksburg.
Stanley, Myron D.	Lieut.	60th Inf.	July 7, '63		Gettysburg.
Sullivan, John	Capt.	63d Inf.	Dec. 15, 62		Fredericksburg.
Smart, James M.	Lieut.	62d Inf.		May 12, '64	Spottsylvania.
Smith, Cadwalader	Lieut.	63d Inf.		Sep. 17, '62	Antietam.
Smith, Harrison T.	Capt.	64th Inf.		Mar. 25, '05	
Sullivan, Daniel R.	Capt.	67th Inf.	June 26, '62		Fair Oaks.
Shanley, Timothy L.	Capt.	69th Inf.	Oct. 1, '62		Antietam.
Stevens, William O.	Col.	72d Inf.		May 3, '63	Chancellorsville.
Shine, Eugene C.	Capt.	73d Inf.		July 2, '63	Gettysburg.
Short, James	Lieut.	74th Inf.		July 23, '63	
Story, Robert	Capt.	76th Inf.	Aug. 6, '63		Gettysburg.
Swarthout, Martin H.	Lieut.	80th Inf.		Sep. 17, '62	Antietam.
Salter, Theodore R.	Lieut.	84th Inf.		July 21, '61	Bull Run.
Scholes, Clayton	Lieut.	84th Inf.		July 21, '61	Bull Run.
Stafford, Michael B.	Lt.-Col.	86th Inf.	Dec. 1, '64		
Stone, Samuel F.	Capt.	86th Inf.		May 10, '64	Spottsylvania.
Stanton, Amos B.	Lieut.	86th Inf.		June 18, '64	Petersburg.
Sparks, John	Lieut.	88th Inf.	May 5, '64		
Smart, John C.	Major	90th Inf.		Oct. 19, '64	Cedar Creek.
Shephard, Sylvester B.	Lieut.	91st Inf.		June 14, '63	
South, Joseph	Lieut.	96th Inf.		June 3, '64	Coal Harbor, Va.
Stiles, James H.	Lieut.	97th Inf.		July 1, '63	Gettysburg.
Spring, Julius	Capt.	102d Inf.		July 9, '62	
Sand, Henry A.	Capt.	103d Inf.	Oct. 31, '62		Antietam.
Sheppard, Charles W.	Lieut.	106th Inf.		June 1, '64	Coal Harbor.
Snedaker, James W.	Lieut.	111th Inf.		May 5, '64	Wilderness.
Smith, John F.	Col.	112th Inf.	Jan. 18, '65		
Sherwin, Samuel G.	Lieut.	112th Inf.		June 28, '64	
Smith, Elisha B.	Col.	114th Inf.	June 19, '63		Port Hudson.
Sheffer, Levi	Lieut.	115th Inf.		Feb. 20, '64	Olustee.
Stone, J. Parsons	Capt.	117th Inf.		June 17, '64	Petersburg.
Stone, John S.	Capt.	118th Inf.		May 16, '64	Drury's Bluff, Va.
Stevenson, Wm. H.	Lieut.	118th Inf.		May 16, '64	Drury's Bluff, Va.

NAME.	RANK.	REGIMENT.	DIED OF WOUNDS.	KILLED.	BATTLE.
Sims, John V.	Lieut.	122d Inf.		Sep. 19, '64	Near Winch'st'r,
Sherrill, Eliakim	Col.	126th Inf.		July 3, '63	Gettysburg.
Sherman, Jacob	Lieut.	126th Inf.	July 26, '63		Gettysburg.
Sherman, Geo. A.	Lieut.	126th Inf.		May 12, '64	
Shimer, Isaac	Capt.	126th Inf.		July 3, '63	Gettysburg.
Stanton, Martin V.	Lieut.	126th Inf.	June 18, '64		
Swift, John W.	Capt.	139th Inf.		Sep. 29, '64	Chapin's Farm, V
Starks, Milo L.	Major	140th Inf.		May 8, '64	
Schenck, Wm. P.	Lieut.	147th Inf.	July 27, '63		Gettysburg.
Scott, Reuben F.	Lieut.	148th Inf.	June 5, '64		Coal Harbor, Va.
Sleight, David B.	Lieut.	150th Inf.		Mar. 16, '65	
Schoen, John C.	Capt.	151st Inf.		June 3, '64	Coal Harbor.
Schuyler, Wm. S.	Capt.	155th Inf.	July 20, '64		
Smith, Herman	Lieut.	159th Inf.	Oct. 14, '64		
Scudder, Theodore A.		162d Inf.		Apl. 19, '64	
Smith, Jr., Abel	Lt.-Col.	165th Inf.	June 23, '63		
Seely, Francis H.	Lieut.	170th Inf.	June 22, '64		
Shea, Morgan	Lieut.	173d Inf.		June 14, '63	Port Hudson.
Strong, Richard M.	Lieut.	177th Inf.	May 12, '63		
Sloan, John Barnet	Major	179th Inf.		June 17, '64	Petersburg.
Saxton, Baker L.	Lieut.	179th Inf.		June 30, '64	Petersburg.
Sweeney, Daniel.	Lieut.	182d Inf.		Aug. 25, '64	Ream's Station.
TAYLOR, RICHARD S.	Lieut.	8th Cav.		May 14, '64	
Tremain, Frederick	Lt.-Col.	10th Cav.	Feb. 8, '65		Hatcher's Run, V
Taylor, Rowley P.	Capt.	19th Cav.		June 30, '63	Deserted Farm.
Thorp, Alexander K.	Capt.	19th Cav.	Sept. 19, '64		Winchester, Va.
Turkington, Joseph	Capt.	5th Inf.	Apl. 6, '65		
Thomas, Gorton T.	Lt.-Col.	22d Inf.	Sep. 7, '62		2d Bull Run.
Thompson, Thomas P.	Lieut.	25th Inf.		May 27, '62	Hanover C. H.
Twaddle, James T.	Lieut.	32d Inf.	July 5, '62		
Tilden, Oliver A.	Capt.	38th Inf.		Sep. 1, '62	Chantilly.
Thomas, Benjamin N.	Lieut.	44th Inf.	July 6, '63		
Tantum, John M.	Lieut.	48th Inf.		Aug. 16, '64	Strawberry Pl's, V
Terry, Seward H.	Capt.	49th Inf.		May 12, '64	Spottsylvania.
Tyler, Mortimer L. V.	Lieut.	49th Inf.		May 12, '64	Spottsylvania.
Throop, N. Garron	Major	57th Inf.	Jan. 12, '63		Fredericksburg.
Thoman, Max A.	Lt.-Col.	59th Inf.	July 11, '63		
Trenor, James J.	Capt.	61st Inf.		June 1, '62	Fair Oaks, Va.
Touley, Thomas	Major	63d Inf.	May 30, '64		Wilderness, Va.
Thurber, Ira S.	Lieut.	64th Inf.		July 2, '63	Gettysburg.
Thomas, Gilbert F.	Lieut.	77th Inf.		Oct. 19, '64	N'r Middletown, V
Tabor, Wm. J.	Lieut.	77th Inf.		Oct. 19, '64	N'r Middletown, V
Tuttle, Squire M.	Lieut.	81st Inf.	Sep. 30, '64		
Tremain, F. W.	Major	89th Inf.		Apl. 2, '65	Near Petersburg.
Tenbroeck, Chas. R.	Lieut.	101st Inf.	Sep. 4, '62		
Townsend, Charles	Lieut.	106th Inf.		June 1, '64	Coal Harbor.
Thrasher, Byron P.	Capt.	108th Inf.	May 30, '63		
Tarbox, David	Lieut.	108th Inf.		Sep. 17, '62	Antietam.
Tucker, Charles E.	Capt.	114th Inf.		June 14, '63	Port Hudson.
Tompkins, Wm.	Lieut.	115th Inf.		Feb. 20, '64	Olustee, Fla.
Tuttle, David W.	Capt.	116th Inf.		July 13, '63	Donaldsonville, L
Thomas, John F.	Capt.	117th Inf.		Jan. 15, '65	Fort Fisher.
Tucker, William H.	Lieut.	121st Inf.		Oct. 19, '64	Cedar Creek, Va.
Timolat, Henry M.	Lieut.	131st Inf.	Sep. 11, '64		
Tresser, Charles F.	Lieut.	136th Inf.	Dec. 16, '63		Chattanooga, Ten
Taft, Joseph B.	Lt.-Col.	143d Inf.		Nov. 25, '63	Chattanooga. Ten
Taylor, Sylvester J.	Lieut.	147th Inf.		July 3, '64	
UNDERHILL, JR. NIMROD	Capt.	14th H. Art.		June 23, '64	Petersburg.
Upham, J. V	Lieut.	102d Inf.		July 2, '63	Gettysburg.
VERMILYEA, ISAAC D.	Lieut.	1st Cav.		June 5, '64	Piedmont, Va.
Van Valkenburgh, D. H.	Major	1st L. Art.		May 31, 62	Fair Oaks, Va.
Vaughn, Henry D.	Lieut.	L. Art.		Oct. 19, '64	N'r Middletown, V

NAME.	RANK.	REGIMENT.	DIED OF WOUNDS.	KILLED.	BATTLE.
Von Buchenhagen, B.	Lieut.	7th Inf.	Jan. 1, '63		Fredericksburg.
Von Apel, August	Lieut.	7th Inf.	Dec. 11, '62		Fredericksburg.
Voelker, Charles	Lieut.	20th Inf.	Sep. 17, '62		Antietam.
Vanderpool, Barrett	Lieut.	40th Inf.	Sep. 3, '62		
Visscher, James D.	Lt.-Col.	43d Inf.		July 12, '64	
Valentine, Henry C.	Lieut.	49th Inf.		May 6, '64	
Venuti, Edward	Major	52d Inf.		July 2, '63	Near Gettysburg.
Von Arno, Walter	Capt.	52d Inf.	May 16, '64		
Von Steuben, Otto	Lieut.	52d Inf.		May 12, '64	Spottsylvania, Va.
Vansteinberg, Benj. V.	Lieut.	59th Inf.	Sep. 22, '62		Antietam.
Van Ingen, Gerritt	Lieut.	89th Inf.	Sep. 26. '62		Antietam.
Vigean, Paul	Lieut.	96th Inf.		June 3, '64	Coal Harbor, Va.
Vandeveer, Garrett	Capt.	115th Inf.	Feb. 24, '64		Olustee, Fla.
Van De Sande, John	Lieut.	115th Inf.	Sep. 3, '64		Deep Bottom, Va.
Van Emburgh, John H.	Lieut.	137th Inf.		July 2, '63	Gettysburg.
Van Dusen, David G.	Lieut.	147th Inf.		July 1, '63	Gettysburg.
Van Dusen, Wm. J.	Capt.	160th Inf.		Apl. 9, '64	Pleasant Hill, La.
Vaughn, A. D.	Capt.	169th Inf.		July 30, '64	Petersburg, Va.
WALTER, JOSEPH	Lieut.	1st Cav.	Apl. 19, '65		
Walters, Charles C.	Capt.	2d Cav.		Aug. 18, '62	Rapidan Stat'n, Va.
Whittaker, Daniel	Lieut.	2d Cav.		June 17, '63	Aldie, Va.
Westinghouse, Albert	Lieut.	2d V. Cav.		Dec. 10, '64	
Williams, Wm. F.	Capt.	2d Mt Rifles	June 19, '64		Near Petersburg.
Wood, Oliver S.	Lieut.	4th Cav.		June 12, '64	Quinlian Station.
Wheelan, William	Lieut.	7th Cav.	Oct. 26, '62		At Blackwater.
Williams, Chas. P.	Lieut.	24th Cav.	Apl. 10, '65		
Wright, Nathaniel	Capt.	7th H. Art.		Aug. 25, '64	Ream's Station.
West, Charles H.	Lieut.	8th H. Art.		Aug. 25, '64	Ream's Station.
Wright, Walter P.	Lieut.	8th H. Art.		June 16, '64	Petersburg.
Wildt, Edward A.	Lieut.	L. Art.		Nov. 20, '64	Honey Hill, S. C.
Wheeler, William	Capt.	L. Art.		June 22, '64	Marietta, Ga.
Wicks, J. M.	Capt.	3d Inf.	Oct. 27, '64		
Wright, Edward O.	Lieut.	5th Inf.	Aug. 30, '62		Manassas Plains.
Winthrop, Frederick	Col.	5th Inf.		Apr. 1, '65	Five Forks, Va.
Winslow, Cleveland	Lt.-Col.	5th Inf.	July 7, '64		Bethesda Ch'r'h, Va
Woods, William S.	Capt.	5th Inf.		Aug. 19, '64	
Weinberg, Constantine	Lieut.	5th Inf.		June 2. '64	
Winter, Andrew	Lieut.	7th Inf.		Dec. 13, '62	Fredericksburg.
Winchester, Salmon	Capt.	10th Inf.	Dec. 16, '62		
Wilson, Andrew	Capt.	17th Inf.	Sep. 18, '62		
Wilson, Geo. S.	Lieut.	17th Inf.	Feb. 7, '63		
Washburn, Jeremiah P.	Capt.	21st Inf.		Aug. 30, '62	2d Bull Run.
Whitney, Wm. L.	Lieut.	21st Inf.		Aug. 30, '62	Bull Run.
Webster, Joseph	Lieut.	27th Inf.	July 22, '62		Gaines Mills.
Whittock, Henry	Capt.	31st Inf.		June 27, '62	Gaines Mills.
Wallace, Edmond	Lieut.	32d Inf.		May 7, '62	West Point.
Wright, Louis R.	Lieut.	32d Inf.		Sep. 14, '62	Crampton's Pass.
Walcot, Harrison T.	Capt.	40th Inf.		May 5, '64	Wilderness.
Wilson, John	Lt.-Col.	43d Inf.	May 7, '64		
Wallace, William	Capt.	43d Inf.		May 6, '64	Wilderness.
Wiggins, Wm. T.	Capt.	49th Inf.		May 5, '64	Wilderness.
Wolf, Louis	Lieut.	52d Inf.		Oct. 21, '64	Near Petersburg.
Walsh, Eugene	Lieut.	52d Inf.	June 15, '64		
Williams, Wm. J.	Capt.	56th Inf.		May 31, '62	Fair Oaks.
Wright, Augustus M.	Capt.	57th Inf.	July 2, '64		Near Petersburg.
Whitney, Chas. H.	Capt.	59th Inf.		Sep. 17, '62	Antietam.
Wade, Edward H.	Capt.	59th Inf.	Oct. 5, '62		Antietam.
Wright, Eugene M.	Lieut.	59th Inf.		May 12, '64	Spottsylvania C. H.
Wilson, John E.	Lieut.	60th Inf.		June 18, '64	Near Golgotha, Ga.
Wiggins, David T.	Lieut.	64th Inf.		May 12, '64	Spottsylvania, C. H.
Wehle, Julius	Capt.	66th Inf.		Dec. 15, '62	Fredericksburg.
Williams, Charles	Lieut.	69th Inf.		Sep. 17, '62	Antietam.
Willard, Darwin	Capt.	72d Inf.		May 5, '62	Williamsburg.
Whiteside, James E.	Lieut.	75th Inf.		Jan. 14, '63	Bayou Teche. La.

390   THE HONORS OF THE EMPIRE STATE

NAME.	RANK.	REGIMENT.	DIED OF WOUNDS.	KILLED.	BATTLE.
Williams, Richard	Lieut.	76th Inf.		Aug. 29, '62	2d Bull Run.
Weldon, Thomas F.	Lieut.	76th Inf.		Aug. 26, '64	
Wheeler, Luther M.	Capt.	77th Inf.		May 3, '63	Chancellorsville.
Ward, Peletiah	Capt.	80th Inf.	Sep. 3, '62		2d Bull Run.
Warner, John N.	Capt.	86th Inf.		July 2, '63	Gettysburg.
Woodward, W. J. M.	Lieut.	94th Inf.	Sep. 15, '62		
Woodrow, Stark A.	Lieut.	95th Inf.		May 1, '64	
Wead, Frederick F.	Col.	98th Inf.		June 3, '64	Coal Harbor.
Wilkeson, Jr, John	Lieut.	100th Inf.		May 31, '62	Fair Oaks.
Warwick, William	Capt.	109th Inf.		June 17, '64	Near Petersburg
Wood, Almon A.	Lieut.	110th Inf.	May 26, '63		
Williams, J. Knox	Lieut.	117th Inf.	Sep. 30, '64		
Wendell, Nelson O.	Capt.	121st Inf.		May 3, '63	Chancellorsville.
Wooster, Frank M.	Lieut.	122d Inf.		June 1, '64	Coal Harbor.
Wilson, Martin L.	Lieut.	122d Inf.	June 10, '64		Wilderness.
Weer, Norman F.	Capt.	123d Inf.	July 26, '63		Gettysburg.
Willard, Geo. L.	Col.	125th Inf.		July 2, '63	Gettysburg.
Wood, Ephraim	Capt.	125th Inf.		July 3, '63	Gettysburg.
Wheeler, Chas. M.	Capt.	126th Inf.		July 3, '63	Gettysburg.
Williams, Oscar C.	Capt.	137th Inf.		July 3, '63	Gettysburg.
Warren, Theodore M.	Lieut.	141st Inf.		July 20, '64	P'ch Tree Cr'k,
Waterbury, Peter L.	Lieut.	143d Inf.	July 24, '64		P'ch Tree Cr'k,
Wilson, Thomas A.	Capt.	146th Inf.	Apl. 25, '65		Five Forks, Va.
Wilcox, Sylvanus S.	Capt.	151st Inf.		Nov. 27, '63	Locust Grove, V
Watters, Charles	Lieut.	164th Inf.		May 18, '64	Spottsylvania.
Williamson, James	Lieut.	177th Inf.		May 27, '63	Port Hudson.
Welpley, Francis	Capt.	182d Inf.		Aug. 25, '64	Ream's Station.
YEARSLEY, CHARLES L.	Lieut.	7th H. Art.		June 16, '64	Petersburg.
Yardley, James M.	Lieut.	10th Inf.		Dec. 13, '62	Fredericksburg.
Young, Elisha S.	Capt.	32d Inf.		May 7, '62	West Point.
Young, John R.	Lieut.	88th Inf.		Dec. 13, '62	Fredericksburg.
ZOLLER, JONAS	Lieut.	2d H. Art.	Feb. 16, '65		
Zenette, Arnold	Lieut.	132d Inf.		Feb. 1, '64	Bachelors Cr'k N

DIED OF DISEASE AND OTHER CAUSES.

NAME.	RANK.	REGIMENT.	DATE.
ARTHERLY, JOSEPH B.	Surgeon	22d Infantry	August 12th, 1862
Ayer, James	Captain	116th Infantry	May 22d, 1863
Aldrich, Daniel N.	Captain	141st Infantry	August 11th, 1863
BENEDICT, JAMES A.	Lieutenant	5th Cavalry	December 11th, 1861
Boudinot, Frank	Lieutenant	7th Cavalry	May 2d, 1864
Brown, John Q.	Captain	9th Cavalry	May 11th, 1864
Bly, Jerry	Lieutenant	9th Cavalry	May 17th, 1864
Burrows, James B.	Lieutenant	9th Cavalry	August 25th, 1864
Baker, Rollin T.	Surgeon	12th Cavalry	October 19th, 1864
Baker, Lewis F.	Surgeon	6th H. Art.	September 6th, 1864
Bell, Matthew	Lieutenant	7th H. Art.	April 12th, 1864
Bickford, William H.	Lieutenant	6th H. Art.	March 9th, 1865
Beach, Alexander J.	Captain	13th H. Art.	August 10th, 1864
Bundy, William	Lieutenant	15th H. Art.	April 26th, 1864
Burt, William J.	Lieutenant	Light Artillery	April 18th, 1864
Bradley, Thomas S.	Captain	1st Bat. Sh'psh't	June 28th, 1863
Backus, Frederick W.	Lieutenant	17th Infantry	August 10th, 1862
Beischeim, Theodore	Lieutenant	41st Infantry	March 6th, 1864
Bullymore, William	Lieutenant	49th Infantry	May – 1862

NAME.	RANK.	REGIMENT.	DATE.
Benton, Orlando N.	Chaplain	51st Infantry	March 15th, 1862
Barstow, Samuel	Captain	64th Infantry	April 20th, 1862
Berry, John	Captain	65th Infantry	May 10th 1864
Bogert, A. S.	Lieutenant	65th Infantry	June 2d, 1862
Bowe, Halsey	Lieutenant	77th Infantry	August 11th, 1862
Berry, D. Clinton	Captain	82d Infantry	May 15th, 1862
Brownson, Amos	Lieutenant	85th Infantry	May 24th, 1862
Bennett, James	Captain	86th Infantry	August 25th, 1862
Brennan, Francis T.	Lieutenant	97th Infantry	May 6th, 1864
Brannigan, Patrick R.	Surgeon	99th Infantry	October 5th, 1864
Brandt, William	Captain	103d Infantry	November 7th, 1862
Baldwin, Lathrop	Major	107th Infantry	July 30th, 1864
Bradley, James H.	Lieutenant	131st Infantry	October 2d, 1864
Brown, Hiram P.	Lieutenant	148th Infantry	October 8th, 1863
Badger John W.	Lieutenant	154th Infantry	June 2d, 1863
Bradley, Wesley W.	Lieutenant	159th Infantry	May 10th, 1863
Brown, Samuel H.	Surgeon	174th Infantry	July 31st, 1863
COYLE, THOMAS	Captain	5th Cavalry	Nov. 24th, 1861
Crafts, William C.	Lieutenant	8th Cavalry	August 29th, 1863
Corrigan, A. McQ.	Major	9th Cavalry	May 28th, 1864
Cobb, Lyman G.	Lieutenant	9th Cavalry	September 6th, 1862
Cole, Daniel	Lieutenant	4th H. Art.	December 27th, 1863
Cornwall, Selah	Captain	9th H. Art.	November 1st, 1862
Cooper, Dealton W.	Lieutenant	10th H. Art.	August 5th, 1864
Cozzens, Henry H.	Lieutenant	Light Artillery	February 18th, 1864
Cassin, Walter S.	Major	15th Engineers	October 8th, 1863
Campbell, John C.	Captain	1st Infantry	May 7th, 1863
Cooper, Marmaduke	Lieutenant	3d Infantry	November 15th, 1862
Clark, Martin C.	Captain	23d Infantry	May 13th, 1863
Coan, William H.	Lieutenant	27th Infantry	September 11th, 1862
Casey, Philip	Lieutenant	30th Infantry	October 24th, 1861
Conkling, William T.	Lieutenant	30th Infantry	November 28th, 1861
Carr, Joseph R.	Lieutenant	31th Infantry	October 4th, 1861
Clark, Johnson	Surgeon	99th Infantry	December 8th, 1861
Cross, William R.	Lieutenant	104th Infantry	March 3d, 1862
Coltier, E. B.	Lieutenant	116th Infantry	August 21st, 1863
Cockburn, William J.	Lieutenant	120th Infantry	July 22d, 1862
Collier, Henry A.	Surgeon	120th Infantry	January 23d, 1863
Cameron, Angus	Lieutenant	121st Infantry	November 9th, 1862
Clapp, Alonzo H.	Major	122d Infantry	June 23d, 1865
Cressy, Charles T.	Lieutenant	124th Infantry	July 14th, 1864
Cooper, Cornelius A.	Captain	127th Infantry	November 26th, 1862
Callahan, Alexander	Lieutenant	139th Infantry	September 14th, 1863
Cooke, Howard	Captain	156th Infantry	March 19th, 1864
DWYER, R. O.	Chaplain	2d Vet. Cavalry	June 30th, 1864
De Forest, Othneil	Colonel	5th Cavalry	Dec. 16th, 1864
Disosway, William W.	Lieutenant	7th Cavalry	October 13th, 1863
De Camp, John	Lieutenant	14th Cavalry	July 26th, 1864
Dalrymple, Theodore	Lieutenant	24th Infantry	April 21st, 1862
Daniel, Robert R.	Major	31st Infantry	April 13th, 1863
Dickinson, Raselas	Captain	49th Infantry	October 10th, 1861
Deitrich, Louis	Lieutenant	58th Infantry	July 2d, 1863
Deming, Eugene M.	Captain	61st Infantry	July 1st, 1862
Davis, Benton H.	Captain	66th Infantry	July 2d, 1864
Dimock, J. J.	Major	82d Infantry	June 22d, 1862
Day, Joseph B.	Lieutenant	82d Infantry	July 21st, 1863
Davis, Edward F.	Lieutenant	85th Infantry	April 10th, 1862
Dutton, William	Colonel	98th Infantry	July 4th, 1862
Dudley, William L	Lieutenant	103d Infantry	August 5th 1862
Donnelly, George G.	Lieutenant	114th Infantry	April 27th, 1863
Davis, George W.	Lieutenant	121st Infantry	October 20th, 1862
Davis, Amos F.	Captain	136th Infantry	November 4th, 1862

NAME.	RANK.	REGIMENT.	DATE.
Dalzell, William	Lieutenant	142d Infantry	August 24th, 1863
Davis, John	Lieutenant	155th Infantry	October 16th, 1864
Donaldson, John	Captain	156th Infantry	September 19th, 1863
Dunbar, Walter O.	Captain	157th Infantry	March 17th, 1863
Dunn, John	Lieutenant	164th Infantry	September 29th, 1863
EDWARDS, GEORGE	Captain	1st Engineers	November 22d, 1864
Ennis, William H.	Lieutenant	9th Infantry	August – 1862
Ellsworth, E. Elmer	Colonel	11th Infantry	May 24th, 1861
Eastman, Henry C.	Lieutenant	60th Infantry	March 8th, 1862
Emnett, Temple	Lieutenant	68th Infantry	August 9th, 1862
Eminett, Richard	Lieutenant	68th Infantry	February 2d, 1863
Elmore, Taylor	Surgeon	137th Infantry	May 25th, 1864
Egbert, Eugene	Lieutenant	141st Infantry	December 18th, 1864
Ellsworth, Asher M.	Lieutenant	165th Infantry	August 14th, 1863
FARR, THOMAS S.	Captain	8th Cavalry	October – 1864
Flower, Byron L.	Surgeon	9th H. Art.	October 24th, 1863
Fullerton, Stephen W.	Captain	3d Infantry	September 11th, 1861
Faxon, Daniel E.	Lieutenant	36th Infantry	June 19th, 1862
Farr, George W.	Lieutenant	36th Infantry	May 17th, 1862
Foye, Michael E.	Surgeon	38th Infantry	June 9th, 1861
Fancher, William	Captain	64th Infantry	May 24th, 1862
Forsher, John M.	Surgeon	66th Infantry	October 25th, 1862
Feeney, John	Captain	73d Infantry	May 24th, 1864
Fox, Charles	Lieutenant	92d Infantry	July 12th, 1862
Farnum, Charles S.	Lieutenant	100th Infantry	May 12th, 1862
Fraser, Marcus	Lieutenant	143d Infantry	November 20th, 1862
Flirt, Henry C.	Lieutenant	147th Infantry	November 4th, 1862
Faucett, Richard W.	Surgeon	155th Infantry	June 22d, 1864
Fowler, Thomas	Lt.-Col.	156th Infantry	July 1st, 1863
GREY, W. C. B.	Lieutenant	4th H. Art.	January 1st, 1863
Gilleo, Richard M.	Lieutenant	6th H. Art.	March 27th, 1863
Gunn, George	Captain	1st Engineers	January 21st, 1862
Gilbert, Edwin S.	Lt.-Col.	25th Infantry	February 22d, 1863
Gleason, Shepard	Major	25th Infantry	June 17th, 1863
Gaul, Charles L.	Lieutenant	27th Infantry	August 20th, 1862
Griswold, Stephen	Surgeon	38th Infantry	December 31st, 1861
Gilder, Sr., William H.	Chaplain	40th Infantry	April 13th, 1864
Grimm, Louis	Lieutenant	62d Infantry	January 30th, 1864
Griffith Walter L.	Lieutenant	90th Infantry	October 1st, 1862
Gardner, Chauncey	Lieutenant	110th Infantry	June 23d, 1864
Gilbert, James E.	Lieutenant	114th Infantry	February 16th, 1863
Gifford, Edward	Captain	128th Infantry	August 8th, 1863
Goewey, John T.	Lieutenant	170th Infantry	May 18th, 1865
HARMORICIER, CHARLES	Lieutenant	1st Cavalry	October 8th, 1861
Hathaway, Henry C.	Lieutenant	12th Cavalry	October 3d, 1864
Hatch, Jeremiah	Captain	19th Cavalry	December 21st, 1862
Harris, Henry G.	Lieutenant	4th H. Art.	September 10th, 1862
Hazen, Charles F.	Lieutenant	6th H. Art.	May 2d, 1863
Hyatt, George D.	Lieutenant	6th H. Art.	July 26th, 1864
Hodgkins, Thomas	Lieutenant	1st Light Artillery	January 25th, 1863
Hillis, David D.	Lieutenant	3d Artillery	September 24th, 1864
Hochheim, Lewis	Captain	7th Infantry	July 13th, 1861
Holt, James	Lieutenant	11th Infantry	—— 1862
Holbrook, Joseph	Lieutenant	16th Infantry	August 28th, 1861
Hart, R. Stewart	Lieutenant	17th Infantry	June 24th, 1861
Hayward, Elisha L.	Captain	21st Infantry	September 9th, 1862
Hank, Ludwig	Lieutenant	20th Infantry	January 28th, 1862
Halsey, Charles E.	Surgeon	40th Infantry	August 30th, 1862
Hogan, Guy	Lieutenant	60th Infantry	August 4th, 1862
Hinman, Richard H.	Surgeon	67th Infantry	May 22d, 1862

NAME.	RANK.	REGIMENT.	DATE.
Howard, Orville C.	Captain	71st Infantry	September 20th, 1861
Higgin, Martin E.	Lieutenant	73d Infantry	July 9th, 1863
Hendricks, James T.	Captain	80th Infantry	September 17th, 1862
Hannahs, Franklin F.	Captain	81st Infantry	August 9th, 1862
Hinds, John M.	Lieutenant	82d Infantry	June 30th, 1863
Hill, William R.	Lieutenant	90th Infantry	October 7th, 1862
Hulbert, Henry S.	Captain	91st Infantry	June 14th, 1863
Helleday, Gustave B.	Lt.-Col.	99th Infantry	August 19th, 1862
Hopkins, James	Lieutenant	106th Infantry	February 22d, 1863
Hull, Egbert B.	Lieutenant	125th Infantry	June – 1864
Hopkins, James A. P.	Lt.-Col.	133d Infantry	November 19th, 1864
Hunter, C. T.	Lieutenant	134th Infantry	March 11th, 1864
Hall, William C.	Lieutenant	136th Infantry	May 27th, 1864
Hine, Franklin T.	Lieutenant	144th Infantry	December 20th, 1864
Huke, George D.	Lieutenant	148th Infantry	November 5th, 1863
Hinds, Josiah	Lieutenant	152d Infantry	August 7th, 1864
Haven, Samuel C.	Lieutenant	162d Infantry	June 25th, 1863
Hermion, George W.	Lieutenant	168th Infantry	September 21st, 1863
Hayes, Mathias	Lieutenant	175th Infantry	October 16th, 1863
Hoyt, William W.	Colonel	189th Infantry	November 8th, 1864
INGALLS, ALBERT S.	Major	40th Infantry	August 11th, 1862
Ives, Samuel J.	Lieutenant	70th Infantry	December 28th, 1863
Irwin, John J.	Lieutenant	90th Infantry	August 20th, 1862
Ireland, David	Colonel	137th Infantry	September 10th, 1864
JERNEGAN, FRANCIS W.	Lieutenant	13th Cavalry	December 2d, 1863
Joachim, Conrad	Surgeon	15th H. Art.	September 4th, 1862
Joachim, Charles	Lieutenant	15th H. Art.	October 8th, 1863
Jeffries, Ulysses F.	Lieutenant	16th H. Art.	November 8th, 1864
Jackson, William A.	Colonel	18th Infantry	November 10th, 1861
Jordan, Albert	Lieutenant	39th Infantry	June 15th, 1862
Jones, William W.	Lieutenant	44th Infantry	May 5th, 1862
Judd, Willard B.	Lieutenant	97th Infantry	February 19th, 1865
Jackson, Rollin C.	Captain	106th Infantry	December 15th, 1862
Jones, Evan G.	Lieutenant	117th Infantry	July 5th, 1863
Jilson, H. H.	Captain	122d Infantry	October 8th, 1862
Jenkins, Isaac T.	Lieutenant	154th Infantry	July 21st, 1863
Jones, Julius A.	Lieutenant	176th Infantry	October 19th, 1864
KETCHUM, JOHN P.	Lieutenant	4th Cavalry	October 8th, 1863
King, John B.	Lieutenant	10th Cavalry	July 31st, 1863
Knight, J. Randolph	Lieutenant	10th H. Art.	November 23d, 1862
Kuchne, Leo	Lieutenant	15th H. Art.	June 9th, 1863
Kimball, Edward A.	Lt.-Col.	9th Infantry	April 12th, 1863
Kane, William	Lieutenant	11th Infantry	— 1862
Kerrigan, Thomas	Captain	25th Infantry	December 12th, 1861
King, Samuel	Captain	30th Infantry	September 1st, 1862
Kennedy, William D.	Colonel	42d Infantry	July 22d, 1861
Kleefisch, John H.	Lt.-Col.	68th Infantry	September 22d, 1862
Kinnear, James	Lieutenant	79th Infantry	June 18th, 1862
Krouth, Hermann	Captain	103d Infantry	June 6th, 1865
Kelly, Samuel B.	Lieutenant	121st Infantry	March – 1865
Kennedy, G. D.	Captain	134th Infantry	August 3d, 1862
Knox, James H.	Lieutenant	140th Infantry	October 13th, 1863
Kane, Patrick	Captain	175th Infantry	September 6th, 1863
Kimball, John F.	Lieutenant	176th Infantry	December 19th, 1863
Kingsley, Henry L.	Lieutenant	185th Infantry	March 31st, 1865
LOWE, JUDSON W.	Lieutenant	9th Cavalry	November 19th, 1863
Laydon, Marshall M.	Captain	15th Cavalry	October 5th, 1864
Louis, John	Captain	12th Infantry	October 21st, 1861
Leonard, George H.	Surgeon	51st Infantry	February – 1863
Littrow, Victor Lud. V.	Major	54th Infantry	April 22d, 1862

NAME.	RANK.	REGIMENT.	DATE.
Lorgan, P. M.	Lieutenant	56th Infantry	August 19th, 1862
Lewis, George T. J.	Captain	62d Infantry	July 14th, 1862
Lynch, Thomas T.	Major	63d Infantry	February 12th, 1862
Lyman, George P	Lieutenant	98th Infantry	May 20th, 1862
Ling, Ferdinand J.	Lieutenant	103d Infantry	September 17th, 1862
Lattin, Jerome	Captain	111th Infantry	July 15th, 1864
Lockwood, John W.	Captain	111th Infantry	
Lewis, Norman M.	Lieutenant	114th Infantry	November 17th, 1864
Lewis, Thomas	Lieutenant	144th Infantry	September 8th, 1863
Lefever, Johannes	Lieutenant	156th Infantry	November 9th, 1864
Lawrence, James R.	Lieutenant	176th Infantry	April 1st, 1863
Leo, John	Major	185th Infantry	December 3d, 1864
MILLIGAN, SAMUEL G.	Captain	2d Cavalry	May 28th, 1862
McMasters, Zolman J.	Captain	5th Cavalry	September 24th, 1863
McVean, Charles	Captain	8th Cavalry	October 26th, 1864
Merrill, Asa B.	Captain	9th Cavalry	June 23d, 1862
Mosher, Henry E.	Lieutenant	12th Cavalry	October 6th, 1864
McAlester, M. P.	Lieutenant	20th Cavalry	September 18th, 1863
McMahon, James	Lieutenant	5th H. Art.	July 3d, 1864
Moss, Edgar S.	Lieutenant	7th H. Art.	October 18th, 1864
Moeller Edward	Surgeon	15th H. Art.	November 10th, 1863
McQueen, James	Captain	15th Engineers	September 18th, 1861
Moore, Theodore	Lieutenant	1st Infantry	June 30th, 1862
Mengersen, William	Captain	8th Infantry	July 12th, 1862
Mattock, William	Lieutenant	17th Infantry	July 31st, 1861
Mattheson, Roderick	Colonel	32d Infantry	October 2d, 1862
McHugh, Francis J.	Captain	37th Infantry	December 12th, 1861
McQuaide, Hugh	Captain	38th Infantry	December 26th, 1861
McGarry, Michael O.	Lieutenant	39th Infantry	May 25th, 1864
Muller, August	Captain	41st Infantry	August 25th, 1865
Miller, William H.	Captain	44th Infantry	April 17th, 1862
Metternich, Germain	Lt.-Col.	46th Infantry	May 13th, 1862
Moss, Charles H.	Captain	49th Infantry	March 25th, 1862
McKibbin, James	Lieutenant	57th Infantry	May 17th, 1862
McDonald, John	Lieutenant	61st Infantry	June 24th, 1862
McNeil, John	Captain	66th Infantry	December 13th, 1863
McDermott, James	Captain	73d Infantry	May 31st, 1864
Morey, George A.	Lieutenant	74th Infantry	June 23d, 1862
Marsh, Moses P.	Lieutenant	76th Infantry	September 26th, 1862
Mulligan, Greig H.	Lieutenant	90th Infantry	August – 1862
Minturn, B. G.	Captain	92d Infantry	August 4th, 1864
McCaffrey, John J.	Lieutenant	104th Infantry	September 17th, 1862
Mitchell, Charles	Surgeon	110th Infantry	August 28th, 1864
Meade, Joseph N.	Lieutenant	119th Infantry	February 11th, 1863
McEntie, Charles H.	Captain	120th Infantry	December 2d, 1862
Meyer, August	Captain	140th Infantry	May 24th, 1864
McMellon, Patrick A.	Captain	140th Infantry	August 23d, 1864
McGraw, Hugh	Lieutenant	140th Infantry	July 9th, 1863
Mayo, DeWitt C.	Lieutenant	144th Infantry	September 27th, 1863
Marshall, Rowland H.	Lieutenant	150th Infantry	September 13th, 1863
McMahon, John E.	Colonel	164th Infantry	March 3d, 1863
McGregor, Thomas H. D.	Lieutenant	169th Infantry	January 16th, 1865
Maguire, John	Captain	175th Infantry	April 14th, 1865
Melhan, William	Lieutenant	188th Infantry	April 17th, 1865
NAZER, FERRIES	Lt.-Col.	4th Cavalry	April 23d, 1863
Nixon, Samuel F.	Lieutenant	1st Infantry	May 26th, 1863
Near, Charles R.	Lieutenant	73d Infantry	September 1st, 1863
Newton, John S.	Lieutenant	90th Infantry	September 13th, 1862
Newcomb, Walter K.	Captain	125th Infantry	August 9th, 1863
O'NEIL, JOHN	Lieutenant	3d L. Art.	August 10th, 1864
Otto, Joseph	Captain	20th Infantry	June 4th, 1861

NAME.	RANK.	REGIMENT.	DATE.
O'Sullivan, Maxwell	Captain	88th Infantry	April 13th, 1862
Oakley, Nehemiah	Lieutenant	162d Infantry	November 10th, 1863
PORTER, JR., GEORGE	Lieutenant	6th H. Art.	June 25th, 1865
Palmer, Albert A.	Lieutenant	13th H. Art.	June 6th, 1864
Parker, Robert I.	Lieutenant	1st Light Artillery	February – 1863
Parker, James C.	Lieutenant	Light Artillery	June 4th, 1862
Perrine, Richard V. R.	Lieutenant	1st Engineers	February 8th, 1862
Pearson, William	Lieutenant	4th Infantry	January 1st, 1863
Pigott, Alfred J.	Captain	36th Infantry	July 6th, 1863
Perry, James H.	Colonel	48th Infantry	June 18th, 1862
Pennock, Horatio B.	Captain	72d Infantry	August 4th, 1862
Parsons, Darius M.	Captain	96th Infantry	June 12th, 1862
Powell, Charles A.	Lieutenant	98th Infantry	May 13th, 1862
Priest, Luther	Captain	106th Infantry	March 14th, 1863
Pettit, Frederick H.	Surgeon	106th Infantry	December 25th, 1863
Poole, Joseph H.	Lieutenant	140th Infantry	July 29th, 1864
Putnam, Charles F.	Major	153d Infantry	September 9th, 1865
Palmer, Charles H.	Lieutenant	169th Infantry	July 28th, 1863
Philips, John P.	Lieutenant	177th Infantry	September 4th, 1863
QUACKENBOS, EDWARD M.	Captain	36th Infantry	August 20th, 1862
RUSHMORE, JOSEPH M.	Captain	2d Mounted Rifles	August 16th, 1864
Roche, Charles H.	Captain	12th Cavalry	October 17th, 1864
Robinson, John F.	Surgeon	15th Cavalry	February 3d, 1864
Richards, Melzer	Lt.-Col.	24th Cavalry	April 13th, 1865
Rundell, Marshall H.	Lieutenant	1st Light Artillery	July 21st, 1862
Rathbaus, Herman	Lieutenant	46th Infantry	August 28th, 1863
Roosa, Isaac	Lieutenant	56th Infantry	January 20th, 1863
Rush, Frank W.	Lieutenant	56th Infantry	December 25th, 1863
Reynolds, Hosea C.	Lieutenant	60th Infantry	October 24th, 1862
Russell, Theodore	Captain	61st Infantry	June 1st, 1862
Rother, Robert	Major	68th Infantry	May 2d, 1863
Rice, A. Clark	Lieutenant	121st Infantry	September 20th, 1863
Redfield, George N.	Lieutenant	126th Infantry	November 9th, 1862
Raymond, Samuel M.	Lieutenant	131st Infantry	April 3d, 1863
Robertson, William	Captain	173d Infantry	August 28th, 1865
Ramsey, Jesse W.	Lieutenant	175th Infantry	October 11th, 1863
Rosche, Francis	Lieutenant	177th Infantry	August 17th, 1863
STUART, ROBERT	Lieutenant	2d Cavalry	September 22d, 1862
Smith, Thomas B.	Captain	2d Vet. Cavalry	February 26th, 1865
Stowe, Don D.	Lieutenant	2d Vet. Cavalry	April 12th, 1864
Sisson, Benjamin E.	Captain	8th Cavalry	February 11th, 1863
Swain, James P.	Lieutenant	8th Cavalry	December 20th, 1864
Stockwell, George B.	Lieutenant	9th Cavalry	October 3d, 1863
Smith, Moses S.	Lieutenant	14th Cavalry	June 26th, 1863
Sherwin, Elbridge S.	Captain	8th H. Art.	July 30, 1864
Swan, Henry R.	Lieutenant	8th H. Art.	June 14th, 1864
Stoyell, George C.	Lieutenant	9th H. Art.	January 21st, 1863
Scott, John	Lieutenant	16th H. Art.	February 19th, 1865
Searle, Tyler E.	Lieutenant	1st Light Artillery	November 3d, 1864
Sahm, Nicholas	Captain	1st Light Artillery	May 1st, 1864
Stone, Henry M.	Lt.-Col.	3d L. Art.	October 2d, 1864
Stahl, William H.	Captain	Light Artillery	September 15th, 1863
Steele, Rodney W.	Lieutenant	23d Infantry	December 7th, 1861
Shay, Cyrus	Lieutenant	25th Infantry	June 20th, 1861
Sawyer, Thomas H.	Surgeon	43d Infantry	August 23d, 1862
Sautter, Frederick	Lieutenant	58th Infantry	April 30th, 1863
Stevens, Gorham P.	Lieutenant	70th Infantry	August 12th, 1862
Silva, Manuel	Captain	73d Infantry	August 17th, 1861
Sittler, Robert	Chaplain	74th Infantry	August 6th, 1863
Shannon, George W.	Lieutenant	82d Infantry	September 15th, 1862

NAME.	RANK.	REGIMENT.	DATE.
Sullivan, John	Captain	90th Infantry	August 16th, 1862
Stackhouse, George W.	Major	91st Infantry	May 27th, 1863
Southwick, James M.	Lieutenant	93d Infantry	May 4th, 1862
Storms, David	Lieutenant	98th Infantry	April 20th, 1862
Stephens, Walter S.	Lieutenant	104th Infantry	April 10th, 1864
Schwerin, Henry R.	Captain	119th Infantry	May 6th, 1863
Simpkins, Edgar	Lieutenant	120th Infantry	March 31st, 1865
Sterling, F. W.	Lieutenant	128th Infantry	December 6th, 1862
Stone, William H.	Captain	144th Infantry	October 17th, 1863
Sisson, George A.	Lieutenant	147th Infantry	May 13th, 1863
Sweet, John	Lieutenant	150th Infantry	August 13th, 1864
Steadman, William	Lieutenant	156th Infantry	August 13th, 1863
Stone, J. R.	Captain	157th Infantry	August 12th, 1864
Stapleton, Michael G.	Lieutenant	164th Infantry	March 26th, 1865
Strong, Richard M.	Lieutenant	177th Infantry	May 12th, 1863
Swan, Edwin	Captain	186th Infantry	February 15th, 1865
TEN BROECK, SAMUEL	Captain	5th Cavalry	July 4th, 1863
Truesdell, Zebedee	Lieutenant	9th Cavalry	September 29th, 1862
Thompson, J. Floyd	Captain	20th Cavalry	July 5th, 1864
Tompkins, Theodore F.	Lieutenant	6th H. Art.	March 16th, 1863
Thompson, John H.	Lieutenant	14th H. Art.	November 20th, 1864
Tillinghast, Henry D.	Lieutenant	49th Infantry	May 31st, 1862
Taggart, George L.	Lieutenant	64th Infantry	May 20th, 1864
Tracey, W. W.	Captain	65th Infantry	May 6th, 1864
Turbagne, George	Lieutenant	66th Infantry	December - 1864
Tarry, Frederick	Lieutenant	91st Infantry	August 24th, 1863
Timpson, Samuel C.	Captain	95th Infantry	December 28th, 1864
Thorp, Lorin L.	Captain	110th Infantry	April 8th, 1863
Thurber, William D.	Lieutenant	114th Infantry	October 27th, 1864
Trumpelman, Otto	Captain	119th Infantry	July 24th, 1863
Tremain, Walter R.	Lieutenant	132d Infantry	December 25th, 1862
Taft, William H.	Lieutenant	137th Infantry	October 31st, 1862
Thomas, DeWitt C.	Lieutenant	144th Infantry	June 5th, 1863
Tanner, Benjamin P.	Lieutenant	151st Infantry	September 21st, 1863
Turner, George S.	Captain	170th Infantry	October 24th, 1864
Trembley, William W	Captain	178th Infantry	May 7th, 1864
VON SCHWENKE, GEORGE	Captain	4th Cavalry	November 1st, 1863
Von Einsiedel, Detler	Lt.-Col.	41st Infantry	August 23d, 1865
Von Gayl, Frederick	Lieutenant	49th Infantry	June 12th, 1863
Von Haake, Herman	Lieutenant	52d Infantry	June 23d, 1864
Von Roserberg, Albert	Captain	58th Infantry	May 3d, 1864
Von Gerber, Gustav	Lt.-Col.	68th Infantry	November 19th, 1861
Van Cott, Leonard B.	Lieutenant	119th Infantry	December 3d, 1862
Van Vleek, Daniel P.	Surgeon	128th Infantry	November 21st, 1862
WARD, GILES F.	Lieutenant	12th Cavalry	January 28th, 1865
White, Charles S.	Lieutenant	7th H. Art.	July 8th, 1864
Willett, Joseph	Lieutenant	8th H. Art.	February 17th, 1865
Wilkie, Chauncey	Captain	14th H. Art.	August 1st, 1864
Westervelt, Minthorne	Lieutenant	1st M. Art.	December 3d, 1862
Wilcken, Charles L.	Lieutenant	1st Engineers	October 10th, 1864
Webster, Calvert S.	Lieutenant	15th Engineers	August 9th, 1862
Wilcox, Charles H.	Surgeon	21st Infantry	November 7th, 1862
Wager, Prentice B.	Lieutenant	32d Infantry	October 22d, 1861
White, Loring E.	Lieutenant	60th Infantry	July 20th, 1862
Woodworth, William W.	Captain	64th Infantry	December 28th, 1862
Walker, J. S.	Captain	65th Infantry	May 27th, 1862
West, William H.	Lieutenant	67th Infantry	August 27th, 1861
Wyatt, James	Chaplain	79th Infantry	July 10th, 1863
Wildrick, John L.	Lieutenant	86th Infantry	December 8th, 1862
Woodward, Jackson A.	Lieutenant	86th Infantry	June 1st, 1863
White, William E.	Captain	90th Infantry	February 4th, 1865

NAME.	RANK.	REGIMENT.	DATE.
Wilson, Hiram S.	Captain	93d Infantry	March 24th, 1864
Webster, Jay	Lieutenant	96th Infantry	August 3d, 1864
Wheelock, Charles	Colonel	97th Infantry	January 21st, 1865
Worden, Monroe C.	Lieutenant	101st Infantry	April 25th, 1862
Waters, Frank	Lieutenant	112th Infantry	October 3d, 1863
Washburn, Charles E.	Surgeon	112th Infantry	April 10th, 1865
Wing, Edgar M.	Lieutenant	118th Infantry	May 16th, 1864
Webb, William J.	Lieutenant	122d Infantry	March 1, 1863
Williams, John W.	Chaplain	131st Infantry	December 15th, 1863
Washburn, A. G.	Captain	134th Infantry	January 26th, 1863
Welling, Edgar P.	Lieutenant	150th Infantry	October 21st, 1863
Wilkes, De Ponthen J.	Lieutenant	162d Infantry	December 6th, 1862
YATES, SQUIRE M.	Lieutenant	22d Cavalry	April 9th, 1865
Young, Edward F.	Major	4th H. Art.	December 22d, 1863
Yates, Henry	Lieutenant	50th Engineers	May 23d, 1862
ZYLA, ANTHONY	Chaplain	58th Infantry	April 5th, 1865

INDEX.*

A.

Name	PAGE
Abeel, Edgar	323
Abernethy, Mrs. Charles	61
Ackerman, William	312
Acton, Thomas C.	123
Adams, Alexander D.	295
Adams, Alonzo W.	254
Adams, George A.	99
Adams, John Quincy	95
Adams, Julius W.	315
Adams, Thomas C.	341
Addi, Thomas J.	30
Agnew, Cornelius R.	40, 61
Agnew, John T.	79
Ainsworth, Ira W.	308
Albans, Charles P.	231
Alden, Alonzo	296, 364
Alden, Henry H.	30
Aldridge, Horace L.	334
Alexander, H.	248
Alford, Samuel M.	241, 243
Allaire, Anthony J.	349
Allen, Joseph H.	365
Allen, William H.	283
Alles, Henry M.	319
Alsdorf, E.	247
Amlet, Carl V.	105
Ammon, John H.	276
Anderson, C. R.	344
Anderson, C. W.	106
Anderson, E. Ellery	235
Anderson, Finley	55
Anderson, Hugh	323
Anderson, John	74
Andres, W. C. H.	263
Angell, Oscar F.	288
Annan, Alexander	344
Anthony, William N.	238
Appleton, D. F.	67
Armon, Robert	321
Armstrong, John M.	330
Armstrong, Thomas	358
Arnold, Henry	30
Arnold, Henry L.	349
Arnold, H. N. T.	119
Arrowsmith, George W.	53, 99, 360
Artand, Theodore	48
Artherly, Joseph B.	46
Arthur, Chester A.	335
Arthur, William	268
Asboth, Alexander	85
Ashby, Charles	308
Ashley, Ossian D.	242
Aspinwall, Lloyd	95, 96, 238, 239
Aspinwall, William H.	67
Aspinwall, Mrs. William H.	59
Astin, William H.	293
Astor, John Jacob	74
Astor, Mrs. John Jacob	59, 289
Atkinson, William	251
Austin, John S.	317
Ayres, Conway W.	261
Ayres, Romeyn B.	94
Axtell, Nathan G.	371

B.

Name	PAGE
Babcock, Charles A.	118
Babcock, Samuel D.	79
Babcock, Willis G.	101
Babcock, Willoughby	319
Bachia, Richard A.	326
Backus, Jason K.	99
Bacon, George	119
Bagley, James	95, 244, 246
Bailey, Benjamin P.	326
Bailey, Guilford D.	275
Bailey, Isaac H.	67
Bailey, Theodorus	118
Bailey, William	345
Baird, Alexander L.	321
Baird, Andrew D.	321
Baird, William H.	343
Baker, Benjamin F.	302
Baker, Joel A.	354
Baker, John A.	26, 30
Baker, Lewis F.	46
Baker, Rollin T.	46
Baker, Stephen	270
Baker, William H.	312
Baldwin, Ambrose N.	105
Baldwin, Charles H.	118
Baldwin, Harvey	340
Ball, J. C.	314
Ballestier, Robert B.	277
Balser, William	50
Bancroft, Conrad	354
Bankhead, John P.	114
Barclay, Thomas	251

* This index does not include names of New York Heroes, mentioned in Appendix No. 1, nor those of our Honored Dead, in Appendix No. 3.

INDEX.

Name	PAGE
Barker, Ayres G.	101
Barlow, Francis C.	52, 94, 97, 234, 310
Barlow, S. L. M.	79
Barnard, F. A. P.	40
Barnes, John S.	118
Barnett, G. A. C.	292
Barnett, John R.	298
Barney, Albert M.	351
Barney, Lewis T.	30
Barney, Matthew J.	369
Barnum, Henry A.	52, 290, 355
Barnum, Mrs. S. M.	60
Barrett, Edward	113
Barry, (Private)	275
Barstow, Wilson	209
Bartlett, Charles G.	357
Bartlett, Joseph J.	295
Barton, Clara	125
Barton, William B.	30
Barton, William H.	305
Bartram, Nelson B.	120, 202
Bassford, Abram	263
Batchelder, William H.	333
Batchelor, George S.	339
Battersby, Jenyns C.	253, 254
Batterson, James P.	340
Baxter, Henry	94
Bayard, Mrs.	61
Bayles, Mrs. H.	61
Beach, Charles	262
Beardsley, John	260
Beardsley, Lester A.	119
Beardsley, Samuel R.	294
Beattie, John	363
Becker, Charles	340
Beecher, Harris H.	338
Beecher, Henry Ward	83
Beecher, James C.	351
Beecher, S. Clark	350
Beekman, James W.	67
Beers, Edmond O.	282
Beers, William F.	289
Begley, T.	107
Belknap, Jr. Augustus	315
Belknap, Jonathan S.	326
Bell, Christopher J.	369
Bell, George W.	289
Bell, Isaac	79
Bellows, Henry W.	61, 62, 120
Belmont, August	67
Belmont, Mrs. August	286
Benbow, Thomas	234
Benedict, Augustus W.	319
Benedict, Lewis	53, 362
Benedict, Lewis J.	318
Bendix, John E.	233, 287
Benham, A E. K.	119
Benjamin, Frank W.	49
Benjamin J. F.	107
Bennett, Augustus G.	323
Bennett, George C.	47
Bennett, John S.	278
Bennett, Michael	95, 241
Bennett, Theron R.	123
Benson, Benjamin F.	344
Bentley, Richard C.	296
Benton, Orlando N.	37
Bergen, John G.	123
Berger, Lewis	95, 229
Bergh, Henry	79
Bernard, George A.	314
Berry, Abraham J.	45
Betje, Robert J.	315
Betts, George F.	286
Bicknell, H. H.	107
Biddle, George H.	98, 330
Bidlack, J. B. W.	49
Bidwell, Daniel D.	305
Biggs, Reuben	330
Birchmeyer, Paul	276
Birdsall, Edgar	250
Birney, William	113
Bissell, George W.	30
Blackmore, Albin C.	313
Blackwell, Henry F.	326
Blackwood, Stephen	123
Blake, Homer C.	117
Blanchard, Justus W.	362
Blenker, Lewis	85, 266
Bliss, Aaron T.	261
Bliss, Jr., George	64
Blume, Theodore	99
Blunt, Orison	72
Bockoven, William C.	313
Bogardus, Charles	357
Bogardus, Jr., Stephen H.	371
Bogart, James Z.	123
Bogert, A. S.	30
Boice, Jeremiah	345
Boice, Theodore A.	258
Bookwood, Charles	277
Boorman, James	67
Booth, Mary L.	60
Borcherdt, Ed.	306
Borcherdt, Julius C.	306
Borden, John G.	305
Bostwick, Henry A.	234, 235
Botta, Mrs. V.	61
Boughton, Horace	290
Bourne, R. Walworth	360
Bowen, C. B.	107
Bowen, Erwin A.	357
Bowerman, R. N.	30
Boyd, Samuel K.	236
Boyd, William H.	254
Boyer, Leonard	358
Bracken, John	116
Bradley, Lemen	313
Bradley, Samuel C.	337
Brady, James B.	79
Brady, James D.	312
Brady, James T.	79
Brady, John A.	288
Brady, John R.	79
Braine, Daniel L.	119
Brainerd, Wesley	281, 282
Bramen, Walter W.	329
Brandt, William	333
Brankstone, George W.	99
Brannigan, Patrick R.	47
Brennan, William D.	351
Brett, E. Augustus	344
Brett, Francis H.	344
Brewer, William I.	107
Brewster, William R.	94, 318
Briggs, Alvah W.	334

INDEX. 401

Name	Page	Name	Page
Briggs, James Henry	267	Byrne, James J.	264
Brincherhoff, John J.	337	Byrnes, John	359
Britt, James W.	309		
Broady, Oscar K.	311	**C.**	
Broas, Benjamin S.	357		
Bronson, Theodore	64		
Brooks, Thomas B.	281	Cady, A. Lester	280
Brooks, William A.	370	Cady, Rush P.	99
Brosero, John B.	278	Caffry, C. W.	123
Brower, S.	123	Calkin, J. S.	107, 256
Brown, David	125	Cameron, Angus	251
Brown, Edwin F.	296	Cameron, James	125, 251, 321
Brown, Franklin F.	351	Cameron, John	123
Brown, Harvey E.	317	Cameron, Robert A.	50
Brown, James M.	331	Camp, Andrew P.	337
Brown, John A.	326	Camp, John G.	24
Brown, Milnor	30, 67, 101	Cannon, Le Grand B.	67
Brown, Jr., Morris	107	Cannon, Madison M.	301
Brown, Jr., Philip P.	360	Canton, Thomas M.	369
Brown, Richard A.	311	Curd, Dayton T.	105
Brown, Samuel H.	47	Carey, Hugh	323
Brown, Stewart	67	Carle, Jason	101
Brown, William C.	293	Carman, Irvine	333
Brown, William R.	237, 247, 354	Carman, W.	107
Browne, Rufus King	45	Carnochan, John M.	45
Browne, William H.	30	Carpenter, Daniel	123
Brundage, Alonzo	293	Carr, Gouverneur	42, 285
Brush, Jesse	43	Carr, Joseph B.	94, 283
Bryan Michael K.	241, 367	Carrington, Edward	53, 352
Bryant, William Cullen	22	Carroll, Howard	334
Bryson, Andrew	119	Carson, Cornelius	247
Buchanan, George A.	354	Carter, Samuel P.	113
Buck, Gordon	45	Cartwright, J. H.	349
Buck, Leander	231	Cary, J.	366
Buckingham, George A.	247	Casler, Marcus R.	341
Buckley, D.	107	Castle, Frederick A.	49
Buckley, S. T.	56	Caswell, Charles S.	340
Buddington, William I.	87	Catlin, Charles M.	242
Buell, Clarence	364	Catlin, Isaac S.	385
Bull, James M.	343	Cavanagh, James	246, 316
Bundy, Henry	278	Chamberlain, Alfred	298
Burhaus, David	303	Chamberlain, Martin J.	334
Burhaus, Henry N.	356	Champlin, Stephen G.	50
Burhaus, John R.	101	Chandler, (Corporal)	303
Burk, M.	107	Chandler, Mrs. Charles	230
Burke, Dennis F.	126	Chandler, Hiram	123
Burke, T.	107	Chandler, Ralph	119
Burleigh, Lemoyne	253	Chapelle, Marcus H.	271
Burnham, Edwin K.	337	Chapin, Edwin P.	339
Burns, (Lieut.-Col.)	241	Chapman, Alford B.	30, 309
Burns, Michael W	318	Chapman, Perry W.	357
Burns, Thomas W.	231	Chapman, William O.	330
Burr, Allen L.	371	Charlier, E.	360
Burrowe, William J.	251	Chase, George P.	289
Burrows, James B.	261	Chatfield, Harvey S.	320, 333
Burton, Christopher C.	107	Cheeseman, Timothy M.	26
Bush, Archibald Mc C.	330	Cherry, William	293
Bush, William P.	47	Chester, George F.	332
Bushee, Andrew S.	314	Chester, Walter T.	329
Bushnell, C. S.	116	Chester, William H.	105
Butler, Benjamin C.	329	Chittenden, S. B.	67
Butler, Mrs. Charles	59	Christian, William H.	294
Butler, John G.	354	Church, Benjamin S.	234
Butler, William Allen	70	Church, Cyrus	262
Butterfield, Daniel	24, 91, 94, 96, 234	Church, Morris H.	342
Butts, Charles A.	341	Churchill, Robert P.	346
Butts, Frank A.	304	Cisco, John J.	71
Byrne, Edward	264	Claassen, Peter J.	250, 348

26

INDEX.

	PAGE
Claesgent, Peter	354
Clark, Charles A.	24, 99
Clark, Charles J.	316
Clark, Frank M.	289
Clark, John S.	277
Clark, Julius H.	323
Clark, Robert B.	236
Clark, William C.	321
Clarke, Johnson	47
Clarkson, Floyd	263
Claxton, Kate	37
Clearman, L. L. S.	26
Clews, Henry	67
Clifton, Edward	366
Clitz, John M. B.	119
Coan, William B.	305
Cochrane, John	53, 89, 91, 313
Coddington, Clifford	308
Coe, George S.	67, 71, 72
Coe, Richard W.	281
Coe, William P.	368
Coffin, James A.	360
Cogeswell, Milton	267, 301
Colahan, Francis	342
Cole, Alonzo R.	341
Cole, Edward	354
Cole, G. W.	256
Cole, Matthew T.	95
Colgate, Clinton C.	281
Coleman, Warren B.	365
Coles, William J.	250
Collier, Henry A.	47
Colvin, Andrew J.	79
Colvin, James A.	365
Compson, Hartwell B.	107
Cone, Spencer H.	37
Cone, Spencer W.	37
Conk, Anthony	350
Conkling, Frederick A.	95, 251
Connelley, John Townsend	43
Connery, John A.	56
Connolly, Richard S.	47
Connor, Patrick E.	85
Connors, J.	107
Connover, D. D.	24
Constable, David	117
Conway, (Private)	275
Conway, William	319
Conyngham, D. P.	56
Cook, Abel G.	356
Cook, Edward A.	323
Cook, Edwin F.	255
Cook, Erastus	360
Cooley, Alfred	360
Cooley, John	354
Coonan, John	369
Cooney, John M.	300
Cooney, Michael	244
Cooper, Alonzo	262
Cooper, Cornelius A.	344
Cooper, Edward	79
Cooper, George H.	119
Cooper, Peter	67
Cooper, Thomas Colden	30
Copeland, Theron S.	123
Coppinger, J. B.	233
Coppinger, John J.	204
Corbett, Boston	235

	PAGE
Corbin, Joseph S.	99
Corcoran, Michael	243
Cornell, M. E.	333
Cornell, Theodore D.	333
Corning, Joseph W.	298, 337
Corwin, B. R.	305
Cossitt, Davis	342
Cossum, Frederick	319
Costello, Edward	245
Coster, Charles R.	349
Coville, Orson	356
Cowan, Andrew	277
Cowdin, Elliott C.	67
Cowdrey, Edward A.	31, 330
Cowles, David S.	53, 345
Cowtan, Charles W.	288
Coyne, John N.	106, 313
Cox, (Sergeant)	304
Cox, Abraham S.	50
Cox, Charles H.	319
Cox, Robert H.	334
Cozens, E. E.	314
Crampton, Henry E.	50
Crandell, Levin	343
Cranston, John	105
Crawford, Mrs. Charles C.	230
Creiger, John A.	280
Creighton, Michael E.	101
Creney, James	330
Crocker, John A.	129
Crocker, John S.	329
Crockett, Le Roy	314
Cromwell, James	101
Cronkite, James W.	341
Crooks, Samuel J.	260, 265
Cropsey, John W.	263
Cross, Amos	270
Cross, Nelson	315
Crounse, George	55
Crowell, Charles	314
Crowley, M.	107
Cruger, Stephan Van Rensselaer	35, 357
Cullen, Edgar M.	330
Cullen, T.	107
Cullum, George W.	61
Cummings, Amos J.	56
Cummings, Francis M.	343
Cunningham, Gabriel	288
Cunningham, William H.	322
Currie, Leonard D. H.	349
Curtin, John G.	286
Curtis, Martin N.	202, 324, 351
Cushing, William B.	117
Cutter, John S.	368
Cutting, Francis B.	79
Cutting, Walter	296
Cutting, William	79
Cuyler, John M.	113

D.

Dada, Miss	60
Daggett, Rufus	91, 339
Dagwell, George A.	262
Dallman, Walter M.	356
Dalrymple, Aaron P.	49
Dalrymple, Henry M.	281

INDEX. 403

Name	PAGE
Dalton, John C.	26, 44
Daly, Charles P.	79, 245
Daly, Mrs. Charles P.	59, 243
Dandy, George B.	332
Daniel, J. Townsend	299
Dare, George H.	107
Darrach, C. B.	237
Darrow, Dr.	230
Dart, William	278
Davey, George W.	278
Davids, S. L.	319
Davies, Edwin G.	333
Davies, Henry E.	240, 255, 285, 291
Davies, Jr., Henry E.	39, 255, 285
Davies, J. Mansfield	255, 285
Davies, Julien T.	240
Davies, Thomas A.	291
Davies, William F.	312
Davies, William G.	240
Davis, Benjamin F.,	113, 260
Davis, Edwin P.	358
Davis, Joshua B.	342
Davis, T.	108
Davis, T. C.	123
Davis, Thomas	267
Davis, William	264
Davis, William	362
Day, Hiram	334
Day, Joseph B.	105
Day, Nicholas W.	91, 247, 348
Decker, Frank	360
De Forest, Jacob J.	323
De Forest, Martin J.	323
De Forest, Othneil	257
De Forest, W. H.	61
Deitrich, Louis	107
De Lacy, William	299, 363
De Landre, George	48
De Lany, John	293
Dennen, George	101
Denning, William H.	238
Denslow, William J.	328
De Peyster, Jr., Frederick	40
De Peyster, Johnston Livingston	40
De Peyster, J. Watts	40, 90
De Peyster, Jr., J. Watts	40
De Russey, Gustavus A.	267
Detmold, William	45
De Trobriand, Regis	85, 300, 308
De Vail, Francis D.	322
Devin, Thomas C.	94, 258
Dewey, George M.	289
De Wint, Arthur	344
De Witt, David P.	351
Di Cesnola, Louis P.	257, 262
Dickel, Christian	257
Dickson, Campbell	261
Dickson, John F.	123
Dilks, George W.	123
Dillingham, Lucius A.	342
Dillon, Garrett F.	344
Dimmock, Robert A.	289
Dingwall, John S.	321
Dinsmore, Samuel P.	24
Dippel, Henry	123
Disosway, William W.	250
Diven, Alexander S.	335
Divine, Michael	314
Divinny, John W.	351
Dix, John A.	89
Dix, Mrs. John A.	59
Dix, Morgan	37
Dixon, Christopher	123
Dockham, W. C.	107
Dodge, Charles C.	67, 259
Dodge, John E. A.	247
Dodge, Stephen A.	327
Dodge, William	351
Dodge, William E.	64, 87
Dodge, Jr., William E.	64, 238
Doherty, Edward B.	249
Donaldson, James	321
Donnelly, Dudley	295
Donnelly, Stewart J.	272
Doolittle, Isaac	329
Doran, (Sergeant)	275
Doran, Jacob M.	370
Doran, James E.	356
Doremieux, Laura	61
Doty, Franklin B.	368
Doubleday, Abner	90, 94
Doubleday, Thomas D.	268
Douglass, Eugene	42, 304
Dowdney, Abram	349
Downer, Edward	305
Doyle, G. E. P.	56
Doyle, James	336
Drake, David	367
Drake, Jeremiah C.	337
Drake, John H.	105
Drake, Marquis M.	341
Draper, John H.	27
Draper, Simeon	308
Drayson, Fordred	31
Drayton, Percival	114
Drew, Charles W.	319
Drummond, Robert L.	337
Duffie, Alfred N.	85
Duffy, James A.	263
Dufloo, Armand	49
Duganne, A. J. H.	367
Duncan, Cecil	41
Duncan, William Butler	79
Dunn, George W.	335
Dunn, James W.	305
Dunne, Patrick R.	366
Durkee, Charles	331
Duryea, Abram	30
Duryea, Jacob E.	30
Duryee, Jacob	312
Dutcher, Silas B.	24
Dutton, Charles K.	353
Dutton, William	330
Duysing, Emil	301
Dwight, Augustus W.	342
Dwight, Charles C.	361
Dwight, John M.	342
Dwight, William	316
Dwyer, R. O.	37
Dwyer, Susan K.	60
Dyckman, Garrett	283

INDEX.

E.

	PAGE
Early, William	289
Eastman, Thomas H.	118
Eaton, John B.	280
Eaton, Samuel C.	281
Eckles, William	366
Eddy, Jr., Edward	305
Eddy, George H.	312
Edgar, Lewis S.	370
Edmerston, Alex. A.	47
Edmonds, Judge	51
Edson, Susan B.	60
Edwards, D.	108
Edwards, Richard	354
Edwards, Roger	305
Egan, Thomas W.	91, 301
Egbert, S. E.	247
Egloffstein, F. W.	333
Elfwing, Nere A.	305
Ellicott, George M.	264
Elliott, Frederick	64
Elliott, Gilbert M.	41, 332
Elliott, John R.	333
Elliott, S. M.	251
Elliott, Samuel R.	49
Ellis, Captain	247
Ellis, A. Van Horne	101, 248, 343
Ellis, Henry C.	314
Ellis, Samuel C.	248
Ellison, John S.	263
Ellsworth, Asher M.	31
Ellsworth, E. Elmer	106, 289
Elmore, Daniel	333
Elmore, Taylor	47
Elwell, John A.	240
Embick, Frederick E.	282
Emerson, William	357
Ennis, John	263, 264
Eno, Amos F.	67
Eno, Amos R.	67
Eno, Mrs. Amos R.	59
Erben, Henry	119
Erhardt, Joel B.	123
Ericsson, John	116
Evans, Robert	101
Evarts, William M.	34, 66
Evarts, Mrs. William M.	59
Everdell, Jr., William	95, 240
Everett, George H.	330
Everett, Robert B.	99, 296
Everson, Adelbert	108

F.

	PAGE
Fairchild, Harrison S.	327
Fancher, Mollie	241
Fardello, Enrico	326
Farley, James M.	325
Farnesworth, Addison	299, 300
Farnham, Noah L.	31, 289, 317
Farquhar, John M.	85
Farragut, David G.	113
Farrell, Christopher	289
Fassett, Louis H.	313
Faucett, Richard W.	47
Faulkner, Lester B.	349
Faxon, Elihu J.	299
Fay, Thomas M.	357

	PAGE
Fergerson, Nelson D.	49
Ferguson, Alonzo	358
Ferguson, Samuel M.	330
Ferrero, Edward	85, 90, 233, 307
Field, Mrs. Cyrus W.	61
Field, Putnam	289
Field, William F.	276
Finnell, Dr.	45
Fish, Hamilton	38
Fish, Mrs. Hamilton	59, 61
Fisher, Henry N.	43
Fisher, N. F. W.	233
Fisk, Harvey	67
Fisk, Henry C.	313
Fisk, John	256
Fisk, Samuel N.	42
Fitch, Amya L.	272
Fitchett, Charles	237
Fitts, James F.	338
Fitzhugh, Charles L.	259
Fitzpatrick, Lawrence	353
Fitzsimons, Charles	265
Flandrau, Thomas M.	49
Fleet, Augustus	31
Fleming, James H.	264
Flood, Hugh C.	359
Flower, Byron L.	46
Floyd, Jr., John Gelston	35
Fogarty, William	246
Folk, John S.	123
Folwell, Mahlon B.	282
Folwell, William W.	282
Foote, Morris C.	328
Ford, George W.	108, 282
Ford, W. G.	314
Forscher, John M.	47
Foss, Charles A.	101
Foster, James P.	347
Foster, John A.	367
Fowler, Edward B.	98, 325
Fowler, Thomas	359
Fox, Watson A.	95
Fox, William F.	87, 125, 335
Foye, Michael E.	46
Franchot, Richard	341
Francis, Henry W.	308
Frank, Harrison	99
Fraser, James L.	304
Freelan, James	366
Freelewick, Frederick	101
Freeman, A.	108
Freligh, William S.	322
French, Peter	323
French, Jr., William H.	311
Friedlander, David	241
Friederich, Otto	101
Frisby, Edward	296
Frost, Emil	101
Frothingham, J. H.	240
Fry, Thomas W. G.	318
Fryer, John	302
Fuller, Henry V.	101
Fuller, James M.	334
Fuller, John W.	85
Fullerton, John H.	284
Fullerton, Stephen W.	284
Funk, Augustus	300
Funk, Ernst	362

G.

Name	PAGE
Gadsden, Charles A.	31
Gage, E. Darwin	354
Gair, Robert	321
Gallatin, James	12, 67, 71
Gallear, Charles W.	305
Galpin, Henry M.	341
Gansevoort, Henry S.	30, 263
Garaghan, Henry T.	305
Gardener, Asa B.	42
Gardiner, Curtiss C.	295
Garland, Franklin K.	101
Garnett, Frederick E.	310
Garrard, Kenner	353
Garrett, Cuyler	333
Garrish, Anna E.	60
Garrish, John P.	45
Gartner, Francis A. O.	340
Gaspar, J. Ward	263
Gates, Theodore B.	98, 237, 322
Gatt, B. F.	367
Genin, John N.	24
Gerry, Elbridge T.	79
Gibbons, Mrs. S. H.	60
Gibbs, Alfred	264
Gibbs, Oliver W.	40
Gibbs, Walcott	62
Gibson, Hansom C.	43
Gifford, B.	108
Gifford, Edward	317
Gilbert, George H.	342
Gilbert, Porteus C.	282
Gilbert, Rufus H.	46
Gilder, W. H.	37
Gildersleeve, Henry A.	357
Gilfillan, William H.	105
Gillem, Alvan C.	118
Gillette, (Rev.)	37
Gillette, David G.	368
Gillette, James	37, 249
Gilmore, James	321
Gleason, John	244
Glendenning, John	321
Glenny, William	313
Goettel, P.	108
Goheen, C. A.	108
Goodrich, Luther	319
Goodrich, William B.	310
Gouraud, Pierre	117
Graef, Frederick E.	281
Graham, Charles K.	94, 318
Graham, James L.	263
Graham, Lawrence P.	113
Graham, Samuel	268
Granger, Erastus M.	105
Grant, Donald	334
Grant, J. Henderson	239
Graves, E. E.	30
Gray, Charles O.	330
Gray, Wm. Cullen Bryant	41
Gregg, William M.	368
Gregory, David E.	353
Gregory, George S.	24
Gregory, J.	366
Greig, Theodore W.	311
Green, C. T.	360
Green, Nelson W.	320
Green, Jr., William N.	366
Greene, George S.	310
Greer, John H.	349
Gribbon, James H.	108
Griffin, Mrs. C.	61
Griffin, Dan S.	351
Griffin, William H.	333
Grindlay, James	353
Grinnell, Moses H.	67
Griswold, Edgar A.	354
Griswold, John A.	116
Griswold, Stephen	46
Grover, Andrew J.	98
Grower, William T. C.	292
Grub, G. M.	361
Grumbach, Nicholas	356
Guion, George M.	298, 354
Gunther, Henry	287
Gurnee, Abram S.	330
Gurney, William	30, 314, 344

H.

Name	PAGE
Hackett, (Sergeant)	302
Hackett, George	289
Hackley, Charles C.	47
Halden, William J.	298
Hagerty, Asel	108
Haggart, Robert	369
Haggerty, James	245
Hague, John	347
Hale, Christopher	305
Hall, George B.	317
Hall, James F.	281
Hall, Miss S. E.	60
Halleck, W. H.	233
Hallett, Henry W.	101
Halpine, Chas. G.	285, 315
Halsey, Charles E.	46
Halsey, Norwood A.	288
Ham, (Sergeant)	275
Hamblin, Joseph E.	30
Hamblin, Joseph H.	313
Hamilton, Charles	336
Hamilton, Frank H.	45, 297
Hamilton, Schuyler	30
Hamilton, Theodore B.	45, 298, 312
Hamilton, Thomas	321
Hammerstein, Herbert	320, 323
Hancock, Cornelia	60
Hanley, Timothy	261
Hanlon, Edward	267
Hannum, Josiah C.	280
Hanson, Frederick	312
Hardenbergh, Jacob B.	237, 322
Harding, William L.	48
Harhaus, Otto	255
Harn, William A.	278
Harney, George	354
Harper, Fletcher	67
Harring, Abram P.	348
Harrison, Edward A.	31
Harrison, Edward	329
Harrison, George	321
Harrison, Napoleon B.	113
Harrower, Gabriel T.	362
Hart, (Captain)	248
Hart, George H.	56

406 INDEX.

Name	PAGE
Hart, George P.	275
Hart, James H.	331
Hart, O. H.	30
Hart, Patrick	279
Hart, Peter	19
Hart, Robert McD.	31
Hartt, J.	123
Hartwell, Charles A.	30
Harvey, H.	108
Hassett, Thos. J.	314, 341
Hassler, J. J. S.	113
Hathaway, Robert B.	333
Hathaway, Samuel G.	351
Hathaway, William M.	237
Havemeyer, William F.	67
Hawkins, Ashley P.	271
Hawkins, Rush C.	286
Haxtun, Milton	119
Hayman, S. B.	299
Hayward, William B.	310
Hazleton, Augustus B.	262
Heavem, John S.	297
Hedden, Josiah	288
Hedden, William R.	314
Heddon, H.	123
Heine, William	333
Helme, John C.	123
Henderson, David B.	85
Hendricks, L. A.	56
Hendrickson, John	30, 324
Henry, Edmund W.	119
Hentsten, Henry R.	314
Herbert, William L.	101
Herendeen, Orin J.	105
Herman, George	297
Herring, Henry P.	320
Hewitt, Abram S.	79
Hewitt, Hiram H.	354
Hickmot, Charles H.	306
Hicks, Jr., Henry W.	31, 364
Hicks, Joseph Lawrence	50
Higbee, Rev. Dr.	37
Higginbotham, Thomas J.	314
Higgins, Benjamin	326
Hill, Charles	288
Hill, Edward B.	23
Hill, J.	108
Hill, Nicholas	23
Hillhouse, Thomas	260
Hilliard, Van Rensselaer K.	305
Hinman, James H.	319, 337
Hinman, Richard H.	47
Hoffman, Henry C.	294
Hoffman, John T.	79
Holbrook, Henry H.	308
Holbrook, M. T.	366
Hollister, Lansing	101
Holmes, Sebastian D.	337
Holt, Guysbert V.	236
Holt, Thomas	319
Homiston, Joseph M.	49
Hooper, Charles W.	329
Hopkins, Hugh J.	231
Hopper, George F.	287
Horgan, Patrick K.	327
Horner, James B.	292
Horner, John B.	322
Hosmer, William M.	319

Name	PAGE
Hough, (Private)	273
Hough, Daniel	19
Hough, A. Barton	282
Houghton, Charles H.	91, 273
Houghton, Horace	352
Houghton, Jonathan	351
Howard, Benjamin	50
Howard, Charles N.	266
Howard, James	361
Howard, William A.	272, 274
Howell, John H.	275
Howes, Reuben W.	67
Howland, Albert F.	305
Howland, Henry J.	238, 240
Howland, Joseph	291
Howland, Mrs. Joseph	60
Howland, Meredith	26
Hoyt, James J.	360
Hoyt, Jonah C.	101
Hoyt, Oliver	67
Hubbell, Cyrus O.	328
Hubbell, Wilson	312
Hughes, Archbishop	37
Hughes, John	346
Hughston, Robert S.	353
Hurlbert, Charles E.	329
Hull, Walter C.	265
Humphreys, George H.	48
Humphreys, Joseph J.	305
Hunt, John W.	49
Hunt, Lewis C.	328
Hunt, Horatio T.	313
Hunt, Sandford B.	45
Hunt, Seth B.	67
Hunt, Wilson G.	67
Hurlaux, Victor	319
Hurley, John	46
Hurst, Frederick	31
Husk, Lewis W.	337
Hustis, H. H.	238
Huston, James	101, 323
Hutchings, Henry	123
Hutchingson, Elbridge J.	305
Hutchingson, Henry	321
Hyde, Joseph	343
Hyland, Jr., George	290

I.

Name	PAGE
Iffla, A. G.	324
Ince, George H.	102
Ingersoll, C. Leonard	237
Ingersoll, Robert G.	53
Ingmire, William F.	330
Inness, Charles H.	298
Inskip, Joseph S.	325
Ireland, David	85, 251, 321, 350
Irvine, William	261
Iselin, Adrian	67

J.

Name	PAGE
Jackson, Daniel D.	341
Jackson, Matthew W.	327
Jackson, William A.	292
Jacobs, Ferris	52

INDEX. 407

	PAGE
Jacobus, John W.	287
Jagger, David	237
James, Courtney H.	260
James, Edward C.	282, 334
James, J. Willis	79
Jardine, Edward	30, 292
Jay, John	35
Jay, John	362
Jay, William	35
Jemison, John S.	48
Jenkins, David T.	353
Jenny, Edwin S.	370
Jennings, Henry M.	330
Jesup, Morris K.	67
Jewitt, Josiah P.	361
Joachim, Conrad	46
Joachimson, Philip J.	310
Johnson, (Adjutant)	236
Johnson, Alba A.	329
Johnson, Charles A.	294
Johnson, Jeremiah	243
Johnson, Nathan J.	339
Johnson, Robert T.	317
Johnson, William	354
Johnson, William H.	67
Johnson, W. H. H.	101
Johnston, James J.	307
Johnston, James W.	341
Johnston, Nicholas R.	354
Jones, Abram	254
Jones, Charles A.	267, 294
Jones, Frank	296
Jones, Henry E.	353
Jones, Ira	337
Jones, John D.	67
Jones, Patrick H.	85, 299, 358
Jones, Samuel B.	30
Jones, William	108
Jordan, Stephen S.	370
Jourdan, James	360
Jourdan, John	123
Judge, Francis W.	108, 321

K.

	PAGE
Kane, (Corporal)	263
Kappesser, P.	109
Kautz, August V.	85
Kay, Joseph W.	289
Kearny, Philip	38
Keech, Willard	311
Keeler, Birney B.	351
Keeler, David B.	231
Keeler, Philip	99, 296
Keese, Francis S.	345
Keese, J. Lawrence	31
Keese, Jr., Oliver	340
Kelly, D.	108
Kelly, Edward	369
Kelty, Eugene	31
Kelly, James	316
Kelly, John	79
Kelly, Michael	369
Kelly, Patrick	327
Kelly, Patrick	366
Kelly, T.	108
Kelly, William	344

	PAGE
Kelsey, William A.	276
Kempsey, Matthew C.	367
Kendrick, G.	366
Kennedy, Charles W.	367
Kennedy, John A.	80, 122
Kennedy, Terence J.	277
Kennedy, William D.	301
Kent, James	237
Kenyon, Delos M.	341
Kenyon, S. P.	108
Kerr, Daniel	85
Ketcham, John H.	356
Ketcham, Edward H.	105
Ketchum, Hiram	79
Ketchum, Morris	67
Ketchum, William A.	281
Keys, Columbus S.	344
Kibbe, George C.	271
Kidder, John S.	344
Kiernan, Dr.	245
Kilpatrick, Judson	257
Kimball, Edward A.	288
Kimball, John F.	361
Kimball, John M.	242
Kimball, Rodney G.	49
Kimberly, Lewis A.	116
King, (Sergeant)	270
King, Alonzo J.	353
King, Charles	40, 233
King, John W.	366
Kingsland, A. C.	309
Kingsland, Phineas C.	41, 333
Kingsland, William H.	31
Kingston, S. F.	256
Kirby, George B.	305
Kirkland, Caroline M.	60
Kirkland, Mrs. Charles P.	61
Kitching, J. Howard	270
Kittinger, Martin S.	47
Kittinger, Samuel	280
Klein, Charles P.	101
Klein, H.	109
Klein, Joe	306
Knapp, Robert M.	79
Knapp, Shepard	67
Knox, Charles McL.	53, 235, 260
Kozlay, Eugene A.	308
Kurz, Richard	301
Kryzanowski, Vlademir	85

L.

	PAGE
Lacy, George W.	267
Ladd, George	109
La Dew, William	298
Ladley, George H.	321
Laflin, Byron	298
Laing, John A.	337
Laing, Joseph	321
Laing, William	361
Lane, James C.	333
Lansing, H. S.	292
Lape, Philip	337
Larish, A. J.	109
Larrabee, Charles H.	53
La Roza, George W.	349
Lathrop, Nehemiah	24

408   INDEX.

	PAGE		PAGE
Lattimore, James M.	274	Lumphrey, Oliver	254
Lawler, Michael R.	85	Lusk, Isaac M.	337
Lawrence, (Corporal)	296	Lutes, F. W.	109
Lawrence, Charles E.	231	Luther, Edward P.	342
Lawrence, Mrs. Henry	59	Lynch, Wm. A.	302
Lawrence, Joseph	67	Lyon, George W.	242
Lawrence, William H.	30	Lyon, Phœbus W.	368
Lazelle, H. M.	264	Lyons, George	230
Ledlie, James H.	276		
Lederer, Charles	289	M.	
Lee, Benjamin F.	42		
Lee, William	236		
Lefferts, Marshall	26, 95	Macay, W. O.	314
Le Gal, Eugene	95	Mace, Guilford D.	99
Le Gendre, Charles W.	308	Mack, James W.	353
Lemmon, John C.	261	Maddox, Samuel T.	243
Lent, Louis H.	31	Maguire, Henry M.	333
Leonard, George H.	46	Mahon, Elam A.	263
Leonard, James	123	Maidhoff, Joachim	95, 233
Leonard, John	317	Malcolm, William	125
Leoser, Charles McK.	289	Mali, H. W. T.	43
Le Roy, William E.	117	Mallon, James E.	32
Leslie, F.	109	Mander, (Captain)	250
Leslie, John R.	322	Mandy, H. J.	109
Lester, Frank	342	Mangin, John	123
Leubuscher, Louis	340	Manley, John A.	313
Lewis, Alfred H.	101	Manning, Frederick L.	354
Lewis, Erastus H.	354	Marble, Manton	79
Lewis, George W.	31	Markoe, Thomas M.	45
Lewis, James	353	Marquand, Mrs.	59
Liebenau, Henry F.	247	Marsh, Samuel	291
Liebenau, J. H.	26	Marsh, Theodore B.	308
Lieber, Francis	40	Marsh, Walter R.	43
Lincoln, Richard F.	313	Marshall, Alexander S.	292
Lippincott, Adon	305	Marshall, Arthur W.	337
Little, Edward H.	314	Marshall, Charles H.	67
Little, George S.	237, 330	Marshall, Elisha G.	272, 290
Littlejohn, Dewitt C.	336	Marshall, John W.	289
Livermore, John R.	250	Marshall, Joseph H.	238
Livingston, Manning	35	Martin, (Sergeant Major)	315
Livingstone, Charles E.	320	Martin, Benjamin Ellis	42, 48
Lloyd, Edward P.	340	Martin, George D.	321
Logie, William K.	351	Martin, Henry P.	247
Locke, Frederick T.	234	Martin, Henry V.	289
Lockman, John T.	340	Martin, William B.	261
Lockwood, Abram L.	341	Mase, A. B.	344
Lockwood, James H.	341	Mason, Joel W.	95, 229
Lockwood, William L.	24	Masset, William Carey	39
Long, Michael	296	Matthews, John	344
Long, William H.	298	May, Robert L.	119
Loomis, Edwin R.	271	McAllister, George	47
Loomis, Henry	353	McArthur, John	85
Lord, Daniel	79	McAssy, Daniel	99
Lord, George DeForest	238	McCallum, Daniel McC.	85
Lord, Newton B.	265, 296	McChesney, W. W.	287
Loud, John S.	263	McClelland, William	101
Loudon, Robert	256	McClenachan, Charles J.	26
Lounsbury, William H.	319	McClintock, John	37
Love, George M.	109, 339	McConihe, John	364
Low, Aaron	263	McCrea, Edward P.	119
Low, A. A.	17, 67	McCurdy, R. H.	67
Low, James	237, 364	McCutchem, Edward T.	313
Low, Thomas	280	McDermott, Peter	365
Lower, Randall D.	99	McDonald, Andrew N.	334
Luce, Stephen D.	118	McDonald, Christopher R.	104
Ludden, Samuel D.	271	McDonald, George E.	49
Ludwick, Ephraim A.	337	McDonald, James H.	282
Ludwig, Charles H.	287	McDonald, John H.	105

INDEX. 409

Name	PAGE
McDonald, W. O.	50
McDougall, Archibald L.	342
McDougall, Clinton D.	319, 336
McEckron, G. M.	238
McEnroe, Patrick	109
McEntee, John	322
McEvily, William	359
McEwan, John S.	270
McFarlan, George B.	319
McGee, James E.	316
McGee, Richard	369
McGriffin, James	321
McGrath, Michael H.	282
McGregor, John D.	284
McIlvaine, Henry B.	268
McIntosh, John R.	113
McIntyre, Martin V.	278
McIvor, James P.	365
McKay, William	252
McKean, James B.	320
McKee, Abram W.	308
McKee, William	236
McKenna, Charles P.	281
McKeon, John	244
McKibbin, Gilbert H.	30, 308
McKinley, William P.	369
McKinstry, Alexander	356
McLaughlin, George H.	358
McLaughlin, N. B.	30
McLaughlin, Robert W.	272
McLelland, David	251, 321
McLeod, Alexander	251
McLeod, Harvey S.	354
McMahon, Daniel	322
McMahon, James P.	359, 363
McMahon, John.	329, 371
McMahon, John E.	363
McMahon, Martin T.	363
McMahon, William H.	53, 295
McMartin, Duncan	358
McMillan, Charles	247
McNary, W. H.	360
McNeill, John	30
McNorton, John R.	354
McNulty, William	289
McQuaide, James	291
McReynolds, Andrew T.	253
McVicar, Duncan	259
McWilliams, Lafayette	360
Mead, Sidney	337
Meade, John	105
Meagher, Thomas Francis	85, 244
Meech, G. E.	109
Meisel, Cæsar	236
Mellick, Simon A.	32
Meredith, Solomon	113
Merriam, William H.	365
Merrill, George	233
Merriman, Truman A.	56
Merritt, Abram	322
Merritt, Henry A. D.	258
Merritt, Wesley	94
Meserole, J. V.	95, 243
Meserole, N. W.	349
Metternich, Germain	304
Meyers, Gus	306
Miles, Nelson A.	310
Millard, James L.	43

Name	PAGE
Miller, Albert F.	305
Miller, B. B.	314
Miller, Charles P.	270
Miller, David J.	314
Miller, F.	109
Miller, Francis C.	98, 354
Miller, Frank	256
Miller, J.	109
Miller, Lindley M. H.	32
Miller, Silas A.	32
Milliken, Charles A.	302
Milliken, Robert H.	316
Mills, Nathaniel W.	123
Millward, James	24
Minor, J. E.	243
Minturn, Robert B.	67
Misner, Elson M.	322
Mitchell, Charles	47
Mitchell, J. F. B.	256
Mitchell, R. Charlton	308
Mitchell, Jr., Samuel L.	332
Mix, Simon H.	256
Moeller, Edward	46
Moesch, Joseph A.	98, 324
Moffit, Stephen	330
Moise, John E.	32
Molineux, Edward L.	30, 361
Monell, C. L.	242
Monroe, James	238
Montfort, Washington J.	344
Montgomery, William S.	321
Monks, George Washington	320
Mooney, Charles	333
Mooney, Thomas	244, 246
Moore, George W.	337
Moore, Henry	304
Moore, James	293
Morey, George A.	32
Morgan, Bankson T.	308
Morgans, Jr., Morgan	367
Morrell, George W.	35
Morren, William J.	99
Morris, (Private)	234
Morris, (Lieutenant)	242
Morris, Edward H.	312
Morris, Henry W.	117
Morris, Lewis O.	35, 270
Morris, Orlando W.	39, 314
Morris, Thomas F.	292
Morris, William	109
Morris, William H.	270
Morrison, David	321
Morrison, James M.	67
Morrison, Joseph J.	26, 30, 273, 276
Moroney, Richard	316
Morse, Henry B.	338
Morton, Charles B.	366
Morton, Charles E.	263
Morton, Charles S.	118
Morton, Peter	278
Morton, W. J.	314
Mosscrop, Thomas D.	289
Mott, Alexander B.	45
Mott, Thaddeus P.	263, 277
Mount, Jacob J.	123
Mowris, James A.	339
Mudgett B. F.	24
Mudie, Archibald F.	49

410 INDEX.

	PAGE
Mulford, John E.	283
Mulford, Sylvanus S.	50
Mulhall, John D.	316
Milligan, Samuel G.	32
Muniford, Lafayette	337
Munn, Elijah T.	102
Munsell, Jane R.	114
Munson, Albert L.	269
Munson, Owen	47
Murdock, Marcus W.	337
Murphy, John McLeod	281
Murphy, H.	109
Murphy, Matthew	369
Murphy, T. J.	109
Murphy, Michael H.	316
Murphy, William H.	234
Murray, Henry R.	354
Murray, Henry S.	343
Murray, John B.	354
Murray, John H.	280
Muschutt, David C.	250
Myers, Aaron B.	343
Myers, Augustus M.	344
Myers, Daniel	370
Myers, George R.	293

N.

	PAGE
Nagle, William J.	52, 327
Neafie, Alfred	360
Near, Charles R.	362
Neighbor, Jay W.	354
Nelson, Adolphus	315
Nevin, David A.	351
Nevin, David J.	312
Newberry, Walter C.	265
Newburgh, Joseph	288
Newman, Leopold C.	297
Newman, L. Howard	119
Newman, William H.	110
Newton, John	113
Nichols, George F.	340
Nichols, George S.	260
Nichols, Isaac	101
Nicholson, Alfred B.	304
Nicholson, Somerville	118
Niven, Robert	109
Nordquist, Charles J.	48
Norton, Charles B.	300
Norton, Franklin	342
Norton, John R.	110
Norvall, James	251, 251
Norwood, Carlisle	67
Nott, Charles C.	367
Noxon, Robert G.	99, 296
Nugent, Robert	30, 244, 316
Nye, Jas. W.	24

O.

	PAGE
Oakley, Henry A.	238
Oakley, Thomas B.	251
Oberteuffer, John C.	260
O'Brien, Fitz James	32
O'Brien, P.	110
O'Connor, Edward F.	316

	PAGE
O'Donnell, John	24
Ogilby, Rev. Dr.	37
Olcott, Egbert	341
Oley, John H.	30
Olmsted, Frederick Law	62
Olmsted, Wm. A.	310
O'Malley, Patrick A.	272
O'Meara, Timothy	301
Onderdonk, Andrew S.	328
O'Neil, James	328
O'Neil, John	276
Opdyke, George	77
O'Reilly, Henry Brooks	316
Ormiston, Robert	49
O'Rorke, Patrick H.	101, 350
Orr, Charles A.	327
Osborne, Galen A.	56
Osborne, Hiram	330
Osborne, John D.	47
Osborne, Thomas W.	275
Osterhaus, Peter J.	85
Ostrander, Charles W.	342
Otis, Elwell S.	351

P.

	PAGE
Paine, Lansing B.	341
Paine, O. Sprague	49
Palmer, Henry I.	99
Palmer, Mrs. Isaac	60
Palmer, John M.	49
Palmer, Oliver H.	335
Palmer, Richard H.	46
Park, Sidney W.	283
Parke, Jeremiah	261
Parker, Professor	45
Parker, Edward H.	238
Parker, Foxhall A.	119
Parker, George	337
Parker, John	345
Parkinson, Edward C.	272
Parkman, Theodore	38
Parks, J.	110
Parmele, Theodore W.	367
Parmelee, Lewis O.	32
Parmenter, S. C.	237, 247
Parish, Samuel B.	43
Parison, Philip J.	251
Parrison, Otto W.	342
Parsons, Jr., A. W.	238
Parsons, Byron	329
Parsons, Charles B.	281
Parsons, Henry	354
Patrick, Marsena R.	94
Patten, Willis	24
Pattison, Thomas	118
Patton, William	26
Paul, E. A.	55
Paulding, Leonard	118
Paush, Theodore	101
Payne, Edward M.	334
Paine, J. C.	110
Peabody, Oliver D.	294
Pearsall, Lewis	344
Pease, Charles E.	303
Pease, Roger W.	49, 262
Pease, William R.	339

INDEX. 411

	PAGE
Peck, Lewis M.	366
Peck, William G.	40
Peisener, Elias	340
Peisener, Francis	340
Penquet, Eugene	249
Per Lee, Samuel R.	338
Perley, Henry C.	287
Perine, Abraham T.	311
Perit, Peletiah	67
Perry, Edgar	350
Perry, James H.	305
Perry, Raymond H.	263
Perry, Robert C.	337
Petard, Felix	48
Pettes, William H.	282
Pettit, Frederick H.	47
Petty, Jeremiah	123
Phelps, Royal	67
Phelps, Jr., Walter	293
Phillips, Charles H.	229
Phipps, Gurdon S.	32
Phythian, Robert L.	118
Pickell, John	290
Pickles, Robert	345
Pierce, Addison	313
Pierce, Samuel C.	257
Pierce, Thomas H.	27
Pierson, Charles H.	302
Pierson, J. Frederick	30, 283
Pinckney, Joseph C.	229
Pinkney, Howard	42
Pinto, Francis E.	297
Piper, Alexander	272
Pittman, G. J.	110
Plaskett, William	353
Platner, John S.	255, 298
Platt, George W.	342
Plogsted, John F. E.	306
Plum, Francis M.	256
Plume, I. Henry	32
Poole, Theodore L.	342
Poole, William H.	353
Porteous, James G.	48
Porter, Burr	266
Porter, John F.	263
Porter, Peter A.	271
Porter, William	24
Post, Philip Sidney	90
Postley, De Van	33
Potter, Edward E.	39
Potter, Edward E.	118
Potter, N. F.	110
Potter, Ray W.	24
Potter, Robert B.	307
Powell, Alfred	49
Powell, Hans	351
Powell, Isaac	354
Powell, William H.	85
Powles, J.	347
Pratt, Calvin E.	52, 296
Pratt, George W.	237, 322
Prendergast, Thomas B.	248
Prentiss, Clifton K.	32
Preston, Reuben M.	306
Prey, Gilbert G.	98
Pride, A. Hamilton	247
Prime, William C.	79
Printup, William H.	358

	PAGE
Pronsens, Augustus W.	105
Pulitzer, Joseph	253
Pulver, Hiram	305
Punnett, James	67
Purdy, Jr., Lovell	319
Putnam, George Haven	368
Putnam, Nathan S.	364
Pyatt, Stephen A.	337
Pye, Edward	329
Pye, John M.	293

Q.

Quackenbush, G. W.	341
Quackenbush, John N.	118
Quackenbush, S. P.	118
Quarterman, George H.	319
Quick, Thomas W.	99
Quigly, Patrick	366
Quimby, Isaac F.	290
Quinlan, James	327
Quinn, Charles A.	329
Quinn, Timothy	254
Quintard, E. A.	247

R.

Radcliff, H. G.	32
Raines, John	326
Randol, A. M.	255
Ranny, Hezekiah B.	264
Ransom, Alfred	280
Rapke, Clara	60
Rathbone, Robert C.	26
Rathbun, Milton G.	229
Raulston, John B.	323
Raymond, George A.	233
Raymond, James P.	251
Read, Brantley G.	323
Read, Mort A.	110
Reed, Horatio B.	265
Reese, William H.	289
Regan, Peter C.	278
Reid, Whitelaw	55
Reilly, Edward	361
Reilly, Michael K.	366
Remington, S. Pierre.	262
Renshaw, William B.	118
Renwick, Jr., James	238
Reynolds, George	110, 261
Reynolds, George W.	289
Reynolds, Gilbert H.	98
Rheims, Leon	277
Rhind, Alexander C.	118
Rice, Dr.	241
Rice, Burrage	371
Rice, Calvin A.	353
Rice, James C.	53, 303
Rice, Pitkin B.	49
Rice, Samuel A.	53
Riddle, Randolph R.	110
Ridgway, Frank	48
Richards, Samuel T.	340
Richardson, Richard H.	294
Richardson, Robert M.	263
Riggs, William J.	276

412 INDEX.

Name	PAGE
Riker, John L.	312
Riley, Charles	321
Riley, Edward	301
Ringold, Benjamin	333
Riordan, Gilbert	299
Ritzens, Henry P.	308
Roberts, Cyrus S.	357
Roberts, Marshall O.	67
Roberts, Samuel H.	350
Robinson, Henry W.	305
Robinson, John C.	94
Robinson, John F.	46
Robinson, Joseph C.	334
Robinson, J. W.	48
Robinson, Wardwell G.	369
Rodgers, C. R. P.	119
Roe, Edward R.	256
Roe, Francis A.	118
Roe, Rozelle B.	319
Roebling, Washington A.	278
Rogers, Edward W.	279
Rogers, Hiram C.	295
Rogers, James C.	342
Rogers, William F.	293
Roller, William W.	313
Ronk, Daniel T.	360
Roome, Charles	95, 242
Roome, W. R.	314
Roosevelt, George W.	247
Roosevelt, James A.	79
Roosevelt, Robert B.	250
Roosevelt, Theodore	64
Root, Adrian R.	98, 293, 329
Root, Augustus I.	264
Root, Henry	48
Root, William H.	319
Rorty, James McKay	279
Rosa, Rudolph	304
Rosencrantz, Frederick	85
Ross, Edward A.	322
Rotherty, Henry	344
Rudd, John P.	334
Ruger, Thomas H.	94
Rulison, William H.	46
Rumsey, Austin B.	313
Rundell, Rufus L.	311
Russ, Charles E.	296
Russell, Charles H.	67
Russell, C. L.	110
Russell, Edmund K.	314
Russell, Mrs. E. J.	60
Russell, Harvey V.	288
Russell, William W.	313
Rutherford, Allen	30, 89
Ryder, (Captain)	234
Ryder, James	237
Ryder, Oscar	26
Ryder, R. H.	326
Ryder, B. Franklin	279

S.

Name	PAGE
Sage, B. Augustus	202
Sage, Clinton H.	336
Salm, Salm Felix	286, 315
Sammon, Simon	339
Sand, Henry A.	32, 333

Name	PAGE
Sanford, Hugh S.	305
Sanger, William H.	42
Sangster, George	243
Sarft, James	241
Satterlee, Livingston	235
Saunders, James	316
Saunders, Thorndike	42
Sava, J. E.	110
Savacoal, Edwin	110
Savage, Henry F.	32
Savage, James W.	262
Sawyer, Frederick A.	304
Sawyer, Thomas H.	46
Sayles, J. L.	292
Sayre, Lewis A.	355
Sayre, William H.	319
Schaffer, George W.	311, 328
Schaffs, Cornelius H.	243
Schell, Augustus	79
Schell, Richard	79
Scheminilfennig, Alexander	85
Schenck, William P.	99
Schermerhorn, F. Augustus	370
Schilling, Eugene	333
Schilling, John	361
Schirmer, Louis	273, 277
Schlacta, G.	110
Schmal, G. W.	110
Schmidt, Adolph	263
Schoepf, Albin	85
Schoomaker, Hiram	237
Schoomaker, Leonard S.	308
Schram, James E.	238
Schubert, F.	110
Schultz, Jackson S.	67
Schurz, Carl	85, 253
Schutt, (Captain)	250
Schutt, Andrew S.	322
Schuyler, Mrs. G. L.	61
Scofield, D. S.	110
Scofield, John S.	357
Scott, George W.	311
Scott, Henry C.	123
Scott, Simon C.	27
Scott, Walter P.	341
Scoville, Frederick	53
Scudder, Henry F.	242
Seabury, Robert	32
Searing, William M.	296
Searles, H. E.	247
Seaward, Benjamin	305
Secor, Mrs. Charles A.	230
Seeley, Aaron	266
Segoine, Jesse	336
Selkirk, Edward A.	326
Serrell, Edward W.	261
Seward, Clarence A.	277
Seward, William H.	83, 104
Seward, Jr., William H.	271
Sewell, Mrs N. D.	61
Seymour, Arba M.	319
Seymour, Joseph	344
Shaler, Alexander	26, 30, 230, 313
Shanks, W. F. G.	55
Sharp, Henry	323
Sharp, George H.	52, 341
Sharpe, Jacob	309, 360
Shaw, Robert G.	32

INDEX.   413

	PAGE
Shaw, Thomas	334
Shedd, J. J.	329
Shedd, John W.	334
Shelby, F.	247
Sheldon, Lionel A.	53
Shenk, Otto	46
Shepard, Elliott F.	307
Sheppard, John T.	328
Sheppard, Thomas F.	274
Sherburne, John P.	262
Sherman, Charles P.	368
Sherman, Isaac	67
Sherman, Jacob	105
Sherwood, William L.	330
Sherrill, Eliakim	105, 343
Shields, James	85
Shine, Eugene C.	101
Shipley, R. F.	111
Shoemaker, (Private)	275
Shufeldt, Robert W.	118
Sicard, Montgomery	118
Sickles, Daniel E.	52, 94, 316
Siebring, Jacob L.	123
Sigel, Franz	85
Silsby, Frank	319
Silvey, John	349
Simmons, J.	110
Simpson, Edward	119
Simpson, George H.	349
Simpson, Jeremiah	328
Simpson, William	321
Sims, Palen H.	307
Sincerbox, Henry H.	344
Sizer, A. J.	314
Skiff, George V.	50
Skilton, Julius A.	49
Shimer, Isaac	105
Skinner, Lewis C.	334
Slaight, James G.	24
Slidell, W. J.	353
Sloan, Samuel	67
Sloat, Charles W.	329
Slocum, Henry W.	52, 94, 102, 295
Smalley, George W.	55
Smart, John C.	328
Smedberg, Charles J.	32
Smith, Abel	236
Smith, Jr., Abel	364
Smith, Abram A.	278
Smith, Albert M.	242
Smith, Alfred B.	357
Smith, Andrew H.	47
Smith, Andrew J.	342
Smith, Bernard N.	365
Smith, Charles H.	250
Smith, Elisha B.	338
Smith, Frank S.	328
Smith, George C.	323
Smith, H. E.	247
Smith, James	345
Smith, James E.	278
Smith, James G.	316
Smith, James J.	316
Smith, James M.	288
Smith, Jesse C.	53
Smith, John Cotton	238
Smith, John F.	337
Smith, Melancthon	117

	PAGE
Smith, M. B.	234
Smith, Stephen B.	123
Smith, Trumbull	250
Smith, William	262
Smith, William M.	332
Smyth, Thomas A.	85
Snee, Patrick	369
Sniper, Gustavus	370
Snow, Asa B.	46
Snow, Henry E.	265
Snyder, Charles	334
Snyder, James W.	272
Solomon, Frederick	85
Spaulding, Elbridge T.	74
Spaulding, Erastus M.	271
Spaulding, Ira	282
Spaulding, Oscar J.	333
Speeding, Samuel	344
Speight, F. C.	123
Speir, S. Fleet	50
Spencer, Mrs. R. H.	60
Sperling, James H.	250
Spofford, John F.	330
Spotts, James H.	113
Spratt, Joseph	275
Spring, Julius	332
Squier, Charles W.	319
Squier, Truman H.	48
Stahel, Julius H.	85
Stamp, Charles E.	320
Stanley, Mary A.	60
Stanley, Myron D.	101
Stark, Isaac	319
Starr, Henry M.	271
Starr, Samuel H.	32
Stearns, Joseph Ketchum	254
Stearns, M. A.	314
Stearns, W. W.	271
Stebbins, Henry G.	67
Stedman, Edmund C.	55
Steedman, Charles	114
Steenburg, Wade H.	357
Steers, Thomas	123
Stephens, Doctor	45
Stephenson, William W.	43, 364
Sterling, F. W.	347
Sternberg, George M.	50
Stetson, John L.	292
Stevens, Hazard	321
Stevens, Isaac I.	321
Stevens, John A.	67, 71
Stevens, Jr., John Austin	68, 71, 75
Stevens, William O.	53, 317
Stevenson, John D.	113
Stevenson, Louis W.	368
Stewart, John A.	67
Stewart, Joseph H.	50
Stiles, James H.	99
Stiles, John W.	233, 324
Stille, Charles J.	61
Stillwell, Silas M.	67, 74
Stimson, E. A.	323
Stocking, Charles D.	288
Stone, David M.	79
Stone, E. L.	233
Storrs, R. S.	58, 241
Story, Robert	99
Strain, Alexander	358

INDEX.

	PAGE
Strong, Mrs. Charles Edward	293
Strong, George T.	40, 61
Strong, James H.	118
Strong, Richard P.	42
Strong, William E.	53, 90
Stuart, Alexander	74
Stuart, Charles B.	282
Stuart, David	53
Sturges, Jonathan	67
Stuyvesant, Mrs. Gerard	59
Suess, John L.	281
Suiter, James A.	298
Sullivan, Dennis E.	316
Sullivan, Dennis F.	42
Sullivan, Timothy	294
Swain, James B.	262
Swalm, William F.	49
Swan, Henry	329
Sweeney, Thomas W.	85
Sweitzer, Nelson B.	264
Swett, H. W. S.	353
Swinburne, John	45
Swinton, William	55
Swords, Thomas	39

T.

Taft, Edward P.	271
Tailox, Ivan	314
Tait, George F.	288
Tanner, James	327
Tappan, John R.	341
Tarbell, Jonathan	328
Taylor, Alfred W.	284
Taylor, Moses	67, 71
Taylor, Nelson	317
Taylor, Robert F.	290, 298
Taylor, Rodney M.	263
Teller, Daniel W.	95
Terry, Augustus H.	345
Terry, David D.	42
Thomas, George H.	113
Thomas, George W.	276
Thomason, Samuel E.	368
Thompson, Rev. Dr.	37
Thompson, Egbert	119
Thompson, John H.	50, 273
Thorne, Thomas W.	123
Thorpe, Gould H.	364
Thorpe, Thomas J.	264
Thurber, Benjamin F.	319
Thurber, Ira S.	101
Thurston, A. Henry	234
Tibbets, William B.	265
Ticehurst, David	293
Tidball, John C.	268
Tidball, William Linn	310
Tidd, Maurice P.	323
Tiffany & Co.	281
Tighe, Richard F.	362
Tileston, Thomas	67
Tillott, David K.	238
Timolat, Henry N.	33
Timpson, Samuel C.	330
Tinelli, Louis W.	328
Titus, Silas	290, 342
Todd, James	123

	PAGE
Todd, John G.	296
Tompkins, G. W.	111
Tompkins, George W. B.	323
Tompsey, James B.	320
Tourgee, Albion W.	295
Townsend, Eben G.	356
Townsend, Frederick	52, 243
Townsend, John D.	79
Townsend, Joseph G.	371
Townsend, Mrs. Peter	50
Townsend, Robert	110
Tracey, Jr., John	264, 350
Tracy, Benjamin F.	52, 335
Tracy, Frederick A.	33
Tracy, William	207
Trafford, Benjamin L.	95, 250
Treadwell, William A.	273
Tremain, Henry E.	30, 41
Tremaine, Walter R.	32
Trimble, Mrs. Merritt	50
Trenchard, Stephen D.	119
Trenor, J. J.	82
Tripp, James M.	42
Trotter, F. E.	30
Truair, George G.	356
Truesdell, Samuel	314
Trumbull, Charles S.	348
Tucker, George	39
Tuller, Anson	310
Tully, James B.	240
Turchin, John B.	85
Turner, George S.	365
Tuttle, George	308
Tyer, Hugh	24
Tyler, A. M.	341
Tyler, Francis E.	319
Tyler, Robert O.	94
Tyler, Rockwell	309
Tyler, Rudolphus D. S.	323

U.

Ullman, Daniel	320
Underhill, Samuel	238
Upham, J. V.	102
Upton, Emory	341
Upton, Henry	341
Urban, Caspar	209

V.

Vail, Henry T.	67
Valentine, Henry C.	306
Van Allen, James H.	276
Van Amburgh, David C.	344
Van Arnsburg, George	304
Van Brocklin, Martin	242
Van Brunt, George B.	24
Van Buren, Barent	333
Van Buren, James L.	41
Van Buren, John	79
Van Buren, T. B.	332
Van Courtlandt, James S.	359
Vanderbilt, Cornelius	115
Vanderbilt, George W.	115
Vanderpoel, Surgeon General	46

INDEX. 415

	PAGE
Vanderpoel, Mrs. Edward	60
Van Deusen, John	286
Van Dusen, David G.	99
Van Duser, Charles F.	33
Van Emburg, John H.	101
Van Hoesen, Garret S.	360
Van Patten, Volkert	302
Van Petten, John B.	361, 371
Van Rensselaer, Cortland	354
Van Rensselaer, Killian	35
Van Rensselaer, Walter A.	322
Van Scoy, Hiram C.	341
Van Slyck, Charles L.	346
Van Slyck, George W.	346
Van Steenbergh, Isaac	333
Van Tine, Charles	344
Van Valkenburg, J. W.	263
Van Valkenburg, Robert	335
Van Vleek, Daniel P.	47, 347
Van Winkle, E.	354
Van Wyck, Charles H.	309
Van Zaunt, J.	240
Varian, Joshua M.	95, 281
Venuti, Edward	101
Vermilye, J. D.	67
Verplank, A. J.	314
Viele, Egbert L.	26, 30
Viele, Mrs. Egbert L.	305
Viele, Henry K.	329
Villard, Henry	55
Vilmar, Frederick	233
Vinton, Rev. Dr.	37
Vinton, Francis L.	302
Visscher, James D.	302
Volks, F. J.	314
Von Gilsa, Leopold	301
Von Schack, George	85, 296
Von Steinwehr, Adolph	85, 296
Von Steuben, Baron	85
Von Vegesack, Ernst	293
Von Weltzien, D.	262
Vosburg, Abram S.	247

W.

	PAGE
Wadsworth, Craig W.	25
Wadsworth, James S.	25, 94
Wainwright, Charles S.	275
Wainwright, Jonathan	118
Wainwright, William P.	320
Walbridge, Hiram	89
Wagner, Adolph	101
Wagstaff, Jr. Alfred	328
Walcott, George B.	322
Walker, William A.	353
Wall, J.	111
Wall, Maurice W.	316
Wallace, Hugh	287
Wallace, Samuel T.	321
Wallace, William	302
Walling, George W.	123
Walling, William H.	351
Wallsch, Thomas	319
Walrath, Ezra L.	289, 330
Walsh, J.	111
Walsh, James J.	299
Walsh, John	123

	PAGE
Walton, Charles W.	308
Wanzer, George G.	295
Ward, Giles F.	328
Ward, J. H. Hobart	24, 94, 300
Ward, Peletiah	37, 322
Ward, William G.	95, 324, 235
Warlow, Jacob B.	123
Warner, Andrew S.	354
Warner, John N.	101
Warren, David	344
Warren, George L.	300
Warren, Gouverneur K.	94
Warren, Robert P.	353
Warren, William S.	305
Wasbburne, Charles E.	47
Watson, Charles	321
Wead, Frederick F.	292, 331
Webb, Alexander S.	35, 94, 104
Webb, Robert	35
Webb, Watson	35
Webber, Max	293
Weber, Frederick	333
Weber, John B.	339
Webster, Calvert S.	281
Weed, Thurlow	23, 89
Weeks, Henry A.	289
Weeks, J.	111
Weer, Norman F.	101
Weinberger, Wm. B.	233
Weir, Robert F.	42, 47
Weismantle, John	306
Weiss, Francis	293
Weller, Charles H.	344
Welles, Edward B.	33
Welling, Joseph	271
Wellington, David G.	308
Wellman, Abijah J.	326
Wells, Amos	351
Wells, George	289
Wells, Henry S.	354
Wells, T. M.	111
Welsh, Thomas	311
Welsh, W. H.	314
Wentworth, Obed F.	281
West, Professor	241
West, Joseph E.	49
West, Rowland R.	263
West, William C.	118
Westbrook, Cornelius D.	341
Wescott (Private)	275
Wescott, Matthew H.	356
Westerhald, W.	111
Weston, Sullivan H.	26, 37
Wheeler, Charles M.	105
Wheeler, John J.	309
Wheeler, Obed	357
Wheeler, William	279
Wheeler, William	351
Wheeler, William	33
Wheelock, Charles	98, 330
Whistler, Joseph N. G.	267
White, Alvin	339
White, Amos H.	258
White, Charles Trumbull	238
White, David B.	323
White, Frank J.	90, 287
White, James B.	85
Whitelow, James	289

Whitman, George W.	308
Whittemore, Harry	123
Whyte, John	321
Wightman, Edward	42
Wilber, John J.	314
Wilbur, R. H.	333
Wilcox, Charles H.	46
Wilcox, J. H.	323
Wilcox, W. H. H.	289
Wilde, Hiram	292
Wilder, John T.	90
Wiley, John	111
Wilhelm, J.	347
Wilkinson, J. P.	346
Wilkinson, Robert F.	347
Wilkeson, John W.	331
Willard, George L.	101, 343, 364
Willard, Orvel H.	313
Willets, Elbert H.	236
Williams, George F.	55
Williams, John E.	67, 71
Williams, Oscar C.	105
Williams, William H.	293
Williams, William J.	33
Williamson, John J.	123, 267, 344
Willich, August	85
Willis, Benjamin A.	340
Willoughby, Richard H.	323
Wilman, Adolph	342
Wilson, Alfred D.	49, 240
Wilson, A. S.	123
Wilson, Henry	119
Wilson, John	302
Wilson, Lester D.	319
Wilson, Philip L.	53
Wilson, Robert P.	292
Wilson, William	285
Winchester, Locke W.	26
Winchester, Salmon	287
Windsor, John	321
Winnegar, William W.	111
Winslow, Bradley	370
Winslow, George B.	92
Winslow, Gordon	61
Winslow, Hiram A.	351
Winslow, John A.	114
Winslow, John F.	116
Winthrop, Theodore	12, 33
Witthaus, R. A.	301
Wolcott, Charles W.	319
Wood, (Sergeant)	259
Wood, Alfred M.	325
Wood, Bradford R.	45
Wood, Charles S.	50
Wood, Ephraim	105
Wood, Fernando	80, 81
Wood, Jr., James	349
Wood, James R.	45
Wood, Willam W. W.	117
Woodford, Stewart L.	39, 344
Woodhall, David M.	368
Woodman, Charles H.	314
Woodward, John B.	98, 236
Woodworth, Selim E.	119
Woolsey, Charles W.	43
Woolsey, Miss	60
Worden, John L.	117
Wright, Benjamin F.	353
Wright, Daniel J.	235
Wright, David F.	307
Wright, Francis M.	49
Wright, John C.	30
Wright, John G.	308
Wright, Joseph	237
Wright, William	333
Wyckoff, Albert	53

Y.

Yates, Austin A.	349
Yates, Jacob L.	294
York, Levi H.	353
York, Robert P.	319
Young, Corporal	303
Young, Edward F.	41
Young, George W.	118
Young, John Russell	56
Young, Mrs. ("Aunt Becky")	60
Young, William H.	293

Z.

Zaft, Rev. Mr.	241
Zook, Samuel K.	100, 229, 309
Zyla, Anthony	37
Zenette, Arnold	348

www.ingramcontent.com/pod-product-compliance
Lightning Source LLC
Chambersburg PA
CBHW030602300426
44111CB00009B/1077